Explaining Traditions

Explaining Traditions

Folk Behavior in Modern Culture

Simon J. Bronner

The University Press of Kentucky

Scholarly publisher for the Commonwealth,
serving Bellarmine University, Berea College, Centre College of
Kentucky, Eastern Kentucky University, The Filson Historical Society,
Georgetown College, Kentucky Historical Society, Kentucky State
University, Morehead State University, Murray State University,
Northern Kentucky University, Transylvania University, University of
Kentucky, University of Louisville, and Western Kentucky University.
All rights reserved.

Editorial and Sales Offices: The University Press of Kentucky
663 South Limestone Street, Lexington, Kentucky 40508-4008
www.kentuckypress.com

The Library of Congress has cataloged the hardcover edition as follows:

Bronner, Simon J.
  Explaining traditions : folk behavior in modern culture / Simon J.
Bronner.
     p. cm.
  Includes bibliographical references and index.
  ISBN 978-0-8131-3406-2 (hardcover : alk. paper)
  ISBN 978-0-8131-3407-9 (ebook)
1. Folklore—United States. 2. Oral tradition—United States.
3. Communication in folklore—United States. 4. United States—Social
life and customs. I. Title.
  GR105.B666 2011
  398.20973—dc23   2011017139
  ISBN 978-0-8131-6586-8 (pbk. : alk. paper)

For Michael Owen Jones,
who challenged me to explain
why we do what we do

Contents

Illustrations

Acknowledgments

I have dedicated this work to Michael Owen Jones, professor emeritus of folkloristics and history at UCLA, to credit him as no endnote tucked into the back of a book can. It is not a single book I cite in honoring his contribution to what he calls a behavioristic approach to the study of tradition, although I admit to having an "ah-ha" moment in my education upon reading *The Hand Made Object and Its Maker* (1975), in which he explains an apparently "strange" rocking chair rooted in tradition with reference to the psychological states of its maker (a concern I carried through to *The Carver's Art* [1996a]). Although I was not his student, his presentations, publications, and dinner conversations about the logic and aesthetics of folklife taught me many profound lessons. I cannot say that he will agree with all the explanations I give in this book, but I hope readers will appreciate his inspiration for the praxis of explaining traditions.

Many generous individuals aided me in depicting the different cultural scenes in this book, and I wish I could list them all. In this limited space, let me at least give notice to the inspiring figures who have been there since I began my intellectual pursuit of traditions in the 1970s. Although not composing a unified school of thought, they are all familiar to one another, and they have commendably unpacked traditions as cultural practices and as modes of thought. Of this group, special mention should be made of senior member Bill Nicolaisen. He was the first professor I encountered who talked seriously and cogently about tradition, and as a folklorist, he presented me with valuable tools of analysis. Spanning the continental traditions of Europe and America, he was the first recipient of the American Folklore Society's coveted lifetime achievement award, and he is a hero to scholars in many fields, including linguistics, philology, geography, history, and literature. Other comrades of various disciplinary stripes with whom I have had many discussions spanning many decades include Roger Abrahams, Ronald L. Baker, the late Mac Barrick, Haya Bar-Itzhak, Dan Ben-Amos, Erika Brady, Linda Dégh, Kurt Dewhurst, James Dow, the late Alan

Dundes, Bill Ellis, Tim Evans, Gary Alan Fine, Henry Glassie, Sylvia Grider, William Hansen, the late Louis C. Jones, Barbara Kirshenblatt-Gimblett, Elaine Lawless, Carl Lindahl, Marsha MacDowell, the late Bill McNeil, Jay Mechling, Wolfgang Mieder, Paul Oliver, Elliott Oring, the late Roderick Roberts, the late Warren Roberts, the late Sue Samuelson, Steve Siporin, Brian Sutton-Smith, Barre Toelken, Patricia Turner, John Vlach, Peter Voorheis, Bert Wilson, and Don Yoder. To this varied lot, let me add my thanks to generations of students and colleagues at Penn State University, Harvard University, University of California at Davis, Dickinson College, Leiden University, and Osaka University, where I have taught and have also learned from their different practices and perspectives.

When not in the classroom, field, or conference center, I am blessed at home with a supportive family. Rather than being a place where I would put my project on the shelf, my household deepened my thinking about tradition. At one end, my Holocaust-survivor mother, in both language and memory, reminds me of folk worlds past; at the other end, my children continually recount nascent traditions projecting the future. In between, in faith and action, my wife, Sally Jo, helps me figure out, in the moment, the beliefs by which we think and act, individually and collectively. These loved ones were the inspiration for many of the topics I investigate in this book, including childhood development; coming-of-age rituals; aging and death; ethnicity and race; masculinity and gender; material and visual culture; the Holocaust; Jewishness; the dialectology of Yiddish and Pennsylvania German, central and eastern European culture; the Internet; sports; and American studies.

To form this book's edifice of tradition, I crafted a number of chapters from previously published materials. All the original work was substantially revised and expanded in light of the theme of this book and updated with new sources and ideas. Chapters 1, 2, 4, 5, and 9 have not appeared in print before. In the best tradition of scholarship, I want to acknowledge the following organizations for their permission to build on my earlier work: Columbia University Graduate School of Arts and Sciences for "Analyzing the Ethnic Self: The Hinkeldreck Theme in Pennsylvania-German Folk Narrative," in *Columbia Journal of American Studies*; Springer Publishing for "From *Landsmanshaften* to *Vinkln*: Mediating Community among Yiddish Speakers in America," in *Jewish History*; Taylor & Francis Group for "Building Tradition: Control and

Authority in Vernacular Architecture," in *Vernacular Architecture in the 21st Century*; University Press of Kentucky for "Left to Their Own Devices: Interpreting American Children's Folklore as an Adaptation to Aging," in *Southern Folklore*; Western States Folklore Society for "Let Me Tell It My Way: Joketelling by a Father and Son," in *Humor and the Individual*, and portions of "The American Concept of Tradition: Folklore in the Discourse of Traditional Values" and "Folk Logic: Interpretation and Explanation in Folkloristics," in *Western Folklore*.

Prologue

Beginning with Tradition

In this book I propose to make sense of tradition. My approach counters the hasty academic relegation of tradition to *non*sense, or the supposed tyranny of the archaic, pastoral past that inexplicably has hung around to the present cosmopolitan day. Well into the modern age, banner-bearers for progress have declared the hindrance of tradition swept away, but the trouble is that despite these pronouncements, tradition is still an ever-present force to be reckoned with—and that persistence merits explanation.

Considering tradition's importance in the here and now, questions also arise whether it really impedes advancement as much as many pundits and politicians would have us believe. Even when some grassroots observers notice tradition's vitality, they often report it as inscrutably ethereal, if not bizarre. Tradition appears mysteriously, mystically, immutably "out there" or out of the limelight. Touting originality as the hallmark of civilization, the highbrow experts often present tradition as something belonging to someone else a distance away and a cultural or class level down. I argue that tradition is a living and ubiquitous, if often neglected or suppressed, process in modern people's lives. Its constancy in, and interaction with, modernity can be explained by its reference to precedence, social connection, consecutiveness, and what I call its "handiness" as well as "folkiness."

What do the intelligentsia have against tradition? For starters, the eighteenth-century European Enlightenment movement to promote freedom, reason, and democracy prompted assorted philosophers to demonize tradition as the enemy of rationality and progress (Adorno 1993, 75; Oakeshott 1962, 1–4). Linking tradition with the vulgarity of the illiterate populace on the one hand and the privilege of aristocracy on the other, they also viewed tradition as a yoke hindering their rebellious or creative imagination. Their scientific ilk has generally not had an easy time pinning down a concept like tradition, which seemed to them elusively fluid. Concerned for outpourings of genius and beauty, aesthetes who were obsessed with showing cultural refinement and renaissance often turned up their noses at tradition's association with the local vernacular, everyday life, and ordinary folk, even if their creative expressions were sources for the hallmarks of the literary circle, the art gallery, and the concert stage (Bushman 1993; Matthiesen 1941). Meanwhile, oriented toward placing a lens on major events and national leaders effecting change, dyed-in-the-wool historians appeared to be unreceptive to questions of continuities through time, characteristic of tradition. Although historians have a major stake in the understanding of the past, in their recovery project, they often derided tradition as unreliable fiction rather than momentous fact.

Speaking for the arts, famed poet T. S. Eliot observed that literary critics seldom referred to tradition "except in a phrase of censure" (1960, 3). Many social scientists, for their part, bemoaned the resistance of tradition to quantification, and rhetoricians grappled with tradition's multiple, often contested meanings from fine to folk art and presumed its opposition to innovation. Tradition appeared suspect to academic purists because it could be primped, trivialized, romanticized, and packaged as nostalgia or exploited for economic or literary gain. Politically, it could be disdained for representing either conservative reactionaryism or liberal radicalism, and it was often connected with romantic nationalistic movements that could be construed as liberating or dictatorial (see Abrahams 1993b; Dow and Lixfeld 1994; Kolakowski 1971; Oinas 1978; Wilson 1976).

As a term and as an idea, tradition has not been treated kindly. In the empirical, recordable form of expressive "traditions," the evidence of cultural practices has not been regarded as hard and fast. Variability, rather than fixity, is tradition's trademark; multiformity has been the source of its complexity and, often, puzzlement. My point in this book is that this feature of lived experience should make it more attractive for considerations of human life and culture. Despite philosophical and political attempts to quash tradition, it keeps coming back into popular realizations of culture because it is still noticeable in life worked by, and on, people in national halls of power as well as at society's grass roots. Tradition may come up in the public discourse of lost heritage or in efforts to revive and invent custom; tradition is wrapped up in talk of technological and social change and the search for solutions to various political problems facing groups and nations cognizant of the force of tradition in the connectedness of citizens or members. Rather than being dispatched to the dustbin, tradition shows up in multiple guises and creeps into major headlines of the day, as I point out in the first chapter.

"We fall for 'tradition,'" an advertising adviser declares, noting that marketers emphasize the idea at times of crisis because "we unconsciously adhere to familiar, comforting rituals" (Lindstrom 2009). In the reference to ritual is an aspect of tradition that communicates behavioral repetition and social bonding—and a lasting symbolism. Yet in lived experience, adults may think of tradition as child's play, mere kids' stuff, if not a survival of long ago, thus evading its impact on markers throughout one's life course. Ironically, children themselves are usually oblivious to the rhetoric of tradition steeped in the passage of knowledge from generation to generation, despite being brought up with traditions at home and on the playground. I rarely see curricula about tradition in the schools, except in relation to "bygone" or "preindustrial" days or the stuff of fantasy such as fairy tales. In fact, children probably harbor negative ideas about tradition because they resent parental claims to authority invoked in proverbs and parables, or they put down their elders as hanging on to old-fashioned "traditional" beliefs and old wives' tales. In sum, tradition can be invoked to prevent and promote change, a point I underscore in the first and last chapters.

Attitudes toward tradition certainly vary. In a place like America, where children are taught to embrace invention, trendiness, and novelty—and a good bit of antiauthoritarian dissidence—students may learn to eschew anything that, like tradition, is tainted by being behind the times and out of style. In contrast, in Japan, where I taught and lived, along with appreciating the latest gadgetry, children report having respect for ancestors, family, and authority drummed into them while their parents bemoan the loss of respect for tradition. If many philosophers want to universalize as well as deride tradition, relativists supporting the "different manifestation" conclusion probably view tradition as less of a hard artifact fixed in place than an idea with variable expressions wedded to cultural context. Adding to the elusiveness, and maybe the trivialization, of the concept, relativists have contended that tradition is perceived through the eyes of the beholder rather than as being capable of objective generalization.

Tradition's role in the life of the mind has, for the most part, been under the scholarly radar, whether because of difficulty with or ignorance of its subject. My purpose here is not just to "fill a gap" in a patronizing "show-and-tell" but to show the objective possibility of cultural study with tradition at its core. To be sure, chronicles of folklore and folklife, ethnographies of social groups, and annals of everyday life have provided much about tradition's whats, if not its whys and wherefores. But overall, tradition presents problems of thought and action that are surely more parried than pondered. I am not the first to point this out, although I cannot say that a swing toward tradition has occurred in scholarship along with the ballyhooed "cultural turn" (more often it looks like a churlish turn *on* tradition). I am encouraged, though, by religious historian Jaroslav Pelikan, who from the revered podium of the Jefferson Lecture in the Humanities, the highest honor the government of the United States confers for intellectual achievement, pounded away at the idea that tradition demands more attention because it has been a primary source of insight, a living faith and force, or, in a phrase he adapted from the writings of Thomas Jefferson, "democracy extended through time and space" (Pelikan 1984, 61).

Using Jefferson to inspire an academic enterprise to grasp tradition is ironic, since he also epitomized America's break with tradition, which he thought of as the imposition of previous generations, particularly from Europe (Boorstin 1993, 204–13). Yet in declaring the presentness of America, expressed in the view that "the dead have no rights" there, he drew attention to the possibility of situating tradition anew according to different conditions and institutionalized by people of the same generation—or, in other words, by transmission within a situated group rather than solely in a family lineage through time (Boorstin 1993, 206). In a distinctively modern voice, Jefferson channeled tradition from a tyranny of the dead into a freedom to choose. Tradition, rather than being a relic set in stone, could be a renewable, malleable resource for the future. The lesson to be drawn from Jefferson is that tradition is relational: instead of being a synonym for the past, tradition brings out the connection of the past in, as well as to, the present.

Additionally, a connection unfolds of tradition's users, or deniers, to one another. Indeed, tradition can be perceived revealingly through the wide-angle lens of the present, allowing a view of social interactions influenced by and generative of varied cultural practices. Tradition becomes meaningful, in the words of contemporary social interactionist Gary Alan Fine, "because of how it is used and the ways to which it is referred" (1989, 264). Unlike terms for human actions such as *habit* or *routine*, which imply unthinking repetition, *tradition* (related to the idea of varied cultural practices) suggests something ideational and symbolic, or, in Pelikan's view, "it points us beyond itself" (1984, 54).

Pelikan's notable role in public humanities was to admonish educators that they had yet "to come to terms with the presence of the traditions from which we are derived," starting with "a knowledge of the contents of those traditions" (1984, 53). That most people are unreflective about tradition does not lessen its importance. Actually, this characteristic indicates that people perceive tradition to be intrinsic to life and an important rhetoric for describing lived experience. By providing the guidance of precedent and collective action, tradition is manifestly the basis of religion, law, politics, and art, among other features of our society that keep us going.

"What's there to know, no less decipher?" some skeptics might ask of tradition's prodders and probers. My quick answer is "life," especially when tradition comes into play as rhetoric and action about behavior or communities that cut against the popular or modern grain. Invoking the terminology of tradition tells people about the ways they think and act continuously as well as connectedly in relation to others in lived experience. The trouble is that explaining tradition might reveal forces and functions people would rather not confront, or else they claim it detracts from the perception of tradition as specially spiritual or ancestral. Too often people assume—indeed, insist—that tradition should work on them without their understanding or interference. They prefer it to be a given of their existence rather than an object of scrutiny.

Pelikan is among those who invite more penetrating work in explaining not only the handed-on content of traditions but also what he calls "the sheer fact" of tradition's existence in modernity (1984, 53). Scholars, oriented as they are to dismissing rather than discussing tradition, did not exactly rush to take the challenge, but time and again, when gusts of technological, social, and economic change in America and around the globe rise up, questions of tradition come to the fore in the shaping of the future (Phillips and Schochet 2004). The period of my writing is certainly one of those times when the idealism of modernism has been challenged by war, ethnic conflict, natural disaster, and economic crisis.

An additional question raised by the gap between scholarship and lived experience with regard to tradition might be: why has tradition been belittled as nonsense if it provides so much insight? My answer is that the derision of tradition supports the constructed image of modernity and youthfulness as progress. It establishes a historical sequence of the new displacing the old, befitting an industrialized power (Childs 2000). Oriented as moderns are to look ahead and consider what is special and new around them, tradition forces an examination of what went on before that is ordinary and social, in contrast to the modern image of accelerated change and chronic aloneness. Modernity favors the prestige of the novel, individual, commercial, youthful, and original production, which in turn exalts a future-oriented capitalist society over communal social structures, folk creativity, and transmitted wisdom.

The image of modernity as the new order sweeping out the old traditions conveys a linear, evolutionary narrative in place of a layered picture of cultural dynamics in a variety of social settings. An assumption underlying this linear narrative is that, in the past, folks unswervingly followed tradition and were therefore stuck in place and mind. Now people, especially youth, are supposedly liberated and in control of their destinies. In the backwoods domains of tradition, popular belief holds, people lack choices, and having options is a hallmark of modern individualism. Alternatively, tradition is condemned for distorting cold, hard facts joined to scientism; in yet another binary, tradition is soft or ineffable, whereas science is solidly certain. A set of associations arises along with these rhetorical strategies: tradition is backward, old, irrational, illiterate, unimaginative, simple, frivolous, ephemeral, irrelevant, limiting, reactionary, and fogyish, whereas modernity is forward, scientific, cosmopolitan, creative, innovative, young, and vibrant. The impression might be that people are naturally attracted to modernity in an imagined competition with the past. Where does that leave tradition? Is there any other answer for tradition besides being shown the door when the hierarchy of culture implicit in educators' binary of traditional and modern is for tradition's intellectual conceptualization as belonging to the lowly, dirty folk and modernity being accorded to the pristine, economically powerful elite?

Raymond Williams, who has been influential on my thinking,

points out that within modernization theory, the words *tradition* and especially *traditional* are "now often used dismissively, with a similar lack of specificity" (1983, 319). In Williams's keyword vocabulary, *tradition* has gained significance as a result of being viewed in intellectual circles as shorthand for the vulgar and ignorant, practices of the common folk that the elite construe as potentially threatening to their social status and control. He is not alone in his estimation that modern things appear to be known empirically when intellectuals place tradition in the realm of the troubling, bizarre, unknown, unseen, and, especially, inexplicable. Compared to *modernity*, he editorializes, *tradition* is the more difficult word to fathom, or maybe scholars have oversimplified it to validate the complexity of modernization. One contribution toward its understanding in this book is to locate different kinds of tradition as modes of thought and forms of transmission and to identify plural traditions as cultural expressions that have a bearing on the times and places in which people live.

Instead of setting tradition in opposition to rationality, progress, and youth, I show examples in which tradition is "with it" rather than without "it"; that is, I analyze traditions that are inextricably intertwined with normative experience. Tradition is a factor, rather than a foil, of modernity as I view it in action. I find the elaboration and variation of tradition rather than presume its limitation and uniformity. I uncover the human agency in tradition and its importance for containing and conveying symbols, deep-seated values, and political and psychological implications in modern culture, often in response to emotional anxieties and social conflicts. Having criticized the privileging of modernity in cultural theory, I strive not to overstate or isolate the role of tradition in practice to the exclusion of other forces. Clearly, my focus is first on making tradition—as a practice in the form of plural traditions and as a keyword in the concept of a singular tradition—visible in complex society, because there are still supposed sages who are touted for declaring that tradition disappeared with the feudal age, the industrial age, the 1960s, or whatever point signaled liberation (Adorno 1993; Lasch 1979; Said 1994).

I find it imperative to analyze the roles tradition plays in cultural process by considering multiple sources—historical, social, and psychological, primarily—in my explanations for the persistent adherence to, and adaptation or decline of, traditions. In many cases, I address the intellectuals constructing images of tradition as well the expressions and scenes characterized as traditions. It will be hard to miss in the subjects I pursue that I ultimately seek cognitive sources of people's actions that have been taken on account of tradition. I find inadequate the defensive (or anti-intellectual), tautological "because we've always done it" as an explanation for the persistence of tradition (Dundes 1994, 85–86; Pieper 2008, 15). I ask why some traditions are chosen to be continued and others are not. I question why the context of events evokes traditions and the realization that participants enact it for themselves. I want to know how traditions gain and change symbolic significance. This means that I often go beyond the empirical evidence to think about the mind, and for some readers, I may go too far with socio- and psychoanalysis to provide explanations of cultural practices and practitioners. I hope readers will stick with me for investigations into a number of cultural "cold cases," for my purpose is to open traditions to closer rationalist scrutiny. If better explanations arise, provoked by my speculations, then I know I have done my job.

Every day people are involved in events they recognize as traditional, and at the same time they look to establish precedents for traditions of the future. They do so because tradition fuels their culture. It provides the precedents by which they make their cultural choices and locate themselves in place and time. Tradition signifies in countless texts of speech, play, and ritual—scripts embedded with values, symbols, and concerns about their lives and the heritage from which they come. In short, tradition informs people where to begin and guides them on how to proceed. But folks may be troubled by engaging in practices for which they lack background. This is why, I think, I so often hear questions about common rituals and customs: How did this start? Why did it last? Why do we do it now? What does it mean? These questions are evidence that tradition is so pervasive that it is hard for people to separate themselves from it so as to recognize it, much less analyze it. And apparently, getting answers to these questions does more than satisfy curiosity. It relates to one's sense of belonging in a mobile, individualistic society. These answers speak to the fit of what people do "naturally" with a world that has been artificially built.

The answers I provide in this book are not so much a Luddite vindication of tradition as a way of analyzing how and why tradition works in modern culture. Despite suspicions by previous reviewers that my analytical concern for folk behavior is a sign of abhorrence for popular culture or a problem with modernity, I am not advocating a return to a simpler era and an escape to a primitive state (Kammen 1999, 6). I am not calling for a turning back of the clock or the bashing of machines, nor am I narrowly standing on ceremony. I am proposing a wider identification and a deeper explanation of why tradition is such a powerful living faith and force, despite philosophers' predictions of its demise. I have designated folk culture not as some exotic entity outside of our experience but as socially constituted frames or registers in which people invoke and enact tradition (Bronner 2010; Mechling 1997; Nicolaisen 1984). In so doing, all people are subject to the force of tradition and engage in expressive traditions in which they project anxieties, conflicts, biases, and desires they find difficult to reconcile or fulfill in everyday life (Bronner 2007; Dundes 1980, 33–61).

The major branch of learning that has admirably developed tools for analyzing the cultural practices in which we are immersed is folkloristics, conceptualized as the "science of tradition" since the nineteenth century, and I have relied on it greatly to uncover the workings of customs. It has been instrumental among the disciplines in disrupting the hierarchical binary of low and high culture. It has also been important in conceptualizing cultural process in everyday endeavors as well as circumscribing the idea of special objects, performances, environments, or circumstances recognized as folk or traditional. Yet I find that many erstwhile folklorists—not to mention most historians, sociologists, and anthropologists—have stopped short of explaining tradition. Underscoring the idea of tradition as hidden, exotic, or unknown, they have endeavored to isolate tradition as nonnormative "in the field," among extraordinary groups, in remote locations, or deep in the recesses of antiquarian archives. Following the pattern of society, they tend to treat it in geometric terms as a given rather than as a problem to be reasoned out or proved (Popper 1949, 36). As I have shown in *Following Tradition* (1998), they may interpret the texts or describe their performances so as to argue for tradition's artistry, but they are hesitant to investigate the cultural undersides of ordinary events or to delve into the nonliteral meanings of expressive texts. They do a marvelous job of contextualizing traditions and observing their consequences but refrain from speculating on why those texts and performances are, or were, enacted in the first place (Bronner 2006a). Many students of folk culture have abstained from exploring causation and correlation not stated by the tradition-bearers they encounter. Preferring literal or dramaturgical approaches that emphasize surface meanings, they have avoided symbolist or psychological reasoning in locating the sources of cultural practice (Dundes 1997c, 2005).

I use the platform of *Explaining Traditions* to argue that tradition is misunderstood as something that is followed blindly, something that everyone does or performs "just to be nice" or even "just for the hell of it." Tradition is enacted for good reason, often outside the awareness of participants in cultural activities, as strategies of maintaining social identities and connections, communicating symbols and values to themselves and others, and projecting and attempting to resolve their anxieties and conflicts. The theory of tradition I am working with is one in which practices (in the sense of being behaviorally repeated and framed culturally) draw attention to tradition as an ideational force by being prescriptive (enacted because of precedent and often varied based on present circumstances), structured (containing a logic and sequence of enactment), and connotative (constituted with associative meanings in addition to an explicit or denotative purpose). Traditions and the folk process they represent should invite explorations beneath the surface of what we see and hear, even if this involves a certain amount of speculation as well as rationalization. In cultural practice, tradition is invoked, evoked, enacted, varied, construed, and constituted with a hidden or sublimated logic that warrants explanation.

I hasten to add that I am not suggesting one grand explanation to account for all of tradition. There are instances when tradition is evoked as an antidote to the accelerating pace of technology (see chapter 4) or as a part of technology, such as the Internet, where it is constructed as a form of social control or what some practitioners call democratization (see chapter 10). Tradition is invoked as the basis of society (see chapter 3) or construed as its antithesis (see chapter 8). I pursue cases in which different versions of tradition conflict in the same group or location or between generations (see chapters 5 and 7). I do not claim that tradition is intrinsically salutary or triumphant; I discuss one case in which a tradition failed as a cultural strategy and analyze the reasons for its decline (chapter 6). The connecting thread is that tradition frames the precedent by which present actions and beliefs are evaluated. It represents continuity in lives and places viewed as discontinuous, or at least unsettled. Tradition is intrinsically prescriptive and socially constituted; it does not carry the rule of law, although it implies authority. By invoking tradition, one offers a pattern that can be repeated, altered, adapted, and indeed broken.

My goal is to present in varying social circumstances symbolist or rationalist models of explanation that draw conclusions from the evidence of objects, texts, and practices in cultural scenes, locales, or frames. Of special concern to tradition's relevance to political and ethical life are scenes of conflict among communities in terms of the choice of actions representing continuity and discontinuity. Often these clashes result from different perceptions of the connotations tradition has or should have. This approach expands the idea of "parabolic meaning of traditional things at moments of deeply felt social and cultural change" I offered in *Grasping Things* (1986b, 213). In that book, I examined the configuration of cultural scenes and objects to communicate symbolic parables designed to persuade and hold moral as well as practical meaning. That book, like this one, presents cultural scenes, beliefs, and activities from different locations and times that raise similar questions of why they do what they do. *Explaining Traditions* broadens the coverage of material from objects to speech, narratives, beliefs, games, gestures, and rituals. It updates the behavioral frames by which people operate, expanding into digital culture as well as revisiting some historic preindustrial sites and scenes.

In this book, I expand on symbolic modes of activity in the conduct of life I call *praxis*, after the Aristotelian distinction of action whereby the doing—the processes involved and the conditions present, rather than solely the end—is paramount. The practice is the repeatable physical event—such as shooting an animal framed culturally as "traditional" hunting—whereas the praxis is the metaphorical sense of hunting, such as being in the woods and relating to nature, representing individual freedom reminiscent of a pioneer heritage, shopping for bargains, or locating lost objects (I elaborate on this example in *Killing Tradition* [2008]). Even if the undertaking does not result in "bagging a buck," in folk parlance, participants refer to the activity as "going hunting" and frame it as well as symbolize it as a distinctive experience.

By denoting fundamental activities imbued with metaphorical potential, praxic activities often refer to political and ethical values. I begin with building and making, material activities that we all engage in, and use rhetorically for creation. Other common actions that serve as cultural metaphors include personalizing jokes, telling stories, gaining ground in football, and logging on to the Internet. Some practices or folk behaviors are special to a group, such as joke telling among Pennsylvania Germans; others are related to a time, such as intergenerational African American storytelling in the post–civil rights era. In either case, they serve to raise broader questions involving continuity and discontinuity in gender, occupational, regional, religious, age, and ethnic settings.

I lay out the basis for my explanations conceptually and methodologically in the first two chapters. From there, the structure of the book proceeds from historical examples of houses, environments, rituals, legends, and folktales to more contemporary activities that are often overlooked as folkloric—sports and the Internet. In addition to showing the content of tradition (*traditum*, or the material transmitted), I give attention to the process of tradition (*traditio*, or the transmission or manner of learning), especially for those activities often presumed to be highly organized and strictly denotative. I am particularly concerned about tradition as an adaptation to the life course, and I give examples among children, adolescents, and older adults of folk culture's logic at life's milestones and in different ethnic and regional contexts.

To sum up the problem, I offer Stephen Crane's brief poem on tradition penned in 1905 as a new century began, filled with worries about the new displacing the old:

Tradition, thou art for suckling children,
Thou art the enlivening milk for babes;
But no meat for men is in thee.
Then—But, alas, we are babes.

Crane understood, I believe, the significance of tradition defining human vitality and serving as the root of mature identity. Tradition is stated as a given in the poem, something known intuitively rather than defined. Puzzled by the denial of the life force of tradition, he reminded readers of their defense mechanisms that may account for their distorted modern self-image. My intention is to explain that force as well as its position today. As you will see, I indeed find wisdom and reason "out of the mouths of babes," from the cradle to the grave.

1

Defining Tradition

On the Meaning and Politics of a "Handy" Concept

Pick up a paper. There you are likely to read columnists who express astonishment that traditions associated with "the way things were" persist, no less get nurtured by folks today. These reporters immersed in and, indeed, promoting events new and now take pen in hand to account for a supposedly improbable situation of a traditional turn. Basing their bewildered reaction on the assumption that modernity sweeps away the past, chroniclers of the present imply that tradition needs to be displaced rather than adapted in order for society to move forward. Representative of this attitude is a headline in the venerable newsmagazine *U.S. News & World Report:* "A Return to Tradition" (Tolson 2007). "Something curious is happening in the wide world of faith," author Jay Tolson observes, and he makes sure to add that it "defies easy explanation or quantification." He elaborates that this "curious" return to tradition in religion means "past practices, observances, and customary ways of worshipping." Several keywords arise in conjunction with this reported tradition: *past practices*, whether in a previous epoch or generation, implying actions recognizable, presumably, as rituals apart from everyday life, *observances* suggesting a continuous belief, and *customary ways* connoting some group's norms.

But hold on. What is this idea of tradition that Tolson assumes his readers know intuitively if not scientifically? Tradition, he implies, went away or was banished, presumably as society modernized, and now it has mysteriously reappeared. In this usage of tradition, characteristics of tradition appear to be collectively understood—it involves continuity in time, it can be seen in actions that draw attention to themselves, and it implies social connections. What makes this "movement" truly curious in Tolson's opinion, though, is that tradition can be new and old at the same time, for he treats tradition as a vestige of the remote past. He writes of the innovation of tradition in the modern context, commenting that "even while drawing on deep traditional resources, many participants are creating something new within the old forms." He mentions self-organizing groups of young Christian adults who may use a piece of bagel for communion or independent or "nontraditional" *minyan* (among Jews, the quorum required for communal worship) in "strangely innovative ways" devoted to "recapturing those traditions that modernizers dismissed as relics." Tolson reports heated controversies about the state of "traditionalism" in Islam as more young Muslims embrace "outward symbols of their devotion—women wearing head scarves, men growing beards," but elders argue whether what has been called "a highly puritanical reformist Islam" runs "contrary to the deeper traditions of the faith." In the context of a secular newsmagazine, it appears that religion is the bellwether of tradition in society. In the end, Tolson reports the phenomenon rather than analyzes it, although he seeks an explanation for what he calls a "new regard for tradition."

Notices of tradition in the news are hardly restricted to the "world of faith," although even in the secular sphere, tradition's hold on its adherents is often questioned. Perhaps the most contentious debate to open the twenty-first century was over "traditional marriage." The public rhetoric of marriage had rarely needed a modifier previously, but in light of the actions of states such as Massachusetts, which legalized same-sex marriage in 2004, a heated public discourse raged over the importance of tradition in establishing marriage as a legally recognized union between a man and a woman. Four years later, the eyes of the nation turned toward California, where voters approved Proposition 8 (known colloquially as "Prop 8"), changing the state constitution to read: "only marriage between a man and a woman is valid and recognized in California." Although the word *tradition* did not appear on the ballot, television campaigns blared the message: "Voting YES means restore traditional marriage." The implication was that nontraditional marriage—that is, same-sex unions—is unnatural and socially disruptive. "Traditional marriage," the message suggested, was pragmatically and ethically "tried and true" because it had stood the test of time.

If traditional marriage has worked for eons and, presumably, has taken on other alternatives in the process, should the practice be changed? What if the rhetoric changed from marriage being a tradition guided by normative custom to being a legal right? One answer to this question came in the courts (Eskridge 1993). Tradition was especially evident in *In re Marriage Cases*, filed on May 15, 2008, which consolidated six separate lawsuits alleging that the City and County of San Francisco had acted unlawfully by issuing marriage licenses to same-sex couples. In that case, an appellate justice who joined the majority opinion pointed out that both same-sex and mixed-sex unions are tied together by tradition:

> The nuance at this moment in history is that the institution (marriage) and emerging institution (same-sex partnerships) are distinct and, we hope, equal. We hope they are equal because of the great consequences attached to each. Childrearing and *passing on culture and traditions* are potential consequences of each. To the degree that any committed relationship provides love and security, encourages fidelity, and creates a supportive environment for children it is entitled to respect. Whether it must be called the same, or supported by the state as equal to the traditional model, only time and patient attention to the models at issue will tell. (*In re Marriage Cases* 2008, 17; emphasis added)

Gay advocates argued that a model for a ritual of marriage, known as "commitment ceremonies," already had the status of cultural tradition tantamount to a wedding after several decades of ritual use (Ochs 2011).

The involvement of children raised the stakes of tradition by suggesting that intergenerational continuity and morals had deteriorated as a result of social innovations. This was apparent in the related argument over "traditional values" and multiculturalism. Implied in the brandishing of "traditional values" as an accusative slogan is a breakdown of filial piety in favor of the individualistic "do your own thing" of modernism. Even monuments to the Ten Commandments, with the admonishment to "honor thy father and thy mother" (indicating an attitude toward the moral authority of the past in addition to social relationships), had been ordered removed from federal government buildings and public schools, leading to a seismic reaction in print and in cyberspace (Dokupil 2005; Lupu, Masci, and Tuttle 2007). In a well-publicized case, Alabama Chief Justice Roy Moore was removed for defying a U.S. Court of Appeals order to remove a 2.5-ton granite monument from the state courthouse in 2003 because it violated the separation of church and state. Blogger Marci Hamilton (2003), a professor at the Cardozo School of Law, defended the decision by writing, "In Judge Moore's world, Alabamians—and all Americans who might have had business in the Alabama courts—who did not share Moore's religious worldview would have had to walk through a courthouse lobby that sent a message that their tradition was, at best, second-class." This is old-fashioned, Old South thinking, she implied, and "fortunately, we don't live in Judge Moore's world." Moore, a supporter of what he calls "moral law," which acknowledges God in law and government, invoked tradition in his appeal to the U.S. Supreme Court by declaring, "Traditionally, the acknowledgment of God was not considered a religious test" (*Moore v. Judicial Inquiry* 2004, 10). This association of tradition with religious belief was significant because of his claim that the state could not force a person to "profess a belief or disbelief in any religion." To underscore this point, he cited the 1946 case of *Girouard v. United States*, in which the court stated, "The [religious] test oath is abhorrent to our tradition." To Moore's way of thinking, it was a "tradition hailed" by the nation's founding fathers (*Moore v. Judicial Inquiry* 2004, 14–15). The reference to "founding traditions" showed up in many letters and blogs on both sides of the issue, viewing the incident as proof of the country's conflict with democratic principles. The popular press, as the epitome of modern popular culture, was culpable, according to one representative letter: "While our news media puts down anyone who stands for the Ten Commandments, our country is slowly deteriorating with a reckless disregard for the very principles our country was founded on" (Fendley and Level 2009). The rhetoric implies that morality is a lagniappe of fidelity to tradition (see Glassie 1983; Vlach 1989).

The aforementioned letter echoes the public brouhaha over Vice President Dan Quayle's complaint in 1992 that "traditional values" had broken down in the United States, referring to the choice of the title character on the television show *Murphy Brown* to raise a child out of wedlock (Bronner 2000a, 148–51). The issue was still percolating years later when, in his short-lived presidential campaign, Quayle contrasted a traditionalist agenda for "middle-class family values" against radical, glitzy "Hollywood values" (McGrory 1997). Tradition in this rhetoric belongs to good God-fearing folk showing fidelity to their lineage; the decadent others, characterized as rich, urban, self-serving, egotistical, and media crazed, have something faddish that subverts the ethical intimacy of a rooted social circle. The use of tradition in "traditional values" connotes what I call *culturalism*, a belief that social stability is gained by a process of sifting out undesirable trends as a result of values being handed down from one generation to another. This kind of tradition provides a sense of belonging to a shared experience judged to be preferable to others. The keyword *multiculturalism* is more present oriented and implies a relativism by which various experiences are tolerated or even encouraged, rather than judged and sifted out, and are then transmitted among peers rather than from parents to children. Groups involved in multiculturalism have their own plural traditions that are not filtered through the cloth of values, even though critics may allege that they are inferior because they lack the tradition of culturalism.

Here is more food for thought on the matter: prompted by the debate, Burger King Corporation bought half-page advertisements in hundreds of newspapers to issue a pointed "Letter to the American People" in which it committed itself to working toward strengthening family bonds. The text trumpeted the company's support of "traditional American values," which the hamburger franchiser swore to support with programs "that reflect the values that they [the American people] are trying to *instill in their children*" (Quillen 1990; emphasis added). Intoning a different take on traditional values from the other side of the political fence, Hillary Clinton made news with her message of social responsibility and equity in a highly publicized book that supposedly took its title from a Nigerian folk proverb: "it takes a village to raise a child" (Clinton 1996, 11–13). Although proverb specialists doubted the African attribution, they could not deny Clinton's rhetorical strategy of invoking a tradition from a folk society to underscore the power of social cooperation (Mieder 2011). Not wanting to have the mantle of tradition removed from her party's political shoulders, Clinton's subtitle, *And Other Lessons Children Teach Us*, was in direct response to the reverence afforded handed-down parental or past wisdom from the traditionalist camp. In presidential candidate Bob Dole's acceptance speech at the 1996 Republican National Convention, he retorted, "It does not take a village to raise a child. It takes a family" (Nnaemeka 2000). For Clinton, a link existed between community and the kind of inclusive tradition she espoused for America's heart and soul. The representatives of various political stripes can agree that, for them, tradition connotes socially constructed ideas of family and community as well as faith.

Some causes are blatantly antitraditional, however, because of the view that tradition stands against social change and cultural diversity. In 2004 journalist Alexandra Robbins scored a popular best seller with a critique of the American college sorority system. She laid the blame for the system's problems squarely on tradition as a club of authority swinging with brutal force on young people. She made news with her charge that sororities' "revulsion to change, euphemized as a devotion to tradition, is what keeps the sororities ignorant and intolerant" (Robbins 2004, 322). She castigated sorority chapters for perpetuating drug use, violence, mental and verbal abuse, prostitution, racism, forced binge drinking, nudity, cheating, and eating disorders—all, in her words, "in the name of tradition" (11). As evidence of the oppressive authority of tradition, she quoted a sorority sister who seemed horrified at the author's suggestion that practices such as running girls through a gauntlet (known as "Pigs' Run," "Running of the Bulls," or "Squeal Day") could be challenged: "you don't even question the tradition. You just do it" (2). In response to the charge that sororities do not embrace diversity and multiculturalism, a campus official told Robbins, "This is a system steeped in tradition, and I think that's part of the problem. Chapters are afraid to go first. I think there's an unarticulated pressure toward sameness, which fosters racism and a homogeneity they'll never see the rest of their lives" (237). In this rhetoric, tradition is both a mode of thought involving fidelity to precedent and a kind of practice that draws attention to itself because of its ritualistic, symbolic content. Either way, it sounds bad, even loony. In the critical context used, it feels static, primitive, unreasonable, and repressive (see Kolakowski 1971). The central complaint from Robbins and other critics is that it is out of step with the enlightened spirit of the modern day.

Many sorority pledges accept, if not venerate, sorority institutions' attachment to the power of tradition, not because of ignorance or intolerance but because of what they view as an admirable process of attaining sisterhood in the midst of a mammoth, often discordant campus culture. Complaining that modernity has also brought an alienating, overwhelming mass culture that makes people feel like small cogs in a giant industrial wheel, organizations such as sororities and fraternities market their "we-ness"—a coupling of social solidarity and mutual aid with a group small enough so that everyone knows one another. Sororities are old institutions featuring social bonding and identity building that routinely occur in a lineage through many generations. This aura of tradition is conveyed through rituals, songs, secret passwords, and initiations that senior sisters pass down to younger pledges in an annual, much-anticipated round of activities known as "rush." Rather than remaining static, the rush tradition had been subject to reform since the late twentieth century, including the increased regulation and, in many cases, elimination of pledging and hazing.

In his own investigation, Alan D. DeSantis found that sorority sisters were dismayed that tradition had eroded rather than, as Robbins tells the tale, intensified. DeSantis reports a reaction from sisters that would have horrified Robbins—a call for a "return to tradition." "We need to start pledging again," a senior Omega told him; "I think we would be much tighter" (2007, 187–88). DeSantis quotes another sister who does not mince words when stating her opinion about the elimination of pledging traditions: "These girls are great, beautiful, blah, blah, blah, but they suck. Nobody pledges anymore, so sororities are nothing more than girls' clubs. They do nothing that makes them respect their chapter; *there's nothing they have to do*" (188; emphasis added). For her, tradition was more than sorority rhetoric or an unwritten guide to action; it gained its significance from practice or purposeful activity. She was not convinced by all the blurbs about tradition being important in the official chapter literature. For her, tradition translated to ritualistic action. It was a vital force for an organization that purported to provide its members with a kind of social intimacy one might culturally associate with a tribe or a family.

In contrast to Robbins's journalistic depiction of tradition as promoting social uniformity, repression, and the status quo in organizational life, most contemporary folklorists (whose main business is to gauge tradition) conceptualize it as a tool of diversity, expressiveness, social change, and tolerance in a homogenizing mass, modern society (Kurin 2002; Mechling 1993; Ó Giolláin 2003; Shimamura 2003). Surveying efforts to preserve endangered minority languages and identify what he calls subaltern or ethnic cultural pockets threatened or dominated by mass societies, Diarmuid Ó Giolláin concludes, "One of the greatest contributions of folkloristics was its engagement with cultural diversity" (2003, 45). It achieved this as a result of attention to, and reverence for, variations of narratives generated by ordinary people in different cultural groups who chose not to follow national or even universalized "master narratives" imposed from above. In relation to modernity, the representation of folklore as indigenous, authentic expressions of ethnic, regional, occupational, and religious groups suggests a heterogeneous culture in danger of being standardized and homogenized. Placing *folk* before tradition could sound redundant in folkloristic work, but it has drawn attention, particularly in Western industrialized societies, to power relationships between traditions generated orally as an instrument of ordinary, often marginalized groups and official or commercial culture (see Bauman and Briggs 2003, 163–96; Bronner 1998, 73–140). In theory, everyone has traditions, and *folk* used as a modifier signals expressive forms such as stories, games, rituals, houses, and crafts that are learned and transmitted in the unofficial social settings of family, play, work, and community. Calling these things *folk* means that they are traditional, but it also has a special naturalistic association with groupness, ordinariness, and often disempowerment, besides the idea of continuity with the past embedded in tradition.

The linkage of folk with tradition to distinguish redemptive cultural artistry emanating from the ground up is evident in the basic folkloristic approach of collecting and exhibiting samples from a naturalistic "field" before the tradition disappears (Ó Giolláin 2003, 3–4). In many Western countries, this linkage is associated with efforts to maintain the idea of community as well as to preserve localized arts produced by social intimacy as a hedge against massification. For example, Mary Hufford, from her vantage at the Library of Congress, wrote that, "in the interest of the general welfare of the Nation to preserve, support, revitalize, and disseminate American folklife traditions and arts," the American Folklife Preservation Act of 1976 "reflects a growing awareness among the American people that cultural diversity, which distinguishes and strengthens us as a nation, is also a resource worthy of protection" (2002, 239).

As president of the American Folklore Society, Henry Glassie produced a socially conscious manifesto for tradition as a keyword of folkloristic practice: "If tradition is a people's creation out of their own past, its character is not stasis but continuity; its opposite is not change but oppression, the intrusion of a power that thwarts the course of development. Oppressed people are made to do what others will them to do. They become slaves in the ceramic factories of their masters. Acting traditionally, by contrast, they use their own resources—their own tradition, one might say—to create their own future, to do what they will themselves to do. They make their own pots" (Glassie 1995, 396). Tradition in this view is able to empower rather than disable groups by being a resource for creativity and social well-being. Tradition allows participants in culture to be directed toward the future because it provides a place to start, a foundation for adaptation and diversification that naturally occurs as people adjust it to their own needs and situations (Popper 1949, 47). Generated from small groups in various locations, tradition in this sense is not monolithic. Instead, it represents multiple socially recognized frames of reference for how things look or how they should be done. In theory, it allows people to choose and to be themselves.

Glassie's reference to ordinary pots is a reminder that, in the hands of art critics, tradition often refers to valued schools or styles of work associated with the past. Renowned twentieth-century poet T. S. Eliot worried that in the rush to claim originality in art, the value of tradition as a timeless presence was unacknowledged. He wrote: "No poet, not artist of any art, has his complete meaning alone. His significance, his appreciation is the appreciation of his relation to the dead poets and artists. You cannot value him alone; you must set him, for contrast and comparison among the dead. I mean this as a principle of aesthetic, not merely historical, criticism. The necessity that he shall conform, that he shall cohere, is not one-sided; what happens when a new work of art is created is something that happens simultaneously to all the works of art which preceded it" (Eliot 1960, 4–5). Philosopher Theodor Adorno, meanwhile, complained that arts in modern society are lacking because tradition is gone. He argued that tradition is downright feudal because, unlike antiquity, divisions between a formally educated elite and a robust, if illiterate, peasantry are more apparent in a medieval age (often thought of as a "golden age" for folklore). Tradition, by

Adorno's account, disappeared when technology displaced the artisan: "In view of the technological modes of production, handicraft has as little substance as the concept of craftsmanship itself, which once ensured tradition, aesthetic tradition in particular" (Adorno 1993, 75).

Writing in the twenty-first century, Michael Owen Jones countered that craft and tradition have crucial functions to perform in modern arts. Though acknowledging that "researchers usually treat tradition separate from considerations of originality in art and individuality in society," he observes that "many people, however, draw upon tradition to create objects or to perform, and thereby fabricate a personal identity and social role for themselves" (2000, 115–16). One notable sign of this in art history is the use of folk art, such as weather vanes, samplers, and signs by the first generation of modernist artists in the early twentieth century, as precedents for the altered perspective and primitivism characteristic of their new abstract art (Rumford 1980).

With the art world's bias toward originality in mind, I was drawn to the newsstand to scour the many art magazines available for public consumption. My eye fixed on the cover of the respected architectural magazine *Dwell*, subtitled *At Home in the Modern World*. The image on the cover certainly bore out this theme, showing a casually dressed woman lounging on furniture with sharp, streamlined surfaces and the open space associated with modern design. Yet the banner for the issue proclaimed: "Mixing Modern with Tradition." The editor's note explained the connection between individuality and modernism at home: "Notably, it's the place where we feel free to be ourselves, make our own judgments, and create a world formed entirely by our own views" (Grawe 2007, 41). More than celebrating the self rather than the collective, *modern*, in the editor's view, is the fashion of the moment with an eye toward what lies ahead; it represents progress as "what's new." Yet, echoing Eliot's idea of the creative spirit, *Dwell*'s editor declared for both artist and consumer: "Truly being in the modern world—as if walking some infinite tightrope—requires a cognizance of the steps that got us here and enables us to maintain a path forward." Instead of referring to tradition as restoration, the examples of *intersection* between past and present include a San Francisco home whose skin exudes "happenstance post-modernism" but whose "bones are 1908 Victorian" and a 200-year-old building in Vilnius, where the tradition is "impossible to really understand if you're not Lithuanian" (Grawe 2007, 41). The implication is that a sense of tradition is culturally ingrained and difficult to articulate, although a localized analogy emerges in the magazine's rhetoric of culture: modern is to tradition as present is to past, and as elite is to folk. Characteristic of a modernist position, the editors refer to tradition as tacit knowledge (McKeon 2004; Turner 1994, 113–18; see also Adam and Hardy 2008; Geertz 2000, 167–234).

Besides relating how people feel at home, the intersection of tradition and modern also arises in what consumers "buy into." Advertisers regularly appeal to shoppers to get the latest model, which is presumably the most modern and up-to-date. The contents are new and improved, and the packaging has been modernized to reflect the change. Yet shoppers are also persuaded by appeals to tradition to form a bond of trust with the product, or, as one marketing adviser postulates, "the more stressed-out we are by the financial crisis and other problems, the more we unconsciously adhere to familiar, comforting rituals" of tradition (Lindstrom 2009, 10). The example this adviser gives under the heading "We Fall for 'Tradition'" is Corona beer, which overtook Heineken as the best-selling imported beer in the American market. How? Consumers came to believe that squeezing a lime into a Corona beer is a time-honored Mexican tradition that enhances the beer's taste or fights off germs. The adviser notes the association of tradition with antiquity and a degree of mysticism in the reported perception that the ritual derives from ancient Mesoamerican folklore. According to the company, however, the ritual dates only to 1981, when a bartender bet a friend that he could start a trend by popping a lime wedge into a long-neck bottle (Lindstrom 2009, 11). Regardless of the practice's origin or the company's advertising campaign, consumers' cognitive associations with tradition play a pivotal role in the perception, as well the practice, of the ritual.

If many marketing appeals familiarize tradition by telling consumers they should do what others do, one prominent advertisement blanketing the airwaves every winter points out tradition as something apart or special. CBS promotes its coverage of the Masters golf tournament with the slogan, "A Tradition Like No Other—The Masters." The almighty voice-over does not elaborate why other traditions do not equal the Masters, but it is clear that viewers are supposed to believe that the Masters has a special aura. It is not because the Masters is the oldest. Established in 1934, the Masters is actually the newest of the four major golf championships; the British Open dates to 1860, and the

U.S. Open and PGA Championship were organized in 1895 and 1916, respectively. The Masters' purse is not the largest, either, but broadcast images suggest that it attracts the best in the game. One ritual connotation is that the Masters is the first of the major tournaments played in the year. Scheduled for the first week in April, it signals the advent of spring as well as the golf season, along with all the associations of fertile greenery and invigorating sunshine. In line with this symbolism, one of the tournament's venerated traditions is the donning of a green jacket by the winner. Caddies traditionally wear green Masters caps and white jumpsuits, and the defending champion can count on being assigned caddy number "1." Honoring continuity with the past, former champions hit a ceremonial tee shot on the morning of the first round.

One thing that sets the Masters apart is the size of the tournament. It is smaller than the other major championship because participants need to be invited to play by its sponsor, the Augusta National Golf Club. Perhaps this association with *Gemeinschaft*-like "we-ness," in the double sense of being small and being a bounded, familiar group (and located in the romanticized, storied American South), raises images of being drenched in tradition (Hostetler 1993, 9; see also Bronner 2005d). The club is known for imposing its own genteel terminology on broadcasters, such as *second cut* for *rough* and *bunker* for *sand trap*. It also worked with CBS to convey a noncommercial image by reducing the number of advertisements aired. With their elite connections, the club and the sport do not support the notion that tradition is something reserved for remote or marginalized folk societies (Cossar 2005).

Yet the Augusta National Golf Club was accused of being nonnormative, that is, not keeping up with the egalitarian times, when it refused to admit women into its membership. Martha Burk, chair of the National Council of Women's Organizations (NCWO), raised a swell of protest in 2002 against the club's male-only membership policy (Nylund 2003). The controversy played out in the media as the NCWO pressured CBS and corporate sponsors to pull out of the Masters and shut it down if the club did not change its policy. The strongly worded answer from club chairman William "Hootie" Johnson invoked tradition in its unapologetic defense:

> We will not be bullied, threatened or intimidated. Obvious-
> ly, Dr. Burk and her colleagues view themselves as agents of

change, and feel any organization that has stood the test of time and has *strong roots of tradition* and does not fit their profile, needs to be changed. We do not intend to become a trophy in their display case. There may well come a day when women will be invited to join our membership, but that timetable will be ours, and not at the point of a bayonet. We do not intend to be further distracted by this matter. We shall *continue our traditions* and prepare to host the Masters as we have since 1934. (Brown 2002; emphasis added)

For Johnson, taking the position of being victimized by feminists holding the mantle of modernization for public culture, and taking the stand of being guided by tradition, held virtue even if it meant being ostracized. And he insisted that holding on to traditions did not mean being averse to change, which would follow its own *natural* course. Despite the rancor raised, Augusta, as a private association, maintained its exclusive policy, and the Masters continued its self-definition as a "tradition like no other."

In modern-as-they-come team sports, coaches and players regularly refer to the importance of tradition in bonding the players together into a unit and providing a motivation for success. They contrast the competitive team to the modernistic expectation of participants acting as self-indulgent individuals going in different directions; the coach uses tradition to fashion a disciplined social interdependence and to build loyalty to a unit bigger than themselves. In my playing days, coaches screamed about tradition to get us to work and move together "as one." Diversity was not a function of tradition in the coaches' minds.

Looking to quantify the special association between sports and tradition, I surveyed headlines containing the word *tradition* in one city daily over a two-year period and found that sports topics had the highest frequency of references to tradition after holidays, local events, religion, and family profiles (Bronner 1998, 48–55). I expected there to be more headlines about tradition attached to national themes, but the numbers suggest that the press prefers *tradition* in conjunction with locality and ethnicity. In sports coverage, teams tend to formalize links to locality and bring tradition into texts to convey pride in the organization over the years. I find this consequential because folkloristic scholarship has tended to neglect sports as too formally organized for an evaluation of cultural tradition. In the public discourse of the press, however, sports teams are the most recognizable location of groupness in modern life. If one goes specifically to "see the Amish" and other communal groups to gaze at tradition apart from modernity, one understands teams as organized groups fostering traditions within modern life. Moreover, there is a kind of functional assumption that players fit certain roles on teams, or players are supposed to sacrifice their individualities for the sake of the team.

Press coverage frequently suggests that players come and go, but the tradition of the team continues. One reporter wondered whether, "in a sports world that is increasingly me-first and money-centric, does tradition and legacy have any real impact on modern athletes anymore?" (Perez 2008). One answer came in 2008, when Bob Stoops tried to explain to reporters why he could not be bought away from his coaching position at the University of Oklahoma, even though he could earn more money and get more media exposure elsewhere. He talked about the backing of the administration, from the university president through the athletics director; the fans; the nice campus; and wanting "to finish what he started." But it appeared that reporters were not swallowing his story. One columnist even wrote, "Who wouldn't take the sun and fun of Florida over the grit and dust of Norman, right?" (Pells 2008). Flustered, Stoops declared that what clinched his final decision to stay was the fact that "the University of Oklahoma *had the tradition*," and it was more than Florida had (Pells 2008; emphasis added).

That emphatic high note was supposed to end speculation about Stoops's departing for greener pastures, but his claim that one school could have more tradition than another also raised the question of how tradition is measured. If the measure is the number of national championships, Florida could claim the crown of tradition. Oklahoma boasted only seven national championships since 1950, whereas Florida had claimed the title in 1996, 2006, and 2008 (when it beat Oklahoma to gain it) and also had the distinction of being the winningest college football team in the nation between 1990 and 2008. For Stoops, though, Oklahoma had a folk or populist spirit (related, perhaps, to what the columnist referred to as folksy grit and dust), and football had been central to the social and cultural life of the down-to-earth region for a longer period. He implied that he perceived a special historical, even spiritual, legacy at the institution (if football can be thought of as a civil religion) and a heightened social connection that added value to his position and pushed his team to victory. Tradition in his rhetoric was not something concrete, but in his mind, it was certainly a force to be reckoned with.

These examples show the need to sort out various terms—*tradition, traditions, traditional,* and *traditionalism*—as well as the layers of meaning for their association with *cultural, multicultural, folk, lore,* and *folklorist.* In this chapter, I address these matters by first evaluating the different senses of tradition in rhetorical use and then by making sense of the politics and scholarship to explain traditions.

Definitions and Perspectives of Tradition

One problem with defining *tradition,* evident in the previously mentioned examples, is that, when used alone, it carries various meanings. When set up at one end of a binary with modernity, law, science, or innovation, it acts as a foil for some other privileged concept. Most linguistic as well as philosophical considerations of the word begin with a singular source, citing the Latin root *tradere,* "to hand over or deliver," and adapting it to the popular idea that tradition is "handed down" from generation to generation, especially by oral means. This gap between the linguistic root and popular discourse raises the question of how speakers moved from the Roman sense of a social act of giving material goods contemporaneously to the dominant narrative of receiving knowledge from a predecessor.

The answer lies in the changing perception of the distinction of knowledge gained by tradition. Historian David Gross shows the source of tradition in Roman jurisprudence, suggesting a literal meaning of tradition as a material transaction (1992, 9). Roman laws of inheritance dealt with goods considered valuable, and meanings arose from the root *tradere,* including *traditio* for the process by which transmission occurs and *traditum* for the thing transmitted. Gross points out that *traditio* implies that "(a) something precious or valuable is (b) given to someone in trust after which (c) the person who receives the 'gift' is expected to keep it intact and unharmed out of a *sense of obligation* to the giver" (1992, 9; emphasis in original). As an inheritance, the gift or *traditum* often comes from a predecessor or ancestor, and with it is the expectation that the thing will be cherished and preserved and considered valuable enough to be passed on to someone else (Gross 1992, 9). The obligation to keep and honor the item is driven, presumably, out of respect for the memory (and wishes) of the predecessor, whose name may be obscured over time as the *traditum* is passed on generations later. This sense of obligation shows up in an alternative meaning of *traditio*, "surrender," and suggests an association with authority because the recipient submits to the sway of the elder.

Getting to the abstraction of tradition from Roman law, a metaphorical shift occurred from thing to knowledge, which was probably based on the symbolic connotations of transmitting the *traditum*. One clue is in the rituals accompanying the transmittal. To mark the transfer of a piece of land, an agent physically handed over a clod of dirt to the recipient; to legally recognize the acquisition of a house or a shop, keys would ritually pass from one person to another (Congar 2004, 9). The earth and the keys not only act as a synecdoche for something larger; they also inspire memory and narrative of the possession and the figures associated with it. Enacting *traditio* drew attention to itself by the use of a repeatable symbolic practice that relied on a shared knowledge between agent and recipient about the consequences of the act. The tradition became noticeable in the flow of life because it was ritualized and framed as time out of time; in that special time, differences between present and past collapsed. One was aware in the tradition that the action had precedent, but especially important was a transcendent concern about what it stood for. Other actions, including telling a story or singing a song that evoked the transference of something expressive or valuable received, could be attached to the process of *traditio*. In this way, both tangible and intangible "gifts" recognized by their expressive and connotative characteristics became equated. Recalling what these things represented constituted a narrated knowledge that was not so much institutionally taught or read as it was socially engaged in, in practice. It was a kind of knowledge, or intangible heritage, popularly designated as *lore*. As medieval English scholars began to gloss Latin texts, they indeed used *folclic lār* ("folklike lore") to designate sayings coming out of vernacular or noninstitutional settings and drawing attention to themselves for being expressive or representative of a locality or group, particularly in contrast to the kind of fixed, widely distributed forms represented by the "modern" spread of printing (Mazo 1996, 107). This usage linked to tradition is an antecedent to the terminology of *folklore* as common "knowledge of the people" introduced by English antiquarian W. J. Thoms in 1846 and *Volkskunde* by German and Dutch literati in the late eighteenth century (Boyer 1997; Margry and Roodenburg 2007, 263–64; Vermeulen 1995).

Setting the process of *traditio* apart is its consecutiveness. In a business deal, an agreement is concluded; it does not have to be reenacted to be valid. The business deal is a matter of record. In tradition, transmittal needs to occur repeatedly, often by word of mouth and practice, which further sets it apart from modernization characterized by the rule of official law and record. The socially communicative characteristic of a transaction in tradition is crucial to the perpetuation of lore. Every action in *traditio* involves a giver as well as a recipient, and the participants are aware that something like it has occurred before and will happen after they are gone. They understand that the action of *traditio* is consecutive from one person and one moment to the next. A commonly used metaphor is that they are links in a chain, each separate but connected to one another in a consecutive pattern. The introduction to the mourner's prayer (Kaddish) in Judaism, for example, states that it is "testimony to that unbroken faith which links the generations one to another." Commenting on the ritual, famed philanthropist Henrietta Szold observed: "The Kaddish means to me that the survivor publicly and markedly manifests his wish and intention to assume the relation to the Jewish community which his parent had, and that *the chain of tradition* remains unbroken from generation to generation" (Lowenthal 1942, 92–93; emphasis added). Tradition requires agency to continue, and part of the obligation to keep the *traditum* intact is to reenact the process. Traditions can disappear and be revived after lapsing, but psychologically, a fear exists that the chain, or the order, of tradition will be broken if it is not enacted consecutively.

Referring to tradition suggests not only that cultural reproduction occurs but also that meaning may be changed through variable repetition of a precedent that creates a situational or local version. This broadening of the social implication of tradition is a semantic development beyond the one-to-one relationship implied in Roman law. As lore, traditions can be transmitted to a crowd and move in different directions with the travels of the recipients. When individuals engage in the process of *traditio*, traditions vary as they are adapted to different settings or are recalled with changes in content and meaning, even if they are structured similarly to the lore that went before them. As populations move and social needs change, traditions inevitably evolve, increasing or altering by fusion with other traditions, or declining in practice and memory. Cognitively, there may be an inclination to believe that traditions, by their nature as valued social artifacts, grow from simpler to more complex forms in an evolutionary pattern, but this may be countered by a devolutionary belief that modernization and the passage of time render traditions fractions of what they once were (Dundes 1969a). The former belief supports the folk idea that "mighty oaks from little acorns grow," with the corollary view that tradition is a living faith and force; the latter belief often reveals the attitude that modernity and industrialization displace ways of life centered on the primary transmission of wisdom from elders to children.

The reverence for the flowering of tradition in the past commonly supports perceptions of a former "golden age" or the "good old days," where traditions are rooted, whereas the devolutionary outlook frequently supports the conceptualization of traditions as relic manifestations of an unenlightened past (Bronner 1998, 73–140). Participants may be unaware of the origins or original meanings of traditions as they take the form of practices and become integrated into everyday life, such as the unself-conscious cultural practices of shaking hands, bowing, and waving. Consequently, the consecutiveness of *traditio* can be expressed structurally as a circle rather than as a linear progression, typical of the arts from creation to imitation, because of the view that persons are joined together as participants in the dual roles of givers and recipients rather than as originators. Theologian Yves Congar understood this structural basis when he offered the circular relay race as a metaphor for tradition, where runners standing at intervals both take and pass batons and, in the process, are bonded as a team (2004, 9–10). A ritual action is embedded in the transfer of the *traditum* to represent continuity, and, as expressed in the idiom "passing the torch," a responsibility is implied in the handling of the *traditum*.

Recognizing that *tradita* can be preserved as relics without the enactment of *traditio*, Congar makes a distinction between active and passive traditions (2004, 45). In active traditions capable of accretion, an expression is passed by agents often called "tradition bearers" (Shils [1981, 13] refers to them as "custodians" or "exemplars"). Passive traditions contain preserved content, often in the form of recorded or remembered texts, but they are not relayed ritually. In this theologi-cally oriented rhetoric, traditions in the plural refer to expressions or practices, whereas the singular tradition, often capitalized, signifies the totality of belief. For Congar, tradition "encloses and dominates" exis-tence by representing a mode of thought held by believers. In contrast to particularized, plural traditions, a capitalized Tradition broadly the-matizes everything a group does (he used it to universalize Catholi-cism) and often carries a sacred connotation (2004, 10). One can view this usage of a capitalized Tradition as a theme in references to "Judeo-Christian Tradition," "Great Tradition," and "Western Tradition." They may not be culturally constituted by participation, but they are identified, organized, and mapped by institutions. Broadly imagined, the capitalized Tradition points to a shared transcendent faith in the understanding of belief as a truth and value.

Rather than categorizing this kind of tradition as *traditum*, phi-losopher Josef Pieper refers to *tradendum* as "what is supposed to be handed down." It is a useful addition to the lexicon of tradition because it differentiates localized cultural expressions from institutional canons, scriptures, or doctrines (Pieper 2008; Berkhof 2002, 105). *Tradenda* are not practices engaged in socially or things passed on; they are the ideals or values connected organizationally. They have a connection to the sense of tradition as a "mode of thinking," which is often the least con-spicuous to observers but the most pervasive in everyday life.

Much of the semantics of tradition, whether as *traditio, traditum*, or *tradendum*, revolves around the process of "handing," and the im-plication is that the thing being handed over metaphorically has tan-gible value. For many people unaware of Roman law, what is relevant about tradition is the symbolism of social and emotional attachment in the hand. The hand is important to tradition because of its capacity to grasp objects physically and intellectually and attach meanings to them. Being "in hand" suggests the tradition's value of being possessed for human purposes. "Handing it over" as the basis of tradition implies a social connection, much like the linkage in a handshake. Giver and recipient come together at that moment and become familiar as a con-sequence. The image of the hand gives it a "personal touch," the ability to "reach out and touch someone" rather than being thought about in solitude. Being "handed down" brings elders or predecessors into the picture, but in a way that implies a familial tie from one generation to another. In other words, a social bond or identity goes "hand in hand" with tradition. Whereas intellectual pursuits are associated with reading, memorization, and individualized study, knowledge to navigate through one's culture is seen as experiential, that is, gained through "hands-on" experience. "Hands-on" or "hand-me-down" shows social continuity with either a mentor in a workplace or an elder in a family, whereas observers attached to vision imply detachment and perhaps apartness from social norms in the odd minds of visionaries.

The "common knowledge" of handed-down lore takes on a vernacular cast because of the association of handwork and domesticity with tradition, especially the perception that handmade, hand-hewn, or homespun materials are naturally traditional (see Bronner 1986b; Jones 1975). The mechanical-sounding action of handing down may not be deemed intellectual or, more accurately, "scholastic," but it suggests active participation and hence authenticity in culture by the passing of something socially significant involving memory and narrative (Bourdieu 1998, 127–40). It is often "practical" in the sense of being applied to lived experience and variable in social situations (Bourdieu 1990, 80–97).

The *Oxford English Dictionary* notes *authenticity*'s derivation from a Greek term for "firsthand authority." As tradition involves authority given to a precedent framing a present action, authenticity lends prestige to an original action before it is subject to artifice or unsatisfying copying. Rather than being deluded by viewing an item, someone may receive satisfaction from authentic, tangible involvement because he or she benefits from direct experience, as in another Greek source for "one who does a thing himself." The shared quality in tradition and authenticity is, in the words of the dictionary, one of "inherent authority" that comes from being handed down.

Unlike intellectualized sight, which allows for looking broadly out on the horizon or reading alone, the sense of touch represented by the hand is immediate, involves bodily action, and implies certitude. Vision associated with a future orientation and the mechanical reproduction of images in photography became emblematic of modernity. Suggesting handiness as materialized and localized, the practical statement of "business at hand" refers to a matter in front of us that demands immediate attention. In conversation, "wanting to see something" with its reference to distance, is weaker than the possessive, gripping imagery of "wanting to get my hands on something." "Seeing is believing," the English proverb states, but it admonishes in the second part that "feeling's the truth" (Bronner 1982a; Dundes 1980, 86–92). "The hand is quicker than the eye," another proverb reminds people, also suggesting that the power of the hand is often overlooked. One might understand the hold of tradition by noting the "tangible proof" provided by touching with the hand. No doubt, one wants to have the certainty of knowing "hands down," or else behold the mistrust of "virtual images." One therefore longs to be "in touch with reality."

In references to being "handy," handwork is often associated with pragmatic concerns about the conduct of everyday life. Handwork accomplishes tasks and orders or changes one's environment. The hand is directly or personally experienced, so one might be assured, "You're in good hands." One might also be reminded that "one in the hand is worth two in the bush," meaning that the thing in the hand is definite, whereas those things one yearns for off in the distance are uncertain. The root of tradition as an inheritance or gift being handed over is relevant because of the idea that practical wisdom is passed along with the touched thing rather than with the artifice of words. From these associations, a place was opened up cognitively for a type of learning and teaching outside of institutional control. In popular usage, it was a vernacular knowledge or lore related to everyday experience. Tradition as a concept to describe the acquisition of this knowledge through repeated, enculturated practice implies a social, often localized, predisposition that informs one's conduct in life.

Handed-on knowledge is more than the delivery of information. By referring to the hand's ability to gesture and touch, tradition is referential, even symbolic, in the actions produced. More than any other part of the body, the hands are images of symbolic actions and feelings: formed into a fist, folded in prayer, or giving an affectionate pat or caress. As a sign of humanity, hands are valued for their special ability to hold tools—as an extension of the body—and thus work as well as play. The hand itself is often viewed as a tool that requires skills to be productive. Overall, hands are perceived as instruments of purposeful activity. They make things happen.

According to psychologist Susan Goldin-Meadow, "Gesture conveys meaning globally, relying on visual and mimetic imagery. Speech conveys meaning discretely, relying on codified words and grammatical devices" (2005, 25). People link handiness with objects rather than with words because of the hand's ability to grasp and form objects that are supposed to stand the test of time, more so than words uttered in a moment. To me, "mimetic imagery" includes not just imitation but also the enactment of intentional representations, which is especially important for the production of culture. Neuroscientist Merlin Donald, for example, notes that mimetic skills basic to toolmaking, child rearing, and custom rest on the ability to produce "conscious, self-initiated, representational acts that are intentional, but not linguistic," and these constitute the foundation of human culture (1991, 168). This "results in the sharing of knowledge without every member of the group having to reinvent that knowledge," or what we think of as tradition (Donald 1991, 173; Wilson 1999, 48–49).

Although people are often unaware of the hand gestures they make to express emotions or provide information, they understand such movements as a basic form of communication, especially when trying to make themselves understood to someone who does not share the same words or when emphasizing a point. In this way, the handy knowledge of tradition is a fundamental communicative behavior that both underlies speech and is independent of it. These associations affect the perception of tradition because of the cognitive categories of thought expressed as reasoned ideas in words by an individual, whereas tradition is construed as emotional action or gesture that is shared socially.

The source of time in handy knowledge is usually less certain than for institutional work because of tradition's imagery of collectivity and continuity. Saying that something is *old* implies that it can be dated, whereas labeling an artifact or a story as *traditional* means that it has been transmitted *through* time. Tradition's time can refer to the last millennium or last week, but in popular usage it suggests "time immemorial" because tradition's nonlinear associations result in uncertainty about how traditions get started. This reference to time is apparent when *tradition* is used as a synonym for *culture* in the sense of representing the totality of arts, customs, lore, and institutions for a group. Thus, when one reads of "Dutch tradition" or "aboriginal tradition," the compound term emphasizes the culture's long, steady existence, which may not be clear from the use of *culture*, with its connotation of a bounded social group in place (Ben-Amos 1984, 119–21; Hultkrantz 1960, 229–31). Individuals are probably conscious of plural traditions that are repeatable activities, but they consider a singular tradition to be an internalized mode of thinking or worldview.

People are said to be born into tradition as well as participating in traditions, but with the singular mode of thinking, there is an added emphasis on the lifelong effect, which people are probably unaware of because it is all around them. Artist Mamie Harmon, for instance, refers to tradition as "comprising that information, those skills, concepts, products, etc., which one acquires almost inevitably *by virtue of the circumstances to which he is born*. It is not so much deliberately sought (like learning) as absorbed. It is not deliberately invented; rather it develops. It is present in the environment, is accepted, used, transformed, transmitted, or forgotten, without arbitrary impetus from individual minds" (1949, 1:400; emphasis in original).

Linked to the life cycle, tradition revolves around generational time. Ever the historian, Gross declared a minimal stretch of time to be three generations (i.e., two transmissions) for a tradition to be authentic, although folklorists conceive of lore as being traditional or "handed over" spatially by virtue of the fact that someone passes it along to someone else (such as telling a joke one has just heard). What appears to be important is that a precedent for action exists; it is traditional because it resembles something that went before and was known among a social unit. Gross distinguishes tradition's "temporal duration" from history's occurrence in time and summarizes this aspect of tradition's meaning as "continuity between the past and the present" (1992, 10). Upon receiving tradition, according to this perspective, people have a feeling of consecutiveness, the sense that they are part of a sequential chain stretching back in time and from one person or group to another. Tradition is therefore prescriptive by virtue of being repeated because it was done before, in contrast to history, which records what occurred previously (Gross 1992, 8).

Habit and custom also rely on precedent, but they are distinguished from tradition by their relative lack of emphasis on intergenerational connection and symbolic connotation. A habit is an action, often a mannerism, that is regularly repeated until it becomes involuntary. Rather than constituting a connotative message, habit is often considered "routine" by being unvarying, an addiction, or a rote procedure for an individual. Its manifestation in individual behavior is often differentiated from custom, which is a repeated social occasion. Although *traditional* and *customary* are often used interchangeably to refer to the prescriptive repetition of activities based on precedent, customary activities do not have the degree of consecutiveness and connotation expected of tradition. One does not hear of the *chain* or *authority* of custom in the way these terms are applied to tradition. Indeed, an event might be intentionally referred to as a custom to imply that it does not have as strong a consecutive hold on its participants as tradition or that it is irregularly enacted.

Both traditions and customs can be symbolic, but the implication of tradition having a hold from the rhetoric of the hand is that it draws attention to itself by its ritualistic connotation of idea and faith. Social psychologist Edward A. Ross includes the criterion of involvement in the distinction he insightfully draws between custom and tradition: "By custom is meant the transmission of a way of *doing*; by tradition is meant the transmission of a way of *thinking* or *believing*" (Ross 1909, 196; see also Clark 2005, 4). The commonality of tradition and custom is their involvement of action in the form of practice, but tradition often brings into play a mode of thought or social learning associated with lore. Tradition—more than custom—brings out the handing on of values.

Separating brushing one's teeth in the morning as a daily routine or custom from the tradition of the tooth fairy is a quality that has been labeled *phemic* by philosophers, particularly those incorporating theories of language developed by J. L. Austin (1961, 1968; see also Warnock 1989). For some observers, the imaginative content of the tooth fairy, along with other beliefs, gestures, games, and narratives, sets it apart as a tradition; however, many utilitarian practices that are socially or geographically situated, such as craft, medicine, and agriculture, would not be perceived as fantasy or play and yet are viewed as noticeable traditions. Phemic material denotes an implicative message that is impelled to be transmitted, and the material becomes associated with the process of its transmission. According to Austin, the analysis of these messages needs to account for the way they are *ordinarily used*, that is, transacted with others, to elucidate meaning. He would call the production of sound a *phone*, whereas a *pheme* is a performative utterance with a definite sense of meaning. Colloquially, a *pheme* is thought to "say something" that might be used on different occasions of utterance with different senses (Warnock 1989, 120).

The term *pheme* comes from Pheme of Greek mythology, who personified renown and was characterized by rumor spreading (Austin was trained in the classics as well as linguistics). Symbolically important to the conceptualization of tradition as consecutive transmission *in vulgus populo* is her status as a daughter of the earth and one of the mightiest, if not the most elegant or beautiful, of the goddesses (Burr 1994, 231; Chisholm 1910, 158). She had a proclivity to repeat what she learned, for better or worse (in art, she is often depicted with multiple tongues, eyes, and ears), to the point that it became common knowledge. Along the way, though, the information varied greatly and was often made larger in proportion to the original bit of news. Pheme did not fabricate knowledge; her skill was in framing material in such a way that it would be passed around. She was a relay station of sorts, serving as both recipient and transmitter of earthy material that drew attention to itself by being shared from person to person. The knowledge transmitted was known as much for the process it went through as for its content. Because it was subjected to this transmittal process associated with earthy rumor, the content invited evaluation of its truth and meaning. In its "larger" form, the material raised questions about its sources and its combinations and recombinations, forming a whole with multiple connotative layers created along the path of transmission.

In Plato's dialogues, *pheme* shows up as a circulating rumor or report, but in repetition, it has religious and political values embedded into speech used by a collective of people. In a dialogue about what constitutes an ideal city, Socrates relates a Phoenician story but points out that the narrative is more than news of an event; it represents the involvement of a whole generation of parents transmitting the material to children with a moralistic message about proper behavior (Grube 1992, 92). He declares, "let us leave the matter to later tradition (*hē phēme agagēi*)" (Ophir 1991, 95). Pheme, in the long term, emphasizes the persistence of the material and the process by which it is preserved. In classicist Luc Brisson's reading, "*Phēmē* in the long term designates collective speech what today we call 'tradition,' whether this tradition refers to a religious sphere—gods, daimons, heros, and even the world of Hades—or to a secular sphere—institutions, heroic military deeds, etc. From this perspective *phēmē* designates collective speech which is destined to be preserved" (2000, 31). This Platonic idea of tradition bridging religious and secular worlds and containing multiple messages

inherent in the process of transmission within a collective group informs the semiotic notion of a pheme as a sign layered with meaning
and "intended to have some sort of compulsive effect on the interpreter
of it" (Ochs 1998, 209).

Phemic transmission can be distinguished from phatic communication in what anthropologist Bronislaw Malinowski characterized as a
"type of speech in which ties of union are created by a mere exchange
of words," such as the greeting formula "How are you?" followed by
"Fine, thank you" (Laver 1975, 215; see also Warnock 1989, 120–22).
As action, phatic speech corresponds to the routine or custom of a
practice intended, according to linguist John Lyons, "to establish and
maintain a feeling of social solidarity and well being" (1968, 417). Tradition often serves this social function as well, but it is distinguished
as purposeful activity with a repeatable, multilayered message that can
be called phemic because it compels "handing on" and variation in the
long term by means of social, especially face-to-face, interaction.

One modern-day example of repeatable or phemic behavior, observable every academic semester, is classroom seating. In most college
classrooms, students choose where to sit. Once a student settles on a
seat, he or she tends to return to the same location. This choice is often
cognitively derived from a number of beliefs and structures: Sitting in
the front increases one's chance of academic success and attracts the
notice of the professor, encouraging him or her to see the student as
an individual; sitting in the back distances oneself from the authority of
the instructor, and the back-wall hugger indicates to others that he or
she is more social or rebellious. Seats are traditionally arranged linearly
in rows. Some students believe that being near the door allows an early
exit or that being near the window is healthier, placing one closer to the
natural outdoors. Students might sit near people they know for social
connection, and many choose a similar location in all their classrooms.
This common practice repeated throughout academe might seem like
habit, except that it is often tied to student identity (i.e., "where I am
dictates who I am"), gender (women tend to cluster in the front), and
belief and value formation, relating action to outcomes. Students, for
instance, insist on sitting in the same seat during finals, even though
classrooms may change. They may even feel discomfort when forced to
relocate. They believe that having the same seat imparts luck and ensures success. As a proctor, I have often heard students explain to others

why certain seats are important to them. Or they assert that being in a certain area and taking the examination in a certain way (suggesting a traditional response to anxiety) constitute a tradition for them.

Associating tradition with precedent, continuity, and convention, scholars rhetorically refer to tradition to direct future action. Whether one wants the future to break with or continue the pattern of tradition dictates judgments of tradition as negative or positive. Especially common in the modernist literature of culture are statements emphasizing tradition as a guide or choice. Many folklorists take the tone that, in the modern push toward novelty, choosing tradition—a social connection hearkening back to the past—is a threatened human freedom. Barry McDonald offers an example in a study of the Archibald family of musicians: "I see tradition as founded upon personal choice. In the Archibalds' case, this translates as the conscious decision to engage in a certain sort of historical relationship, involving a network of people and a shared musical activity and repertoire" (1997, 58). Hence, folk musicians, folk artists, and folk tradition-bearers may appear to be touted as exemplars of free will in a mass society that applies pressure to conform. There is noticeable irony in the invocation of tradition, a social connection to the past, as a sign of individualism. In political usage, as discussed later, tradition may variously refer to individual autonomy and social authority. It can suggest a so-called conservative virtue of stability through continuity and deference to previous authority, whereas supposedly liberal views may credit tradition for encouraging a constant reshaping to form new, or "progressive," directions.

Reacting to the modern ability, or pressure, to create a personal identity to differentiate oneself from the mass of society, Jay Mechling and Michael Owen Jones suggest that tradition can indeed be formed for oneself rather than for a collective. Mechling, for instance, regards "talking to oneself" as a folkloric practice because it involves a cultural frame in which an exchange occurs (2006). Jones describes artists who create apparently unique objects intended to express their personalities, yet they self-consciously draw from different traditions (Jones 1995, 266–68; 2000). Although the social component of "handing" may not be as apparent in this conceptualization of traditional transactions, the folklorization of the self nonetheless brings to the fore the handiness of constructing (or hybridizing) an identity out of the materials of tradition.

Handy knowledge conceived as "natural" or "earthy" may be devalued by academicians positioning themselves outside of tradition as fantastical old wives' tales, bawdy (or dirty) ditties, or irrational superstition because, in modern terms, such knowledge stands outside the rule of law and the reign of (clean or sacred) gentility. Yet by relating directly to experience and being perceived as accompanied by down-to-earth wisdom, it may be popularly viewed as a force or power because, in Gross's words, it carries "a certain amount of spiritual or moral prestige" (1992, 10). An emotional or even spiritual connotation to tradition exists that may belie objective chronologies or social inventories. To claim tradition, after all, is to bring into play the presence (and guilt) of countless generations of ancestors and perhaps the gaze of present-day neighbors. In political usage, it allows for a natural state. It refers to the givens of public practice and suggests, problematically, that the long-standing character of a practice is justification for its continuation.

For religion, following tradition may be construed as keeping the faith. To break it is to risk apostasy. Hence, there is a vibrant legacy of writing on tradition from the view of how religion draws its meaning from continuities of shared ritual and belief and how individual expressions of art and literature respond to socially inherited aesthetics, symbols, and themes. This is not to say that attempts to clinically objectify tradition have not been made, particularly in folkloristics, which above all other disciplines claims tradition for its sense of being. Tradition can be calculatedly viewed as a biological specimen and given the look of a genealogical chart. It can be stolidly computed as a series of motions and minutely analyzed bit by bit or frame by frame. Traditions can be "collected" as empirical evidence of everyday practice, or tradition in the singular can be described as some conceptual, almost mystical whole, often outside the awareness of individuals. In both directions, scientific and humanistic, the problem of tradition questions the sources on which people base their actions and attitudes.

Thus far, a number of discrete senses of tradition can be discerned. I have listed them below with the corresponding definitions often cited by scholars of tradition.

1. A temporal process (*traditio*) of handing down valued material, often cast in intergenerational time, and the handy or practical knowledge (*traditum*) associated with this process

that exists in the present but was inherited from the past.
This sense is placed first because it represents, according to sociologist Edward Shils, tradition "in its barest, most elementary
sense . . . it is anything which is transmitted or handed down
from the past to the present" (1981, 12). This global sense of tradition is often tempered by the *traditum's* ability to draw attention to itself because it provides continuity with the past or, as
folklorist Randal S. Allison states, it is "something passed down
from one generation to the next, generally by informal means,
with little or no change in the transmission of that item or in
the item that is transmitted" (1997, 800). Shils also gives a more
exclusive definition of tradition that still focuses on the handing-
down process but characterizes tradition as malleable by its
bearers or custodians: "Traditions are beliefs, standards, and
rules, *of varying but never exhaustive explicitness*, which have been
received from the preceding generation, through a process of
continuous transmission from generation to generation" (1958,
154; emphasis added). When contrasted to modern means of
transmitting knowledge scholastically or electronically, this kind
of tradition may sound fragile, precious, or even rare, whereas
the other forms of tradition enumerated below that emphasize
repetition underscore the pervasiveness of tradition.

2. **A spatial or performative process of handing over imaginative material drawing on collective wisdom or noninstitutionalized "lore," typically enacted creatively and
strategically in face-to-face interactions within localized or
small groups (pheme).** Because this material is often performed
orally and festively or involves handwork passed on by imitation and demonstration, the presumption is that the knowledge
draws attention to itself with imaginative content, in contrast to
the mundane routines of everyday life. Inevitably, it varies across
space and its elaboration stabilizes over time as it is passed,
whereas nontraditional material is often associated with fixity
across space and variability over time (Glassie 1968, 33–34). Answering the question "what is tradition?" for example, musicolo-
gists Phillips Barry and Fannie Hardy Eckstorm differentiate a
tradition in space from a tradition in time: a tradition in space
comprises songs that are "widely distributed, so that one who

sings it [a particular song] may expect to find an indefinite number of persons, over a large territory who know it" (1930, 2). Their attention, like that of many others concerned with lore as manifestations of the process of tradition, is on the imaginative content of songs as traditional or on songs as a genre constituting plural traditions. Folklorist Richard Bauman contrasts the naturalistic view of the singular tradition as temporal continuity with what he calls an "emergent reorientation . . . toward an understanding of tradition as symbolically constituted in the present. Tradition, so reconceptualized, is seen as a selective, interpretive construction, the social and symbolic creation of a connection between aspects of the present and an interpretation of the past" (1992a, 31–32). In line with the performative aspect of using imaginative material to invoke a sense of the past, social historian Eric Hobsbawm popularized the concept of "invented tradition," by which he means a "set of practices, normally governed by overtly or tacitly accepted rules and of a ritual or symbolic nature, which seek to inculcate certain values and norms of behaviour by repetition, which automatically implies continuity with the past" (1983, 1). Anthropologist Jocelyn Linnekin expands this idea with the notion of the constructiveness or reflexivity of tradition: "Tradition is not a coherent body of customs, lying 'out there' to be discovered, but an a priori model that shapes individual and group experience and is, in turn, shaped by it. . . . The invention of tradition is not restricted to nationalists and intellectuals, who characteristically manipulate symbols of collective identity, but is an intrinsic part of social differentiation" (1983, 241, 250). She defines tradition as a kind of strategy, "a conscious model of past lifeways that people use in the construction of their identity" (Linnekin 1983, 241). This use of traditions to construct as well as reflect identity is important in folklorist Alan Dundes's definition of *folk* as "*any group of people whatsoever* who share at least one common factor. It does not matter what the linking factor is—it could be a common occupation, language, or religion—but what is important is that a group formed for whatever reason will have some traditions which it calls its own. . . . A member of the group may not know all other members, but he will probably know the common core of traditions belonging to the group, traditions which help the group have a sense of group identity" (1965b, 2).

3. **The total sum of knowledge associated with noninstitutionalized oral transmission, artisanship, and performance and associated with continuous preexistence (often described as antiquity, medieval, or time immemorial).** Tradition is also cited as a fount of wisdom stretching back in time, as in the phrase "known in tradition." The statement may be respectful of this wisdom because it has been around for so long and among so many people, but it can also be used derisively to cast doubt on the reliability of the information. Tradition as a totality of knowledge can be global, but it is more often categorized nationally, regionally, and ethnically or is contextualized in an era, life age, or environment. Related to the concept of culture as a totality, tradition thought of in this way is often conveyed as folk culture or folklife. In *General Ethnological Concepts* (1960), Åke Hultkrantz defines tradition as "very close to the concept of culture" (230), which is "the sum total of ideological premises, learned behaviour and transmitted mental, social and material traits characterizing a human social group" (69). In his usage, folk culture rhetorically draws attention to "culture that is . . . characterized by its conformity to tradition and primary types of organization" (129). Even if tradition is not broadly construed as a totality, it is still treated as an aggregate of cultural elements, such as in Gross's definition of tradition as "*a set* of practices, *a constellation* of beliefs, or *a mode* of thinking that exists in the present, but was inherited from the past" (1992, 8; emphasis added).

4. **In a modern context, a guiding principle as well as material associated with subcultural, marginalized, or isolated groups denoted as tightly knit communities.** This designation includes ethnic, rural, religious, familial, organizational, and occupational groups that are especially considered to possess tradition because they emphasize groupness in a modern world deemed individualistic, elitist, or alienating. Sociologist Gary Alan Fine, for instance, observes, "Given that adherence to tradition tends to establish a group as peripheral to 'rationalized' activity, such a social definition attaches to those groups without

power" (1989, 267). In addition to tradition operating as a factor of groupness in these definitions, with the implication that tradition is generated by social connection as a contrast to the dominant modern tendency to emphasize individualism, tradition enters into theories of social conflict of race, class, and gender in which tradition is repressed or appropriated by a dominant elite or relegated to groups with certain traits (e.g., darkness, lower or working class, women). For Marxist thinker Antonio Gramsci, tradition is a "mosaic" made up of material from such groups, and he looks to folklore to provide evidence of tradition as a "conception of the world" of particular social strata that are untouched by modern currents of thought (1999, 134). Cultural elements might be especially associated with tradition if they display aesthetic qualities perceived to be nonacademic or unofficial, such as folk songs, folk art, and folk literature, or if they are connected to communitarian groups such as the Amish, Hasidim, and Shakers. In this communitarian version of tradition, tradition is a rare, endangered phenomenon.

5. **A proclivity by individuals for the repetition of actions and speech, often ritually enacted or even invented, and used to form identity, relate memory, build confidence, create resistance, or provide stability.** In this orientation toward repeatable practice, tradition pervades everyday life and is an abundant renewable resource in the present. Supporting this view are a number of behavioral experiments in the repeated reproduction of information showing that what people think of as tradition is compulsive, is channeled into various social conduits rather than being global, and is characterized by serial recall and incremental changes as information gets passed (Anderson 1951, 1956; Bartlett 1965; Dégh and Vázsonyi 1975; Fine 1980b, 1992; Lowie 1965; Oring 1978; Rubin 1995). Asking why people rely on ritualized activity thought of as traditional or "superstitious," another type of laboratory observation tries to establish a correlation between repetitive behavior and belief, suggesting that the tradition is emotionally reinforced because of the anticipation of benefits (Bachrach 1962; Ketner 1971; Rachlin 1990). The implication is that tradition constitutes a fundamental, even dominant human behavior rather than being

a factor of modernity and social marginalization, as emphasized in the fourth conceptualization of tradition. The opening of the textbook *Folkloristics* by Robert A. Georges and Michael Owen Jones underscores this view when it states:

> As we interact with each other on a daily basis, we continuously express what we know, think, believe, and feel. . . . Much of what we express and the ways we do so have the behaviors of our predecessors and peers as sources. We learn most of the stories we tell and the games we play not in the classroom or through print or other media, but rather informally and directly from each other. *With time and repetition,* some examples of human expression become pervasive and commonplace. When they do, we conceive them to be traditions or traditional; and we can identify them individually or collectively as folklore. (1995, 1; emphasis added)

One significant implication of this view is that "time and repetition" can allow a process of "handing up" traditions from youth to adults (as I discuss in chapter 10 on the Internet as a folk system) rather than presuming that elders hand down age-old wisdom to innocent, childish receptacles.

6. **Standards, figures, norms, or ideals often prescribed in texts and identified as scripture, canon, pantheon, reputation, or order (tradendum), which form the authority and basis of an organization or institution.** This issue has produced heated discourse in theology and philosophy, and the authority of tradition channeled into canons and norms is part of several commentaries on the meaning of tradition. Pieper, for example, observes that "accepting tradition has the basic structure of belief, i.e., relying on someone else. This amounts to saying that we cannot think of tradition without authority" (2008, 23). He cites the precedent of philosopher Karl Jaspers, who wrote, "The crystallization of tradition into fixed authority is unavoidable. It is . . . existentially necessary, since it [tradition] is the first form of certainty about existence for every awakening being" (Jaspers 1948, 263). H. B. Acton also cites authority as

a defining characteristic of tradition: "A tradition is a belief or practice transmitted from one generation to another and accepted as authoritative, or deferred to, without argument" (1952–1953, 2). Religious historian Jaroslav Pelikan softens the blow of authority, particularly in the common attachment between tradition and religion, by declaring, "Tradition is the living faith of the dead" (1984, 65). This perspective may imply, however, that some groups have tradition and others do not, by virtue of their adherence to such standards or by being more modern. Anthropologist Ruth Finnegan criticized her own academic field, for example, for locating tradition as the exclusive property of non-Western or nonmodern groups, thereby providing "a rationale and a set of ideals that could be associated with Western imperial, commercial, and business expansion in other countries of the world and were apparently supported by anthropological findings about the traditional institutions in those countries; and it provided a vision and a sense of confidence for the newly integrating nations of the nineteenth and twentieth centuries, first in Europe, then in Africa, Asia, and the Pacific" (1991, 109).

7. **A mode of thought or a set of ideas often presumed to be conservative (resistant to change), collective (stressing uniformity of the group), naturalistic (opposed to the artificiality of technology), religious (or faith and belief based), or ethical (stable, tried-and-true values).** The mode of thought may refer to working with older approaches or content, or it may suggest respect for predecessors, whether in scholarship or in creative achievement. Reading Secretary of the Interior Franklin Lane's address on "A Western View of Tradition" for George Washington's birthday, one gets the impression that the mode of thought represented by tradition is one of holding a lofty principle. He asked the gathered throng:

> Why are we here? What is our purpose? These questions will give you the tradition of the American people, our supreme tradition—the one into which all others fall, and a part of which they are—the right of man to oppose injustice. There follow from this the right of man to govern himself, the right of property and to personal liberty, the

right to freedom of speech, the right to make of himself all that nature will permit, the right to be one of many in creating a national life that will realize those hopes which single could not be achieved. (1912, 6)

Lane thus spoke of tradition as "sacred," reflecting beliefs that are "so much a part of ourselves" in a collective consciousness (1912, 6). Such statements of principle are not only nationalistic; they can also refer to other types of organizations, such as advertising for businesses that claim traditions of excellence, quality, and service.

Sociologist S. N. Eisenstadt, in an oft-cited statement on the dynamics of tradition, writes of its limiting function: "Tradition not only serves as a symbol of continuity, it delineates the legitimate limits of creativity and innovation and is the major criterion of their legitimacy" (1969, 452). In political discourse, Edmund Burke is often cited for being a "traditionalist" and important to the development of conservatism in opposing the French Revolution. According to Kenneth Zaretzke, Burke's philosophy rests on the view that "we are pleased that things should merely work, and if they have worked for a long time it is more likely than not that they will continue to work well and be useful: whether they remain socially operative is something we must find out by experience" (1982, 87–88). In the arts, a set of ideas may constitute a school or style of work whose practitioners are presumably connected and gain status by their aesthetic or social ties. Such sets are often relative to historical periods or places, leading Finnegan to observe, for example, that "it is scarcely surprising that this emotive concept—that is, the complex *set of ideas* clustering under this umbrella term—should be related to its times, deployed to serve cultural, intellectual, and political purposes. But the point is worth noting, if only because it gives more critical perspective on the term, reminding us to pay attention to its contexts of use and to those who used it, rather than just taking it at face value as a neutral and self-standing concept" (1991, 109–10; emphasis added).

8. **Rhetorically, a negative category meant to act as a foil or contradiction for progress, modernity, industrialization, rationality, innovation, and novelty.** A classic statement of this

view comes from Adorno, who claims that "tradition is opposed to rationality" and that a progressive country such as the United States lacks tradition. "The absence of traditional aspects of culture in the US and of those experiences linked with them thwarts a consciousness of temporal continuity," he writes (Adorno 1993, 75). Folklorist Don Yoder disagrees that the United States lacks tradition, but he still establishes a binary between folk culture standing for tradition and popular culture representing modernity. He states, "Folk culture is traditional culture, bound by tradition and transmitted by tradition, and is basically (although not exclusively) rural and preindustrial. Obviously it is the opposite of the mass-produced, mechanized, popular culture of the twentieth century" (Yoder 1990, 25). In Europe, Kosta Mihailović writes of situations such as postwar Yugoslavia, where "industrialization operated as a direct or indirect cause of the weakening or even abandonment of tradition. The project of industrialization implied not only the modernization of the economy, but also the modernization of a traditional society" (1989, 28).

Feelings about authority, about the virtue of the past, and about the state of the present shape the positive and negative values given to tradition. Max Radin wryly remarks about tradition in the *Encyclopedia of Social Sciences* that "in all its aspects it retains enough of its primary characteristics of vagueness, remoteness of source, and wide ramification to make it seem peculiarly strong to those who have recourse to it and peculiarly weak to those who mean to reject it" (1935, 67). Vehement argument can arise over whether following tradition means unconsciously following a severe form of cultural authority or choosing from tradition that which one finds appropriate. When celebrated writer Lafcadio Hearn described in the early twentieth century how "every act of domestic life" in Japan was "regulated by . . . tradition," he suggested to Americans that this structure provided an admirable social model. He emphasized "the law of duty"—"obedience absolute to . . . tradition" (Hearn 1984, 287). For Hearn and other commentators of the time, America was the place of the fresh start; it was the ideal global location to break tradition. It was young among the nations, lacked a shared racial stock or peasant class, and had too large an expanse of land to bring cultural unity, or tradition, to its people.

The *Oxford English Dictionary* impartially notes the value placed on the practices or collective wisdom deemed worthy of the label *tradition*. In the sense of practice, narrative, or wisdom passed through the generations, *tradition* can be found in print well back to the Middle Ages, but the more recent call of traditionalism rings harder, with an air of harsh authority from the past. In *Keywords*, his widely known vocabulary of culture and society, Raymond Williams suggests that the time-honored process of inheritance from an older generation implies respect for elders and a certain duty to continue the process. But he warns that persistence through time is not necessarily a mark of honor if it is enforced irrationally. Williams's Marxist critique is that the labels *traditionalist* and *traditionalism* suggest authoritarian enforcement and are therefore negative (1983, 318–20). Pelikan correlates the stigma of traditionalism with a historical antagonism to tradition, writing, "it is traditionalism that gives tradition such a bad name. The reformers of every age, whether political or religious or literary, have protested against the tyranny of the dead, and in doing so have called for innovation and insight in place of tradition" (1984, 65). Amitai Etzioni, another prominent scholar concerned with the charge of authority implicit in traditionalism, draws a contrast between modernity, associated with an emphasis on universal individual rights, and what he considers the unfortunately detrimental view of traditionalism conjuring up the rigidity of an imagined Dark Ages. In fashioning what he calls a communitarian movement for the future, he hopes to recover the legitimacy of order and the claim of appropriate social virtues from traditionalism (Etzioni 1996, xvii).

Even if tradition has various meanings, a primary characteristic is the transmission of material or action that, through the process of being handed on, is socially framed and imbued with connotative meanings. The perception of tradition as informal, everyday, handy, commonsensical, authentic, or earthy is conveyed by its attachment in most senses of the term with *folk*. This folkness can represent the "we-ness" of a small group, a peoplehood defined by region, nation, language, age, gender, or ethnicity; or it can refer back to the folk process of transmission through generations or among peers. The rationality of tradition is consistently expressed as a folk logic, generated out of social interaction. Small groups associated with folkness constitute the logic of folk tradition structured as belief and handy knowledge. Headlines in the popular press and scholarly discourse manifest a tension in modern societies over whether this logic is anachronistic, senseless, pragmatic, or wise. The stakes associated with resolving this tension are nothing short of directing the course of everyday life and the behavior, faith, and metaphors by which people live. With this in mind, I now examine more closely the politics of American traditionalism.

Perceptions and Politics of Tradition

Having reviewed scholarly concepts of tradition, a critical question remains: what does the public think of all this? Opinion polls embedding tradition within hot-button political issues suggest some surprising results concerning the popular perception of tradition in modern nations such as the United States. For most Americans, tradition is a personal, intergenerational matter relating to one's relation to family and locality. Yet another strong trend is to relate tradition in the singular to a concern for a national common culture and traditions in the plural to the diversity of ethnic identities.

Major polling organizations such as Roper, Harris, and Gallup make a habit of asking about tradition in the context of (1) attitudes toward family and religion, (2) relations among the different generations, (3) opinions about values education and school curriculum, and (4) perceptions of immigration and multiculturalism. Issues of tradition appeared to occupy the minds of pollsters as a new century and millennium approached in the 1990s, probably because of the occasion to reflect simultaneously on the past and the future as the milestone event drew near. The millennium, known popularly as Y2K, turned out to be a signal moment for people to think about the importance of their traditions in what seemed to be an acceleration into a changeful, technology-filled future epitomizing modernization.

One significant poll showing that the idea of tradition was weighing heavily on the public's mind was conducted by the Public Agenda Foundation in 1998. It posed this question: "If you had to choose the one thing we should be trying to accomplish as a nation, which of the following four things would you choose: lowering taxes, improving the public schools, preserving America's ideals and traditions, reducing crime and violence?" Despite the expectation from previous polls that issues related to the economy and safety would predominate, the responses were fairly evenly distributed, showing that tradition was higher on Americans' agenda than the pollsters had anticipated. Twenty-seven percent thought that lowering taxes should be the highest priority, but 23 percent chose preserving America's ideals and traditions, one percentage point higher than reducing crime and violence and only three points lower than improving the public schools.

Reading the Public Agenda Foundation's question, one might infer that presenting "traditions" together with "ideals" suggests that tradition is a lofty, desirable goal in need of preservation because it has been eroded or lost. Although the linkage between ideals and traditions was not clarified in that poll, the role of family in upholding traditions was specifically included in other polls. In 1992 Roper asked parents of children through age seventeen the following:

> We hear a lot these days about family values. Family values can mean a number of different things to people. Taking that into account, please tell me which of the statements on this card best describes what family values mean to you personally? A. Are a set of beliefs that promote togetherness or unity among members of one's immediate family. B. Are a set of beliefs which emphasize the importance of the conventional family structure, that is, a mother and father who are married to each other living with each other living with their children. C. Mean adherence to traditions that have been passed down from one generation to the next. D. Mean putting the desires and needs of one's children before one's own desires and needs. E. Mean adherence to religious beliefs. F. Mean the same thing as basic American values, like hard work, responsibility, and working to make life better for your children than it was for you.

The selections that received the most affirmations were probably the broadest: beliefs that promote togetherness (54 percent) and basic American values (47 percent). But a significant percentage, 19 percent, chose adherence to traditions. Another indication that *family* means *tradition* to most Americans was revealed in Mass Mutual's American Family Values Study, which asked adults to what extent the phrase "has traditions" described their families. More than 80 percent answered "very well" or "pretty well." Only 19 percent responded "not too well" or "not well at all." Americans thus told pollsters that they value tradition for raising a family.

Likewise, when the Institute for Social Inquiry in 1996 asked a sample of American parents of children younger than eighteen to rate the importance of "a sense of local history and tradition" for raising a family, 76 percent answered "very important" (26 percent) or "fairly important" (50 percent). Yet generational differences are apparent. The perception is strong in America that one's parents' generation follows traditions more closely than the present generation. A *Rolling Stone* survey in 1987 revealed that 77 percent of respondents thought their parents' generation "follows traditions," whereas only 8 percent described their own generation that way. When the Veterans Administration polled Americans about the "Vietnam Generation" (those between twenty-five and thirty-five years old in 1979), more than 63 percent thought its main characteristic was being "not willing to keep traditions, too interested in changing things."

If Americans told pollsters that tradition is indeed desirable, that it means family, and that their parents have more of it than they do, they also felt they came up short on tradition compared with other nations. When Harris pollsters asked whether the Japanese have a stronger sense of family tradition and parental authority than Americans, an American sample in 1982 overwhelmingly responded yes (87 percent). When asked in the same poll whether the description "has a unique culture and tradition" characterizes Japan, China, and the United States, 63 percent of the American sample applied that statement to Japan, 45 percent to China, and only 29 percent to the United States. Americans felt deprived and typically blamed mass media and technology for displacing the sense of togetherness provided by traditions. They firmly believed that no other nation was as modernized—that is, as hooked on gadgets and mobility—as the United States. Pollsters found that Americans were concerned enough to make concerted efforts to keep traditions going or to change their technological habits.

Considering this uneasiness about America's claim on tradition as a social resource, the matter of whether American traditions should be presented and interpreted to schoolchildren as multicultural or as part of a national experience became a critical issue in several politically driven polls from the 1990s into the early twenty-first century. Back in 1974, Roper asked a national adult sample, "Generally speaking, do you think people in this country who are from different cultures, religion and countries should try to maintain in their family lives a good many of the traditions and customs of their particular heritage, or try to maintain a few of the traditions and customs, or that people should concentrate on adopting the customs of this country?" Although 38 percent answered "maintain a few traditions and customs," about the same number (34 percent) chose "concentrate on adopting the customs of this country." The split continued into the 1990s. In 1996 the National Opinion Research Center posed the following: "Some people say that it is better for a country if different racial and ethnic groups maintain their distinct customs and traditions. Others say that it is better if these groups adapt and blend into the larger society. Which of these views comes closer to your own?" Forty-three percent chose "adapt and blend into the larger society," while 31 percent said "maintain distinct customs and traditions." The breakdown by race showed that whites chose blending into the larger society over maintaining customs by a margin of 45 to 29 percent; blacks also preferred adapting and blending, but by a smaller margin (36 to 33 percent). The connection between customs and traditions in this line of questioning suggests that tradition is a way of doing things that draws attention to itself as different or robust and therefore appears to the group as exceptional or even exotic.

When asked whether the schools should give equal emphasis to "one common cultural tradition" and "diverse cultural traditions," more than 70 percent of Gallup poll respondents answered affirmatively in 1994. Blacks more than Hispanics and whites thought that both should be emphasized (81 percent of blacks, as opposed to 71 percent of Hispanics and 70 of whites). Only in the West did more respondents prefer an emphasis on one common cultural tradition (19 percent) over diverse cultural traditions (10 percent); 70 percent in the West thought both should be emphasized. The basis for a common cultural tradition was in dispute, however. For instance, the Anti-Defamation League sponsored a poll in 1992 questioning Americans' agreement with this statement: "Christianity has always been the dominant moral and religious tradition in America, and it should continue to be that way." Twenty-six percent of respondents mostly or completely disagreed, and 71 percent completely or mostly agreed.

The discourse of "traditional values" became complicated when religion was thrown into the mix. Demographic information from polls showed that there was less variation in responses by class, region, and gender than by religion. Yet the trends were arguably inconsistent. Jews and Catholics in the previously mentioned 1994 Gallup poll were more likely to favor an emphasis on diverse cultural traditions than on one common cultural tradition (32 and 20 percent, respectively). Although Protestants were more likely to favor one common cultural tradition over diversity (14 to 13 percent), the same percentage of Jews and Protestants (14 percent) favored one common tradition.

The subject of religion was extremely sensitive, especially in a political system adhering to the separation of church and state and in a society given to extensive denominationalism. Perhaps in response to the headway made by Democrats through the early twenty-first century with their criticisms of economic and immigration policies that disrupt families, Republican leadership observed that religious faith keeps families together through time, and government policies should respect this faith, such as by allowing prayer in the schools. Countering liberal criticism of a hegemonic social elite, Republicans revived the charge that an irreligious "cultural elite," primarily in the media and academe, conspired to spread a radical liberalism and contributed to the dissolution of basic American moral guides (see Medved 1992; McDonald 1994; Smith 1995).

Associations such as the Coalition for Traditional Values, Toward Tradition, and Concerned Citizens for Traditional Values took on the "traditional values" label to represent conservative religious groups in lobbying for prayer and religious programming in the schools, public support for parochial institutions, and school voucher programs (Yoachum 1993).[1] Although sounding secular and broad based, the "traditional" in these organizational titles came to stand for an orthodox morality upholding the centrality of religion in public life. It invoked the merit of "traditional" in describing "values" proved worthy by time and by popular usage. In 1997 the Christian Coalition announced that no issue would be higher on its agenda than passing a proposal by Rep. Ernest Istook (R-Okla.) for a constitutional amendment to ensure "the right to pray or acknowledge religious belief, *heritage or tradition* on public property, including public schools" (Stoll Report 1997; emphasis added). Taking exception to the coalition's conservative representation of Christians in this campaign, a less publicized religious Left countered with the keywords *community* and *dignity of the individual*. James Davison Hunter made his mark on the national scene in *Culture Wars* (1991) by interpreting the alignment of religious groups advocating for public policy as being at the heart of culture wars that preceded shooting wars (Hunter 1994, 4–5).

Although the culture wars were originally declared by defenders of traditional values to rally troops to the cause, the term was also picked up by sentries for multiculturalism, who announced that *they* were the embattled ones. In the construction of culture war rhetoric, it was an advantage to proclaim that one was losing. Another strategy was to characterize the public as the voice of tradition and to portray the artificial institutions of education, media, and government as the organs of transformation. Set up in this way, the contest invited the crowning of a winner, even though the wars were part of a long-standing struggle in the definition of American culture. During a lull in 1997, a year without national elections to galvanize opinion, the *New York Times* offered the consensus that the "conservatives" had won the hearts of the public in the battle of ideas, and the "liberals" had triumphed in the "battle of institutions," especially in academia (Scott 1997). Although anxious to have an end to the story, such press accounts of an Appomattox in the culture wars typically missed the historical significance of the battles over American tradition and the uncertain alliances they represented. The simultaneous tendencies toward diversity and union in the discourse of the 1990s did not represent a new struggle in America, which has redefined its nationhood several times in relation to social changes within its leaky borders and proclaimed its unity, in various degrees of looseness, out of its plurality (Kammen 1991; Barone 1994; Glazer 1997). Americans apparently recognized this paradox, based on their responses to a 2010 Gallup poll that asked whether "taking strict measures against illegal immigrants would go against the American tradition of welcoming those who come to the US to find a better life?" (64 percent were very or somewhat "concerned" that this would be true).

With the Y2K dust settling but tensions over immigration kicking up, a number of national surveys repeated the question about a common tradition, in different ways. In 2002 the National Opinion Research Center (NORC) asked a sample of adults how strongly they agreed with the following statement: "If we want to help create a harmonious society, we must recognize that each ethnic group has the right to maintain its own unique traditions." An overwhelming 83 percent agreed, indicating the importance of multiculturalism. But two years later, when the Associated Press reworded the statement, a higher proportion of respondents called for a common culture. More than a quarter of respondents to the Associated Press's survey agreed with this statement: "It is better for a country if almost everyone shares the same customs and traditions." Illustrating the political division in the United States on this issue, half of all respondents to a 2005 NORC poll felt that "it is better if groups adapt and blend into the larger society," but 47 percent thought "it is better for society if groups maintain their distinct customs and traditions." Indeed, almost a quarter of the NORC respondents agreed that "ethnic minorities should be given government assistance to preserve their customs and traditions." Conversely, the same poll found that a third of respondents believed "it is impossible for people who do not share American customs and traditions to become fully American."

The NORC poll did not identify those distinctively American customs and traditions, but the tone of the answers indicates that they were nonethnic. When National Public Radio specifically asked about the traditions of "recent immigrants," almost a third of respondents answered that "people who have come to the United States to live and work in the past ten years or so" have kept "too much" of their "culture and traditions." Respondents appeared to assume that immigrants maintained their separateness by preserving traditions from their native lands; however, a poll conducted by CBS News/ New York Times in 2003 found that a large proportion of immigrants in fact wanted to "adopt traditions and values of the United States" (33 percent, compared with 36 percent who wanted to preserve their "native traditions"). This is not to say that immigrants encountered significant obstacles in the United States to the maintenance of their native traditions. The Public Agenda Foundation found in 2009 that 84 percent of foreign-born adults agreed with this statement: "It's easy for me to hold on to my culture and traditions in the United States." One might reasonably ask whether immigrants can both preserve their ethnic traditions and participate in an American common culture, especially in light of scholarly models for the performance of different identities that vary with the setting. Yet close to 70 percent believe that immigrants ultimately have to choose one or the other. An overwhelming percentage of respondents agree on one point: traditions are important to maintain, especially within a family and religious context.

Several explanations can be posited for the tension over America's alleged fragmentation in the twenty-first century. First of all, the number, if not the percentage, of foreign-born people residing in the United States reached an all-time high in 2010. Second, the increased array of nationalities and ethnicities present in America is staggering. Politicians have declared border controls ineffective and are frustrated by the monitoring of immigrants who overstay their visas (Fischer and Mattson 2009; Lamm 1985; Schlesinger 1998). In 2010 an Arizona law intended to identify, prosecute, and deport illegal immigrants raised a firestorm of protest over potential racial and ethnic profiling in the law's enforcement. The law reignited debate over the changing cultural composition of America as a result of immigration in a modern era characterized by some pundits as "postnational"—marked by mobility across borders and transnational citizens (Phillips 2000; Rowe 2000; Su 2010). The perception that this wave of immigrants is not assimilating, nor do they need to, in multicultural America, has led to questions about the management of diversity in a modern nation-state. In some widely noticed cities—Los Angeles, New York City, and Miami—new immigration has contributed to the rise of seemingly self-contained foreign-language communities within metropolitan areas, as well as public discourse about whether they are bellwethers of national trends. An array of persistent traditions in these communities, including foodways, religion, music, and dress, has added to the perception of heightened fragmentation. The gulf between inner cities and orbiting suburban communities, representing political and ethnic differences, is more apparent. Predictions abound that the percentage of racial minorities will accelerate into the mid-twenty-first century, adding to a sense of social upheaval (Wattenberg 1995, 209; Roberts 1995, 71; Spencer 1994).

With the promotion of ethnic, sexual, and racial consciousness in multiculturalism, it is worth contemplating whether other forms of identity have been displaced. The most striking contrast between American cultural studies of the 1950s, for example, and those of the twenty-first century is the diminishing presence of region as an American cultural priority. The *Journal of American Folklore* featured five articles indexed under "regionalism" in the postwar decade but not another one for twenty-seven years. In contrast, sixteen were indexed under "ethnicity" or "ethnic identity" during that interval, while only one article on that topic appeared during the 1950s (Jackson, Taft, and Axlerod 1988). The 1963–1978 index for the *Journal of the Folklore Institute* listed eleven entries under the category "regionalism," whereas the 1979–1993 index did not have a single entry for "region" (Braid and Smith 1993; Mordoh 1981). The later index also replaced "ethnic folklore" with "ethnic identity" (eighteen entries).

There is indeed evidence for an American vagueness about the "home place" as a social root. The U.S. Census estimated in 1990 that about one in six Americans, or more than 40 million people, moved from one residence to another in a single year, and one in six of those moved to another state. Most moved to suburban areas that had a tenuous hold on community tradition between the firm historical and literary realms of city and country. Americans lived increasingly at the edges of communities, both figuratively and literally. In 1990, for the first time, half the nation's population lived in the orbit of thirty-nine metropolises of 1 million or more persons (Roberts 1995, 122). With major population shifts toward the West and South occurring during the 1980s, by 1990, more than half the residents of eight states had been born in other states. As one census expert acknowledged, "this degree of mobility is unique in the developed world" (Roberts 1995, 144). Nonetheless, regional loyalties, particularly in the South and New England, remain lodged in the literary imagination throughout American history, and the mythology of small-town America being the nation's backbone raises its head in every political campaign.

Arguably, an important function of scholarship on plural traditions for public discourse has been to recognize areas, such as Appalachia or the Ozarks, where *place* as a locus of tradition really matters. In the burst of regional romanticism in the early to mid-twentieth century, town and region provided a desirable folk sensibility of a social identity below the nation (see Allen 1996; Allen and Schlereth 1990). More socially intimate than the political nation, the region was a model for *E Pluribus Unum*. The region apparently tolerated myriad ethnic, religious, and occupational traditions and integrated them into a sense of place, giving America a lasting image of diversity (see Dorson 1964; Jones 1976). A search for, as well as a sense of, place did not go away, but it gave way in the culture wars to other competitors for American social priorities. Crucial for views expressed in the new century is that cultural critics and educators have promoted ethnicity and race as the most mobile and symbolic marker of identity for citizens on the move. Set against the background of the unstable institutions of family, company, church, and community, Americans have increasingly turned to ethnicity and race as portable ways for individuals to be counted in mass culture.

The popular press has also reported popular associations between childhood and tradition, since childhood is presumably the time when beliefs and customs are transmitted and absorbed. Childhood's images of continuity with the past include children playing games like hide-and-seek that are supposedly based on a peaceful pastoralism, but the press set off alarms with reports of danger from video games and social networking sites used by children that purportedly displace traditions of the past. Folklore, long hailed as a "natural" educational repository for "traditional" moral lessons conveyed to generations of American children, came under the multicultural magnifying glass with the dawn of the new millennium. The underlying issue in the new scrutiny of childhood texts is, as stated by *U.S. News & World Report*, "how to raise decent kids when traditional ties to church, school and community are badly frayed" (Herbert 1996).

It had been widely accepted in American education that reading folk and fairy tales provided engaging educational and moral lessons in the early grades and at home. This transmission of folklore was not only elementary in the schools but also fundamental to the growth of cultural literacy in children. In *The New Dictionary of Cultural Literacy*, E. D. Hirsch, Joseph E. Kett, and James Trefil (2002) place folklore before art, history, and philosophy, in recognition of its place at the foundation of culture (see also E. D. Hirsch 1987, 1989). Classic mythology and European folktales are there as well, familiar figures such as Zeus, Snow White, and Cinderella. They are the hallmarks of civilization, and at one time, every schoolchild knew the legends of Davy Crockett, Johnny Appleseed, and John Henry. They were part of a "culturalism" in which stable social institutions of family, religion, and community offer continuity with the past by passing "traditional" moral lessons in the form of folklore from one generation to another.

Change became apparent in education circles during the 1980s with the rise of sensitivity to ethnic and religious representation, a kind of relativism that encouraged tolerance of alternative lifestyles, and a multiculturalism that enhanced wide social inclusion (La Belle and Ward 1994; Glazer 1997). Multiculturalists encouraged teachers to avoid authoritatively drumming the legacy of Western civilization into children's heads. In keeping with a relativistic perspective, teachers opened students' awareness to an array of moral codes and cultural identities from a number of legitimate alternatives—Eastern civilization, African societies, and possibly even New Age philosophies. Often accompanying this self-determination of identity was a cultural criticism of Western "isms"—racism, sexism, classism. Many of the tales of the Brothers Grimm were scornfully reevaluated as presenting females in a bad light or being too violent or irreligious or privileging European ancestry (Katz 1991). A wire story in 1993 about the banning of Snow White in Jacksonville, Florida, led to the realization in many localities that formerly revered folktales had now been condemned. Halloween customs increasingly came under attack from religious groups for encouraging Satanism, and many schools forbade traditional decorations of ghosts and goblins as well as trick-or-treating (Marlow 1994; Swinson 2000). At least one folklorist stood up publicly in the popular press to question, "Can't We Pass on Fairy Tales without Being Accused of Satanism?" (Bulger 1992).

Conservative advocates of "traditional values" answered the rush to mine folktales for multicultural ore with adaptations of their own. Spreading the message that schools and libraries had been stormed by irreligious multicultural agendas, some writers reached out to parents to use folktales to teach moral lessons at home. Christine Allison published a "parent's guide" called *Teach Your Children Well* (1993) that includes fables and tales meant to "instill traditional values" and bolster a "moral imagination" (Guroian 1996). Calling herself a "thoroughly modern woman," Emyl Jenkins compiled the hefty *Book of American Traditions* because, as a mother, she worried that "our children often spend more time sitting alone in front of a computer or TV screen than they do playing and chatting with one another" (1996, 2–3). Concerned that children do not have traditions to carry into adulthood, she recounts stories of holidays, rites of passage, and family customs that can be called distinctively American. She writes of the need for traditions "in today's political[ly] correct world" because "as we search for a sense of direction and permanence in our hurried lives today, traditions provide an anchor, a guidepost" (1996, 3). Contrasting the naturalness of tradition with the artificiality of technology, which holds more than its share of power in modernity, she notes that "traditions, like wisdom, spring from history and people, not from the machines that rule our lives today" (1996, 3).

Perhaps the biggest surprise in the publishing world of the inter-millennial period from 1990 to 2010, when the rhetoric of tradition was in the news, was the success of William Bennett's *Book of Virtues* (1993). The unwieldy, 832-page anthology appeared to many literary pundits an unlikely choice for a pivotal book of fin de siècle America, but it enjoyed a spectacularly long run at the top of the *New York Times* best-seller list. An audio version, children's edition, and wall calendar—and a host of parodies—followed. The original book is a compilation of stories, including many Euro-American folktales meant to teach the moral virtues of compassion, responsibility, self-discipline, courage, honesty, friendship, and faith. Bennett bemoans the erosion of traditional values of family and faith and calls for a renewal of the tradition of storytelling drawn from Western civilization. Bennett's use of the buzzword *treasury* in his subtitle (*A Treasury of Great Moral Stories*) raises images of B. A. Botkin's best-selling American folklore treasuries of the 1940s and 1950s (Botkin 1944, 1949, 1951). Botkin's 1944 *Treasury of American Folklore* promotes cultural pluralism with the subtitle *Stories, Ballads, and Traditions of the People* (see J. Hirsch 1987). In *The Book of Virtues*, Bennett culls "moral" stories from classic folklore collections of the Brothers Grimm, Andrew Lang, and Joseph Jacobs and gives his own brief ethical commentaries. The hugely successful book spawned a television series, *Adventures from the Book of Virtues*, on PBS.[2] The choice of PBS for a conservative answer to HBO's controversial multicultural series had its ironies: in budget hearings, some lawmakers accused the beleaguered Public Broadcasting System, supported with public funds, of being too liberal in its programming.

One needs look no further than the furor over the popular uses of folktales to find political divisions involving the character of American tradition. Opponents in the culture wars found it essential to locate a folklore that would legitimize a claim to an authentic tradition at the heart of an American culture. It would provide a foundation of the past for the constructed edifice of the future. Whether Right or Left, conservative or liberal, Democrat or Republican, tradition had been shaped to the goals of an imagined society. In the public realm, tradition became coded for the moral education of children in the midst of social upheaval.

Squeamish about references to the past and associations with traditionalism, scholars shifted their ground from the continuity of tradition and custom to the future-oriented "dynamics" of community and identity. The concern for locality and place evident in indexes of folkloristic publications during the 1940s and 1950s was replaced, with American folklorists leading the way, by the engagement of identity and difference as a matter of choice, evident in situated expression. These scholars worked in their outreach to the public to emphasize tradition representing a strategy by localized or marginalized groups to maintain transnational or counternational social markers of ethnicity, race, sexuality, and class in the face of mass or commercial national cultures that would wipe the subcultural canvas clean (see Oring 1994; Kirshenblatt-Gimblett 1994). Tradition, whether defined as handed-down or handed-over knowledge, could be construed politically as a force of either the past or the future. Popular perception of tradition as a threatened commodity met up with scholarly efforts to recover traditions as signs of social vitality. Many scholars wanted to emphasize tradition as a renewable resource and adjusted the definition of tradition to arise from social interaction, whereas public forums of the press and municipalities maintained, perhaps for political reasons, a notion of tradition as a resource of a pastoral past, a socially bound and rooted community, and a coherent family. The common ground for both was the handiness of tradition, although they differed on tradition's grasp over their lives.

2

Explaining Tradition

On Folk and Folkloristic Logic

Not long after antiquarian William Thoms coined the term *folklore* in 1846, to spur the collection of British "manners, customs, observances, superstitions, ballads, proverbs, etc., of the olden time," fellow Englishman Edwin Sidney Hartland clarified—indeed, encouraged—the professional pursuit of folklore as first the "study of tradition" and then the "science of tradition" (Thoms 1965; Hartland 1894–1896, 1968). For Thoms and Hartland, swept up in a rush toward industrial capitalism and the rule of scientific reasoning, tradition emblematized an authority and logic characterizing communal societies that stood in contrast to their modern age by being preindustrial and superstitious. Even as methods and theories changed drastically from the Victorians to the Americans, framing tradition as arising out of the contemporary interaction of postindustrial individuals, the flag of tradition continued to be waved over the territory of folklore. If that banner was not conspicuous enough, American scholar Richard Bauman declared at the end of the twentieth century, "there is no single idea more central to conceptions of folklore than tradition" (1992a, 30).

An argument exists that the association of folklore with tradition gained the most ground in America (Margry and Roodenburg 2007, 262). Surveying the concepts of folklore in 1986, Elliott Oring reflected that the reformulation of folklore with reference to living tradition rather than as an anachronistic product of a caste or class of people in the United States was probably inevitable. With the absence of a peasant class or a native ancestral population (Indian tribes were native but not ancestors), and given the desire to identify a genuine, renewable American folklore, Oring points out that the conceptual shift from "survival" and "relic," emphasized by Europeans, to an "oral tradition" found ready acceptance among American folklorists for their materials of recent vintage (Oring 1986, 10; see also Hofer 1984). The emphasis on transmission in the concept of tradition allowed the demotion of characteristics such as antiquity, level of society, and remoteness for Americans immersed in a progressive, supposedly classless society.

In the American concept of folklore, "folklore then may crop up in any subject, any group or individual, any time, any place," according to Mamie Harmon writing in the *Standard Dictionary of Folklore, Mythology, and Legend* (1949, 400; see also Dundes 1966). During the 1970s, American updates of folkloristics as the study of folklore were frequently defined as "scientific in the study of human traditions" (Ketner 1973, 1976; Georges and Jones 1995). Surveying folklore's study at the midway point of the twentieth century, American folklorist Stith Thompson proclaimed, "the idea of tradition is the touchstone for everything that is to be included in the term folklore" (1951, 11). Surveys of folklore studies after the 1980s showed an even greater consensus among folklorists about the emphasis on tradition than had been evident during the 1950s. Dan Ben-Amos, a leader of one of the American doctorate-granting programs in folklore, declared in 1984, "Tradition has survived criticism and remained a symbol of and for folklore" (124). At another such program, Michael Owen Jones concluded, "what appeals to folklorists is the study of traditions—something in which all people of every time and place engage" (1989, 263). This kind of tradition, which epitomizes folklore, typically highlights the processes of handing down and over (the first and second "senses" from the previous chapter), along with the characteristic repetition and variation of imaginative material in group life (the third through fifth senses).

Thoms's imaginative nineteenth-century call for "a good Saxon compound, Folklore," only indirectly referred to tradition. He announced folklore as a replacement for "popular antiquities" or "popular literature" and located folklore in "that interesting branch of literary antiquities" (Thoms 1965, 6). He objectified tradition as an observable custom steeped in the past rather than as a process or transmission. He asked the editor of *Athenaeum*, "How many readers would be glad to show their gratitude for the novelties which you, from week to week, communicate to them, by forwarding to you some record of

old Time—some recollection of a now neglected custom—some fad-
ing legend, local tradition, or fragmentary ballad!" (Thoms 1965, 5).
Folklore is, he wrote, "a mass of minute facts, many of which, when
separately considered, appear trifling and insignificant, but, when taken
in connection with the system into which his master-mind has woven
them, assume a value that he who first recorded them never dreamed
of attributing to them" (Thoms 1965, 5). That value, he implied, is in
charting a national tradition, if one acknowledges his desire to extrapo-
late from English folklore a spiritual core similar to what the Brothers
Grimm had suggested for Germany.

As British folklorists transplanted Thoms's literary folklore into the
location of science, Hartland articulated for them the empirical foundation of tradition. He wrote, "Every people has its own body of Tradition, its own Folk-Lore, which comprises a slowly diminishing part,
or the whole, of its mental furniture, according as the art of writing
is, or is not, known" (Hartland 1891, 34). With reference to tradition,
Hartland altered Thoms's emphasis in folklore on literary antiquity to a
social application of natural history that follows a hierarchy of progress
in civilization. Tradition, as he later publicized it for his fellow folklorists in various guides, is a process of transmission characteristic of the
level of "savagery" among unlettered, isolated groups that survives into
civilization. In his words:

> It is now well established that the most civilized races have all
> fought their way slowly upwards from a condition of savage-
> ry. Now, savages can neither read nor write; yet they manage
> to collect and store up a considerable amount of knowledge
> of a certain kind, and to hand on from one generation to an-
> other a definite social organization and certain invariable rules
> thus gathered and formulated are preserved in the memory,
> and communicated by word of mouth and by actions of vari-
> ous kinds. To this mode of preservation and communication,
> as well as to the things thus preserved and communicated, the
> name of Tradition is given; and Folklore is the science of Tradi-
> tion. (Hartland 1904, 6–7)

Although Hartland was influential in the professionalization of
folklore around tradition as the knowledge of surviving lore, the mod-

ern conception of tradition in folklore, as it developed in the twentieth century, owes more to another British folklorist's social-psychological emphasis on the "folk" (see Fine 1987). In an oft-cited essay titled simply "The Folk," Joseph Jacobs (1893) blasts the natural history model and asserts several principles that add the individual to group, and space to time, as crucial factors in analyzing the significance of folklore. He views the diffusion of folklore, and its suggestion of a multiplicity of cultures, as negating the assumptions of a singular hierarchy of civilization. His points are as follows: (1) because folklore is continuously being updated and invented, folklore involves innovation and, consequently, individual initiative; (2) folk is not a level of society but a group sharing tradition that can be of any stratum; (3) tradition is not a body of knowledge but a process understood by following spatial and psychological patterns. He declares:

> We shall have to go more minutely into the modus operandi of tradition if this conception of individual origin of folk-lore be firmly grasped. Just at present, we are content to say such and such a creation is spread from John-o'-Groat's to Land's End. The assumption is usually made, if only implicitly, that it arose independently in all the places of its occurrence, owing to the similarity of social conditions and the like. From the new standpoint we shall want to know how it thus spread, and where it took its rise, since from that standpoint it must have originated in one mind in one spot. And when we learn how it spreads in one country, we may get to know how it spreads from one country to another. (Jacobs 1893, 237)

Folklore in Jacobs's perspective became contemporaneous, spread by technology such as telephones and books as well as by word of mouth. Linked to individual needs and social conditions, folklore lost the racial taint applied by the survivalists. Tradition, he implies, is chosen as well as followed; it is created anew as well as inherited from yore. Calling for the study of the lore of the present, Jacobs observes, "We ought to learn valuable hints as to the spread of folk-lore by studying the Folk of today" (1893, 237). Hartland was willing to concede the point by establishing the study of folklore as a science rather than an antiquarian pursuit. He broke with his fellow Victorians, who viewed folklore's "subjects only in the remains of a distant epoch, preserved less perfectly in Europe, more perfectly in Africa" (Hartland 1885, 120). Capitalizing *tradition* to denote a body of knowledge in contrast to the customary manifestations of the plural *traditions*, Hartland presaged future scholarly thought by pronouncing, "I contend that Tradition is always being created anew, and that traditions of modern origin wherever found are as much within our province as ancient ones" (1885, 120).

In late-nineteenth-century America, similar definitional debates ensued, and like those in Britain, they often referenced the dramatic changes brought by mass industrialization and immigration. The underlying issue driving the concern for folklore as a vernacular product was the effect of rapid social and material changes on national traditions and values as perceived by the white Protestant elite. Folklore was not the only location for this issue. As abstract art, inspired by primitivism, took hold in the early twentieth century in response to modernization, art critics raised the issue of a tradition of art. As new forms of writing—realistic and popular—spread, literary circles took up the matter of vernacular or "local color" tradition in literary production. But arguably, tradition was most discernible in the persistent quality of folklore and the groups it represented. In the first issue of the publication of the Folk-Song Society of the Northeast, Phillips Barry and Fannie Hardy Eckstorm were among the few folklorists to directly address the matter in their title "What Is Tradition?" They were acutely aware of changes in popular musical tastes and the rise of the urban recording industry. They well understood the preservation instinct behind the desire to save the songs of tradition they called folksongs, even as they recognized "that ballad making is still going on" (Barry and Eckstorm 1930, 2).

Following Jacobs, Barry and Eckstorm significantly distinguished two kinds of tradition: "tradition in time and tradition in space." Their important explanation, excerpted previously in my discussion of the entrenchment of "handing over" as well as "handing down" in tradition, merits a full citation:

> A song may have come down through the ages, like "Hind Horn" or "Johnny Scot," traditional in the sense that many generations of singers have sung it. Or, it may be, like "Willie the Weeper," or "Fair Florella," merely widely distributed, so

that one who sings it may expect to find an indefinite number of persons, over a large territory who know it. Such is tradition in space. Both types of songs are equally traditional; both are species of folk-song. For, despite all that has been argued to demonstrate the contrary, it is tradition that makes the folk-song a distinct genre, both as to text and music. (Barry and Eckstorm 1930, 2).

Still, the problem of how tradition fit into technological or mass culture remained, along with the additional question of whether "authentic" traditions in modernity needed the qualifier "folk."

MacEdward Leach addressed these issues when he observed, "America is rapidly developing a new cultural stratum—alas for folk story and song. This is mass culture, a product of a society ordered and regimented by a technology working through mass media, such as radio, television and graphic advertising; and master-minded by hucksters selling goods, ideas, social behavior, religions—hard and soft commodities. Perhaps the society that emerges will have the homogeneity of a folk society; if so, that will be the only common trait" (1966, 395). Leach foretold the rethinking of tradition as the emblem of folklore. He observed that, in the midst of the dramatic rise of mass media, mass culture, and mass communication emphasizing novelty and uniformity, tradition came under suspicion.

The classic statement of doubt is Ben-Amos's "Toward a Definition of Folklore in Context," first presented in 1967 and published in 1972. With the goal of understanding folklore as a process, Ben-Amos offers a postindustrial definition of folklore as "artistic communication in small groups." By this definition, not all folklore is "traditional," if persistence of form through time is indeed the standard of tradition. Referring to the "tradition of time" as a "burden" on folklore studies, he worries that folklore defined by tradition prevents the folklorist's subject from expanding to emergent performances in mass culture. He writes:

If folklore as a discipline focuses on tradition only, it "contradicts its own raison d'etre." If the initial assumption of folklore research is based on the disappearance of its subject matter, there is no way to prevent the science from following the same road. If the attempt to save tradition from oblivion remains the only function of the folklorist, he returns to the role of the antiquarian from which he tried so hard to escape. In that case, it is in the interest of folklore scholarship that we change the definition of the subject to allow broader and more dynamic research in the field. (Ben-Amos 1972, 14)

Ben-Amos wants to emphasize the process of transmitting lore in the form of expressive communication rather than the preservation of material. Yet the transmission still entails the social exchange or "handing over" of tradition, conceived as a transaction of expressive knowledge. Writing a dozen years later, Ben-Amos reflects that tradition "has been one of the principal metaphors to guide us in the choate world of experiences and ideas" (1984, 124).

The experiment to deny or mask tradition in the conceptualization of folklore reflects an effort to emphasize the contemporary performance of folklore and thus remove the popular association of folk material with a relic, irrational past and its bearers with a backward or primitive reputation. To Oring, one of Ben-Amos's contemporaries, the emphasis on the artistic element of folklore—evident in "verbal art" as a modernist (and, he adds, characteristically American) definition of folklore in lieu of "oral tradition"—"reflected an anthropological preoccupation with the cultural present as well as the effort to explain social and cultural forms in terms of the larger social and cultural systems in which these forms play some part" (1986, 14; for examples of "verbal art" conceptualizations, see Bascom 1955; Bauman 1977). Although designed to expand the categories of folklore to include intermingling with modern popular culture, the terminology of *verbal art* removes the sense of cultural practices not involving speech. An alternative view is that those practices are tied by a process of transmittal that can be called traditional; tradition is the structure that connects different genres under the category of folklore (Bayard 1953; Bronner 2000a, 2000b; Dundes 1964a, 1965b). Without the burden of tracing transactions back in time and over space, however, the analyst can assume a unique or emergent meaning within a particular context or situation (see Kirshenblatt-Gimblett 1975; Toelken 1995, 48–68). This often leads to a problem of disabling comparison or generalization; it precludes an explanation of locating a precedent in a series of transactions or a cognitive response and social agency in the construction of symbols (Dundes 2005; Oring 2006). It frequently replaces the analytical implication of tradition constituting meaning outside the awareness of participants with an empiricist stance that the participants' views represent the only reality.

Although definitions emphasizing artistic communication with the conspicuous absence of tradition made many rounds, the concept of tradition was revised rather than swept aside (Bronner 2000c; Glassie 1995; Noyes 2009). One contribution of folklore studies to the philosophy of tradition, in fact, is the integration of creativity and emergence into the idea of tradition. In the literature of American folkloristics, especially, traditions are chosen and adapted, not merely followed (see Bronner 1998; Dorson 1978a; Dundes 1966). They are indeed invented and individualized. They are strategically selected and performed for the purpose of changing modes of persuasion and identity. In this reformulation, tradition is perceived by individual and group rather than objectified as a culture. For instance, Richard Dorson's well-known separation of an objectively conceived "folklore," assumed to be authentic, and a fabricated "fakelore," presumably ersatz, came into question, since both could be viewed as strategic uses of tradition in cultural production (see Bendix 1997; Dorson 1976; Doyle 2009; Kirshenblatt-Gimblett 1988).

Worth considering in recollecting the period of doubt in the 1960s and 1970s is the influence of political turmoil at the time. Upholding tradition in public discourse was often associated with conservative forces blocking progressive social movements such as civil rights for African Americans, labor causes, and equal rights for women and other groups. While folklorists hailed folk traditions as lending integrity and value to disadvantaged groups—including ethnic, racial, religious, and regional—in an imposing power structure, a growing unease with tradition (and related words such as *heritage* and *legacy*) as the politics of the past was apparent (see Denisoff 1971; Hanson 1995). To the chagrin of the restless baby boomer generation, tradition could represent perpetuation of the political and social status quo and control by elites of an older, intransigent generation. G. K. Chesterton anticipated this view when he observed, "Tradition means giving votes to the most obscure of all classes, our ancestors. All democrats object to men being disqualified by the accident of birth; tradition objects to their being disqualified by the accident of death" (quoted in Walzer 2000). The question for many folklorists in the wake of the civil rights era was how to renew traditions to serve progressive values (see Dorson 1975; Green 1983; Keil 1978; Williams 1975). Guy and Candie Carawan, active in the southern freedom movement, recalled that "folklorists— Alan Lomax and Willis James, in particular, met freedom fighters at these conferences and intense discussions took place about the value of older cultural traditions to contemporary struggles" (Carawan and Carawan 1990, 6). In 1967 Lomax compiled *Hard Hitting Songs for Hard-Hit People* and commented on the possible reinterpretation of tradition represented by these newly composed songs of protest based on old forms. While criticizing folklorists for presenting their findings "as a quaintly phrased view of a bygone time or as a fantasy escape from life," he offered that "most of our traditional American songs can be considered songs of complaint or protest about the main economic and social problems that have always faced the mass of the American people as they struggled for a living." And he took "literary scholars" to task for neglecting folk songs "as relevant to the real problems of everyday life" (Lomax 1967, 365).

Dorson (1972, 45–47), meanwhile, derided young folklorists for embracing social sciences on ideological as well as methodological grounds. Advocating for folklore studies as a nonideological discipline and profession, Dorson chastised do-gooders and popularizers for knocking or altering authentic tradition (Dorson 1971, 1976; see also Bronner 1998, 349–412). Folk tradition, thought of as literary antiques, had a sanctity that Dorson swore to protect (see Dorson 1971, 1978b). Several analyses from outside the American folklore profession took note of the rancorous debate between popularizers and professionals regarding the authenticity of tradition as well as the application of folklore to political causes. They noted that the stands taken had political undertones of a conflict between either "reactionary and progressive forces" or "rationalism and radicalism" (see Zemljanova 1963; Williams 1975). In line with this political analysis, Raymond Williams claimed *tradition* to be a loaded keyword of culture and society that was frequently manipulated to keep the establishment in power. In the midst of modernization, he reflected, tradition became associated with respect for the establishment and the duty to follow precedent. In his view, tradition stood in the way of "virtually any innovation" (Williams

1983, 318–20). In the reformulation of tradition advanced by folklorists, however, the term became intertwined with creativity as an expressive or artistic form of communication. It was often presented as the intellectual property of disempowered groups hanging on to tradition as a form of resistance to official authority or to bolster claims for social recognition (Bronner 1992a; Limón 1983; Norkunas 2004; Silverman 1983).

The Logic of Tradition in Folkloristics

Whereas *tradition* had a popular, sentimental meaning in both public and scholarly discourse dating back to at least the Victorians, in postindustrial, postsentimental society it appeared elastic, even protean, and individualized (see Oring 2003, 71–84; Pleck 2000). In the rhetoric of modernity, folklorists used *tradition* to designate a more contemporaneous, spatially spread, and strategically applied and manipulated tool of individuals. In the reformulation of tradition characterized by acceptance of a present accelerating into the future, the standard of persistence through generations no longer held fast. The spread of jokes in short-lasting "cycles," carried through loosely connected "networks," "conduits," and "communities," was one oft-cited example of a "new" or "emergent" tradition (Dundes 1987). Indeed, the late-twentieth-century folkloristic attention to jokes as a narrative genre was itself a sign of expansion of the concept of tradition. Formerly, according to folklorist Elliott Oring, jokes—a prominent example of a performative "living tradition" used by people in all walks of modern life—"were considered neither to reflect the spirit of the ancient folk-nation nor to indicate the survival of primitive belief and thought" (1986, 9–10).

If tradition as the basis of folklore is indeed both invented and inherited, individual and social, stable and changing, oral and written, of past and present, of time and space, about both authority and freedom, then what does it exclude? Is it shorthand for a feeling of connection rather than a process of transmission? Is it possible to make it empirical if it depends so much on judgment and perception? Or is that its strength—to point to the ways that spiritual and social connection can be subjectively invoked? The term *traditions* references discrete texts and observable activities that are empirically documentable; *tradition* sounds like an overarching force, pattern, or authority—often outside of awareness. Traditions are identifiable in cultural expressions and behavior, while tradition is often described as unself-conscious, ingrained, and unthinking.

For anthropologist William Bascom, folklore's significance is its contribution to culture, and this can be objectively analyzed "in the same way as other customs and traditions, in terms of form and function, or of interrelations with other aspects of culture" (1965, 28). As part of culture, folklore comprises traditions meant for expressive and social purposes; hence the repeated anthropological reference to folklore as "verbal art" or "literary art of a culture" in definitions of folklore included in the *Standard Dictionary of Folklore, Mythology, and Legend* (Leach 1949, 398–403). In this line of thinking, a *cultural tradition* is presumably an item or pattern that represents a culture, whereas a *folk tradition* can be either an item going through a folk process or a pattern standing for a folk (culture). Yet other statements equate culture, particularly in complex societies, with tradition, such as in the connection of folklife and folk culture with "American tradition," "Pennsylvania German tradition," or "urban tradition" (see Yoder 1990; Paredes and Stekert 1971; Ben-Amos 1984, 119–21). Anthropologist Melville Herskovits, in fact, tersely proclaims that "one synonym for culture is tradition" (1948, 17). Judging by Herskovits's definition of *folklore* published a year later in the *Standard Dictionary, tradition* has a broader, more spiritual meaning than *folklore*: "Originally the study of cultural curiosities, and held to be the survivals of an earlier period in the history of 'civilized' literate peoples, folklore has come more and more to denote the study of the unwritten literature of any group, whether having writing or being without it" (Herskovits 1949, 400). Ben-Amos reflects on this major thrust in folklore studies as essentially an American anthropological reformulation of Hartland's "science of tradition." According to Ben-Amos, for Hartland, "folklore is 'the science of tradition'; for them [anthropological folklorists in America], it can be only the science of part of tradition—anthropology bites off the larger slice" (Ben-Amos 1984, 120). As the subject of a discipline, folklore represents the study of tradition as culture; in anthropology or literature, it is a body of material signifying a portion of culture.

A glance at major introductory textbooks from the past five decades and into the twenty-first century shows that students are led to understand the social basis of tradition as being essential to folklore.

Probably the most popular introductory text, published in four editions beginning in the late 1960s, is Jan Brunvand's *The Study of American Folklore*, which opens: "Folklore comprises the unrecorded traditions of a people" (1998, 3). The meaning can be interpreted as items persisting in time framed by groups. In avowing folklore as a form of action, Barre Toelken's *The Dynamics of Folklore* (1979, 1996) emphasizes that "variation within a tradition, whether intentional or inadvertent, is viewed here simply as a central fact of existence for folklore, and rather than presenting it in opposed terms of conscious artistic manipulation vs. forgetfulness, I accept it as a defining feature that grows out of context, performance, attitude, cultural tastes, and the like" (Toelken 1996, 7).

Robert Georges and Michael Owen Jones's *Folkloristics: An Introduction* underscores "traditional" along with "expressive" as the key descriptors of folklore. With a slight rhetorical shift, they raise for discussion the effect of people's perceptions of tradition on their view of culture. By stating that folklore denotes "expressive forms, processes, and behaviors . . . *that we judge* to be traditional," they offer both the empirical and the subjective experience of folklore as legitimate (Georges and Jones 1995, 1; emphasis added). They observe repeated forms, processes, and behaviors distinguishable as traditional because they represent "continuities and consistencies through time and space in human knowledge, thought, belief, and feeling." According to their account, traditions characteristically have precedents and are "customarily" enacted during face-to-face interactions. Hardly an obscure relic, traditions as folklore "become pervasive and commonplace." Folklore, they underscore, is a living tradition enacted every day; it is, in their words, "an integral and vital part of our daily lives" (Georges and Jones 1995, 1).

To get at why people use traditions, Brunvand, Toelken, and Georges and Jones all advocate the documentation of expressive practices that, by being repeated in cultural settings, are often unself-consciously linked to social identities. In observing practices, the analyst looks for tradition as prescriptive action because, by being done traditionally, it is assumed to have a precedent. Rather than taking repetition for granted, a practice-oriented analyst asks why or how that action is repeated and varied. In addition to looking for prescriptive action, an analyst with a concern for the function of tradition queries ascriptive thinking that attributes, consciously or unconsciously, values or meanings to the practice and its frame.

French sociologist Michel de Certeau, in *The Practice of Everyday Life* (1984), argues for the identification of the rules of operation in daily life, which he dichotomizes into practices of making and using. Advocating for a structuralism of cultural behavior, he declares, "There must be a logic of these practices." Folklore can be read in the reference to "local stabilities," which, he argues, "break down . . . , no longer fixed by a circumscribed community." Cultural analysts might infer from de Certeau that folklore is a form of marginalized cultural production that is, in his words, "massive and pervasive" (1984, xv, xx, xvii). Another place for folkloristics is in the logic (construed as a process in the sense of *traditio* differentiated from *traditum*) communities devise for themselves. Inasmuch as logic suggests constraints as well as forms for improvisation and variation, this invites analyses of power because one set of rules may be in conflict with another as local stabilities come up against dominant systems.

Folklore as *traditum* is the primary evidence used by analysts to produce findings and generalizations about tradition as process (*traditio*). Victorian authors were well aware that since the materials of folklore are not easily perceived as particles of physics or specimens of biology, there could be skepticism about their application as scientific data. Hartland's important popular tract *Folklore: What Is It and What Is the Good of It?* (1904) addresses the issue of whether folklore studies constitute science by stating, "But here you will tell me: It is impossible to have a science of anything which does not fall into method, and is not capable of being classified and reduced to rule. Tradition is admittedly shifting, uncertain, chaotic; and how can you have a science in tradition?" His answer is that folklore obeys laws and follows patterns. "The aim of the science of Tradition," he writes, "is to discover those laws, by the examination of their products, the customs and beliefs, the stories and superstitions handed down from generation to generation, to ascertain how those products arose and what was the order of their development" (Hartland 1904, 11). The modern reformulation of folklore takes into account more flexibility in the authority of tradition and shifts interest from the development to the generation of folklore. A driving force in the reformulation of folklore arising in the present day, Alan Dundes calls for the identification and interpretation of folklore's "patterns" (1980, x). Brunvand refers to folklore's "common qualities" and proposes that the "findings of such folklore research are applicable to many fields" (1998, 24). Georges and Jones's hallmark of tradition as "continuities and consistencies" suggests a discernible structural pattern similar to Bauman's "regularities," which he describes as "discoverable uniformities in folklore behavior" (Georges and Jones 1995, 1; Bauman 1969, 169). The choice of words such as *patterns, qualities, continuities,* and *regularities* to describe folklore conveys the notion that folklore can be objectified as material or "content." It can then can be ordered and compared, and work with it can be replicated. In this model, the analyst records or *recovers* phenomena and renders them manageable as data. Then he or she *discovers* connections among aggregate data. Reflecting on this occupational praxis, Bauman boasts, in fact, that folkloristics is the most "documentary" and "aggregative" of the social sciences (1969, 168–69).

The rhetoric of discovery appears to be especially important in folkloristic discourse past and present. Brunvand relates the Victorian background of folklore's study this way: "The *discovery* of the historical depth and the geographical breadth of some of these traditional 'survivals' (as they were once called) is what first gave the study of folklore much of its fascination" (1998, 23; emphasis added). Referring to late-twentieth-century folklore studies, Dundes notes, "At a moment in American history when multi-cultural diversity is being celebrated, this is precisely when enlightened university administrators ought to be encouraging practitioners of an international discipline which goes back to Herder and the Grimms, a discipline which has been ahead of its time in recognizing the importance of folklore in promoting ethnic pride and in providing invaluable data for the *discovery* of native cognitive categories and patterns of worldview and values" (2005, 387; emphasis added). Amy Shuman and Charles L. Briggs's introduction to *Theorizing Folklore* cites different objects of discovery, but discovery all the same: "the study of folklore and folkloristics can play a significant role in the postmodern effort to *discover* modernism's various 'Others'" (1993, 109; emphasis added). Toelken opens his textbook by announcing that newcomers to the field are "surprised to *discover* that the scholarly discussion of the subject has been taking place for over two hundred years" (1996, 1; emphasis added). The use of the word *discovery* implies that enterprising labor is required to unearth folklore and that popular conceptions about it are undermined. Although the point is often underscored that folklore is everywhere and renewable in modernity, its documentation, according to folklorists, is daunting. Perceived as "shifting, uncertain, chaotic," to reiterate Hartland, folklore needs to be, as the manifesto *Toward New Perspectives in Folklore* states, "controlled and studied" (Paredes 1972, x). Textbooks describe the recovery and control of folklore as a procedure of collection followed by classification and *encoding* of the material.

But toward what end? Dundes complains that "little or no attempt was made in comparative studies of folklore to *explain* why the item may have been created in the first place or why it continued to be transmitted by bearers of tradition. To put it another way, the 'meaning' or 'meanings' of folklore were not investigated to any great extent by folklorists" (2002, ix; emphasis added). Oring earlier warned that "the development of theory in folkloristics will be ages in coming if we believe that the task of *explanation* has already been accomplished" (1976, 80; emphasis added). The implication is that folklore may be illuminated by scholars—that is, they may draw attention to its characteristics and patterns—but its existence has not been explicated (see Bronner 1988b; Dundes 1980; Ketner 1976; Oring 1996). In other words, these authors complain that reasons have not been given for what people do (see Tilly 2006). Explication—giving sources and causes of phenomena—requires, in their view, the organization of systematic investigation that results in findings.

Dundes's complaint is that the structured procedure does not advance to *decoding*, or what he calls "interpretation." He calls for "true grand theories" that "allow us to understand data that would otherwise remain enigmatic, if not indecipherable" (2005, 289). He derides poststructural theories of performance and feminism as "simply pretentious ways of saying that we should study folklore as performed, and we should be more sensitive to the depiction of women in folkloristic texts and contexts" (2005, 389). This critique echoes, ironically, performance-oriented folklorists' belittling of the older Finnish historic-geographic approach of collecting texts for a determination of their origin and diffusion. As Américo Paredes states, the modest revelation from the Finnish school's labor-intensive text-centered approach is that "folklore travels" (1972, x). The goal of theory building around contextualized performance was to develop "understanding" and "insight," although typically, a method by which these attributes are gained was not delineated, and this was not seen as a detriment.

In his important theoretical survey "Structuralism and Folklore," Dundes observes, "there is no theoretical trend which has had more impact upon both the humanities and the social sciences than structuralism" (1978b, 178). He conceptualizes structuralism in folkloristics as "the study of the interrelationships or organization of the component parts of an item of folklore," related especially to Ferdinand de Saussure's linguistic concept that meaning is defined within a generative system or structure (Dundes 1978b, 179; see also Dundes 1980, 36–37). The significance of this idea is that speakers are frequently unaware of the generative system, and the analyst gets at meaning by identifying underlying structures used by a language community (Tallis 2005). Making the shift from linguistic to folkloric structures, Dundes notes that the materials of folklore had inspired structural inquiry well before the narrative analytical systems of Claude Lévi-Strauss and Vladimir Propp gained currency in the mid-twentieth century. The concept of *rites de passage* introduced by Arnold van Gennep, for instance, and the Finnish school of comparative studies (utilizing etic units of motif and type) championed by Stith Thompson can be viewed as structural because they describe minimal units of analysis and use these units as the basis for some manipulation of data (Dundes 1978b, 192–97; Dundes 1962b; Krohn 1999; van Gennep 1960, 1999). Further, they establish a linear procedure from identification of the phenomenon under study to an outcome. The outcome can be framed as a proposal or finding that invites confirmation of the study's data or testing with different evidence.[1]

Although Dundes espoused structuralism in service of discipline to define the genres that constitute folklore, the concept has philosophical implications of humans' creativity guided by underlying cognitive structures. In reaction to the evolutionists of the Victorian era, Dundes, as a folklorist, was skeptical of universal claims for psychic unity, and he therefore saw the separation of structural approaches in the mid-twentieth century from the superorganic tendency in evolutionary theory to posit principles "which are presumed to operate independently of human emotion and volition" (Dundes 1978b, 185; see also Kroeber 1917). The modern folkloristic adaptation of structuralism is therefore to make it culturally relative and contextualized, represented by the idea of *oikotypification*—that is, changes to a "text-type's content style, or structures it adapts to the preferred patterns of a particular locality or culture group" (Clements 1997; see also Cochrane 1987; von Sydow 1948, 1999). Outlining a method of empirical analysis, Dundes states: "Either there will be locally popular structural patterns and thus structural oicotypes or the identification of cross-cultural structural patterns will greatly assist researchers in concentrating upon local oicotypical content differences within a common structural frame. In other words, there may be oicotypes of a structural nature or oicotypes of content. The point is that whether a folklorist employs the comparative method or structuralism, he is concerned with 1. defining similarities, and 2. delineating differences" (Dundes 1978b, 187). In sum, although Dundes cites precedents for the structural analysis of folklore, he considers structuralism an explanatory movement sparked by professional folklorists' desire to show "how folklore contains and communicates the central metaphors of a society" (Dundes 1978b, 200). Structural analysis in folklore is "a means to an end," and that end is the explanation of the logic of practice. Structuralism thus characterizes an approach that can potentially draw on a number of theories, such as psychoanalysis and Marxism, to achieve its goals (Bronner 1986a, 112–16; Dundes 1978b, 199–200; see also Burns 1977, 128–33).

One can detect a structuralist tone pervading the shift from the items of folklore to the doing of folklore in the groundbreaking book *Toward New Perspectives in Folklore*, edited by Paredes and Bauman (1972). Bauman, in his "Differential Identity and the Social Base of Folklore," states, for example, "As a form of social behavior, artistic verbal performance is subject to the same kind of implicit and explicit cultural rules which govern all human behavior, and the relevant questions become where, when, for what purposes, and to whom does a person with a particular set of attributes, or identity features, employ (or not employ) a particular form of verbal art" (1972, 40). Yet one can also discern a post-structuralist doubt about the analytical conclusion. For instance, although Roger Abrahams notes in the same volume that the functionalist approach "does allow us to test some basic hypotheses through direct observation," he sees problems in a "frame of reference" that proposes to identify a "sole purpose" (1972, 27). This refers to the ability to generalize from specific performances. Understanding that folklore is enacted by tradition-bearers or organizers for specific purposes, supporters of the "new perspectives" are tempted to answer the question of meaning with the particularistic statement, "it depends on the context." And even then, the context is understood by the participants in the situation, thus rendering the continuity of tradition an intentional act. Carried to the extreme, this dependent post-structural interpretation asserts that generalization is impossible because every tradition is a singular event and each performance is unique and incomparable.

Oring utilizes folklore to demonstrate that using context as interpretation is problematic (I would replace *humor* with *tradition* to make the same point):

> There is a joke about a man who describes to his friend a cocktail party he attended. "At the party, I met this guy who just talked, and talked, and talked, and talked." "What did he talk about?" his friend inquired. "I don't know. He didn't say." Too often humor is treated like this cocktail party conversation. We know it is there, we know who participated, we know it occurred in a particular space and took up time, we know it was funny. Nevertheless, because joke tellers and wit makers don't usually tell us what their comic performances are about, it is easy to assume that they aren't about anything. I presume, however, that humor *means* something. For me, humor studies is fundamentally an interpretive enterprise. It is an attempt to say what people are talking about even when they don't say so themselves. It is an attempt to wrest meaning—sometimes significant meaning—from ludicrous and seemingly discountable expressions. (Oring 2003, 146)

To be sure, knowing the context for tradition is significant, especially, in Oring's view, to reduce the ambiguity that typically permeates a traditional expression. It clarifies the rules, conventions, and understandings of the culture in which tradition is communicated and the roles and attitudes of participants and observers of tradition (Oring 1992, 15).

Dundes argues similarly that post-structural perspectives express control over specific experiences transformed into data, but they do not derive "deep" (i.e., cognitive), generalizable meaning from aggregate patterns. Underlying this plaint is his use of a structured method of identification and interpretation designed to discover a latent cognitive or social meaning after describing manifest content. Dundes was known for using psychoanalysis to get at latent meanings, but other analytic schema can certainly be employed to get to the bottom of why and how tradition is enacted, including positing social functions and behavioral reinforcements. Oring is concerned about positing functions as scientific explanation because it makes lawlike statements in theory but may be logically flawed in practice. To say that a tradition has the function of bonding a group presents the consequences, often unintended, of actions as causes. The goal of explanation demands that the analyst still has to present sources or causes of actions. Oring gives the example of a joke: "the fact that a joke may be used to embarrass and subsequently control a particular individual is an important observation so long as it is not regarded as an explanation for the presence of the joke in any particular social system" (1976, 77). Oring observes the confusion of functionalism as explanatory deduction with interpretation as the perception of patterns. Therefore he advises that the post-structural preoccupation with situating the emergence of lore cannot serve as the basis for a science of folkloristics, defining it as the formulation of "testable hypotheses in an effort to construct those empirical generalizations which provide the higher level of understanding that we seek" (Oring 1976, 80).

One source of post-structural anxiety is that functionalism and structuralism suggest meanings or consequences outside the awareness of participants. The analyst's logic, and his or her authority to posit meaning, must therefore be critically examined. The founding narratives of Victorian folklore studies, in contrast, frequently questioned the logic of tradition-bearers. Victorian folklorists rendered a service to rationalize what appeared to be "meaningless." Hartland's prime example is of folk cures for warts, which were quite familiar to his readers. He editorializes, "Now, this is a very silly superstition; quite meaningless, you may think, founded on nothing; and you are astonished that any one can believe it. But there you are too hasty." By saying that "no belief, no superstition in this world is founded upon nothing," he offers a structural explanation. He emphasizes that indeed a logical system is at work, but "while very often the reasoning is accurate, the premises only are insecure." He criticizes the folk logic of *post hoc, propter hoc* ("after this, therefore because of it"), evident in "from not taking into account all the possible causes of an effect; and, on the other hand, from not testing the supposed cause by other evidence" (Hartland 1904, 13).

Hartland's commentary uses the strategy of explanation to show, in Hartland's words, "that the science of Folklore is one of real importance, full of interest, full of surprises to those who are unacquainted with it." The expectation of a paradigm shift arising from the identification of causation is evident from his comment that folklore "has vast possibilities that will revolutionise our conceptions of human history" (Hartland 1904, 44). History is especially pertinent, not just because of the attraction of evolutionary models in Hartland's era but also because of the logical presumption of presumptive causation—what went before explains what occurred later. Even if the discipline of history is not the locus of contemporary folkloristic activity, replaced often by human behavior and experience, the idea persists that folklore needs to be rationalized. Interpreted, folklore's patterns are uncovered; explained, its sources are analyzed.

From where does the commanding rhetoric of interpretation derive? Intellectually, reverence as well as citation is often given to Clifford Geertz's *The Interpretation of Cultures* (1973) and his concept of "thick description" in an "interpretive theory of culture." He distinguishes his "description" from "explanation" by stating that rather than generalizing across cases characteristic of explanation, description generalizes "within them."[2] Using the analogy of a patient being diagnosed, Geertz is particularly concerned that interpretation will not be predictive but will anticipate a specific situation. Geertz states that his subjective interpretation gives special attention to "the meaning particular social actions have for the actors whose actions they are, and stating, as explicitly as we can manage, what the knowledge thus attained demonstrates about the society in which it is found and, beyond that, about social life as such" (1973, 27).

To be sure, Geertz suggests a structuralist task for the ethnographer: to "uncover the conceptual structures that inform our subjects' acts, the 'said' of social discourse, and to construct a system of analysis in whose terms what is generic to those structures, what belongs to them because they are what they are, will stand out against the other determinants of behavior" (1973, 27). Yet Geertz leaves doubt about the structuralist endeavor by suggesting that knowledge of culture need not be cumulative: "Rather than following a rising curve of cumulative findings, cultural analysis breaks up into a disconnected yet coherent sequence of bolder and bolder sorties. Studies do build on other studies, not in the sense that they take up where the others leave off, but in the sense that, better informed and better conceptualized, they plunge more deeply into the same things" (1973, 25). The structuralist challenge to this notion is whether disconnected and particularized ethnographies can be made coherent. The appeal of Geertz's interpretative "sorties" to post-structuralism, I propose, is the importance placed on describing cultural practices as unique actions and the relation of meanings as expressed by actors in a performance. Geertz's interpretation also refers to his background in literary study, because he conceives of actions as "texts" that can be read differently by various observers as well as by participants. Therefore, the post-structural possibility of different, even simultaneous meanings exists. Geertz's textual readings have in fact been criticized methodologically for being arbitrarily derived and essentially unprovable (see Hammersley 1992; Schneider 1987; Yoshida 2007).

Dundes's structural source for *Interpreting Folklore* (1980) is Sigmund Freud's *The Interpretation of Dreams* (1900). Freud studied both dreams and folklore and in fact related the two (Freud and Oppenheim 1958). Both are often viewed as "unintelligible and absurd" and carrying little significance, although Freud ventured to show that they are important psychologically (Freud 1999, 128). In his essay "The Method of Interpreting Dreams: An Analysis of a Specimen Dream," Freud calls for a "scientific treatment of the subject," involving the materialization of dream content into comparable texts (1999, 132). He warns that "the object of our attention is not the dream as a whole but the separate portions of its content" (Freud 1999, 136). Freud describes the analysis of the dream's portions as a "decoding method, since it treats dreams as a kind of cryptography in which each sign can be translated into another sign" (1999, 130). The interpretation posits "hidden" meanings that the actor is not aware of. They are deduced from general principles, such as "a dream is the fulfilment of a wish" (Freud 1999, 154). Both Geertz's socioanalysis and Dundes's psychoanalysis involve the conceptualization of tradition as symbolic texts, but the former relates them to social structure, whereas the latter relates them to mental processes.

Even if modern folklorists on the whole did not embrace Freudian analysis as Dundes did, they nonetheless largely adopted the rhetoric of interpretation from Dundes's oft-repeated statement of folkloristic methodology in "The Study of Folklore in Literature and Culture: Identification and Interpretation" (1965a). The significance of this statement is its articulation of a distinct folkloristic method. It locates a disciplinary space for scholars examining expressive traditions, especially related to the problem of identity—the correlative relation of worldview to expression and the idea that this outlook is learned or inherited through tradition. Dundes narrates this distinction by observing, "If it is true that folklorists too often identify without going on to interpret whereas literary critics and anthropologists interpret without first properly identifying folklore, then it seems obvious that some changes are needed. Either folklorists are going to have to educate their literary and anthropological colleagues in the mechanics of identifying folklore or they will have to undertake some of the problems of interpretation themselves" (Dundes 1965a, 142). Often overlooked in the rush to dismiss symbolist interpretation as subjective is Dundes's demonstration of empirical analysis, that is, some operation on data—whether structuralism, historical reconstruction, or cross-cultural comparison—as a prerequisite to interpretation. Indeed, critics of psychoanalytical interpretation, such as Oring, also apply analysis, often structural and contextual, although they arrive at different conclusions about causes of folkloric phenomena (Oring 1975).

The use of hypotheses is not restricted to testing previous results. This method is frequently used to analyze new data to determine whether a predictive proposition applies. A startling example is Oring's "The Humor of Hate," in which his explicit goal is to test the Freudian hypothesis that "if the function of joke technique is to overcome the resistances—both internal and external—to aggression, jokes should be absent in situations where that aggression is open and direct" (Oring 2003, 42). His data were drawn from a concentrated sample of humor circulated by a single neo-Nazi group, and his finding negates Freud's hypothesis that humor is a disguising strategy. To test the explanation of humor, he generates a new hypothesis: "When humor is hostile, the motive is more than likely to be conscious and the effects deliberate" (Oring 2003, 57). In setting out this hypothesis, Oring implies methodologically that folkloristic problems can in fact be stated as testable propositions, with the goal of explaining the presence of material or actions that people perceive as traditional or that appear demonstrative, repetitive, or bizarre (Oring 2003, 146).

Toward an Explanatory Method
for the Study of Traditions

Considering that the role of accruable, generalizable findings in an explanatory method of folkloristics is central to the development of a "science of tradition," I now address the adaptation of folkloristic methodologies from the scientific method. Arguably, labeling this method "scientific" is a rhetorical strategy to point out that the study of tradition should be empirically based and contribute to explanations of human behavior rather than a simulation of experimental laboratory science (Brown 2008; Glassie 1983, 124–26; Samuelson 1983). The four-tier ethnographic methodology I outline moves from problem statement, identification, and annotation to analysis, explanation, and implication. This is a far cry from the Victorians' natural history, in which traditions were collected and classified as biological specimens to construct an evolutionary periodization from savagery to civilization. In the outline presented here, folklore is key evidence of the process of tradition acting as a causal force in culture while still inquiring humanistically into the faith and insight that tradition provides as a type of knowledge or mode of thought (D'Andrade 2008; Pelikan 1984, 65–82). In answering basic questions of why people cling to traditions, why some traditions "catch on" or "die out," and why some people defend or attack traditions as things or values that are "traditional," the outline is intended to guide the investigation of tradition's connotativeness—its encapsulation of meanings that may vary as traditions are enacted by participants and perceived by insiders and outsiders.

Returning to the "science" in the "science of tradition," I find that the basis for a laboratory version of the scientific method is typically summarized as follows:

1. Observation and description of phenomena.
2. Formulation of a hypothesis to explain the phenomena. The hypothesis often takes the form of a causal mechanism or a mathematical relation.
3. Use of the hypothesis to predict the existence of other phenomena or to predict, quantitatively, the results of new observations.
4. Confirmation of the hypothesis through experimental tests by several independent experimenters (Wilson 1991; Gower 1997).

What happens when the controlled conditions of a laboratory are transferred outside, to the wildness of a cultural "field" with human subjects? Kenneth Goldstein's *A Guide for Field Workers in Folklore* (1964) was a landmark work that proposed an answer to the question by adapting "scientific inquiry" to the study of imaginative expressions collected from human subjects in their "natural contexts." His guide was, according to both humanities and social science indexes, the most frequently cited folkloristic fieldwork guide up to the end of the twentieth century, but it is significant that his method of scientific inquiry is left out of fieldwork chapters in the discipline's post-structural textbooks.[3]

A comparison of Goldstein's procedure with that of laboratory science reveals that the use of hypothesis is similarly emphasized, but it appears late rather than early in the process:

1. Problem statement: setting up a problem to be solved.
2. Analysis of the problem: determining the relevant data and the most appropriate methods for obtaining them.
3. Collection of data.
4. Presentation of the research findings.
5. Postulation of hypotheses, based on the analysis and interpretation of data. (Goldstein 1964, 16)

Note that the keyword *interpretation* singularly appears in Goldstein's outline. It is relative to the scientific use of prediction and causation but suggests a subjective statement of meaning from the viewpoint of the analyst that differs from *findings*. Goldstein makes a connection between inference and interpretation and warns, "since inference involves a considerable amount of interpretation, it is less to be preferred as a field method than interviewing" (1964, 105). Goldstein suggests that findings are evident from direct observation, whereas an interpretation is deduced from general principles and may not be apparent from the literal content of the collected material. As a narrative structure, Goldstein's method follows a sequence of solving a puzzle, from the opening problem to a concluding solution. This procedure implies that in resolving an enigma, the analyst rationalizes folklore together with tradition, since its persistence and use seem irregular or unusual, or tradition draws attention to itself in some other way.

An especially trenchant inquiry into folkloristic method by Kenneth Laine Ketner (1973, 118–20) revised Goldstein's schema for scientific inquiry with the following:

1. Recognize a puzzling question or doubt.
   A. Unsaturated questions—those that begin with words such as *what, when, where, why*, or *how*.
   B. Saturated questions: those that take the form "Is S a P?"
2. Develop one or more hypotheses.
   A. If the inquiry begins with an unsaturated question, the first step is to propose a hypothetical answer.
   B. If the inquiry begins with a saturated question, we already have a hypothesis and can proceed to steps 3 and 4.
3. Deduce consequences.
4. Test the hypothesis.

One basis of this revision is a move beyond folklore materialism in Goldstein's emphasis on collecting. According to Ketner, materialism "insists that folkloric phenomena are to be understood as if they were objects, which means that folklore is seen as a static entity, a thing that can be transmitted from one person to another." The negation of this philosophy, seen in post-structuralist approaches, is "folklore interactionism"; this view "urges that folkloric phenomena are basically dynamic processes of interpersonal interaction" (Ketner 1973, 122). By referring to the processes as "dynamic," Ketner implies that they defy categorization and generalization. If that is the case, how is knowledge cumulative? One realizes that the inventory of "instances" has replaced the objectification of events in interactionism, but general concepts are not advanced.

Ketner's revision also suggests the use of explanation rather than interpretation, or the idea that the collection of objects and the observation of dynamic processes are ends in themselves. The inquiry may not follow the scientific method, but it is scientific in tenor by following from hypotheses that are confirmable (Ketner 1973, 122–23; see also Ketner 1975). If hypotheses are confirmed that, in Ketner's terms, "provide a statement of general lawlike relationships between phenomena," then one can posit an *explanation* of the connection between phenomena as a matter of observable fact (Ketner 1973, 126). The model for explanation would look like the following (with *explanans* represent-

ing the material used in explaining and *explanandum* being the matter
to be explained):

> Premises, such as . . . Statement of one or more general lawlike
> regularities, and Statement of one or more specific conditions
> Constituting *Explanans* (all statements true), leading to . . .
> Conclusion . . . Which logically implies that which requires
> explanation
> Constituting *Explanandum.* (Ketner 1973, 127)

By emphasizing the phenomena rather than their location, this
model removes the essential prerequisites of a "field" as a special place
with unusual people and fieldwork to "discover" them. With the addition of a scientific "mode of inference," according to Ketner, the implications are that "folkloric behavior is not a curiosity, not a symptom of
inferiority and ineptitude, not a mass of error, not the exclusive property of the stereotyped 'folk,' but a sign of one's humanity" (Ketner
1973, 130). The objection to the use of hypotheses as somehow inhu-
mane in post-structural approaches is obviated, although there is still
recognition of a special folkloristic sensibility to confirm and explain
the phenomena. That sensibility, as defined by Dundes and Dorson,
among others, involves a description of folklore's minimal units and
genres connected by processes of tradition, an appreciation of folklore's multiple existences and variations and its symbolic, connotative
characteristics.

Returning to Dundes's binary structure of identification and interpretation as a folkloristic research procedure, one can discern a division
between description and analysis. Dundes's critique suggests that post-
structuralist approaches are locked into description, although the textbooks claim that they apply analysis. There is a way to double Dundes's
binary, however, to create a more systematic linear methodology than
is denoted by identification and interpretation alone. Before identification, the folklorist has a *problem statement* that is often expressed
as a puzzling question. Working from the assumption that cumulative
scholarship begins where others end, the problem statement involves
an extended survey of bibliographic sources on the subject and variations of the material under consideration. This opening establishes the
significance of the query by reconsidering a previous interpretation

stated as a hypothesis; questioning a monocultural limitation that can be addressed with cross-cultural comparison or contrast; pointing out an action that had not been considered as a subject for inquiry (e.g., collecting as a praxis by folklorists); showing that an unlikely, usually learned or elite, group (e.g., scientists, mathematicians, physicians) is "folk" in the form of a saturated question; considering the effects of changing units of analysis (e.g., etic to emic units); or correcting nonfolkloristic treatment of folkloric material (e.g., Lévi-Strauss and Campbell on myth).

What follows is an *identification* predicated on the description of the item and the genre or genres to which it belongs. For Dundes, identification often involves showing material that was left out or minimized in previous collections, especially that involving the extent of an item's variations, its various cultural contexts, behavioral (or performance) information, or the available metafolklore. Distinctive to the study of folk traditions is the *annotation* that is often included in the identification project. Related to the conceptualization of folklore resulting from the process of *traditio*, the annotation positions the *traditum* in time and place and relates it to, or even categorizes it with, similar forms of practice. Oring considers the annotation essential to the analytic process because it uncovers "some sense of this web of relations"; it illustrates that folklore collected in "the face-to-face encounters at home, in the dormitory, or at work are often related to traditions that have been reported by other collectors in other times and in other places" (1989, 361). The annotation addresses issues that, according to Oring, involve the spread of tradition beyond a single group, class, or level of culture to avoid "cultural parochialism"; the identification of sociocultural change and variation, particularly in response to the tendency to view tradition as a sign of stasis; and the psychological or social importance of tradition—in other words, its force and function for individuals and groups as members of society.

Dundes constantly points out that previous scholars stopped short of "analyzing" the descriptive data, or they analyzed the wrong thing. He thus moves to the *analysis*, which he defines as conducting an operation on the data to signify cultural patterns. This is where underlying structures are exposed or other procedures come into play, such as extracting symbols from a text for closer examination, presenting contextual descriptions of an item's use, using cross-cultural examples to draw comparisons and contrasts, finding significance in etymologies and names as signs, or constructing the developmental chronology of an item or culture. Partly as a response to Victorian evolutionary models, analysis as it was pursued in the 1960s concentrated on the "immediate" context of the moment rather than reaching back into the past (see Bronner 1982c; de Caro 1976; McNeil 1982). At times, this analysis was not just ahistorical but also antihistorical, preferring the idea of folklore as unique performances emerging from the social situation to the idea of folklore as a sequence of events in time (Kapchan 2003). This presentist tendency shows, at least in part, a discomfort with tradition being construed as a bygone or survival, but in constructing a modern conception of tradition as a living force, it misses the significance of precedence to the notion of tradition as prescriptive. An important "context" I advocate for arriving at explanation is consideration of the continuities of practices and settings back in time, especially when they involve the diffusion of ideas and cultural adaptation in different places and conditions. In an orientation on tradition, the role of the past in the present should be ascertained, in addition to determining historic sources for, and reactions to, cultural practices (see Abrahams 2005; Bronner 1982b; Knight 2006). The "text" analyzed has expanded from the utterances and objects to the event as a whole and the behaviors that shape the event. Such texts have categorizable forms, patterns, and structures that can be described, annotated, and compared.

The *explanation* in a structural or rationalist approach is the critical leap from identifying textual or behavioral patterns to recognizing cognition. It typically involves discerning meaning with reference to generalizable statements that can solve intellectual enigmas, resolve apparent paradoxes, and uncover hidden motivations. Frequently the conclusion constitutes a final phase that I call *implication*, although others may call this step *application*. Implication is different from many folklorists' application (the basis of applied or public folklore) because in the latter one usually proposes programming to edify the public or procedures implemented by professionals (see Jones 1994). Analysis can be used, for example, to consider the social and political significance of the outlooks one uncovers or symbolic relationships among apparently diverse forms or traditions. Dundes provides a model of the analysis in his famously controversial *Life Is Like a Chicken Coop Ladder* (1984; the title derives from a well-known German folk proverb). He *identifies* a pattern of obsession with cleanliness and order in German folk speech and narrative; then, with *annotation*, he determines that the theme is not universal but is distinctive, if not unique, in German expressive traditions. He psychologically *analyzes* the material by noting the relation to anal erotic personality traits and posits a social pattern that *explains* the emphasis on authoritarian hierarchy and homogeneity in folklore as a mirror of national culture. He concludes by pointing to the *implication* of "elaborate purges" carried out by governments on the basis of a comparison of enemies to feces and suggests that such Holocaust-like events could happen again (Dundes 1984, 141).

The causal propositions of explanation invite testing and checking, and certainly Dundes's finding of a national character drew criticism for both over- and undergeneralization as well as selectivity of data (Bottigheimer 1985; Decker 1986; Eidson 1984; Tucker 1985). I take up his challenge in chapter 4 on Pennsylvania German narrative and consider his causal propositions elsewhere (see chapter 9 on football, which diverges from his anal-erotic explanation). The point here is that the structuralist procedure Dundes outlines is a methodological basis for a folkloristic explanation of traditions and provides options for the leap from identification to explanation that do not necessitate a psychoanalytic reading. Findings can be checked for validity and consistency by determining whether the explanation holds in other settings and ascertaining that the metaphoric claims are not contradicted within the scene examined (see Fine 1984; Mieder 2006). In my presentation of various scenes encompassing a range of cultural behaviors such as building, narrating, joking, crafting, and playing, I elaborate the inquiry into cognitive, historical, and social sources of repetitive, connotative content and practices identified as traditions. Readers will note a contrast to post-structural, performative arguments, where they do not receive a set of causal propositions as much as a set of contextual relations. This is not to say that I dismiss considerations of performance and textual comparison. The trouble is that the typical conclusion in performance-centered "interrogation" is not an answer to the question of why the event originates or persists, as in explanation, but rather a description of how the event proceeds and affects. In explanation, we find principle and action; in post-structural interpretation, we contemplate incidence and act. Interpretation can never be complete because it depends on inductive reasoning from ultimately unrepresentative examples or unique instances, whereas explanations are often deductive, subsumed under or covered by some regularity of culture or mind (in Dundes's case, psychoanalytic propositions; see Gensler 2002, 267–304). We might say that explanation samples, that is, compiles evidence to make a case or reach its object, while interpretation ensamples, that is, creates its subject. The logic of interpretation is modal, in that it uses inferences and possibilities rather than propositions or hypotheses in the sense of extrapolating predictive statements and analytical definitions.

In sum, folklore objectifies tradition and allows for its rationalization. It presents tradition as meaningful, purposeful activity that is an instrument of knowing and navigating through social life. In contrast to presentations of tradition that emphasize its ethereal, mystical, or ancient characteristics, the modifier *folk* clarifies this tradition as measurable, comparable, analyzable—and explicable. It is at once timeless and of the moment in a web of relations that includes modernity, the past, and the future, because it is continuous. It therefore does not presume that tradition is anachronistic or restricted to faith and falsehood (unlike the writer reporting an inexplicable "return to tradition" quoted at the beginning of the first chapter). If folk logic often proceeds according to the idea of handy knowledge in pragmatic response to local conditions, folkloristic logic generalizes the process into a fundamental behavior that is necessary to being human (Wilson 1988, 2006). Observed, collected, identified, annotated, and analyzed as practice or expression, folklore provides challenges to being translated into the data of tradition, not the least of which is its potential politicization. Overall, folklore problematizes tradition. Tradition in folkloristics is revealed as both continuous and changing, obvious and elusive, and therefore in need of explanation. In the chapters that follow I try my hand at explanation by showing why people do what they do—from getting one's hands dirty in raising a barn to barnstorming around the Internet.

3

Building Tradition

On Control and Authority in Vernacular Architecture

Eminently visible, persistent, and complex, buildings are objects that enclose people rather than objects they grasp with their hands, but residents often claim to be handy not only by maintaining their structures but also by gaining a sense of ownership (see Goldstein 1998; Jones 1980b). People use bodily rhetoric to refer to their enclosures; their frontal exteriors are said to have public "faces" that project dwellers' personalities to passersby (they also have "rears," where privacy, and waste, can be found). Viewing large edifices, especially, raises issues of control for people about to cross thresholds—the human ability to create anew and alter the old. Bound up with control is a question of authority: by whose standards, by what precedents, and with whose skills will creation, maintenance, and alteration occur?

Because buildings commonly combine a public facade with a private interior, the mind anticipates in advance the kinds of practices allowed as one navigates across space. After all, buildings rise above human scale, have public faces that people respond to, and typically shelter people coming together for dining, work, and play, which suggests culturally framed social interactions. The problem I deal with here concerns the human need to materialize traditions around those interactions, particularly when "handy" control of building is removed from dwellers. The evidence of persistent American grassroots building despite architectural pundits' predictions of its doom merits explanation. I hypothesize that some communities and individuals engage in building as an intentionally intrusive cultural behavior that draws attention to the social need for identity based on a handwrought connection or response to place. Given contemporary American practices associated with vernacular construction, it appears that people who view a sense of place and social belonging as running counter to modern edifices seek security and control in the claim to have built something "with their own hands" and associate that process with tradition.

Vernacular is an analytical term for those buildings that belong to a place, that express local or regional traditions. The linguistic analogy of the vernacular speech of building and dialect is significant because it allows a comparison of grammar and syntax, as well as style or manner of expression in material and verbal forms (Oliver 1997a, xxi). It names a category of expression for the majority of the world's buildings that come into being without schooled architects and that, in fact, offer long-standing reminders of the labor and resources in a cultural environment. Drawing on the Latin root *vernaculus*, or "native," these buildings tell what is indigenous, common, and shared in a community or region. *Vernacular* identifies buildings as social representations and links them to coherent cultural systems of values and beliefs. This point is evident in Paul Oliver's influential definition of vernacular architecture in *Encyclopedia of Vernacular Architecture of the World:* "Vernacular architecture comprises the dwellings and other buildings of the people. Related to their environmental contexts and available resources, they are customarily owner- or community-built, utilizing traditional technologies. All forms of vernacular architecture are built to meet specific needs, accommodating the values, economies and ways of living of the cultures that produce them" (1997a, xxiii). This definition is apparently an answer to the problem of visibly locating vernacular architecture in the broad global landscape. It emphasizes, after all, the building as a text within environmental contexts and available technologies. The last sentence, however, suggests another question of process, for if buildings represent the cultures that produce them, how and why are they produced? The answer emanates from the ways in which a people's values, "ways of living," and modes of building are transmitted and inherited. In short, we are led to issues of tradition to explain the visibility, persistence, and complexity of architecture as a problem of continuity and change. Considering tradition should allow us to answer not only textual questions, such as why buildings look the way they do and why they are located where they are, but also process-related questions, such as why they came into being and how they changed along the way.

These thorny questions often carry a reference to tradition because decisions about the shape of the future are based on the influence of precedent. Lest one assume that vernacular architectural texts are static points on the globe, tradition takes into account the balance of individual innovation and social custom in the generation of material culture (Bronner 1992b, 2000b; Martin 1983; Glassie 1993). Concern for the traditional in architecture therefore poses not only the question of what tradition is within a society or community: even more importantly, it asks what it *does* (see Riesman 1961; Shils 1981; Milspaw 1983; Glassie 1985; Rapoport 1989).

Tradition, Transmission, and Creativity

Oliver readily acknowledges that the concept of tradition and transmission has been neglected in vernacular architecture studies. This situation is surprising and perplexing, considering Oliver's contention that "in architecture it is the transmission of traditions that is . . . most essential to its understanding." He points out that "in spite of the vast quantity of studies of vernacular buildings—measured, drawn in plan, section and elevation, or described in technical detail, the fewer, but still numerous, studies of their use, and the occasional analyses of their symbolism, the verbatim record of how the traditions involved in them were transmitted is exceptionally rare" (Oliver 1989, 53, 74). In this discussion, Oliver implies a duality to tradition as it has been applied to vernacular architecture. Tradition can refer to both a cultural context and a performed text. He offers an analogy from linguistics whereby *parole* as the "rule system" (or competence) governs *langue*, the expression or performance (see de Saussure 1972; Hymes 1972; Jakobson and Bogatyrev 1980; Ben-Amos 1984, 121–24; Bauman 1992b). On this basis, tradition can be both subject and object; tradition shapes building, and buildings entail traditions. The common use of *traditional* to describe building is a reference to the structure as an object within a broader category of vernacular or indigenous, although as a subject, all vernacular dwellings embody traditions.

If the vernacular implies a culturally based, generative grammar for material texts, then tradition is a reference to the learning that engenders cultural expressions and the authority that precedent holds. This construct of tradition as a process of socially shared knowledge and transmission across time and space is the source of conceptualizing a model of explanation in vernacular architecture. Oliver underscores this direction for explanation by suggesting the usage of "vernacular know-how" or the "faculty of knowing." He writes, "within the context of vernacular architecture it embraces what is known and what is inherited about the dwelling, building, or settlement. It includes the collective wisdom and experience of a society, and the norms that have become accepted by the group as being appropriate to its built environment" (Oliver 1986, 113).

Tradition in vernacular building is not equal to "rule"; in fact, it implies unwritten or even unconscious codes of doing things that foster variation, because a single tradition, as it has been interpreted (especially in religion), can spawn many versions (see Shils 1981; Glassie 1974; Bronner 1986a). Tradition as a reference to precedent is therefore not fixed, and as a social construction, it is often renegotiated in every generation and in every community. Tradition as an idea invites commentary and interpretation and negotiation of allowable innovation, which, with repetition, might later come to be viewed as "traditional." As folklorist Henry Glassie observes, "Tradition's detractors associate it with stasis and contrast it with change, but it is rooted in volition and it flowers in variation and innovation." In relation to control and authority, tradition "opposes the alien and imposed" (Glassie 1993, 9).

Just as the individual (or, in reference to control, the "owner") responds to the perception of tradition as belonging to the group or community and works identity into this relationship, creativity is another necessary component of tradition because the possibility of change is inexorably linked to continuity of form and process over time (Evans 1982; Kristeller 1983; Santino 1986; Jones 1989; Bronner 1992a, 2000b). In Glassie's study of Turkish traditional artists, for example, he observes tradition as "the collective resource, essential to all creativity, and in adjective form it can qualify the products of people who keep faith with their dead teachers and their live companions while shaping their actions responsibly" (1993, 9).

The linking of creativity and tradition suggests a modern philosophy of the arts in which "the ability to create is not limited to artists or writers but extends to many more, and perhaps to all, areas of human activity and endeavor" (Kristeller 1983, 106). This broadening of artistry suggests creativity as a social ideal. This ideal succeeds the Romantic notion of art and architecture as the sole domain of exceptional cultivated minds, existing free of tradition, and as an expression of originality or genius that can create something where nothing existed previously (summarized as "creation"). There is not one capitalized Tradition in architecture in a modern philosophy of the arts but a multiplicity of traditions to explore, for tradition in its multiple, abstract existence does not form a simple contrast with creativity. We may recognize situations and societies in which the pressure to repeat precedent is strong, when tradition may be reintroduced or reestablished as a creative contribution. In any case, innovation is based on an understanding of precedents, many of which will be perceived as traditional. Creativity and tradition are intertwined and represent the complex processes of humans expressing themselves to others in ways that carry value and meaning. Tradition demands attention to form and fidelity to cultural continuity, while inviting alteration and extension for social needs.

An assumption of the vernacular as part of a modern philosophy of the arts is that tradition tends to dominate at the social grass roots, by which is meant that choices are restricted. Stating that there is a vernacular implies the existence of a shared social understanding of cultural standards, customs, and norms. But choices are nonetheless apparent in the performance of customs and the enforcement of norms. Geographer Yi-Fu Tuan describes the process of tradition as one of "constraint" rather than repetition. The question it begs is critical to the reformation of culture: "Out of all the things that have been handed down to us and that we now possess, what do we choose, and what are we compelled, to pass on?" Tuan reflects that "perhaps what we must seek to retain are not so much particular artifacts and buildings (though we should try to do so in exceptional instances), but rather the skill to reproduce them" (Tuan 1989, 33). Amos Rapoport picks up this theme in his effort to define the attributes of tradition in relation to the analysis of the built environment. Whereas Rapoport associates tradition with "conservatism" in the sense of accepting the past, continuity, and repetition, Tuan offers the less politically loaded (and often negative) sense of "waiting." I prefer the idea of "expectation" coupled with "reliance," implying social connection and trust, and a notion of "security" (as I discuss later with some native descriptions of tradition). "Dependence" does not offer choice, but "reliance" does, and the sense of reliable connotes the rationality of being time-tested. What is significant in the modern concept of tradition is that the past becomes part of the present as a guide to future action. Avoiding the word *past* as well as its sense of a distant time, Rapoport considers the prevailing question to be "what is repeated, through what mechanisms it is repeated, and what, if anything, makes it meaningful" (Rapoport 1989, 82).

Using the linguistic model of vernacular, we might think of tradition as the local saying that gains credit by long and frequent use. Structured as a proverb, the saying offers the wisdom of many expressed by one person, but it may not need a long precedent (Taylor 1994). Its wisdom is a result of an important aspect of tradition: social acceptance. As an adage, the saying takes on significance because of being transmitted, and tested, through time, and it may be variously influenced by the performer's perception of certain situations and surroundings. *Adage* implies wisdom that one may choose to follow or at least recognize, in contrast to *maxim*, which is more of a rule of conduct. The differences among these types of sayings show that tradition covers a range of control and authority and can become contentious for a community as a result. In the modern concept, it is important to take note of the enactment of the tradition and observe that traditions of proverbial performance can be customary, such as a practice followed as a matter of course among a people or a community or by an individual as part of that person's experience and way of living. In this analogy, builders can use forms and techniques they recognize from tradition as socially accepted and time-tested, and residents alter and apply their experiences in the house. To be sure, the house is not an utterance, and in its persistence as a form and its complexity as a process, it stands boldly on the landscape. It frames experience and custom by providing shelter, a basic human need, and by symbolizing social existence. Sheltering people as well as symbolizing them, elevated above them and enclosing them, the house rhetorically stands for tradition.

As Oliver, Glassie, and Rapoport have all pointed out, the concept of tradition is a distinct analytical tool. It lacks an exact synonym or meaning and, being a process rather than a thing, requires abstraction. Tradition is not the same as the broader category of culture, with which it is often allied, because tradition is presumably selected for transmission and can be enacted in specific instances, such as the construction of a building (Rapoport 1989, 98; Ben-Amos 1984, 119–21). Although both concepts are seen as patterns for behavior and actions, culture in the literature is often used in the broader sense of the "superorganic," in that it is an analytical concept describing a condition over which humans have little control (Alfred Kroeber [1917] gives the analogy of culture being akin to water for fish; see also Sapir 1917; Bauman 1972; Ben-Amos 1984, 119–21).

Tradition as a concept that humans manage and adapt represents a native category. Rapoport comments, for example, that "many environments seen as chaotic are only incomprehensible to, disliked by, or inappropriate for the outside observer" (1989, 97). There are many traditions, therefore, only some of which are called traditional or folk—if one applies Rapoport's criteria for traditional as widely accepted "models or schemata" that are usually culture specific—and are persistent through time. As Rapoport explains, "one can like some aspects of tradition and not others, so that traditions do not disappear or change all of a piece; some aspects may persist, while others disappear or are modified. Even when traditions continue rather than being rejected, adherence to them today is not as it once was. Both rejection and fervent attachment to pastness, as well as acceptance of only some aspects of tradition, are the result of choice, of decision. These responses are no longer non-reflective, 'natural' or self-evident, qualities which constitute one of the major attributes of traditionality" (1989, 98–99).

If tradition is viewed as a process, then an eye toward tradition in the vernacular landscape takes in several significant implications:

1. When consistencies among buildings are apparent at a single time, the question arises as to the force of tradition as a social construction in dictating the similarities. The understanding is that there is a perception of cultural precedent by which forms are generated. The interrogation of tradition reveals the process of learning or direction from tradition-bearers to others or the socially shared events in which tradition is invoked.

2. When inconsistencies are apparent in different periods, the question arises as to the forces in tradition that allow builders to change and innovate. The understanding is that the vernacular, being rooted in tradition, is less apt to change; therefore, when significant change occurs, it indicates major social struc-

tural shifts. Implied in this understanding is that communities perpetuate their traditions from one generation to another in various and often culturally specific ways—in apprenticeships, in rituals and festive events, and in family and community institutions, for instance.

3. When variations are apparent in communities or regions, the question arises as to the communication of tradition across space. The understanding is that tradition diffuses in traceable patterns and cultural influences. The implication is that various influences affect diffusion, including geographic, social, and economic opportunities and barriers; technology and economic connections; linguistic connections from one group to another; political organization; self-perceptions of insiders (what may be referred to as "identity"); and attitudes toward outsiders.

4. When variations are apparent among the dwellings of different builders and residents who have physically adapted the structures for their use, the question arises as to the dynamics of creativity and tradition in individual decisions about the appearance of buildings. Implicit in this question is the role of individuality within a culture. Whereas tradition itself suggests an ethnographic focus on the "performance" or enactment of a building, the question of variation often adds the behavioral issues (i.e., those based on personal, material enactments of ideas and involving the communication of symbols) of technical competence (culturally developed skills and talents), decoration and style, use and function, arrangement, and aesthetics to the more textual methodology associated with a comparison of the form (floor plans and elevations) and materials of construction.

In sum, traditions draw attention when they are enacted, and oral traditions can be traced to other performers by attention to the style and variation of singers, speakers, and tellers. Indeed, with songs, speech, and tales, tradition as a behavioral process is frequently invoked because the performer is more apparent than in architecture. It appears, in fact, that in uttering (rather than building) material texts in situational and cultural contexts, the performer is more in control of tradition in the shaping of a performance (Evans 1982; Bauman 1992b; Jones 1997). One reason that tradition as an explanatory concept has not been more often applied to building is that scholars typically approach the building as text rather than as event or process (see Upton 1979, 1985; Herman 1985; Glassie 1972a; Jones 1997). It can be argued that *vernacular* rather than *traditional* became an appealing adjective for architecture because it allows the viewer license to identify cultures through consistencies in building styles without full knowledge of the human mediation and customs involved (see Bronner 1979a; Heath 1988). *Vernacular* suggests the distancing of people as agents of their own artifacts. Thus we can understand Oliver's frustration with the neglect of tradition, since the link between past and present requires an analysis of tradition in the consideration of human agency. "In all societies," Oliver writes, "traditions are valued for the continuity that they symbolize between the past and present. The means by which traditions are transmitted between generations are therefore fundamental" (1997b, 117).

With tradition as a consideration in material culture, it is not just the skill or procedure of construction that is in question; also at issue is the way that knowledge—of design and values—is inherited, adapted, and transmitted. From a textual point of view, variation in architecture is assumed to be across space, thus lending itself to the identification of types and the mapping of regions. The impression is that an organic progression, apart from the volition of human builders, occurs as one surveys patterns across the landscape (see Noble 1984; Ensminger 1992). But with more inquiry into tradition, the relations of self to community, continuity to change, and innovation to conformity come to the fore to explain technological choices that lead to variation.

One way to signify the performative aspect of shelters is to refer to building as an integration of the action of constructing with the resulting form. Architecture, in contrast, connotes a value judgment about the look of structures to authorities, rather than to owners. The frequently invoked term *process* is useful as a differentiation from text, but it may sound overly behavioral without encompassing the symbolic, cognitive implications of actions by participants in tradition as they negotiate with their cultures about innovations and variations. I have used the concept of *praxis* to extend the ethnography of cultural practices to a philosophy of cultural action (Bronner 1984, 1988b, 2010). The term, a root of *practice*, is intended to draw attention to the symbolic qualities of doing things that have social and cultural significance. Building as practice is the physical act of constructing with materials. But what about the phrase "building a family" after marriage? Is that building? Is it the same as making? No, because it is symbolically important to express the solidity and display of building for a new, fragile social unit. In proverbial usage, one might hear, "When we build, let us think that we build forever," to reinforce the cognitive association of building with a lasting edifice for future generations (Mieder 1992, 73). People choose the rhetoric of building to convey a cognitive concept that others in their context can understand and probably associate with various images inculcated through tradition. The rhetoric reveals their thinking and translates it into symbolic behavior.

An important query involving the praxis of tradition is the way it relates to modern pluralistic societies in which, as Tuan claims, individual choices are more abundant and innovation is encouraged. Although it may appear that tradition is "lost," arguably, the number of available and emergent traditions is greatly multiplied. Indeed, a complex question is the changing nature of tradition within modern industrialized states. Although tradition, following Robert Redfield's paradigm of the "little community" and "folk society," is associated anthropologically with small, homogeneous groups and a limited space and is assumed to be passively received, tradition in modern society is still at work on a mass scale as a cultural reference to a way of doing things or an appeal to the authenticity provided by "roots" (see Bauman 1983; Bronner 2002b, 2005d; Foster 1953; Kirshenblatt-Gimblett 1983, 1995; Redfield 1947, 1960; Sider 1986). Rapoport sees contrasts in the survival of traditional groups and products in centralized states such as France in comparison to the diverse United States (Rapoport 1989, 99). This survivalistic concern is understandable, considering the cultural historian's worry about the preservation of vernacular environments in mass culture. However, the query that reveals the dynamic process of transmitted, inherited tradition, as well as modernity, is about continuity and change. The focus is on the creative choices made as individuals perceive the external authority of tradition.

Representations of Dynamic Traditions in Twenty-First-Century America

As examples of the incorporation of tradition in the vernacular architecture of complex societies, I offer three representations of the dynamics

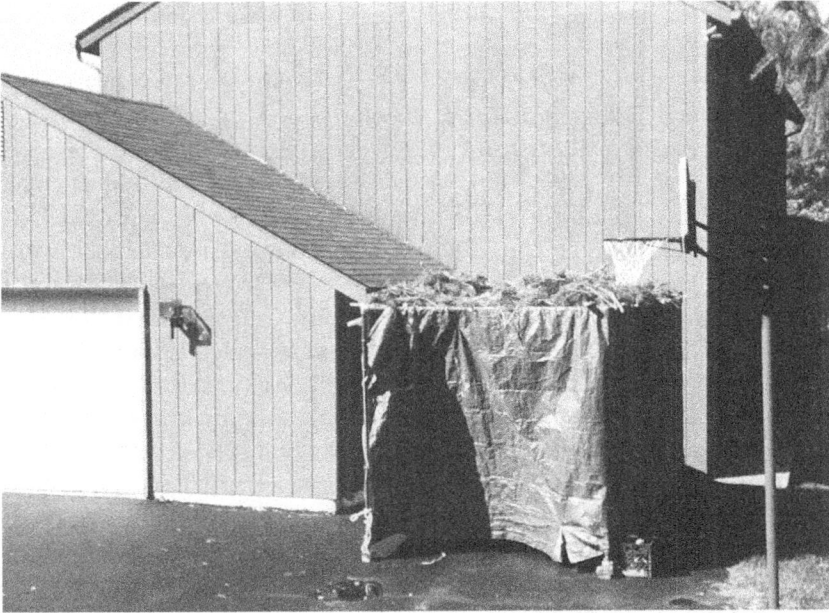

Family sukkah built in a suburban development in Harrisburg, Pennsylvania. (Photo by Simon Bronner)

of tradition in twenty-first-century America: seasonal construction of the Jewish *sukkah*, Amish community barn raising, and Houston's "recycled" houses. I order them based on their historical reach: the sukkah is an ancient structure codified in a religious text; barn raising among the Amish originated in Europe and developed over the last 200 years; and the "recycled" houses, or homemade environments, date to the late twentieth century. With each, the control individuals exert over their environments in response to mass society, and therefore the meaning of tradition, is frequently at issue.

The *sukkah* (plural, *sukkot*), translated roughly from Hebrew as "booth" or "tabernacle," is central to the Jewish thanksgiving holiday *Sukkot*, or the "Festival of Booths." It drew my attention because the holiday revolves around the construction of a primitive dwelling, intended to be temporary. The building of this structure is an annual reminder of the Israelites' exodus from ancient Egypt. Every year, Jews are called to reconstruct the historical vernacular architecture of their nomadic period in the desert. The biblical description in Leviticus 23:42 makes it plain that the purpose is to reinforce the transmission of values from one generation to another: "You shall dwell in sukkot seven days . . . in order that future generations may know that I made the Israelite people live in sukkot when I brought them out of the land of Egypt, I the Lord your God." In modern American society, with its individualistic pursuit of wealth and materialism, orientation toward the future, and reliance on a service economy, the creation of a simple dwelling and giving thanks for nature's bounty are supposed to have a leveling effect socially and a humbling one personally (United Synagogue 2003). Even if a resident lives in a modern prefabricated house, he or she can build the sukkah to represent Jews' handwrought roots in the ancient Middle East. One man recalled (apropos of my previous analogy, with a connection between the structure and a proverb):

> It has been said that the pleasures we make for ourselves are fuller and fairer than the pleasures which are given to us. Perhaps this is why we loved our *sukkah*—for we made it ourselves. We did not employ a professional carpenter to put in a single nail or plane a single beam. We bought rough logs and boards at the city timber yard. We planed the logs and grazed our fingers, but the pain did not count. Though all these preparatory stages occurred a fortnight beforehand, the actual building operations never began until the night, when the Great Fast was over. Old traditions clung to us, and somehow we knew it as a special merit to close the Day of Atonement, hammer in hand, putting in the first nail of the *sukkah*, passing as the psalmist has it "from strength to strength." (Abrahams 1958, 145)

For seven days during autumn, five days after the solemn observance and fast of Yom Kippur, many Jews celebrate Sukkot as one of the most joyous days on the Jewish calendar. As part of the Diaspora, American Jews consider the first two days of the holiday to be *yom tov*, that is, a major festival during which work is prohibited. The sukkah is the major symbol of the holiday and is referenced in the Hebrew Bible: "After the ingathering from your threshing floor and your vat, you shall hold the Feast of Booths for seven days" (Deuteronomy 16:13–17). Although most American Jews do not have agrarian occupations, as referenced in the Bible, many use the occasion to connect with nature and emphasize "ingathering" to identify observant Jews. Some Jews explained to me that in the absence of a harvest, they consider it preferable to build their own sukkot to symbolically mark labor (and the "fruits" thereof), followed by the celebration.

Representing a thanksgiving harvest festival, the booths abound with symbols of nature's bounty, but even more evident is the sukkah's function to encourage close relations within family and community. The holiday is associated with hospitality and the charitable spirit of sharing. Accordingly, it is customary to invite one's Jewish neighbors and friends to share a meal in the sukkah. Reinforcing this spirit is a symbolic ritual known as *ushpizin* (Hebrew for "guests"), in which a blessing is read to mark the invitation to an ancient Jewish patriarch, such as Abraham, Isaac, Jacob, Joseph, Moses, Aaron, or David, to sit with the participants in the sukkah.

Against the backdrop of a sukkah built at the Jewish Community Center, students from the Harrisburg Hebrew School (front row) show models of sukkot they made. (Courtesy Historical Society of Dauphin County)

Once considered an individual's obligation among the many American Jews of eastern European ancestry, building the sukkah in the United States was increasingly relegated to Jewish community institutions, including synagogues and Jewish community centers, through the twentieth century. The sukkot of such institutions tend to be large, often holding as many as 100 people. Some orthodox critics consider this trend an undesirable result of assimilation, as individuals give up their piety and treat the synagogue as a convenient service. During the 1990s there was an effort, especially among the Lubavitcher wing of orthodoxy, to publicize among Jews the need to restore the obligation of the household sukkah.

Few Jews I interviewed consulted the Talmud, the written code drawn from rabbinical oral tradition, for the design of the sukkah, although it is specific on many of the structure's aspects. Most commonly they used a "blueprint" drawn from two sources—participation in the sukkah's construction as a youth, and the prevailing design of other structures in their community. Building the sukkah is usually a family project: parents place the poles, the father erects the walls, and the mother and children decorate the interior. Most builders understand the significant features of the structure to be the dimensions and the roof covering. The structure thus invites variation and identification with the family who builds it. In Harrisburg, Pennsylvania, where I made my ethnographic observations, the majority of sukkot were built in a single neighborhood populated by Jews who affiliate with the Orthodox synagogue and self-identify as "traditional" Jews (about 10 percent of all Jews). Beyond this neighborhood, I found scattered examples in a suburban area north of the city, where many residents were affiliated with the Conservative synagogue (Bronner 1999).

Sukkah builders have several choices related to the extent of the exterior walls and their composition. The structure is usually rectangular, with at least three walls typically made of wood or cloth (the use of canvas is prevalent in America). Other choices include aluminum, metal, and fiberglass. If precut lumber is used, builders commonly leave it unpainted to evoke a connection with nature and a vernacular style. The most dramatic recent development in America has been the use of plastic tarp, typically in a conspicuously unnatural blue color, which can be tied to metal or bamboo poles to create a wall. The most common site for the sukkah is in the backyard of a suburban house, although some are located by a side entrance. The fourth wall may be left open, but it is customary to build the fourth wall with an opening entrance or doorway. Some apartment dwellers leave an end open so the family can erect the structure on a terrace or porch. In some European communities, one room of the house has a removable roof so that *sekhakh*, or "freshly cut branches with leaves," can be placed over the opening. In the northeastern United States, where the American Jewish population is concentrated (about 40 percent of America's Jews reside there, and Jews constitute about 2 percent of the total U.S. population), the festival dates can fall in October, when chilly temperatures and winds arrive. Therefore, most sukkot in the Northeast tend to be enclosed, whereas in tropical southern Florida, another Jewish population center, airier constructions are more common.

Although the wall material varies, Jewish custom as outlined in the Talmud is more demanding about the roof covering, or *sekhakh*. The covering material must grow from the earth (excluding animal skins), must be cut down (excluding metal and cloth), and must be ritually pure (excluding food and fruit). Jews commonly choose branches cut from trees (cedar is a favorite), reeds, bamboo poles, straw, and bushes and place enough of the material over the top so that the inside of the sukkah is shady. Some families buy bamboo mats, which can be rolled up, stored, and reused the following year, but several builders mentioned the joy they feel when collecting branches and creating a crude roof from them. Some booths use the side of the house for support, but the prevalent custom is to have the booth separable from, or separate within, the house and to place it under open skies to represent the distinct tabernacles or "feast of ingathering" in the Jewish biblical experience.

As I watched several sukkot being built, families commented that putting on the roof is the most important part because it is the most vivid reminder of tradition. Although other parts of the sukkah have been commercialized and the walls might be made of nonnatural materials, the roof is still constructed with natural materials gathered by hand. As a praxis, building the roof last represents a "topping off" (or "topping out") ceremony, common in the building trades: when the structure reaches its maximum height, the event is celebrated by placing an evergreen tree on top (Robinson 2001). This is not to say that the sukkah tradition is linked by cultural diffusion. The custom of topping off has been traced to northern European roots, but it is connected symbolically by the perception that evergreen materials identify the process of building as a kind of planting and ensure a permanent future. Another modern feature of topping off is the addition of a national flag, indicating building as a patriotic production representing participation in some progressive national effort.

Although no flag is raised in the sukkah, I argue that it has become a symbol of intense identification, showing ethnic loyalty. The placement of the roof as a protective praxis, a sign of completion and security, reinforces this message to participants if not observers. The importance of the roof is evident in the stringent guidelines prescribed in the Talmud, and it is customarily a special roof that allows the inhabitants to see the stars. Even with the form of the sukkah looking more artificial, the praxis of creating the roof makes the building traditional in participants' minds. The praxis is also gendered, in the sense that the father is usually expected to apply the natural materials, emphasizing patriarchal protection of the family and maintenance of the domestic tradition as a dwelling house (see Lehman 2010). One final ritual that recognizes the structure as a home is the attachment of a *mezuzah* (a small case containing a scroll with biblical passages that is fixed to the doorpost of Jewish homes) to the entranceway of the sukkah.

By the dictates of the Talmud, a household sukkah, which must accommodate a family for meals and sometimes for sleeping, has to be larger than 7 by 7 *tefakhim* (65.4 centimeters, or 25.75 inches). It is usually a few feet long by 7 to 8 feet (2 to 2.5 meters) high. The dimensions of 7 by 7, even in a measure that is no longer used, symbolically reinforce the magico-religious significance of the number seven as the length of time God took to create the world. Other reminders of the quality of seven are found in the holiday. On the seventh day of Sukkot, seven circuits are made around the *bimah* (the pedestal where the Torah is read in the synagogue). For this reason, the seventh day of Sukkot is known as Hoshanah Rabbah (the "great supplication"). Following biblical directive, the sukkah must be higher than 10 *tefakhim* or 94 centimeters (36.88 inches) but lower than 20 cubits or 11 meters (36.25 feet). The standard of ten is a common mark of official counting, thus emphasizing the structure's conformity to a standard. Sukkot in the United States are commonly rectangular structures measuring 6 by 8, 8 by 10, 8 by 12, 10 by 12, or 10 by 16 feet. Because the structure is temporary but is built annually, many sukkah builders today construct the walls of collapsible or prefabricated parts that can be easily stored and reassembled, and they add the *sekhakh* anew when the holiday occurs. Although the sukkah may have permanent walls of brick and stone, for example, it must be lower than 20 cubits to qualify as a temporary building, and it must have the *sekhakh*. Most builders construct their sukkot to accommodate eight to ten diners, although some prefabricated kits are advertised as "portable" and can be set up for only one or two diners. In any case, once the structure is erected, the owner must gather natural materials for the roof.

If the exterior has shown increased variation because of the use of commercial products, there is even more variability in the interiors. Families individualize the interiors of the structures to represent their identities. Orthodox rabbis occasionally sermonize on the Talmudic reference to "make a beautiful *sukkah* in His honor" (Shabbat 133b), based on the biblical verse "This is my God and I will adorn Him" (Exodus 15:2). In a separate section entitled "Sukkah," the Talmud describes the possibility of decorating with embroidered sheets, nuts, almonds, peaches, pomegranates, grapes, corn, wine, oil, and fine flour (although it forbids eating any of the fruit until the last day of the festival). In the United States, apples are abundant in the Northeast during the season and are common decorations, along with gourds, cranberries, and dried corn. The interior commonly holds a small table and chairs for eating in close quarters. Around this furniture, the family decorates the sukkah to be a cheerful place, with reminders of nature and harvest. Parents invite children to help decorate the interior with paper chains and garlands, pictures, sticks, and crafted decorations. Sometimes Jewish New Year cards are hung to remind visitors of the previous High Holy Days. Sephardic Jews from Arab countries often hang tapestries. Fruits, nuts, and evergreen boughs frequently hang from the roof covering. Importance is placed on the activity of decorating because it engages participants in the process of belonging to the Jewish tradition. One editorial suggested hanging dried squash and corn in the sukkah, since "these vegetables are readily available at that time for the American holidays of Halloween and Thanksgiving. Building and decorating a sukkah is a fun, family project, much like decorating the Christmas tree is for Christians. It is a sad commentary on modern American Judaism that most of the highly assimilated Jews who complain about being de-

Interior of an Orthodox synagogue's sukkah, with homemade decorations and an emphasis on roof hangings. (Courtesy Historical Society of Dauphin County)

prived of the fun of having and decorating a Christmas tree have never even heard of Sukkot" (Rich 2002).

Sukkot stands alone for Jews in late September or early October, whereas Hanukkah, a minor holiday according to ancient sources, has grown in observance because of its timing around Christmas. Thus Jews are more aware than non-Jews whether one celebrates Sukkot. As the aforementioned editorial implies, the issue of following tradition and maintaining a Jewish identity frequently compares "assimilated Jews" and "traditional Jews." Even as demographic studies show an increasing number of assimilated Jews who have largely abandoned the observance of Sukkot, they also reveal a growth in the number of Orthodox or traditional Jews (Goldstein 1992; Mayer, Kosmin, and Keysar 2003). This statistic suggests that Jews are either adopting tradition or revitalizing it. It is the middle, representing a compromise between tradition and modernity, that appears to be losing ground. Reinforcing this perception is my count of structures in Harrisburg over a twelve-year period from 1998 to 2010, in which I noted a 10 percent increase in the number of sukkot. Membership in the Orthodox and Reform synagogues grew during that period, while the Conservatives (representing a middle-way approach) suffered a decrease.

Although the sukkah is commonly described as representing thanksgiving and serving as a reminder of the exodus experience, for many Jews in the United States, the construction of sukkot signifies an enactment of and fidelity to tradition. As a result of a dramatic rise in intermarriage, secularization, geographic dispersal, and suburbanization in the late twentieth century, American Jews are well aware of the importance of following religious tradition and living in a Jewish community to maintain religious identity. In erecting the sukkah, households visibly declare their identity as "Jewish Jews," to use the phrase uttered by some Orthodox residents, choosing to follow all the customs and showing a preference for living within a Jewish community (Schertz 2005). Many Jews affiliated with Reform or Conservative Judaism elect not to observe Sukkot or erect a sukkah and confine their observance to the High Holy Days of Rosh Hashanah and Yom Kippur. Orthodox critics complain that this type of Judaism is an occasionally expressed gesture rather than a total identity of faith. In an effort to bolster the holiday, many synagogues and Jewish community centers have offered construction "kits" and have organized children's programs in large community sukkot. Yeshivas often train children in the building of sukkot by involving them in a craft activities in which they create small booths out of popsicle sticks and participate in the decoration of community sukkot. In sum, the act of building the sukkah has become more than observance; it has become an affirmation of an identity connected to Jewish religious tradition (common alternatives to religious or synagogue Judaism are ethical, emotional, and cultural affiliations to a feeling of Jewishness).

Once an obligation, building the sukkah in twenty-first-century America has become a signal of involvement. It pronounces the continuity of family ties and Jews' proximity to one another in the conceptualization of Jewish identity. It states that the family—by manually building a primitive structure that stands out in modern suburbia, by being willing to work for it, and by laboring together rather than individually—is a key to Jewish continuity. By dining outside, often in the cold, the family is stepping out of the comfort of modernity and engaging tradition that is vital to their lives. Yet the flexibility that allows the use of new materials and modern conveniences, such as tarps and electric lights, provides integration with the times. Apart from the synagogue, families who elect to build and gather in the sukkah as their mode of dwelling are inviting notice.

Whereas Jews are concerned about the decline of not only their numbers but also their fidelity to tradition, the Amish are experiencing growth. Nonetheless, leaders of both groups worry about the effects of dispersal and the impact of mass society on their sense of community. Today, Amish barn raisings are signals of community identity, concentrated in places such as Lancaster County, Pennsylvania, Holmes County, Ohio, and Elkhart County, Indiana. In these three contiguous states, the Amish account for around 180,000 individuals, divided into 907 small districts; about 80,000 more are spread out in settlements through the United States and Canada, mostly in the Midwest, Upland South, New York, and Ontario. The large number of districts ensures that the number of members in any community is small, thus encouraging face-to-face interaction in a limited locale. In addition to differences in dress, transportation, language, and religion, the Amish are distinguished from their neighbors by their commitment to agriculture. In Lancaster County, 44 percent of Amish adults are employed in farming, whereas only 4 percent of their non-Amish neighbors are (Kraybill 2001, 81). Despite scholarly predictions of their demise in the twentieth century because of their insistence on separation from the modern world, their tradition directedness, and their reliance on horse and manual power, both the Amish and their settlements have dramatically increased (Glassie 1968, 4). In Lancaster County the Amish have doubled their population every twenty years since 1960, numbering more than 22,000 in 131 districts in 2000, or approximately 4 percent of the county's population. Unlike their neighbors, whose children younger than eighteen account for less than a quarter of the population, children constitute 52 percent of the Amish population in the county. The number of Amish in Lancaster County was expected to exceed 30,000 by 2010 (Kraybill 2001, 16–21).

Unlike the building of the sukkah, barn raisings have become spectator events for outsiders. Once a common American practice in pre-industrial times, barn raisings have been appropriated by the Amish. Amish communities tolerate their neighbors' gaze and sometimes exploit it for commercial gain. This odd combination of barn raising as a practical use of donated labor and an event to be consumed by outsiders suggests the process of symbiosis in the perpetuation of traditions. For Americans, the Amish barn raising suggests America's pioneer heritage and expansion of the rural western frontier, but for the Amish, the barn raising has functions that are distinct from the American popular imagination (Weaver-Zercher 2001).

Throughout nineteenth-century America, barns grew in size as well as importance to the farm, and the social response to the challenge of building a large barn was to turn the task of construction into a community event. As American settlements expanded westward in the nineteenth century, the large, imposing structure of the barn often dwarfed the farmhouse and became a symbol of growth and abundance on the American landscape and of the accessibility of individual property (Vlach 2003, 1–22; Hubka 1994). The dimensions of American barns grew throughout the nineteenth century, and in Pennsylvania, structures in the style of German bank barns with English entrances on the nongable end emerged as an expandable, hybrid form often called the Pennsylvania barn (see Ensminger 1992; Hubka 1994). It featured at least two levels—one below the bank, often to house animals, and one above for the storage of grains and vehicles. The tradition of building these large structures could not be perpetuated, however, without substantial labor. Many travelers remarked on the palatial dimensions and finish of the Amish barn compared with the simplicity of the house. Elmer Smith, an early scholar of the Amish, observes, "The Amish barn is the keystone of the farm itself, and it was among such people that the saying, 'The barn will build the house, but the house will never build the barn' gained meaning, for the Amish and other Pennsylvania Germans valued the barn when other farmers in America were still entrusting their livestock and crops to crudely constructed huts and lean-to's" (1960, 262–63).

The American vernacular term *raising* refers to the task of lifting into place erect "bents," or large vertical frames that form the skeleton of the barn, and connecting them with cross-girts (Mathews 1966). This task—visually, the most exciting part of barn building—requires many men working cooperatively and using ropes and poles (or "pikes") to erect the heavy wooden bents (Price and Walters 1989). The expectation arose that the community would create a festive family atmosphere around the laborious work. These events featured large

The early stages of an Amish barn raising in Lancaster County, Pennsylvania, showing the erection of a bent. (Photo by Mel Horst)

communal dinners, sometimes liquor and cider, and play opportunities for children. Sources describe this kind of festival in medieval England and continental Europe, but evidence suggests its association with preindustrial America because of the increased frequency of barn building on individual farms (see Glassie 1974). Although the image of the rugged, independent male pioneer building his home by himself is common in American popular iconography, the visual culture of the barn emphasizes the spirit of community offering mutual aid and generosity in expanding America.

Later stage of an Amish barn raising showing construction of the roof. (Photo by Mel Horst)

Despite the communal image, there was usually a hierarchy involved in organizing the barn raising. A master carpenter or foreman was hired to direct the construction and supervise the crew. The typical procedure was to connect tie beams to end posts below the roof plate (Price and Walters 1989). In addition to building the bents on the ground before lifting them into place, the crew constructed temporary scaffolding, laying boards across horizontal beams to provide platforms from which to work. An alternative to raising completely assembled H-bents in Pennsylvania was to join the tie beam over the roof plate and end post (Ensminger 1992). Workers laid long planks against the uppermost girts at the rear of the frame to serve as ramps or skids on which the upper frame parts could be slid to their proper height. They rotated the tie beams after moving them up the skids and secured the barn frame. They then erected the roof framework and rafters and completed the barn with roofing and siding. By most accounts, the raising process usually took a day. Women prepared an abundance of food for the event and often served it at a large communal dinner. It was common to have a dance at the house after the raising, and many accounts recall the prevalence of drunkenness at these parties.

The introduction of individual fire and disaster insurance plans, growth of agribusiness, invention of mechanical devices for raising bents, use of lighter presawn timbers, and professionalization of farm construction in the twentieth century resulted in the decline of barn raisings as festive communal events. The tradition of barn raising was no longer necessary because the farmer did not need the community for his success or, in the event of a disaster, his recovery. The farmer, increasingly centered on monetary capital, was not rewarded for providing social capital. The application of technology, and the reliance on professional specialists and services, allowed for more individualism. Among agrarian groups that retained the values of mutual aid, however, such as the Amish and Old Order Mennonites, barn raisings became increasingly important to maintain interpersonal connections in their communities. They encouraged residents to remain in close proximity to one another to take advantage of the labor required for complex tasks such as the building of barns. Social capital became even more significant to the Amish as modernization intruded, putting highways and technology between them and their neighbors. Increasingly individualized modern Americans, unfamiliar with community-built structures, flocked to and consumed images of barn raisings as spectators to provide symbols of social connection (see Weaver-Zercher 2001). The Amish, a German-speaking group that believes in separation from the world, ironically became transformed in Americans' imagination to their pioneer ancestors. Barn raising became intimately associated with the Amish because of its inclusion as a significant symbol of wholesome communal values in the Broadway hit *Plain and Fancy* (1955), the movie *Witness* (1985), and numerous popular magazine features (Weaver-Zercher 2001; Walbert 2002, 89–100; Tortora 1980). For outsiders, the large, visible architectural statement of a barn raising encapsulated the significance of tradition as a kind of consumed morality (see Walbert 2002; Weaver-Zercher 2001). The Amish at first resisted this attention, but as land prices and the costs of farming increased, catering to spectators by selling food and crafts added to their finances. The skills of barn raising also applied to carpentry and construction jobs contracted by the "English," or non-Amish, especially as farming opportunities declined. According to the authors of *Amish Enterprise*, woodworking trades constitute the largest clustering of enterprises, and residential and commercial construction amounts to 10 percent of all Amish business activity. The association of the Amish with barns is notable in the prominent production of "little red barns" used as storage sheds by the "English" (Kraybill and Nolt 1995, 45).

The Amish share with their non-Amish farming neighbors the feature of individual ownership; they are not a communal sect that shares property among its members, like the Hutterites. But barns fulfill community functions that distinguish the group from its English neighbors and help barn raisings to persist, even as the number of Amish involved in agriculture declines (see Kraybill 2001). Ethnographies of Amish societies show that the barn is important not only because of its function for farming activity but also as a space for religious services (the Amish do not have churches; instead, they gather in members' barns for services). The religious connection of the barn raising goes beyond providing a space for services, because the idea of mutual aid is considered a spiritual value of *Bruderschaft*, or "brotherhood." It is coupled with the spiritual value of manual labor in close proximity to the land, and the barn raising is an especially dramatic reminder that everyone in the community is involved in handwork. Although barn raising is an especially visible example, many activities in Amish life follow this principle, including community care for the sick and aged, help with moving, relief after a flood or drought, and benefit auctions to help families burdened by excessive medical bills or injuries. Several analysts of Amish traditions observe that the provision of security by the community allows the group to maintain its separation from the world. John Hostetler, in his classic sociological study *Amish Society*, reflects, "Security is therefore assured to the Amish individual by the concern of the whole community. If a member is sick, in distress, or is incapacitated, the community knows about it. While the Scriptures admonish the believer to do good to all men, the Amish are especially serious about the advice with respect to their own 'household of faith'" (1963, 146). Smith adds:

> The practice of group barn-raising, although a social activity, is not engaged in for that purpose; the same holds true of other activities of a similar nature, such as when the neighbors har-

vest the crops of a sick member. Such an activity is a great mo-
rale builder for a small sect-group and has a real social value,
but its major underlying function is to create a feeling of security in the minds of all the members, who, when they give their
time for others' welfare, can expect the same treatment from
others if such a need should arise in their own lives. (1958, 176)

Realizing this value of mutual aid supporting the tradition of barn
raising helps illuminate the outlook of the Amish man who told Don
Kraybill, "When I am plowing in the spring, I can often see five or six
other teams in nearby fields, and I know if I was sick they would all be
here plowing my field" (Kraybill 2001, 154). Especially important is
that the barn raising became part of a system of disaster insurance for
a group dependent on mutual aid rather than worldly professional services. The Amish believe that church members should be accountable
to and responsible for one another; therefore, commercial insurance
would undercut aid within the community (Kraybill 2001, 155). After
a fire, the community pitches in by restoring the barn or raising a new
one. With the features of a communal meal, visual excitement for spectators, and a festive atmosphere, the Amish barn raising is a productive
integration of pleasure and labor serving the needs, and underscoring
the importance, of the community. In sum, the barn raising is the most
dramatic example of "social capital" among the Amish, which includes
face-to-face relationships, extended family, and long-standing traditions and rituals that support them (see Kraybill 2001, 142–60; Putnam
2000, 234–35).

The Amish barn raising is different from other forms of barn construction because of the speed of the process and the labor involved
(often between 100 and 300 members). Although the foundation may
be laid by contractors beforehand, the construction is usually completed in one day (Smith and Stoltzfus 1959; Tortora 1980). To save
time, the Amish allow the use of electricity for power drills to make the
holes into which hickory pegs will be hammered. These pegs hold the
flush and mortised beams in place. Power tools may also be used to cut
planks. A foreman is usually in charge of the whole operation, but different crews work together to prepare planks, beams, and rafters for the
walls and roof. Young boys are usually given the task of carrying nails
to prepare them for the adult job of nailing panels. While some crews

take rest periods, others take over. Although the operation appears to be demanding, there is time for socializing over meals. "There's a lot of visiting going on here," as well as work, many Amish informants report (Kraybill 2001, 155).

The building praxis that most differentiates the Amish barn raising from "English" construction, according to Amish carpenters, is the use of poles to raise the bents. In modern construction, a crane would be brought in, and the operator would lift the bent and lower it in place from *above*. The Amish demonstration of social capital and the value of their place in the land is in gathering a group and lifting the bent from *below*. It is not so much the use of machinery that bothers the Amish, since, as noted earlier, they have been known to use power tools for barn raisings; rather, it is the crane's displacement of the group and its symbolic descent from above, which makes it seem above human scale or ostentatiously assuming a divine position from the heaven to the human level. More than any other component of the barn raising, the use of poles pushed up by human power coming from the earthy ground retains the function of tradition as the Amish conceive it in the construction of their culture.

The barns are usually of a substantial size, built to house animals as well as for storage. One non-Amish observer reports, "Nor were the barns the usual modern, one-story metal boxes hung on poles. They were huge buildings, three and four stories high, post-and-beam framed, and held together with hand-hewn mortises and tenons. . . . Some 400 Amish men and boys, acting and reacting like a hive of bees in absolute harmony of cooperation, started at sunrise with only a foundation and floor and by noon, *by noon*, had the huge edifice far enough along that you could put hay in it" (Logsdon 1989, 78). The Amish insider's view tends to dwell not on the speed of the operation or the size of the building but on the quiet effort (placing value on humility) of a total community acting in unison. In the following Amish man's description, the contrast of the Amish barn raising to modern commercial construction illustrates the importance of tradition and the spiritual dimension of a dramatic gesture toward heaven:

There isn't a crane poking its long boom skyward, hook dangling. There are no white-hatted foremen dashing about with squawking radios. Now watch as, just as for the last 500 years, a forty-six foot long line of straw hatted men, facing east, bend down. Forty-six feet of rear ends face westward, with all hands on the top timber of the assembled frame. All are ready to push it skyward. The moment is dramatic, everyone is quiet as several late comers rush up the barn hill to help. Reuben says, "Take her up"—not a holler, but a positive command—in a voice filled with experience. With some minor grunts the ponderous frame moves up, hands outstretched. (Kraybill 2001, 155)

We can read in this statement that barn raising gains importance because it is recognized as both a need and a symbol of the community, and it is related to other practices as a tradition in the sense of being socially shared and continuous over time. Tradition allows for change, the Amish recognize, but as one Amish man observes:

We consider tradition as being spiritually helpful. Tradition can blind you if you adhere only to tradition and not the meanings of the tradition, but really maintain a tradition. . . . We have some traditions, that some people question and I sometimes myself question, that are being maintained just because they are a tradition. This can be adverse, but it can also be a benefit. Tradition always looks bad if you're comparing one month to the next or one year to the next, but when you're talking fifty years or more, tradition looks more favorable. (Kraybill 2001, 49–50)

Some Amish old-timers note the changes that have occurred, such as the toleration of drink coolers, electric drills, and portable toilets at barn raisings, but the process of a brotherhood using its labor to build a symbolic working barn remains and will likely continue. John Hostetler, a sociologist who grew up in the Amish sect, emphasizes, "Tradition and experience tend to become highly symbolic in structural acts such as a shared style of dress, language, limited education, and mutual-aid practices." The Amish, he reports, are successful in staying bound by tradition because they have maintained "substitutionary forms of intense sharing but also by meeting the social needs of the individual" (Hostetler 1963, 147). Symbols such as the Amish barn raising express the group's social unity in material form. In Hostetler's phrase, "it clarifies the sentiment a society has of itself" (1963, 147).

A sign of individualistic modernity and mass industrialization is that traditional vernacular structures such as the human-built sukkah and the Amish barn have drawn attention to themselves because they stand out as symbols of the social integration of a community. As a result, in modern journalistic accounts they are often referred to as *art*, with the implication of being uncommon or even exceptional, rather than a *craft* of everyday living (see Ames 1977). Although apparently elevating the status of these traditions, *art* also implies cultural weakening. Whereas some critics such as Kosta Mihailović claim that "the abandonment of traditional production and the traditional way of life is an unavoidable consequence of industrialization and urbanization" (1989, 36), the above examples show that modernization can also result in the revitalization of traditions as a response to maintain community and identity. This revitalization raises the question of how conspicuous emergent traditions of homemade built environments, often categorized as vernacular, folk, outsider, informal, or grassroots art, comment directly on modernization by the use of manufactured materials in striking assemblages (Blasdel 1968; Brackman and Dwigans 1999; Cardinal 1972; Manley 1989; Margry and Sánchez-Carretero 2011; Rosen 1979; Santino 1986; Walker Art Center 1974; Wampler 1978; Ward 1984). Unlike the sukkah and the Amish barn, their tradition is not connected to ethnic and religious roots; it is more of an approach to the built environment that may have class or occupational connections and a cultural stance of resistance to modern commercial culture. Many vernacular architecture scholars might dismiss such structures as idiosyncratic, marked more by individual oddity than by vernacular criteria of a common parlance rooted in place and community (see Marshall 1982; Vlach 1985a, 1986). In another sense, however, as hand-built environments tolerated within certain locales, are they a sign of the future of the vernacular in complex, industrialized societies?

To begin answering this question, consider the following native description that raises the question of tradition in modernity: "Nowhere but Houston does outsider art enjoy such insider status. Folk art icons like the venerable Orange Show, postman Jeff McKissack's mini-Disneyland of recycled machinery and salvaged building materials, or upholsterer John Milkovisch's "Beer Can House," a Memorial

Park bungalow sheathed in approximately 50,000 flattened empties, are as much a part of the city's cultural profile as the Rothko Chapel or the Cullen Sculpture Garden" (Ennis 2002). The environments gain the label "outsider art" because they contrast sharply as hand-built decorative structures amid a landscape of white frame buildings. Perhaps they enjoy the "insider status" and folkness of the vernacular in Houston because of the lack of zoning ordinances, which typically restrict owners' enhancements to properties. In fact, Houston is the largest city in the world without zoning restrictions, partly due to its nineteenth-century heritage as an open western frontier inviting new settlement and development. Its climate is fairly temperate year-round, enabling builders to work outdoors continuously. Journalist Michael Ennis also refers to "a state of mind peculiar to Houston," based on the lack of a tie to one culture. He explains it as a distinct local recipe: "Take a pungent mix of Latino, African American, and Cajun influences, combine with a surprisingly resilient blue-collar ethic, wildcatter individualism, and Southern eccentricity, and stir it all up with Houston's storied absence of zoning regulations; the recipe has encouraged exuberant public displays of art rarely seen elsewhere. The *tradition is a living one*" (Ennis 2002; emphasis added).

The reference to tradition as living suggests that there is social toleration of the creation of these environments and an ongoing adaptation of practices and forms as builders become aware of one another's work. That certainly was the case with the rise of the "art car" movement in Houston during the late twentieth century, which has resulted in an annual parade and a museum showcasing working cars festooned with welded decorations (McClusky 2003). It is a celebration of working-class creativity and the grassroots transformation of corporate productions, since the makers are usually not schooled artists. The object itself is significant as something that people allow to enclose them, and therefore the transformation of this object becomes a powerful symbol of human control. The artists start with commercial objects as the basis for their creativity and produce whole environments out of the machines. This process says something significant about vernacular production in an industrialized society: in the absence of natural resources, makers employ a type of assemblage and bricolage, whereby the materials of construction are often manufactured objects that are altered, assembled, and arranged so that their original functions are transformed.

One can see many examples of this transformation in front yards, where tires, rain gutters, and milk cans become planters and mailbox supports (Abernethy 1985; Bronner 1986b; Nicolaisen 1979; Sewell and Linck 1985; Sheehy 1998), and in urban settings, where the sidewalk is appropriated for recreational or even religious purposes with recycled furnishings and equipment (Bronner 1985a; Sciorra 1989). On highways, mourners erect spontaneous roadside shrines with mementoes of car accident victims (Everett 2002; Santino 2006a). In the most total change of the environment, the *bricoleur* may add layers to a house, so as to essentially refabricate the structure (Bronner 1986b, 63–86). The items added may be significant to the *bricoleur* not only because of their material, color, and shape in the overall design but also because they represent the transformation of the process of disposal (and obsolescence), which is intrinsic to commercial culture, into a cultural ecology associated with the folk cultural use of local resources.

The praxis referred to in this process is one of recycling, which, as some critics observe, is akin to the ecological value many folk regional groups place on avoiding excess and waste in the relation between the built environment and nature (Ferris 1974; Greenfield 1986). The transformation of dwelling in these producer cultures occurs from the natural resources in the environment; the argument is that this kind of ecology is still taking place in a consumer society, but the resources are manufactured. Fieldworkers find old bathtubs used for Madonna shrines, bleach bottles for weather vanes, soda bottles for tree structures, egg crates for herb planters, and mailbox supports created from welded chains, and they interpret these uses as either replacement for unavailable natural resources in an urbanizing society or an answer to the standardization, specialization, and disposability of labor and technology (Greenfield 1986; Jencks and Silver 1972). Analysts often find in the bricolage structures an artistic outlet for the need to create by hand, driven by the urge to express a rooted identity in a mass society (Bronner 1986b, 63–86; Jones 1987, 1995, 2001; Sheehy 1998). Others who view consumerism as a middle-class movement sometimes comment on how members of the lower or working class meet their needs through emergent forms of industrial folk crafts (Dewhurst 1984; Lockwood 1984). Anthropologist Julius Kassovic (1983) dubs "folk recycling" a refabrication out of industrial scrap, but rather than viewing it as a folk cultural value, he understands it as a function of poverty. Some studies

Section of "The Orange Show," built by Jeff McKissack of Houston, Texas, showing construction using wheels. (Photo by Simon Bronner)

of the makeshift structures of the homeless, apparently following patterns learned from one another, comment on the reassemblage of discarded cardboard boxes, corrugated tin, vinyl tarp, and plastic milk crates (Daniels 1981). The refabrication can also be occupational, as in the case of factory workers who create artistic pieces, sometimes called "homers" (from home crafted), out of materials smuggled out of the factory or rescued from the dumpster (Lockwood 1984). A notable architectural example is small buildings made out of sewer tiles drawn from a conduit factory (Dewhurst 1986; Dewhurst and MacDowell 1983).

In Houston, postal worker Jefferson Davis McKissack (1902–1980) called his handmade environment "The Orange Show" to materialize his belief that long life results from manual labor and the consumption of fruit (Lomax 1985a). He used ceramic tiles, recycled metal wheels, and welded iron to create a shrine, covering two city lots in a residential neighborhood, to the healthy benefits of eating oranges. Born in Georgia, McKissack made a living trucking oranges from the Atlanta farmers' market to locations throughout the Deep South. After serving in the U.S. Navy during World War II, where he learned to weld, McKissack moved to Houston and worked for the post office. He began to build a fairly conventional frame house with his own hands, but in the early 1950s he bought some land with the idea of building a plant nursery. He got as far as constructing the exterior walls, but as the project developed in his mind, it took a different direction. Influenced by the rise of roadside attractions and amusement parks throughout the South as automobile ownership increased, he instead created an environment to demonstrate to the public the healthy uses of oranges. Between 1956 and 1979 he accumulated objects and incorporated them into the site. Metal wheels were the central elements in the design, appearing on staircases, fences, and walls. The recycling of metal and wooden wagon wheels (perhaps inspired by the shape of rolling irrigation systems on the dry plains) to create welded fences, barriers, arches, gates, and mailbox supports is common throughout the West and evokes a sense of place tied to the frontier (Abernethy 1985; Cannon 1980).

Although The Orange Show did not become the roadside attraction McKissack envisioned, Houstonians often pointed to it as an example of residents' personal determination tied to a western vernacular spirit and the city's fostering of handmade grassroots environments.

After McKissack's death in 1980, skyscrapers began to sprout up in the "Skyline District," including such notable architectural showcases as the J. P. Morgan Chase Tower (built in 1981 as the Texas Commerce Tower, the tallest five-sided building in the world, designed by I. M. Pei & Partners) and the Wells Fargo Plaza (completed in 1983 as the Allied Bank Plaza and First Interstate Bank Plaza, the tallest all-glass building in the Western Hemisphere, designed by Skidmore, Owings & Merrill). With this, McKissack's structure symbolized less the lessons of healthy living and more the working-class hand skills perceived to be constrained by consumer prefabrication, and it became a vernacular answer to Houston's rising image as a global center for Fortune 500 companies. Preservation-minded Houstonians organized the Orange Show Foundation in 1980 (renamed the Orange Show Center for Visionary Art in 2003) to maintain the site and organize public programming. Its website declares, "The Orange Show Is a Folk-Art Environment: A Monumental Work of Handmade Architecture." Instead of separating McKissack from his grass roots as an eccentric, weirdo, or genius, the center interprets the structure as celebrating "the Artist in Everyone" (Orange Show 2010).

Folklorist Michael Owen Jones argues that building practices such as McKissack's suggest a shift in attention by scholars of folk art—a shift from repeated forms to individuals' behavioral models as ways of organizing identity and fulfilling psychological needs (Jones 1980b, 1993, 2000). The attention to expressive activity constituting tradition, rather than the uniformity of the expression with a relic form, he proposes, "would not assume that models are normative, restrictive, limiting, or serving as binding forces of conformity" (Jones 1980b, 360). He views modern traditions as chosen practices, perhaps strategically enacted in response to certain situations or psychological states (Jones 1997). Instead of the *outsider, naïve,* or *visionary* label for personal environments, Jones urges vernacular art and architecture students to understand the continuities and consistencies in *material behavior* (Jones 1993, 1997). This approach is a move away from the insistence on a social community for the understanding of tradition, but it nonetheless focuses on the formation of identity and the creative enactment of perceived tradition (Vlach 1985a). It suggests that individuals consciously shape their own traditions by repeating framed activities that ritualize and materialize their values and identities.

"Beer Can House," built by John M. Milkovisch of Houston, Texas. (Photo by Simon Bronner)

Houston residents point out that The Orange Show is hardly alone in representing a grassroots building project that materializes the gap between the corporate and folk city. The Houston dwelling known as "Beer Can House" raises especially provocative questions about material praxis. Covered in decorations crafted from thousands of beer cans, it appears at first glance to have little precedent as a form, but the process of folk recycling that informs its construction is familiar. When its maker, Houston native John M. Milkovisch (1912–1988), was asked why he used beer cans as his building material, he remarked, "I hate to throw anything away" (Lomax 1985b). Milkovisch and his wife drank the beer, and then he used the cans to create curtains, fences, windmills, and wind chimes. The result, however, is not an advertisement for any particular commercial label, because only on close inspection does one realize the source of the house's metal shell. Milkovisch had been in the habit of saving cans, anticipating some use for them, before he got the idea to decorate his house with them. His neighbors engaged in similar behaviors, such as saving egg crates (to make planters and jewelry holders), cheese containers (reused for food storage), bleach bottles (for liquid storage or scoops), baby food jars (to store nails and other small items), and bread wrappers (reused as bags or woven into rugs). Although the Milkovisch house extended the "home" use of recycled materials, it was related to other familiar house structures in the twentieth-century West, which used hay bales, railroad ties, and stove wood (Graham 1989; Tishler 1982; Welsch 1970, 1976). Milkovisch was aware of a number of houses that used for recycled bottles as either a building material or decoration (Seltzer 2000; see also "Bottle Houses" 2010; Greenfield 1986, 55–90; McCoy 1974). In fact, Milkovisch first decorated his property with glass marbles and parts of bottles before turning to beer cans.

Milkovisch sliced off the tops and bottoms and split the seams of the cans with homemade tools. He bundled stacks of fifty flattened cans and filled his attic and garage with them. He was an upholsterer for the Southern Pacific Railroad, but like many working-class residents, he engaged in various hobbies such as woodworking and home maintenance. He lived in the house with his wife, Mary Hite, whom he married in 1940. The modest frame house had belonged to his parents, and he bought it in 1942. It was not unusual for the neighborhood men to build their own patios and loan one another material. Milkovisch's project began in 1968 with the installation of a concrete patio and driveway. Looking to enhance the backyard patio, he used marbles and other small objects such as broken glass, tiles, and old keys to decorate it. As he worked on this project he drank beer and continued to stack the cans, which he had been saving for about seventeen years. He loathed the constant routine of cutting the grass and decided to pave over his front lawn as well, which he also enhanced by pressing marbles, tiles, and other objects into the wet concrete. He was encouraged by compliments and even contributions of materials from his neighbors. His assemblage of diverse, readily available materials into a unified work followed a common process that anthropologist Claude Lévi-Strauss called *bricolage*, which means working with whatever materials are available rather than producing a craftsmanlike transformation from nature to product (Lévi-Strauss 1966, 17–18). The significance of this process is its commentary on the surroundings; it takes materials from the surroundings and reconstitutes them into a construction that draws attention to itself or to the maker. The materials are often outside the control of the maker, but in the process of reconstitution, those forces

(*Above*) Patio shelter with bottles and inlaid marbles built by Milkovisch. (*Below*) Section of Milkovisch's patio that shows bottle construction. (Photos by Simon Bronner)

threatening to restrain the handiness of the maker are countered or domesticated (Lévi-Strauss 1966, 19–20; Hans 1987, 145–46). Bricolage
often comments on modernity by taking commercial consumables and
transforming them into resources for traditional construction, suggesting the maker's handiness and creating a hedge against being swallowed
up by mass culture (Bronner 1986b, 63–86; Herman 1997; Nicolaisen
1979).

Given the positive reinforcement from his neighbors for his decorative use of recycled materials, Milkovisch remembered the stacks of
flattened beer cans in the garage. He first hung them as streamers in
trees, where they reflected the sunlight, similar to the wind chimes he
had seen in other yards. Looking to frame the open driveway, he built
an arch over it with unflattened cans. Enthused by their malleability as
a construction and decorative material, Milkovisch applied the cans to
the house itself as a substitute for repainting, creating a ribbon of silver
metal around the bottom. Then he kept going, since he saw an incon-
sistency between the old siding and the cans he was applying. This gave
him other ideas about the possibilities of transformation, and he hung
streams of cans from the eaves to create a curtain effect, like a second
layer over the siding; then he made window shades out of them. According to his supportive wife, "he did it all before I knew what was going on" (Lomax 1985b, 18). Although she respected the outside as her
husband's domain, Mary did not allow him to apply his can decorations
to the house's interior.

Milkovisch added assemblages that helped explain some of his
values to curious passersby. One striking sculpture in the garden is a
"ladder of success," which he completed after the house was done. As
Milkovisch said in an interview, "Painted one rung black because most
people don't make it. They say every man should always leave something to be remembered by. At least I accomplished that goal" (Lomax 1985b, 21). Although Milkovisch appreciated being recognized for
the skill and creativity that went into the house, he became irritated
at interviewers who questioned his drinking or the idiosyncrasy of the
house (Lomax 1985b, 19). To be sure, he wanted to be noticed, but he
declined to call it art. In his mind, it was his home project after years
of unrecognized labor (he refused to upholster at home upon his retirement), and this productive handwork using recycled materials gave
him and his family satisfaction. His locus was familial and local, as he

Milkovisch's "ladder of success" behind his front-yard assemblage of beer cans and stone. (Photo by Simon Bronner)

related with this anecdote: "Like I told one foreman over there at the railroad, he asked me where was I going on my vacation. We could see downtown Houston from that roundhouse. I says, 'You see them tall buildings up there?' That was uptown. 'That's where I'm going.' He says, 'That's where you're going?' I says, 'Yeah'" (Lomax 1985b, 20).

Likewise, Milkovisch was not interested in using his retirement as a time for distant travel and exotic experience; he was more inclined to root himself in the familiarity of place as he aged. The city he knew had

(Left) Cleveland Turner, the "Flower Man," talking to passersby in Houston, Texas. (Photo by Simon Bronner)

(Below) Turner's "Yard Show" in Houston. (Photo by Simon Bronner)

changed dramatically, with high-rise development and urban sprawl. He would relate his memories of old Houston as a kind of urban village, where neighbors related closely to one another. Thus he erected a large sign near the entrance of his house that was as much a social reminder as a religious reference: "Live by [the] Golden Rule." His building displaced some personal concerns about suddenly feeling "out of place" by drawing attention to the processes he was familiar with as a longtime working-class resident. He did not join forces with other environmental builders, but he understood their motivations for creating meaningful personal spaces (Lomax 1985b, 21).

Section of a wall constructed of beer cans, labels, and wood by Ronny Milkovisch of Houston, Texas. (Photo by Simon Bronner)

Beer can houses did not spring up all over Houston, but as the press began to notice Milkovisch, reporters often made the connection between his structure and other grassroots home environments in the area. For example, Cleveland Turner (b. 1935), known as the "Flower Man," invokes the tradition of votive offering by using elaborate bricolage on his property to invite his neighbors to know his experience of being saved from alcoholism and to announce his new appreciation for life and his intention to give back to the depressed community (Editors of Roadside America 2003). Whereas he once scoured dumpsters for food in misery as a skid row resident, he now searches for refuse to create beauty. In addition to the decoration of his house, inside and out, he built a dome out of bicycle rims in a vacant lot across the street, which attracted the attention of many neighborhood children. Befitting his nickname, he displays many plants and flowers in front of his house, along with parts of bicycles, bottles, and knickknacks. Wagon wheels, a common sight in many Houston yards, also appear toward the top of his house front. Turner intended his environment to be a gathering place for adults and children in the neighborhood to instill a sense of community support, which he felt had been lost. His actions had an impact, as others in his African American neighborhood took up decorating their plain shotgun houses. In one cluster of houses, children participated in creating a play area out of concrete, paint, and recycled materials. Unlike some of the other builders, Milkovisch and Turner intentionally transmitted their project, and their vernacular spirits, to another generation who took up the task.

Milkovisch passed his love of handiwork on to his sons Ronny and Guy, and after he died, they maintained the house and the various structures on the property for their mother, Mary, who still lived there. They even added some fences made out of cans that line one side of the property. Proud of carrying on their father's work, in the 1990s they completed a television commercial in support of recycling (Theis 1998). In November 2001, when Mary, who had always expressed pride in the structure, could no longer live without assistance, the Orange Show Foundation bought the property, with the idea of preserving the house for future generations.

The use of cans as a building material is not unique to Houston. "Can City," created by Joshua Samuel in Walterboro, South Carolina (Stanley 1984), is constructed of discarded quart oil cans collected from gas stations. What began as border trim for Samuel's yard became decorations for trees and an assortment of rooms running a tenth of a mile long. In Silver Spring, Maryland, Richard Van Os Keuls personally flattened 15,000 beer and soda cans to use as shingles on his modest 1950s-era ranch house. Its colorful "carnival-like surface" stands out from his neighbors' residences, he said, suggesting a commentary on the dullness of suburban material culture. "It's not just the riot of color," he told a *Washington Post* reporter, "but the way the sun hits it in different ways. On sunny days, it sparkles" (Rogers 2003).

Samuel and Keuls, like many folk recyclers, began their endeavors as extensions of their vocations or as demonstrations of their hand skills, starting late in their careers when they took stock of their lives and had more leisure time. To be sure, one often finds religious, visionary, or moralistic reasons for the undertaking, as well as the hope of inspiring others to create. The analysis of tradition in these environments takes in the life story of the creator and the symbolism of the expressions. Unlike the ideal of vernacular as the prevalent common expression of the people, most of these folk recyclers are well aware that they stand apart in their elaborate structures, although in interviews, many of them refer to grassroots skills and processes that are, or should be, part of modern culture (Foster 1984). Their recycling is familiar, although the forms may not be, and sometimes they even draw attention to the biblical phrase "silk purses from sows' ears" to add spiritual force, and perhaps a communal allusion, to their constructions (Greenfield 1986; "Tinkering" 1984). As *bricoleurs*, these do-it-yourselfers shape structures and identities that appear human rather than industrial, and they offer reminders of a lost vernacular.

Traditions as Models for Action and Commentary on Control and Authority

Inquiries about these structures often center on the individuals who created them, but questions persist about the connections of form to place and society, raising the issue of tradition as a model for action. The behaviors that generate various environments as grassroots, hand-built productions in a consumer society invite analysis as a transition from the vernacular of Redfield's "little community" to the "mass society" (Bronner 2005d; Brunkhorst 2004; Redfield 1960). In the Midwest, several religious grottoes made from geodes by devoted Catholic priests invite commentary on their special individual nature and their relation as traditions to similar constructions (Brackman 1999; Mordoh 1989; Niles 1999; Ohrn 1984; Stone, Zanzi, and Iversen 1999). In Los Angeles, the Watts Towers left by Simon Rodia appeared to be out of place and without precedent or model, until the connection to Rodia's Italian background of processions with pyramidal Giglio was understood (Posen and Ward 1985). On the Great Plains, gates made of horseshoes and structures built from wagon wheels lead to discussions of grassroots efforts to embellish the flat, dreary landscape (Abernethy 1985; Fife 1969, 11–16). I could go on, but suffice it to say that traditions need not be anonymous.

On the surface, the three examples of living traditions examined in this chapter refer to the continuities they maintain, often with distinct challenges. The continuity, in the case of the Jewish sukkah builders, is to an ancient place and form, and their personal involvement in the construction of these structures has become increasingly symbolized as a revitalization of a community of faith. The Amish barn raising is also

about community strengthened by participation in a social construc-
tive act, but complicated by the ambivalence toward the outside society
from which it seeks distance yet at the same time relies on for its prosperity. The continuity for the grassroots environments in Houston is
less to the forms erected than to the processes and values that many of
the builders feel has been displaced by consumer society. All the examples remind us of the constant of change in traditions. Social discourse
is rampant on the tools, the materials, and, significantly, the changing
functions of the Jewish and Amish traditions. For the homemade environments, the discourse of change is based on the mass society that
now views the act of building personal space as "out of place." Whether
the two millennia of the sukkah or the two generations of the "Beer
Can House," the builders had to take into account the transmission
of the skills and motivations for constructing the structures, lest they
became relics rather than continuing experiences or customs.

Less obvious in the examples is the matter of control and authority suggested by engaging traditions, especially in the United States,
where there is supposedly a democratic belief in individual liberty and
a future orientation, rather than social obligation and fidelity to the
past (Bronner 2002a, 2002b; Dundes 1969b; Kluckhohn and Strodtbeck 1973). The examples remind us of the negotiation inherent when
traditions are enacted, including the questions of who dictates which
traditions will be followed, how they will be followed, how traditions
may be discouraged or even proscribed by external forces (i.e., authority), and how traditions are adapted by their participants (i.e., control).
Concerns about maintaining vernacular building in the twenty-first
century as keys to the welfare of migratory and disaster-struck populations imply an accounting of not only what happens to the forms left
behind or swept away but also what happens to the ideas of traditions
themselves. For Oliver, the modernist assault on traditional housing in
favor of the "up-to-date" has contributed substantially to the problems
of urbanization (2006, 383).

Oliver points out that to perpetuate professional authority over
the built environment, modernists have publicly promoted a view of
tradition "which is no more than habit or mere repetition; tradition
that is principally a vehicle for sentimental associations; tradition that
promotes stereotypical imitation and the 'neo-vernacular'" (2006,
383–84). From the vantage of *bricoleurs*, tradition involves the trans-

mission of technical know-how that gives meaning to the utilization of accumulated experience. Oliver argues that when it is viewed this way, with the values of a society embodied in its built structures, "tradition is a complex continuity inherited from the past, lived in the present and sustained in the future. It encompasses the concepts, processes and meanings of those aspects of praxis and materiality whose persistence ensures durability, reliability and identity" (2006, 384). In a call to architects and planners who wield professional authority, Oliver declares, "We need not despair of the end of tradition: on the contrary, we need to acknowledge, celebrate and actively promote it, if unimaginable misery is to be averted" (2006, 392).

But one has to wonder whether new conditions allow *bricoleurs* to operate adequately. "Much can be learned from traditional builders, who willingly pass on their know-how and skills as they have in the past," Oliver admonishes, and it is well worth remembering that the physical as well as political environment that supports the process of tradition may also be critical to addressing the "massive problems of housing in the next century" (1999, 1). Insofar as many housing crises result from political campaigns against traditional ecologies, social structures, and economies, as well as from natural disasters and wars, I would add that these problems are often cultural matters that entail the way people control, or are prevented from engaging, tradition in their lives. Scholars can assist in responding to crises, then, by questioning in vernacular architecture the traditions that encompass, vitalize, and emblematize identity to people. Maybe then we will not only see vernacular architecture for what it is but also grasp the feeling of what it does.

4

Making Tradition

On Craft in American Consciousness

Americans' complicated attitude toward tradition is wrapped up in the connotations of craft in the transition from a preindustrial to a postindustrial society. The *Oxford English Dictionary* asserts that the transference of *craft* from the Teutonic root for "strength" or "force" to "skill, art, skilled occupation" appears to be exclusively English. My argument is that it has gone through another move in American usage to one of "traditional, rural, old" in the service of modernity. It has done so because of an emergent progressive worldview among Americans that associates craft with America's founding in the wilderness. Its naturalistic and communitarian associations came into conflict with modernization, played out in the rise of industry, the city, nationalism, mobility, and capitalism in the nineteenth century. If craft in American thinking took on a negative cast because nation builders wanted to leave behind the past-oriented image, they also embraced it as praxis to retain values representing a rooted democratic society. In the rhetoric of craft broadcast by literature, media, and education, I find a dilemma played out between tradition and modernity, past and future, local and global. To explain the conflicting meanings of *craft*, I observe that craft has been culturally located in traditions as a naturalistic sign of social belonging and a commentary on mechanical displacement engendered by modernity.

The admiration of renowned American writer Nathaniel Hawthorne (1804–1864) for the old wood-carver in his short story "Drowne's Wooden Image," the idealization of the pioneer house builder by Henry David Thoreau (1817–1862) in *Walden*, and Henry Wadsworth Longfellow's (1807–1882) nostalgia for the blacksmith in his poem "The Village Blacksmith" epitomize the historical symbol-ism of craft set against the backdrop of industrial and social change in American thought. The pioneer craftsman was a significant character for American writers interpreting the American experience, especially in the decades leading up to the Civil War. Nineteenth-century writ-ers typically portrayed the American craftsman sympathetically in New England rural or village scenes, set in a time before the industrial revo-lution supposedly swept away the intimate feeling of community. In countless American museum exhibitions, school textbooks, and stories following this legacy, American craft echoed the virtues of America's founding in the preindustrial past.

Longfellow, writing during the 1840s, when Americans experienced industrial change and rapid expansion, deserves particular credit for in-fluencing the image of the moral purity and physical prowess of the old craftsman in American letters. In "The Village Blacksmith" (probably sec-ond in popularity only to Longfellow's "Song of Hiawatha"), he writes of the physical enormity and strength of the archetypal American craftsman:

> Under a spreading chestnut-tree
> The village smithy stands;
> The smith a man is he,
> With large and sinewy hands;
> And the muscles of his brawny arms
> Are strong as iron bands.

As rough and tough as this figure is, the village blacksmith has a certain moral purity and therefore a special appeal to the innocence of chil-dren. Longfellow likens him to masters of other rural brawny skills, such as farmers threshing, because of the revered values associated with Americans who possess a rugged individual initiative, vernacular aes-thetic, and community spirit:

> And children coming home from school
> Look in at the open door;
> They love to see the flaming forge,
> And hear the bellows roar,
> And catch the burning sparks that fly
> Like chaff from a threshing-floor.

Longfellow concludes:

> Thanks, thanks to thee, my worthy friend,
> For the lesson thou has taught!
> Thus at the flaming forge of life
> Our fortunes must be wrought;
> Thus on its sounding anvil shaped
> Each burning deed and thought.

In contemporary America, the image of craft has regained significance, but its meaning has shifted. It commonly reemerges as a potent symbol in media, exhibition, and literature to give sincerity to industrial production or offer ethnic significance within a mass culture. In contrast to the aestheticism of poetry and fiction, the reigning forms of craft imagery are now found in the down-home realism of documentary, festival, do-it-yourself production, and exhibition (Levine and Heimerl 2008). Crafts workers appear not as the idealized and generalized rural American but as the ethnically or regionally tinged man or woman marked by a concern for heritage. Indeed, the craft metaphor has notably emerged as a rhetoric of ethnic and regional difference for a way of living effectively in a multicultural society. The qualities of craft—its physical enormity and strength, its handmade and often rough-hewn intimacy, its democratic spirit of enthusiasm and participation—continue from the poetry of the nineteenth century to the rhetoric of the new millennium. It is this distinctive American conception of craft that I examine here, with reference to advertisements, essays, exhibitions, ethnographies, and other expressions of persuasion.

Because of the historical background of colonial crafts and industrial revolution usually inculcated in American education, the rhetoric of craft and industry in America normally offers contrasting images. Craft, simply put, is usually thought of as practical skill, especially handwork for making or shaping household objects. To emphasize the use of handwork, especially detailed work for domestic items, one might occasionally hear the term *handicraft* being used, although *craft* is the simplest, most widespread, and probably most ambiguous term in circulation. The kinds of objects covered by *crafts* are usually thought of as having utilitarian and often domestic use—woven baskets for carrying, candles for lighting—although broader objects such as landscapes and houses can be said to be crafted by farmers and builders. The signifi-cance of craft utility may explain the vagueness of commercialism in the image of craft, since objects can be made for one's own use or to serve community needs, as well as being sold for profit or trade. Although craft can involve multiple workers, the common image is one of a lone skilled artisan using simple tools to control the process of creation from nature to product—from "sheep to shawl," as the saying goes. Because of the importance of transformation in craft—turning the wild shapes and materials of nature into small, formed objects for human use— emphasis is often placed on crafting in rural environs. Although a ma-terial dimension to craft predominates, there is also an abstract sense emphasizing skill rather than product. Even in the abstract, craft con-veys an idea of specialized tools or processes used for transformation. Americans speak of a lawyer's or teacher's craft, signifying the methods and materials used in the profession. Use of the term *craft* connotes individual expertise requiring training, patience, and care.

In school texts such as *America, Our Country* (Burnham and Jack 1934), *The American People and Nation* (Tyron and Lingley 1927), and *Our Nation's Heritage* (Halleck and Frantz 1925), students absorbed abundant references to the crafts workers of the frontier past as in-dustrious but not part of industry. Crafts workers were busy and pro-ductive, but they did not manufacture commodities on a large scale. Although industrial workers may use their hands to create objects in the manner of crafts, the connotation of industry in America is that workers manage machines rather than shape materials from nature. Workers' roles in the American industrial system, typically conceived as consisting of factories, is that they are machine-like in their ac-tions, measured by time rather than outcome. A common conception is that such toilers do not control the multiple steps of transforma-tion. They labor and are part of a uniform labor force, rather than individual artisans. Industry commonly means having a "laborious" task rather than a special expertise. The emphasis is often on the ef-ficient means of production rather than the careful process of creation. Although mining or lumbering can be—and once were—thought of as crafts, for example, they became industries when they were trans-formed into large-scale, mechanized enterprises with the objective of shipping products to distant markets. Society became industrialized when its economy became dependent on the commerce produced by such large-scale enterprises and culture relied on the consumption of their commodities.

In the late nineteenth and early twentieth centuries, Americans were given popular reminders that craft remained in the midst of mass industry. In mountain regions, by rough shores, and in desert climes, writers located places that had not shared in the nation's "progress" toward industry. As Americans wondered what would be lost and gained in the push for an industrialized future, authors who could be considered "romantic regionalists"—John Fox Jr. (1863–1919), James Lane Allen (1849–1925), and Henry W. Shoemaker (1880–1958), among others—embarked on fresh voyages of discovery, looking for pockets where rugged families maintained a hardscrabble existence and provided for themselves through craft. Judging by the imaginative accounts of America's handwrought ancestors in Appalachia and the Ozarks, life was homespun and had a charming, earthy, rough-hewn quality. The perceived values of craft became social concerns for proud individuality nurtured by family, community, and nature. In narrative and exhibition, quilts and coverlets became front-cover testimonies to the persistence—indeed, the dignity—of handwork. In story and song, they were metaphors for the old-fashioned life. In the Southwest, native blankets and pottery became the symbols for a regional-ethnic identity sprouting in the sand. On New England coasts, bird decoys and weather vanes appealed to the nostalgia for handwrought rural life not far from America's largest mills and factories. In bounded Pennsylvania German valleys, painted dowry chests and colorful fraktur manuscripts symbolized a picturesque life in sight of smokestack America.

The symbolism of old-time craft became visible in conspicuously public settings. Sometimes it was called "folk craft" to emphasize the continuity with the past, encompassing traditions that supposedly thrived in isolated locales. World's Fairs, the grand industrial spectacles of the late nineteenth and early twentieth centuries, regularly featured an "old-tyme" or "New England" kitchen or "farmer's" home. Costumed in colonial dress, demonstrators showed traditional food preservation and pointed to the spinning wheel as the epitome of American existence before modernity came in the nineteenth century and caused a sharp break with the past. In 1913 the new first lady, Ellen Axom Wilson, acknowledged craft's connection to the American spirit by redecorating the president's bedroom as the "Blue Mountain Room," fitting it with homespun rugs and coverlets. Ernest Thompson Seton (1860–1946), meanwhile, offered lessons on the disappearing American wilderness and the natives who lived in harmony with nature, and he fashioned a program of youth activities to enliven generations weakened by industrialization. Seton promoted among the nation's youth the "principles of woodcraft"—values of self-government, manhood, picturesqueness, competition, and heroism—which guided the activities of his Woodcraft Indians. His series of nature and woodcraft books were best sellers at the turn of the twentieth century, and he had a hand in the development of the Boy Scout movement, with its system of acquiring "craft" badges (Mechling 1989).

Often setting art apart from utility in America's most vigorous industrial era and conceiving of it as decoration or recreation, popular magazines carried feature stories linking craft in the late nineteenth century to a special vernacular American contribution to high art. In the search for a distinctive American design to rival Europe, the commercial Arts and Crafts movement drew attention by producing furniture that emulated the simplicity and hardiness of traditional craft. The plain forms of the furniture, designers proclaimed, marked a renewed aestheticism that retained the compassion of handwork in a machine age. With "modern art" all the rage, the Ogunquit School of Painting and Sculpture in Maine gained notice for inspiring its prominent modernist artists by decorating their studios with traditional bird decoys, rustic weather vanes, and homemade rugs. Famous figures from the school, such as Robert Laurent, Bernard Karfiol, and Niles Spencer, were moved to create avant-garde art based on "primitive" craft design and subsequently influenced the collection of Americana. They elevated their traditional craft sources by calling them folk painting and folk sculpture, supposedly produced by intrepid, anonymous New England artisans of the colonial era.

Many museums picked up on the glorification of early American crafts as art and therefore representing a worthy tradition for modern-day design and production. Hailing the abstractness of decoys and weather vanes, vocal museum leaders pointed to the artistry of American craft as the unself-conscious production of vernacular beauty. In these presentations of folk craft and art, America's simplicity and ruggedness, the democratic ideology of every man as his own creator, shone through. Louis C. Jones, director of the New York State His-

Louis C. Jones in the folk art gallery of the New York State Historical Association, Cooperstown, New York, 1967. (Photo by Milo V. Stewart)

torical Association (NYSHA), often related the event that inspired the association to begin its folk art collection in 1949. Walking through the Farmer's Museum, Jones stopped at an exhibit of home-crafted farm tools. He picked up a wooden barley fork and admired it, apart from the working scene. He praised its smooth lines, the patterned grain of the wood, its solid form. He told his curator it appeared to be "a beautiful, flowing rivulet of wood" (Jones 1982, 153). It became the centerpiece of a new gallery celebrating artistry in American everyday life. Craft, ever American, stood on the pedestal of art.

As a folklorist, Jones thought his reconceptualization of the barley fork as art could elevate the standing of traditions and their hardscrabble bearers. Before assuming the helm of the NYSHA, he had been a professor with avowedly socialist political leanings during the 1940s at the State Teachers College at Albany (later the State University of New York at Albany). He worked for civil rights for immigrants and African Americans and viewed folklore as the voice of the common people. Within the folklore field, Jones set himself apart by advocating a folklife approach developed in Scandinavia and central Europe that incorporated material culture research, documentation of folk communities and their everyday lives, and museum interpretation. These intellectual credentials and Jones's solid New York State roots were attractive to corporate mogul Stephen Clark as he developed the Farmer's Museum in Cooperstown as part of the NYSHA to represent the everyday folklife of upstate New York heritage. However, after sharing a podium with Clark at one event, Jones wrote, "I am against everything he stands for," referring to Clark's imperious acquisitiveness as one of America's richest men. Jones was surprised, and then rethought his position, when he was offered leadership of the NYSHA: "It means a new kind of work in which I shall use all my past experience, with large funds for expanding a vigorous set up—including one of the finest folk-life museums in America" (Jones 1946).

For Clark's part, he was an avid connoisseur of fine art, amassing an astounding collection by the likes of Picasso, Renoir, Matisse, van Gogh, Homer, and Eakins that became centerpieces at the Metropolitan Museum of Art, Whitney Museum of American Art, and Museum of Modern Art. His status within high society was elevated by his acquisitions, which drew awe from the wealthy set declaring an affinity with the new modern age of the twentieth century, including Electra Havemeyer Webb, Abby Aldrich Rockefeller, and Anson Conger Goodyear. Though residing in New York City, Clark summered in Cooperstown, where his country lawyer grandfather had helped build a fortune around the industrial empire of Singer Sewing Machines. The Clarks had a paternalistic relationship with the village and helped sustain it through the Great Depression with projects that boosted American traditions, such as the Baseball Hall of Fame. This was followed by creation of the Farmer's Museum from one of Clark's properties. He was less interested in upholding folk traditions than in giving something back to the village residents (Weber 2007, 258–383). The sites and collections Clark built, however, did not blare his name and its association with the power elite; instead, they reflected a democratic spirit and were intended to be public services for and about the common people.

With Jones in tow, Clark bought up folk art collections from New York dealers to fill the Fenimore House at Cooperstown and realized Jones's proletarian vision. Jones wanted to elevate the status of the folk in the post–World War II era, when the products of crafts workers were quickly being displaced by mass-produced goods. He hoped that in this distended society, the handwork of the community's crafts worker would provide a moral lesson for visitors, teaching them the value of grassroots self-reliance and social sustainability. If the revised interpretation of craft as folk art reinforced the idea of tradition as relic in a modernizing society, Jones still had his Farmer's Museum to show crossroads life as the backbone of American enterprise. Yet by accepting Clark's corporate patronage for the craft as art paradigm, Jones also encouraged a hierarchy of value for craft. The rhetoric of folk art joined a competitive commodity system, with curators and collectors contending to own the best and most valuable pieces. Longfellow's nineteenth-century characterization of the anonymous village blacksmith as part of the craft world became, in the twentieth-century American art world, a name-driven catalog of elaborate ironwork to be hung on the wall.

Put on display, craft as art also became increasingly symbolized as a worthy American past, even as it showed an inferiority complex about things American alongside the European classics and masters. American visitors could replicate at home the enshrinement of craft on a pedestal to announce, on the one hand, that American progress builds on a homegrown foundation and, on the other (perhaps a sleight of hand), that it makes a connection to tradition requiring no labor or social commitment. At the Village Crossroads of the Farmer's Museum, representing the period between 1790 and 1840—called the "Golden Age of Homespun" in a text Jones admired—one first encountered a large blacksmith shop, emblematic of hardy utilitarian craft at the center of preindustrial America (Van Wagenen 1953, 10). But across the street, the stately Fenimore House (a former home of Stephen Clark's brother) was fitted with modern trappings and featured a folk art gallery to remind visitors of the symbolic place of folk art as a relic of the past, while highlighting the advancement, and modern taste, of the present.

Folk art as a label repackaging the craft of community and utility into upper-class commodity and fashion became linked to modernism when wealthy patrons such as Abby Aldrich Rockefeller and Stephen Clark, serving as trustees of the Museum of Modern Art (MOMA, established in 1929), validated folk art as aesthetically contemporary by collecting American decorative craft objects for their skewed perspective alongside the work of French impressionists and American abstractionists. Rockefeller later founded the folk art center at Colo-

Ethnic textile exhibition designed by Allen Eaton at "Arts and Crafts of the Home-lands" exhibition, Buffalo, New York, 1919. (Courtesy Albright-Knox Gallery)

nial Williamsburg, while Clark, as noted earlier, was the driving force and financial backer of NYSHA's famed folk art collection. With the trustees' support, acting MOMA director Holger Cahill mounted a groundbreaking exhibition in 1932 called "American Folk Art: The Art of the Common Man in America 1750–1900," which began to shift the emphasis in folk art to the fine art categories of painting and sculp-ture (Bronner 1998, 413–74; Jones 1982, 152–53; Vlach 1985b). Louis Jones reflected that it "marked the arrival of folk art on the major art scene in New York" (1982, 152). Despite the fact that the exhibition's frame of reference in painting and sculpture was drawn largely from Rockefeller's collection, Cahill tried to differentiate folk art from fine art by pointing to the "craft tradition": "It does not come out of an aca-demic tradition passed on by schools, but out of a craft tradition plus the personal quality of the rare craftsman who is an artist" (Cahill 1932, 6). In his mind, the craft tradition linked folk art to America's "older communities," an ethic that is "honest and straightforward" coming from the "spirit of the people," a location in the "local," and a quality of "quaintness" (Cahill 1932, 3–28). If the skewed perspective of folk art held an aesthetic appeal for the modernists, it was nonetheless part of the past, set in community, and refreshing in its simplicity and untethered expression; in contrast, modern art was a complex, abstracted "art of our time" for a globalizing world.

Seven years later, MOMA was instrumental in both burying and promoting craft as America's romantic past in a blockbuster exhibition called "Art in Our Time" to celebrate its tenth anniversary, which coincided with the opening of the New York World's Fair in 1939. The show's accompanying book, which became a best seller in the art world, opened with a section on American folk and popular art, noting that "modern artists have been its 'discoverers,' finding in its clear childlike vision and straightforward technique qualities which they value" (Miller 1939, 17). As modern art was a protest, in many ways, of the harsh realism of industrialization, so folk craft and art stood for the preindustrial, even if social activists at the time, such as Allen Eaton working for the Russell Sage Foundation, argued that folk craft was persistent and relevant in regional and ethnic communities, especially during the Depression of the 1930s (Eaton 1932, 1937; Bronner 1998, 418–24).

Dorothy C. Miller, MOMA's assistant curator of American painting and sculpture, wrote in the "Art in Our Time" exhibition catalog:

> Today machine civilization tends to destroy this background of folk tradition. But in art the vision of the common man continues to find expression in certain talented but untrained and isolated individuals—men who have found in themselves a kind of common pictorial language which links the American carpenter Pickett (no. 2) with the French gardener Bauchant (no. 203); Hicks, a Pennsylvania sign painter who died ninety years ago (nos. 5, 6) with the living color lithographer Peyronnet of Paris (no. 204); Bombois (no. 202) with the unknown master of the *Quilting Party* (no. 3); Kane's masterpiece (no. 1) with Rousseau's (no. 84). (Miller 1939, 17).

Hinting at some kind of psychic unity or emotional motivation that could explain the rough-hewn character of artists labeled folk and modern, Miller gave an American primitivist cast to the definition of *modern* in modern art exemplified in the displayed works of European artists

Marc Chagall, Salvador Dali, and Pablo Picasso along with Americans Thomas Hart Benton, Charles Sheeler, and Edward Hopper.

Despite MOMA's promotion of the idea of craft and folk art's spiritual opposition to and displacement by "machine civilization," the art of craftsmanship occasionally entered the rhetoric of industry to show a tradition of individual care—indeed, humanity—in new technologies. Advertisements for Stevens-Duryea Motor Cars of Chicopee Falls, Massachusetts, for example, touted artists and craftsmen as the kind of people who "live to work" rather than "work to live." They are masters, the advertisements emphasized, not only of their trade but also of their spirit. Themes of earthiness, ruggedness, regionalism, and especially time-honored tradition—touchstones of folk craft's image in modern America—come through in the advertisement's copy. This campaign was meant to offset the American view that working in industry was a faceless job measured by time rather than a life's devotion with individual pride in the product. "Due to the rugged character and natural creative genius of its people," a similar advertisement from 1920 read, "New England has for nearly three hundred years offered the most fertile soil in America for the development of craftsmanship. Generation after generation, New England artisans have been imbued with a spirit of mastership—independent, individualistic, proud, unshaken by industrial and social upheavals. For nearly thirty years this spirit has governed the building of Stevens-Duryea Motor Cars." Seventy years after this advertisement appeared, General Motors featured assembly-line workers on television boasting craftsman values of individual concern for the products they build. For many viewers, however, the American industrial image of assembly, rather than creation associated with craft, undermined the persuasiveness of the pitch.

Symbolic of twenty-first-century global corporate expansion, Starbucks Coffee Company hoped to humanize its commercial behemoth image by advertising that its coffee is "handcrafted all the way from the farm to you" and "handcrafted from us to you." In one magazine advertisement, thirty white cups of coffee are arranged assembly-line style against a burlap-bag background, but only one of the cups has the colorful Starbucks logo. The message is clear: Starbucks is different; it has life. In 2008 it continued this theme with a line of "handcrafted tea beverages," accompanied by the reminder that Starbucks is "steeped in coffeehouse tradition." This appeal to tradition evokes localism and, as Starbucks' press releases suggest, a break from the stress of modern cosmopolitan life (Starbucks Newsroom 2008). Not to be outdone, the global fast-food giant McDonald's has emphasized its down-home praxis by declaring that Big Mac sandwiches are "handcrafted for that one-of-a-kind taste." The commercial even tries to folklorize the commercial brand, a metaphor for mass culture, by labeling the food "legendary."

Earlier in the twentieth century, the rhetoric of craft and tradition made a contrast between immigrants, who had an earthy, often exotic tradition, and native-born Americans, who supposedly did not. Images of industry and craft took center stage in public discourse regarding immigration's effect on the American spirit. Immigrants of diverse backgrounds—Russian Jews, Italian Catholics, Greek Orthodox—and black migrants moving from the South to the North changed the social map of America. Would they change its cultural configuration? Many came to find work in industry, and Israel Zangwill's (1864–1926) play *The Melting Pot*, produced in New York in 1908, suggested the industrial "melting pot" image for what happened to these people in machine-age America. In this view, their backgrounds melted together in the huge national cauldron, and unity was retained. Considering that many references to American craft emphasized the colonial (indeed, mostly English) roots of craftsmanship that supposedly developed into American tradition, how would the diverse "foreign" cultures coming to urban America in the twentieth century change the view that America's ancestors could be seen in crafts in isolated regions?

One response to the idea of the melting pot and the colonial revival was provided by settlement houses and social agencies. Eaton, for example, had this to say:

> Among the efforts . . . to assimilate these peoples from many lands, some were prompted by fears that old and tried values which had come to be prized in this country might be submerged or completely lost. . . . Some of the efforts at Americanization were without doubt shortsighted and ill-considered, particularly those which assumed that the immigrant had nothing to contribute, that on landing he must discard all the values precious to him in his homeland. A better approach and one which has gained support through more recent years springs

from an appreciation of what he has brought to his newly chosen country, not only the myrrh and frankincense of his tribute,
but treasures in the form of beautiful skills and crafts. By this
approach his gifts were gladly received and cherished in the
hope that their roots might strike deeply into the new soil to
which they were being transplanted. (Eaton 1932, 10)

After World War I, Eaton organized the "Arts and Crafts of the
Homelands" exhibition, designed to show the diverse color, vitality,
and worthiness of immigrant crafts and therefore immigrants themselves in America. He had no doubt that immigrants would be Ameri-
canized, but he insisted that their craft traditions could continue the
process of building a national life, much as the historical colonial experience had. The hands of Hungarian Americans produced intricate
embroideries on pillows and bedspreads, from Old Bohemia came
festively decorated Easter eggs, and from Holland came gaily painted
chairs and tables.

    In addition to material skills, performing arts were featured in the
exhibition as equally enriching. Bulgarian dancers and Ukrainian musicians, among others, filled the hall. The objective was to show immigrant life as a full community very much a part of the present day. In
dance, music, and craft, urban immigrants were energetic, productive,
full of life. The exhibition traveled widely and still holds visitorship
records in New York City. Other "homelands" programs with similar
goals swept America, with names such as the International Folk Festival, Folk Festivals of the Homelands, and America's Making Exposition. The frontispiece of Eaton's book on these festivals and exhibitions
illustrates a magnificent doorway, conceived as "Some Experiments
in Appreciation of the Contributions of Our Foreign-Born Citizens
to American Culture." The Philadelphia door (actually a door to an
inner-city church) encapsulates the modern ethnic idea: it is an urban
entrance to the opportunity of America, raising comparisons to Independence Hall. The door contains fancy ironwork by Samuel Yellin
from Poland, relief wood carving by Edward Maene from Belgium,
and colorful stained glass by Nicola D'Ascenzo from Italy, all against
a red backdrop. The exhibition's displays included the surroundings
of immigrant residences, with the intent of showing that art was part
of the newcomers' everyday lives, not the rare outburst of expression

described by MOMA. Thus, the exemplification of folk arts in Eaton's effort to shape American consciousness was a far cry from the humble, singular spinning wheel of the New England kitchen or MOMA's gallery of abstractionists.

Portraying immigrants as diverse crafts workers who could work together on a door as well as a nation, rather than as ingredients in a melting pot, verified their cultural value, their individuality, their integrity. It also allowed a duality of identities implied by the compound labeling of ethnic Americans. Immigrants could display compelling skills—such as embroidery and carving—while accepting American dress and food and, of course, American work. Settlement houses, established to ease immigrants' transition into the new society, used this image extensively. They often displayed traditional crafts brought or made by immigrants in a historic museum setting. To show the ways these crafts enriched the American future, they presented immigrants demonstrating new arts and industrial skills in a modern context. At the well-known Hull House in Chicago, Jane Addams underscored this point in 1910 with the example—indeed, the parable—of a young Russian immigrant:

> The Hull-House shop affords many examples of the restorative power in the exercise of a genuine craft; a young Russian who, like too many of his countrymen, had made a desperate effort to fit himself for a learned profession, and who had almost finished his course in a night law school, used to watch constantly the work being done in the metal shop at Hull-House. One evening in a moment of sudden resolve, he took off his coat, sat down at one of the benches, and began to work, obviously as a very clever silversmith. He had long concealed his craft because he thought it would hurt his efforts as a lawyer and because he imagined an office more honorable and 'more American' than a shop. As he worked on during his two leisure evenings each week, his entire bearing and conversation registered the relief of one who abandons the effort he is not fitted for and becomes a man on his own feet, expressing himself through a familiar and delicate technique. (Addams 1990, 216)

Eighty-five years after these words were written, I received a letter from the Pennsylvania Heritage Affairs Commission announcing an

Rosemaled bowl made by Judith Nelson of Minneapolis, Minnesota, 1988, from the touring exhibition "Circles of Tradition: Folk Arts in Minnesota," organized by the University Art Museum, University of Minnesota, 1989. (Courtesy Frederick R. Weisman Art Museum)

innovative program for new immigrants, or refugees. Although its bureaucratic rhetoric had the ring of new policy, it essentially reenacted the social uses of craft of Addams's day. "The goal of this endeavor," the letter read, "is to focus attention on the strengths and resources of refugee communities with respect to their cultural and arts traditions in order to improve their resettlement success and ensure more stable, economic development in our refugee communities."

With the post-1965 wave of arrivals in the United States after the lifting of immigration restrictions, socially conscious essayists took great pains to show that ethnic crafts did not necessarily fall away as immigrants, migrants, natives, and their children took on industrial jobs and professions. A survey of Wisconsin folk crafts, for example, revealed ongoing traditions of Ojibwa feather work, Croatian *tamburitza* making, Slovak Easter egg decorating, Norwegian wooden shoe making, African American cane carving, and Hmong needlework. The immigrant arts represent the expression of persistent community within the uniformity of America's emerging mass culture, and "they help to create a sense of continuity and belonging" (John Michael Kohler Arts Center 1987). This and other ethnic surveys of the post-1965 immigration wave altered the connotations of *folk*—from an association with antiquity to the importance of learning skills in a community or group. In this view, craft had a vital role to play on the contemporary scene. Even crafts that had not been continuously active might be revived to perform social or community functions. Rosemaling, for instance, a style of painted decoration used in eighteenth-century rural Norwegian homes, enjoyed a revival in the 1930s in the Upper Midwest as part of a regional-ethnic consciousness. It spread so widely that some late-twentieth-century writers claimed it was more popular in the United States than in Norway (Ellingsgard 1995; Martin 1989; Nelson 1995, 96–97).

Other examples that drew attention because of their use of tradi-

Yolanda Rosenschein weaving a tallith (a Jewish prayer shawl) for her grandson on a loom at her synagogue in Harrisburg, Pennsylvania. (Photo by Simon Bronner)

tion brought the continuity of time and the authenticity of place into question. During the 1970s, when "Black Pride" became a public slogan, hair braiding and head wrapping based on African sources came into fashion. Jewish mothers, meanwhile, began weaving prayer shawls for their bar mitzvah boys, bringing a handwrought meaning of tradition to the event, even though the weaving custom and the grand celebration of the bar mitzvah itself were relatively recent innovations (Bronner 2008–2009; Joselit 1994, 89–118).

Charles Rebuck, a self-described "Dutchman through and through," saw a sign of the times in the things he made. For years his baskets boasted a Pennsylvania German design, but in the 1990s he started making them smaller and sometimes more elaborate. He thought people tended to pick them up and notice the tradition even more than when he had made his baskets as full-size utilitarian objects. As a Dutchman concerned about the erosion of Pennsylvania German traditions, Rebuck created evocative reminders of the region's woven traditions. He no longer sold his baskets but made them for people he wanted to reach with his ethnic message—old cronies, his children and grandchildren, assimilated professionals with "Dutchy" names. Craft in these instances became a sign of recalling or even creating tradition to provide communal identity in an imposing mass society.

In the American rhetoric of craft, the works of some ethnic and regional groups have a special attachment to craft. Pennsylvania Germans, known for their furniture, baskets, redware pottery, hex signs, quilts, and paper arts, are one such group. Among people living in the southern Appalachians and Ozark Mountains, associated with a rough-hewn life and English and Scots-Irish ancestry, wood carving, textile weaving, and chair making are commonly hawked as "authentic" signs of regional and American heritage. Native Americans have relied on their image as a people who live close to the land and use crafts to peddle native-made rugs, jewelry, and pottery to tourists, especially in the American West. In the area around Charleston, South Carolina, the nearby Sea Islands are known for an isolated African American community where living plainly has boosted a cottage economy of basket weaving from sweetgrass. Some of these baskets, such as the rice baskets, have traditional designs with origins in Africa, but others, such as those serving as glass coasters and flower planters, are adaptations to the modern trade.

Charles Rebuck weaving a basket,
Klingerstown, Pennsylvania,
1992. (Photo by Simon Bronner)

Rebuck with finished baskets.
(Photo by Simon Bronner)

Pang Xiong Sirathasuk holding up her Hmong *paj ntaub tib neeg,* or "story cloth," Upper Darby, Pennsylvania. (Photo by Simon Bronner)

Another sign of adaptation is the use of textiles by the Hmong, who originally arrived in the United States from Laos. The women turned the elaborate embroidery and cloth designs on their dresses into quilt blocks and "story cloths" (embroidered with characters from Hmong folktales or illustrating experiences from the Vietnam War) for an American audience familiar with a quilt aesthetic (Conquerwood 1992; MacDowell 1989; Peterson 1988a, 1988b). In areas of Hmong resettlement, such as Minneapolis, Philadelphia, and Los Angeles, Hmong textile designs have turned up on pillowcases, vests, and hats. Although many of these products are meant for a consumer market, the production of traditional dress is reserved for holiday celebrations such as New Year (Lynch 1995). In Pennsylvania, Hmong needleworkers produce white quilts with Amish designs, but aesthetically, they favor light pastel colors to the traditional Amish use of dark, deep purples and blues (Henry 1995).

The appeal of the Hmong women's designs is part of the perception of Asian work as ancient, delicate, and precise. Chinese calligraphy and scissors cutting are featured at many crafts fairs, where the work is framed, similar to photographs, and sold as small gift items. Coinciding with the boom in Japanese electronics in the late twentieth century was an interest in Japanese crafts, bolstered by some aspects of popular culture, such as the film *The Karate Kid* (1984), which shows the Japanese master quietly at work pruning his bonsai. I should emphasize that this trend is no threat to the normative Euro-American craft aesthetic apparent in pioneer quilts, heavy wood carving, and forged ironwork. But as privatization becomes more apparent in modern life, with an inward turn rather than socialization in the public arena, and with the growing awareness of Asia as a rising force in the globalized economy, the contemplative features of Asian craft draw more people. Perhaps they are attracted by Asian economic success, on the one hand, and by an anti-industrial quest for spiritual serenity through craft (absent in Euro-American production), on the other. For some American home owners, Asian craft creates a cultural difference between their homes' interiors and the exteriority of public life; it establishes the domestic sphere as an exotic island of serenity in a vast sea awash in modern Euro-American homogeneity. Without ever stepping foot in China or Japan, a number of Americans have gone beyond the general fascination with large-scale gardening to the minimalist approach to flower arranging and ikebana pottery and the minimizing praxis of bonsai, in contrast to the "bigger is better" American mentality. A blockbuster exhibition of Japanese screens at the Art Institute of Chicago in 1996 sparked national interest in the use of these items to lend a sense of craftsmanship to the otherwise mechanized American home. For years afterward, the gift shop promoted *Japan: The Art of Living* (Katoh and Kimura 2003) as its primary Japanese art volume, which is intended to offer "exciting new ideas and inspiration for [American] home décor" from the use of Japanese folk crafts.

Arguably, the appeal of Japanese craft differs from the European-centered inheritance in American colonial heritage and is still marginalized, to an extent, within American culture. Japanese craft, together with its generalized link to Chinese cultural traditions, expresses a meditative, spiritual aura around the activities of pruning, cultivating, and decorating. Whereas craft in an American mode is made to extend outward by giving it to someone else to use, the intensity by which trees are miniaturized or space is abstracted in Japanese craft connotes that the self as an object is being improved. This inward direction has been called a key to the "compact culture" of Japanese life, in contrast to the emphasis on outward thinking that translates into value placed on large, expansive objects that allow mobility and their externalization as utilities (Lee 1992; Yoshida, Tanaka, and Sesoko 1982).

When I was in Japan, I realized that my Japanese hosts looked at the screens I admired differently. Whereas I saw the decorative motif on the screen, they focused on its use as a divider that serves to create space. Similarly, Americans may wonder about the "craft" in compact Japanese rock gardens, a contrast to the naturalistic idea of the growing American garden. One notices, of course, that crowds gather in temples throughout Japan to look meditatively at these arrangements of rock and sand, and Americans figure that they have a spiritual meaning. Often lost in translation is the idea that these arrangements gain importance because they encapsulate larger concepts. A rock surrounded by raked sand symbolizes—indeed, metaphorically focuses—the relation of a mountainous island to the ocean. For many Americans, oriented generally toward the West, the Japanese represent two ends of a spectrum: at one end, Japanese work is associated with the large-scale electronics industry and the ultimate realization of a mass society, and at the other end, folk crafts such as bonsai represent the extreme of solitary, patience-requiring, small-scale intensity. There may be a connection, however, in the commonly held American perception of a craftsman-like attention to detail in Japanese industrial products.

A broader issue of the nationalistic function of craft is raised by the contrasting economic and cultural protections available in the United

States and Japan. Since 1950, the Japanese government has designated individuals or groups who embody intangible national cultural values as living human treasures, and this designation accords their craft traditions and styles economic and cultural protection. Officially, the protected traditions are deemed by law to be "important intangible cultural property." By honoring crafts workers, this program encourages bearers of traditions of national significance to continue to ply their trade, including pottery, decorated screens, and lacquerware. Protection is different from preservation, in the sense that crafts workers are not expected to slavishly churn out copies of familiar relics. As one such honored crafts worker, potter Kaneshige Michiaki (1934–1995), explained, "Tradition is sometimes confused with transmission. Copying Momoyama pieces is transmission. Producing contemporary pieces incorporating Momoyama period techniques is tradition. Tradition consists of retaining transmitted forms and techniques in one's mind when producing a contemporary piece. Tradition is always changing. A mere copy of an old piece has not changed; it is nearly the same as its prototype of four hundred years ago. Tradition consists of creating something new with what one has inherited" (Japanese Pottery Information Center 2005). The Japanese view craft as rooted in the past in a lineal descent from masters and evolving into the present. This Confucian perspective on craft, related to the perception of filial piety as a high virtue, lacks the democratized vernacular of American craft and its association with a prior, unrecoverable stage of industrial progress.

Many of the individuals designated "living treasures" are centered in Miyajima, which ties folk crafts to national religion and naturalistic spirituality. Promoted as the "historic and cultural crossroads of Japan" and "an island where people and gods live together," Miyajima is famous for its Itsukushima shrine, which sets the theme for the folk crafts celebrated and protected on the island. UNESCO, which designated it a World Heritage Site, explains its significance as a "holy place of Shintoism since the earliest times. The first shrine buildings here were probably erected in the sixth century. The present shrine dates from the thirteenth century and the harmoniously arranged buildings reveal great artistic and technical skill. The shrine plays on the contrasts in color and form between mountains and sea. It illustrates the Japanese concept of scenic beauty, which combines nature and human creativity" (UNESCO 2007; see also Bonneville 2006, 440).

Nature and creativity are indeed apparent. When I visited Miyajima, I was struck by the deer that roam freely on the island, placing the various crafts shops in a naturalistic as well as spiritualistic setting, which is so important to the tradition-centered sense of Japaneseness. There seems to be no need to elevate crafts to a class-based definition of art because the aesthetic as well as cultural importance of craft is assumed. The island has a traditional crafts center, a treasure hall for the crafts associated with the shrine, and a museum that combines history and folklore. Although Japanese visitors admire the skill of the masters, revered as elder parental sensei, they also relate the environment of craft to their own development into adults. Paper folding (the making of cranes, for example, as symbols of long life), calligraphy (characters are taught by handling brushes dipped in ink), and the tea ceremony are living traditions in their everyday experience.

To be sure, the United States has a program of National Heritage Fellowships awarded by the National Endowment for the Arts (NEA) to recognize master "folk and traditional artists . . . to recognize recipients' artistic excellence and support their continuing contributions to our nation's traditional arts heritage" (National Endowment 2007; Siporin 1992). I took pride in nominating one of those recipients, Earnest Bennett, for his chain carving, which I document in my book on wood carving (Bronner 1996a). Much as Bennett appreciated the one-time payment from the government, I observed from the aftereffects of his honor that this program is not intended to perpetuate his craft or even to call it a craft. The program underscores the recipients' status as artists rather than as bearers of tradition to elevate their work to the level of fine art. Reflecting American progressive individualism, the program highlights their outstanding past achievements as individuals rather than the future of their evolving tradition or their perpetuation of a school of work. Although it shares with the Japanese a nationalistic goal, it is an honors program rather than a protectionist initiative. Whereas the Japanese program functions to create a unified soul for Japanese identity, linking religion, nature, and craft as national icons, the American fellowships strive to represent the democratized diversity—regional and ethnic—of American experience.

As the NEA program illustrates, traditional crafts workers are suspect because they operate in contemporary society, which is assumed to have progressed from a hand to a machine civilization, from

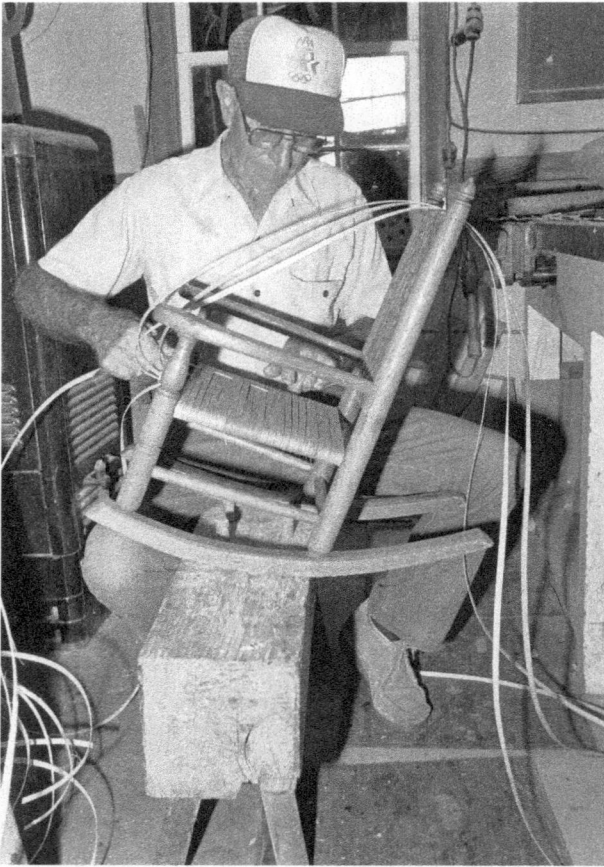

Charles Starry
making a child's
rocker, East Berlin,
Pennsylvania.
(Photo by Simon
Bronner)

a group-centered world of tradition to an individualistic society oriented toward the future. Yet craft holds an appeal and has the desirable
connotation of community and nature. Arising from this conflict is a
struggle to symbolize craft in the workaday world. For most Americans, craft serves aesthetic purposes to offset the shadow of mass society, especially in the home, and crafts are harnessed in American life to
provide public community roles, if not to integrate instrumentally into
everyday life. In Ferdinand, Indiana, a local hardware store manager
told me that he needs his traditional blacksmithing skills to fill difficult requests to repair metal tools and fences. He maintains a forge
behind the store and keeps his hammer ringing. In Louisiana, crafts-

men keep busy making flat-bottomed bateaux and pirogues, necessary to maneuver the tricky bayous. In New Orleans, specialized artisans supply many of the ornate feather costumes and beaded patches used during Mardi Gras.

In Adams County, Pennsylvania, Charles Starry, a third-generation chair maker, is no longer actively engaged in making the "porch rockers" that graced houses throughout the Middle Atlantic before air-conditioning brought people indoors during the summer. However, he still gets many orders from seaside resorts, and he fills seat-weaving requests from local residents (Zercher 1992–1993). His shop resounds with more power equipment than his grandfather had, and he no longer gets his slats from Penn's Woods (the "reeds" come from a supplier, who gets them from China). His craft has adapted to new times. He makes more children's rockers than ever before, for a clientele that associates old-time craft with parental nurturing. "I sell a lot of those for gifts," he told me. And many of his orders for bigger rockers come from men who want the chairs for their hunting cabins or porches, connecting them to nature or heritage. For many customers, handmade furniture reminds them of tradition and holds the appeal of human involvement, of a special custom touch. Starry appears annually at a colonial arts fair near his home and sets up his wares against a backdrop of a log cabin erected by the local historical society. Yet for Starry, there is a personal motivation of continuing a workaday schedule past retirement in a garage converted to a manly workshop away from the feminized interior decorated and controlled by his wife.

Lewis Reinhart, who comes from a long line of German Gypsy basket makers, collected willows from riverbanks in Pennsylvania and traveled widely during the 1930s, selling willow baskets to farmers for carrying potatoes and eggs. By century's end, he was still on the road, keeping his family together by attending the crafts fairs that dotted the region and responding to consumers' interest in willow hampers and flower stands (Staub 1988, 169–71). His son Willie, who grew up traveling to these shows, learned to weave willows into baskets from his father and made an alteration for the new trade—putting wooden skids on the bottom to make the baskets more stable on tabletops and spray-painting the finished baskets to add flowery colors. He continues the legacy of seasonal trade in his family and supplements his income with another manual trade—paving.

(*Above*) Lewis Reinhart weaving a willow basket, New Oxford, Pennsylvania. (Photo by Simon Bronner)

(*Left*) William "Willie" Reinhart with willow baskets at a crafts fair in East Berlin, Pennsylvania. (Photo by Simon Bronner)

Whereas industry was once the foil for crafts as the spiritual side of America, in postmodern America, mass media is presented as the spoiler. Craft is something active and wholesome, promoters say, as opposed to the stupefying effects of television and video games. One point made by numerous contemporary ethnographies about religious or folk communities is that craft serves special, sometimes ritual, needs that cannot be provided by hypnotizing high-definition screens. Again associated with naturalistic praxis, craft is constructed as peaceful and contemplative, in contrast to the violence and shallowness of remote-controlled electronics. In popular culture, the critically acclaimed movie *Witness* (1985) and lesser films such as *Kingpin* (1996) and *For Richer or Poorer* (1997), along with the television productions *Saving Sarah Cain* (2007) and *Amish Grace* (2010), show the Amish engaged in craftwork as a defining example of tradition-centered activity. The film portrayals of plainly dressed Amish eschewing electronics bear out the redemptive quality, in the modern view, of an ethnic-religious group in modern society that maintains craft as an everyday pursuit. In most of these movies, Amish characters are tempted away from their tradition, and moderns feel guilty for their seductive ways. Although usually unwilling to revert back to tradition, conceived as the "simple life," moderns want the Amish to remain traditional and thus be available for symbolic and sometimes consumable purposes.

Other ethnic communities that fulfill the redemptive function of craft as metaphor for traditional life are less popularized than the Amish, but they must still deal with the symbolization of their practices by moderns. In many Jewish communities, ambivalence is expressed by liberal, secularized Jews toward ultraorthodox Jews or Hasidim. The Hasidim's conspicuous black hats, earlocks, and strict kosher observance seem out of place in modern society, yet they are also celebrated for maintaining ancient crafts that provide a sense of continuity. For example, a *sofer*, or sacred scribe, is required to prepare and repair stylized inscriptions on Torah scrolls and is often touted as essential to Jewish authenticity. This calligrapher, facing the daunting task of producing precise lettering on parchment using a feather quill, must endure many years of training for this delicate work.

Not all ritual tasks are ancient or religious. College fraternities and sororities also have traditional sacred objects and symbols, and in a society that often questions the exclusive club, these craft features are used to show that such organizations have social purpose. Members may be required to make medallions, paddles, and amulets to represent the bonds of brother- or sisterhood. During homecoming celebrations, many fraternities and sororities exhibit their crafting abilities by creating elaborate displays paraded past the college community.

Many reasons, often personal in nature, can account for the pursuit of traditional crafts in mass society. The movie *Best Little Whorehouse in Texas* (1982) features Burt Reynolds as a backcountry sheriff who is carving a chain from wood to convey his southern leisureliness and down-home ways. My ethnography of the craft, *The Carver's Art* (Bronner 1996a), led to some fame for one carver, as noted earlier. Earnest Bennett drew special notice, probably because of the rustic image of a Kentucky farm boy transplanted to a big northern city. Bennett, a gifted wood-carver, moved to Indianapolis from the tiny hamlet of Fairplay. As a child, he learned wood carving—a useful skill for a man to have around the farm and at home—from relatives. Later in life he turned to carving again to relax after his labors. He found solace in using his skill and received kudos when he shared it with others. He was proud that a tradition he associated with his "country boy" ways was valued. Yet his carvings did not follow past designs. He worked around the patterns he knew and created innovative designs that included belt buckles, snakes, and pillars on basic chains.

Bennett's wife found an outlet in a different medium; she quilted and created family treasures to hand down to her grandchildren. Quilting was a social activity that gave her time with her friends, and she liked to point out that the very process was something of a metaphor for her family. She picked out ordinary pieces of cloth, brought them together in a pleasing pattern, and created something beautiful and warming.

George Blume, a wood-carver in Indiana, had his own reasons for taking up carving. Faced with aging and feeling that his skills had been maligned, he showed his fellow workers at a furniture factory in Huntingburg what he could do by creating intricate wooden chains made out of one piece of wood—some as small as a matchstick, others as long as a city block. He liked the process of chain carving, he said, because it made him think that his hands and their old ways still had power. He beamed as he pointed out that the chains were made by *cutting in* rather than cutting out, emphasizing his contribution to creation (Bronner 2005b, 274–84).

Blume's connection of cutting praxis and social acceptability reminds us that technical and ethnographic studies of crafts often leave
out the larger context of mass society to explain the symbolic significance of handwork to crafts workers. Craft has been perceived as a
type of labor associated with preindustrial life, and its documentation is
pursued to preserve a piece of the past rather than to examine its commentary on the present. Historically, the search is typically for people
who draw their identity totally from their labor. We want to know why
all those with the common surnames of Smith, Wright, and Cooper
have little connection to their laboring legacy today. They were once
attached to a place or a natural setting and represented a long line engaged in a certain handicraft.

So what about the Russian lawyer engaged in silversmithing, or the
black professional donning a head wrap? Or what about the writer who
is also a weightlifter and a home owner, crafting an argument, sculpt-
ing muscles, or tending the yard? These questions imply that multiple
identities, many of which are only occasionally enacted, are possible. In
the mass society that suggests free mobility, mass communication, and
consumer economics, craft can have a personal significance by shaping,
building, and constructing social meaning. Even if someone doesn't
make baskets, can he or she be said to be using the structure and aesthetics of craft in everyday activity? Are there processes at work that
link or divide the way things are done in the factory and farm, house
and office?

The proclivity for craft begins in childhood, despite the parental
urge to keep children occupied with the latest electronic toy. Yet around
sand and snow, children mine raw materials for crafting. Among their
favorite activities is taking a stone and dropping it softly into the water
to make concentric circles; another is building mountains, forts, and
castles out of rocks. In these examples, children play with form and
display their aesthetic sense, turning natural shapes into human-made
constructions. At the Susquehanna River near Harrisburg, Pennsylvania, I observed Neva building with rocks, and her sister Sadie followed suit. The children compared their constructions and discussed
what they were: castles, islands, volcanoes. After finishing one, they
started to arrange their constructions in rows, creating a neat landscape of forms. They stepped back to see if it looked right—from their
child's-eye sense of aesthetics. With this shared idea of what was be-

ing constructed, the girls worked together. Their little brother, Jonah, meanwhile, worked off at a distance building a rectangular fort made of rocks. The forms themselves were not necessarily traditional (although the Western tendency to arrange forms in rows and rectangles is), but the process involving informal learning, repetition, and variation shows the kind of praxis common to the folk craft of children. The conventional tendency to arrange forms linearly and symmetrically is balanced by the sculptures' imaginative, almost magical, quality imparted by their pyramidal shape. Such constructions are not normally displayed in museum galleries or folk art collections, but they are worthy of discussion as culturally based design. In city sections where the landscape has been altered—indeed, crafted—by children making the most of their environment to create playthings, milk crates become basketball hoops, police barricades turn into carts, telephone wires are transformed into jewelry, and hangers into weapons of attack.

Forms created of folded paper are more comparable, perhaps, because one can recognize the shapes children craft (for example, airplanes). They defy some of the assumptions of the rural craft working from sheep to shawl, however. The modern prevalence of paper folding among youth suggests socially significant implications when contrasted to the wood and cloth constructions more common in previous generations. In the past, these folk constructions commonly prepared youngsters to use technology they would need in the material culture of adulthood. Such constructions developed certain kinds of activities, differentiated perhaps by sex or region or occupation, such as rural boys who carved wooden puzzles with pocketknives to prepare them for outdoor work and farm labor. Emphasized in the woodworking was the conversion of natural three-dimensional materials by cutting, splitting, and sanding into an industrial tool. The prevalence of paper folding suggests something different. The conversion does not rely so much on tools, and the process of altering nature is missing. The flat paper is folded to produce a new shape, but the paper itself keeps its integrity, and it can be returned to its original appearance. The productions are often technological, with successive steps to be followed and geometric shapes to execute. The materials emphasize visual cues more than the textured feel of wood and cloth productions. To be sure, the scale of both wooden and paper productions is smaller than in the adult world, but the paper products are often more secretive and tem-

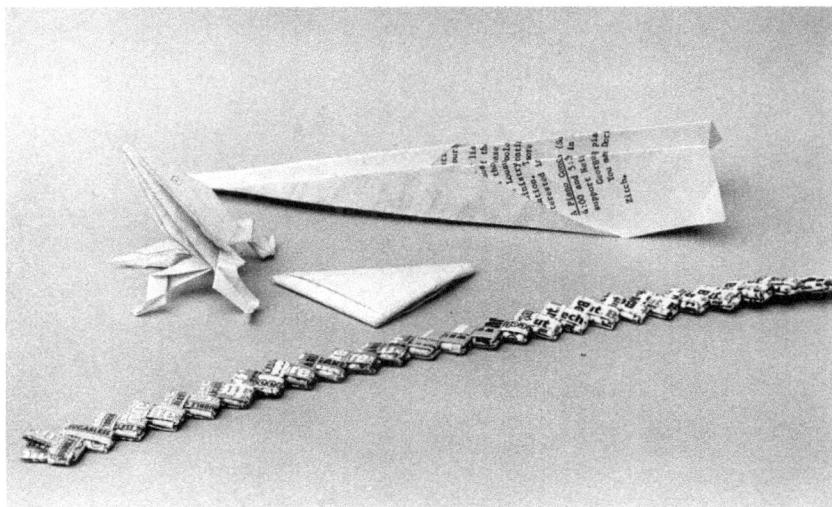

Paper crafts made by fourth-grade children in Harrisburg, Pennsylvania. (Photo by Simon Bronner)

porary; they are also more quickly made. Commonly arising out of the school experience, paper-folded constructions in this context reflect the heavy influence of institutional life on today's youth and convey the importance of an information economy, with its emphasis on paperwork and disposal. For the child, the thrill of the conversion is in taking the plain, sober paper and turning it into something playful, maybe even rebellious.

Crafting is hardly just child's play. Examination of household environments often reveals adult craft at work. Begin with the mailbox. Many American home owners are not content with the official, public look of the mailbox fronting their private homes, so they personalize it by crafting a base or making a covering for the box itself, and they often follow conventions of design. A common sight is a welded metal chain holding up the box. It seems to magically stay up and can take on different shapes and sizes, such as being bent to indicate the first letter of the family name. Besides the chain, a support can be made from horseshoes and spikes, if the maker desires. Many of these are made by the home owner for his or her own use, but I found one industrial welder who constructed lots of them for his neighbors and friends. When asked

(Above) Driveway lined with wagon wheels, Logan, Utah. (Photo by Simon Bronner)

(Left) Front gate crafted with a wagon wheel, Logan, Utah. (Photo by Simon Bronner)

why the designs are appealing, he answered that the mailbox is standardized and official, and the do-it-yourself look of the support makes a statement about the residents' control over their property. As the sentry for the yard and the house entrance, the mailbox can be imaginatively embellished through a handwrought support or box casing to express the personality of the owners.

Many residents told me that their "craft" is tending and decorating the yard. Objects in the yard are not necessarily made from scratch, but for the residents, the arrangement is a crafted work. With the prevalence of consumer behavior, the process of arranging consumed items and converting their functions has become a common craft. Tires become planters, bottles hang from trees, and rakes become figures in a homemade landscape. In some parts, the designs are regionally distinctive. In Utah, I noticed gates and fences made from irrigation wheels and horseshoes that extended far down the lane; mailboxes had western themes of cowboys, plows, and wagon wheels. All over America, homes announce seasonal celebrations with crafted displays of arranged objects. At Easter, Pennsylvanians hang colored eggs from the trees. At Halloween, stuffed effigies sit on porches, ghostly creations hang around the yard, and carved pumpkins smile eerily at the street.

Given that these craft traditions are normative, what happens when someone uses craft in an oppositional way? That is, if craft from the vantage of moderns is redemptive as long it stays in its place to be observed and consumed, then it is also possible to take the offensive, using craft as a tool to show the corruption of modern life. During the "back-to-the-city" movement of the 1980s, when municipal governments lured young professionals to reclaim dilapidated brownstones, for instance, I recorded the behavior of Clarence "Cal" Yingst—someone people recognized as a craftsman (Bronner 1986b, 63–86). He fit squarely into his Harrisburg, Pennsylvania, neighborhood, which was home to many tradesmen who worked with their hands, but as many of them became displaced by gentrification, Cal stood out more. Back in 1972, Cal and his working-class neighbors had reclaimed the area after a disastrous flood. Using techniques of bricolage—making overlays of paint and wood on their houses from the wreckage of buildings abandoned in the flood—residents of the midtown area not only repaired their dwellings but also gave the neighborhood a vernacular patchwork look. Cal was especially active in making the houses habitable through woodworking and painting skills, learned from his father. Cal's work was in the neighborhood, and he knew all his clients personally. His work encouraged residents to sit out in front of their homes and talk to one another.

During the early 1980s, the back-to-the-city movement brought middle-class professionals to the midtown region, and they demanded refurbished houses that were made to order by professionals. As these rehabilitated houses came to dominate the landscape of the neighborhood, Cal's artistic work on his own housefront increased, to the chagrin of the middle-class residents, who preferred restraint when it came to public displays. The professionals wanted housefronts in the neighborhood to look "clean" and uniform, in keeping with the conception of professionalism as unearthly, free of the grime and exuberance associated with the working-class trades.

When the local newspaper praised the "fine art" of the renovated houses owned by the professionals and ignored the handiwork done by the working-class residents, Cal recognized a threat to the environment he had shaped. He responded by dramatizing the social nature of his surroundings, extending his living space forward into the street.

Housefront constructed by *bricoleur* Cal Yingst out of paint, wood, mats, and found objects in Harrisburg, Pennsylvania. (Photo by Simon Bronner)

Yingst holding a crafted bird in his backyard filled with environmental art and homemade furnishings. (Photo by Simon Bronner)

He built boxes around street signs, carpeted his front steps in a bright color, dug a garden into the sidewalk, and painted his shutters in a bold design. When one of the professionals had the sidewalk in front of her house replaced with brickwork, Cal painted images of bricks on his sidewalk, using bold white lines for the grout and deep browns for the bricks. Then, thinking it seemed too much of an imitation, he varied the colors to create a bright checkerboard look that gained more notice. Complaints by the professionals only heightened Cal's efforts. Working-class residents praised his work and gathered to talk in front of his house. Events took a turn when one working-class resident died and another was evicted. Then, rather than pushing his work forward, Cal turned his efforts inward. The constructions in front of his house created enclosures for Cal to view his environment, protected by layers of wood.

My study appeared to end when the rootedness of the working-class residents triumphed over the essentially mobile character of the middle-class professionals. Although the professionals complained, they did not press their advantage of power because they always planned to move on, whereas the working-class residents operated on the assumption of stability. But since my story was published in 1986, additional changes had occurred in the built landscape. More houses became rehabilitated as the working-class residents left their homes. In response, Cal's house became more enclosed; he created a closed-in entranceway, whereas once it had been open and invited visitors. He gave more social attention to the back of his house than to the front, creating structures in his own private space.

The use of craft and decoration became more pronounced in the months following a changeover in the neighborhood. Whereas Cal had once mimicked urban building styles in his construction, the new work conveyed a feeling of whimsy through color and cement. Eventually, several working-class houses, including Cal's, were condemned by city authorities for building code violations. The gentrified houses remain dominant. In a new location near the old neighborhood, Cal still expresses his social priorities through the praxis of structuring the environment. He has built colorful whirligigs of birds and other animals, arranged colored stones on the ground, and made yard furniture. His work is more private and smaller in scale, but still expressive and symbolic. He has moved his craftwork to the back of the house because of restrictions against working on the facade, but at the official street sign, one can detect his handiwork: colored stones surround the bottom of the pole.

This process is related to an essential point made by Zygmunt Bauman in *Culture as Praxis:* "the generic notion of culture is coined in order to overcome the persistent philosophical opposition between the spiritual and the real, thought and matter, body and mind. The only necessary and irreplaceable component of the concept is the process of structuring, together with its objectified results—man-made structures. The continuous and unending structuring activity constitutes the core of human praxis, the human mode of being-in-the-world" (1973, 56). The creation of objects, the arrangement of structures, signals a way of doing things that allows informal learning and communal relations. The concept of praxis helps describe how cultural actions such as craft translate into potent symbols of identity and being because of their association with the hand and body and their provision of shelter and labor.

Cal's case is a classic example of crafting as a symbolic social praxis because it speaks to an expressive response by a member of a powerless group to the empowered. Power in this case was revealed by the ability to consume craft rather than produce it. But this is only one of many possible responses represented by the arranging and structuring of the home environment. For comparison, I present another environment in Harrisburg, this one completed by Jack, a retired chemist. Jack came to his corner lot east of the city during the 1950s. As the city grew, the area began to look more suburban, and ranch houses and imitation Cape Cods surrounded Jack's lot. Eventually, his children left home to pursue careers, and shortly thereafter, his wife left him for another man. Inspired by the suggestion of a builder friend, Jack created a landscape of gates and designs on his corner plot to express his control over his life. Once he started building, Jack could not rest. His "garden" as he calls it, is a naturalistic metaphor for something cultivated by hand in the mode of craft rather than prefabricated in his suburban environment; it has become an ever-changing laboratory for his designs. The results appear chaotic, but as Jack explains to people who inquire, what is important is the process used to create the landscape. A response to loneliness and grief, a response to his changing environment, Jack's creations dramatize techniques he used during his working career. Using bricolage, Jack looks to beautify the everyday, bringing material order to his life of the mind and using the arrangement of found objects from his occupational and personal experiences to construct an identity he can display. Although Jack and Cal do not know each other, they share an urge to express and a need to create, not just for themselves but also as a cultural register to persuade others of their legitimacy.

Like other older men, Jack is attracted to the symbolism of the carved chain, which he places in conspicuous locations on tables and by entrances. The technique of "cutting in" required to make it relates to the perception that these men are being cut out of society because of their lack of usefulness and creativity. Like other older retired men who were emotionally invested in their work, he wants to show that he is still vital, still productive. And although he feels marginalized by a youth-oriented society that seems to change too quickly for him, Jack has found license in his old age to speak his mind more than when he was young and to act out desires to find meaning for himself before he dies. Like Cal, he reminisces about a time when people made things for themselves and were more connected socially.

(Left) Bricoleur "Jack" working with stone in Harrisburg, Pennsylvania. (Photo by Simon Bronner)

(Below) Jack sitting in his yard with his environmental art and suburban houses in the background. (Photo by Simon Bronner)

(Left) Jack with his crafted religious shrine. (Photo by Simon Bronner)

(Below) One of several crafted gates in Jack's surrounding property. (Photo by Simon Bronner)

(Above) One of several "tool sculptures" made by Jack. *(Below)* Jack's cement wall is topped with found objects, including baseballs, bowling balls, bricks, teapots, bowls, mugs, cups, bottles, statues, and toys. (Photos by Simon Bronner)

Jack's fundamental constructions in cement have Westinghouse logos (he worked for Westinghouse as an engineer), steps for climbing, pedestals for displays, and enclosures for protection from the elements. In addition to these constructions, the most conspicuous features of his garden are the numerous gates spread up and down both sides of the corner lot. Lions and cement constructions typically flank these gates. On the gates themselves, Jack has added symbols of duality, such as Janus masks of tragedy and comedy. When I first asked Jack about the gates, he seemed surprised. Attracted to their form, he apparently did not realize he had crafted a dozen of them. He reflects that the gates are appealing because they are both entrances and exits. He envisions a place where people flock, where they come in and leave from all angles.

Reinforcing this idea are many seats and benches strewn over the property. Jack likes to sit and contemplate his creations before he changes the landscape once again. Alongside the seats are various symbols of his work—beakers, burners, and dials—combined with designs he admires, such as carved chains and globes. He also has stools reminiscent of lab work in his garden. One stool near the entrance sits in front of a broken-down typewriter painted silver—a monument to his wife, who was a writer. Crafting for Jack has become a form of creation that he likens to giving birth, and interspersed in the garden are reminders of the male appropriation of female procreative abilities in maternal symbols.

As Jack's garden grew, his neighbors were aghast. This was no romantic farmscape of crafted work reminiscent of preindustrial life in textbooks and open-air museums; this was a disruption of their Pax Suburbia. Their efforts to make him dismantle the garden failed. The township, typical of most American localities, gives residents leeway to create such constructions on their property (if he had renovated or built on to his house, he would have needed a building permit). The only recourse Jack's neighbors had was to enforce an ordinance against tall grass. Because of the growing number of structures on his lot, Jack found it increasingly difficult to mow the grass, so he responded to the complaints by enclosing his space with a wall. At first, this prospect pleased the neighbors; then they discovered that Jack's idea of a wall was an elaborate creation made of cylinders and squares. From the front of the wall, small semicircles contain mini-gardens. Other walls are found inside the garden, where they act as pedestals for small sculptures and globes. Atop one wall stands a line of elephants. Jack built this after one of his daughters came to visit after an absence of two years and complained that the place looked like a circus. This behavior, which can be thought of as a literalization of metaphor, shows Jack's ability—his "craftiness," as he calls it—to translate images into reality. This is significant because of what he perceives as the malaise of suburbia—its repression of creativity in prefabricated houses and neatly trimmed yards.

Readers may be thinking, as his neighbors did, that Jack is crazy. There is no evidence of a clinical problem, but he has certainly raised for discussion the cultural issue of what is normal. To be sure, he has some exaggerated notions of a built home environment, but placed in context, Jack did not feel the need to express himself this way before his surroundings changed. He has built an enclosure even more than a yard environment. He realizes that what he has created stands out and draws attention to himself, but he resists the idea that he is unique or nuts. He points out other yards that seem to be packed with objects, both crafted and manufactured. Most of these yards express some identity, such as the former coal miner's shrine bemoaning the demise of the regional coal industry or a firefighting assemblage by a fireman. Others are holiday displays, especially for Halloween and Christmas, that go well beyond the singular season's greeting. Like his, their signs of tradition are crafted and, ironically, testify to their individuality. Jack cites an American libertarian value when he places a facsimile of the Declaration of Independence on a pedestal near one of the entrances to his garden. Besides associating his construction with a free spirit and linking it to a do-it-yourself ideal, it also castigates his neighbors and their suburban mind-set. Making things, he says, gives him a sense of accomplishment and self-reliance. In Jack's mind, suburbia represents a postmodern tyranny of uniformity that takes away from a local sense of belonging.

Several of the influences on Jack's garden are local. He points this out to refute the notion that suburban houses dictate the "normal" look of the neighborhood. One influence is the local garden shop, which in addition to plants and flowers contains gates and globes. Another is the Byzantine Catholic Church, which influences his placement of various religious sculptures throughout the garden, including Eastern Orthodox crosses with various necklaces, icons, and amulets hanging from them. The religious connection may not be apparent to onlookers, but it has symbolic significance that Jack can explain. The church is an example, he contends, of a firm insistence on holding on to distinct forms (different from both Latin forms and those of other Eastern Catholic churches) of liturgical worship and practices. He can recount the historical background of the emergence of the church in the context of cultural differences between the Greek-speaking East and the Latin-speaking West. Additionally, he relates his stand for tradition to a modern-day schism between a soulless existence in a prefabricated environment and the spiritual need to create and express one's vitality through handwork. He takes inspiration in the busy, mixed Byzantine architectural style composed of Greco-Roman and Oriental elements on the exterior and handmade icons on the interior. He is especially drawn to the aggregation of domes, which is a vivid contrast to what he calls the boring boxes that dot the suburban landscape.

Jack's landscape, he insists, creates links to cultural features of the locality, whereas the suburban houses could be found anywhere. "There's no sense of belonging with them," he complains, and he indicates that in his crafting of an environment, he seeks belonging, or at least he wants to display its possibilities. To show the work that goes into the garden, Jack makes sculptures of the tools themselves. At least three of these stand in different sections of the garden. "That shows that I'm a craftsman," he tells me, lest people think he is hauling in "junk."

Jack's garden is still changing. He is not done yet, and he probably never will be. He reminds me during several visits that as long he can craft, he feels alive. Slight of build and getting more frail with age, he expresses pride in the manual lifting and heaving he has accomplished. When I give him my customary parting line of "Take care of yourself," he shoots back, "You'll know I'm still living if you see my stuff hasn't been cleared away." The forms he builds do not mean as much to him as the process of making and arranging them. He has even extended some of the constructions to the home of a woman friend of his. In his garden, he is rooting himself; in his constructions, he is creating an environment for his ideas. This praxis is wrapped up in a saying he likes to use to instruct, but it also refers to himself: "There's no shame in your craft." He means to say that it is all right to be different, and that craft binds what one does with what one is thinking. His moral is that rather than keeping creative behaviors private, one should display them as signs of freedom as well as tradition. This attitude sets Jack apart from his neighbors. His saying also has an American context: "Think no shame of your craft" (Mieder 1992, 124) indicates that craft as a preindustrial pursuit differentiates a person, but rather than being displaced as old, one should think of craft as skill gained by tradition.

Jack's work raises the issue of what people in this part of the world are expected to do with their yards and whether this constitutes craft. Several commentators have noted the American obsession with the front lawn, beginning with Thorstein Veblen, who in *The Theory of the Leisure Class* remarks that "the close-cropped lawn is beautiful in the eyes of a people whose inherited bent is to readily find pleasure in contemplating a well-preserved pasture or grazing land" (1899, 134; see also Jenkins 1994; Steinberg 2006). In his view, the lawn is a mark of "well-to-do classes" because it represents the ownership of property reminiscent of grazing land, which signified wealth because it was expansive. It also required workers to maintain it, so the pasture represented a separation between the supervising overlord (expressed in the traditional saying "a man is king of his castle") and the laboring force. A lawn is unnecessary for sustenance and demands a great deal of attention, which suggests it has no practical purpose, thus raising its status as a luxury on which surplus money can be spent.

With its field of green, the lawn gives the impression of an aristocratic English manor, which seems contrary to American ideals. The lawn in front of the manor was tended by servants and made the house look bigger because it rose out of the flat land. In the suburban development, the lawn reinforces the demeanor of restraint and human domination over the environment. The lawn's uniformity and the machinery required to keep it "under control" make it seem more industry than craft. Even though it requires a great deal of manual work to maintain as a symbol of valuable property, residents perceive the lawn as unproductive in contrast to craft. What modern residents "produce" is often an arrangement, indicating a consumer praxis because objects are placed rather than made.

Yet the act of arranging simulates the identity building and sense of place connoted by craft. Placing animal figures around the yard to create the feel of a house in the woods is one common arrangement; another is to use globes and statues to reinforce the English country manor image. Some residents place whimsical figures such as "little Dutch boys" or girls bending over, showing their bloomers. They render the lawn a park for play, a sign of the leisure that, according to Veblen, marked aspirations to a class above laboring but was hardly acceptable as elite. In the privatized world of the American suburban house, craft is thought to go on privately, inside spaces designated for use rather than show. These can be the garage or basement workshop, the family room, or the privatized backyard.

Jack and Cal have brought their work forward into public space that has become restricted. Although both live in the Harrisburg city limits, they have different backgrounds and live in different neighborhoods. They reverted to techniques of shaping an environment that appeals to them because doing so dramatizes personal control and social belonging. Cal's work comments on the social system that once stressed production and communal aid. Jack's work uses techniques of production as a statement of defiance and as a way to rebuild himself. Here are individuals making traditions but not constrained by them. Here are men entering into social dialogue through intentional expression. Here are men demonstrating through their production the modern tendency of social structures to locate boundaries and centers, to privatize and consume traditions.

Prominent do-it-yourself intrusions on the paved landscape that are not individualized but represent a communal arrangement of objects that engage in social dialogue are the roadside markers that spring up at the sites of fatal auto accidents. Although they can be found internationally, journalists report that there are tens of thousands in the United States, where they are especially popular because of their commentary on the nation's massive consumer cultural development (Burger 2002). They usually consist of crosses inscribed with the names of the deceased and the date of the accident. Often a carver also leaves a saying such as "Only the Good Die Young" or "You Will Be Missed." People attach messages and photographs to the cross and leave a variety of objects at the base, including flowers, stuffed animals, candles, and trinkets. Rising above may be helium-filled balloons tied to the horizontal part of the cross. Similar markers have been erected at the sites of other shocking and tragic events, such as the bombing of the federal building in downtown Oklahoma City in 1995; the Columbine High School shootings in 1999; the collapse of the Aggie Bonfire at Texas A&M University in 1999; the 9/11 terrorist attacks in New York City, Washington, D.C., and Somerset, Pennsylvania; and the Virginia Tech massacre in 2007. At each of these sites, permanent memorials were eventually erected by formal organizations, but the first images of mourning were vernacular material expressions of grief.

Originally, organizations such as Mothers Against Drunk Driving (MADD, founded in 1980) and Students Against Destructive Decisions (originally Students Against Driving Drunk, or SADD, established in 1981) placed crosses at crash sites involving drivers under the influence of alcohol and drugs (Everett 2000, 92–93). They did not consider the crosses Christian symbols but conceived them more broadly to remind viewers of death (Everett 2000, 92). The crosses also drew attention to the anonymity of accident victims and the invisibility of death in the modern world. The handcrafted crosses personalized the accidents with names and individual messages. Sympathetic mourners added items such as stuffed animals and balloons, particularly for young casualties, and created what appeared to be crudely crafted assemblages. Cars slowed to gawk at the growing constructions, and municipal officials ordered their removal to prevent traffic problems. In a number of localities, authorities imposed steep fines for the placement of memorials along public roadways. Journalists took notice of these sites and described them with rhetoric emphasizing their unofficial nature— calling the memorials "makeshift," "spontaneous," and "grassroots"— and they reported conflicts between mourners and public officials. As more markers popped up in other places, such as sidewalks, parks, and alleys, journalists called on professorial authorities, including me, to explain the phenomenon and asked a crucial question: "Is this totally new, or is it some kind of tradition we haven't noticed before?"

My answer was to point to a number of precedents involving beliefs about marking the deaths of travelers, youths, soldiers, or martyrs. Visitors to American memorials, such as the Vietnam Veterans Memorial, often leave objects, sometimes as a form of protest (Hass 1998). Folklorists describe the older Latino tradition of placing a cross or *descanso* to mark the place where a coffin was set down during a funeral procession (Collins and Rhine 2003; Everett 2002, 21–29; Nance 2004). *Descansos* would be decorated at holidays and to mark the anniversary dates in the life of the deceased; generally, they stand for places of human loss. A connection to this tradition in Mexico may account for the popularity of early roadside crosses erected by MADD in Texas beginning in 1984. The typical two-foot-high white MADD cross includes a red plastic plaque at the crosspiece containing the accident victim's name and dates of birth and death. Yet these official organizational crosses do not predominate the roadside memorial landscape. Most memorials are installed by family members or friends, and they have expanded beyond auto accidents to other sites of tragedy, including street murders and building accidents, often with plaques and arrangements of candles, flowers, and signs (Everett 2000, 93).

The assemblage traditions are not universalized, however. After the 2006 Amish school shooting in Nickel Mines, Pennsylvania, neighbors created a memorial at the site, but the Amish did not participate because of prohibitions against elaborate public display. Jews, with their religious emphasis on home mourning in the custom of *shiva* and their aversion to presenting flowers, rarely support roadside memorials. When government officials responded to the proliferation of homemade roadside memorials by issuing guidelines for approved markers, they often ran into church-state conflicts. The Florida Department of Transportation, for example, received protests from Jewish residents and legislators for endorsing a religious preference when it prescribed an official white marker in the form of a cross (Bradbery and Fields 1997). Defenders of the marker called it a secular symbol of death. The Utah legislature went so far as to pass a joint resolution in 2006 declaring the cross a nonreligious symbol of death. That resolution served as background for a federal court ruling, based on the disestablishment of religion clause of the Constitution, that forced the removal of fourteen twelve-foot-high crosses erected by the Utah Highway Patrol along public highways to commemorate fallen troopers (Associated Press 2010).

The politics of the roadside markers reported in the newspapers is related to an explanation given by folklorists and ethnologists—that is, that the markers spring up because of an urgency felt at the grass roots to draw attention to social and political issues that are not sufficiently out in the open. Jack Santino states, "I suggest that the shrines personalize public and political issues, and in personalizing them, are political themselves" (2006a, 12). They extend the grieving for an individual to a social message for a viewing public. Indeed, motorists buzzing by are more likely to notice the intrusion of a marker than the name on it. The extent of the assemblage, with toys, photographs, balloons, and trinkets, is often a clue to the social identity in crisis and the tragedy of loss for the locality. The fact that the assemblage is crafted unofficially, rising out of the grass or ground and sometimes at great risk, adds to the urgency.

The novel aspect of these markers is their ability to create public recognition of cultural as well as human loss, outside of graveside rituals. The markers appear out of place along the side of the road and stand in the way of forgetting that a preventable tragedy has occurred. The cemetery is too out of sight and seems to be meant for occasional visitation rather than constant viewing. Additionally, the cemetery landscape is corporately controlled, and its mass-produced stones are not sufficiently personalized, unlike a handmade marker and the personal act of adding an object to an assemblage that in its growth represents the event's social impact. Auto accidents in particular have attracted grassroots markers, I contend, because the car symbolizes qualities of everyday mass culture—faceless, corporate, hedonistic, accelerating, unavoidable—implicated in the tragedy. Mourners resist the official signs of an accident because the homemade or makeshift markers emphasize the compassion of manual social practice and thereby evoke the importance of communal structures and practices.

I witnessed one example of the process from accident to display involving an alcohol-related crash resulting in the deaths of six persons under age twenty-two. On Saturday evening, July 13, 2002, on a state road north of Harrisburg, Pennsylvania, a twenty-year-old with a blood alcohol level more than six times the limit of 0.02 for drivers under age twenty-one collided with a sedan carrying five young people on their way to a movie. Four of the moviegoers died, as did two of the passengers with the drunk driver (Decker 2002). One swerving car snapped a telephone pole, and pieces of both cars flew deep into the nearby woods. Less than a week after the accident, eighteen handmade crosses appeared where trees had been knocked down and bushes had been flattened by the careening cars. Car parts, including hubcaps, tail lights, and dashboard scraps strewn along the ground, had been moved to the bases of the crosses. The boards of the crosses had the names of victims and messages inscribed; several had "In Loving Memory" on the vertical piece, while the horizontal one had the victim's name. Flowers, candles, pictures, stuffed animals, and key chains had been laid around the structures. Some items appeared to have been crafted by a *bricoleur*, such as a plastic stool hand-inscribed with the message "R.I.P." and a candle, Jesus statuette, key chain, and "America the Beautiful" sticker attached to the top. Paper messages were left, including one that became the front-page headline in the city's newspaper: "Life can change in the blink of an eye and around any corner could be the end" (Lewis and Bothum 2002, A1). I did not see any mourners at the site I passed every day, but drivers slowed down to get a better look.

State police tolerated the display for two weeks, but with the number of objects growing, authorities cited safety concerns and asked the victims' families to scale down the memorial. The families responded that they were not organizing the assemblage but expressed their preference for the memorial to remain (Burger 2002, A1). "I understand why they're there, why they did this," one family member told a reporter. "They don't know what else to do right now. You just have to do something" (Burger 2002, A20). The mourner understood that people outside his family circle were affected, that the dead represented youthful victims of a dangerous world. None of the signs or messages in the

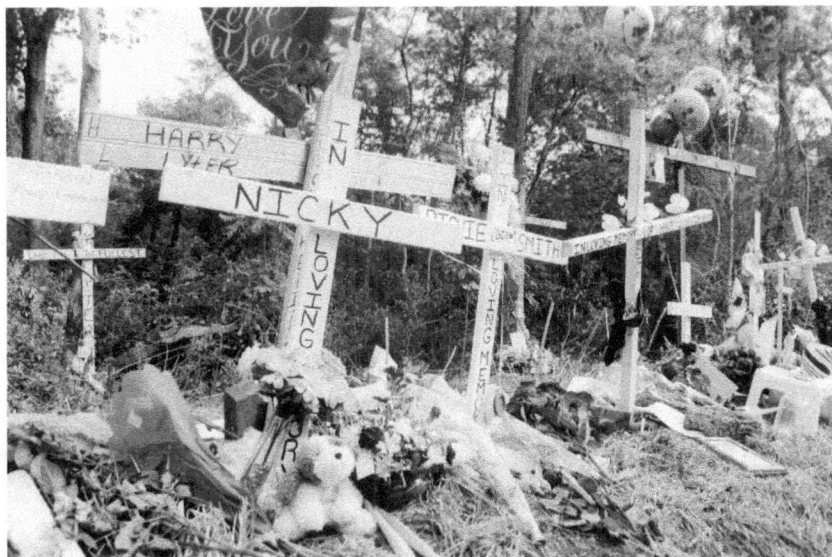

Memorial assemblage for six accident victims on Linglestown Road (State Road 39), Harrisburg, Pennsylvania, July 2002. (Photo by Simon Bronner)

Decorated stool left in front of a cross for Harry Lyter, seventeen years old at the time of his death. (Photo by Simon Bronner)

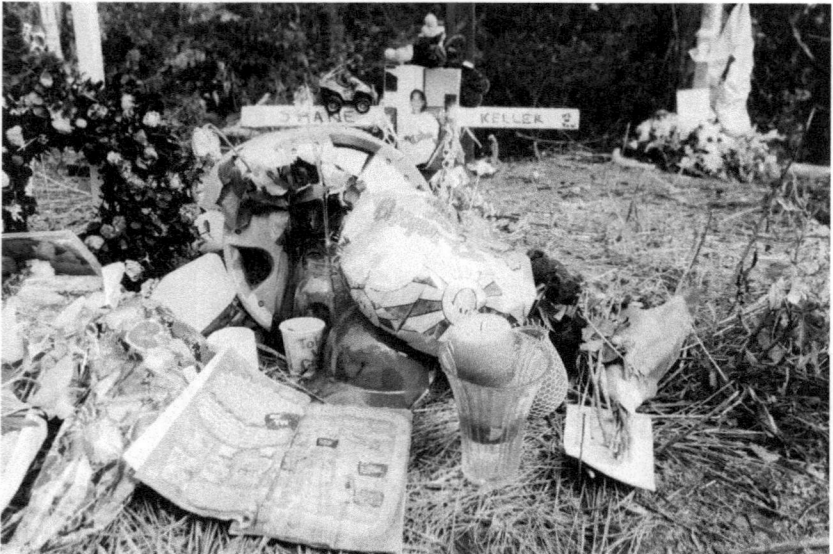

Memorial assemblage, including a hubcap, a comic book, and a batting helmet, in front of a cross for eight-year-old Shane Keller, the youngest victim in the Linglestown Road crash and the one with the smallest cross but the largest collection of left objects. (Photo by Simon Bronner)

assemblage referred to drunk driving laws, however. They were more concerned with the premature cessation of life and the end of innocence; the accumulation of car parts drew some comments about killer machines. MADD's office in Harrisburg issued a statement indicating that "this is among the highest, if not the highest number of alcohol-related crash deaths in one incident in Pennsylvania," but it was not involved in the display (Klaus 2002, A1).

More than a month after the crash, Pennsylvania Department of Transportation (PennDOT) workers cleared the site. PennDOT did not issue a press release, but the local paper reported the change. Asked for comment, a spokesman for PennDOT reminded readers that "it's illegal to place an obstruction within the right of way." Realizing that this sounded heartless, he added, "We recognize that people have a need to grieve, and this is one way to do that. An exception is when the memorials cause a hazard, such as rubbernecking, that pose a danger of more accidents at a fatal crash scene" (Burger 2002, A20). Letters protesting the move poured into the newspaper's editorial office, often with the rejoinder that the assemblage was more than a mourning site. For many writers, the vernacular arrangement conveyed a personal message from ordinary folks about protecting youth or about the danger of the roads and society (Burger 2002, A20). Many of the comments were concerned about a modern society composed of strangers and the possibility of instant death. Crosses went back up at the site after the initial clearing and were removed again. The PennDOT spokesman spun the issue as one related to the need to maintain the roads: "I do let them know it won't be a permanent installation, eventually we may have some maintenance work to do, and, in the course of that, we may remove it" (Burger 2002, A20). By the end of September the assemblage was gone, and cars again zipped by the woods. I talked to some students from the area, who said they still felt a need to mark the site but thought that with Halloween coming, the assemblage might be mistaken for playful decorations rather than a sobering message. Ten years later, handcrafted markers and objects placed around them can be spied on downtown streets, commemorating young victims of drug-related shootings, and along other roadways to remember the victims of other auto accidents. Most people in the area have only a faint recollection of the horrific crash on that hot July night that sparked the largest vernacular display I have recorded in central Pennsylvania. They certainly do not remember the names of the victims, but they often recognize the themes of untimely death represented by the tradition of grassroots markers, unabated by PennDOT regulations, and find in the contrast between crafted object and the paved landscape a commentary on modern life.

Particularly in postmodern settings, attention commonly shifts from traditional creative work as symbols of community to dramatizations of identity. The South Carolina Sea Islanders, for example, no longer need to make baskets for fanning rice, but these baskets represent the Gullah identity that has largely been eroded by resort development. Duck decoy makers continue their trade on the Eastern Shore of Maryland, but they sell most of their decoys not to hunters but to collectors of Americana. As a result of the ambiguity in modern life of inheriting one's cultural identity, the American festival has become the organized setting that most contextualizes craft in terms of regional and ethnic identities. Apparently meant to celebrate craft, the festival is a condensed space of time with an element of fantasy and play. It is also a sign of cultural weakening because of the implicit view that the activities featured in a festival need bolstering by presenting them in a framework that is symbolically separate from normative life. At many folk festivals, such as the Smithsonian Folklife Festival on the Mall in Washington, D.C., symbolically held around Independence Day, or at community versions of craft festivals, continuity with the preindustrial period is preferred. On the East Coast, many communities host "colonial crafts fairs" to make a social connection to the locality's founding in the colonial period, with the implication that the handwork and sweat of hardy white pioneers of British Protestant origin ensured the present prosperity. This is where the village blacksmith, wood-carver, quilter, and broom maker represent the American craft ideal. With this trend as the baseline, many communities have introduced separate festivals labeled multicultural, folk, or ethnic to show the presence of immigrant and ethnic groups in the symbolism of craft as signs of skill and usefulness.

At the Michigan Folklife Festival, organizers make a special effort to represent industrial crafts, especially in the state known as the center of the auto industry. When the festival included a display of bricklayers at work, it raised eyebrows for being unusual, even though interpreters explained that skill and folk wisdom are inherited through an apprentice system. The festival even had ironworkers raise beams and place an evergreen tree on top to mark a traditional "topping off" ceremony, when a building reaches its maximum height (Robinson 2001). I personally worked on an exhibition in which teenagers demonstrated the process of making a homecoming float, a skill passed down from one class to another (Dewhurst 1996). As the teens crafted the structure out of paper and wire, it quickly became apparent that onlookers had another definition of craft besides historical and preindustrial; they thought craft was something done by older adults. The homecoming demonstration did get some passersby to participate in the process of making the float, rekindling memories of other traditional youth crafts they had engaged in, such as making friendship bracelets, folded paper constructions, and platted gum wrappers, which they had not thought of as craft at the time. The display disrupted their assumptions about craft as something naturally plied by workers in remote times and places.

Festival crafts are also supposed to be sanitized and public, exuding a redemptive wholesomeness. In industrial settings, however, the idea of craft is often surreptitious. For instance, assembly-line workers may craft objects on the job, such as bookmarks and signs, to show their ability to make things for themselves as well as for the company (Dewhurst 1984). These objects might also be obscene, such as outlines of genitalia made of metal or wood, thus making it clear that they are not company made. In the Pennsylvania coal industry, miners identified with their occupation by taking chunks of coal and carving them into sculptures with themes related to coal occupations. Some brave souls also engaged in a folk industry—or industrial craft, depending on how one sees it—opening so-called bootleg mines, where they pulled coal from the earth in solo shafts of their own building. Is it going too far from our colonial craftsman idolized in history textbooks to point out the use of computers and copiers to create signs and constructions for social purposes around the office? At my institution, one crafty colleague extended a sign draped in pink that announced "It's A Girl!" down a long hallway. It was a human celebration that he wanted, maybe needed, to share with the office, made out of the materials of his labor.

Arguably, craft as a process of transformation pervades much of everyday life, although cognitive denial occurs, particularly among middle-class workers in the service and information economy. This denial has its roots in the perception of a working class as urban manual laborers or rural agrarian laborers who engage in "dirty" jobs as opposed to "clean" professions. Yet from dressing in the morning to cooking at night, handwork is involved in shaping objects and designs. More abstractly, crafting in our lives can involve words and gestures. The stories people tell have a crafted quality because they take the raw materials of words and shape them into a story that people recognize as a distinctive creation. In their occupations, people want to believe they have the control and autonomy, the pride and passion of the crafts worker. Even in supposedly intellectual pursuits, an experienced professor such as Thomas Schlereth, serving duty in the information economy, publicly declared that he could not claim affinity with traditional artisanship through family heritage, vocational training, or a personal ability to work wood or metal, glass or clay, or any other object in a creative way; however, he thought of himself as engaging in the material behavior of polishing his skill, shaping ideas, and forming meaning. It was important to him to conceptualize his writing, his approach to life, as crafting a structure from the substance of knowledge (Schlereth 1990, 420–28). How many of his intellectual colleagues feel the same way is hard to say, but the point is that one can discern crafting cognitively applied to reformulate the expectations of a service and information economy (see Jones 1980a).

In a more material sense, consumer culture has mediated the crafting impulse as the fulfillment obtained from doing things for oneself. Whether this comes from the old American value placed on self-reliance or a capitalistic notion of property that constantly requires expansion, the home improvement superstore that swept away Main Street hardware stores in the late twentieth century has encouraged a craft ethic (Goldstein 1998). Even before Home Depot and Lowe's expanded their consumer home craft lines, Sears was advertising its "Craftsman" tools as products with a lasting power greater than industry. Consumers may not be able to build a house by themselves, but they gain a sense of ownership by repairing and enhancing their homes. Lowe's invokes the social aspect of craft by the slogan, "Let's build something together." Like Home Depot, it offers classes on "transforming spaces," as its advertisements frequently blare. This has had a democratizing effect because, unlike the hardware store, which exudes a manly aura, the superstores make projects available to men and women and depict women involved in heavy craft work.

What about American craft stores? What is their role in reflecting or shaping a consciousness of craft? It is noteworthy that Ben Franklin Crafts advertises, "We carry the creative products you need to add personal flair to your home or to create gifts for your family and friends—needlecrafts, florals, wicker, paints, fabrics, yarn, and much more." Craft is defined here as a way to use creativity socially. Although it does not promote craft as utility, it allows control and identity by inviting customers to "add personal flair." A strong holiday and seasonal theme is apparent in the store, because craft is being mediated corporately to fit into the naturalistic seasons. Holiday crafts mark seasonal change and family memories. By making something oneself, even if the materials come out of a kit, a gift has warmth as well as "personal flair." The very name Ben Franklin conveys a vernacular ingenuity and colonial reference. Michael's, another major crafts chain, uses the slogan "Imaginate," a portmanteau that combines *imagine* with a number of active verbs such as *create* and *fabricate*. Craft has been made decorative, turning personal flair into flights of fancy. There is a decided emphasis on decorative crafts for women to preserve memory, such as scrapbooking and other keepsake paper crafts. On a regional level, commercial quilt stores, a subset of the craft store, are concentrated in areas such as Utah to respond to Mormon values of family nurture and ties to the pioneer past promoted in the region (Eliason 2004). In other regions of the country with pioneer legacies, such as New England, Appalachia, and the Ozarks, quilting supply stores abound, according to Quilt.com. On the Internet, do-it-yourselfers have created a marketplace in Etsy.com, which includes forums and blogs proclaiming the virtue of "this handmade life." Entering *quilting* in the site's search engine results in more than 67,000 hits, more than rugs, furniture, and baskets (pottery and jewelry are also strong contenders in the craft market). The keywords *tradition* and *folk* carry significance for this crowd: more than 11,000 and 26,000 items, respectively.

In online marketplaces, quilt stores, and national craft supply chains, many of the craft projects involve activities for children. Many modern-day advisers tout craft projects as a way to engage family values, impart problem-solving skills to youth, and bridge child-parent communicative divides. For example, by the end of the twentieth century, craft stores had tapped into the fame of Martha Stewart as a reviver of domestic craft to promote do-it-yourself projects for the entire family.

I find it significant that the product line of Martha Stewart Craft was organized around behaviors that suggest social maintenance: cherish, celebrate, share, play. Responding to the middle class's expectation that it had risen above the manual trades to serve a corporate, information economy, Stewart urged suburban parents to view craft as an enrichment of life rather than as toil that gets one's hands dirty. She branded do-it-yourself kits as a middle-class way to impress as well as connect to others. Much of the Martha Stewart Craft line is about paper, a sign that the modern office or children's work can be domesticated through guided handwork.

In contrast to the feminized actions of cherish, celebrate, share, and play provided by Martha Stewart in 2007, Longfellow in 1841 exacted a more morbid tone in "The Village Blacksmith":

> Toiling—rejoicing—sorrowing,
> Onward through life he goes;
> Each morning sees some task begin,
> Each evening sees it close;
> Something attempted, something done
> Has earned a night's repose.

Craft in Longfellow's imagination conveys routine and need. Craft stores and Stewart's various enterprises have been instrumental in making craft playful in the postmodern age. Even the home improvement stores encourage patrons to try creative "projects" rather than needed repairs. Longfellow, like the craft stores, appeals to continuity into the next generation:

> And children coming home from school
> Look in at the open door;
> They love to see the flaming forge,
> And hear the bellows roar,
> And catch the burning sparks that fly
> Like chaff from a threshing-floor.

Nonetheless, traditions in the twenty-first century take on a more individualistic, futuristic cast. Enacting them is a way to remake oneself, but can they also be used to engage children and teach a lasting lesson for the future? The mediated version of craft is less past oriented and compromises the vernacular.

As Americans today contemplate the ways they use, and sometimes lose, the transformative process of craft in their work and in their lives, they can also reflect on the past and view again the crafts of history as more than production in antiquity. From childhood to old age, from one end of the country to the other, crafts help define what people do and have done in as well as to America. In the United States, education in the form of schools and museums has built craft as a colonial, nationalistic legacy; movies and festivals have shown craft's redemptive and social potential; craft and home improvement stores are the latest chapter in the conceptualization of craft, this time a corporate way to individualize, domesticate, and enliven craft. With great human ingenuity, crafts have been adapted to the various scenes and traditions, the many personal stories, the very human needs and desires that have gone into the shaping of the American experience. Craft as an idea, as a form of American rhetoric, evokes differences—traditions—between now and then, us and them, seen through things that are made.

5

Adapting Tradition

On Folklore in Human Development

What are we to make of the startling variety and intensity of folklore among American children today? Was not this material supposed to be dead and gone, replaced by a swirling array of electronic devices to keep children isolated and glued to screens, partaking of entertainment dished out by corporate America? Rhymes, taunts, jokes, and games familiar to previous generations can still be heard when children gather, and these forms are imaginatively adapted to new circumstances. If parents are not aware of what their children are saying or playing, it seems as if there is a folklorist or a reporter willing, with a bit of censorship, to spill the beans on the latest joke or legend cycle sweeping through the grades. There is often a note of surprise that children still engage in oral tradition, rather than having all their expressive culture imposed on them by mass media and toy manufacturers.

Even if parents remember telling some of the same stories and playing similar games in their youth, they are sure things must be different now, as they schedule another organized activity for their children. Forgetting about play dates, recess, and plain old socializing, they may even wonder aloud when children have the time (after school and lessons) to come up with these things, or where children get these traditions if their parents have not left instructions for them. As they bemoan the travail of administrating children's schedules, they imagine that it is the parents' job alone to didactically "hand down" traditions to children. They do not realize that children create their own traditions out of the cognitive structures and images they gain from participating in culture.

Americans in particular may dismiss the deep impact of play and lore on psychosocial development because adults apply the culturally reinforced distinction between work as serious activity and play as non-serious praxis (Sutton-Smith 1970, 5). Crafty, and needy, as they are, children may use that bias to say or do in play what they cannot normally express under the authority of parents, dealing with serious developmental issues. In the usual cognitive association of adulthood = work and childhood = play, putting lore to use in games, customs, stories, rhymes, crafts, gestures, speech, and ritual is the work of childhood.

That the continued vitality of lore goes against the common assumption of folk traditions dwindling in the face of modernization can be explained by children's inclination to use the material among themselves, away from watchful parents, to establish their own cultural space. Although parents may believe they provide for all their children's developmental needs, children's "secret" lore fills an important cultural niche. Psychologist Brian Sutton-Smith describes it simply as "the excitement it brings children." Commenting on adults' surprise that children possess an active lore-producing culture, he notes, "this wisdom appears strange only because adults spend so much time trying to cure children of their childhood." He adds, "If adults thought of children as being more like themselves, they would say of children's play, 'Of course, they enjoy the same as we enjoy'" (1979a, 5).

Yet adults rationalizing what happens in childhood have designated the prepubertal years as a developmental stage, a time of innocence spent playing and learning. Once imagined as a time when the previous generation passed its wisdom and values down to the young, childhood is now constructed as a break from what went on before. This is the result of a certain American evolutionary mind-set that mass-mediated popular culture is all-consuming, a result of machine civilization inexorably replacing the social needs of face-to-face imaginative communication. Connected to that developmental attitude is a historical one: in a modernizing, progressive society, culture in a new generation is sui generis, and therefore continuities with previous traditions are not expected. Adults past and present are well aware that children "grow up" rather than age or gray as adults do, and they are in awe of how quickly that maturation occurs. They should not be surprised at the extent of traditional communication among the young, in light of the fact that children constitute the largest semiliterate group in society and thus need an expressive and informational outlet through song, story, gesture, and game. Parents may be unsure exactly when this period of childhood ends and how adolescence figures into the mix, even though it is often structured by the school years K–12. But one thing is sure: children are paradoxical, for they represent the ultimate change—rapid physical, social, and cognitive development—and the epitome of cultural continuity through the direct inheritance of cultural values.

Children probably do not call their lore "traditions." To them, it likely constitutes play and, as such, should be recognized as intelligent adaptation (Sutton-Smith 1971, 9–10). Analysts notice the precedents and the multiple versions of the games, rhymes, and stories that children enact as the basis of traditions, usually unbeknownst to youths in their localized existence. Sutton-Smith thinks that tradition "introduces the notion of history to the notion of custom, or if you will the self-consciousness of history to the praxis of custom" (1992, 13). As a result, it is commonplace for analysts (as adults) to neglect what the child is going through and observe their own culture through the prism of children's games and, in Sutton-Smith's words, to *"enhance the national, cultural, or individual status* of those who had once played them and perhaps should continue to play them" (1992, 14; emphasis in original). This bias may be responsible for the intense scrutiny given to compiling texts to be read literally, tracing the origins of customs deemed strange or cryptic, and locating social and geographic contexts when it comes to the study of childhood, often at the expense of developmental factors. Interpretation therefore follows literary, social, or historical lines derived from the observation of externalized behavior rather than being connected to psychological processes (Dundes 1997c). A methodological orientation to collecting contemporaneous data is also relevant to the lack of developmental attention to tradition: analysts do not follow lore over the course of a life because they are typically wresting information to represent a moment or a place, not a person. Lore is categorized as belonging generally to children or to an ethnic group or region, rather than noting the variability of expression by age, especially in middle childhood (usually defined as between five and twelve years of age) or at the beginning of puberty.

Correlating age-related development to the use of folk expressions addresses several issues in the study of childhood. One is the observed pattern that children, more than other age groups, regularly discard their lore, and this process is subject to "curricular generations," whereby an appropriate age context is structured by school grades (Fine 1980a). Children often categorize their lore by the grade in which it is enacted, and they seek new lore associated with a new grade, making sure to point out that they are no longer identified by the old material. This discarding of lore has caused puzzlement because of the adult assumption that lore is a permanent fixture of a culture. This view of cultural permanence is evident in the frequently used rhetoric that "folklore is a mirror of culture," and it translates into the description of tradition as "age-old" or as being a celebration of the elderly or some other group that has preserved tradition for eons (Dundes 1969b; Mullen 1991). It may account for the cultural amnesia that parents develop about their children's traditions, and it suggests to analysts that children are a more differentiated group in social theory than are regional, occupational, and ethnic groups.

Children have their place, and those borders set them apart from other age groups. Several settings are bounded cultural scenes that are dominated by children, even if they are ostensibly supervised by adults. A good deal of attention, for instance, has been given to playground behavior and the way it responds to the material culture of swings, fences, and nooks and to social organization by gender and sometimes by race and class (Bishop and Curtis 2001; Frost 2010; Mergen 1999; Sutton-Smith 1981). The playground is imagined as a festive, liberating place where children can really be themselves, rather than being controlled and routed through school and home (Sutton-Smith 1990b). Cordoning off play in a playground may also show adults' fear of children being true to their nature. Following an evolutionary metaphor, children act like savages before becoming civilized, and the playground can appear more like a zoo than a festival (Roud 2010, xi–xii; Sutton-Smith 1980). Although the playground is recognized as children's space, children also appropriate, mark, frame, or even construct other protected play locations, such as stoops, streets, alleys, tree houses, pools, beaches, and yards (Bronner 1977; 1988a, 199–236).

Children's lore may become secret because of youths' perception that adults frown upon free play and organize institutions to restrain and segregate children. A prominent institutional feature in America is the summer camp, which frequently generates its own institutional lore in which children dominate (Mechling 1999). Other organized child-centered institutions that facilitate the transmission of children's lore are community centers and clubs, sports teams, and after-school facilities. Sometimes adults express the topographic attitude that the countryside is more folkloric than cities and the no-man's-land of suburbia, but many collections have demonstrated adaptations of tradition across space, as well as distinctive associations with play in a locality (Dargan and Zeitlin 1990).

Many of these institutions are devoted to middle childhood, suggesting a fear of rapid maturation by both adults and children. As a period in the life course, the years between six and twelve often seem ambiguous to analysts and parents. The main theme of this period is its betwixt and between status; children at this age are between infancy and adolescence, both of which are considered sharply defined cultural periods, at least in America. People understand the infant and toddler years as a generally unstructured "preschool" time marked by rapid physical growth and the attainment of linguistic competence. For parents, this is a time when children are largely dependent on adults for their basic physical needs. Learning appears to be unidirectional from the parent to the child, with finger and guessing games, storytelling, and gestures. At the other end, adolescence is clearly marked physically by puberty and by the expectation of teenagers preparing for independence. The main physical demarcation for change in middle childhood is an object loss—teeth (identified significantly as "baby teeth," colloquially as "milk teeth," and scientifically as deciduous teeth)—accompanied by bleeding. Children begin losing their front teeth at around age six, a point usually thought of as the beginning of middle childhood, and they lose the last of their back teeth before puberty, from ten to twelve years old, or at the end of the developmental period.

In America, one sign of hurrying children through middle childhood and enculturating them into a consumer culture is offering a reward for lost teeth, compensating them for (and commodifying) the lost object and encouraging the process of growth. The reward is masked in magic and constitutes the baby tooth's metaphorical change into something of value associated with adulthood: money. Placed under a pillow or in a container by the bed, the tooth magically disappears in the dark of night, taken away by a feminized tooth fairy representing infancy and thus encouraging the child to embrace the new day with an adult sign of status—that is, acquisitive, reproducible wealth. It has often been noted that the American adaptation of the tooth fairy tradition emphasizes commercial gain and independence from the maternal bond, whereas Japanese society encourages children to make the tooth an offering to spirits by throwing it outside the house, and a number of cultures in Europe offer it up to a mouse (to ensure growth of a new and better tooth, characteristic of the rodent's growing incisors), replace the tooth with sweet food (in a form of sympathetic magic, to ensure a sweet future), or dispose of it in a fire (to prevent an animal from finding it and causing the growth of an animal-like tooth in place of the lost one) (Clark 1995, 5–21; Granger 1961, 54; Roud 2003, 456–60; Tuleja 1991; Wells 1991).

In adolescence, change is marked more by object gains—facial and pubic hair, breasts, muscles—but much of the preadolescent lore involves loss in the form of separation, recovery, and quests in guessing and chasing games. Beliefs during the period are epitomized by the replacement or exchange process circulating around the loss of teeth. We can surmise that before puberty, the protrusion of teeth is the most publicly visible bodily change, and it draws comparison in lore to sexual attraction and potency (Biedermann 1994, 347; Kanner 1968, 62–65). Much is made by parents and children of the wiggling and removal of baby teeth as a sign of growing up (Clark 1995, 5–21). Common folk phrases involving teeth and biting include "I want to bite into that" (or "I want to eat or gobble her up"), "dressed to the teeth," and "sink my teeth into her." In children's early courtship behavior, a red bruise on the neck caused by sucking and biting is referred to as a "bite mark," "nibble," or "hickey," and it is considered a sign of possession as well as seduction. Pulling one's tooth out, rather than letting it fall out, is commonly interpreted as a manly trait or a sign of maturity because of the pain endured and the aggressive control it exudes. Boys threaten others with "kicking [knocking] their teeth in," implying infantilization of the opponent.

Children's folk sayings and stories refer to the teeth as bodily protrusions, and they are often thought of as phallic (such as the vampire's fangs in popular culture), although a feminine association is evident in the *vagina dentata* motif (Thompson 1955–1958, F457.1.1). It has been argued, though, that the idea of vaginal teeth in lore is a revenge fantasy in which the woman takes a male castratory role (Legman 1975,

434–46). An example of this theme from my collection comes from a ten-year-old boy in Indiana who set the scene in a medieval fantasy:

> King Arthur was going off to war and he wanted to make sure that Guinevere would remain faithful. He put a little chastity belt on her with a set of teeth [a guillotine in some versions] that would bite down if anyone tried to go in her. When he came back, he checked on his knights of the round table by telling them to drop their drawers. All of them except for Sir Galahad had his dick cut off. He praised the loyalty of Galahad and asked him to speak for himself. Galahad replied, "ah, wah, yah, uh" [imitation of someone speaking with his tongue cut off]. (Compare Dodson 1969, 74; Dougherty and Cohl 2009, 233–34; Legman 1975, 580; Weidlich 1974, 50; Shubnell 2008, 94.)

The implication is that King Arthur inserted the teeth (or guillotine) as revenge rather than as protection. But it should be noted that the young teller can relate to the story because of the competition with his father as he anticipates puberty. As G. Legman notes, "the woman—who does not even appear in the story—is only the stalking-horse or shooting-box of the father-king's vengeful concern with the penises of other, younger men" (1975, 580). A contest for Guinevere, as the domesticated mother-queen, is apparent among the knights under Arthur's charge while the king is, in a symbolic equivalence of manly aggression and virility, "off to war." The loyalty as well as the orality of Galahad (and the association with the name "Kid" Galahad) indicates an intimate relation characteristic of a son and points to Galahad's infancy in contrast to the manliness of the other knights (in variations, Lancelot is the most trusted knight of legend). The familiar action of sticking out the tongue, a common physical taunt in middle childhood, could be an infantile phallic replacement; the tongue, like the penis, is a hidden member that is "let out," does not grow back, and is associated with wetness.

Yet the story is often reported without reference to the age of the teller or presented as a humorous text about grown-up adultery rather than children's developmental concerns and conflicts projected into folklore (Dodson 1969, 74; Dougherty and Cohl 2009, 233–34;

Shubnell 2008, 94). Maybe adults believe that ten-year-olds are not supposed to relate these stories; yet I collected multiple versions of the Galahad story in age-segregated camp settings where the boys were acutely aware of developmental differences in their bodies, penis size, and amount of pubic hair. Another favorite story was the "hairy pickle," popular among nine-year-olds and recited as a comic routine between two boys or as a joking monologue: "There was this town named Hairy Pickle. Everyone in the town was named Harry Pickle. But there was this one man who was not named Harry Pickle. So they hanged him by his hairy pickle." Built on the repetition of "hairy pickle" and word-play—confusing a person's name (Harry Pickle) with a bawdy reference (hairy pickle—or a man's penis)—the story centers on an adult phallic image that ends with an apparent castration by hanging. To the boys, *pickle* sounds more erect and masculine than *peenie*, the slang for an infantile penis symbolized in the rhyme "Wee Jeanie had a nice clean peenie" (Roud 2011, 19378). The story's significance for prepubescent boys (in their betwixt and between state) is its expression of the fear of not maturing (being hanged for not being named Harry Pickle) and the simultaneous dread of the hairy adult image and leaving childhood behind. When older boys were in earshot, they sometimes deemed the formulaic routine not funny or childish, although they recalled per-forming it a few years earlier. Adults thought it was nonsensical and missed the developmental connection because they gave primary at-tention to the literal rather than symbolic content of the narrative. The boys could be observed, however, using folklore to provide commen-tary on the anticipation of puberty while looking back at the social ex-pectations of being a kid.

Middle childhood is a transitional time of growth marked by grad-ual physical, cognitive, and emotional maturation. The most profound aspect for human development is that this is a crucial period during which children emerge as unique individuals while aligning themselves with multiple social networks of peers, teachers, neighbors, and rela-tives. Children at this age think more autonomously but are still rooted in families. Learning that takes place during middle childhood goes beyond what psychologist Nancy F. Cincotta encapsulates as the "re-petitive 'why' question" of toddlers to an exploration of "who, what, where, when, and how" (2002, 69). Within this betwixt and between developmental period are several challenging transitions, including

adjustments to schools and new siblings, parents' changing expectations and often mixed signals about their children's self-sufficiency (a
coupling of "don't act like a baby" with "you're not old enough"), the
beginning of various kinds of social relationships, and the expansion
of territorial and emotional space. According to psychologists, growth
during middle childhood is relatively gradual, yet in modern America, children are often hurried through it, before they are emotionally
ready. Culturally, they receive simultaneous messages about staying a
cute kid but adopting the cool of an adult (Cross 2004; Cincotta 2002,
71). Pointing a wagging finger at mass media, many critics complain
that there is more exposure to the adult vices of sex and violence during middle childhood than ever before in history, and at the same time,
discussion of these topics is repressed.

Theoretically, gaming and humorous lore responds to these developmental conditions because, more than other forms of expression,
it enables a socially sanctioned outlet in the frame of play, fantasy, or
tradition to symbolize, project, and confront various conflicts, ambiguities, taboos, and wishes that cannot be easily expressed in everyday
conversation. Arguably, the vitality of lore during middle childhood
owes to the intensity of transitions during the period and the reliance
on oral, visual, and gestural media rather than on written communication. Yet American children lack elaborate rituals for leaving infancy
and entering middle childhood or, for that matter, any stage prior to
puberty. Games and narrative are found in abundance, though, and as I
will demonstrate, they serve adaptive functions. Lore tends to be shared
among peers at the same developmental stage and can be protected
from the intervention of authority. Folklore can therefore be analyzed
in light of the age or developmental stage at which it is enacted. Dispute rages over what these stages are and their concerns—whether the
psychosexual content of Freudian movement through infantile anal and
oral stages or Piaget's ideas of a period of concrete operations followed
by formal operations that stress thought structures (Bidell and Fischer
1992; Oates, Wood, and Grayson 2005, 9–88).

Whereas psychologists deduce an expressive profile from various
developmental stages and transitions, folklorists who work with cultural variations of texts recorded in social contexts make more inductive use of the lore to identify and explain the images and practices used
to deal with conflicts and ambiguities of an age. They are attentive to

subcultural differences as well as to textual and performative variation, often leading to resistance to the developmental generalization of social science (Bronner 2006a). Like many social scientists, however, they are influenced by Erik Erikson's notion of a "latency" period between the ages of six and twelve years in the categorization of a children's folklore (Erikson 1950; Mechling 1980; Mulhern 1980; Sutton-Smith 1972). The term *latency* suggests that sexual urges remain dormant and development is concentrated on taking initiative (and creating guilt over taking control from elders), mastering skills (and dealing with failure), and forming identity through social relationships (with attendant fears of fitting in). Implicit in the idea of a latency period is that social concerns predominate, as evidenced by the period's association with the social tradition of games; along with these social concerns is a certain prepubescent innocence, which comes through in collections of clever and quaint material, often romanticized or bowdlerized, exemplifying children during the middle childhood period. Critics have called *latency* a misnomer, however, because significant cognitive, social, and emotional development is occurring, and sexual and bodily awareness becomes intensely symbolized (Cincotta 2002, 70). In a developmental approach to folklore, the transitional (if not latent) nature of the period generates the need to project problematic issues onto the playful screen of folklore in interaction with peers. Mere "child's play," in this view, becomes paramount to the emergence of a socially situated identity and the development of a person's relation of self to society, individuality to authority, and tradition to modernity.

One important developmental thesis linking lore to age is Brian Sutton-Smith and John Roberts's contention that games, stories, and toys are models of power and provide agency through which the developing, uncertain child learns to cope in culture (Sutton-Smith and Roberts 1972; Sutton-Smith, Roberts, and Kendon 1972; Sutton-Smith 1986). The significance of this argument is that it extends the "projective" psychoanalytical idea that the fantasy in lore disguises anxieties and ambiguities (Dundes 1976). Analysts' observation of projected symbolism to protect the self from disturbing thoughts can explain why the meanings of and motivations for the generation of folklore lie outside the awareness of tellers and players. Going further, analysts might then look to lore as a tool of adjustment rather than as a mirror of culture. Enacting folklore becomes an adaptive strategy whose usefulness is tested and negotiated in social situations. Tradition becomes a factor in the enactments because a recognition of precedents for these expressive forms makes them appropriate at that age and allows their repetition to be shared socially rather than remaining idiosyncratically personal.

If folklore provides intrinsic evidence of cognitive process and social agency in response to transition-related anxiety, one might ask about the extrinsic factors that make the use of lore an appealing adaptive strategy for children. One significant answer is the historic trend, since the early twentieth century, of less involvement with children by parents and communities (Mintz 2004, 335–71). To be sure, children are monitored, but this is often care from a distance, because another trend is toward greater segregation of and independence for children. Children spend more and more time away from their parents as two-income households and variable workdays have changed the patterns of child care prevalent in America. At the same time, institutions such as day-care and after-school centers have fostered more cultural unity among children, a unity that has helped preserve old folklore and perpetuate new. Contributing to the unity is greater integration of the sexes at these centers and the removal of gender restrictions from children's playground and school activities.

Other social changes affect children where they live. The U.S. census shows a trend among the nation's households: they are leaving large cities and moving, often across great distances, to the suburbs and the countryside. The size of American families, on average, has been decreasing since the twentieth century to less than two children per family. Children have fewer brothers and sisters than they used to, but they are likely to have more out-of-household chums. The landscape of children's groups is leveling out, giving rise to more interconnections among children across the street and across the country. Moving around as much as their parents do, most American children have a basic repertoire of lore that comes into play when they have to adjust to different places and different groups of children.

Increasingly left to their own devices, American children rely on folklore as part of their adaptation to aging. As children mature, folklore is the backdrop for much of childhood socializing and communicating. Children go through a succession of physical and emotional changes, and most children cannot wait to grow up, for adulthood is held up as the standard of power and status. But this headlong rush into an ambiguous realm brings anxieties about security, ability, and identity. Folklore steps in with many rituals and lessons to ease the passage through these early years, and it provides benchmarks for growth to order the passage. Annual birthday celebrations, insisted on by rapidly developing children, are the norm through childhood (less so in adulthood) and mark cultural passage. Childhood also encompasses most of life's celebratory rites: baptism, graduation, confirmation, and even more modern inventions such as the sweet sixteen party.

As children age, they have more questions about the adult world they are about to enter. Although eager to be grown up, children express anxiety about the prospects of sex, marriage, work, and mortality in adulthood. When reality blends with imagination in folklore, children confront uneasy situations before they happen. They learn by symbol and parable from stories heard from a friend of a friend, who heard them from a second cousin.

Although many of my statements apply to other national experiences, the prevalent American attitude encouraging independence in children compounds the reliance on folklore as an adaptive device. Parents expect a child to develop a unique personality, and young people's individualized volition is emphasized by the constant question from an early age, "What do you want to be when you grow up?" Parental responses to maturing, especially puberty, tend to be relatively lax. Whereas other societies, notably those in England and Japan, respond with the imposition of intensive schoolwork and discipline during these years, American adolescents generally fend for themselves or utilize the time to "find themselves," to use a popular phrase, personally and socially. The social side of high school—its clubs, rites, and events—often predominates (see Burnett 1969; Coleman 1961; Eizuru 1983; Hufford 1970; Ueda 1987). In Japan and England, by contrast, academic pressure is highest at the secondary school level. Indeed, college is often viewed as a time for social pursuits after a repressive secondary school experience.

The contrast between attitudes came home to me when I was in England and tried to explain the tradition of the American slumber party to an astounded twelve-year-old girl. In America, groups of preadolescent to adolescent girls make an event of sleep. They gather in groups of three or four in the host girl's room, and the parents' role is to keep their distance. The expectation is that the girls will stay up late trading stories, commonly of the urban legend type, and indulge in rituals such as séances and levitations (Tucker 1984, 2007–2008). The slumber party is a common setting for folklore transmission, and the themes of such folklore touch on independence, the dangers of courtship, and other matters concerning adulthood and the mysterious world (Oxreider 1977). The twelve-year-old English girl looked at me in shock. Although she was familiar with folklore, the slumber party concept seemed alien to her. Given her school pressures and society's watchful attitude toward these years, the lack of regulation—indeed, the frivolity of the event—placed it outside the norm. And she was not alone in expressing this opinion. In conversations with numerous students from England, the message was clear: during the secondary school years, such laxity, such lack of directedness, seemed inappropriate. In their testimonies, these students emphasized individual study, concentration, and more than a hint of sexual displacement. Yet in England, students reported jovial social activities after "exams"—that is, in college. The situation in Japan, exacerbated by a heightened competitiveness, is even more extreme, to the point that the laxity and frivolity typical of college years are a national reform issue (Doyon 2001).

To explain the use of childhood lore in America, I give examples primarily from social traditions that provide an adaptive strategy for human development. Although these traditions signal only one part of the range of folklore, they identify matters of emphasis in children's lore. Social traditions such as games and customs, greatly heightened during middle childhood, stress interpersonal relations of various types. Although conducted among peers, social traditions can encompass relations between parents and children, gestural modes of activity, and behavioral tools of persuasion; they test limits and societal and community models. Oral traditions, relying on speech and often incorporated into social traditions, are rhetorical modes of persuasion and typically flaunt verbal taboos; they confront areas of ambiguity through creative expression. Material traditions, and their association with shelter and tools, represent economic and technological relations, although social relations are revealed through the exchange of goods. Manipulation of form and substance is itself a form of persuasion that also comments on human adaptation.

An early manifestation of a social tradition is the game hide-and-seek.

It is often the first organized game children learn and continues to be popular until the age of eight or nine. The prevalence of hide-and-seek in America is indicated by Norma Schwendener's sweeping study in New York City entitled *Game Preferences of 10,000 Fourth Grade Children* (1932). In a survey of games learned outside of school, hide-and-seek had the highest frequency for a folk game and was second in total references only to the organized playing of baseball. In 1896, a survey of 2,000 children in Worcester, Massachusetts, from kindergarten to high school age produced similar results (Crosswell 1899). Tag and hide-and-seek headed the list of chasing games and were found in similar ranges among boys and girls. In Michigan in 1981, I asked several hundred children to collect their favorite traditional games from one another, and they reported that besides being the most commonly reported chasing game other than tag, hide-and-seek was the first organized game the children had played.

My survey revealed that most children avoid becoming "it" because of the low status it affords. Often a young or weak child in the group is assigned the role of "it." In a more democratic spirit, there are various ways to choose "it," such as with counting-out rhymes or the screaming of "not it," although these rituals can be easily manipulated to effect the desired outcome (Goldstein 1971). When "not it" is screamed by a child taking a leadership role, the other children immediately join in the chorus. The last to scream the words becomes "it." He or she then counts, and this ritual, too, can vary. Some count backward from 100 or count "one-Mississippi, two-Mississippi," up to ten. As soon as "it" is finished counting, he or she may call to the hiders, "Apple, peaches, pumpkin pie, Who's not ready, holler I!" or "Ready or not, here I come!" or "All not hid, holler I!" If no one yells, folklorist Paul Brewster points out, "it" often calls out, "A bushel of wheat and a bushel of clover, All not hid can't hide over." When "it" finds a hider, Brewster writes, "there is a race between them back to a preannounced spot. If the player who is 'It' succeeds in reaching the spot first, he strikes it and says, 'One, two, three for —!' If the other is the first to reach it, he calls, 'One, two, three for me!' or simply 'Home free!'" (Brewster 1953, 45–46; see also Newell 1963, 160; Opie and Opie 1969, 154–55). In other versions, the person sighted is "caught" and is out of the game or has to go back "home." Sometimes the person who is "it" does not have to tag the hider but rather announces, "One, two, three, I spy [hider's name]," and the race begins. In the versions I observed in Harrisburg, Pennsylvania, when one child is seen, all must run for home base (a wooden pole) and touch it before being tagged by "it." In these games, one girl, a victim of taunts from the other children, was consistently "it." A particular feature of the American variant of the game is the calling in of the players with the words "All in, all in, come in free," "Olley olley oxen free," or a number of other possibilities on the same theme. According to Brewster, the call can occur "when a player has been caught to take the place of the first 'It'" (1953, 45–46). I have also observed "it" give up the chase.

Hide-and-seek is particularly appealing to young children because it has simple rules that allow them to organize themselves into a running and chasing form of play. It also follows from infants' common delight at peekaboo, which establishes the concept of being there but not being there by hiding behind an object. Hide-and-seek operates on a similar concept and invites children to explore their surroundings— a prospect that is especially appealing when they find themselves in an unfamiliar situation, such as visiting relatives or attending summer camp. Because this game is familiar to many different children, players feel that they are on equal footing; they usually do not perceive an advantage to children at the host site. The game can be played at dusk to add to the challenge and to give the players the joy of delaying having to go inside. Players are aware that the game is highly adaptive to a variety of locations and can serve to frame ordinary (or adult) spaces as children's play areas.

Some experiences gained from hide-and-seek may be outside the players' awareness. In early childhood, the game replicates characteristics of the parent-child relationship. The player who is "it" operates from "home," while the others, in a gesture of independence, scatter to find hiding places from the authority of "it"; the children prefer to join the anonymity of the group rather than stand out as the parental "it." Yet they still operate within set boundaries, and when they hide they are soothed by the fact that the person who is "it" will look for them, try to bring them back, and eventually call them all in. Richard Phillips, in his study of games, adds that "children routinely stop playing hide-and-seek about the time of puberty. This coincides with the time when children leave home by train, bus, airplane, or on long hikes without adult supervision, confident of their ability to find their way to a destination and to return home" (1960, 203–4). Hide-and-seek has strong connections to prepubescent stages, and a scan of the surveys mentioned earlier shows that hide-and-seek is more prevalent today in younger age groups than it was a hundred years ago. Today, it is typically played among those aged four to seven, whereas the survey of Worcester children found that the game was most popular between the ages of eight and ten (Crosswell 1899). Apparently, the playing out of parent-child relations in a setting where the child is outside of parental watch and gaining independence is now occurring earlier.

This interpretation of hide-and-seek in the American context—that is, bearing out the separation of children from parents as part of an individual-centered society—may seem to be negated by other popular games played during the early part of middle childhood such as "Mother may I" (also known as "steps") and "red light, green light," which ostensibly inculcate obedience to authority. The texts of both these games depend on players obtaining an objective by following the directives of a high-power "it." In Mother may I, players line up at a distance from "it" and ask questions of him or her, such as how many and what kind of steps they may take. "It" can reply "three baby ones" or "two giant ones," for instance, allowing the players to get closer (Brewster 1953, 164). In contrast, red light, green light involves a counting "it" whose back is turned to the players lined up a distance away. As "it" counts, the players mover closer to him or her, thus representing a return home rather than a departure. When "it" turns around, the players are supposed to freeze and stand still. If "it" sees a player move, he or she penalizes that player a number of steps. Yet when one watches children playing these games, it is quickly apparent that the thrill comes not from obeying the leader but from defying him or her. The expected praxis in these games is to cheat to get ahead. While "it" points out the player caught moving in red light, others sneak forward. In Mother may I, players try to escape the notice of "Mother" while "she" gives one player permission to take baby steps forward.

The preponderance of a narrative structure involving the separation from and return to home underscores the linear plot of many social traditions, reminiscent of Vladimir Propp's structuring of folktales according to a plan of a lack established to a lack eliminated—or, in other words, a journey away from home and a return after tribulation (Propp 1968; Dundes 1964a, 1964b). A form of hide-and-seek involving animal figures, variously called fox and hounds, hare and hounds, and hunt the fox, underscores this plot development and the creation of dramatic tension in the chasing game. This game can involve as many as twenty children, divided into two groups. The group identified as the hares gets a head start on the group identified as the hounds. The race is not directionless, however; the hares are supposed to pack together and follow a course that will take them, often circularly, back "home." On occasion, the hares leave items, such as scraps of paper, to mark their trail. The hounds chase the hares and try to capture them before they reach home. Comparing this game to Propp's folktale structure, a linear progression is evident from a lack established (the absent hares) to a lack eliminated (the hares captured), at least from the point of view of the hounds. From the point of view of the hares, they want to go home, or, in folktale terms, the hero is pursued and is rescued from a pursuit. The hares progress from a lack (the desire to go home) to an interdiction (doing so without being caught by the hounds) to a violation (being caught) to the consequence (losing the game); the hounds also progress from a lack (the desire to catch the absent hares) to an interdiction (doing so before the hares arrive back home) to a violation (not catching the hares) to the consequence (losing the game, unless the hares are caught, in which case the hounds win) (see Dundes 1964a; Opie and Opie 1969).

The structuring of the game suggests a comparison to rites of passage that proceed from a separation stage, in which initiates are isolated from the community or elder group, to a transitional stage, in which a task or ceremony is performed, to an incorporation, in which the initiates are united with the community. The therapeutic function of such rites is that they ensure smooth transitions at life-changing moments such as puberty, marriage, and death. Often the social function of such rites is that they remind the initiates of the fundamental symbols and values of a society (see Myerhoff 1982; Van Gennep 1960). Although not celebratory in the same sense as the rites marking birth and marriage, the structure of the rites incorporated into an everyday social experience offers an important instrument of adaptation. In the everyday lives of children, especially when they are rapidly developing physically and socially, games work outside parental guidance to provide stages for growth and passage. Following the structure of rites, games provide oft-repeated devices of social reassurance and transition; they condense adaptive passage into everyday praxis (Bronner 1988b; Bauman 1973; Bernstein 1971). The expressive profile of chasing games during middle childhood suggests that its structure has an instrumental purpose. It may involve, as Sutton-Smith has pointed out, power relations, such as the often gendered relationship of male hounds pursuing female, if not feminized, hares as the chased objects. Like hide-and-seek, hare and hounds is based on the departure from and return to home. In the often repeated fantasy of play during the early part of middle childhood, children realize their newfound autonomy by enacting the structure of a rite of passage. In the praxis of chasing, they use play to extend their territorial domain and face challenges (interdictions in the narrative of the game) outside the safety of home.

Although the example of hare and hounds has a long lineage, new forms of chasing games that fit into the expressive profile of the early part of middle childhood emphasize an adaptation to historical events and fears. The most striking example to my mind is "cooties tag." The term *cooties* is thought to derive from *kutu*, a word used throughout Polynesia for "body lice." It entered British military slang by the start of World War I (Brophy and Partridge 1965, 105; Partridge 1970, 179). One theory about how it spread so quickly in America during the 1950s is that U.S. military personnel who joined British allies in the South Pacific during World War II brought the term back home (Samuelson 1980, 199).

Cooties tag joins a complex of activities revolving around the concept of cooties as ritualized affliction. Thus, with the announcement that someone has cooties, children are associating that person with an inferior social position or physical appearance. Children give each other cootie shots by pretending to inject a pen into an arm; they make cootie marks, usually an *X* on the upper arm; and they construct "cootie catchers," folded paper contraptions that look like scoopers. Similar to the paper-folded "fortune-teller" reported widely in many collections, the cootie catcher has little black specks on one side, instead of numbers or the names of colors. When the child opens the catcher with his or her fingers, the blank side shows up—hence the cooties are gone, flushed. In this sanitary metaphor is an example of the "cooties complex," emphasizing cleanliness achieved by washing away, like the action of a toilet (Samuelson 1980, 201; Bronner 1988a, 210–17). Cooties tag sometimes takes the pre-courtship form of boys chasing the girls, or what appears to be a mock enactment of the fairy tale prince awakening or curing the princess; in "cootie kissing," girls run from boys and suffer kissing when caught (Samuelson 1980, 199). Various beliefs have arisen about cooties as well, such as the idea that certain signs (e.g., wearing glasses, being fat) are evidence of cooties, that crossing one's fingers prevents one from catching cooties from another child, and that only children of the same sex can inoculate one another or that only children of the opposite sex can pass cooties to one another.

Cooties came into play among American children during the early 1950s, the time of the polio epidemic.[1] The greatest sustained outbreak of the disease in the United States occurred between 1942 and 1953; in 1950 alone, it affected 33,344 persons, most of whom were children older than ten. Before much was known about the disease, the prevalent belief was that polio fit into the germ theory of disease—that is, invisible creatures that liked to dwell in dirty, hot, and damp places were the gritty culprits, indiscriminately causing ailments that could strike anyone who was not careful. The polio epidemic was especially disconcerting to many Americans because even the healthy and wealthy, who should be immune to such afflictions because of their clean and honorable living, contracted the disease, and distrustful, blaming eyes turned toward the lower classes. It turned out that the disease was probably spread from person to person (the virus normally attaches to living tissue cells) by intimate human contact, although unsanitary conditions, especial fecal and sewage contamination, could support the virus, which entered the throat, spread to the nervous system, and could paralyze or even kill its victims. During the polio scare, parents kept their children out of swimming pools for fear of contagion and told them to avoid touching other children. The cooties complex fit into the expressive profile of middle childhood, but it was adapted as a specific strategy to deal with a threat to children at an already vulnerable time. My argument is that rather than play "polio," which was disturbing to both parents and children, cooties became metaphorically refocused as infection.[2] It represented a projection into play of the autonomous child's finding that invisible danger lurked in the places one went and the company one kept. The cooties complex, incorporating a host of beliefs and play activities, became children's way to dramatize the dread of the disease while also bringing out social relations underlying the modern emphasis on cleanliness and appearance—relations important to adult ways of dealing with one another.

The game was still played even after the polio epidemic ended because it continued to comment on the importance of cleanliness and appearance. But by the 1980s, cooties tag had lost much of its popularity, and when it was enacted, it usually took the form of pre-courtship play. During the late 1980s, the game, with its association to disease, enjoyed a resurgence in the wake of the AIDS epidemic, suggesting again an adaptive strategy related to the developmental stage of middle childhood by which fears of contagion are projected into the socially sanctioned outlet of play. Supporting this observation is Holly Outten's (1988) study of third and fourth graders in a Camden, Delaware, elementary school, where cooties tag was prevalent in a new form known as "the touch." According to Outten, "The game is initiated with one player, usually a male, claiming he has the germs of the 'Touch' of a girl close to him. He passes 'It' to a boy standing nearby, and the game is under way. All of the players cross their fingers to ward off infection." In addition, children might spray themselves with an invisible disinfectant to temporarily end the game, but the "game is never over." The infection lingers, and children remember who had the infection from the day before. As with cooties tag, the child who is "it" is usually "dirty, overweight, or seen as non-conforming. To be a perpetual 'Touch' carrier is an unpopular status and is one that the other children work very hard to avoid." In a version of freeze tag, the children freeze in place "until disinfected by a fellow playmate." Common variations of the game concern bodily emissions: spit touch, booger touch, poop touch, and grease touch. One form even referred to a specific person who was obese—a reminder of the strong connection between popularity and conformity to standards of appearance and manner.

The concern for bodily emissions also suggests a modern fear of infection, especially considering beliefs about the AIDS virus being carried in bodily emissions. Indeed, Outten (1988) collected one manifestation of this fear in children's folklore: "One girl told of a game she played at a slumber party where three bowls were filled with ketchup, mustard, and water, and then placed behind a box. The players reached over the box and put their finger into one of the three bowls. If they touched the mustard, they were said to be infected with rabies; if they touched the ketchup, they were said to have the AIDS virus; if they touched the water, they were said to be free from all diseases."

Related to the fear of contagion is the game's emphasis on avoiding contact among males. As Outten (1988) observes, "Males do not touch other males because of the inbred social sanction which forbids bodily contact by hands. Instead, males infect by tripping each other. Upon infection, the boys would squeal in an effeminate manner and make a mocking face at the female he was infected by. To rid themselves of 'the Touch,' a male must show a masculine trait of knocking a fellow player down, or tripping them—and in the process, restoring his maleness and/or cleanliness. Newly cleansed males, as well as other players, taunt the infected male until he cleanses himself also." Consider, too, the different responses to the touch: "Most females infect one another by touching each other on the arms or back. Upon infection, they walked in a zombie like fashion with their arms outstretched, and moaning 'I got it.' The other children run from her." The boys symbolically show decay or homophobia, while the girls reveal more of the metaphors of contamination. Although I have inferred metaphors of disease in the playing of the game, Outten stresses a concern for gender roles and pre-courtship behavior in her observations. The game allows play that involves touching the opposite sex; the girls' chasing role reinforces the boys' standard of athletic ability, according to Outten, and suggests that girls must force boys to commit to them. The boys in the game are given a higher status than the girls. Females are associated with the filth, and males play in fear of them. Those males who are touched by females are considered to have a worse infliction because the girl must catch the boy in order to "touch" him.

In some cases, it is less desirable to be caught by a female than to actually carry the "infection of the germ, because of the concern of the male that he will be seen by his peers as weak." Working further on the metaphor of disease, however, we can see a childhood form of projection; the afflicted, in the aggressor role, blame the "weaker" girls for their problem. "This game is a vicious one," Outten asserts, "but is looked at as essential by the children in order to be self-assured."

Smaller groups of children, typically girls, participate in games that also conspicuously use rhyme to advance the game. The advantage of boys in large-group games is not surprising in light of their behavioral tendency to "gang" rather than to develop the intimate dyadic relationships that are characteristic of girls' play. The pattern in girls' play is to value cooperation and small-group interaction rather than the aggressive expression of social dominance (Sutton-Smith 1979b). Hand clapping and jumping rope require the cooperation of peers, although collectors have typically extracted rhymes apart from these routines. As girls play, the social tradition stresses emotional adaptation, especially as courtship and commitment become more important for girls' socialization as they mature. Hand clapping typically precedes jumping rope; indeed, as jumping rope has declined in popularity, many of the jump-rope rhymes can be heard predominantly in hand-clapping routines, which remain strong. Let me discuss two of the more popular routines: "Miss Susie Had a Baby" for hand clapping, and "Cinderella Dressed in Yellow" for jumping rope.

"Miss Susie had a baby" is the first line of a rhyme typically heard from girls in the early years of middle childhood (Roud 2011, 4835). In older versions, the rhyme continues: "His name was Tiny Tim. She put him in the bathtub to see if he could swim. He drank up all the water. He ate up all the soap. He tried to eat the bathtub but it wouldn't go down his throat. Miss Susie called the doctor. The doctor called the nurse. The nurse called the lady with the alligator purse. Out ran the doctor. Out ran the nurse. Out ran the lady with the alligator purse. And now Tiny Tim is home sick in bed, with soap in his throat and bubbles in his head." Peter and Iona Opie in *The Singing Game* (1985) list this rhyme as "The Johnsons Had a Baby": "The Johnsons had a baby. They called him Tiny Tim, Tim, Tim. They put him in a bathtub, to see if he could swim, swim, swim. He drank a bowl of water, and ate a bar of soap, soap, soap. He tried to eat the bathtub, but it wouldn't fit down his throat, throat, throat." These lines, the Opies offer, "can be recognized as part of a bawdy song about a whore called Lulu." They report that the song appeared as a joke verse during the 1920s and later became a game rhyme. They list the first recording of the child's verse in 1938 in Westchester County, New York (Opie and Opie 1985, 472–73; see Abrahams 1969; Brown 1979; McCosh 1979; Fowke 1969). But the old bawdy meaning (few singers recognize that Susie—or Lucy or Lulu or Virginia—is unmarried) has been converted into children's adaptive concern about the appearance of new siblings. In fact, today the rhyme's opening line is frequently changed to "My mommy had a baby" or "I had a little brother" (Abrahams 1969, 79; Brown 1979, 31–32).

Folklorist Alan Dundes states the case for the symbolism of sibling rivalry this way: "Precisely where is it that the newborn baby gets so much obvious physical attention? In American culture, it is the bath"

(1969b, 479). Girls especially feel some ambivalence, because even though they are socialized to provide nurturing to younger children, they may also be jealous of the attention directed away from them toward the younger child. So Miss Susie becomes the singer, the older child.

The name of Tiny Tim for the baby, meanwhile, imbues the role of the younger child with symbolic significance. Tiny Tim is well known to children from the many versions of Charles Dickens's *A Christmas Carol* adapted to television, film, theater, and print. In the story, Tiny Tim is the youngest son of Bob Cratchit, Scrooge's poor toiling assistant. Tiny Tim arouses sympathy because of his youthful charm and innocence and because he is crippled. The story climaxes with Scrooge showering gifts and attention on Tiny Tim. Further underscoring the theme of sibling rivalry, Dundes observes:

> It is during and after bathing that the baby is fondled, powdered, played with, etc. So the older child takes things into his own hands. He puts the baby into the tub pretending to teach him how to swim. What does the baby do in the tub? He tries to eat everything. Babies are in fact orally inclined as it is this body zone which provides the initial point of contact with the world, a body zone which operates by incorporating what is needed, i.e., mother's milk. From the older child's point of view, the baby is always being fed—hence it appears to have an insatiable appetite. What then is more appropriate from the older child's perspective than to have his baby brother choke to death from eating something he shouldn't be eating, from trying to eat too much, that is, symbolically speaking, from trying to take too much, more than his share of their common parent's bounty. (1969b, 479)

The attachment of the "Miss Susie called the doctor" verse, which is taken from a separate literary tradition, affords another opportunity to underscore the sibling rivalry theme. Frequently, the opening line becomes, "Mother, mother, I am ill, send (call) for the doctor over the hill (quick)." These lines signify a request for attention away from the baby and toward the singer. The theme of sibling rivalry appears in other girls' rhymes as well, such as "Fudge, fudge, tell the judge, Momma's gonna have a newborn baby. Wrap it up in tissue paper. Send it down the elevator" (see Browne 1955, 7; Dundes 1980, 39–40; Bronner 1988a, 71–72; Roud 2011, 19318). I kept a journal of folkloric expressions used in a play group of five-year-olds, one of which was a well-known taunting rhyme: "X and Y sitting in a tree, K-I-S-S-I-N-G." But at this age, it was common to personalize the rhyme as "Me and Mommy sitting in a tree, K-I-S-S-I-N-G. First comes love, then comes marriage; then comes Mommy in a baby carriage" (Roud 2011, 19216). The text at this age shows mother-child bonding typical of early childhood, but more characteristic of middle childhood is an awareness of the procreation of more children or siblings "in a baby carriage." Nonetheless, the displacement by a new child indicates a desire to retain a singular relationship with the mother. Among first graders, the most common counting-out rhyme was "Bubble gum, bubble gum in a dish. How many do you wish?"—indicating an acquisitive desire, as if the child does not have to share treats with others (Roud 2011, 19256). A symbolic equivalence between bubble gum and infancy can be seen in a derisive rhyme found in the early part of middle childhood: "Baby, baby, suck your thumb. Wash your face in bubble gum" (Bronner 1988a, 74). As a form of adjustment, the rhymes in this expressive profile playfully project the growing child's concerns about competition, yet they also allow a release for undesirable feelings of hostility.

Apart from sibling relations, what about the child's self (not considered by Dundes in the expressive profile of children)? A parent of an only child reported to me her daughter's frequent singing of "Tiny Tim," which emerged as her favorite for a period of months. About to turn eight years old, the child, according to the parent, "was suffering the growing pains of turning from a kitten into a cat." The child longed for her "baby" years because, as she said, "everyone likes you then." As she became older, adults were less tolerant of her mischievous behavior and less attentive to her presence. The child culturally expressed this transition from the idolized baby to the disciplined kid, in her native categorization of developmental stages, with "Tiny Tim." Another indication in her expressive profile was her most commonly used birthday song parody: "Happy birthday to me, I'm one hundred and three, I still go to school, and I want my mommy." To be sure, she knew another parody that externalized the expression: "Happy birthday to you, happy birthday to you, you look like a monkey, and you smell like one too." But significantly, during this transitional period, when she perceived that autonomy, though desirable, had a downside—that is, diminished attention from her mother—she blurted out the "happy birthday to me" rhyme in a frame for an event about aging. The parody expressed a desire not to age and, in a projective inversion, placed the mother in the position of the child. This move implied that the child still wanted her mother to be maternally affectionate even as she got older, underscored by the exaggerated age of 103. This rhyme was quickly discarded the next year, although the externalized parody about appearance and body image, an ongoing concern in preadolescence, continued. As fantasy, the "happy birthday to me" and "Tiny Tim" rhymes allow a child to acknowledge the attention once bestowed on him or her and to realize that those awkward days are over.

"Cinderella Dressed in Yellow" represents young girls' relation to the Cinderella character, who, as a popular culture figure, is more prevalent than other Disney characters such as Snow White or Sleeping Beauty. Whereas the other figures have motifs of courtship by a handsome prince, resulting in a wedding, Cinderella has more transformative symbols and a greater suggestion of the sexual awakening representative of puberty. Cinderella of fairy tale fame is young and is repressed by the older stepsister and stepmother characters. With her father absent, she longs for some male attachment, replacing the loving parent with a romantic interest. Despite feeling ugly in this awkward stage, Cinderella triumphs because of her youthful beauty and material surroundings. Her maturity and sexuality are awakened by the handsome, mature prince, who promises a bright future that allows Cinderella to leave the past behind. The jump-rope rhyme, however, follows a different plot, pointing to the sexual undertones of the original fairy tale: "Cinderella dressed in yellow (yella), went upstairs to kiss a fellow (fella). Made a mistake and kissed a snake. How many doctors did it take? One, two, three, etc." Or alternatively: "Cinderella dressed in yellow, went upstairs (downtown) to kiss (see) her fella. How many kisses did she get? One, two, three, etc." The popularity of this rhyme is indicated by the fifty published sources between 1926 and 1966 listed by Roger Abrahams in *Jump-Rope Rhymes* (1969, 30–32; see also Roud 2010, 178; Roud 2011, 18410). Collector Marice Brown, writing in *Amen, Brother Ben*, adds, "this rhyme was the one most commonly cited by informants under twenty. It also had the widest regional spread" (1979, 22). These collectors, working in the third quarter of the twentieth century, reported that the rhyme was more popular in the later part of middle childhood, whereas rhymes expressing physical skill and the infantile "teddy bear" image were prominent during the early part: "Teddy bear, teddy bear, turn around. Teddy bear, teddy bear, touch the ground" (Roud 2011, 19264).

Yet I found that the rhyme was reported among children as young as five years old in journals I collected from parents in the early twenty-first century. One connection I noticed between the two most popular rhymes was the inclusion of "stairs," because after children "touch the ground," they often "walk (climb) the stairs" as the next physical challenge. The suggestion is that climbing stairs symbolizes maturation, as if the teddy bear in the rhyme moves from crawling (touching the ground) to walking or climbing the stairs in an upward ascension. Cinderella, an older feminine figure, replaces the stuffed animal associated with infantile security; she too goes up the stairs, but unlike the teddy bear, her climb suggests a journey to the upstairs bedrooms. The binary of upstairs as a place for bedrooms and downstairs as a place for maternal or domestic care is indicated by the following jump-rope rhyme:

> I went upstairs to make my bed
> I made a mistake and bumped my head
> I went downstairs to milk my cow
> I made a mistake and milked the sow
> I went into the kitchen to bake a pie
> I made a mistake and baked a fly
> How many flies does it take to make a pie.

The first "mistake" sets the stage for the others, and there appears to be a causal link between going upstairs and bumping her head. This is followed by a milking image, suggestive of nurturing a baby, and the preparation of food (the communal pie) for a family. The symbolic equivalence of bedroom and upstairs is reinforced by the image of Cinderella's castle in popular toys and images. Cinderella finds her dreams by ascending to the top of the edifice where there are private bedrooms, indicating, on the one hand, her fulfillment in a man's home and, on the other, the independence of being given her privacy.

The symbolist question is whether girls are aware of the connotation of sexual awakening in the rhyme, especially since this meaning seems to defy the idea of sexual latency during middle childhood. A key developmental factor is the awareness of gender difference that occurs around five years old in differentiating between possession of a penis and possession of a vagina. Parents increasingly segregate boys and girls to protect their "private parts" at this time, and they dress children to show gender distinctions more sharply than they do during infancy. Psychologists argue whether this emerging cognitive binary between boy = penis and girl = vagina creates an inequality of power whereby the male pole is purer and more dominant than the female side. One piece of evidence in expressive profiles is the reference to receiving kisses as a positive value in girls' rhymes, whereas being kissed is viewed as negative in boys' lore, implying an awareness of pre-courtship behavior. Here is an example of a derisive rhyme typically hurled at boys in the early part of middle childhood: "Jack is mad and I am glad, and I know how to please him. A bottle of wine to make him shine, and a great big kiss from Jill." Kissing is a sign of maturation for the girl, as indicated by the following rhyme: "My mother gave me peaches, my father gave me pears, my boyfriend gave me fifty cents, and kissed me up the stairs" (Bronner 1988a, 62). It presents a narrative sequence of nurturing by the parents, followed by the appearance of a boyfriend (and money), who kisses the girl "up the stairs." The awareness of kissing as a girls' praxis is indicated by a boys' anti-rhyme I collected: "Cinderella dressed in yella, went upstairs to see her fella. She killed herself." This indicates boys' awareness of the rhyme's association with girlhood. The boys would not recite the rhyme as their tradition; rather, they referred to it in a subversive way. The startling replacement line is for the start of kissing and suggests either death as the end of childhood or a resentment of girls' newfound power.

Girls in Cinderella rhymes frequently initiate kissing with the hope of reciprocity. This symbolic praxis is not unique to Cinderella. One popular representation of the male-female binary occurs in rhymes that begin, "Not last night but the night before." This jump-rope rhyme is typically finished as follows: "Two little rats came knocking at my door. I went to let them in, and this is what they said, 'Butterfly, butterfly, turn all around. Butterfly, butterfly touch the ground. Butterfly, butterfly, throw out a kiss. Butterfly, butterfly, get out before you miss'" (Bronner 1988a, 70). Butterflies are commonly used as symbols for girls because of the suggestion of extreme transformation from a crawling caterpillar to a butterfly taking flight; in contrast, boys are symbolized as rats or robbers. (Little Orphan Annie takes up the motific slot held by the butterfly in another reference to the extreme transformation from rags to riches.)

Girls' extreme transformation is contrasted in the expressive profiles with the gradual development of a generalized male character in "Billy Oh La." Usually performed as a hand-clapping rhyme, the routine takes Billy through ages one to ten:

When Billy was zero
He went to be a hero
Here Billy oh la
Here Billy oh la
Half past two, cross down

When Billy was one
He learned to suck his thumb
Thumb Billy oh la
Thumb Billy oh la
Half past one, cross down

When Billy was two
He learned to tie his shoe
Shoe Billy oh la
Shoe Billy oh la
Half past two, cross down

When Billy was three
He learned to climb a tree
Tree Billy oh la
Tree Billy oh la
Half past three, cross down

When Billy was four
He learned to shut the door
Door Billy oh la
Door Billy oh la
Half past four, cross down

When Billy was five
He learned to seek a hive
Hive Billy oh la
Hive Billy oh la
Half past five, cross down

When Billy was six
He learned to pick up sticks
Sticks Billy oh la
Sticks Billy oh la
Half past six, cross down

When Billy was seven
He learned to go to heaven
Heaven Billy oh la
Heaven Billy oh la
Half past seven, cross down

When Billy was eight
He learned to clean his plate
Plate Billy oh la
Plate Billy oh la
Half past eight, cross down

When Billy was nine
He learned to break his spine
Spine Billy oh la
Spine Billy oh la
Half past nine, cross down

When Billy was ten
He learned to start again
Again Billy oh la
Again Billy oh la
Half past ten. (Bronner 1988a, 65)

Instead of going up the stairs, Billy climbs a tree in an apparent display of male bravado. Unlike girls, who get fed, Billy consumes food, cleaning his plate. He shows strength in breaking his spine, but there is no shape-shifting into a butterfly or bodily change with a rising belly.

Unlike the images of courtship in girls' rhymes of middle childhood, the content of boys' speech play eschews intimacy and often implies sexual bravado as a sign of maturity. This pattern is especially evident in the apparent male praxis of taunting and insulting, often ritualized in "ranking" or "cutting" contests, as they are known among whites, or "dozens" or "sounding" among blacks. Both forms involve insults aimed at the opponent's mother, but lest this attack lead to fisticuffs, it is framed in play as a contest of quick thinking and fast talk. In the early twenty-first century, MTV even institutionalized the older folk tradition by organizing a competition with formal rules called *Yo Momma*. As the name implies, much of the speech play involved insulting the other person's mother. Dozens are often expressed in rhymed couplets, especially using the following formula: "I (saw, screwed) your mama (on, in, by, or between) —. / She —." The subcategory of snaps or rank-outs often follows this formula: "Your mother's like —; she —," or "Your mother's so —, she —." For example, "Your mother's like a doorknob; everyone gets a turn," or "Your mother's so low, she could play handball on the curb." According to folklorist Roger Abrahams, dozens represent a striving for masculine identity at a crucial preadolescent stage for black boys seeking to assert power in a matrifocal society. They represent a symbolic rejection of the woman's world—or, indeed, the black world they see as run by the mother—in favor of the male gang life. The structure of insulting one's mother is significant because it puts the boy in the position of simultaneously separating from the mother figure by aggressively dominating her and defending her honor from outsiders' attack (Abrahams 1970, 39–60; see also Abrahams 1962).

Is this really so different from ritualized white enactments of insults? I have argued, based on ethnographic observations of contests in insults, that preadolescent whites share a desire to exhibit separation from the feminine, which dominates the early nurturing years of middle childhood (Bronner 1978). Independence is symbolized in phallocentric fantasies in which the mother is violated; after this developmental stage, joking tends to focus on sex with other women in the same age cohort. A noticeable difference along racial lines, however, is the presence of more insults related to physical appearance, gender distinction, and intellectual ability in white repertoires (Bronner 1988a, 42–43). For example, "If brains were dynamite, you couldn't blow your nose," or "You're so ugly, when you were a kid your parents fed you with a slingshot." Arguably, the adaptive strategy suggested for maturing white males is oriented toward achievement by appearance and intelligence, whereas a more fatalistic attitude is expressed by blacks in dozens, which are often associated with inner-city settings where status is accorded to the aggressive, hypermasculine man of action and words (Abrahams 1970; Franklin 1992).

Sexuality in girls' expressive profiles also represents a departure from and often a rejection of home and mother, but it more often involves a protective father figure and a desire for intimacy with a partner, coupled with the fear of being exploited or abused in the new relationship. Even if the girls performing the rhymes are unaware of the sexuality implicit in transformation, an argument can be made that this transformation is bound up with uncertainty for maturing girls, who expect greater changes with puberty than do boys. One obvious sign of change that differentiates girls from maturing boys is the ability to procreate, conceptualized as a rising belly with pregnancy. This is related to the concern about menses as a visible sign of change for girls, whereas boys' maturation is more ambiguous, except as fantasized by hypermasculine phallic display. Whereas Cinderella and other naïve or needy princess avatars seeking intimacy are the dramatis personae of girls' rhymes, superheroes representing social dominance are ubiquitous in boys' rhymes. In dozens, one might hear, "I screwed your mother between two cans. Up jumped a baby and hollered 'Superman'" (Abrahams 1962, 211). A number of insult rhymes collected from boys also bring up superhero icons in relation to phallic awareness, such as this one:

> Here comes Batman
> Swinging on a rubber band,
> Stronger than Superman,
> Here comes King Kong
> Beating on his ding dong. (Sherman and Weisskopf 1995, 49)

One might speculate whether Batman's ascendancy is a result of his bat or vampire image, and whether King Kong is appealing as a phallic symbol because of the growth of body and facial hair associated with puberty. Batman and Robin are feminized in one of the most frequently collected parodies in children's lore: "Jingle bells, Batman smells, Robin laid an egg. Batmobile broke its wheel and Joker got away" (Bronner 1988a, 105–6). Many parodies of popular songs subvert the values of society as a sign of separation from parental or institutional authority, along with a display of or wish for social dominance. Boys also express fantasies of gun play as part of phallocentric bravado, such as in the following verse (to the tune of "Jingle Bells"):

> Jingle bells, shotgun shells
> (name) on the run
> Oh what fun it is to shoot (name) with a gun.
> A day or two ago I thought I'd take a ride
> And take my father's gun and shoot (name) in the hide.
> Jingle bells, shotgun shells
> (name)'s on the run
> Oh what fun it is to shoot (name) in the bun. (Bronner 1988a, 105)

One example of the importance of menses as a marker of the end of middle childhood for girls is a ritual often referred to as "Bloody Mary." (Boys acknowledge this marker by a spate of "what's grosser than gross?" jokes centering on the symbol of the tampon, as discussed later.) The features of the Bloody Mary ritual—gathering séance-style in a dark room (usually a bathroom, where sanitary napkins would be applied) and trying to call forth the spirit of a tormented, bloodied youth—suggest the adaptive use of a fantasy of a bloody girl to project anxiety over the onset of menses and anticipate the future. According to Alan Dundes, "As a prepubescent fantasy about the somewhat fearsome but inevitable onset of menarche, it is enacted usually by an individual girl (or an all-girl group), it takes place in a bathroom, it involves a bloody image, sometimes a bloody self-image appears, and the ritual may conclude with the flushing of a toilet" (2002, 91).

Dundes generalizes the girls' anxiety as stemming from the negative cultural attitude toward menses and the association of blood flow with pain, but arguably, their trepidation may be developmental. In addition to menses representing a clear physical marker of a new, independent stage of life, it symbolizes a readiness for sexuality. Unlike the role of sexuality in boys' lore, which emphasizes male bravado without responsibility, sexuality in girls' lore is coupled with the possibility of motherhood and the attendant obligation. The suggestion of motherhood—shown in boys' folk sayings such as "Old enough to bleed, old enough to breed"—also emphasizes separation from the mother by replacing her. The new mother nurtures the child yet worries whether she will still be cared for. If she cannot depend on her mother, the lore suggests, then she must be more reliant on the commitment of the undependable male, causing distress. This developmental context may explain the many appeals of "Mother, mother I am ill" in rhymes of middle childhood, especially for the consequences of a belly rising. In the extreme, the girl may even fantasize her mother's death, as in a variant of "I'm a little Dutch girl," which relates, "I am a little orphan girl. My mother she is dead" (Abrahams 1969, 69). Associating the "queen" with maturity and the cutesy Dutch girl with her braided blonde hair, exaggerated hat, and wooden shoes with infantile innocence, yet another variant of the Dutch girl rhyme proclaims: "I'm a girl dressed in green. My mother didn't want me, so she sent me to the Queen. The Queen didn't want me, so she sent me to the King. The King said, 'Shut your eyes and count sixteen'" (Abrahams 1969, 69). Shutting the eyes implies sexuality, and the count is for the age usually associated with blossoming, recognized, for example, in the "sweet sixteen" party usually reserved for girls.

A series of jump-rope rhymes that do not have comparable counting-out versions start with "Down in the meadow," "Down in the valley," or "Down by the river." In the most frequently collected version, the girl is surrounded by green and is then identified by the red rose before being kissed by a boy:

> Down by the river
> Where the green grass grows,
> There sat (any girl's name)
> As pretty as a rose.
> She sang herself to sleep,
> And up came (any boy's name)
> And kissed her on the cheek. (Abrahams 1969, 40–41; Browne
>   1955, 7; Roud 2011, 12967)

One parody changes the green grass to purple, suggesting the color of dried blood, and connects it with a witch figure replacing the innocent girl:

> Down in the desert
> Where the purple grass dies,
> There sat a witch with
> Yellowish-green eyes.
> Nobody came to see her
> Because she always ate them
> One by one, two by two, etc. (Abrahams 1969, 42)

A number of parodies relate this scenario to a sexual praxis. Here is an example from Texas collected by Abrahams:

> Down in the valley where the green grass grows,
> There sat little (girl's name) without any clothes.
> Along came (boy's name) swinging a chain,
> Down went his zipper and out it came.
> Three months later she began to swell,
> Six months later you could really tell.
> Nine months later, out they came,
> Two little (boy's names) swinging a chain. (1969, 43)

The above verse, which Abrahams calls a "common bawdy rhyme," implies anxiety about the boy's predation and undependability and the responsibility that must be borne by the girl. There is also a hint of continued harm in the junior forms of the phallocentric boy "swinging a chain." Notable in girls' characterization of boys is a series of rhymes about "a boy's occupation" collected from sixth- to eighth-grade girls:

> A boy's occupation
> Is to stick his preparation (boneration, information)
> Into a girl's separation (communication)
> To increase the population
> Of the younger generation.
> Do you want a demonstration? (Sherman and Weisskopf 1995,
>   51–52)

Unlike Cinderella in the jump-rope verse, who goes to the bedroom, this crude adolescent boy "mates (gets)" the girl "on the floor, floor, floor" (Sherman and Weisskopf 1995, 51). Other rhymes mask the male's sexual penetration of the female in the active play frame of the jump-rope game and rhyme:

> Charlie Chaplin sat on a pin (tack)
> How many inches did it go in?
> [Jumper jumps until she misses, counting the jumps.]

> Rooms to let (House for sale). Inquire with*in*.
> Let me move out, let John [or any name] move *in*.
> [Jumper jumps in and out while the rope turns.]

> Rooms to let (House for sale). Inquire with*in*.
> A lady was put out for drinking *gin*.
> If she promises to drink no *more*
> Here's a key to Anna's back *door*. (Abrahams 1969, 25–26, 66–67;
>   Roud 2011, 19223; Roud 2010, 184; Smith 1926, 83)

By middle childhood, youths already recognize the bedroom as a private, often sexualized location, and they use the house and other buildings to symbolize the body (as in the rhymes above). Well known among children, for instance, is the rhyme about the old woman who lived in a shoe and had so many children she didn't know what to do (Dundes 1969b, 480). They learn that homes have faces, and obese friends can be "as big as a house." The selling of space, such as "rooms to let" or "house for sale," suggests that the body is available for action. Boys tease one another if their pants zippers are open by saying, "Your barn door is open." This frontal reference suggests a feminine symbolism of the "backside," as the buttocks in "Anna's back door" (Brunvand 2001, 457–58; Richter 1987, 93). The reading of jump-rope verses as the projection of the chanting girl is defensible, I maintain, because of the preponderance of girls' performances that personalize the lore as a first-person narrative, in contradistinction to boys' jokes, which are typically told in the third person about someone else. Jump-rope rhymes performed in all-girl groups therefore contain material about sexuality and courtship that are not found in the related genre of counting-out rhymes, which are played in mixed-gender groups, also in middle childhood. The comprehensive dictionary of counting rhymes prepared by Roger Abrahams and Lois Rankin (1980), for instance, contains no entries for Cinderella. Often the narrative in jump-rope rhymes performed by girls concerns growth and a parent's ire at the suggestion of fertility. "I am a little girl just so high," a popular rhyme relates, "I can make donuts, I can make pie. I broke a platter right in two. Mother came to whip me, boo, hoo, hoo." Or, more explicitly, "Over the garden wall, I let the baby fall. My mother came out, and gave me a clout, over the garden wall" (Abrahams 1969, 71, 156). Or the appeal is directly to the mother, in a kind of warning that the girl has grown to the point of being capable of being domestic: "Mother, mother, I am able, to stand on a chair and set the table. Daughter, daughter don't forget, salt, vinegar, and red hot pepper" (Abrahams 1969, 125–26).

Another indication of the role of jumping rope and hand clapping in expressing sexual anticipation during middle childhood is their simulation of excitable, often sensual behavior. Whereas counting out is often done in a stationary position, reflecting on the outcome of the count, jumping rope and hand clapping involve jumping, twisting, and rapid hand movements. Jump rope features a girl enclosed by the linear rope, which could represent the contrast between the circular, vaginal girl and the linear, phallic male (see Dundes 2004, 184). In fact, one could argue that jumping rope metaphorically enacts the attractiveness of the girl's physical appeal while warning that this results in her prolonged entrapment in a confined space as she embraces courtship and marriage. The more active she is, the longer she stays in the twirling ropes. Several rhymes reinforce this image of moving rapidly and being sensuously kept "in place": "She can wiggle, she can wobble, she can do the split. But I bet you five dollars, she can't do this." There is often the suggestion of a developmental as well as an expressive transformation from one home to another in the play frame of jump rope. For example, the goody-two-shoes "Shirley Temple went to France [a place associated in the public imagination with loose morals] to teach the girls the hootchie-kootchie dance. First on heels, second on toes. Do the split and away she goes" (Bronner 1988a, 72; Roud 2011, 19102). Girls also appeal to authority when they chant, "Policeman, policeman, do your duty, for here comes (child's name), the bathing beauty. She can wiggle, she can waddle, she can do the kick. And I bet you all the money, she can do the split" (Bronner 1988a, 72; Roud 2011, 19335). Or they announce, "Here comes (child's name) with the tight skirt on. She can wiggle . . ." (Bronner 1988a, 72).

At least one popular rhyme refers to the iconic couple Blondie and Dagwood, of comic book fame:

Blondie and Dagwood went to town,
Blondie bought an evening gown,
Dagwood bought the evening news,
And this is what it said,
Blondie jump on one foot, one foot, one foot
Blondie jump on two feet, two feet, two feet
Blondie jump on three feet, three feet, three feet
Blondie jump on four feet, four feet, four feet
Blondie jump out. (Bronner 1988a, 72; Roud 2011, 19212)

The narrative in the verse starts with the excitement of going to town and staying out late in an elaborate evening gown. But it then describes stereotypical marital behaviors: the man settling in with the newspaper while the woman, represented as the attractive Blondie, performs various physical feats on command. This interpretation of the sensual actions coupled with the courtship texts of jump rope may explain the feminist discouragement of traditional girls' play and the reported decline of jump rope in favor of organized, supervised competitive sports associated with male team play such as soccer, softball, and basketball in twenty-first-century America. Granted, not everyone will see the praxis of jump rope this way, but my point is that although there is ethnographic evidence of the adaptive function of jump rope for girls to divine the future, the feminist perception of the action of jumping rope as confining and essentializing girls has fostered a negative attitude toward the texts and actions of traditional activity. If not displaced, jump rope in the hands of adults has been reorganized to turn its cooperative spirit into aggressive competitive sport in the form of fancy double-Dutch tournaments and aerobic contests. Nonetheless, traditional jump-rope play can still be readily observed among girls on the street and in the playground, indicating its persistent sociopsychological as well as physical appeal.

Whereas jump-rope verse deals mostly with courtship as a sign of girls' flowering, jokes told by prepubescent boys treat menstruation as a deflowering, implying the girl's transformation into something more powerful than the boy. Asking the question, "What's grosser than gross?" the boys' jokes treat menses with a combination of jealousy and disgust, for it represents a visible sign of differentiation in the two genders' development at the end of middle childhood. It is viewed as a source of both power and weakness, and the lore acts to direct its place for the male who is uncertain about his own maturation. Examples of answers blurted out to the question include "two vampires fighting over a bloody tampon," "drinking a glass of tomato juice and finding a bloody tampon at the bottom," or "finishing a bottle of ketchup and finding a tampon" (Bronner 1985b, 39). Related to this cycle are elephant jokes in which the huge, powerful animal is feminized:

What do elephants use for tampons? Sheep.
How do you know when your pet elephant is having her period? There's a quarter on the dresser and your mattress is missing.

The tampon in folklore has become symbolic of ritual dirt that connotes taboo. Folklorist Lydia Fish (1972), for example, reports the modern persistence of beliefs among adolescents that the touch of a menstruating woman spoils milk, meat, and pickles or can kill plants and cause illness in baby animals. The menstruating woman, according to slang, is said to be "on the rag," "falling off the roof," "having the curse," or "getting a visit from Aunt Flo from Red Bank." The tampon is grosser than gross at one level because its bloody image is a tangible reminder of imbalance and danger, but on another level, it causes anxiety, particularly in males, because of its suggestion of female empowerment. The tampon is related to the new freedom proclaimed by the women's movement since the late twentieth century. Indeed, a well-known sanitary napkin product is called "New Freedom." The grosser than gross jokes told by prepubescent males suggest that this freedom involves a ritual violation. One joke asks, "What do you do when Kotex catches on fire?" Answer: "Throw it on the floor and tampon it." This raises the image of bra burnings, whereas the earlier example of the elephant using a sheep for a tampon suggests social power. In contrast is the joking question, "Why don't midgets wear tampons?" Answer: "They trip over the string" (Bronner 1985b, 39). Here, the midget is a symbol for the prepubescent child.

The elephant joke is often traced to the 1960s, when it was thought to be an embodiment of the civil rights struggle because the elephant is conspicuous yet somehow invisible or mistreated (Abrahams and Dundes 1969). Tellers of the feminized elephant cycle represent the elephant as powerful yet awkward with its strength, and sometimes vulnerable because of the need to menstruate. An example showing the novel ascendancy of the woman is, "Where is an elephant's sex organ?" Answer: "In her foot; if she steps on you, you're screwed!" Yet in at least one joke, collected from an eleven-year-old boy in Harrisburg, Pennsylvania, the male remains the standard by which women are judged: "How do you shoot blue and pink elephants?" Answer: "You shoot the blue one with a blue elephant gun. For the pink one, you hold its nose until it turns blue and then you shoot it with the blue elephant gun." The color blue symbolizes the standardization of the man's world. The pink—that is, feminine—elephant has to become blue and masculine to participate.

Boys in a feminist world are made aware, through education, of women's political rise at the same time they are recognizing girls' rapid physical development (i.e., the growth of breasts). In addition, there is the belief that girls mature faster than boys. Through humor, boys who are insecure about their own maturation turn a developmental milestone for girls into a source of embarrassment and weakness. The underlying opposition in the cycle of big and small, powerful and weak, becomes important in the boys' answer to what's grosser than gross?— namely, "When a short man walks up to a tall lady and says, 'Gee your hair smells terrific.'" The "little man" one-upping (and "topping," I might add) the woman through a faux pas also occurs in a related joke: "What did the blind man say when he passed the fish market?" Answer: "Good morning, ladies!" Such comical situations are violations of the social order because they depend on an understanding of a socially or- dained code of manners that comes with human development. When the man innocently shows "bad" manners, he reveals the woman as a sexual object and also strikes a blow at her special fear of odor or discharge.

The character of the vampire, feminized by the boys' humor into

the image of a menstruating woman, projects a male fear of the contaminated woman as a bloodthirsty, revengeful predator associated
with aggressive biting. At the same time, in the popular imagination,
menses marks a coming-of-age both physically and sexually, which
may contribute to the vampire image's transference into an attribute
of feminine kissing or maternal sucking. The image suggests an ambivalence in its representation of the vampire as simultaneously powerful and vulnerable, dangerous and seductive, repulsive and attractive
(Dundes 2002). There is evidence that the conspicuous "biting" in
boys' preadolescent characterization of the vampire may be related to
a maternal fear of separation during middle childhood. One source
of the perception may be rhymes used by mothers. In a play group I
observed in Harrisburg, Pennsylvania, several mothers liked to chant
to their toddler sons:

> I see your peenie
> It's very teenie,
> You better hide it,
> Before I bite it.

The rhyme was affectionately rendered, suggesting attraction, but it
could also create castration anxiety at an infantile stage when fantasies
are understood literally. Cognitively, children at that stage are aware
of biting as an aggressive act resulting in penetration of the skin, as
children may resort to biting during fights with siblings. Suggestive of
castration anxiety for boys and domination or seduction by the mother, the rhyme linguistically presents children with a structural model
for their own folkloric constructions in taunts and in jump-rope and
counting-out rhymes, but I noticed that the particular text was not
incorporated into their expressive profile. From the mothers' viewpoint, it was meant to be part of gender awareness in the transition
from infant to toddler, centering on the boy's awareness of his penis
and its relative size. It was an early instance of having the child make
a cognitive separation between private and public parts of the body.
In the toddler stage, mothers want their children to cover up their
"privates."

   I heard a variant of the biting rhyme from the mothers of girls that
associated females with anality rather than the vagina:

I see your hiney,
It's very shiny,
You better hide it,
Before I bite it.

There was no similar rhyme for the vagina, suggesting a taboo or, as some psychologists have argued, an inferior status or inequality associated with girls that manifests at around age five, when gender differentiation is reinforced for girls and castration anxiety is commonly expressed by boys (Carroll 1987).

A narrative that offers some evidence of the castration threat from the mother and repression of the vagina in folkloric fantasy came to me from a seven-year-old boy, who said the story was frequently repeated among his fellow second graders:

> There was this little boy and he was peeing out the window. When his mother saw him she said, "Johnny, if you do that again I'm going to cut it off." Not too much later, his mother caught him again, peeing out the window. And she said again, "Now Johnny, I mean it. If I catch you doing that again, I'm going to cut it off." Again it happened. His mother said, "All right, it wouldn't be too bad of an idea. The little girl across the street had hers cut off and it looks rather nice, neatly folded under." (Bronner 1988a, 137)

Among middle childhood storytellers, "Little Johnny" is the symbol of the foul-mouthed, rebellious child who knows more about sex than his teachers, siblings, and parents would like. The name Johnny represents the diminutive of the standard British and American everyman character of John. It is worth speculating whether "Little Johnny" has a thematic if not a historical relation to "Little John" from the Robin Hood legends. "Little John" and "Little Johnny" both suggest an impudent character in the shadow of a larger hero (metaphorically, a parent or an authoritarian adult) who draws attention to himself within a group by being feisty, outspoken, or impetuous and represents a potential challenge to the leader's authority over the group. I collected a number of "Little Johnny" jokes, which I found to be the most frequently given narratives among middle childhood youths, and they often concerned power relationships with older siblings or teachers, with Johnny acting as a naïve and transgressive trickster. Rather than turning the tables on authority with his wits, he often triumphs with his gall.

Another exemplary narrative with reference to gender development and subordinate impudence is the story of Johnny's counterpart, "Little Susie." She comes to Johnny because she is worried about getting her period for the first time, and when she shows him, he exclaims, "Damn, it looks like someone just ripped your balls off!" In a joke that reinforces male primacy, Johnny's mother gives him an anatomy lesson and points to her vagina, saying, "Johnny, this is where you came from." Johnny goes to school the next day and tells his friends how lucky he feels. When asked why, Johnny holds up two fingers an inch apart and says, "Because I came this close to being a turd." In the narrative, feminine anality is connected to an infantile anal stage of development characterized by fecal play. Related to this symbolism, for example, is the joke about Johnny seeing his older sister on a swing without underwear. She notices Johnny looking up her dress, spreads her legs, and asks him, "Johnny, what do you think of my wildcat (or hellcat—which is also the name of a CW series about sexy cheerleaders premiering in 2010)?" Johnny responds with an observation about the wildcat's meanness or repulsive appearance, and a puzzled Susie asks him why the wildcat is repelling. Johnny answers, "Because that pussy's got blood in one eye and shit in the other!" The compensation for the developing girl's sexual attractiveness in the boy's fantasy is the defiance of social norms about urination, as seen in the joke about Johnny peeing out the window. In a related narrative, a lifeguard warns Johnny about urinating in the pool. When Johnny protests that everyone pees in the pool, the lifeguard answers, "Sure they do. But not from the diving board!"

Convinced of social phallocentrism as middle childhood begins, boys respond with shock to the ascendancy of girls' power—both sexual and physical—as adolescence approaches. It may be argued that one compensation is for boys to turn a sign of feminine strength into weakness or to signify a duality of strength and weakness to seek comment on an appropriate reaction, denoted by the challenging question, "What's grosser than gross?" The frequent reference to biting and vampire symbols may trigger castration anxiety instilled by the mother, especially as preadolescent boys are experiencing guilt over separating from the maternal bond to establish their manhood. Both boys and girls commonly lose their pointed "canine teeth," also colloquially called "fangs," between ten and twelve years of age, and the incoming replacements first appear as sharp protrusions. When preadolescent subjects were shown pictures of children with their new teeth coming in, they thought the children looked like vampires. Children also mentioned the vampire in references to hickeys on the neck associated with early courtship behavior, saying they looked like a vampire's bite. Suggesting a phallic fear, girls commented on biting as a predatory male impulse, while boys imagined the bloodthirstiness of girls who looked like vampires.

Although Bram Stoker's literary Dracula presents the vampire as a male predator, he has feminized attributes, such as his affectation of regal refinement. Many makeovers of the seductive night figure in movies and fiction have made the idea of a she-demon appropriate, and folklorists have pointed out the ancient roots of a feminine succubus, sometimes connected nominally to "bad girls" Lili and Lulu (forms of Lilith), used in variations of jump-rope verses and bawdy verses (e.g., "Bang Bang Lulu") (Dundes 2002, 16–32; Bronner 1988a, 59; Roud 2011, 4835). In folklore, the childless, vengeful figure is significant in terms of male anxiety about inadequacy because, as part of her sexual dominance, she drains men of their semen. Many modern athletes report abstaining from sex before a competition, based on the belief that such activity with women will weaken them. In folklore, the actions of the "sucking woman" have a moral lesson: to punish men for their lewd thoughts and for not taking responsibility for family (in classical texts, she is also said to steal or harm children). Rather than being a sign of coming-of-age in succubus stories, boys' sexuality is presented as a sign of immaturity. According to folklorists, the Mexican La Llorona is a variant of the childless, fearsome Lili/Lulu/Lilith succubus, and it is commonly related in preadolescents' belief narratives in response to the social expectations that boys will be sexually promiscuous while girls will be chaste (Cantú 2002; Hawes 1968; Jones 1988; Kearney 1969; Kirtley 1960; Leddy 1948; Pérez 2002). In the Mexican context, girls are the more common tellers of La Llorona stories; boys' genre during the developmental stage is the Pepito joke about a diminutive sexual male trickster who bests his parents, teachers, and other adults, comparable to the precocious "Little Johnny" figure of Euro-American children's jokelore (Cantú 2005; Sullivan 1987).

In the cautionary tales told to children, the witch takes the form of a withered elderly figure, a stranger who hunts children and drains mother's milk and is to be avoided. This witch figure is usually part of the expressive profile in the infantile stage. In contrast, the preadolescent's vampire is more familiar in age and appearance. Blood defines the figure and gives it life, more so than other monstrous figures in children's expressive profile, which suggests a connection to the disgust associated with menses. An advancement beyond the authority figure of the bogeyman in the infantile stage, the preadolescent's vampire image may therefore be significant as a sign of the new masculinized woman in boys' lore. Whether the vampire is a feminized man or a masculinized woman, the point is that it has a betwixt and between quality—a coming out, if not a coming-of-age—that marks it as transitional, much as the preadolescent stage is demarcated as a threshold period.

The vampire's symbolic renewal through drinking blood suggests a transition or passage. The figure emerges after being dead, a process representative of leaving an old stage and entering a new one. Dundes, in fact, observes that the process enacts an infantile rejection of parents because the vampire is "debirthed" and then reborn with the projective symbolism of infantile sucking, or sustenance, from the maternal breast, followed by vicious, vengeful biting (Dundes 2002, 28). More so than other scary characters in children's expressive profile that appear grotesquely monstrous or ghoulishly old, the vampire is comely, even familiar, and in oral tradition it has the attribute of attacking its own family. This also figures into preadolescent anxieties about close siblings or cohorts separating from, and then turning on, the ones left behind. The evidence of the person's vampiric nature is found at home—at the dinner table in the ketchup bottle or the tomato juice—as if a profound, potentially dangerous change is being hidden from the family.

Although boys may notice hair growth and sexual arousal to mark their own maturity, they lack the sharp demarcation that menarche represents, at least in their minds. Indeed, an insecurity arises about one sign of maturity that boys are not supposed to show one another: sustaining an erection. In aggressive taunts such as "giving the finger" or "flipping the bird," with the middle finger outstretched in imitation of an erect penis, or grabbing the crotch and challenging the taunted feminized target to "bite me," "eat me," or "blow me," boys are investing emotional capital in the mature ability to hold an erection (see

Mechling 2005a). An age-related aggressive behavior that uses a play frame to draw attention to phallic vulnerability is what nine- and ten-year-old boys described to me as "popping" or "socking": one boy hits another in the groin lightly to show that the tap can be painful and to get a loud, defensive rise out of the victim as his friends laugh. One boy referred to the popping practice as more than delivering a shot in the groin; he indicated growing phallic awareness among his peers by saying, "If it sticks out, it's going to be a target." This genital play appears to show that even if a boy's physical development is not obvious, he is aware of the growing importance of his phallus, which the play frame teaches him to protect. Boys at this age are also comparing themselves in stature and power to their fathers. Because of their height, these boys are particularly aware of their fathers' midsections, and they report with great glee "getting away" with smacking their dads in the groin.

Dundes suggests that if the phallus becomes the primary symbol of manliness, separating the boys from the men, the unavoidably temporary nature of the erection translates into a need to repeatedly prove one's manhood. This is often accomplished in all-male combative contests that replace chasing games and in which the player gains ego by feminizing or emasculating an opponent again and again (Dundes 1997d, 41). The advantage of feminizing a male metaphorically rather than defeating a female in reality is that the risk of rejection and embarrassment is reduced. The player can view the activity as a male contest even though the consequences can be punitive, such as running defeated players through the mill or through the gauntlet and allowing triumphant players to hit the losers on the rump, or forcing them to assume a submissive, female, "asses up" position and having the winners throw balls at their buttocks. There may indeed be menarche envy at this time because the girl does not have to prove her femininity the way the boy has to prove his masculinity, and one expressive response is to construct fantasies in which the girl is contaminated and the boy is hypermasculine. In one example of a narrative about menstruation from a ten-year-old, the boy is able to have sex—indeed, he desires it as a sign of maturity—but the girl needs to wait for menarche:

> Once upon a time there was a boy and he was thirteen. He went to a girl and all of a sudden he said, "You wanna do it?" And she said, "No, I have my period." And he said, "I don't

believe you." And she says, "Okay, I'll show you." And she went to the store and she got some red paint and painted her panties red and he said, "Okay." And he asked a girl who was younger. And it was the same thing. And he asked a girl who was about eleven. And she said the same thing and she did the same thing. There was a girl who was ten, and he asked her and she said, "No I have my period." And he said, "I don't believe you, you're too young." And she said, "Okay, I'll show you." And she went to the same store that everyone else did. And she said, "You have any red paint?" And he said, "The only colors we have left are purple, yellow, and green." And the girl said, "I'll take green." And she painted her pants green. And the boy said, "That's not the color it's supposed to be." And she said, "Can I help it? Mine hasn't ripened yet." (Bronner 1988a, 139)

The implication in the narrative is that the boy is already mature; he is unemotionally and easily able to have an erection. But in a naturalistic metaphor, the girl must wait to "ripen."

Sexual undertones are apparent in sayings that associate aggressive behavior with manliness, such as "the bigger the hit, the bigger the man," or the claim that some feat of toughness will "separate the men from the boys." Some of this lore may be a direct response to the conventional wisdom expressed through American proverb tradition that boys are instinctually immature or do not "blossom" physically as girls do: "The only difference between men and boys is the size of their toys" and "Boys will be boys."

An example in which the binary between the erect penis and nature is vividly expressed is this coming-of-age joke told by an eleven-year-old boy who thought the punch line was hilarious because of the mention of "Peter"—slang for *penis*:

There was this boy that was born, and his mother and father didn't know what to name him, so they finally decided to name him the next commercial that came on TV, and the next commercial that came on was "Mountain Dew" so they named him Mountain Dew. And he kept *growing and growing* until he got to the first grade, and his first-grade teacher said that "If you give me something that rhymes with your name or a hint of

your name, then I'll guess your name and tell you where to sit."
And this little girl said, "A flower." And the teacher said, "Rose,
you sit there." And this little boy said, "Tiny." And the teacher
said, "Tim, you sit there." And then it finally came along to
Mountain Dew, and Mountain Dew said, "It'll tickle your in-
nards." And the teacher said, "Peter, you sit there." (Bronner
1988a, 135–36)

The teller constructs the adjective "tiny" in the infantile "Tiny Tim"
character with the implicitly large, sexually potent "Peter" of the boy
who is set apart from his first-grade cohort as precocious because he is
"growing and growing." Meanwhile, the girls are represented as pretty,
dainty, and innocent as flowers, a sharp contrast to the contaminated,
dangerous vampire image of the menstruating girl. Thus it is significant that the feminized vampire pattern separating the bloody, polluted
female from the male phallocentric sphere is coupled at the same developmental stage with the rise of jokes among boys about male genital
size and inadequacy. An example is the story a ten-year-old boy told me
about the man who went to see the doctor about crabs in his crotch.
The doctor tells him, "Those aren't crabs; those are fruit flies—your
banana died!" During this developmental stage, it is common to use
food and machinery symbols to safely distance the teller from the reality of the situation, while also relating to it through the anxieties presented (Zumwalt 1976).

An example of boys' lore about genital development that appears
during the later part of middle childhood and is then unceremoniously
discarded as childish is the "can I shower with you?" scenario. It shows
boys' insecurity about the manifestation of their sexual development
compared with girls' clear physical change. This example is from a
nine-year-old:

One day a boy said to his dad, "Can I take a shower with you?"
"Okay, but don't look down." So, of course he looked down
at his dad and he said, "What's that?" And his dad said, "My
snake." So then he went to his mom. So then he said to his
mom, "Can I take a shower with you?" And she said, "Yes, but
don't look up or down." So he looked up and said, "What's
that?" She said, "My headlights." And he looked down, and

said, "What's that?" She said, "My grass." So then that night the boy was scared of monsters and so he said, "Can I sleep with you, Mom and Dad?" And they said, "Okay, but don't go under the covers." So he went under the covers, and he said, "Mommy, Mommy, turn on your headlights, Daddy's snake is in your grass." (Bronner 1988a, 136).

Besides confirming the snake as a phallic image, the story is about boys' physical development. The boy in the story appears infantile because of his fear of "monsters" after noticing the difference between his parents' fully developed "privates" and his own. He shows the autonomy typical of middle childhood by disobeying all his parents' directives. He ends up embarrassing his parents, apparently warning his mother of the danger from his father's powerful "snake." In so doing, he arguably identifies with the father dominating the mother after comparing himself with both naked parents in the shower.

The presence of an expressive profile is evident from the collection of jokes that invariably present the central character as an inquisitive boy rather than a developing girl (Bronner 1988a, 136–37). Sometimes the psychosexual transition of the prepubescent boy in the narrative is shown by a move from the bath to the shower, and the adult-oriented shower is inhabited by the more fully formed woman. Although the teller of the following narrative is close to the age of puberty, he tells the story from the infantile perspective of a six-year-old to underscore the change from sexual innocence to cognizance:

There's this boy, he's about six years old. He goes in and he asks his father, "Can I take a bath with you?" He says, "Okay, but don't look down." He takes a bath with him and looks down, "Daddy, what's that?" "Oh, that's my submarine." And so, he says, "Mother, can I take a shower with you?" And she says, "Okay, but don't look up or down." And he looks up and down. First he looks up and he says, "Mother what are those?" She says, "Oh, those are my bombs." And so, he looks down and he says, "Mother, what's that?" "That's my tunnel." And then, he says, "Daddy, Mommy, can I sleep with you?" And they said, "Okay." And so, they were sleeping and the little boy's awake, and he says, "Mommy, Mommy, drop your bombs, Daddy's submarine is going into your tunnel!" (Bronner 1988a, 137)

A change occurs after the infantile need to seek security by sleeping with the parents, with the expectation that they will provide nurturing to the child. In the conclusion, the child realizes that the new parental model that comes with heightened awareness of physical development involves having sexual urges, with the father asserting dominance, somewhat to the chagrin of the mother-raised boy.

For the young girl, jump-rope rhymes are replete with the divination of courtship and sexuality as evidence of transformation. Whereas the chasing praxis in early childhood games resembles the relationship between authoritarian parents and increasingly independent children, in rhymes, boys chase girls in references to courtship, and fear of this pattern is often expressed. One of the most common rhymes that personalizes an avatar for the young, innocent girl is this: "I'm a little Dutch girl, as pretty as can be, And all the boys around the town, are chasing after me." Or, alternatively: "I am a pretty little Dutch girl. My home is far away. And when the boys start kissing me, I always run away" (Bronner 1988a, 59–60; Roud 2011, 12986). Indicating the symbolic significance of the bellyache as a reference to pregnancy (and the snake as a phallic symbol) is the reported coda to the little Dutch girl rhyme: "I heard my boyfriend call, and this is what I said to him. I love you very dearly, I love you most sincerely. So I jumped in a lake, to swallow a snake, and came out with a bellyache" (Bronner 1988a, 60).

Another reference connects the bellyache to the doctor in a motific slot: "I met my boyfriend at the candy store. He bought me ice cream, he bought me cake, he brought me home with a bellyache. Mamma, mamma, I feel sick. Call the doctor, quick, quick, quick. Doctor, doctor will I die? Count to five and you'll be alive. 1, 2, 3, 4, 5, I'm alive" (Bronner 1988a, 60). In a variant reported in North Carolina, the doctor is called because "Little Mary swallowed a stick" (Belden and Hudson 1952, 269; Roud 2011, 21048). Feeding as a prelude to courtship "up the stairs" is also vividly imagined in this jump-rope rhyme: "I fell in love with the grocery boy, and there I stayed all day. He gave me all his peaches. He gave me all his pears. He gave me fifty cents, and chased me up the stairs." The ambivalence of literally taking this upward step is indicated by the coda: "I ate up all the peaches. I ate up all the pears.

I held on tight to the fifty cents, and kicked him down the stairs." But if the girl enacting the rhyme is not empowered to kick the boy away, the fear of courtship is frequently projected into a situation in which a rising belly resulting from being fed in a penetrating way requires a doctor's care, much in the fashion of giving birth. Because this involves a visit to the hospital, the child might logically conclude that the mother could die. The rhyme has an optimistic ending, but the feeling of ambivalence about being "fed" by a boy's advances is evident. Besides the equation of feeding and marriage found in the ritual of smashing cake into one's spouse's mouth at a wedding, it is also found in a common coda added to many rhymes: "Shave and a haircut, two bits. Who you gonna marry, Tom Mix. What you gonna feed, buckbones. Who you gonna marry, Spike Jones" (Bronner 1988a, 60). If feeding suggests nurturing, then food's replacement with money represents ownership, and rhymes used by children in the latter part of middle childhood more vividly describe the bellyache or rising belly as a pregnancy image: "Three boys came my way. They gave me fifty cents to lay across the bench. They said it wouldn't hurt. They stuck it up my skirt. My mother was surprised to see my belly rise. My father was disgusted. My sister jumped for joy. It was a baby boy. My brother raised some shit. He had to babysit" (Bronner 1988a, 62).

Cinderella is not unique in terms of performing domestic chores as a sign of repression. Perhaps looking to an older sister as a preview of what the younger child will go through, a popular rhyme declares: "My mother gave me a nickel. My father gave me a dime. My sister gave me a lover boy, who loved me all the time. My mother took her nickel. My father took his dime. My sister took her lover boy, and gave me Frankenstein. He made me do the dishes. He made me mop the floor. I got so sick and tired of him, I kicked him out the door" (Bronner 1988a, 62). Just as girls relate to the character of Miss Susie, they also relate to Cinderella in this rhyme around puberty, when girls are becoming aware of their sexual potential or preparing for the onset of menses (Mechling 1986, 101). One sign that reinforces the image of the rising belly as pregnancy to be avoided is this rhyme: "Cinderella, dressed in yellow, went downtown to meet a fellow. On the way her girdle busted. How many people were disgusted?" (Dundes 1969b, 478). A symbolic equivalence is suggested between "upstairs" for the bedroom as a location for sex and "downtown," representing the fast life and vice of the city.

Reinforcing the relation of sexual development to the Cinderella rhyme is the observation of gestures accompanying it. The girls turn, stoop, and throw kisses between the ropes. The prevalence of rhymes with references to courtship and sexuality corresponds to the fact that girls experience puberty earlier than boys do, and it tends to cause them more profound emotional and physical changes. An example of a rhyme addressing early development is this: "Two years old, goin' on three—I wear my dress above the knee. I walk in the rain, I walk in the snow. And it's nobody's business, if I do have a beau." Others refer to sexual awakening at set times or on journeys from home to town: "Nine o'clock is striking. Mother, may I go out? All the boys are waiting, for me to take out" (Browne 1955, 17–18; Yoffie 1947, 33; Roud 2011, 12986); or "Cinderella dressed in yellow, went down town to buy an umbrella. On the way she met her beau, who took her to a five-cent show. When the lights were turned down low, how many kisses did he give her?" (Britt and Balcom 1941, 299–300; Browne 1955, 6; Roud 2011, 12986). Following this line of argument, one might read the "made a mistake and kissed a snake" line as a warning about the limits of courtship. Ed Cray collected this variant: "Cinderella dressed in yellow, went to the ball with a handsome fellow. The handsome fellow was dressed in blue. Poor Cinderella lost her shoe" (1970, 121). This reinforces the idea of the loss of something after a date. A similar rhyme was recorded earlier by Brian Sutton-Smith: "Cinderella at a ball, Cinderella had a fall. When she fell she lost her shoe, Cinderella, Y-O-U" (1959, 77). In light of the common association between the shoe and fertility symbolism in folklore—because of the satisfying fit of the protruding foot into the new, alluring shoe (sometimes referred to as "breaking in" the shoe)—the loss is arguably of virginity (Bettleheim 1976, 266–72; Dundes 1976, 1516–17; Freud 1963, 158).

Of significance to the contextual argument that children are more exposed to sex and violence than ever before by television and the Internet is an apparent change in the developmental association of Cinderella rhymes. Whereas folklorists of the mid-twentieth century found Cinderella in rhyme and game to be popular in the later part of middle childhood, I have observed her, along with the bellyache and snake symbolism, among children as young as five. Perhaps popular culture has had an influence because of the prevalent "princess" fantasy theme among girls this age in terms of room decoration, costumes, school supplies, and family vacations (Orenstein 2011). Part of that popular culture trope is the "dream" of the princess living happily ever after with the handsome prince in a magical castle of her own, apart from her family, and folklore may still serve to caution girls at play in a general way about the consequences of relationships, if not express anxiety over maturation and pregnancy. This pattern is also consistent with the lower age of participation in hide-and-seek, if the game is viewed as a signifier of children's independence from parents and an awareness of life outside the home.

I contend that with children's increasing independence, with the length of childhood expanding, and with puberty coming earlier in childhood, American children of the twenty-first century rely on cultural models for adjustment to the significant, if often overlooked, emotional, social, and physical changes associated with development in middle childhood. Folklore, with its ritual passages, symbolic tools of expression and persuasion, and lessons for social relations and roles, takes on an extraparental role. With change as the one constant of modern life, folklore provides a familiar, reassuring type of learning, a cultural register where children can anticipate the future and express concerns about the present. Modern American children want to declare their own identity, and lore is their protected expression of cultural connection to one another. Increasingly independent, American children fiercely hang on to their cultural property to express their distinct personality and social separation from other ages. Increasingly left to themselves, children use folklore to help them grow and cope.

6

Fading Tradition

On a Dying Language and Lore

Why would a group transplanted to a new place and concerned about preserving its traditions not pass down its lore to the next generation? That question troubled me because I had to account for a situation that broke with the prevalent presumption among professional observers of traditions, or ethnographers, that elders in a community seek to engage youth in a natural cycle. A preservationist appeal that typically resonates from ethnographic writing is that the senior bearers of traditional wisdom seek young apprentices to carry the torch of tradition into the future. After all, is not the power of tradition its ability to carry on the values and meaning of one's cultural life? Do not people gain a sense of immortality by knowing that they are part of an unbroken chain from the past to the future? This question especially concerned me, as an educator looking for continuities in language and lore over time, because my own mother was part of an immigrant cohort that, despite their pride in their language-based Yiddish culture and their efforts to enact it in everyday life, preferred that it die with them. Yet, as a son of Holocaust survivors, I was taught the importance of saving precious cultural roots to renew the tree of life.

Much of the speculation about the death of Yiddish and the culture revolving around it was assuredly triggered by the end of the millennium. With the beginning of the twenty-first century and its metaphor of a fresh start in sight, many linguistic pundits declared that moment to be a terminus for Yiddish in Jewish history. Benjamin Harshav's book *The Meaning of Yiddish* (1990), for example, closes with the headline-like chapter title "The End of a Language." His proclamation frames a tidy historical evolution from origins in medieval Europe to development in eastern Europe and transplantation in America. Following were various artistic revivals in twentieth-century America in response to modernization and, ultimately, demise under the weight of assimilation. This historical outline commonly has a social reference to "secular" Jews—or, more accurately, nonpietistic Jews—for whom Yiddish is a primary mark of identity, a form of ethnic and artistic expression outside of religion. In the United States, it has a more focused reference to the generation of immigrant Jews who came from eastern Europe between 1884 and 1924, particularly in the momentous "great wave" years of 1904 to 1914. A set of social associations with this Yiddish-speaking group arose: they were wage laborers, urban (especially in the Northeast, including New York, New Jersey, and Pennsylvania, which accounted for 86 percent of the foreign-born Jewish population between 1899 and 1910, with New York alone accounting for 64.2 percent), and artistic (through Yiddish films, novels, drama, and poetry). With the announcement of Yiddish as history, the implication is that assimilation to America among second- and third-generation Jews transformed Jewish culture and brought the language down. With this implication is the corollary that Jews' geographic horizon shifted from eastern Europe to Israel, along with a linguistic shift to Hebrew and "ethnic" expression within English.

One complication of charting a devolution of Yiddish in the late twentieth century is the contribution of Holocaust survivors from eastern Europe to a revitalized American Yiddish culture in the second half of the twentieth century. One indication is that the U.S. census between 1960 and 1970 recorded a 33 percent increase in the number of people claiming Yiddish as their mother tongue. In succeeding decades, the number dwindled. In the 1980 census, 315,953 persons acknowledged that they used Yiddish at home. That number dwindled by 157,000, or a drop of 50 percent, twenty-seven years later (Shin and Kominski 2010, 6). In 2007 Yiddish was seventeenth among languages other than English used at home in the United States—a sharp drop of eleven places from the 1980 census. Although the New York metropolitan area was still the leading center for Yiddish usage (76 percent of all Yiddish speakers), Miami and Los Angeles had concentrations as well (4 and 2 percent of all Yiddish speakers, respectively). Only a dozen of the fifty states had more than a thousand Yiddish speakers. A prominent symbol for the emblematic use of Yiddish among Holocaust survivors, and in fact for the movement from New York to Florida, was the public accolades from non-Yiddish speakers given to writer Isaac Bashevis Singer (he arrived in New York in 1935 and later moved to Miami), who composed and published work in Yiddish and had his fiction translated into English for a mass audience. Accepting the Nobel Prize for Literature in 1978, Singer admitted, "there are some who call Yiddish a dead language," but, he insisted, "Yiddish has not yet said its last word." Yiddish, he proclaimed, "has been revived in our time in a most remarkable, almost miraculous way. . . . In a figurative way, Yiddish is the wise and humble language of us all, the idiom of frightened and hopeful humanity" (Singer 1978, 9).

In addition to reminding the world of secular Yiddish themes, Singer incidentally pointed to his Hasidic religious roots deep in the soil of the Polish past. But in fact, Hasidism in America is a major factor in reevaluating the master narrative of Yiddish in Jewish history as the expression of "secular" immigrant Jews. The growth of "the pious ones" (the English translation of *Hasidim*), particularly in New York, began after World War II with the arrival of Holocaust survivors from Poland. Sociologists estimate that if their high birthrates continue, the Hasidim (who educate their children in Yiddish) are likely to double their population every decade (Mintz 1992). Given these trends, Sol Steinmetz, author of *Yiddish and English* (1986), remains hopeful for the continuance of Yiddish in America. He estimated a 20 percent rise of Hasidic children fluent in Yiddish to 26,000 (still a small portion of all Jews) by 2000. Although Steinmetz finds consolation in the "gratifying news to Yiddish speakers who, having listened to the doomsayers for years, have grown despondent over the fate of their language," he charts a devolutionary history of the language based on its social and artistic foundations in the great wave of immigration to America. He summarizes, "the language has undergone three stages in its 100-odd years of existence in the United States: it flourished during the 'golden age' of Yiddish, from the last two decades of the nineteenth century through the 1920s; it declined as the primary language down to the present, with a slow but continuous decline in the number of its speakers but with a marked renewal of interest in its preservation since the post–World War II period" (Steinmetz 1986, 28–29).

Set against the background of this common narrative of historical devolution, the progression from immigrant arrival to cultural assimilation may appear, deceptively, to follow natural laws. The diversity of Yiddish-speaking groups in the 100-year history under consideration, along with the processes and organizations by which Yiddish speakers have maintained community and, indeed, have constructed signs of resurgence, deserves closer inspection. I present one portion of the Yiddish-speaking world as a case study: Holocaust survivors from eastern Europe, who are concentrated in southern Florida and New York. I am attracted to them as a means of addressing the problem of the dissolution of traditions because their cultural history within the narrative of Yiddish in America is commonly underestimated and falls outside the master narrative of historical devolution. I have access to this group because I am a child of survivors who participated in Yiddish social organizations for the last forty years. My scholarly purpose is to question the mechanisms by which language is historically and culturally linked to society by the use of organizations called *vinkln*, or "corners," to give members a sense of cultural association outside of synagogues. My historical inquiry is into the continuities and links between these organizations and *landsmanschaften*, or "hometown associations," used by the "great wave" immigrants of an earlier generation to maintain traditions. The survivors have a word for the cultural flavor of this tradition; they call it *Yiddishkeit*, which roughly translates to "Jewishness," but its clear central image is a sense of belonging to an eastern European heritage imparted by speaking Yiddish.

Within American historical studies, more so than Jewish historical studies, it is not uncommon to find guides to communities as social systems that omit language. Irwin Sanders's classic *The Community* (1958) sets "place" as the primary determinant of community, followed by shared social characteristics, a communication network, and traditions and values. Its contribution to the discussion here is the recognition of a set of "intense social activities" representing "community life" as a behavioral category separate from the aggregate data of a group's demography. Robert Redfield's influential *The Little Community and Peasant Society and Culture* (1960) refers to community as a "settlement" with observable and distinctive characteristics, but he adds the psychological idea of a group's self-consciousness. In light of the diaspora experience, Jewish scholars have understandably been more sensitive to language used in everyday life as a crucial bond for a Redfieldian community within communities. In the report *Jewish Social Research in America*, published in 1949, editors Harry L. Lurie and Max Weinreich predicted a shift from a preoccupation with anti-Semitism and locating the global characteristics of the racialized "Jew" to an exploration of the diversity of Jewish community life and experience (154–71). Addressing the uncovering of the cultural and psychological formation of "Jewishness" in addition to or without Judaism, ethnographic and folklife techniques of forming cultural histories became more recognizable in later studies of individual identity and small-group dynamics (see Abrahams 1980; Bronner 1999; Kirshenblatt-Gimblett 1996a).

Moshe Becker and the Crisis of Tradition

Especially relevant here is Barbara Myerhoff's *Number Our Days* (1980), which examines organizational life at a Jewish senior center in California and confronts the role of age and gender among Yiddish speakers to examine the continuity of Jewish values. Myerhoff understands the importance of the leadership of emblematic figures in establishing continuity among an aging community. Although identifying herself as Jewish, she points curiously to the reverence accorded tradition by elderly speakers from eastern Europe as a formula for living in the present. In observing their contemporary behavior, she recognizes in her American Jewishness the historical development of a future orientation and a desire to integrate with mainstream society. In the organizational rituals she records in banquets and classes, she acknowledges the importance of bestowing honor and worth in the aging Jewish community linked to pre–World War II eastern Europe. She admits her inability to penetrate Yiddish in her study and relies on collecting life histories in English. Although her informants speak fluent English, she can hear that "Yiddish binds these diverse people together, the beloved *mama-loshen* of their childhood. It is Yiddish that is used for the most emotional discussions" (Myerhoff 1980, 5). Although aware of "poetry and discussion groups," she does not (or cannot) explore their significance in the expression of community and continuity by Yiddish speakers. Myerhoff's study has had a great scholarly impact (and rightly so) in encouraging the use of life history and cultural considerations of aging. However, she omits the pivotal roles of the emerging "culture clubs" in what she refers to as "Yiddish culture." As I argue, it is in these clubs that Yiddish culture is expressed and, indeed, ritualized.

Myerhoff is methodologically instructive in dealing with historical process as it unfolds, particularly by participants within the culture. The anthropological stance, she admits, is based on the outsider position, which allows one to record what insiders may not recognize as cultural or historical. This position may be limited, however, because it does not allow one to experience the culture and analyze the processes of change and stability. For Myerhoff, the "reflexive" position is one that takes "into account our role in our own productions" and results in the fusion of subject and object (1992, 307–40). In her questioning of her contemporary sense of ethnic integration against the graying of Old World Jewishness, the reflexive position became as much a part of her analysis as the ethnography of her senior citizens' center. In my observations—which became a study only when I began conducting interviews and recording events in south Florida, the Catskill Mountains region of New York, and central Pennsylvania from 1997 to 1999 and again a decade later from 2007 to 2010—I realized that I had become part of the historical narrative, for my "subjects" had questions for me, and for my generation, as representatives of the future that had sprung from their experience. More than Myerhoff, I use the codes of language I understand from my subjects to probe the past and analyze the break from it.

My historical evidence is compiled from documents of the Works Progress Administration (WPA) Yiddish Writers' Group and the International Association of Yiddish Clubs, in addition to oral histories of Holocaust survivors. To bring out "texts of difference" that could illuminate the significance of the central group meeting in *vinkln*, I examined the "World Wide Yiddish Community" of the Internet and comparable information on other American folk communities, such as the Pennsylvania Germans, with an integral tie between language and culture. My thesis to account for the turn toward cultural expression and the use of Yiddish to represent Jewishness, though often presented as a united revitalization movement, involves diverse forms of community—indeed, recovery of community—in response to American conditions and, to a large extent, a weakening of social structures and a sense of placelessness. My explanation of the paradoxical veneration of Yiddish as a symbolic center of ethnic identity and a denial of its future is based on immigrants' disjuncture between their investment in the new land as a fresh start and their connection to one another as a memory culture.

An emblematic figure in my study, comparable to Myerhoff's search for cultural leaders as the key to community, was Moshe Becker. Becker's death in 1999 at age ninety-two caused more than the usual sense of crisis among Yiddish speakers in south Florida. That he died toward the end of the century, when there was much talk about the passing of Yiddish culture, did not help the image of cultural continuity. Becker's regional association with south Florida is often represented in conversation as simply "Miami," even though it covers numerous communities outside that city, and it is probably the most concentrated area of Yiddish speakers in North America. The connection of Yiddish speakers to Becker and to one another is more than likely that they were Holocaust survivors; that they came to the United States from eastern Europe, especially Poland, after World War II; and that they did not affiliate with the ultra-Orthodox Jewish sects. Becker had a special position among these people, even if he lived in Miami for only a few months of the year.

Becker was the longtime editor of *Der Onheib* ("The Beginning"), reaching members of Yiddish "culture clubs" throughout Miami. The title denies the "end" of secular Yiddish culture predicted by many sociologists and even by Jewish leaders. By collecting poems, songs, essays, and art, Becker and his colleagues presented proof, they thought, of the vitality of the culture and their sense of community in Miami. The clubs and their cultural production provided *vinkln*, or private "corners" to congregate and imagine Yiddish as a total experience, even with the understanding that other corners of their lives existed in another cultural register. Polish-born Chaim Lewin, secretary of the Coordinating Committee of the Yiddish Culture Clubs in Miami, offered a stirring eulogy in *Der Onheib* and reflected on Becker's signification of the history of Yiddish from Poland to America. Becker's death was a harsh dose of reality, judging from Lewin's plain admission: "*Lomir zogn dem emes: undser gantzer 'minyon' bashteyt fun eltere mentschen*" ("Let me tell you the truth: our whole minyan is composed of old people") (1999, 2). His reference to minyan was a touch of irony coupling the community-forming mission of the secular culture clubs with the synagogues, equating Jewishness with Judaism. Thinking of the clubs

Becker tirelessly promoted, Lewin poignantly editorialized that Becker's passing was a reminder to all Yiddish speakers that not only their lives but also their culture would soon be gone forever. *"Farliren mir di gelegnheit oystzudricken undser meynung in der richtiker zeit,"* he wrote, and his choice of words must have penetrated those who read it, for the text refers to the loss of "the possibility of expressing our thoughts at the appropriate time" (1999, 2). Instead of calling for a new generation to take up the cause, he urged the old ones to bond as a group and to donate generously to its cultural mission. At once bemoaning and celebrating the exclusivity of the group's age cohort, Lewin equated that mission with constructing self-consciousness rather than building a future.

Shortly after Lewin's editorial appeared, another publication called attention to a far less intimate and more heterogeneous community than the one reached by *Der Onheib*. *Der Bay* (standing for "Bay Area Yiddish," the origin of the publication, but also signifying a Yiddish preposition meaning "at" or "near") has historically called attention to *Der Onheib's* successor, a "World Wide Yiddish Community" connected over the Internet. Emblazoned across the top of the publication was this headline: "Extra! Extra! Extra! Yiddish Survives the Millennium!" "Despite the vocalized nay-sayers of academia," American-born editor Philip Kutner proclaimed, "our beloved mame-loshn is thriving . . . Yiddish is alive and well!" One difference between Lewin's and Kutner's announcements was Lewin's reference to community as a face-to-face group linked by language, age, ancestry, and place—indeed, a community entered by birthright—and Kutner's reference to community as a faceless, placeless "network" joined by an online interest, regardless of ethnic or religious background. Kutner explained his optimism as follows: "One of the major reasons for the continued interest in Yiddish in outlying areas is the wonderful ability to communicate over the World Wide Web." He mentioned the discussion list of Mendele, serving 2,000 members worldwide; websites such as the "Virtual Shtetl"; and conferences of the International Association of Yiddish Clubs, which claimed more than 60 member organizations. A database he compiled extended the number of Yiddish organizations to more than 300 clubs, mostly in North America (Kutner 2000).

Der Bay's break with the past is in its placelessness. Although the members of Becker's world were Holocaust survivors, they shared with an earlier immigrant generation a reliance on hometown associations. A central issue in examining historical links between the hometown associations shared by Holocaust survivors and the "great wave" immigrants of the early twentieth century is the function of cultural activities in promoting *Yiddishkeit* as Jewishness. In 1938, the Yiddish Writers' Group of the Federal Writers' Project published a survey of Jewish *landsmanschaften*, or immigrant hometown associations, in New York. In American Jewish chronicles, many scholars cite these organizations as the main social agencies for immigrant Jewish communities prior to World War II. Although omitting any mention of culture clubs as one of the forms of Jewish immigrant organization, the survey asked more than 2,000 societies comprising 256,924 members, "Do you carry on cultural activities?" The result was almost evenly split, with 904 replying no and 898 answering yes. Among those that did schedule cultural activities, fraternal workers' orders, such as the Workmen's Circle or International Workers' Order, constituted the highest percentage. Overall, the *landsmanschaften* relied mainly on Yiddish as their lingua franca. The survey reported that 76 percent of all societies recorded their minutes in Yiddish, and the percentage for fraternal orders reached an overwhelming 96 percent. Yet the survey uncovered a language problem that the report called a "Babel of tongues" at society meetings. According to the report, the effects of assimilation could already be felt: "The old generation speaks a rich Yiddish interspersed with Hebrew phrases and Talmudic proverbs; the second generation delivers itself of a melange of Yiddish and English, and the new generation speaks a fluent English, using occasional Yiddish sayings the way the patriarchal grandfather interpolates Hebrew sayings" (Kliger 1992, 38). The point here is the decline of Yiddish as the binding language of Jewish immigrants with each successive generation, although it should be noted that the organizations were intergenerational. In fact, 15 percent of the members of hometown organizations were American born, as were almost half the members of family circles. The lowest percentages were posted by the fraternal workers' orders, whose members had a working-class association with the New York industries that drew the bulk of immigrants between 1900 and 1920. But even in 1938, the Yiddish Writers' Group complained that the Yiddish speakers in the *landsmanschaften* were graying quickly and that new, young recruits were lacking.

The rise of *landsmanschaften* in America led to a close competition, in their heyday in the early twentieth century, with an American Yiddish culture to describe secular cultural expressions of drama, film, poetry, music, humor, journalism, and literature in a language brought to America by eastern European immigrants, primarily a laboring class, and attached to certain locations such as New York, Miami, and Los Angeles (see Doroshkin 1969; Shepard and Levi 1982; Moore 1994). The symbolism of Yiddish was that it provided a social connection in terms of tradition and values that allowed one to have different identities at home, at leisure, and at work in response to pressures to Americanize. Yiddish could continue as an American language because it was supposedly an outlet of art and a reminder of home and family. This was the main argument for an unsuccessful effort to introduce Yiddish in New York City public schools. Subsequently, Yiddish community instruction became associated with the literary hero Sholem Aleichem in private schools named after him or in the progressive and populist sounding *folksschulen* (literally, the people's or folk schools). The social interpretation of Yiddish was particularly promoted by fraternal workers' orders, such as the Workmen's Circle, and by artistic agencies, such as the Yiddish Writers' Group.

The cultural concern for legitimacy among Yiddish-speaking Jews prior to World War II arose within "sub" or "little" eastern European communities inside the predominant community of western European Jews. Although Yiddish-speaking Jews were concentrated mainly in New York City, they subdivided into little communities represented by the regular meetings of *landsmanschaften* and family circles. By some estimates, there were as many as 10,000 hometown associations. By the 1930s, the WPA survey claimed, one out of every four Jews living in New York belonged to a hometown association. Ties of hometown ancestry and family lineage predominated as differentiating characteristics of Jewish identity, whereas the Yiddish language and Jewish religion were perceived as part of the superstructure of tradition. Yiddish was not yet distinctive or endangered enough to constitute the main trait of a folk group, and in fact, collections of American Jewish folklore in Yiddish as secular *Yiddishkeit* were hardly mobilized until the 1950s (Cahan 1952). Some early hometown associations, called *anshey* (from the Hebrew for "our people," as in fellowship), were in fact congregational groups that established their own synagogue buildings.

By the 1930s, however, the religious organizations declined and made up only a small portion (15 percent) of the total number of hometown associations. The largest number was represented by independent societies and ladies' auxiliaries (55 percent), followed by the fraternal orders (17.5 percent). The WPA survey also mentioned eighteen miscellaneous centers and clubs that were left undefined. Although some of these miscellaneous organizations were political action groups, others were likely the beginnings of cultural clubs that met in "neighborhood centers" (Kliger 1992, 30). Although the report recognized that the hometown associations were threatened by the lack of new, young members, it predicted the continuation of these organizations, albeit in different forms, for the purposes of self-help and "concern for the weak, the oppressed, and the needy" (Kliger 1992, 43).

An idea of the intense social activity of hometown associations can be gained from the minutes of their meetings. Meetings were typically held twice a month and concerned mainly social welfare issues related to residents in America—sick benefits, strike funds, and immigrant aid. A major point of discussion in many meetings was assistance to the hometowns, including contributing to children's schools, Talmud Torahs, and homes for the aged. The greatest obligation of members of hometown associations in America was attending funerals and providing plots and memorials in the organizations' burial grounds. References to cultural activities included "theater benefits," which involved renting theaters to sponsor musical performances to raise funds, and "souvenir journals," which were typically published in Yiddish and included songs, poems, and anecdotes written by members. Yet the organizing principle of these journals was to provide reminiscences of the hometown and news of its former residents in America. They also provided community news to complement the national and international coverage of several Yiddish daily newspapers and monthly literary magazines.

Landsmanschaften are still around, although they do not have the impact of the organizations described by the WPA report. Many Holocaust survivors from Poland revitalized hometown associations in America and used them mainly as burial societies. In many cases they were regionalized so that survivors from surrounding communities could more readily form a critical mass. In addition to providing plots and memorials for members, the organizations made contributions for the maintenance of Jewish cemeteries in eastern Europe and community memorials in Israel. The cultural functions of the theater benefits and journals, however, were channeled into the *vinkln*, which began to form in the 1970s. Some of the impetus for these groups was the loss of institutions devoted to Yiddish entertainment. Yiddish theaters closed, and mass-distribution Yiddish publications became scarcer. Therefore, privatized events at the community level became necessary if Yiddish entertainment was to be sustained. The children of Holocaust survivors were less likely to speak Yiddish, and many familiar public meeting places catering to Yiddish conversation, such as tea rooms and cafeterias, closed down.

The impetus to celebrate Yiddish was not immediate, however. My interviews with *vinkl* members revealed that retirement, and often relocation to Florida, triggered *more* social connections in Yiddish, rather than fewer, which had been predicted by many Jewish cultural scholars. Separated from their children and reconcentrated by age as well as ethnicity in their high-rise condominiums, they turned to one another and revitalized Yiddish in their daily social encounters. Less divided by their European hometowns than by their ethnic status within the Florida Jewish community as Yiddish-speaking, nonpietistic Jews and often Holocaust survivors, they used non-Orthodox dress and the Yiddish language as their main communal signifiers. A common motif in their oral explanations is that, during their working lives in the northeastern United States, they were more concerned with learning English, but after retiring to Florida, they returned to Yiddish and its symbolic provision of home and an intimate community. With Florida's emergence as a constructed location attracting elderly migrants, they often felt a reduction in the perceived conflict between Americanization and *Yiddishkeit*.

Language, Religion, and Holocaust

Yiddish is often referred to as a language without a nation, but for most of the *vinkl* members I interviewed, the language raises a mental map of Jewish eastern Europe with Poland at its center. This image frequently comes with self-doubt, since Yiddish connotes to interviewees the language of the Holocaust, an irrecoverable and undesirable past. Others express ambivalence about Yiddish because of its contemporary association with the Hasidim, whom many connect with Jewish passivity and communal control during the Holocaust. They commonly explain their fidelity to Yiddish by referring to its special expressiveness rather than to the fact that it was the language of their childhood. One way for nonpietistic Yiddish speakers to deal with these conflicts psychologically is to tout their membership in Zionist organizations. The organization mentioned most commonly is the Ben Gurion Culture Club. Founded in 1975 (with 1,000 members), the club is named for a Polish-born Zionist leader who emerged to lead Israel after World War II, at a time when Jews were reforming their lives. Although conversations at the club's dances and other events are conducted in Yiddish, the Miami-based club is devoted first to support for Hebraized Israel by Holocaust survivors and secondarily to the celebration of American holidays and the provision of charity. It also sponsors memorial meetings on Yom Hashoah, usually at the Miami Holocaust Memorial. The Yiddish component consists of songs of the ghettos and camps (see Flam 1992, 170–77). Thus, the Holocaust connections are kept separate from Yiddish as a form of cultural expression. In this American context, Yiddish is simultaneously placed in a future haven in Israel and in a future-oriented *kholem*, or "dream" land, of the United States, even while representing an organization referencing the Holocaust. Another way to separate the connection to an undesirable past is to maintain membership in a *landsmanschaft* so as to categorize loyalty to the hometown, or the death "benefit" of Jewish burial, separately from the vitality of Yiddish expression in America.

In Florida, many organizations for Yiddish speakers are known formally as *kultur klubs* ("culture clubs"), whereas the small theatrical meetings are informally referred to as *vinkln*. Yiddish speakers have other places to congregate for informal conversation, especially the Waterways Shopping Center, which is outdoors by the waterfront, but the understanding is that the *vinkln* are for theatrical cultural performances. One can also find notices in Jewish newspapers for a *leyenkrayz* for reading, *schraybkraz* for writing, or *schmoozkrayz* for conversation, but these groups take the form of community center seminars or therapeutic support groups rather than local organizations. The Yiddish language they speak and the structure of their meetings are indeed different from those the survivors—or *greena* (referencing "greenhorn"), as they refer to themselves—know. References to speaking, writing, or reading are signs that the membership comprises mostly children of immigrants who are recovering their Yiddish literacy rather than survivors and other immigrants participating in culture. One such group I witnessed in Harrisburg, Pennsylvania, during the 1980s was typical. Members were all over forty-five, and the sessions were preoccupied with readings of Yiddish literature or journalism and discussion of the passages' meanings. Led by American-born Abe Gottlieb, who had been educated in Yiddish by the Workmen's Circle, the group of ten to fifteen members met in his home. There was great concern for standards of Yiddish and the understanding of Yiddish terminology. After the "study" session, tea and sweets would be served, and the conversation returned to English. When Gottlieb tried to expand the meetings to include Holocaust survivors and recent Russian immigrants, the group unwound. The Holocaust survivors had little patience for the linguistic discussions and agitated for a cultural or conversational outlet centered on their Old World connections.

Rakhmiel Peltz's ethnography of a culture club in a Philadelphia neighborhood contextualizes the late-twentieth-century formation of Yiddish conversation groups: "Elderly Jews, preponderantly children of immigrants, have formed hundreds of Yiddish cultural clubs in a variety of institutional settings. Some are connected to synagogues, Jewish community centers, and residential centers for the elderly. Others take the form of adult education courses or informal meetings of friends. Since most Jewish communal institutions are not accustomed to offering any Yiddish-language activities, this new interest in Yiddish on the part of children of immigrants is perhaps the major shift in Jewish cultural programming in the United States in recent years" (1998, 191–92). This movement is interpreted as a recovery of "culturalism," a longing for the transmission of oral tradition from one generation to another as a sign of family continuity and social identity. Peltz's insight is that "the strong attachment to Yiddish language as a component of yiddishkeit is a sign of identification with an oral culture of the immigrant household. The fundamental transmitters of Jewish tradition are not the synagogue, the local federation of Jewish agencies, or Zionism and the state of Israel, but family members, who pass on the immigrant cultures of the kitchen, of holidays, and of Yiddish (1998, 193). For the Florida speakers who differentiated themselves in their *vinkln*, the association was less with family, with whom they felt a cultural break, and more with their lives as members of a minority culture and speakers of a minority language within a religious minority.

The function of the *vinkln* is more about proving vitality and according worth, especially among those who are elderly survivors and unlikely to transmit their *Yiddishkeit* to a younger generation. The play of youth, the depth of art, and the emotion of performance are more at work in the *vinkln*. In *vinkl* performances, participants partly relive teenage outings in a Yiddish world and recall the many social clubs that encouraged artistic expression as social pride, as well as signs of struggle. The *vinkln* are arguably not about nostalgia because of the intentional referencing of contemporary life and the surrounding American environment. But they are used as the characteristics of settlement rather than as defining traits of identity. The *vinkln* offer immersion in *Yiddishkeit* without reference to the Holocaust or to Europe, for that matter, and they therefore remind participants of a Yiddish cultural identity that cannot be displaced. To be sure, their *Yiddishkeit* is indirectly, and ironically, connected to Israel (albeit not to Israelis), but it is basically bound to wherever Yiddish speakers gather as a homogeneous group.

The *vinkln* are independent of Jewish institutions and emphasize the intimacy and spontaneity of a "neighborhood," even if it has to be carefully organized. In Miami, Florida, and in Monticello, New York, the organizer, or *forsitzer*, typically informs members, usually numbering less than a hundred, about weekly meetings by phone. By speaking directly to each potential participant, the *forsitzer* reinforces the orality and communal spirit of the event. It is "sort of like getting people to a *bris* [circumcision ceremony]," Chaim Lewin half joked to me, but his reference to a ritual gathering to proclaim continuity is significant.

Beforehand, the *forsitzer*, usually a man described as *kovedik* ("honorable") and *kluge* ("wise" or "smart"), invites individuals to read or sing at the meeting, and he arranges a program designed to last two hours. The performers are often the same from one meeting to another. The meeting places are typically the social halls of condominium buildings, where many Yiddish speakers reside in south Florida, or the "casinos" of bungalow colonies in the Catskill Mountains of New York during the summer. The "colonies" are differentiated by religious piety: the ultra-Orthodox have bounded intergenerational settlements, while the nonpietistic survivors have their own set of bungalows. There is little mixing between the two, even though the colonies are contiguous.

People come handsomely dressed to the *vinkln*, which are usually scheduled for the afternoon (so the elderly attendees do not have to drive at night), and they often arrive early to socialize before the event. The *forsitzer* calls the meeting to order, and several "officers" come to the front. It is not uncommon for the meeting to commence with the singing of the Israeli and U.S. national anthems. The organizer, typically seated in front of posters or props of Israel, opens the event with announcements of anniversaries, special visitors, publications, social events, and, rarely, members' deaths (however, one can count on hearing gossip among the audience about fellow members' illnesses and deaths from week to week). From start to finish, the proceedings are in Yiddish. Every performer is introduced, including where that person resides and where in eastern Europe he or she is from. Many members spend winters in Florida and summers in Monticello, and at the meetings in the Catskills, the organizer often states the *kultur klub* the person belongs to or other places the person has performed, such as the Ben Gurion Club. The performances may consist of a poetry reading, anecdotes by classic Yiddish authors, or original compositions.

The highlight of the afternoon is usually considered the singing portion of the program, which may be unaccompanied or, on occasion, include a pianist. Unlike the Orthodox synagogue setting, in which men preside at the bimah, both men and women perform. The songs usually come from the secular repertoire of the Yiddish theater or from the folk song tradition. Performers can expect a responsive crowd, and members of the audience regularly sing along from their seats. Rarely quiet, the audience is capable of expressing displeasure as well as approval. On one occasion, an orator read an excerpt from the Yiddish newspaper *Forverts*, and after the presentation had dragged on a while, several shouts of *tsu fil* ("too much") could be heard. Yet the crowd rarely carps about Yiddish pronunciation. Although the proceedings I attended were dominated by speakers of the Litvak dialect (usually from northeastern Poland and the Baltic area), nonstandard Galitzianer attendees (usually from southwestern Poland and the former Austria-Hungarian empire) spoke freely without comment. The programs are designed to end with a singing performance, usually by the person considered the best singer.

The structure of the event has parallels with the Jewish religious service. The *forsitzer* has a rabbinical character, and his male associates select individuals to play honored roles during the meeting. Being invited to sing or speak is one important way that honor is accorded; worth is also assigned to the organizational role. In the *vinkln*, as in Myerhoff's Jewish senior center, "men were invariably ceremonial leaders, and all the important leadership positions were held by men" (1980, 247). Women assert themselves through performance and do not hesitate to instruct the organizers about which direction the program should take. Women hold creative power and are venerated for producing an abundance of essays, stories, poems, and songs for the events. Again using the model of the Jewish service, portions of the program devoted to singing alternate with recitations, and the audience responds to the leader. Indeed, speakers may introduce their recitations of poems by classic authors with a reminder of the author's *Yohrzeit*, or ritual mourning on the anniversary of his or her death.

The fusion of literacy and orality in the performance of text is another connection to the Ashkenazic Jewish service, which the Yiddish speakers know well from their religious backgrounds. When performers "read" poems, especially by classic authors, they often have them committed to memory and may even break into a chant. Indeed, many audience members know the material but appreciate hearing the pieces performed, especially if it gives a member of the community time in the honored position of leader. Just as the Jewish service has prayers and passages that are performed by a cantor and often intoned by the audience, and just as being invited to "read" at the Torah accords honor, the "readings" at the *vinkl* are more like chanted recitations given a special status. The service reinforces bonds of community not only by common prayer but also by designating traditions to be regularly performed in front of the gathered group and by assigning special roles for those performances. The ample representation of poetry and song at the *vinkl* may reflect an orientation toward the Jewish service. Further, it is a sign of orality, since these forms invite community reenactment. The intersection of orality and literacy in the performance of text signifies the position of Yiddish as an orally transmitted and varied language with the literate aspirations of art. Week after week, the *vinkl* reenacts traditions designed to keep Yiddish speakers performing for one another in community.

The place for members of the *vinkl* to read alone is *Der Onheib*. It is published entirely in Yiddish, and it contains texts that remember the past. Largely replacing the "souvenir journals" of an earlier generation, the culture club magazines have little of the mutual aid content of the earlier format. They bring to the fore poems, songs, and anecdotes, signifying a cultural bridge between oral and literary traditions. As many as 100 entries are included in a typical 130-page issue, but essays rather than poems tend to predominate, in contrast to the content at a *vinkl* meeting. Each entry is short, and variety is stressed. The entries are easily absorbed, and an image of abundant vitality is conveyed through the quantity of production. Although original compositions are favored, it is not unusual for the editor to reprint poems and songs by classic Yiddish authors. Mention of the culture clubs in the Yiddish *Forverts* takes the form of announcements in the magazines. Since dues are usually not collected for the *vinkln*, donations are accepted in exchange for the magazines.

The *vinkl* events and their products mediate community by performing culture. When I began going to the *vinkl* at the behest of my mother, I could feel the suspicions of the organizers, for even though I was in my forties, in their eyes I was a *boychik*, a mere child. At the time, I thought it was shortsighted not to extend this performance to youths, but I began to realize that doing so would taint the total experience the members imagined. Surprisingly few of them felt guilty about not passing Yiddish on to their children. They thought of English or even Hebrew as preferable for their offspring, but they realized the social connection Yiddish gave them. Although they spoke English and lived in close proximity to Miami or Monticello, they needed to perform Yiddish to center their liminal identity. Their revitalized cultural use of Yiddish was a strategy of isolation to maintain the boundaries of their age, class, and ethnicity.

Few members of the *vinkln* I talked to participated in Yiddish groups on the Internet. The Internet Yiddish "community" does not carry the burden of a past that requires social interaction. Members of the Internet community admit to multiple, often separable identities (read as interests), rather than the overlapping identities surrounding the central feature of homegrown *Yiddishkeit* among members of the *vinkln*. The social functions of the *vinkln*, related to members' cultural identities, have come to dominate the mutual aid purposes of the *landsmanschaften*. Less connected to their hometowns yet still linked to a foreign culture, even within their Jewish identity, the Yiddish speakers have organized a ritual performance of the expression of their thoughts. More economically individualized yet more reliant socially, they think of Yiddish as a way to reveal themselves to one another. Yiddish is their object. For the Internet community, Yiddish is a subject, a classical language, that does not require "settlement."

The position of Yiddish as representing a class of people beyond borders is distinctive in America. Yet Yiddish invites comparison with other folk communities for which language serves a function of age and settlement. Perhaps paralleling the development and revival of Yiddish is Pennsylvania Dutch (a dialect emerging from *Plattdeutsch*, or low German, of the Rhenish palatinate), a language that identifies a group living in America since the late seventeenth century. In the wake of twentieth-century modernization, elderly Pennsylvania Germans responded in the 1930s with *Versommlinge* (gatherings of dialect speakers, along with entertainment) and "groundhog lodges" to provide immersive performances of culture that symbolized older forms of community (Kemp 1944; Wieand 1984; Yoder 2003, 65–84). Although the lodges are typically larger than the intimate *vinkln*, observers can witness religious tension between the "church people" (primarily Protestant denominations of Lutherans and the United Church of Christ) and the pietistic Amish, for whom the dialect thrives through the continuation of "culturalism." Among Pennsylvania German descendants, there is much optimistic talk of "revival," especially given the public displays that draw tourists to artistic emblems of folk culture and the dramatic spread and growth of the Dutch-speaking Amish (Louden 2008). The Yiddish-speaking communities of Florida and the Catskills have probably reconstructed the face-to-face community more successfully than the Pennsylvania Germans have, but they have resisted more effectively the tourist's gaze on their anachronism.

The Use of Legend as Cultural Strategy

The Yiddish speakers do not foresee a future for their language in the American setting, and they have a hard time envisioning *vinkln* as encounters of tradition with younger generations for the purpose of creating continuity. They underscore this view by using the *vinkln* to enact lore that tightly frames the communication of Yiddish in the experience of the Holocaust. In the custom of serving tea and cakes after *vinkl* meetings, legends are frequently told that on the one hand recall the past and on the other hand question its significance to life today. Consider one such narrative frame I recorded in 1993 that was used by speakers to discuss the bridge between their tradition and the present: A group of Yiddish speakers had gathered in the dining room of Holocaust survivor Ed Dunietz in Harrisburg, Pennsylvania, after a formal *vinkl* program of readings in the living room. Dunietz had placed a tantalizing array of pastries, fruit, tea, and coffee on the table, and the move to the dining room signaled the start of informal conversation among the members. Everyone in attendance, except for me, had been born before World War II. Several had been in concentration camps or had escaped to Russia from Poland during the war. Leo Mantelmacher, who was born in Poland but had not been back since the liberation, pressed Ed to describe his trip there the month before. Ed, born not far from Cracow, had been hidden for much of the war. "Did you go to Kazimierz?" Leo asked. The question implied the specialness of this section of Cracow as a Jewish place. Ed nodded and described what seemed to him an astounding development—Jewish tourism in downtrodden Kazimierz. A museum had been made from the old synagogue, and there was a restaurant that featured Jewish and Russian entertainment. His tone softened when he talked about the Remu synagogue. The name Remu (or Remah) was familiar to all of Ed's listeners, referring to renowned Talmudist rabbi Moses Isserles (born in Cracow in 1525 or 1530; died in 1572). In 1553 the Remu built a small synagogue in Kazimierz to memorialize his wife, who had died in 1552 at the tender age of twenty. A cemetery lies beside the synagogue, and its major attraction is the grave of the Remu himself. Before World War II it was a pilgrimage site for Jews from every part of Poland, who visited the grave of the wonder-working rabbi on the holiday of Lag b'Omer. Although the holiday is officially the thirty-third day of the counting of the Omer (the period from the second day of Passover until the holiday of Shavuoth), it is known colloquially as a "scholar's festival" by Talmudic students and is marked by merrymaking, including the lighting of bonfires (Zerubavel 1995, 96–113). The holiday coincides with the anniversary of the Remu's death, and pilgrims to his grave leave written wishes there. "It's still there? The Nazis didn't destroy it?" Leo asked incredulously.

"That's right," Ed replied. He knew that many of his listeners could recount stories of the destruction of synagogues, cemeteries, and ye-shivas in their hometowns in Poland, so he felt the need to explain the survival of this structure revered by Jews. "I'll tell you what people say," he said in Yiddish. "The Nazis went to burn the shul by the Remu's grave [the stone is situated next to one wall]. But the sparks blew back, they got scared and left it alone."

"Dos iz a mayse" ("that is a story"), Leo said dismissively. By *mayse*, he meant an intentionally false narrative. "No, that's what the people there say," Ed repeated in his defense. "A legend," someone else in-terjected in English. *"Nischt emes"* ("not true"), Leo blurted out. Leo was irritated because the discussion had deviated from the hard facts and numbers of the Jewish catastrophe. Ed turned from the issue of whether it was true and tried to impress on Leo the importance of be-lief. "If you were there," Ed challenged, "you would feel it was a magi-cal place." Then a lively argument ensued about the ruthlessness of the Nazis, with Leo taking the position that they would have destroyed the structure, and anything Jewish, if they had wanted to. Others were not so sure. Or else they did not want to discount a host of legends about the magical powers of wonder-working rabbis in Poland. "Maybe it is a *mayse*," Ed finally offered, and he emphasized in Yiddish, *"Die geschichte bringt mir a sach wichtigkeit . . . bedaitung"* ("the narrative has impor-tance, meaning, for me"). His choice of *geschichte* implied a matter of immediacy, a matter Ed referred to as *richtig epes* ("something real or meaningful").

It was not the first time I had heard the story told as a *geschichte* ("narrative") and witnessed the argument that followed. In Los Angeles that same year, I attended the regular Sunday brunch hosted by Henry and Lola Bornstein, my uncle and aunt, for Yiddish-speaking Jews from Oświęcim (known during the war as Auschwitz), Poland. The conver-sation drifted, as it had many times before, to wartime Poland. My aunt sighed when she said to me, "No matter how we start off—the weather, taxes, traffic—the talk always comes back to the Holocaust. We're still trying to figure out how Auschwitz happened to Oświęcim." At one brunch, my aunt recounted her experience in Cracow after leaving the smaller town of Oświęcim during the 1930s. She was asked, "Was Ka-zimierz *frum* [religious] then?" She acknowledged the Hasidic presence and recalled the pilgrimages to the Remu grave. "The Nazis cleared out the old quarter," she said, and some of her family members had been caught in Cracow. Her husband, Henry, piped in that it was "incomprehensible" that the Remu synagogue survived. "You know why it remained?" he asked in his typical cue that a narrative was coming. "I tell you. It was said that if the stone was touched then your family would mysteriously die or disappear. So the Nazis were scared."

"You know, I heard that too," Nathan Littner replied. "But I thought the Nazis tried to burn it, but the fire flew back at them." One guest at the brunch was a Yiddish speaker from Romania; he emphasized the importance placed on burning the synagogue among the Nazis in his town, and he found it strange that they would spare the Remu structure. This led to an excited conversation about the Nazi destruction of Jewish sites in Poland. Some attributed the Nazis' actions to senseless cruelty, while others saw a method in their madness. Accentuating the devilish traits of the Nazis, Nathan remarked that they were "superstitious, into occult," and could have been scared by the curse.

When I made a query about the legend over the Internet, I received a note from Jonah Bookstein, living in Cracow. He recalled that a Jew in the city had explained to him that the Nazis were aware of a curse on vandals of the grave: "When the first Nazi refused [to vandalize the grave] because he was scared (he had been told by a Jew the power of the Rabbi), a second Nazi stepped up. He swung at the matzevah [Hebrew for "gravestone"] with a sledgehammer which bounced off the stone and hit him in the head. He was killed instantly" (Bookstein 1995). The significance of the story is the local awareness that stones around the Remu's grave were destroyed, and the cemetery was in disarray after the war. Historian Earl Vinecour has commented, in fact, that "*miraculously*, the only tombstone to survive the war totally unimpaired was that of Rabbi Moses Isserles" (1977, 22; emphasis added). Part of the miraculousness of the grave, besides its towering size, its position right next to the eastern wall of the synagogue, and its elaborate inscription, is the boastful Hebrew phrase connecting the Remu with Moses himself: "From Moshe until Moshe, there was none like Moshe. May his soul be bound in the bond of eternal life."

My Internet query also produced an incredulous reply, similar to Leo's at the *vinkl*. In his message to me, Bernard Sussman of Washington, D.C., underscored his displeasure upon hearing the legend. He drew my attention to the work going on at the concentration camps in the region. "It is very probable that all the energies and facilities of the German troops in the area were devoted to the extermination camps, with nothing left over for pointless gestures such as desecrating a cemetery that Jews couldn't see anymore." What especially bothered him was the supernatural motif of the story: "This 'legend' about a Remu Stone supports the sympathetic notion of those poor ignorant, sentimental Nazis, so easily frightened by ghost stories, like little children; can't really hold them responsible for the Holocaust. That's why I am very unsympathetic to such 'legends'" (Sussman 1995a). He could not explain, however, why the Remu's stone survived when the rest of the cemetery was in disarray. He believed the stone's survival stemmed "partly from its superior construction and partly from the veneration of the spot which may have been known (if imperfectly) among local Christian Poles" (Sussman 1995b).

The only published account of the "protection from the Nazis" narrative is by Moshe Weiss, a Bobover rabbi who grew up in Oświęcim: "Legend has it that the Nazis spared the Remu Synagogue after being told that it was a holy place inhabited by the spirit of a holy man, and should they attempt to burn it down, they would fail in their mission" (Weiss 1994, 38). Weiss offers the narrative to emphasize the spiritual importance of the Remu, and he recounts other legends about the great wonder-working rabbi. One includes a commentary on German destructiveness: "There is also another story about a wedding celebrated on Ulica Sheroka near the Remu Synagogue until late one Friday afternoon. The rabbi implored the guests to end the festivities lest they violate the Sabbath. When the guests went heedlessly on their merrymaking, the rabbi placed a curse on them. According to one account, they all died; another version has it that they were swallowed alive. In any case, after the Sabbath a fence was installed around the entire area. This fence remained standing until the Germans invaded Krakow and destroyed it" (Weiss 1994, 38).

This last narrative was also given by a Polish Catholic tour guide when I visited the site, but she did not relate the story of the Remu grave. The "wedding cemetery" story also appears in the memoirs of Jacob Seifter in the Oświęcim Jewish memorial book (1977, 355–61). Seifter emphasizes the magical quality (what he calls *epes tsoiberhaftes*) of places such as the Remu synagogue for Jews in that area (see Bronner 1996b). For many survivors from the region, Kazimierz symbolizes old Jewish Poland, and the Remu synagogue is its spiritual center.

The Remu grave story, as far as I can determine, was told largely by Jewish survivors of the Holocaust from western Galicia, which includes Oświęcim and Cracow. It is not a story that their children have inherited.

Use of the story raises several questions about the emergence and function of such narratives among Jews removed from their former homes and dealing with the memory of the Holocaust. In terms of the imaginative response to issues of desecration, one can locate magical motifs in the narrative (Thompson 1955–1958, Q556 Curse as punishment, Q558.14 Mysterious death for desecration of holy places, D1299.2 Magic sepulchre). A specific context affecting the interpretation of the Remu grave belief-legend in the *vinkl* scene I observed is the shared concern for the continuity of a language and a culture removed from their original setting. The debate among speakers at the table, representing a memory culture versus historicity, raised the issue of whether Yiddish culture has any relevance in a new American setting.

The Remu grave belief-legend can create controversy when it is told because of public sensitivity about relating the hard facts of the Holocaust. As my experience shows, there may even be attempts to suppress the telling of the story. But as Ed Dunietz said, the story is important for survivors to relate because of the *bedaitung*, the "meaning," it conveys. In the manner of legend, it connects consequences to actions in real-life places considered to be mysterious zones. It is not a ghost story, although it suggests a protective spirit. This is significant, given the common discourse among Holocaust survivors about the role of God in combating evil. Leo Mantelmacher's denial of supernatural motifs is part of his bitterness at orthodoxy for promising divine intervention; for Bernard Sussman, it represents resistance to the characterization of Nazis as blameless Germans. For the tellers I heard relate the story, the point is to find vindication, because justice can never be served. By presenting the legend as an explanation of how the grave survived, they are questioning how they miraculously survived. By not stating directly that a ghost or divine intervention was involved, the legend invites contemplation of and commentary on the persistence of Jewish lives and traditions. Again, without directly including the details of Nazi crimes against humanity, the narrative questions whether murder and destruction will go unpunished. The saint figure symbolizes the power of righteousness taught in Judaism, which seems ineffective against weapons. Set in the cemetery, the story raises images of whole-sale death, and the key action of destroying a stone gains significance as the ultimate desecration.

The story may be heard in Freudian terms as a form of wish fulfill-ment through magic, but as legend, it questions whether fulfillment can be achieved. Frustrated that they cannot avenge the deaths of loved ones, tellers frequently relate variant punishments that affect the Nazis' families, just as the survivors' families have been disrupted by death. In some stories, there is a reciprocal relationship between the deed—hitting the stone—and the consequence—being hit—but more often, the justice rendered appears to go beyond the moment. A curse acts to affect generations afterward and move beyond the perpetrators to all their accomplices. Sparks and fire as punishment are particularly apt because of the connection between veneration of the Remu and the lighting of bonfires on Lag b'Omer, but even more so, they are signs of mass destruction in Holocaust iconography, such as synagogue burn-ings. Summoning fire is often considered a divine power and is gen-dered as a masculine strength in war (Thompson 1955–1958, Q552.13 Fire from heaven as punishment). The Remu grave belief-legend is ultimately a story of power and triumph for the vanquished. The in-troductory phrase "I heard it said," though, casts some doubt on the supernatural source of the action and invites commentary from listen-ers on historical vindication at one level and belief in divine protection at another.

If the Remu legend is a Holocaust narrative adapted from tradition-al Jewish themes of cemeteries and synagogues as magical sites, wishes fulfilled by saintly *tzaddikim*, and Poland as the storied "old country," more can be said in colonialist terms of the "vengeance from the grave" trope in the "curse of the pharaohs," also known as the "mummy's curse." It is connected to archaeologist Howard Carter's discovery of the tomb of Tutankhamen in the Egyptian Valley of the Kings in 1922. Probably influenced by the British nineteenth-century literary fascina-tion with mummies as scary bogeymen who exact revenge after be-ing unearthed by colonialist discoverers, the King Tut legend claims that team members connected with excavation of the tomb died under mysterious circumstances soon afterward (Stephens 2001). The theme was the basis for Hollywood films such as *The Mummy's Tomb* (1942), in which a mummy kills an archaeologist after a high priest has vowed revenge on the men who entered the tomb years before (Lant 1992, 104). Interest in the "curse" remained through several blockbuster King Tut exhibitions in the early twenty-first century, and the documentary *Curse of King Tut* (2006) aired on the History Channel.

No empirical evidence suggests that the mummy's curse legend popularized during the mid-twentieth century is a direct antecedent of the Remu legend. Nonetheless, its structural similarities suggest some symbolic equivalences between grave and tomb, saint and pharaoh, and ancient site and sacred space in the narratives. Especially notable is what Antonia Lant (1992) calls the twentieth-century "cult of the ruin" in mummy narratives, in which connections are found between contemporary and ancient civilizations, even though the moderns assume that the ancients are physically and culturally dead. In the movies, the curse often follows the archaeologists from Egypt to modern-day America; in *The Mummy's Tomb*, for instance, the mummy travels to the unlikely location of New England. The insult added to injury, or the life force given to the ancient mummy, is shown to be the use of modern tools such as electric lights and recording equipment. Following this line of inquiry, a subtext referred to by tellers in America can be discerned in the Remu legend concerning the continuity of medieval Polish *tzaddikim* and religious piety in modern life in a new place. Tellers seem to be asking: Are they, and the tradition they represent, to be left behind with the Holocaust? Or do they still have a place, even if they let us down? The reference to these elements, after all, is an esoteric knowledge that needs contextualization. The legend is not just about the Holocaust, then, but also about the disjuncture of Jewish tradition.

A remaining structuralist question is the symbolic equivalence of Nazis and archaeologists. Both are presented as violating sacred ground for irreligious reasons that are shown to be exploitative—anti-Semitism by the Nazis, and scientific inquiry by the archaeologists. Both are blinded by their obsessions and suffer personal tragedies for their more public triumphs. Both have a colonialist implication because they represent forces involving, in Edward Said's words, the "implanting of settlements on distant territory" (1993, 8); significantly, both represent orientalized groups, for Jews as Hebrews were referred to as "Orientals" in European literature (Said 1994; Kalmar and Penslar 2004). Yiddish speakers were also derided as backward *Ostjuden* (Eastern Jews), a reference to their primary location in eastern Europe. Both Jews and

Egyptians were racialized or "othered" as inferior by Western imperial powers. In the legends, their domination is shown by references to modernity, whether warfare or science, which allows the displacement of their Eastern roots. But the stories remind listeners of the fearsome spiritual force, and the often neglected wisdom, in those ancient or traditional societies.

I am not discounting the impact of the Nazi dramatis personae as genocidal evil in the Remu legend, and whereas the archaeologists may have good intentions, they are shown to be exploitative by venturing where they have no place. Arguably, different psychological processes are at work. In the Remu legend, as I have discussed, wish fulfillment for vindication is coupled with guilt about survival; the storyteller's vantage point is that of the minority. In the mummy's curse, guilt is also apparent, but the raconteur is a member of the colonialist majority and is worried about the consequences of tampering with spiritual forces and ancient tradition that his or her own culture has denied. This may explain why, in the popularized King Tut legend, the othered mummy is a monster instead of being a wonder-working saint in the expression of the collective self.

The Remu legend also deserves consideration as a statement, or a question, of Poland's position in Jewish sacred space. The holy places of Israel are venerated as pilgrimage sites, and for Polish Holocaust survivors, stories of the Remu invite commentary on the significance of their religious legacy in eastern Europe. The old age of many synagogues and the representation of generations in cemeteries are reminders of Jewish persistence in the Polish landscape, but not necessarily in Jewish memory. Kazimierz is a fitting legendary context for Holocaust survivors, however, because of one unusual feature: it has two synagogues that date back to the sixteenth century or earlier. Although the Polish government's official guidebook notes that "the 15th century synagogue in Cracow, one of the oldest in Poland, miraculously escaped destruction," it was Remu's later one that gave rise to legend, probably because of the renown of the Remu himself. A guidebook by Polish historian Michał Rożek observes: "Moses Isserles is regarded by Jews as a miracle-worker. They come to his grave on pilgrimages from all over the world and leave notes with requests round the matzevah. Nowadays, [a] special metal box for the requests has been put on the grave. Rabbi Remuh's intercession eases suffering and hardship of everyday life and the belief in his might works wonders" (1990, 71).

Polish Jews indicate the special roles of synagogues and cemeteries in religious ritual as centers of spiritual activity, and in narrative as belief centers of the activity of spirits. They are related because spirits from the cemetery often gather in synagogues as "spirit congregations," according to frequently collected legends from eastern Europe (Seifter 1977, 355–61; Sherman 1992, 76–77; Trachtenberg 1979, 62; Weinreich 1988, 348). Jacob Hennenberg in Cleveland related to me in 1995 the following narrative of a spirit congregation:

> I remember hearing a legend as a youth about the Great Synagogue of Oswiecim. It was told that there were ghosts inside. Going home from *cheder* [religious school] I had to pass the Great Synagogue, and I became scared sometimes when it was an especially dark night. According to the legend, when someone passed the synagogue, the ghosts could call you to the Torah and you had to go in. The whole city knew the legend that one time this happened and some people walked by at night, and the doors of the Great Synagogue opened. The lights went on and the people were ordered to go in backwards and to say the "Brucha" [blessing] and walk out the same way.

Like other tellers, Hennenberg distances himself from the belief by using the rhetoric "it was told," although he indicates that he was affected in the Polish setting by being "scared." The story expresses for him the power of faith in the Polish Jewish social structure that was disrupted in the new setting of America.

Joshua Trachtenberg devotes a full chapter in his classic study *Jewish Magic and Superstition* to the "spirits of the dead," most of whom, according to tradition, dwell in synagogues and cemeteries. Whereas the Jewish cemetery is an unclean place, as indicated by the ritual cleansing of one's hands upon leaving the grounds, and a place apart from life, as shown by the traditional absence of flowers and plant growth, it may also be a site for magical beseeching. Trachtenberg points out the custom of visiting deceased relatives and scholars to request their intercession to avert evil on earth. Indeed, the Remu grave site is a place where people leave written notes with prayers and wishes (*kvitl*). Cemeteries,

Trachtenberg observes, are places to visit on certain occasions so "that the dead may beseech mercy on our behalf" (1979, 64–65). Befitting the power of spirits of the dead, grave inscriptions in Ashkenazic tradition became elaborate and, in the case of renowned scholars and tzaddikim, their graves became shrines. Dov Noy identifies the perception of the meaningfulness of the grave in Jewish culture with the Talmudic motif of "Return from dead to punish disturber of grave" (1954, E235.6).

That the spirits did not provide protection or return to punish Nazi destroyers of graves and synagogues is one of the running commentaries that pepper many conversations among Jewish Holocaust survivors. The Remu legend may have sparked the arguments I recounted here because it features magical intervention through Jewish spirituality, whereas many survivors report feeling disenchanted with religious faith. If survivors often contest the supernatural content of narratives about the Holocaust, they are nonetheless drawn to the often personalized stories about lost communities and notable figures. There is a sense, in their reminiscences, that their communities lie outside of history, especially in relation to the settings of the concentration camps; therefore, in memorial books and oral gatherings, they use narrative to signify their experience. Reflecting on her collections of narratives from Holocaust survivors, for example, folklorist Haya Bar-Itzhak writes, "the survivors' sense of commitment to their dead and their community produces a sense of obligation to tell their stories and that of the community, which includes the story of its synagogue" (2001, 155). She gives as an example a narrative collected in Israel that recalls the glory of the Jewish synagogue on the Polish landscape and laments its destruction:

> The ancient synagogue in our town was built more than 900 years ago. They built it over a period of several years but were unable to finish it. Suddenly a Jew appeared from far away. No one knew who he was or where he had come from. He pledged to the community leaders that he would complete the synagogue. When the construction was complete the man abruptly disappeared. The next day the congregation found all the money the community council had paid him for his work in a corner of the synagogue. People said he was none other than King David, may his merit defend us and all Israel, who built

this splendid synagogue, for it was impossible that normal flesh and blood, a *gevayntlikher mensch* [common man], could build such a glorious holy place. I myself cannot believe that I ever merited to see with my own eyes this remarkable and magnificent synagogue, which had all the hues and colors of the sun and the moon and the rainbow. And when I remember and call to mind the Great Synagogue, the ancient synagogue in our town, which was destroyed by the Germans, may their name be blotted out, then my eyes shed tears because the enemy has overcome; my sighs are many and my heart is sick. (Bar-Itzhak 2001, 155–56)

Although the teller is removed from the place of the synagogue, it is important to narrate the structure to give, in Bar-Itzhak's words, "a spiritual and theological seal of approval to the community's presence in Poland" (2001, 156). King David as a dramatis persona is ancestral; he is the greatest king and hero of Israel and is aggressively powerful. The Remu legend also provides an ancestral reference to somewhere the narrators have been, and it assures listeners that even if Jews are now most visible on the Polish landscape as graves, they are still protected from opponents. Bar-Itzhak contextualizes the telling of miraculous events in a post-Holocaust setting, far removed from Poland, as narrative efforts to tell about survivors' self and community with the themes she identifies as "destruction, eulogy, and lament" (2001, 156).

Yet when I heard the Remu stories told, they offered less separation from the past than the stories Bar-Itzhak summarizes as "destruction, eulogy, and lament." The Remu narratives certainly refer to the destruction of the Holocaust and the separation of pre- and post-Holocaust experience. They also offer a parable of Jewish persistence. And whereas Bar-Itzhak heard in her tellers' performances an editorializing about Jewish revival in *Eretz Yisrael* (the "land of Israel"), I understood from the commentaries on the Remu story a connection to the diaspora. I heard the Remu narrative most often from Yiddish speakers who still felt some sense of connection, culturally and religiously, to their Polish Jewish past. The locations and characters in the story were significant, for they represented in the speakers' minds the oldest Jewish section with the most ancient synagogues and the most revered religious figures. Yet it was not uncommon for listeners to counter these stories with narratives that echoed Bar-Itzhak's theme of final destruction from which one can never return. Folklore thus acquires *wichtigkeit*, or "weighty importance," because it is a strategy of memorializing the dead and at the same time commenting on the new cultural milieu of the living. Arguments over its content are often about whether closure can be achieved, whether Poland can be left behind or whether it still holds significance as a Jewish place to which tellers feel compelled to relate.

The attachment of the post-Holocaust narrative to the Remu is not incidental. He has attracted a host of legends set in the pre-Holocaust period, and the location of his synagogue and grave in the vicinity of the most notorious region of the Holocaust—Auschwitz and Plaszow—adds to his post-Holocaust significance. That his synagogue was built as a memorial to his wife, who died prematurely, is significant for its relation to Holocaust victims who died prematurely. Offering Hasidic tales of the Holocaust, Yaffa Eliach writes, "As I walk down the streets of Cracow I feel as if I am stepping on the dead. Each cobblestone is a skull, a Jewish face. Cracow's violated synagogues are habitations of ghosts. Cracow, the first Jewish settlement on Polish soil, the center of Jewish creativity, of law and Hasidic lore, is now a town with virtually no living Jews. Only a handful remain here, more dead than the clouds above Auschwitz and neighboring Plaszow" (1988, 210). Within pre-Holocaust legendry, the Remu, as a religious figure who studied Kabbalah and commented on magical powers, added to his mystique and the perception of his power (Shulman 1991). Although he could be critical of unlettered people who engaged in mystical speculation, the Remu wrote on the roots of magical arts from God and nature and observed that material things can be endowed with occult virtues and powers (Trachtenberg 1979, 20–21; Unterman 1991, 101–2). One can still hear the numerological commentary that the Remu lived thirty-three years, wrote thirty-three books, and died on the thirty-third day of the Omer, and the rabbis who eulogized him listed thirty-three merits (Weiss 1994, 101–2). Beyond the Remu's association with magic, he was also the codifier, sometimes called the "Maimonides of Polish Jewry," and was known for his commentaries on the customs of Ashkenazic Jews. He thus represented the carrying on of life as a Jew in Poland.

The Remu and his grave occupied a special place because of his stature as a tzaddik, or miracle-working rabbi. The renowned Yiddish folklorist Y. L. Cahan collected a legend in Poland concerning a poor man who asked to buy a plot near the Remu's grave because of its magical association. The caretaker took the man's money but buried him in a different plot, far from the Remu. The dead man's ghost appeared in the caretaker's dreams and disturbed him. After consulting with a rabbi, the caretaker honored his promise and reburied the man near the Remu. Mysteriously, the grave of the buried man collapsed in on itself (Cahan 1938, 152–53; see also Weinreich 1988, 338).

The Remu's saintly role is significant, according to Bar-Itzhak, because whereas "the divinity . . . is an amorphous force in Judaism, the saint serves as a means of religious identification for the members of the community who are unable to identify with the divine force or can do so only through the saintly mediator" (1990, 207). Thus the poor man in Cahan's story seeks a place near the Remu. Frequently, a key feature of such legends about Jewish miracle-working rabbis is the saint as a hero who offers passive but profound resistance to persecution. The saintly hero uses spiritual or intellectual power to act for a people who are apparently powerless to combat violent attack themselves. There can be a range of legendary explanations of resistance, from Rabbi Akiva Ben-Yosef's martyrdom, which inspired an insurrection against the Romans, to Yemenite Rabbi Shalom Shabazi's turning from his plowing to destroy the governor's palace. In the latter narrative, which Bar-Itzhak uses as an example of the Jewish saint's legend, "The governor, who was secretly plotting to deal unjustly with the Jews, saw the great power of Shabazi and recanted, and abandoned the wicked plot he had intended to carry out (1990, 209).

The Remu story combines reference to the saintly intervener with the pre-Holocaust legend of place. Like many pre-Holocaust narratives of synagogues connected to the place legend, it brings out the "uniqueness, beauty, and sanctity" of community and its religious center (Bar-Itzhak 2001, 134). It also locates a shadowy, extrareligious realm of belief connected to life in Poland. It offers an experience of a specific location. But in its post-Holocaust context, the story relies on a memory of place and the realization of a community's destruction. Its reference to the Nazis is not unique or final, being only one of many parables of Jewish persistence in the face of persecutors from the Romans to the Crusaders. It is a contested narrative, however, when the Holocaust is offered as a historical finality that marks the rise of a new

Jewish identity. Its countering version is as much a narrative of explanation as the Remu story is. The *bedaitung* in both cases comes from the struggle of memory. Not meant to be passed on to youth, the Remu story is told in conversation among elderly Yiddish speakers to record a connection to spiritual resistance, if not continuity with a younger generation.

Tradition as Beginning and End

In the intimate communities represented by *vinkln*, crises such as Moshe Becker's death can seriously unnerve a community and threaten its historical continuity, especially when it is structured so locally. One cultural response was to make Becker a hero to inspire maintenance of the *vinkln* as a total experience. *Der Onheib* was, in fact, filled with poems as well as eulogies for Becker. Because he turned their aging *vinkln* into secular youth organizations with a religious function and structure, much of the rhetoric regarded him as *undser lehrer Moshe*, "our teacher Moses" (Applebaum 1999). Psychologically, the elderly *vinkl* members became students who need to carry on the mission. Although socially weakened, the community has used cultural expression and its ritual organization to sustain its members. Reflexively, it promises itself that other men of letters will follow, and culture will be produced as a sign of new life, even if the products come primarily from the past.

Myerhoff describes Jacob, one of the men at the Jewish senior center she studied, as someone who became "a symbol perfected in death." This description can also be applied to the Miami Yiddish community's response to Becker's passing. Myerhoff recognizes Jacob as an organizer, a man of letters who was identified with *Yiddishkeit* and success. She writes, he "was not only a symbol of and force for continuity, but also he was to Center members a symbol of the possibilities of aging well. Extreme age had not cost Jacob clarity of mind, determination of purpose, or passion in life" (1980, 206). A poignant ethnographic moment was provided when Jacob died shortly after speaking at a public banquet in front of gathered center members. Myerhoff makes a great deal of the symbolism of Jacob "willing" his own death. Beyond the growth of his legend as a result of an event interpreted as mystical, Jacob held a post that was apparently crucial to the fragile Yiddish community. She interprets his "organizer" role as providing continuity, at least a version of continuity that connects life in eastern Europe to Jewish tradition in America, but more of the conflicts between little and great communities can be realized in the context of *vinkln*.

From *landsmanschaften* to *vinkln*, a process is evident from hometown association to community signifier. The organizer of a *vinkl* has a leadership role in the community that, unlike a religious role, can entail social bonding without a future. As *redaktor*, or "editor," Moshe Becker exaggerated the social power of Yiddish by his use of the printed word, but he did not encourage Yiddish linguistic practice or cultural performance based on it by a new generation. Becker and his comrades were gratified that Jewish heritage would continue, even if Yiddish traditions did not. For Becker's contemporaries, poems, folk songs, and stories expressed in the social frame of the *vinkln* provided an emotional base to the memory culture and constituted a set of signs of their past that could be remembered only in Yiddish. The American future in their minds, however, did not mesh with Yiddish. Their children would know the lessons of the Holocaust, but they would not inherit the Yiddish culture associated with it. In Miami and Monticello, Chaim Lewin, now in his nineties, continues Becker's work of organizing *vinkln* and editing *Der Onheib* for the dwindling number of Yiddish-speaking survivors. He dispenses honor and accumulates worth as if he were in a shtetl synagogue, but he does not invite younger members in America to join his group or broadcast its traditions beyond his circle. He stands by the idea that the "beginning" he edits marks an end.

7

Personalizing Tradition

On Storytelling by an African American Father and Son

Eugene Powell answered my knock on his rickety door with little emotion. He had not known I was coming just then, but he confidently said to me, "I've been expecting you. Come on in and sit." The row of black faces assembled in his parlor looked suspiciously at us. Eugene felt their stares and offered, "He's here to learn about me!" With that, the men broke into quips and smirks. Once Eugene had vouched for me, they relaxed, and as happened so often that summer, Eugene stepped forward from the crowd. I heard one man remark, "Yeah, he should figure you out, 'cause you sure are different, Red." That elicited laughter. A quiet man in a corner interjected, "Talk to him, Red; you're a talker when you get rolling with them stories!"

Why tell stories? The question seems basic, but we have far more inventories of tales than explanations of why they are told. Venerated for being passed down from generation to generation, folk narratives recorded in collections rarely if ever account for what one generation does with the previous one's legacy or how the narratives become part of individual tellers' personality profiles. *Collection*, the common scholarly term for the data of oral tradition, implies the gathering of stories as static objects that can be accumulated. Collectors typically offer stories as representations of the whole society; narratives are seen as common knowledge rather than a source for the psychological response of a few. One reason for this bias is the intellectual construction that telling stories is instinctual—that is, people tell tales because they have to, and they rely on an accessible storehouse of information. If this is the case, then it is not crucial to show the special circumstances in which story-telling is needed or the people for whom it is necessary. It may even lead to the false universalist conclusion that a limited number of plots exist, and tellers adapt them to the culture of which they are a part. To show that folklore is an expanding, living force, instinctually minded scholars point out that everyone tells some form of story as plotted narration in the process of making conversation and relating events of the day—so much so that many people are unaware that being a storyteller is a distinctive part of being human (Nicolaisen 1990, 9–10). Stories thus appear to be diffused through a culture instead of being performed by ritual specialists on structured occasions.

In the vernacular, most people reserve the *storyteller* label for folks who draw attention to their stories or themselves. Often, the connotation of storytelling is the performance of a fictional set piece that listeners appreciate as a "good story." The question "Have you heard this one?" or the cue "I've got a good story to tell you" braces the listener for a narrative with a beginning, middle, and end. There is a sense that stories attach to certain places, situations, and people (and, as I argue in chapter 5, ages) more than others. As authorities on traditions, folklorists position stories, help identify when and how people break into stories, and often classify them by the group in which they are told. The narratives they collect might fall under ethnic, regional, occupational, or religious groups, but the social-interactional assumption is that the praxis we might call *storying* provides an esoteric consciousness that lends identity to those in the know.

Stories in the social-interactional view are a result of people coming together and a reason to get together. In this social frame, stories are appropriate to occasions and settings such as holidays, "sessions," or bars to comment on the group's tradition and to bond the people participating in that tradition to one another. If storytelling has a social function, that is not to say that the consequence of bonding explains storytelling in the sense of providing a cause for narrative behavior. As part of the understanding of function as purpose rather than as cause, though, stories serve the group's desire to define itself culturally, and they serve the needs of an occasion (Bascom 1954; Oring 1976). Life without stories would therefore be unimaginable. Folklorist W. F. H. Nicolaisen even asserts, "Without stories we could not survive; without stories we would be disoriented; without stories we would be lost;

without stories we lack assurance as to who we are or who we could be" (1990, 10).

The defensible philosophy that humans are fundamentally *Homo narrans* is undermined by a prevalent modernist notion that stories told in our presence are relics (Niles 1999). People think that electronic technology has displaced the passion of an orally performed narrative and that aesthetic modernization has encouraged folks to pass information dispassionately rather than giving an imaginative face-to-face telling. The traditionalist view is that wisdom and cultural literacy are embedded in narrative and hence play a central function in the maintenance of a society. In postmodern thinking, story has been unhinged from knowledge and construed as inconsequential, as "mere" entertainment, even though there is an etymological connection in the Latin root *historia* between story as tradition and knowledge and wisdom attributed to its imaginative teller (Nicolaisen 1990, 5–6; see also Bacchilega 1997, 19–25). Story can seem superfluous compared to tidbits of data scrolling across a screen in today's information society. Nonetheless, it is possible to cite many instances of narratives having a profound impact on modern public discourse (see Dégh 1994; Ellis 2000; Fine and Turner 2001; Goldstein 2004; Whatley and Henken 2000). In addition, psychologically minded folklorists give numerous examples of the way stories interpret experiences and provide socially sanctioned outlets for conflicts, anxieties, and ambiguities that are repressed in everyday conversation or the reporting of facts (Bronner 2007; Dundes 1987, 1997c; Mechling 2005a).

Stories in the vernacular, when told in face-to-face sessions, are loaded with words or images that people imagine would never get into print, being too titillating or obscene; therefore, they retain the role of something people heard or picked up somewhere. Being nonnormative, folk narrative's risky content gets to comment on the normal or restrained state of things in relation to the margins—socially and psychologically. *Storying* in fact suggests the play of imagination and evokes a psychological perspective as an expression of an idea, drawn from the root of both *history* and *story* in *id-* (to know) (Nicolaisen 1990, 6). This nominal root suggests *story* as a signifier for the projection of ideas in a verbal form that people recognize as separate from other types of discourse. If people express themselves in story, if narrative allows for fantasy as well as truthfulness that is not acceptable in normative conversation, then we should know its ideation. We should know those special people, whom John D. Niles calls "strong tradition-bearers," who work in story, as well as the process of storying, which varies by group and circumstance (1999, 173–93).

Even as folklorists aver that storytelling is a living tradition, a requisite artistry of life, they often fuel the antiquated status of lore by turning stories into measurable objects of the past for preservation as well as comparison. They give them titles, generic labels, and numbers in a literary museum that materializes stories as the dusty stuff of history (Dundes 1997b). Objectification and classification of oral material are not without intellectual benefit, but when captured as an expression of mind, stories flow rather than being pinned down. In trying to answer the question "why tell stories?" Nicolaisen agrees and points out the "lack of definitiveness" of story in oral tradition, in contrast to the formalism of art literature. A point that Nicolaisen makes—and one that I have tried to expand on—is that storytelling is significant for what he calls "creative risk-taking and fulfillment. Its audible actualization depends completely on the performer's skill and inclination to create a text that channels the story's potential into performer- and audience-friendly forms, made for the occasion. Like all expressive manifestations of folklore, it derives its very existence from the tension between repetition and variability" (1990, 7). To be sure, I, too, have engaged in the classificatory exercise to organize my aggregate data into units of analysis, but when I walked through Eugene's rickety door that summer day, I entered his private world very much of the present that I sought to explain. To know why he told stories, and maybe why others did, I needed to know him as a person. I had to comprehend his ideas as he projected them onto the fictive plane of tale. I needed to participate in those occasions that required storied practice.

An illiterate man, Eugene said he always had a head for remembering stories. One might surmise that he compensated for his inability to read and write by impressing others with his capacity for oral recitation. His knack for storytelling earned him accolades for his memory and creativity. There were racial differences, though, for he was more expressive among his black cronies than among whites, who typically had the role of superiors. He was well aware that his stories, which often contained pointed or subversive humor, had the potential to be offensive and might affect his hierarchical social relations. Eugene's primary source for his repertoire was his black cohorts on the plantation and roadhouses of his youth, more so than his unstable family. Being illiterate was not uncommon among African Americans of his generation in Mississippi, but that did not mean they all engaged in storytelling the way Eugene did. Among his primary social world of African American friends born in the early twentieth century, he welcomed the reputation of storyteller. It was a familiar scenario in African American lore of the plantation South. Evenings were spent on segregated front porches and in juke joints filled with humor intended to get a laugh and provide more than a hint of protest against white domination. In a world where few writers were employed to give their sentiments, the expressive oral "man of words," whether preacher or street talker, was accorded honor (Abrahams 1970, 1983). Women told stories too, but men were known as the talkers and jokers who drew an audience in public.

Around Eugene's house, I found that storytelling, usually in the form of jokes told by men, invited competition. As one joke led to another, a discourse formed in a register apart from the everyday. Men were prime characters in the guise of tricksters and heroes who mocked the master and the reverend, and they demonstrated sexual bravado, at least on the fictive plane of oral narration. In the play frame of story, these men, who in real life were repressed by whites and dominated by women, could shine. Eugene was at the center of attention in his living room and out on the street among his friends in their sixties. Eugene's son Ernest recognized and admired that quality in his father. He also wanted to be known as a good talker, and he tried to develop the talent of being ready with a joke or a rhyme whenever the occasion arose. Ernest wanted to be both like his father and not like his father, because in post–civil rights Mississippi, his father's stories seemed too country, too much of John and Ole Massa, too uncool.

To answer the question of why people tell stories, I began with a person. To get at the praxis of storying, I strove to comprehend the strategies underlying an individual's storytelling and to see what would happen when storytelling as perceived in this particular situation was adapted from father to son. It provides a perspective on what Nicolaisen offers as explanation: "We tell stories because, in order to cope with the present and to face the future, we have to create the past, both as time and space, through narrating it. If these stories are autobiographical in nature and sometimes if they are not, we create, in the process, the illusion of identity and of a continuous self by inventing ourselves in true stories of a past than never was" (1990, 10). Here, I focus especially on the praxis of coping and the personality of self between father and son to uncover the process of narration in time and place.

I was drawn to Eugene Powell because he had been a prominent bluesman of the Mississippi Delta (Bronner 1979b; Lomax 1993, 367–73). Another blues musician, Sam Chatmon of Hollandale, Mississippi, first told me about Eugene as a contrast to Chatmon's self-conscious development of a concert persona. He described Eugene as someone who was immersed in his community, personifying the blues ethos of "laughing to keep from crying." Chatmon had observed Eugene's cathartic use of lore and noted it was one reason Eugene could not leave his home situation. I knew of some blues recordings Eugene had made in 1936 for Bluebird Records, but he had been largely overlooked by the wave of enthusiasts who descended on the South during the 1960s seeking pre–World War II blues artists. One reason he was missed was that his recording name threw blues sleuths off the track; his records had been issued under the name Sonny Boy Nelson. Eugene knew that fellow bluesmen of the 1930s, like Chatmon, had toured college venues and festivals in the North during the 1970s, but he felt trepidation in following their path. He had been coaxed into performing at the Smithsonian's Festival of American Folklife in 1972 and reported feeling uncomfortable on stage in unfamiliar surroundings. After that brief experience in the spotlight, he stayed at home. When I arrived in Greenville, Mississippi, to spend time with him on his home turf, he was anxious to tell me what I wanted to know.

I expected that music would be the center of my documentation, but Eugene's neighbors told me to get his "stories," that is, his jokes, which were his claim to fame. It often came as news to them that before the war, Eugene had been a musician of note. "I didn't know he played guitar, but he sure can tell them stories," I would hear. Lounging in front of his house with his friends, I had the opportunity to watch and hear Eugene "tell 'em," and in quieter moments inside, when it was just the two of us, Eugene told me his favorites and reflected on his life.

After about two weeks, Eugene made a point of telling me, "If you want stories, you should get Little Man. He knows gangs of them. He thinks of all of them *all* the time."

"Little Man?" I asked.

Eugene and Ernest Powell outside Eugene's home in Greenville, Mississippi, 1978. (Photo by Simon Bronner)

"Yeah, he's my son," Eugene answered, "but he's in jail now."

Little Man, sometimes called just Man, is Ernest Powell, and he is hardly little. He is a large hulk of a man easily tipping the scale at over 300 pounds. Both father and son are known as exceptional joke tellers, and although bound by a family name, their styles are markedly different. Ernest learned some jokes from his father, but he picked up many more from friends at the bars he frequented.

After Ernest was released from jail in the summer of 1976, he came regularly to see his father and hang out with friends in front of the house. But tension often arose when both men were out in the front yard with friends and stories were called for. On one occasion, Ernest started a joke and Eugene piped in with alterations to the story during Ernest's narrating. Annoyed, Ernest turned sharply to his father and said, "You going to let me tell it? Let me tell it my way, huh? You get a chance with your old friends." Ernest's rebuke was meant to tell his father that, much as they both appreciated a good joke, age separated them, and to Ernest's thinking, Eugene was old-fashioned. Ernest had no desire to impress his father's friends, whom he connected to

Men gathered with Eugene for outdoor storytelling on a hot summer day in Greenville, Mississippi, 1978. (Photo by Simon Bronner)

Mississippi's Jim Crow past. He was fond of them as his cultural forebears, but he was also repulsed by what he thought of as their submissiveness and backwardness. Later, when the tapes of our conversations spun before me, I saw an opportunity to examine Eugene and his son as more than carriers of some abstracted African American tradition or community aesthetic. I could look at them as individuals in a historical moment who used narrative to project their personal styles and backgrounds—and their personalities.

Eugene Powell was born in 1908 in Utica, Mississippi, a small town southwest of Jackson. His father was white and his mother was half Native American and half black. Eugene was raised by a black stepfather, Sid Nelson, from whom he got his recording name Sonny Boy Nelson. Because of his light complexion, he was also dubbed "Red." As a young boy, Eugene moved with his family to a plantation in Lombardy, in the heart of the Delta region, where he learned to play the guitar and performed with his half brother Ben for black and white picnics and suppers. At Lombardy, the family suffered two serious misfortunes. Eugene lost an eye when a playmate accidentally hit him with an arrow shot from a bow, and Ben was killed mysteriously by gunfire. Violence was no stranger to Eugene Powell.

Eugene and his parents then moved to another plantation in the Delta, and he gave up schooling to toil on the land. Once he was grown, Eugene began sharecropping on his own and supplemented his meager income by playing music and selling home-brewed whiskey. Eugene was an entertainer. Besides being a deft musician, he also gladly told stories, especially when male friends gathered, and he could perform acrobatics with the guitar. Sam Chatmon referred to Eugene's antics as "clowning," and Lewis Buchanan, another fellow musician, remembered that Eugene liked to "steal the show." Eugene was hesitant about singing, but he cultivated a wealth of jokes and legends to impart. He went on to open a roadhouse where music, drinking, and bawdy storytelling were regular fare, along with occasional violence.

Eugene usually found singers to front his deft playing. One was Matilda Witherspoon from Hollandale. They played together in clubs and cafés around the lower Delta, and in September 1935 they married. Another music-making friend was Bo Chatmon, who recorded under the name Bo Carter and performed with his brothers as the popular Mississippi Sheiks. Bo arranged for Eugene and Matilda to come to New Orleans in 1936 for a recording session. Arriving at the studio sick, tired, and nervous, Eugene was dissatisfied with his performance and gave up any hope of having a recording career, so he returned to picking cotton and performing around the Delta. It was not until the 1960s that he discovered records from his 1936 session had been released.

Like many people in the rural South of the 1940s, he moved to nearby cities looking for better pay and opportunity. He had eight children to raise, including young Ernest, whom Eugene called a "worrisome child." Upon his return to Mississippi, Eugene found a job as a mechanic for a John Deere tractor outlet. In 1952 Eugene's wife left him for the bright lights of Chicago, and he fell into a depression. Eugene told me, "I was sick. I thought I was going to die." In his mind, he had failed in his marriage and in his responsibility to support his family.

Eugene went north to Decatur, Illinois, but quickly returned when he could not find a job. He settled back in Greenville and married again. Although most of Eugene's children journeyed north in the "great migration" from Mississippi to Chicago, Ernest stayed behind in Greenville. Eugene pushed aside his music. With rock and roll and rhythm and blues dominating the airwaves, country blues—like Eugene—was now old-fashioned in the eyes of the baby boom generation. Many of his old music-making buddies had moved north, but for those friends who remained, Eugene's house became a gathering place. A regular crowd came on weekends to sit under the shade tree, swap jokes, drink, and listen to Eugene.

Powell's life changed in the late 1960s when his second wife suffered a stroke that effectively paralyzed her. Eugene fed her, clothed her, and otherwise cared for her. For income, Eugene took to hiring out his truck to haul trash. While friends like Sam Chatmon were being "rediscovered" and traveling to college campuses to play the old music, Eugene stayed at home, barely noticed except by his local friends, who still liked to come by for stories and songs to pass the day.

On a hot June night I recorded one of these story and song sessions. I sat on the couch in the living room, while Eugene took up a chair in front of the window. George Hitt (GH), a friend of Eugene's from their days together at John Deere, came in, beer in tow. Eugene introduced him as a good joke teller, to which George answered, "Not like you, Red." George took up another chair in front of the window, and a neighbor came in and sat across from George and Eugene in a lounge chair. George and Eugene began talking about joke telling during their working days. "We're just hillbillies, I guess, Red," George said. George and Eugene traded jokes ridiculing preachers, women, and rubes. Their exchange then became more competitive. "OK now, you come on with one now," Eugene would say, daring George to top his joke. Finally, two jokes told by Eugene (EP) climaxed the evening.

> EP: Well, now, here we go again. This old preacher, he was fucking the deacon's wife. He went to work he did. Went over there that day, wanted to fuck. Well they caught the deacon broadcasting. He was broadcasting. Deacon's wife—the preacher went over there and old deacon breaking up his land over there. He was broadcasting it and sowing oats. His wife was sowing the oats. She out there sowing the oats, you know, and going on. He got there, he says [in a low-pitched voice], "Well, how you doing, Deac?" Deac says, "Oh doing pretty good, Reverend. How are you?" "Oh, I'm doing just fine." Says, "Uh huh." "Well," he says, "where you going, Deac?" Says, "Well, I'm going to run up to the store and get me a little chaw of tobacco. I'm going

to rush on back home." Said, "I'm going up there in a few minutes. You can wait, I'll go up there with you." Well, he didn't want him with him. He wanted to catch him absent where he could crank his wife. So all right. He went on up there and rushed up and got his tobacco. Come on back. Old Deac suspicious some. He said he was going up to get some tobacco in a few minutes. His wife had done got through sowing the oats so she went on to the house. It's real hot like it is today, you know. Going to the house. So old Deac, he stood around there in the woods a while. When mind told him, "You go to the house and get you some bricks and kill that old preacher." And so he went to the house and got some bricks. Stayed in old upstairs house. He went upstairs and hid himself up there. Preacher come back along. He wanted to know, said, "Where's old Deac?" Said, "I left him, he still down there. Trying to cover up those old oats I planted." Says, "I stop by, came by to see if I could get a little piece." *And she snatched up her dress right quick* [Eugene emphasizes the words, and he makes a gesture of pulling up a dress]. She said, "Whooo, I'm just as hot as I could be. Been out there sowing them oats all day." And says, "I'm just as hot as I could be. I hope every one of them seeds come up is thick as the hair on this."

GH: Oh my goodness.

EP: And the old preacher he hauled his great big dick out. He said, "Yes, I hope I can get this in right now so I can do some good." The old preacher said, "And I hope the stalk will be the size of this." That what the old preacher said. Old Deacon upstairs commence to putting them bricks 'side his head. He said, "God damn! I hope the seeds would be the size of these too." [Everyone laughs.]

GH: He putting the bricks on him.

EP: Yeah. He said, "I hope the seeds would be the size of these." [Everyone laughs.] Yeah.

GH: Oh Lord!

EP: All right, come on with your'n now.

GH: Oh Red, I got to think a while.

EP: Well, they say an old boy carried his wife uptown. She's a great big fat woman, you know. Carried her uptown and she got uptown, she wanted some grapes. "Why don't you call for what you want, I'll pay for it." So she got her some grapes and got about two pounds and a half, three. Went back home to eat them that night.

GH: Oh no!

EP: Kept on till she ate them all up. He kept to her, said, "Now wife, don't you eat all them grapes. They going to make you sick." "No they ain't either." She just kept eating them. So all right. He messed around. They went to bed that night and she taken sick over the bed that night. She messed around and twist around. She thought she was in the bed right. She had her head down to the floor [George laughs]. Messed around there. Every once in a while she said, "Foooo," fart you know. He said, "Wife, wake up and turn over. Your breath smell like shit!" [Everyone laughs.] So she didn't hear him because she was sleeping bad [George claps his hands]. Way after a while she said, "Fooo," she farted again. "All right, wife. I done told you to turn your head the other way." Said, "Your breath smelling just like shit. I'm tired of your smelling." So she laid on there. He said now she done it again. He said, "No I done asked you nice to turn. If you don't, I'm going to slap your goddamn eyes out!" [Everyone laughs.] After a while she said, "Fooo." He hauled off and slapped the hell out of them there. One of them grapes jumped out of her ass, hit him back there. Said, "Lord, I didn't mean to knock your eyes out!" Commence kissing in the ass. He said [makes a kissing sound], "Whooo, baby, you sure in bad shape because your jaws—you must be got the mumps." [Everyone laughs; George claps his hands and stomps his feet.] Must be got the mumps. He kissing them big fat jaws in her ass![1]

In the first story, the men laughed at a comic situation of infidelity among religious figures. Eugene used farming metaphors for sexual parts, relating the work of persons to social domination. The preacher represents an authority figure, who is humanized by having sexual urges and is then subverted by being exposed, literally and figuratively. The penis becomes a stalk; continuing the extended wordplay, the bricks used against the preacher are seeds. Because the seeds come from the earth, they symbolize the ordinary toilers of the land, whose power may not be as visible as the preacher's stalk. Discounting the psychological significance of the joke, folklorist D. K. Wilgus (1983) suggests that the story is an example of using folklore as a mirror of culture in which old rituals survive in narrative. He claims that the language derives from an agricultural ritual in which a man and his wife would wander through the fields and slap a part of their bodies to encourage the crop to grow to that body part's size or height. In a form of sympathetic magic, whereby a like action produces a like effect, human copulation results in fertile fields. Even if this belief has a historical basis, it does not explain Eugene's position in the structural binary between holy and profane that is projected in the story. Eugene used the story to comment on the fallibility of a religious authority that would degrade him.

How did Eugene's mind make the leap from the first story of infidelity to the second story about mistaking the anus for the mouth? Eugene explained that the symbol of the ejective seed is associated with the dirt of the earth, and the expelled grape comes from the "dirty" anal zone. "Both reminded me of some kind of shit," he cackled. There was a transition from a story that externalized a public ritual to a story of a more personal conflict. In the second story, the anus is mistaken for a mouth, grapes for eyes, and buttocks for jaws. For Eugene, the story seemed to make light of his experience with his wife, who was an invalid and had to be cared for—symbolized by being taken "uptown"; she was "sick" and not in control of her bodily functions. Eugene felt embarrassed about having to take her to the bathroom and help her like a child. The expression of that embarrassment in the story was outside of his awareness, yet it was consistent with the way he used humor to deal with awkward situations. Its relevance also came from his references to his wife's child-like needs, because of the Freudian association of the anal phase with the second stage of libidinal development, following an oral stage. The man in the joke mistakes his wife's anus for her mouth, and he thinks she has the mumps, which is commonly considered a childhood disease that causes soreness in the face. At first expressing aggressive desires by slapping her, the man concludes by "kissing . . . her ass," a sign of submission and feminization.

Evincing laughter, though, gave Eugene the satisfaction of knowing that his words had an effect. Joke telling helped raise his prestige and fulfilled a need for recognition. Eugene's self-esteem was generally

low because of the condition of his wife and their house and his me-
nial job as a trash hauler. He felt alienated from an unfamiliar world
of changing values. He was "old" and "country," whereas many of his
neighbors were young and had been raised in the city. For solace, he
savored compliments from his friends about his stories. He expressed
this need for recognition in a statement he made to me midway into
the summer. While we were talking about my coming to see him, he
said, "I wish more people around here would notice me." Although he
thought well of his narrative and musical skills, he did not feel useful,
and he felt confined by the demands of caring for his wife. One sign of
that outlook was a preponderance of scatological tales, such as the one
about the farting woman. The link is the repression and entrapment
symbolized in the retention of feces. As much as storying—"talking
shit," in his words—gave Eugene pleasure, suggestive of the gratification of anal ejection, the tales often seemed to convey a measure of
self-hatred. Eugene's jokes often ridiculed the naïveté of sheltered or
simpleminded country boys, and it was no secret that Eugene could not
read or write and hailed from the plantation.

When not rattling off his jokes to friends, Eugene Powell was
quiet. He was not known for chatter or loud outbursts. Jokes let him
say more about himself than he volunteered normally. He touched on
themes close to his experience. As a bluesman, he was on the other side
of religion, which was a matter of concern in the Delta because the
church held a powerful social position. Eugene mistrusted and resented
preachers, yet he felt guilty about his feelings and often regretted his
barbs. He talked of going back to the church, of having more respect
for church leaders, but he resented the way they used the image of
devil's work to condemn blues playing. He also thought of churchgoing
as a feminine activity, championed, for example, by his first wife, who
had turned to gospel music and evangelism.

Violence was a regular part of Eugene's jokes, too, but compared
with the jokes of his son, Eugene's renditions came off as passive and
reserved. On violence, Eugene told me, "All right, if you would be in a
gang, and a bunch of people don't want to act right and you see there's
going to be trouble, well you walk away. Where peace don't abide, dust
your feet and flee. Even if it's at your mother's house. He [God] don't
say fight him, he says dust your feet and flee." His jokes dramatized
the ambiguity about whether violence should evoke pride or loathing.

Often Eugene projected a passive outlook coupled with the glee of striking out at an antagonist. In the preacher joke he told at the session with George Hitt, for example, the deacon proudly throws bricks, but harm is only implied.

Another indication of this ambivalence was Eugene's fondness for "bad man" legends. The legends were generally offered to support two separate philosophies: the religious and virtuous life as supreme, by showing the trouble and hatred the bad man aroused, and the defiance of whites, by pointing out their fallibility in the bad man's presence. I witnessed Powell telling such stories to a teenaged neighbor who had been involved in local violence and carried obvious scars from the incident. Eugene told him legends of a figure he called "Bad Man Monroe." Eugene seemed to be moralizing to the boy, but he reduced the effect of condemning Monroe's violence by showing pride in the black character's exploits. He began with a narrative that extolled Monroe's strength and his defiance of whites:

> He sure hurts, boy; he ain't scared of nobody. I don't care who he is. Now the main place he's on, Mr. Smith. Mr. Smith had a .38 special, nickel plated. He wore it on his hip like a police—big old man. Mr. Smith would always call on himself. Monroe got there, and them folks got to tell Monroe about picking. Monroe would pick seven, eight hundred pounds of cotton, and Monroe would get that cotton so bad—told him, "Monroe, don't you pick that cotton like that; that [white] man going to get on you." Say [defiantly], "Who?" Monroe then commence to stripping that stalk, put everything in his sack. All right, went up there, weighed it. Mr. Smith got up there and got on the wagon; that fellow was showing him about how them fellows was getting the cotton. He said, "Who's doing this?"—tall fellow. He wasn't long before he had a sack full again. He went up there with it. They weighed it up. Mr. Smith said to him, "Son," says, "This is your sack?" "Yeah" [said defiantly]. "Well, try and get it a little better" [said meekly].

Powell commented, "If it had been anybody else, I don't know—I reckon he just felt he would do wrong fooling with him." From this avoidance of violence because of the hero's badass reputation, Eugene moved on to the story of a fight:

> Henry Brown done killed a boy and went to Parchman and stayed maybe about two years and Mr. Smith got him out. He raised him from a little boy. He got him out, and after which . . . that evening, him and Henry were riding around. And Henry jumped on to Indianola and tore at Monroe quick about a woman. Said, "Don't do that woman that-a-way. Quit that fighting that-a-way. Stop that!" Henry be a bad man. Killed one man, you know. He had a .32 Colt automatic in his pocket. He hauled off and hit her again. When he hit her again, Monroe out with that .38–40. When he come out with that .38–40, Henry reached—he was a church hog too, partner! Went back there to get that Colt—that .32 Colt. When he went back there to get that .32 Colt, he busted him right in the arm right there. Hit that muscle, knocked a hole in the arm that big [cups his hand]. When the doctor come to him, put some medicine on that cotton and run it through from this side and pulled it out from that side! Took his pistol, draw to his head, and pulled that pistol out of his pocket. Put it in his pocket and went on down the road and the folks was begging him, "Don't give him his pistol; don't give him his pistol." And he carried way down the road, then took the bullets out of it and kept the magazine and laid the pistol down there and told old Jim, "Don't pick it up." Say, "If you pick it up, put a bullet between your eyes." He shoots that good. So all right, Jim was following him begging him for it. He carried him about as far as here to that light over yonder [about 500 yards]. He lay down some and then he lay down in some other place and he said, "When I holler for you, you pick it up; you can pick it up." That's what he done. So Henry got his pistol back.
>
> Then [Monroe] went on by a fellow's house—Amos Roberts—he had got in some trouble. He hurt a man, killed a man. Well, that was his friend. I didn't know nothing about him being his friend. Well, Amos done been to Parchman because he killed seven men. Little black nigger with a mouth full of gold—sure shoot you, sure as iron. But Monroe a little too

tough. A little too tough. Monroe went by there, didn't know nothing about the man. Just heard that he killed. After he shot him [Henry Brown], he said, "I'm going by and see this Amos Roberts and you all say is so bad." Say [in a loud, gruff voice], "I'd rather be in a God damn pistol part than be in a God damn candy breaker, God damn it!" He says, "I tell you about me." He says, "Trouble I crave, God damn, and peace I do despise." That what he say all the time. Tall nigger with good hair. Smile and long pretty mustache and never was dressed up but nice-looking fellow. He had gone by Amos's house looking for him, and Amos wasn't there. Sat out there in the yard waiting for him awhile. I reckon he decided he better get up; the law might come or something. So he got up and left, but he told Amos's wife, said, "Say, I don't know your husband, but tell me he pretty good with a gun. Tell this is Monroe; tell him he back to see him." Say, "Tell him I wants to meet somebody that can handle a gun good." Say, "You tell him I'd rather be in a damn pistol part than be in a damn candy breaker. Tell him this is Monroe!" He went on. Well then he left. Afterwards wife come to the house and his wife got to talking. She said, "Lord," she said, "I ain't never had no peace." Said, "Man took me around schoolgirl once, put a pistol on her, got her." He say, "Had to wade the water to keep the dogs from running his track with me sitting straddle his shoulders." She said, "I ain't seen my peoples in thirteen years." And she had a boy thirteen year old. Boy bigger than you, and he be only thirteen. And she had them—she was a heavy-stock woman then. Said, "Took me when I was going to school." I asked her how old she was. I think she said she was fourteen. Yeah, fourteen. My wife said, "Well, how come you want to stay with him?" She said, "No, because I never would have nothing." Said, "Hurt somebody or kill somebody everywhere we ever been." His wife told just like he did. Like it was at a picnic and Henry Brown shoot him there and that bullet plowed him that-a-way. A pistol knocked him down raggedy like that. When it staggered him like that, fellows were running looking back and Monroe jumped up over the crowd. The fellows run looking back. Monroe jumped over the crowd. Said, "Pow!" between the eyes. Killed him.

Well, I say, "I didn't believe"; she was telling it, you know. I didn't believe him. I didn't thought he could do that good. She say, "Yes, he can too." He hunts squirrels with his pistol. Shoots a .38–40. You know it's the biggest pistol you can have. And so you know I didn't want to be around this fellow.

Powell conveyed truthfulness in the legend by providing names and narrating in the first person. Yet he elaborated the narrative by the repetition of boastful phrases such as "Trouble I crave, God damn, and peace I do despise," reminiscent of the giant's fearsome chant "Fee, fie, fo, fum, I smell the blood of an Englishman" in the "Jack and the Beanstalk" tale. In the narrative he added the props of guns and suggested the bad man's phallic power by his having the "biggest pistol you can have," especially in competition over a woman. With it, he dominated women, as indicated by the next story Eugene told about Monroe looking for his wife:

Monroe come back there looking for his wife. [That caused] her to hide. But somehow or another he found out where she was and went there that night. Now Ben Bushey one of those knife men—believe in knife. You understand, that's what he believe in. He don't believe in gun. He try you; if you had a gun, he had a knife. He try you. Monroe came there that night and set a big fire. He say Monroe must have been standing around, heard his wife talking. He came up there and knocked on the door. Say [makes knocking noise], "Who is that?" Say, "Monroe." Say, "This is Monroe; nobody hurt you." She tipped up there run under the bed. So he come in there, he big man. Sit down smoking his pipe. Come around there and have a seat. "Well, how's the time in the Delta?" Said, "Well," Monroe says, "been a little tough. I'm on a little business, kind of a little hurry." Says, "Is my wife here?" Ben told him, "No, she ain't here." He says, "I'll go if she ain't here," and he went out the door and he got to the door and he had that .38–40 pulled up like that. Said, "Well, Mr. Bushey, *I always tell people good night with this!*" Ben told him, "Come back in here! Your wife is there under the bed!"

Powell concluded with the story of Monroe's capture, lest the boy think that defiance of the law goes unpunished. But in legendary fashion, he cloaked the outcome in mystery:

> The police the one that told me uptown there. Police said, "Do you know that son of a bitch?" He says, "That's a mean son of a bitch out there." He said, "You know how many it took us to get him?" I said, "No." Said, "Had to get police out of Rolling Fork and police out of Hollandale, Glen Allan, and then that son of a bitch shot—had heavy shots would have killed a bunch of us. He shooting man!" They captured him when he shot out of bullets. Brought him to jail. Now what they done with him, I don't know. I ain't seen him or heard from him no more.

Whereas Eugene's humor invited the exchange of another joke, distancing tellers from the ability to relate the fiction to their real lives, his legendry sparked philosophizing about himself. "Don't fool with nobody like [Monroe]," Powell told the boy. Then he personalized the message: "Anytime a man put himself up against the lid, I don't fool with him. Shucks, I don't fool with them kind of folk, man! See, I ain't got in my head to try to do nothing to nobody. I wants to live my life out and do right by people. What you want to take away from a poor man; he ain't got shit. Ain't got nothing." To relate the stories of Monroe to other outlaw legends, Eugene compared him to Jesse James. "Now Jesse James was the baddest man in the world," he started, "and they didn't do that [take advantage of poor folk]. They would take money and then buy some poor peoples out, give them money! Make them cook them something too. Get through, give them four, five hundred dollars. Six, seven hundred, a thousand—jump on a horse and go. That's what they said they did."

Eugene's narratives of Bad Man Monroe epitomize what folklorist John W. Roberts has observed in the creation of the African American bad man as an outlaw hero in the post-Reconstruction South. Monroe, like the better-known black bad men Stagolee and John Hardy, represents the economic as well as legalistic victimization of blacks. Although Roberts notes that the black bad man in the fantasy of the narrative exaggerates the gun to break up the order of co-constructed white hegemony and black submissiveness, "reality demanded" that, "in transmitting a conception of behaviors embodied in badman folklore as heroic, the consequences of these actions be made clear" (Roberts 1989, 212). Black bad men in legend were typically caught and punished by whites, although these bad men were also depicted as a threat to African Americans because they jeopardized socioeconomic progress by disrupting the black community, convinced nonblacks of African American brutishness, or brought retribution down on black heads (see Dance 1978, 224–46). Roberts explains this ambivalence as the influence of Christian religious values, which condemn the morality of the bad man's actions, versus sympathy for aggression born of frustration (1989, 213). In legend, bad men fear no one and instill dread; they are oblivious to restrictions placed on them. In folklore, Roberts points out, "the badman emerged as an outlaw folk hero whose characteristic actions offered a model of behavior for dealing with the power of whites under the law that created conditions threatening to the values of the black community from both within and without" (1989, 215). In relating these narratives to his young neighbor, Eugene was thinking of his own son, who had developed a reputation as a troublemaker among blacks as well as whites and had become a threat to both. He was sympathetically portrayed as one of "us" to Eugene and was viewed as heroic because he defied the socioeconomic hierarchy that would victimize him, but in the legendary end, Ernest could not avoid a tragic fall.

Legendry was Eugene's vehicle for discussing violence and his son's future, but his jokes dealt with women and Eugene's social role. Eugene told jokes to and for men, whereas legends could be discussed with women. The sexual segregation of his storytelling allowed him to engage with other men in this matrifocal society in a domination over women. Yet it would be unfair to say that his jokes showed a singular distaste for women. In Eugene's jokes, the woman was an object of scorn and desire simultaneously. In real life, Eugene bore a tremendous responsibility for his wife that he both accepted and resented. Chained to his invalid wife, Eugene wanted to leave no doubt about his manliness. His view of manliness—the appearance of dominance over women—came out in his jokes and was also set against the background of black and white depictions of black males as irresponsible and hypersexualized. In jokes, sex was equated with aggression that showed power.

Eugene told his jokes like he sang the blues—with an intensity that exuded a cathartic expressiveness. His words came out slowly and deliberately. He punctuated his narration with puffs on his cigarette, and he altered his voice regularly to imitate children, women, and animals. He stressed to me how easily learning stories came to him. He got the stories from others, but in elaborating them for retelling, he emphasized, he made them his own. Not being able to write them down for memorization, he recalled plot outlines that he elaborated with character names and actions. When he could not tell stories and had to face an unfamiliar social situation, he felt uncomfortable. Jokes, familiar and relaxed, gave the insecure Eugene a sense of confidence.

Eugene's insecurity spilled over into his relationship with Ernest. Eugene saw much of himself in his son. Ernest was more rebellious and aggressive, but like his father, he cultivated creativity and popularity, and he too had trouble dealing with women and finding success. Eugene worried about his control over Ernest. Talking to his cousin and me, Eugene said, "The reason why they got my boy locked up down there [in jail] now 'cause he went too far. He didn't do like I tried to get him to do. He never do like I try to get him to do. He never do like I try to get him to do. It had been me letting him out when he get into something, he do no stealing or nothing. But when he would get into it, they [the police] turn him loose and let him go on back to the job and tell him to pay on some that he owe. Well he wouldn't do it. You understand—*he wouldn't do it.* One fella come in there, hit him setting up in the chair, knocked him plumb out of the chair there cause he used be a police. He long tall nigger and he went for a good man. My boy picked him up in the air to tell me and [pause] put that squeeze on him. Know he good on that squeeze. He put that squeeze on him and hollered then to get him off. Little Man sitting up there drinking along the chair; he come up there and knocked him out with another chair." To Eugene, Ernest was commendably strong and prideful, but Ernest's tendency to overreact was his downfall. Like telling a bad-man legend, Eugene's account of his son's exploits exaggerated his strength and size, underscored his obstinacy with repeated phrases, and assured his path to ruin.

Ernest's aggressiveness quickly became apparent to me. When Eugene and I went to jail to get Ernest released, the sheriff warned me about his past: "He'll be in here so fast with just a hint of trouble." Ernest talked fast and cursed regularly. His bulk added to the fear he could muster. He often seemed angry at some unknown force and thought strangers and friends alike were out to do him in. I asked Eugene about Ernest's mistrust, and he replied, "City done that to him—fast life." Once he was out of jail, Ernest returned to a woman with whom he shared a trailer, but Eugene reported that his son's relationship with her was not good. A welder by trade, Ernest had trouble holding a job and found himself unemployed once again. He had been arrested several times for fighting and disturbing the peace, and his most recent incarceration had been for not paying fines owed.

The day after he was released, Ernest and his friend Elton visited Eugene's front lawn. A neighbor joined the group. Ernest saw my tape recorder and, without comment, picked up the microphone and began speaking into it. With little body movement but in a rapid-fire vocal delivery, be began a toast:

> Say I went to a shit called the Bucket of Blood, I walked in the door.
> I seen this fast stinking asshole you know.
> I walked up to the bar, I said, "Bartender, bartender, give me a drink."
> Said, "Bartender, bartender, give me a drink."
> That son of a bitch stood there and he had to think.
> He walked over there and he come back; I asked him for a dinner too.
> That son of a gun gave me a muddy glass of water and a nasty piece of meat.
> I looked at him and said, "Bartender, bartender, you don't know who I am."
> That motherfucker looked at me and said, "In fact, I don't give a God damn."
> I said, "Bartender, bartender, don't you know?
> You got to come here and move over some of this floor."
> He said, "I tell you what, Man. You nice fella but you're talking too fast.
> I wind up kicking in your dirty black ass."
> I said, "Let me tell you something before you go too far."
> I said, "This shit you talking ain't worth a damn.
> Last motherfucker who told me that, I kicked between his motherfucking legs,

And he wound up going to the hospital for about three or four years."

He said, "Yeah?"

He said, "But I'm going to tell you something."

He said, "In other words, I'm not the man who you did that way,

And I'm just passing my time away fucking around with you."

He said, "The best thing for you to do is hit that door and don't be too slow,

Because I've seen a lot of motherfuckers you going on to another shore."

I started out the door and I began to think.

I said, "This motherfucker here got me on the rink."

I said, "I'm going to step back and tell him a thing or two."

I stepped back and I said, "You know what?

You're a long-living motherfucker and you mustn't don't mind dying."

That's when I rushed back there and got that heavy piece of iron.

I cocked it in his face, he began to grin.

I said, "Oh baby," I said, "I'm going to stay out long as you whine."

That son of a gun looked at me a long time.

And he started talking slow.

"In other words, baby," I said, "That shit you talking got to go."

I made two shots up in the top.

That's when that motherfucker dropped.

I left out the place and I ain't been back again.

But they always told me, says, "You know what?

You a bad motherfucker and *you had to win*."[2]

Elton smiled, but Eugene looked pained. This kind of bad-man narrative "toast" is associated with prison and harsh street life. Unlike Eugene's bad-man legend, Ernest's "bad motherfucker" toast does not include retribution for violence; he is not fatalistic. The narrator in Ernest's story regenerates by killing another person; he will never back down from a fight. Ernest's bit of folklore was told poetically, but its images were drawn from experience. It was recited like an overstated oral autobiography. The bars were Ernest's domain, and violence often followed him in. Eugene had mentioned Ernest's habit of getting into bar fights with people who "didn't treat him right." Ernest lacked Eugene's old country sentiment about avoiding trouble. Yet he and his father used humor and folklore similarly—as personal outlets of emotion and as ways to elevate their prestige. Competitive and fearsome, Ernest ended his toast pridefully, saying, "You a bad motherfucker and *you had to win.*"

Ernest's storytelling also lacked the social requirements of Eugene's. Whereas Eugene needed prodding from an attentive face to tell his jokes, Ernest told jokes as if delivering a soliloquy; that is, his jokes revealed his thoughts to himself. They were often more personal and independent, even bordering on the limits of the usual social standards of performance. Ernest asked me what his father had given me in the way of jokes, and I told him about the many preacher jokes Eugene had offered. "Yeah, I heard him tell 'em all right, but listen here," Ernest said. And with that he put his head down, brought the microphone to his lips, and raced through a joke:

> This preacher was screwing this woman and it got good to him. So he looked at her. Said, "You know what, baby, you sure got something good." She said, "I want to tell you something." He said, "Don't talk, it's too good." She said, "I just got to tell you. You know what? There was a guy screwing me last night. Whooo, he sure did make me feel bad. He had a big one, and it was hurting me." He said, "A grand rascal." She said, "You know what?" He said, "Don't talk, baby. It's so good to me. Don't talk. Wait till later." Said, "No I got to tell you." She said, "And the other night—night before last, another guy screwing me." Said, "Just about time I got ready to get a good feeling, that son of a gun jacked off and got up." He said, "A grand rascal." Said, "Now baby, don't talk. It's so good to me." She said, "You know what?" Said, "Don't talk." She said, "But this son of a bitch gave me the clap." He said, *"A dirty motherfucker!"*[3]

Ernest's story brought out the casualness with which the preacher accepts the woman's affairs, since he appears to be interested solely in the physical sensation of sex. He reacts severely only when he learns that another man is getting to him by passing him a disease, thus emasculating him. In the telling, Ernest enjoyed imitating the soft, breathy sounds associated with sex and contrasting that with the final earthy exclamation, "dirty motherfucker!"

Ernest had little patience for the subtleties of Eugene's preacher jokes. To Ernest, women lacked depth or use. Ernest's jokes dramatized directly some of his paranoid feelings that both women and men were out to get him or to screw him over, and his reaction was to fight back or to use sex to show his manly dominance. With glee he told this story about a sexual contest between two men as we sat out on Eugene's front lawn with two of Ernest's friends who were around his age:

> Sam and Shine had 250 women lined up along the wall. The boss man had a bet on them. The one that fucked the most women would get so much money. They bet money or prizes or whatever. The boss said, "OK, well let's get it going. We got the bet." The women had their dresses up; you could see the thing there, you know. Old Shine said, "I'm going to go first." Sam said, "No, let me go first." Shine said, "All right Sam, if you want to go first, go on." Old Sam got up there and every time he said, "Bip bam, thank you ma'am," he had fucked one. Old Sam was up there—"bip bam, thank you ma'am; bip bam, thank you ma'am; bip bam, thank you ma'am; bip bam, thank you ma'am." He went on till he fucked 150. Old Shine said, "Goddamn Sam, you sure went on in there." Sam said, "I don't believe you're gonna make it there." Shine said, "I don't believe I'm gonna make it myself." Boss man said, "Old Shine, you know you can do it." Old Shine got up there and pulled his big black greasy thing out. He grabbed them women up there right fast. "Bip bam, thank you ma'am; bip bam, thank you ma'am [said very quickly]; bip bam, thank you ma'am—*sorry Sam!*" He fucked *all* them women, and fucked Sam before he knew it.[4]

The black trickster Shine was victorious through an aggressive social posture. The men found this story funny because Shine adds insult to injury by winning the contest and then feminizing Sam. Ernest's point was that sex as a weapon and an activity is more important than the object of sex. Indeed, Ernest freely showed annoyance by shouting "fuck you" and "motherfucker," and on occasion he would refer to having sex with a woman he *did not like* to get back at her.

Male rivalry and dominance through sex were only part of the story. Ernest was easily offended, and his friend Elton told me of "brushes he got in because he thought someone was putting him down." Ernest had gone to jail for fighting and drunkenness. One incident that especially angered Ernest involved a fellow worker who had asked him kiddingly, "Do you fuck your wife?" Ernest shouted to us on the lawn, "He's a dirty motherfucker. If that boy had any sense, I'd a knocked him—I'd a knocked him out hot as I was. That son of a gun come there and ask me, 'Hey.' I said, 'What you want, boy? I got to finish this job here.' Man, come five o'clock I want to finish this job because I want to be outside! I says, 'What you want?' He asked me, 'Do you, do you. . . .' He can't talk good. 'Do you fuck your wife?' Yeah, that's what that son of a bitch told me." The boy had challenged one of Ernest's last sources of prestige—his manliness. But it would have been below him to hit the boy.

Recounting the incident led Ernest to think of some dozens: "I fucked your momma on a train, her drawers fell out and she killed a man; I fucked your momma behind the door, shot her in the ass with my .44." This was unusual, because dozens were typically limited to adolescents, and Ernest was in his thirties. Besides, he was telling them to himself rather than engaging in a play frame with someone else. He liked the rapid repetition of risqué words, and the outward aggression of the rhymes released some of his tension. But to Elton and Eugene, the dozens were unnecessary; Ernest, however, appeared to be fixated on that one incident. Ernest would become excited when criticized by his father, telling him angrily to mind his own business or hurling an insult at him. He could not take kidding about his weight or submission to the law, yet he liked to insult others. Folklorist Roger Abrahams, in his observation of African Americans in Philadelphia, also found that dozens are occasionally recited by adults, and he corroborates Ernest's psychological response by stating that when adults use dozens, it "indicate[s] flatly that the players are in some way victims of a fixation, needing a kind of release mechanism that allows them to get rid of some of their tensions" (1962, 215).

For Ernest, folklore was more than simply release. It told others who he was, as he told the bartender in the toast. His folklore informed others how he wanted to be treated and what the consequences might be if they failed to treat him correctly. Folklore was a way to gain prestige and convey his emotional state. Ernest's folklore told others to fear him and laugh with him at the same time.

Ernest had trouble with authority. For example, he ran afoul of the law for not responding to police instructions or questions when stopped on the street, and on the job he got into trouble with his bosses for insubordination. Unsurprisingly, defiance was an especially strong theme in his jokes, and he used them to affirm his independence. Joke telling often identifies the teller as a rule breaker, since the content is commonly unanticipated or risqué. Ernest's jokes touched on "brushes" with bosses and his father. Consider, for instance, two of his favorites, which he called "The Son Who Wouldn't Listen" and "Lucille from Mobile":

This old guy had three sons, one died—the one he liked the most. He kept wanting his other son to carry him out to see his dead son's grave. He'd pray and ask the Lord to let him see his son. He never did see him. One night the son carried him out to the grave around twelve o'clock. He was over the grave praying, "Oh Lord, please let me see my son, please Jesus. I've been asking you for five or six years and you ain't let me see my son at all. Oh Lord, please let me see him just one more time." The other boy was sitting in the car and said to himself, "I know what I'm gonna do, I'm gonna stop Dad from this." He got a white sheet and put it over his head, eased out there while his dad was kneeling and praying by the grave. "Oh Jesus, please let me see my son one more time. Oh Jesus, please." The son raised up from behind the grave with the sheet over his head and said, "Oh Daddy, here I am." The daddy said, "Huh?" The boy said, "Oh Daddy, you've been wanting to see me, here I am." The daddy said, "Yea son, you look the same, now go on back in your grave. I done seen ya, the Lord done answered my prayer." The son said, "No Daddy, you been praying to see me and I wanna hold you one time." Daddy said, "No son, I don't wanna hold you, now go on back in your grave, go on now." His daddy was backing up away from him, kinda scared. The son said, "Daddy, I just got to hold you one time." Daddy said, "Boy, won't you listen to me, I told you to go back in your grave. Now I don't wanna argue. Man, I told you to go back." The son said, "No Daddy, I just got to hold you." Daddy said, "Yea, well that's why you're dead and in that damn grave then. *You never would listen to nobody!*"[5]

There was this guy coming from Chicago. He was driving one of these new Oldsmobiles. He pulled in at a gas station. Before he did he stopped along the road and picked up a lady. When he got to the gas station, the guy asked could he help him. The fella said, "Yea, fill my tank up with gas." The gas station attendant said, "You want me to check your oil too?" The fella said, "Damn right, check my oil too. That's your job, isn't it?" Attendant said, "Yea." So he checked his oil and gas and everything. He peeped in there and see this pretty woman in the car with him. He said, "Who is that you got in the car with you?" The fella said, "Oh, that's Susan Haywood." Attendant said, "Where you from?" Fella said, "Hollywood." Attendant said, "What kind of car you drivin'?" Fella said, "A Fleetwood." Attendant said, "What's your occupation?" Fella said, "Drive good." Attendant said, "Oh, you a pretty smart guy." Fella said, "Yea." Attendant said, "I'm gonna see if you can like that when I come back." He went in there and got his blue steel .45 and come back out there and threw it up in the fella's face and said, "Now who did you say you got in the car with you?" Fella said, "Lucille." Attendant said, "And where you from?" Fella said, "Mobile." Attendant said, "What kind of old car you drivin'?" Fella said, "Oldsmobile." Attendant said, "What made you change your mind?" Fella said, "Blue steel." Attendant said, "Now what's your occupation?" Fella said, "Cotton field." Attendant said, "Where you buy your clothes from?" Fella said, "Goodwill."[6]

Ernest told the first story in the same style as the story about the preacher who gets the "clap" (gonorrhea). He used a soothing tone of voice until the final line, when he broke into a loud, angry insult. The story is related to Ernest's experience. It is about a son reaching out to his father, yet the father rebuffs him for his rebelliousness. Ernest resented his father telling him to heed authority and to quiet down. Ernest was proud of talking loud and defiantly. Ernest told the second story as if it actually happened to him. That feeling of empathy helped make Ernest's stories effective and distinctive. Ernest showed glee, for instance, when reciting the gun-toting attendant's questions. With a tool of violence and a forceful posture, the attendant reverses his subordinate role and exposes the driver's pretension. Ernest, frustrated by his lack of success, felt that aggression was one way to put himself on top. The structural formula of rhymed one-word replies is usually reported in folkloristic literature as a frontier yarn about a city slicker in the backwoods who gets terse replies from a settler:

"Whose house?"
"Nog's."
"Of what built?"
"Logs."
"Any neighbors?"
"Frogs."
"What kind of soil?"
"Bogs."
"Your diet?"
"Hogs."
"Dogs." (Boatright 1949, 61)

Whereas the answer "hogs" could be interpreted as civilized, suggesting "living high on the hog," the practice of eating dogs, implied in the last line, invites contempt. Folklorist Mody Boatright views such yarns as having the function of separating the offspring (who usually tell the story) from the parents, with the young storytellers ridiculing the rusticity and backwardness of the past they hope to leave behind (1949, 61). By teasing out the truth in the last line, the teller declares that he has progressed in manners beyond the oldster's crudeness and ties to the land. He also undermines the authority of the elder. One difference in Ernest's story is that the setting is not the frontier but an urban locale, where the rube is unmasked and subordinated. The demeaned figure in Ernest's story turns out to be from the "cotton field," suggesting Ernest's attitude toward his father's maintaining his country ways in the city. The critical addition to Ernest's narrative is the power of "blue steel," which forces the driver to admit his true socioeconomic class. Ernest seemed to relate to the attendant, who resents his servile role, but in the context of his frustration over finding success, Ernest performed both ends of the dialogue as a projection of himself. Although one could hear in Ernest's rendition a wish to invert the master-servant relationship, there was also a fatalism about his station in life, which he attributed to his race.

I asked Eugene whether he knew "The Son Who Wouldn't Listen" and "Lucille from Mobile." Although he did not know them exactly as Ernest had told them, Eugene had an "Old John" tale to match Ernest's first story. In Eugene's tale, a boy hides up in a tree with a sheet over him. John says, "Lord, if you call me tonight, I'm ready to go; any time you call I'm ready to go." When the boy comes down covered by the sheet, John runs. As a punch line, his wife exclaims, "Listen Lord, I'm gonna tell you what, John can run fast with his shoes on, but he done pulled them shoes off. You can't catch him now—he's barefooted." The joke came off rather weakly, and Eugene admitted he did not tell it too often. Ernest's joke packed more power because he organized its symbolism clearly and related it to his experience and personality. Eugene like the rhyming formula but not necessarily the content of "Lucille from Mobile," and he offered as similar this joking dialogue: "What's your name? My name is Needin' Peter. Where you from? I'm from Alaska. Well what did you do up there? I done plenty things. I bet you can't screw. Yes I can too. No you can't. I can do it more neater and more sweeter and with less peter than any man you ever saw from Toleder [Toledo]." The play on words delighted Eugene, whereas Ernest stressed action and reality in his jokes. Eugene's jokes were passive by comparison, more innocent and less cynical.

Ernest had learned the forms from Eugene, but the two men's individual personalities led them to select different tones and textures for their jokes. I noticed their selectivity within similar forms when they began an exchange of jokes out on the lawn. They both had their friends there, resulting in some rivalry for attention. It was a hot day, and talk about the heat turned to "getting hot" sexually. Eugene told a joke first, followed by Ernest's telling of two more vivid jokes:

> EP: Three girls sitting together talking. One girl said, "What does your old man do to get you hot?" The other one said, "Well,

he doesn't have to do too much to me, 'cause I stay hot all the time." The third girl says, "If he just touches my titties, it just makes me so hot I don't know what to do." The colored girl that was sitting there didn't know what else to say. She said, "Do you know what, the only time my old man can make me hot is when he fucks me all night and I don't have a nickel to buy a God damn bar of Big Ben soap to wash my ass with the next day." [Laughter.][7]

LM (Little Man): Oh hey then. These three women was lined up thanking the Lord for what he done for them. The white woman said, "Oh Lord, I thank you for my pretty hair, my pretty face, my pretty color." The China woman said, "Oh Lord, me thank you for me pretty hair, me pretty legs, me pretty color, and me pretty eyes." The colored woman said, "Say J.C., I don't thank you for a God damn thing. I thank you for how you fucked me up. Short black nappy hair, big funky [stinky] ass, big cock [vagina]—and it's wore out—but I don't thank you for a damn thing." And she walked out. Then this guy and gal was out at this old run-down barn. He said, "Hey, let's fuck a little." So they went up in the loft. They was really fuckin' away and the board cracked and busted. They fell out of the loft. She hit the floor first and said, "Oh Lordy, my back." He said, "You God damn bitch, hollering about your back. You don't see my nuts hanging up there on the nail do you?" [Groans from the men.][8]

Elton laughed while Eugene winced at Ernest's verbal picture of impaled testes. Ernest smiled broadly. He had bested his father, he thought, not necessarily by telling the more creative joke but by garnering the stronger reaction. Ernest's jokes, like his presence, were stronger, cruder, and angrier. Whereas Eugene's character merely laments the lack of soap to wash her ass, Ernest's stormily exclaims, "I don't thank you for a God damn thing." Giving the line even more effect is the fact that it is said to Jesus Christ. The story about testes hanging on a nail is a strong joke because of its image of mutilation, but it also shows Ernest's hostile attitude toward complaining women. Indeed, he often expressed his annoyance at the nagging of the woman with whom he lived, along with his complaint about being in a servile position: "They all think they're superior or something!"

As good joke tellers, Ernest and Eugene knew what structure to use for spinning out humorous narratives, but they displayed strong differences in delivery. Ernest's rapid-fire style and tendency to look away from his audience sometimes shut people out from his narratives. He stressed deviance and aggressiveness in sexual relations, violence as an everyday occurrence, and manliness as a basic value of dominance that had to be constantly proved. Ernest also had a striking concern for persecution in his jokes. His protagonists hurled abuse at others in reaction to an overwhelming prejudice, and they sometimes directed that antipathy at themselves. In real life, Ernest felt hounded too—by his father, by his common-law wife, by the police. Ernest's jokes became platforms to beat back the hounds and scoundrels. In narrative, he delighted in subterfuge to foil the powerful and violence to smash antagonists. In real life, he was more often locked up in jail than triumphant on the street.

When Eugene and Ernest told the same narratives, it dramatized their differences. Both of them had a special fondness, for example, for a story Eugene called "Oink Is Ugly" and passed on to his son. It is commonly reported in collections of African American folklore and was known by others in Eugene's circle. Nonetheless, friends frequently asked him to tell it, even though they knew the punch line. In their view, it was "a good one" that was worth hearing again as Eugene performed it. It was this comic story that caused Ernest to castigate his father for trying to alter Ernest's version. In the process of learning and personalizing the story, Ernest had become protective of his repertoire, or perhaps he was jealous of the honor accorded Eugene's rendition. Feeling threatened again, Ernest seemed to think that besting his father was a way to show his manhood. After his burst of anger, Ernest returned to his narration, using the names of people in his audience for the characters in the story:

> These three guys went out and stole this hog and they was on their way back, and the road man was stopping everybody and checking for licenses and things. One guy said, "What we gonna do y'all?" The second guy said, "I'm gonna put my coat on him." The third guy said, "I'll give him my hat." The other guy said, "Well I'll tell you what I'm gonna do. I'll give him my shade glasses." So they did. They pulled up the road and

the man said, "Hey, hold up there." He went over to the car and said, "What's your name?" The first guy said, "My name is Simon." He asked, "What's your name?" The second guy said, "Old Joe." He asked again, "And what's your name?" The third guy said, "Tom." The road man said, "Who's that you got there in the back with you?" One of the guys said, "Oh, that's a friend of ours." The road man said, "By the way, buddy, what's your name?" He was talking to the hog. The hog didn't answer. He said, "Man, don't you hear me talking to you? I said what's your name." The one guy sitting beside the hog nudged him in the side and the hog said, "Oink Wig." The road man said, "Oh, your name's Oink Wig, huh? Where you on your way to?" One guy said, "Well, we taking Oink Wig to the doctor." The road man said, "Well, you mostly got to go to the dentist. You ain't got to tell me no more. I can see you got to go to the dentist, the way his teeth look in that mouth. Them teeth real bad. Y'all rush him on to the doctor 'cause he need them teeth pulled bad. He looks rough." They pulled away and said, "Boy, we sure was lucky." The road man went on back to his car and said to the other guy, "You know what, man? You know I pulled them guys over and checked them out? They had a guy in that car they called Oink Wig. That son of a bitch looked just like a hog."[9]

The power of this story in the African American section of Greenville comes from the black characters outsmarting whitey. The black narrator knows the absurdity of disguising a hog as a person, but to the white person in a position of authority, the teller underscores, all African Americans are metaphorically in the same category. If that is a harsh message, the humor derives from the blacks fooling the road man. But unlike other jokes, this narrative lacks a clear, striking punch line. Instead, it depends on a comic delivery to emphasize, on the one hand, the ludicrousness of the ruse and, on the other, the road man's folly. The audience on the lawn laughed at the creation of a comic situation and at Ernest's boastful delivery of the scene where the rebels "get away with it." Ernest told the story as if he were the one being stopped by the "man" and had to explain what he was doing.

Two days later I recorded Eugene's version, which I had heard him tell before:

Some black folk went in the country and stole a hog. When they was going out there, one of 'em said, "Now we don't want to go out there and get no shoke. We gonna go out there and get a big hog, 'cause we got to eat." He went out there and got a hog and he caught the wrong one. He caught a big old bull hog. He wanted to turn him loose. His buddy said don't turn him loose. He said, "He's meat too, man. We can eat him." So he got him and put him in the car. They let out [highway] number one with him. They got to the red light. The police was behind them. They was running red lights, kinda scared. They stopped. The policeman come up and asked them, "What y'all running that red light for? What's a matter here?" They said, "I'll tell you what. This man is so sick in here we was trying to get him to the doctor." So the other boy pulled off his coat right quick and slipped it on the hog and slid his hat up on his head. The policeman come over and looked at him and mumbled and then said, "That man is *sick*. We'll try and make it to the hospital with him quick." The policeman said, "You go on 'cause damn, he don't look like he's gonna be here much longer. He's the ugliest son of a bitch I ever seen in my life. He needs a shave, he needs his teeth fixed; he's in *bad* shape." One of the fellas said, "His name is Oink." The policeman said, "I don't give a damn who them other people was but that god damn Oink sitting there in the back, that's one ugly son of a bitch!"

Ernest's narration effused hostility, with the road man and the car passengers showing little regard for each other. Their theft of the hog was deliberate and defiant, whereas Eugene used their search for food to justify the act. Eugene's story used misunderstanding and duping for its dramatic impact. Ernest, in contrast, boldly told his joke and took more of a risk, extending his marginality by immediately following "Oink Is Ugly" with a graphic joke called "Reverend Fucking a Hog":

One day the old preacher was on his way to church. He got up by the church and saw this old sow out there. She was in heat, and her pussy was swelled up real big. He wanted some of it. He decided to go out there and screw her. He went out there and was screwing her. A little boy come along and caught him fucking her. The little boy said, "Aw Rev, I'm gonna tell everybody in church you was out there fuckin' that hog. Sunday when you come to church, I'm gonna tell everybody you was out there fuckin' a hog." The Rev said, "Son, I don't give a damn what you tell them folks. You can tell them any God damn thing you want to when you go to church Sunday. But just don't tell this damn hog!"

This joke did not get as many laughs, maybe because bestiality went beyond the norms of ridicule for the group. Or perhaps because of the symbolic equivalence between hog and black person established in the previous narratives, this story represented a repugnant violation. In the position of narrator, Ernest appeared to be saying that he didn't give a damn about restrictions—moral or physical. He would be, at least in the fictive plane of narrative, unrestrained.

Both Eugene and Ernest demonstrated their abilities and expressed themselves through jokes. Neighbors would ask what led them to "tell 'em like that." The tellers could not be said to represent a community, except that their stories attracted gatherings of small groups, and they applied the characteristics of tricksters outsmarting whitey and Deep South life tied to African American tradition. Many of Ernest's narratives, told as jokes and toasts, came from jailhouse and barroom settings, whereas Eugene's stories derived from talk sessions and, before that, his plantation youth. Although garnered from various local sources, the individuality of the joke teller remained essential to the gatherings in which they performed. Eugene and Ernest wanted to elevate themselves above the crowd. They told their jokes in different styles and for different purposes, but similarities occasionally surfaced because of a shared technique of learning jokes and their family bond. They personalized their jokes and selected stories that were appropriate to their personalities. From my vantage point, I noted that Ernest's exhibition of paranoia and aggression drew him to jokes with related themes of persecution and violence. Eugene's insecurity and passivity drew him to jokes stressing predictable linguistic structures and awkward social situations.

Eugene was right when he told me that Ernest was thinking of stories all the time. Often, Ernest's jokes blended with reality, whereas Eugene set reality and fiction apart more readily. Eugene enacted storying in framed "sessions," but Ernest roamed in settings—bars and prisons—where his creativity and bold words took on extra importance. Eugene needed spoken words because he could not write and was homebound. They both chose jokes to build symbols of personal experience within the themes of the society around them. As individuals, they both told stories in a personal style that others recognized, but Ernest violated one of the norms of their tradition. He made the stories his property, which others infringed on; in Eugene's social praxis, the stories were intended to be exchanged and shared. Ernest used stories to exert social dominance; Eugene made social connection with them.

My observations of unstated norms for tradition bear out Mary Douglas's proposal that joke telling as a special form and as a predominantly male genre of storying "could be saying something about the value of individuals as against the value of the social relations in which they are organized" (1975, 104). The structure of jokes involves working up to a surprising conclusion, and the content of jokes depends on a shared understanding by tellers and listeners of the references being used or an ambiguity being addressed. When tellers control that structure and content, they manipulate fiction to bring listeners around to their way of thinking. Jokes' appeal to men is the control they afford and their intrinsic aggression and frequent sexual bravado as a sign of male vitality. Told by African American men in this Mississippi context, the jokes had the extra significance of subverting the submissiveness and degradation attributed to them in a matrifocal black culture and the white hegemony in the wider society. Although the teller maintains some distance when setting up a joke, the telling is expected to garner social support through the content of the story while projecting the self in the process of storytelling. Joking normally violates rules or expectations; the teller must take some risks to draw attention to the narrative and the narrator. Joke telling means that limits are being tested, sensitive topics are being broached, and hidden feelings are symbolically being exposed. Why tell stories? One answer is that, to the teller, the risk is worth it, and listeners encourage the performance. Storying is not merely a behavioral response, however, for the content of jokes on a fictive plane allows one to broach subjects and take attitudes that are distinct from everyday discourse. Whether admitting fatalism or posturing aggression, jokes take positions that demand a response—aesthetic and moralistic.

Receiving attention is one reward reserved for the teller. The other is a sense of immunity. When telling stories, Ernest and Eugene exhibited more freedom to elaborately fantasize and insult than in everyday conversation. Because their audiences considered them accomplished at storytelling, they were given license to embellish their stories and take risks. Douglas points out that the joker "appears to be a privileged person who can say certain things in a certain way which confers immunity" (1975, 107). But she is too ready to see the joker as a representative of the consensus of a social structure. The jokes told by Ernest, for instance, were intentionally disruptive and risqué; his unnerving jokes had become his trademark. They extended the manliness, and often the aggression, implicit in the praxis of telling jokes. Jokers as men are intrusive; for these black men, jokes' use of play frames to invert and subvert power relations added to their appeal in a hierarchical social world distinguished by the binary of black and white.

What I call folklore, and what Eugene and Ernest called their stories, is a powerful vessel for creating and using symbols of self as well as society. Eugene and Ernest used storying to publicly exhibit and affirm their needs and positions. Storying involves "being lively," according to Eugene. By this, he means that it invigorates the teller and excites the listener. In that emotional state, and in the encapsulated symbolic system of narratives, messages are pointed and responses are invited. I find that portrayal useful to think about storying as action and tradition. For Eugene, "telling it his way" established his presence; it conveyed his vitality and his experience. Storying connected him to, and separated him from, his son.

8

Symbolizing Tradition

On the Scatology of an Ethnic Identity

Mahlon Hellerich strode to the podium to talk about Pennsylvania German (or, in his folk usage, Dutch, from the dialect *Deitsch*) culture to a gathering of the Pennsylvania German Society in Allentown, Pennsylvania. The audience did not need lecturing about the history of the group, since it comprised many people who, like him, had grown up with "Dutch" traditions. So he decided to focus on how the Dutch identity had changed from the mid-twentieth century of his youth to this twenty-first-century moment. In his eighties at that point, Hellerich was a well-recognized speaker on Pennsylvania German topics. Calling himself a proud "Dutchman," he drew on his experiences growing up in East Texas, Pennsylvania, which he described as a Pennsylvania Dutch hamlet. He began his lecture with a story that, he said, encompassed what being Pennsylvania German was about:

A Pennsylvania German mother tells her daughter that she would need to go to English school to register. And she tells her daughter to take her little brother because he would need to register next year. She goes to the teacher and the teacher asks for her name. The little girl answers *Waggeraad* ["wagon wheel"]. The teacher asks again, "OK, what is your real name?" *Waggeraad*, the girl emphatically answers again. "And how did you get that name?" the teacher follows up. The little girl explains, "My mother told me that when I was born the first thing she saw out the window was a wagon wheel by the barn." Still skeptical, the teacher tells her to go home and get a note from her mother confirming the story. The teacher then asks the boy, her little brother, to come forward. But the little girl exclaims, "Don't bother, if she didn't believe me, she's not going to believe you, *Hinkeldreck* ["chicken shit"].[1]

The story got a good laugh, and several persons in the audience glanced knowingly at one another, indicating they had heard that one before. At first, the joke may seem like an odd choice to represent the Pennsylvania German experience. Besides its off-color reference, some people might interpret its crude characterization of Pennsylvania German bumpkins as unflattering. Hellerich, however, recalled the narrative fondly from his childhood and appreciated the way it related the ethnic identity, and especially the rural consciousness, of Pennsylvania Germans, in contrast to the "English" outsiders (English-speaking Americans) viewed as part of the formal establishment. He lamented that this identity, arising largely out of an agrarian lifestyle, was on the wane.

It is a story I had heard regularly at the annual all-male *Fersommling* ("gathering") in Lykens, Pennsylvania, featuring an after-dinner speaker who related humorous jokes and anecdotes to hundreds of dialect speakers. It was usually part of a series of narratives the Pennsylvania Germans euphemistically refer to as earthy *Bauer* ("farmer") stories revolving around the feces of farm animals, especially chickens and horses. The narrative's anal theme was echoed in the joyous singing of "Schnitzelbank" with various barn images:

> *Ist das dein schnitzelbank?* [Isn't that your carving bench?]
> *Ja, das ist mein schnitzelbank?* [Yes, that is my carving bench]
> *Oh, du schoene,*
> *Oh, du schoene,*
> *Oh, du schoene*
> *Schnitz-el-bank!* [Oh, you wonderful carving bench]
>
> *Ist das nicht dein waggeraad?*
> *Ja, das ist mein waggeraad?*
>
> [Chorus]

Is das nicht dein haufen Mischt [manure pile]?
Ja, das ist mein haufen Mischt.

Outside of the *Fersommling* hall, I solicited descriptions of such narratives as a fieldworker. The most common comment I heard was, "That's earthy stuff," connecting manure with farm life and suggesting that the motif of animal feces was a defining feature of Pennsylvania German humor. It was what folklorists might call an "esoteric" expression, because it was intended to be communicated from one member of the group to another, rather than shared with outsiders or used by outsiders about Pennsylvania Germans (categorized as "exoteric") (Jansen 1959). To be sure, it was not the sole theme, as published field collections of oral tradition by John Baer Stoudt (1915) and Thomas Brendle and William Troxell (1944) indicate. For public audiences, Pennsylvania German collectors might recount trickster tales of Eileschpigel, the cycle of Swabian jokes related to ethnic "moron" humor, ghost and treasure tales, accounts of stolen goods retrieved, and a number of *parre* legends and anecdotes about notable ministers (Barrick 1969, 1987b). But as I will show, the feces theme provides more of a connecting thread among these Pennsylvania German narrative types than may be apparent at first.

Aware of this earthy repertoire, I began to suspect that previously published collections (the largest of which was Brendle and Troxell's), amassed in the early to mid-twentieth century, had understated or omitted these earthy stories because they were off-color and might be embarrassing to Pennsylvania Germans if they were read by outsiders. Or the tradition-bearers might have selected a "clean" repertoire to relate to Brendle, who was a man of the cloth. Apparently, Brendle was not oblivious to this material, for when Richard Beam mined his journals (57,124 items spread over approximately 24,000 pages) for a posthumous compendium of folklore, he found a number of scatological expressions recorded in Brendle's hand as "Excrementa" (Beam 1995, 47–48). Nonetheless, either Brendle or the publisher had chosen not to print that material for public consumption. Brendle's linguistic comments about the abundance of terms for excrement among Pennsylvania German speakers suggest that he was thinking about a cultural connection. He found *dreck* to be the most common term, but a round-shaped dropping could be called a *gnoddle*. *Scheissdreck* represented excrement of all kinds, Brendle observed, but the "vulgar" *scheiss* was normally reserved for humans, and *dreck* was reserved for animals, as is the linguistic usage in Germany. Pennsylvania German speakers differentiated among different types of *dreck*, most notably *hinkeldreck* (chicken), *geilsdreck* (horse), and *kiehdreck* (cow)—connected to Pennsylvania German pastures and barnyards.

Likewise, Brendle noted that the Pennsylvania Germans identified an abundance of manure as *mischt* but differentiated the various types of manure as *geilsmischt* (horse), *hinkelmischt* (chicken), and *haasemischt* (rabbit). The last term could also be used as a synecdoche for a rabbit farm. Brendle was apparently impressed by the Pennsylvania German penchant for designating places and implements as belonging to dirt, as in *mischthof*, that conspicuous part of the barnyard reserved for the collection of manure during the year (collected in Montgomery County as *mischtpen*, or a pile of manure, and as *mischthaufe*). *Mischtbrieh* was a special name for the liquid manure that collects around rotten manure heaps. Farmers typically had a *mischtschlidde* (sled), *mischtgawwel* (four-pronged fork), and *mischtwagge* (wagon) containing *mischtbanke* (planks). Pennsylvania German speakers also used a form of *mischt* as a verb meaning "to spread manure" and "to defecate" (Beam 1995, 47–48).

Even if Brendle and other collectors had published the scatological lore, they probably would not have applied a psychological analysis or, as I propose, a psychology of anality as an ethnic strategy expressed through fantasy narratives.[2] The folkloristic project of the early to mid-twentieth century for the Pennsylvania Germans was to record what they assumed would be a passing tradition, reflecting the decline of a self-contained rural Pennsylvania German folklife with the coming of industrialization and urbanization. The typical folkloristic presentation was to organize stories by themes and list them under these thematic headings as a series of relic texts associated with a once vibrant expressive culture. In the introduction to *Pennsylvania German Folk Tales, Legends, Once-upon-a-Time Stories, Maxims, and Sayings*, Brendle and Troxell comment, for example, "We have felt the greatest service we could render toward a study of our folk stories was to make a faithful record of what we heard and thus afford a true source for future comparative study" (1944, 10). Although they seemingly disavowed any analytical or anal interest, they made theoretical assumptions by organizing their collection to show the historical progression from the supernatural and wonder tales associated, they claimed, with the distant past to the "humorous anecdote and the tall story" in the living tradition of contemporary Pennsylvania German culture. Because their generation of Pennsylvania German scholars emphasized recovering the past rather than interpreting the adaptation of the present, they published what they considered the more "traditional" material of a memory culture. As Brendle and Troxell explain, "Our collection consists, therefore, in large part of stories that arose in the past and *belong to the past*" (1944, 8; emphasis added).

The stories published by Brendle and Troxell were all originally recorded in the dialect, and the idea of producing their collection in the tellers' own words owed to the German legacy of the Grimm brothers, Jacob (1785–1863) and Wilhelm (1786–1859). In fact, the publication of Brendle and Troxell's collection, according to Pennsylvania German Society president Henry Borneman, was to be "regarded as a tribute to the Brothers Grimm" (Borneman 1944, 5). While praising the Grimms' collections for their "scientific basis," thus initiating modern folklore scholarship, Borneman suggests an anal-ejective reference in reporting, finding great satisfaction in the "exhaustive" collection and dissemination of the once-private stories from the lips of earthy peasants to a general audience through publication.[3] He even claims that stories have the "spirit of childhood" (Borneman 1944, 5). Although this reference does not outline in Freudian terms an anal stage of development preceding latent and genital stages in maturity, he concludes his praise of Brendle and Troxell's collection by using the metaphor of a bygone age as childish or earthy: "They are gone and the spring choked up. The fashion, they tell me, is gone by and these things are esteemed childish. Why not then gratify children by letting them stand? Why must everything smack of man and mannish? Is the world all grown up? Is childhood dead? Or is there not in the bosoms of the wisest and the best some of the child's heart left to respond to its *earliest enchantments?*" (Borneman 1944, 6–7; emphasis added). One can interpret this quotation not just as nostalgic sentiment but also as pride in material that overly sober intellectuals understate as childish and earthy—that is, in psychoanalyst Otto Fenichel's view, the collector's "continuation of his infantile-narcissistic pleasure in his own feces" (1954, 148).

Commenting on the significance of Brendle and Troxell's collection, Borneman alludes to the importance of the memory culture:

"Fortunately, their work was done in the very nick of time; for, with the vanishing use of Pennsylvania German dialect, these tales will be no longer told by the descendants of this racial group" (1944, 6). Lacking an expressive outlet, the editors imply, descendants of the farm-raised, preindustrial Pennsylvania Germans will lack a meaningful social tie and a distinctive cultural identity. The impression Brendle and Troxell give, therefore, is that the culture has dissipated with the passing of this folklore. In their view, the "humorous anecdote and the tall story" are less important and less aesthetically pleasing to the reading public. These new narratives, which they mistakenly assume will be novel rather than part of a long-standing tradition, are presented as an unfortunate devolutionary development for the culture.

What is the historical background for the development, evolutionary or devolutionary, of the culture? The Pennsylvania Germans first arrived as a wave of immigrants in the late seventeenth and early eighteenth centuries. They were attracted by William Penn's promise of land and religious tolerance as his agents recruited settlers in the Palatinate Rhineland region of what is now southern Germany and north-central Switzerland. Most of them were Protestant (Lutheran and Reformed) or members of Anabaptist and Pietist groups such as Mennonites, Amish, and Brethren. Moving beyond Quaker and Welsh areas in southeastern Pennsylvania, they sought farmland in the mountain valleys farther west. They followed the valleys across the Susquehanna River into western Maryland and Virginia. Many of these areas were isolated from urban centers and transportation corridors by natural mountain and river barriers. The Pennsylvania Germans formed closed farming communities and relied on mutual aid. A dialect drawing on the Plattdeutsch of their homelands dominated, although there were regional variations in the eastern and southern parts of the culture. They differentiated their workaday, "low" German speech from the "high" German of prayer and church service, and linguistically, they perceived themselves as ordinary or "low" folk. Their concentrated settlements and the persistence of a traditional agrarian life inland helped foster the formation of a cultural region—often called by geographers and folklorists the Pennsylvania Culture Region or, more familiarly, "Dutch Country" (Bronner 2006b; Glass 1986; Zelinsky 1977).

In the early nineteenth century, as the government attempted to make English the standard language through compulsory public education, a cultural and linguistic awareness of ethnic difference grew among the Pennsylvania Germans, unifying them and distinguishing them from the English "other." Visual displays of this emergent identity became prominent in a range of artifacts, such as hex signs, gravestones, and prints conspicuously decorated with traditional Pennsylvania German signs and designs associated with the founding generation of settlers (Bronner 1992b, 1996c; Nolt 2002, 129–44; Yoder and Graves 1989, 12–15). By the late nineteenth century, organizations such as the Pennsylvania German Society (1891) were established to document and promote the folk culture as well as to raise its standing in the eyes of the general public (see Diffenderffer 1891; Egle 1892; Weaver-Zercher 2001, 21–34). By using the colloquial identity label "Pennsylvania Dutch," they also distinguished themselves from other German immigrants moving to the cities through their religion, dialect, art, and folklore. Estimated at more than 300,000 in 1950, the number of active dialect speakers was less than 80,000 in 1995 (Louden 2008). Many nonspeakers of Pennsylvania German in the region converse in what is popularly known as "Dutchified" English—also called a "Dutchy" or central Pennsylvania accent—featuring the use of phrases in the dialect and rhythms and grammatical formations based on Pennsylvania German patterns (Huffines 1984).

A break in tradition appeared to occur during World War II, when many Pennsylvania German parents stopped teaching their children the dialect. They often professed embarrassment over their accents as their children made their way into the wider world, but they were probably also responding to lingering anti-German sentiment in the nation. An additional factor was the out-migration of youths from Pennsylvania German–speaking agrarian communities to urban centers for industrial and professional work. After the war, a number of organizations sponsored festivals and programs to promote the culture, leading to the rise of cultural tourism in Lancaster County (primarily for the Amish farmlands) and America's largest folk festival (the Kutztown Folk Festival) celebrating Pennsylvania German culture. Into the twenty-first century, Pennsylvania German identity has gained stature for its expressive arts, but it still suffers, according to Pennsylvania Germans, from images of the "dumb Dutch"—referring to the perception of backwardness because they continue to hold on to the folk past. Moreover, Dutchiness is often viewed as less visible or less socially relevant in a multicultural society compared with other ethnic movements in the United States, such as racialized movements for Latino, African, and Native American groups.

To contextualize Hellerich's narrative culturally as well as historically, I turn to examples of the "humorous anecdote and the tall story" circulating in, and commenting on, contemporary Pennsylvania German culture. The culture is an enigmatic ethnic identity in America—one consumed by outsiders through constructed tourist symbols but known differently, and ambivalently, by insiders. Relying on the historical precedents of Brendle and Troxell's collections, I reinterpret the narratives told to them as reflections of anality in the culture and show how this trait is used in later generations as an adaptive strategy with the decline of the culture. I focus on the *dreck* motif because, based on fieldwork, it appears to be the most conspicuous theme that Pennsylvania German tradition-bearers associate with their own folklore, and I explain it in contemporary esoteric discourse as a social construction of an ethnic self.

In addition to being found in narrative, the *hinkeldreck* theme can be seen visually in a number of T-shirt designs with sayings such as *"Heila, Heila, Hinkel Dreck,"* proclaiming pride in Pennsylvania German identity. Significant to my thesis, these T-shirts are sold not to tourists, who typically do not understand the reference, but to people who grew up in the culture. Another expression of this theme is the annual Hinkelfests in Lebanon, Pennsylvania, and Fredericksburg, Maryland—community festivals that are apparently unique to the Pennsylvania German region and that celebrate the chicken as an ethnic symbol of Dutchiness. Although my analysis emphasizes the symbolic readings of texts within cultural contexts, I also include a comparative component prompted by Alan Dundes's (1984) characterization of continental German culture as anal, examining its prevalent scatalogical humor to evaluate sources of the *dreck* theme in Germany.

The *"Heila, Heila, Hinkel Dreck"* saying comes from a chant that is often reported as being used in powwowing rituals (a form of magical healing). The full text is typically *"Heila, heila, hinkel dreck, Bis morgen (marye) frie iss alles veck"* or *"immer morgen (marye) iss alles weg,"* meaning "Holy, holy, chicken shit, in the morning, all has gone away" or "is on its way." It did not have to be uttered by powwowers, judging by the commentaries of Pennsylvania Germans. If a child got hurt, it was common for the parents to pretend to heal the bruise with the anally suggestive chant, much as the oral "kissing the boo-boo" is common in American popular culture. In the Pennsylvania German chant, the powwowers substitute *dreck* for holy water. An example is this general charm using religious images:

> *Die Wasser und dis Feuer* [This water and fire],
> *Die Wasser und dis Feuer*,
> *Die Wasser und dis Feuer*,
> *Die ist eine grosse Dinge* [This is a big thing],
> *In dies grosses geheilige Land* [In this big holy land],
> *Unser yunge frau Maria* [Our young lady Maria],
> Father, Son, and Holy Ghost, Amen. (Bronner 1996c, 551)

Narrative evidence is provided by Brendle and Troxell, who recorded the story of a *braucher*, or powwower, sprinkling holy water on scrawny cattle every morning and evening to fatten them. After three months, the powwower reports to the farm servant that the cattle will be free of evil and they will grow. The servant answers, "Your cattle need less holy water on the outside and more feed on the inside" (*Was des do Vieh brauch is wennicher heilich Wasser uff di haut un mehner schrod im Bauch*) (Brendle and Troxell 1944, 151–52). The story suggests the pragmatic concerns of the servant, who is closer to the land than to heaven. It implies, in fact, that the reference to *hinkeldreck* as a powwow chant is itself a parody, inverting the heavenly water into earthly dirt. A symbolic opposition is created not only between water and dirt but also between *heila* (from the German *heilig*) and *hinkel* (from the German *henne*).

The opposition of clean and dirty materials can be interpreted as creating separation between sacred and profane categories. This is necessary partly because the human body may be viewed as unclean, and in forms of fantasy, the dirt is removed from the self and projected onto outside objects and places (Kubie 1937). Brendle notes, for example, that *naus misse*, meaning "having to defecate," originally meant "to go out of the house to void the bowels." A traditional German riddle expressing the problem of differentiating dirt in the bodily interior and the physical exterior is this: "*Was ist draussen und doch drinnen?* (What is outside and yet inside?)" Answer: "*Der Dreck, wenn man sich in die*

Hosen beschissen hat (Dirt when a person has shit in his pants)" (Dundes 1984, 32–33). The psychological implication, as Lawrence Kubie explains, is that "the body, must despite its own uncleanliness shun as dirty anything in the outside world which resembles or represents the body's own 'dirt,' and that above all else it must never allow its own relatively 'clean' outsides to become contaminated by contact with the filthy interior of itself or of anyone else" (1937, 39). Applying this idea to the *hinkeldreck* image, it appears that the human body (the inside) becomes cleaner by noting the extraordinary dirt created outside by the chickens.

Another implication of constructing separate categories of clean and dirty is the analogy between up and down, short and long, and narrow and broad. In each case, the latter represents the earthy, anal side. Dundes, in fact, bases his analysis of the German worldview on the German proverbial expression *"Das Leben ist wie eine Hühnerleiter—kurz und beschissen* (Life is like a chicken coop ladder—short and shitty)" (1984, 9). In a common variation, a connection is made to infant toilet training, reinforcing a cognitive connection found in Hellerich's narrative: *Das leben ist wie ein Kinderhemd—kurz und beschissen* (Life is like a child's undershirt—short and shitty). The ladder, or life journey, is metaphorically climbed step by step to success or to heaven. In one of the most popular Pennsylvania German religious broadsides called "The Broad and Narrow Way," for instance, the broad, easy path on earth is the one filled with temptations of vice, whereas the narrow, more difficult path is directed toward heaven (Yoder 2005). Even Pennsylvania German baptismal certificates are often clearly divided between the earthly and the heavenly, with flowers and animals associated with the land lining the bottom of the form, while angels and eagles grace the top (Bronner 1992b, 289–93). In the "Schnitzelbank" song, which is still popular among Pennsylvania Germans, the lyrics emphasize some of these oppositions, related to the inclusion of the wagon wheel and the manure pile mentioned earlier: *"hin und her"* (here and there), *"kurz und lang"* (short and long), and *"krumm und grad"* (crooked and straight).

Other oppositions may be implied by the holy-*hinkel* substitution. The patriarchal heaven is contrasted with the matriarchal chicken, often expressed as the "mother hen" laying eggs and watching her chicks (Davis 2002). The chicken, as a domesticated bird controlled by humans, is frequently infantilized in narrative imagery, as in the designation of the little boy as *Hinkeldreck* in Hellerich's story. A Pennsylvania German folk rhyme reinforcing the infantilized feminine connection to *hinkel* is "*Haahnekamm, Hinkelbiebs, Frehlich Maedchen, du warscht hibscht*" (Cockscomb, hen peep, cheerful maiden, you were lovely) (Beam 1995, 21–22). In the case of Brendle and Troxell's story of the scrawny cattle, the powerful *braucher*, in the patriarchal provider role, is bested by the subordinate servant, in a feminine role but shown to be more in touch with the day-to-day care of the child-like cattle. The feed has more substance than the water, but instead of having spiritual value, it descends through the body to the ground as *dreck*.

The symbolic opposition of heavenly and earthly approaches can be read in a widely known Pennsylvania German story of a farmer who wants to protect his cattle. The *braucher* recommends closing openings in the roof *above* the cattle, but when the cows' milk turns sour in the pots, the answer to the problem comes from *below:* the pots are laid out on the manure heap and shot to pieces with a gun. The pragmatic advice is to get new crocks and keep them clean (Brendle and Troxell 1944, 142–43). Another narrative that Brendle recorded but declined to publish—maybe because it makes a cleric the butt of humor—also involves manure and the offering of pragmatic advice. Brendle identifies the narrative in his journal as an "anecdote," with the comment that he heard it often: "A farmer who was unable to raise good crops went 'zum Prieschder' [to the priest] and asked him to pray that he might have good crops. He received the answer, 'Do bade Bede nix; do muss Mischt bei!' [Here prayers are of no avail; manure is the answer.] 'Do batt Bidde un Bede nix; do muss Mischt bei!' [Here asking and praying are of no avail; manure is the answer.]" (Beam 1995, 71–72).

Whereas manure produces results in the preceding story, the tails of cattle and chickens appear in German lore to eject or lay bodily objects. One indication of this ejective function is the euphemism *machen*, or "making," for defecation. There may indeed be a veiled wish for a pleasant defecation experience in the typical Pennsylvania German parting phrase "*Mach's gut*" (literally, "make it good"). Brendle found other examples relating the tail or anus to production; for instance, he collected the belief "*So as die Hinkel lege, glob uff ihre Schwenz* [To make the chickens lay, beat on their tails]" (Beam 1995, 95). Although the cow does not lay eggs, its ejective function creates manure, as in this German children's riddle: "*Wie kommt Kuhscheisse auf das Dach?* [How did the cow shit get on the roof?] *Hat sich Kuh auf Schwanz geschissen und dann auf das Dach geschmissen* [The cow shit on its tail and then threw it up on the roof]" (Dundes 1984, 12). The humor derives from the manure being out of place—on the lofty roof, rather than on the ground—but there may be an implied association of the residents with the cow and its feces.

Pennsylvania German folk narrative can be read as expressing ambivalence toward the ritualizing of manure as lowly, profane "dirt" and contrasting it with lofty, sacred "cleanliness."[4] The dirt-profane association is an important way that ethical choices and cognitive categories are culturally constructed (see Bourke 1891; Kubie 1937; Sabbath and Hall 1977). Both insider and outsider observers have commented about the fixation on—even obsession with—cleanliness inside the Pennsylvania German home and its contrast with the *mischt* in the surrounding barnyards (Baver 1953a, 1953b). The affinity with the chicken in Pennsylvania German culture suggests a specific complicating context, since the separation of dirty and clean is more difficult to imagine with a bird immersed in its own feces and associated with living in roosts, suggesting its own community. Since the chicken does not fly, it is seen as being docile, stupid, and "grounded." It is a domesticated bird linked not to the wild but to the farm, where it is exploited by humans for its meat and eggs. Its feces, then, are one of its few natural defenses, since humans would rather avoid the smell and substance of the material.

The Pennsylvania Germans' association with raising chickens elevates their self-perception of toughness, since they realize that outsiders view it as a dirty and disgusting activity. This use of the power of chickens' *dreck*, enlarged by the strength of chickens in numbers, subverts the symbolism of the chicken as cowardly and feminine in American popular culture. It nonetheless makes reference to mainstream American culture's perception of the chicken, in keeping with attitudes toward the Pennsylvania Dutch, as unbecoming and marginalized, but it also gives the bird trickster qualities and allows it to prevail. Furthermore, whereas the main motif of chickens in American popular humor is a variation of "Why did the chicken cross the road?" and the catch answer "To get to the other side" (suggesting its simplicity or stupidity), in Pennsylvania German folklore, chickens are a metaphor for control of the farm because they are frequently described as having, in Beam's words, "the run of the barnyard" (1995, 22). The implication is that chickens have a dominant role within the landscape, although that environment may not be recognized outside of the culture.

The symbolic connection of Pennsylvania Germans with chickens is evident from non–Pennsylvania German versions of Hellerich's story of *hinkeldreck*, which typically leave out the chicken image. The joke can be found in several sources, both African American and European American; the boy's name is reported as "Shitass" in a second-generation immigrant family in New York (Legman 1968) and as "Motherfuck-er," "Shit," and "Sonovabitch" among African Americans in Virginia (Dance 1978, 297). A representative example in America is the follow-ing oral version collected in Indiana:

> It was the first day of school and the children filed into the classroom and took their seats. Teacher says, "All right, boys and girls. Now I want you all to stand up one at a time and tell everybody here your name, so we will all get to know each other." First little boy stood up and said, "My name is John Brown." "Very good, John, you may be seated." Next a little girl stood up and said, "My name is Nancy Jones." "Very good, Nancy, you may be seated." Next a little girl stood up and said, "My name is Pissy Smith." The teacher said, "You mustn't talk that way. We're in school, you know. Now tell us your real name." "My name is Pissy Smith," the little girl said. The teacher again reminded the little girl where she was and again asked her to give her real name. The little girl for the third time said, "My name is Pissy Smith." Okay, the teacher said, "one more chance to tell us your real name or leave." The little girl again said, "My name is Pissy Smith." "Get out," the teacher said, "until you can learn to talk right." As Pissy left the room, she said to a little boy in the back row, "Come on, Shit Head, she won't believe you either!" (Bronner 1988a, 135)

Both stories revolve around the prudish authoritarian teacher who is skeptical about the child's name. In both narratives, the first child is a girl, and the second, whose name invariably refers to excrement, is her little brother. A social hierarchy of dirt—from the feminine to the mas-culine, and in age from the older to the younger (presumably closer to the age of toilet training)—is suggested. In contrast to Hellerich's story, however, the above narrative lacks the ethnic associations of *hinkel* representing the Pennsylvania Germans' farm life. Hellerich also indicates a linguistic and cultural difference, not just a moralistic one, concerning German-sounding names and the English teacher.[5]

Of significance in Hellerich's narrative is the boundary between inside and outside the house. It is not only the name the teacher disbelieves but also the human association with earthly dirt. Inside the house is presumably clean, while outside is dirty, but the mother relates to what she sees as the surrounding context for her onomastic texts and perhaps implies the pre–toilet-training status of children. The teacher fails to understand the wagon wheel as a clue, for as Brendle's abundant examples of excrement show, the wagon wheel in the yard is associated linguistically with *mischt,* or "mess." The *hinkel* is significant because the fowl, and their droppings, cover the yard. The children appear to occupy a middle position between the clean inside and the dirty outside. For example, among Pennsylvania German children, the popular game known in English as ring-around-the-rosy differs from the English version by its reference to *dreck:*

> *Ringe, Ringe, Rosen*
> *Die Buben tragen Hosen*
> *Die Maedeln tragen Roeck*
> *Un fallen dann in Dreck*

> [Ring around a rosy,
> The boys wear pants
> The girls wear skirts
> And fall in the dirt/shit] (Beam 1995, 106)

In the English version, the children merely "fall down," rather than specifying the *dreck* as a pleasant destination.

In Hellerich's narrative, the mother can be viewed as relating to the *hinkel* outside as a hen would relate to her chicks, but the English teacher cannot understand the inclination and, in fact, judges it negatively. The humor, then, carries an indictment of the English establishment as harshly judging or suppressing the Germans as different, but also as dirty. The story absorbs the exoteric judgment and turns it into an esoteric source of pride. The name *hinkeldreck* signals ethnic separation for the boy as a symbol of his group (and its culture handed down from his mother), and it can also be viewed as an act of verbal aggression, hurling "shit" at the establishment that "looks down" on the group like dirt.

A traditional tale I collected in the Mahantango Valley area of central Pennsylvania further connects *hinkel* with *dreck* and contrasts it in an indicting way with the sacred establishment. It concerns a man who is on his way home and cannot hold his bowel movement. Thinking that no one can see him, he goes to the side of the road and defecates. But when a minister comes up the hill, the man quickly covers the pile with his hat. The minister asks him what he is doing on the side of the road, and the man explains defensively that one of his chicks escaped from the barnyard and he has caught it under his hat. The minister offers to buy the bird, and the man agrees only if the minister picks up the hat after the man is out of sight. The priest bends down to grab the bird and gets feces on his hands (Aarne-Thompson [AT] Tale Type 1528 in Uther 2004). The AT index shows that the story was originally documented in Germany as a moral tale as early as the fourteenth century, but it was most often related in the twentieth century as a joke (Uther 2004, 2:257–58).

The other animal associated with the production of feces in the Pennsylvania German world is the horse, and it, too, is pervasive in Pennsylvania German folklore. An example is this common parody of the "Our Father" prayer in the dialect:

Unser Vadder, wer du bischt
Marye faahre mer wider Mischt
Freidaag faahre mer die grosse Load
Bis Samschdaag faahre der Schimmel dod

[Our father, who you are
Tomorrow we haul manure
Friday we haul the big load
Until Saturday the horse is dead] (Beam 1995, 55)

Like other references to ritualized dirt, this parody contains a contrast to the sacred category of cleanliness to connote a difference between the spiritual and the earthly. Like the chicken, the horse can benefit humans, but people may express ambivalence toward the animal because of its immersion in feces, and for male tellers, the horse may be perceived as a male rival. The dialect linguistically associates *geilsdreck* (horseshit) with manure that is particularly abundant and potent. The size of the animal, its muscular appearance, and fantasies about its sexual organ suggest a more masculine symbol compared to the chicken.

One indication of the symbolic association of the chicken with the feminine and the horse with the masculine, affecting their characterizations in storytelling, is a contemporary-sounding pseudo-fable or "shaggy dog story" told about a chicken and a horse playing together in a barnyard. Tellers describe the horse falling into a mud pit and yelling to the chicken to get the farmer to help. Unable to locate the farmer, the chicken gets the farmer's fancy car (described as a BMW, Mercedes, or Porsche) and drives it to the mud pit, throws a rope to the horse, and ties the other end to the car to pull him out. The horse is grateful to the chicken for saving his life. A few days later, the two animals are playing again, and this time the chicken falls into the mud pit and exclaims, "Help me, go get the farmer!" The horse says, "No, I think I can save you." The horse stretches across the mud pit and tells the chicken to grab on to his penis. The chicken clutches it, and the horse stretches back and saves the chicken's life. The moral of the story, male tellers like to say, is that if you are hung like a horse, you don't need a fancy car to pick up chicks.[6] Both animals fear being submerged in dirt, or feces, suggesting a projection of the male teller's concerns to the animals' plight. Although both the masculine and the feminine animals become stuck in the dirt, it is the masculine horse—an alter ego for the farmer or the storyteller—that becomes the hero.[7] In another way, the story is unusual in Pennsylvania German lore, owing to its sexual content. Unlike American popular culture, the German repertoire of risqué narrative emphasizes "earthy" themes of excrement and anality over phallocentric motifs (Dundes 1984, 87). The narrative probably came from outside the culture in the style of the "shaggy dog joke" and was incorporated into the twenty-first-century Pennsylvania German male joke telling repertoire because of its chicken and horse imagery and because of a resentment against societal pressures exerted by popular culture for ordinary folk (characterized by farm animals) to conform or aspire to nonproductive wealth represented by fancy foreign cars (Brunvand 1963, 65).

One way Pennsylvania German folk humor mediates between the

animal as benefactor (as well as metaphor for the culture) and its as-sociation with masculinized dirt is to show the farmer's obliviousness to the *mischt*, suggesting the normative "earthy" existence. Here, for example, are two versions of a joke I heard at a Pennsylvania German gathering in Lebanon, Pennsylvania, in 2005:

> A farmer was a little lazy, and he didn't clean out the horse stable. The manure got so high that the horse hit his head on a beam about the door. This made the horse dizzy, and he couldn't work. The farmer hired a carpenter to raise the beam so the horse wouldn't hit his head. When the carpenter asked why the farmer hadn't removed the manure, he replied, "The horse hits his head, not his feet."

> Bob went to see an Amish friend. When he got to the house, the man's wife answered the door, "Hello Bop, what do you want?" He says, "I came to see Abie." "Vell, he's at the barn verking." Going to the barn he sees Abie on a ladder with a hatchet, chopping at the top beam of the door to the horse stable. "What are you doing, Abie?" "Vell hello Bop, you see I have this horse whose ears are too long, and they rub the beam and getting sore." "Well, Abie, why don't you take some of the manure away at the bottom?" "You vern't listening, Bop, I said his ears were too long, not his legs."

The second narrative was told by a Pennsylvania German man in his sixties, and he used the Amish to intensify the connection to farm life and the Pennsylvania German dialect. Reflecting on the story after he told it, he expressed the view that the Amish are living the life the Penn-sylvania German "church people" (Lutherans and Reformed) used to live. He felt that the Pennsylvania Germans had lost their identity with the decline of the dialect and of their agrarian lifestyle.

The Pennsylvania German obsession with cleanliness comes up in a joke I heard often about a farmer dealing with his sickly horse. The farmer wants to avoid going to the veterinarian, so he asks a neighbor (sometimes identified as non–Pennsylvania German or "English") for help. The neighbor says he has something that has worked wonders for him. So he goes to see the sickly horse and sticks a tube in the horse's rear end. He proceeds to blow into the tube, but the horse still will not stand. The farmer says to his neighbor, "Here, let me try." The farmer takes the tube out of the horse's butt, turns it around, and sticks the tube back into the horse's anus. "What did you do that for?" the neighbor asks. The farmer replies, "I wasn't going to blow in it after you had your mouth on it!" (see McNeil 2005, 267).

In a common variant, the farmer does go to the vet and says, "My horse is constipated." The vet advises, "Take one of these pills, put it in a long tube, stick the other end in the horse's ass, and blow the pill up there." But the farmer returns the next day, and he looks sick. The veterinarian asks, "What happened?" The farmer says, "The horse blew first" (see AT 1862D, The Constipated Cow, in Uther 2004, 2:465). In both versions, reversals occur between human and animal, triggered by the insertion of a tube physically linking man and horse. In the first narrative, the theme of obliviousness to the ritualized dirt coming out of the anus recurs, while in the second narrative, this dirt, in the form of flatulence, is the expression of the animal's potency. Given the many German folklore texts that confuse oral and anal, Dundes suggests that the oral action (expressed as *Leck mich am Arsch*, or "ass licking") implies "eating shit . . . the ultimate degradation" (Dundes 1984, 48). Brendle documents a Pennsylvania German children's custom that verifies this view: When children pass excrement on the ground on their way to school, they spit. The last one to spit or a child who does not spit at all will be accused of metaphorically eating "shit" (Beam 1995, 98).

Corroborating the confusion of the oral and the anal in German cultural sources is the devilish German character Eulenspiegel (often rendered in Pennsylvania German as Eileschpigel). A literal interpretation of the trickster's name is "owl mirror" (*die Eule* and *der Spiegel*, respectively), suggesting that he provides wisdom through a distorted reflection of society. A metaphorical interpretation, however, traces the name's meaning to forms of *Leck mich am Arsch*. According to this theory, *ulen* in the first part of the name also means "to wipe" or "to clean," and *spiegel* colloquially refers to the posterior (Collofino 1939, 1048; Dundes 1984, 49). In a Pennsylvania German story recorded by Brendle and Troxell that supports this theory (and relates to Hellerich's association of the mother with manure and to the *dreck*-water substitution in the powwow parody), Eileschpigel is said to be baptized three times in one day: once by a pastor with water in the church, a second time when his mother brings him outside and he falls into the *mischt*, and a third time when she washes him clean (Brendle and Troxell 1944, 176).

The anal Eileschpigel appears in Pennsylvania German folklore in a variant of the tale type mentioned earlier about the minister who thinks he is getting a bird under a hat but gets feces instead. Brendle and Troxell collected this story from Mrs. Emma Faustner of Bath, Pennsylvania:

> When Eileschipijjel's end drew near, he filled a box with worthless things and nailed it up tightly. Then taking the box he went to his pastor. He asked the pastor to preach a good sermon over his remains.
>
> "As a reward for your services you will receive this box which I have filled with things for you," said Eileschipijjel.
>
> The pastor conducted the funeral with an eye to the reward that was coming to him. After the burial he was given the box that Eileschipijjel had made ready. He hastened home and eagerly opened the box, and found in it nothing but rubbish.

The "rubbish" in the text represents waste, and it may very well have been *dreck* in the original but was edited by Brendle and Troxell or cleaned up by the teller. Worth noting is the rhetorical strategy also found in Hellerich's story of shocking the establishment (or sacred) figure with ritual dirt, echoing an infant's act of defecation as an unwelcome gift for the mother (Dundes 1984, 34).

In contests, usually with the devil, Eileschpigel shows his superior ability with the aid of trickery to haul loads, make piles, and throw sheaves. These actions suggest an infantile, anal ejective function, and when portrayed in this way, Eileschpigel figuratively soils the profane devil and wipes himself clean. He typically gloats after completing his task, finding pleasure in his discharge, which is usually done, he emphasizes, without exertion. In a tale reminiscent of the confusion between the oral and anal actions of human and horse in a narrative given earlier, Eileschpigel goes out hunting with an old musket. As Brendle and Troxell record the story:

> The devil came along and seeing the musket asked, "What is that?"

Eileschipijjel answered, "A smoke pipe" [*schmokpeif*] and turning the end of the barrel to the devil, said, "Take a puff."

The devil took the end of the barrel into his mouth and began to suck. Thereupon Eileschipijjel pulled the trigger and the bullet and the smoke flew into the devil's mouth.

The devil, coughing and gasping for breath, spat out the bullet and said, "You—you surely use strong tobacco." (Brendle and Troxell 1944, 161; cf. Tale Type 1157 in Uther 2004, 2:53)

Although Brendle and Troxell attribute this narrative to Anson Sittler of Egypt, Pennsylvania, they comment that it was told by "many others," suggesting its wide circulation.

One theory explaining the male fascination with anality in folk narratives is that it represents ejection as a form of creation, simulating the female ability to give birth (Dundes 1962a). A striking part of the Pennsylvania German corpus that may invite this interpretation is the story "The Mule's Egg," which was "quite widely heard" by Brendle and Troxell:

Eileschipijjel came across a pumpkin and did not know what it was. As he was looking it over, a man came along and asked, "Do you know what that is?"

Answered Eileschipijjel, "I do not. I never saw anything like it."

The man said, "That is a mule's egg and if you sit on it for three weeks there will be a young mule."

Eileschipijjel reflected upon the matter and decided that it would be worthwhile to sit on the mule egg for three weeks. He proceeded to sit on the pumpkin.

Becoming tired in a short time, he arose and rolled the pumpkin down the hill. The pumpkin rolled on until it hit a boulder and flew into pieces. At that very moment a rabbit that had been nesting at the boulder scurried away. Seeing the rabbit, Eileschipijjel cried, "Hee-haw little colt, here is your mammy" [*Hie-ha Hutchehelli, Do is dei Mudderli*]. (Brendle and Troxell 1944, 169–70; cf. Tale Type 1319 in Uther 2004, 2:121–22)

The trickster character, who is able to take risks, squats on the pumpkin in an anal position, but as he rises, the pumpkin—in a kind of discharge—descends the hill and breaks apart. There is an apparent transformation into a rabbit, an animal associated with the abundant production of dung pellets.

A connection is frequently made in German lore between the taint of money and the dirt of feces, and this is sometimes used to link values placed on the traits of being orderly, parsimonious, industrious, and obstinate (Dundes 1984, 80). All these traits are attributed in literature and lore to Pennsylvania Germans. Dundes points out that, "While the money-feces equation is found outside German culture, it is nowhere more explicit than in German folklore. One thinks of the goose that laid the golden egg (Motif B 103.2.1, Treasure-laying bird) or the donkey which defecates gold (Motif B 103.1.1, Gold producing ass) or perhaps even [a] German version of Aarne-Thompson tale type 500, The Name of the Helper (Uther I, 285–86). In that folktale, the heroine's parent boasts that the girl can spin straw into gold—is it the straw found in the stable? If so, it would very likely contain animal manure" (Dundes 1984, 81–82). An Eileschpigel cycle that utilizes the money-feces equation is the story titled "The Devil Wants Eileschipijjel's Soul," recorded by Brendle and Troxell:

> Eileschipijjel sold his soul to the devil on the understanding that the devil was to fill a room with gold for him.
> The devil was willing and a hole was made in the ceiling of a large room. Thereupon the devil began to pour gold into the room.
> Eileschipijjel, however, had made a hole in the floor of the room. When the devil found that it was impossible to fill the room, he disappeared. (Brendle and Troxell 1944, 158)

The trickster triumphs because he directed the devil to pour gold into the top of the room, like a mouth, which then falls through a cavity in the bottom that could be called anal. The trickster derives great pleasure from the evacuation of the room's contents, suggesting, if one accepts the metaphor of the anal cavity, an equivalence of gold and feces. The trickster's crossing of a boundary, adjusting the defecation process to create wealth and pleasure, can be taken as a sign of the culture's adaptability, particularly to an uncomfortable environment.

In a comparison of global trickster tales, psychologists David M. Abrams and Brian Sutton-Smith observe that, in a complex society, the trickster genre expresses an emotional ambivalence toward the success orientation or privilege of the dominant society and expresses a value placed on adaptability and flexibility as an alternative (1977, 45). This view brings into relief Dundes's example of the chicken coop ladder as conveying ambivalence toward the drive toward success and the German signification of *dreck* to show pleasure and independence. The violation of taboo is a particular form of culturally symbolic reversal that contributes to cultural stability, not to its downfall. As Abrams and Sutton-Smith observe, "Dealing in such symbolic contraries appears to deliver the group from the frustrations that arise out of the entrapment in a particular form of adaptation" (1977, 45–46); mocking authority figures and exaggerating trickery, the trickster remains autonomous.

The money-feces equation can be viewed as a cognitive reaction to a preoccupation with things that are unclean or associated with corruption, and the cultural context of rural life, with its earthiness, intensifies the need for order. Indeed, Pennsylvania Germans, like Germans, indicate in folk speech a sense of satisfaction or normality by saying, *Alles iss in ordnung* ("everything is in order"). Folklore provides an outlet to symbolize the drive to be fastidious about cleanliness, perhaps derived from early toilet training and culturally inherited values, even though one desires to revel in defecation as a source of pleasure and, in the German context, often a sense of identity. In the fantasy of the story, one may read the transformation of feces as something pleasurable but dirty into something valuable and clean. Immobility is viewed as a form of constipation and anal retention, and it is often associated in barnyard stories with efforts to force ejection. The most common type is about horses that get stuck, and as I have pointed out, in the social hierarchy of animals constructed by humans, the feces produced by horses are considered especially abundant and potent. Brendle and Troxell give six versions of a story relating the insertion of an implement into the horse or, symbolically, the *rear* of the wagon, followed by a human falling dead to the ground. They report this example from Bucks County, Pennsylvania:

A farmer, hauling hay and grain to Philadelphia, found that, whenever he was passing a certain inn, his horses stopped. He was advised to take a revolver along and, should his horses to stop again at the same place, he was to get off the wagon and walk around the rear, and shoot into the hub of the hind wheel on the other side. This he did, and his horses immediately went on. The next day he learned that a man sitting in the bar-room had fallen over dead. (Brendle and Troxell 1944, 98–99)

Related to narratives about animate objects that cannot move are those about inanimate items that have been stolen. Brendle and Troxell are at a loss to explain why so many narratives revolve around theft (often humorously described as the owner's misplacement of objects mistakenly thought to be the result of a burglary) when the strong social bond among Pennsylvania Germans would seem to imply a trusting community. Following the previous interpretation, the theft story may reflect an anal order because the objects, like emissions from one's body, are out of place—indeed, taken away, as if they are still connected to the body. The story treats this misplacement as a serious violation not just of property but also of personal well-being. In many narratives, the humor serves to remind listeners that objects or piles of them can be easily recovered, often to the embarrassment of the neurotic owner (suggesting the equation of anal-retentiveness with protectiveness). In supernatural tales, a wheel associated with a natural circle shape (or anus) causes the thief to return the stolen goods. In the first of four versions published by Brendle and Troxell, a farmer discovers that a bag of corn has been stolen. The farmer goes to his wheelbarrow (used to haul manure) and turns the wheel backward. At first he moves the wheel slowly, "then faster and faster, all the while repeating some mystic words. When the wheel was revolving at its highest speed, the thief came running breathlessly from behind the barn with the bag of stolen corn" (Brendle and Troxell 1944, 177). In a more direct signification of the Pennsylvania German farmer's anality, a farmer's purse is stolen in Brendle and Troxell's published version from Allentown, Pennsylvania:

To discover the thief, he went into the stable and rubbed balsam on the tail of his donkey.

Then he called his men together and said, "One of you stole my purse, and I am going to discover which one of you is the thief. One by one you must go into the stable and rub your hands upon the donkey's tail and when he who stole the purse touches the tail, the donkey will bray."

All the men went into the stable, one by one, and all came out, but the donkey didn't bray. Thereupon the master lined the ten men against a wall. He went along the line, took their hands and smelled at them. He came to one whose hands were free from the odor of balsam. To him he said, "You are the thief. Your hands betray you." (Brendle and Troxell 1944, 181–82)

The hands are supposed to have an earthy odor connected with the donkey, known in colloquial speech as an ass—the same name given to the human posterior. And the recovered goods are coins kept in a sack (*tasch*), substituted magically with an anal odor, suggesting again the money-feces equation.

Another form involves guns that will not shoot, and as the previous Eileschpigel story shows, whereas the gun is often interpreted as phallic in psychoanalytical treatises, in Pennsylvania German stories, it appears to be anal. In the "Schnitzelbank" song, for example, there is a lyrical reference to a "shooting gun" (*schiess gewehr*), playing on the resemblance between *schiess* ("shoot") and *scheiss* ("shit"). The *bank* image itself, with a craftsman sitting on the plank ejecting shavings while carving, suggests an anal ejective function (in Pennsylvania German, a *bank* is often associated with a manure wagon). In Brendle and Troxell's collected narratives, there is some force that takes away the gun's power to shoot. In the following example, a woman's curse is the culprit, and it is lifted by destroying a cat (associated with feminine power):

In the days of muzzle loading guns, it was believed that envious people could and would "take the fire from a gun."

Two men of the Perkiomen Valley, while out hunting, passed a cabin. An old woman who was in the yard looked at them intently, and then tucked a corner of her apron under her apron strings. The hunters went on, but had no success.

Game was plentiful, and the shots were easy, but the hunters were unable to hit whatever they shot at. Then, they concluded that the old woman had put a spell on their guns.

One of them suggested that they leave the open fields, and take to the road, and if perchance they would come upon a cat, they would shoot her; and that would restore the killing power to the guns.

They took to the road, and shot a cat. Thereafter, they easily shot whatever game they saw. (Brendle and Troxell 1944, 101–2)

Evidence of the anal metaphor is the collectors' contextual explanation that a charm would cause the shot to fall to the ground as soon as it left the barrel. A similar narrative motif is found in another "widely heard" version in which a man boasts that "he could take the shot from a gun; that is he could cause the shot to drop straightaway to the ground as soon as it came from the mouth of the barrel" (Brendle and Troxell 1944, 203).

Another type of distress is created by cream that will not turn to butter, suggesting the bodily transformation of food into feces. A common motif is a bag that magically helps the transformation and destroys the curser. In one of five versions collected by Brendle and Troxell, for instance, a family is told to take "a flour bag [*Mehlsack*] and pour a dipperful of cream from the churn into the bag and beat it well with a stout cudgel. This was done, and thereupon the cream readily turned to butter." The family subsequently discovers that an "old lady" has fallen and broken a leg. The bag simulates the action of a digestive bladder that has been "stopped" by the charmer. The flour or "meal" is connected in Pennsylvania German proverbs with the fertile field, as indicated by "*Der Hawwer sucht sei Mehl uff em Feld* [Oats looks for its flour in the field]" (Beam 1995, 56).

The other side of the lack of movement in the money-feces equation is the finding of treasure. But this can also imply a lack of order or regularity in life, since it involves a massive change of fortune. Most Pennsylvania German stories about treasure are about fortunes buried in the ground or down a hole, again linking earthiness and anality. And in most stories the fortune is not found, as if to warn against the irregularity of a lack of ejective production until one finds the fortune and of soiling oneself in the process of digging. One can see the connection to concentrated defecation in the motif of maintaining silence while digging a hole. Brendle and Troxell give seven different variants of the motif that hidden treasure must be sought in silence. In the first story, given by Edwin Long of Geryville, Pennsylvania, searchers dutifully

remain silent while digging until they look up and see the devil, identified in one version as *dar Mann mit em Mischdhoke*, or "the man with
the manure hook" (also connected with the animal symbol of *der mit de
Gloee fies*, or "cloven feet") (Brendle and Troxell 1944, 46). In another
version with a possible money-feces connection, the searchers open the
chest after digging and find it full of gold pieces. In a violation of anal
retention, one digger is "unable to restrain his joy" and yells, "Now,
we'll be rich," which causes the chest to disappear (Brendle and Troxell
1944, 46).

The social hierarchy of animals in relation to literally working in
the dirt occurs in a version from Laurys, Pennsylvania. In it, the motif
of the searchers digging within a ring adds to the anal symbolism:

> N. N. heard that a treasure was buried at the Sand Bank, not
> far from Hellertown. He and several others went to a braucher
> who told them to draw a ring around the spot where the trea-
> sure was supposed to be, and then, in absolute silence, they
> were to dig within the ring.
>
> Soon after they began digging, a flock of blackbirds flew on
> a tree nearby. The birds whistled and sang, but the men kept
> on digging.
>
> Then a hen with a flock of chicks came to the ring, but the
> men paid no attention to her, and kept on digging.
>
> Then came an ugly ferocious looking boar up to the ring,
> and one of the men became scared and cried out, "Huss!" [ex-
> clamatory word used when driving pigs]
>
> The boar immediately vanished. The men ceased digging
> for they knew that it would be impossible for them to find the
> treasure after one had broken the injunction of silence. (Bren-
> dle and Troxell 1944, 49)

Sometimes the pigs, representing animals that root in the dirt, are replaced by money. In a story from Lehigh County, Pennsylvania, the
searcher hears that he needs "seven brothers" to find the treasure. He remembers that his sow had a litter of seven, so he takes the seven little pigs
down into the cellar. The next morning he finds them torn to pieces, and
on the floor is a large pile of money (Brendle and Troxell 1944, 52, 53).

Treasure found in bed suggests defecation as the soiling of sheets or one's pants, often with the mother in view. The German counting-out rhyme relates, for example, *"Herbert hat ins Bett geschissen, Gerade aufs Paradekissen, Mutter hat's gesehn—Und du kannst gehn!* [Herbert has shit in bed, Right on the good pillow, Mother has seen it, And you can go out]" (Dundes 1984, 33). Finding treasure in bed (suggesting feces as a gift or reward) is known by folklorists as a widely circulated tale type (1645B Dream of Marking the Treasure in Uther 2004, 2:352–53). A man (e.g., a farmer, poor man, miser, fool) dreams that he finds a treasure or is told (often by the devil or a spirit) where a treasure is buried. It is too heavy for him to carry, so he marks the place with his own excrement. In the morning he finds that only the end of this dream is true: he has defecated in his bed. In Brendle and Troxell's collection, a Pennsylvania German narrative involves a mother guiding her daughter and a subservient character to treasure:

After old mother N. N., who died at the home of her daughter, had been buried, the daughter asked her maid whether she would occupy the bedroom where the old lady had slept.

"Surely! Why not?" answered the maid. "Your mother was a good woman and harmed no one while she was living, and now she has found rest and will never come back to this world."

The first night that the maid slept in the room, she awoke around midnight and saw the mother sitting at the foot of the bed. The next morning she told her mistress, who smiled and said, "That was only a dream. Nothing more."

Several nights later the maid again saw the mother sitting at the foot of the bed and again she told her mistress. Unwilling to believe that the maid had seen her mother, because she could not understand why her mother should come back from the grave, the daughter resolved to sleep with the maid, and should her mother appear, to ask of her what she sought.

That very night the mother appeared. The daughter asked, "What is your desire?" The mother answered that the bedpost where she was sitting had been chiselled out and much money concealed in it, and then disappeared.

They searched and found a large sum of money. The old woman never reappeared thereafter. (Brendle and Troxell 1944, 54–55)

Related to this symbolic equivalence of money and feces is the linguistic use of *deposit* for both finance and excrement. Common in the United States are variations of this riddle-joke: "What is the difference between a bankrupt lawyer and a pigeon?" Answer: "The pigeon can still make a deposit on a Mercedes." To show the German variation of the gold-feces equation, Dundes gives the following Wellerism from oral tradition: "*Es is nicht alles Gold, was glänzt! Sagt der Herr—da war er in einen Haufen Kleinkinderscheisse getreten* [All is not gold that glistens, said the man as he stepped into a pile of baby shit]" (Dundes 1984, 103–4).

Although this equivalence is widespread, a German distinction recorded in ethnographic chronicles is the high status accorded to the display of piles of manure. According to Dundes, a pile of manure in front of a house served as a public proclamation of wealth in Germany as early as the seventeenth century. This assessment was based on the greater amount of manure created when a family owned more farm animals. In the nineteenth century, a chronicle of Saxony announced that "boys and girls in the streets, with a barrow, broom, and shovel, gathering up the horse-dung for the increase of the much-prized muck-heap at the back of every dwelling" (Mayhew 1864, 2:611). In the late twentieth century, anthropologist Ethel Nurge studied village life in the Vogelsberg region of Germany and found, "One of the symbols of household wealth is the size of the manure pile. The manure pile stands in the front yard. Decades and centuries ago it must have been a more important symbol of the industry and wealth of a family than it is today but even today, when a family builds a new house and could put their manure heap in the back by changing floor plans and work routes, they do not; they put it in the front" (Nurge 1975, 137). In Hellerich's narrative is the implicit contrast of looking out the window in the Pennsylvania German world and seeing the barnyard, with its manure, as a sign of ejective prosperity versus the American cultural standard (or obsession) derived from the English heritage of the grass lawn, suggesting a manorial presence and the anal-retentive maintenance of a close-cropped appearance (i.e., representing human control rather than natural, dispersed growth) (Jenkins 1994; Steinberg 2006; Teyssot 1999).

Another related puzzle that may be solved by an understanding of anality is the insistence on separate "water closets" for toilets throughout the Rhineland, in contrast to the American bathroom with toilet and bath. It may appear to be another example of a Continental cultural construction of clean and dirty zones, since this segregation of the toilet is not shared in the United Kingdom. But another possibility is that there is also a reveling in defecation or the material representation of a tight anus by being enclosed by walls with one's stink (even looking at one's results in popular "platform" toilets and focusing on it as it is wiped away). If this interpretation is applied to Hellerich's narrative, the symbolic opposition of German and English in the story is made even greater by the possibility of a German attribution of value and identity association to manure, while the English view it as a sign of depravation. Further, the symbolic opposition in Hellerich's story can be read as one between the anal-ejective children, whose ethnic birth names represent a "natural" anal stage of development, and the anal-retentive character of the rules-oriented teacher, imposing practical and societal assimilative pressures on the children to "grow up" into the phallic stage. Thus, the joke is used to express a conflict in Freudian terms between the natural or pleasure-seeking id and the societal control of the ego. The ethnic composition of the narrative is indeed enmeshed in anal references.

Having argued that the Pennsylvania German "earthy" attitude toward manure as a marker of rural identity is rooted in German cultural sources, the question arises whether there are differences between Pennsylvania Germans in the American setting and in the European homeland. The essential distinction is the ethnic status of Pennsylvania Germans in the United States and, particularly, the collective memory in the middle Atlantic region of homogeneous settlements where a German dialect was the workaday language before modernization broke down the isolation and self-contained folklife of Pennsylvania German farming communities. Especially expressive in the onomastic details related by Hellerich is the Pennsylvania Germans' identity as a linguistic community tied to the land. When performed among Pennsylvania Germans, the story serves to question the sources of identity once these two important markers disappear. Brendle's corpus does not reference ethnic status as much as it does a separate world that is apparently homogeneously Pennsylvania German. Beam observes, for example, that in 1942, when Brendle was collecting in Lehigh County, "the PG culture was the dominant one in many of the rural sections of southeastern Pennsylvania." Into the twenty-first century, Beam bemoans, "Among the non-sectarian Pennsylvania Dutch only the oldest generation speaks the dialect fluently and not all of those are bearers of traditional sayings and beliefs" (Beam 1995, vii, ii).

Brendle, in fact, lamented as early as 1937 that "our folk-life has truly been diluted" (Brendle 1985, 33). He worried that, with this dilution, the Pennsylvania German "folk character of our ancestors" would disappear, and central to this character were the traits of work and determination, related to the "earthy" endeavors of farming folk. Indeed, to underscore his point, he directed the audience to look at the land. "Look at the great barns, the beautiful houses, the marvellous fields, the handsome churches," he advised. "All this has come about through work!" he declared, and he offered the evidence of bodily emissions, or droppings: "industry and drops of perspiration" (Brendle 1985, 27). The nonearthy or non–Pennsylvania German "others" for Brendle were the intellectual "lazybones" who did not produce or eject. They have misunderstood the dialect as a sign of ignorance, he reflected, and went on to pronounce that they failed to see the whole cultural landscape, the "deepness," symbolized by the language. "We have more than a language. We have a special character, a folk-character," he told his Pennsylvania Dutch audience (in the Pennsylvania Dutch language), and to his mind, that "industrious" character was a function of the people's attachment to the land (Brendle 1985, 31).

A dialect folklore, rather than a folklore in the dialect, continues for a contemporary generation that understands its relation to a rural heritage and an ethnic identity. This dialect folklore resolves cultural conflicts through symbols in folklore's fictive plane. Without that heritage, since many Pennsylvania Germans have left the land, and without the dialect, the ethnic identity revolves around the perception of a cultural difference in values and the collective memory of a common historical experience. The big difference between Brendle and Troxell's corpus and mine, accordingly, is that the mid-twentieth-century repertoire barely mentions outsiders to the culture. The anecdotes and jokes in today's material are preoccupied with what it means to be Pennsylvania German in relation to modern American society, symbolized as the authoritarian establishment in the center and Pennsylvania Germans at the margins, and they draw liberally on earthiness, signified in the *hinkeldreck* motif, as an identifying Pennsylvania German theme.

The *hinkel* is unique in Pennsylvania German folklore because it draws attention to the chicken as a metaphor for the esoteric Dutchman. Proudly, the chicken has the run of the farm, but it is viewed as dirty by English outsiders and as an anachronism by twenty-first-century descendants of German American settlers. If contemporary Dutch ethnics assign blame for the Pennsylvania German decline on the English, and if their stories show the suppressed Dutch emerging triumphant in their identity, at least for a moment, they also reveal a projection onto the English of guilt by the Dutch speakers for not perpetuating their linguistic and cultural tradition. Telling a story *with* dialect rather than *in* it, Hellerich expresses a disjuncture between the contemporary feeling of being Dutch in a modern society and the language and culture in the homogeneous society of his forebears (Brandes 1983; Dorson 1949; Kemp 1978–1979; Nusbaum 1979; Salmons 1988). Its fictive setting in the school is significant because of the historical association between the implementation of compulsory education in English during the nineteenth century, which presaged the death of the Pennsylvania German language, and the twentieth-century failure of Dutch speakers to pass the heritage on a younger generation, which sounded the death knell for the culture (Egle 1892; Beam 1995).

The telling of the dialect story, as Hellerich proclaimed, reveals what contemporary Dutchiness is about by, on its surface, reporting the struggle to maintain a Pennsylvania German identity under English pressure to assimilate. At a deeper level, it becomes imperative to tell the story to symbolically express the conflicts, and the guilt, felt by allowing the loss of the language, land, and identity. Moreover, the inside-outside distinction for ethnicity seems to be more blurred in modern consciousness, and the dialect folklore acts to bring order and boundary to a non-racial status for Pennsylvania Germans and, indeed, to show that they are different by type as well as by heritage. Although the Pennsylvania Germans are not alone among American groups in using dialect folklore to deal with conflicts in identity, their modern verbal art is distinctive for the significance of anality. Even if Pennsylvania German individuals are not anal in their contemporary practice, particularly the late-twentieth-century generations that followed the perceived decline of a *folklife*, they can be heard using anality symbolically in their lore. Represented as *hinkeldreck*, the anality speaks to adaptability under changing conditions and the importance of a Pennsylvania German past to the creation of an ethnic self in modern culture.

9

Sporting Tradition

On the Praxis of American Football

Ironically, people refer to play as a chance to "let go," meaning the suspension of the usual, even as the guidelines they apply to their fun and games derive from everyday life. In modern culture, characterized by corporate routine and the passive reception of entertainment, many traditions are cognitively perceived as special occasions for participatory play in which "fun time" can be used to comment on what one does during serious or ordinary time (Abrahams 2005, 96–110; Bascom 1954, 336–38; Dundes 1969b). It might even be said to take one back to childhood because traditional play often appears to be "child's play." As a childhood preoccupation one engages in before beginning to work, play holds a critical developmental role in transmitting culture from one generation to the next and preparing children for work in the society (Denzin 1975). An assumption in such a "cultural mirror" perspective relates to the social construction of play frames that apparently keeps them separate from the reality of usual practice: by compacting deep-seated symbols into a tightly framed event, such as a game usually of short duration, play brings into relief the broad experience of life (Sherzer 1993; Sutton-Smith 1997).

Yet there is also a prevalent counternotion drawing attention to play and tradition. It holds that play is configured in a separate space and time to facilitate distortions, even subversions, of society (Sherman and Weisskopf 1995; Sutton-Smith 1986, 252–53). Play can be seen as a form of fantasy in which people take license to do and say what they cannot in everyday life. In the form of sport taken so seriously by fans that they blur the lines between fantasy and reality, such distortions have to be managed, and social worlds have to be organized hierarchically to prevent the practice of sport from being perceived as a threat to society. Sport involves masses of people who engage in the praxis of playing without participating in play, yet they help determine the frame by which the messages of play are perceived and allowed to occur repeatedly as traditions.

Take the case of American football—America's colossal spectacle to behold, if not to play. The seventeen most-watched programs in television history are all football games, and Super Bowl XLIII set a record for U.S. viewership of 151.6 million people, or half the country's entire population (National Football League 2009, 2). No other spectator sport commands that kind of intense popularity; opinion polls taken in the first decade of the twenty-first century show that fans name professional and college football as their favorite sport by a margin of more than three to one over other sports (National Football League 2009, 12). "Are you ready for some football?" That is the opening theme hollered by country music performer Hank Williams Jr. for *Monday Night Football* beginning in 1989, implying that other sports are fine, but football is the ultimate contest, at least for Americans. The theme song is unapologetic in its celebration of the sport's violent appeal—"Time to get all the hits, the bangs, and the blocks"—and its macho context— "All my rowdy friends are back for Monday Night!" Is that message a reflection or a distortion of everyday life?

Football imagined as a grand festival, or spectacle, emerged in the twentieth century as an American tradition, with connotations of football's being essential to an understanding of American modern culture. In 2010 the superstore chain Walmart launched an advertising campaign to encourage consumers to stock up for the weekend and the "big game." A maternal voice narrates a domestic scene: "Game time is all about the tradition. It's all about the tackles, the touchdowns, and watching my boys do what they do." Everything else going on in the house pales in comparison to watching the football game. With the invocation to tradition, promotional videos for individual teams often feature rabid fans as well as players. Two representative examples are the University of Michigan, which blares the message "Tradition Lives Here," and Purdue University, which hails its toughness and competitiveness represented by football's "One Tradition."

In its unabashed staging of hypermasculine contests of strength and speed, and in its dramatic rise to prominence in terms of attendance and media coverage, football appears to deny the thesis that play involving manly values of aggression and social dominance have been sublimated or eliminated as American culture became feminized from the nineteenth century to the twenty-first century (Douglas 1978). Despite the egalitarian spirit heralded by Title IX in the 1970s and the rise of women's sports, football is dominated by men as both players and spectators, yet broadcasters hail it as "America's game," with its crushing hits, bangs, and blocks eclipsing the public's fondness for the more leisurely, and sanitary, actions of baseball out at the pastoral park (MacCambridge 2004; Mandelbaum 2004; National Football League 2009). The mixed message for boys is that American society disapproves of the veneration of brute force to exert social dominance, but it nonetheless makes heroes of the game of football and the mass spectacle of its battles royale.

Despite its tremendous popularity in America, football has not been exported to the rest of the world the way baseball and basketball have. So it is not only manly but also somehow American in its profile. The cultural puzzle of football as a distinctively modern American obsession is to find the source of its popularity, which appears on the surface to defy social historical trends. The scholarship proposing that football is not "merely a game" but a prime cultural metaphor, or antimetaphor, dates to the sport's emergence in the late nineteenth century as the trophy event of college athletics, coinciding with the start of the academic year (Krout 1929, 232–58). Youths' fondness for the sport's brutality sparked harsh newspaper editorials and banishment by some college presidents, especially among the elite institutions of the Northeast, where football had become all the rage among student bodies. Much of the critical concern was related to its ferocity and gore, which appeared to go against the image of the life of the mind in advanced education. Yet many pundits viewed it not as a reflection of life but as a necessary release from reality for adolescent boys making the transition to adulthood. They promoted its roughness as a necessary antidote to the enervating effects of modernization and industrialization on American manhood, particularly among the sedentary upper class. Offsetting teenagers' tendencies toward self-absorption and laziness, they mused, football would also transmit the values of teamwork, perseverance, and grit, which were supposed to be the keys to success in the professional world (Watterson 2000, 9–98).

Nineteenth-century stereoview of boys playing "football," issued by Kilburn Brothers, Littleton, New Hampshire.

The late-nineteenth-century public understood football as a participant sport associated with the high school and college years. However, with media coverage of professional football played in huge stadiums before national audiences, football played by college graduates rose to the pinnacle of spectator sports during the 1960s. With replays of head-on collisions on the field and scans of rabid fans in the stands braving the elements to cheer their team on, football appeared to be tailor made to the visual medium of television (Mandelbaum 2004, 175–79; Oriard 2001, 11–12; Rader 1999, 255–56). In 2010, football again took the lead among major American sports by being broadcast in 3-D, a viewing experience fans embraced for its ability to make the action "jump off the screen" (Pucin 2008). Viewers reported that the close-ups made them feel like they were in the midst of the battle, and they praised the exaggeration of the bulk of fast-moving, grappling bodies (Staples 2010). Unlike baseball and basketball, with many games stretching over a long season, football's relatively few games carry high stakes, and each one is cast as a major spectacle with "make or break" consequences (Oriard 2007). The inauguration of the Super Bowl in 1967 and the consequent construction of Super Bowl Sunday as a national festival sent signals that football deserved the crown as America's obsession as well as its prime-time sport (MacCambridge 2004).

Reports of football scores and standings took on unprecedented public urgency. Meanwhile, congressional hearings dragged on about the fairness of the Bowl Championship Series and concussions suffered by players; football coaches and star players became glitterati admired for their tough, aggressive attitudes, yet they were also mercilessly incriminated for bad behavior off the field; and pundits contemplated whether the bruising game of football was a better metaphor for America than other sports were (Austin 2008). Disagreement prevailed among scholars, however, about what it was a metaphor for. The following is a list of the most common views:

1. Football is a metaphor for war and violence. As a distortion of culture, it became especially popular as America became less powerful militarily; alternatively, as a reflection of culture, it became more popular as America prepared for war (Cunningham 2004; Davison 2008; Mandelbaum 2004, 128–42; Stempel 2006; Trujillo 1995). A subset of this argument is that football was tied historically to the Cold War culture, and the sport became culturally crucial to magnify American distinctiveness and tout American values in response to communism and other perceived antidemocratic threats (Kemper 2009).
2. Football is a metaphor for corporate organization, drawing on its historical connection to industrialism and urbanism (e.g., the specialization and management of a large number of players, attention to the clock, a platoon system, ethnic participation, and collective rather than individual performance). As a reflection of culture, football became especially popular as the American economy became more service and information oriented, and football sustained the excesses of capitalism (Belliotti 2008; Hartmann 2003; Lindquist 2006; Mandelbaum 2004, 119–27;

Norwood 2004; Riesman and Denney 1951; Robertson 1980, 253–57).

3. Football is a metaphor for mass society. As a distortion of culture, it became an outlet for individuals to express local loyalties. Football grew in popularity as people expressed their frustrations with a society distended beyond the community scale, or the mass media seized on football (more so than other sports) as a way to construct a mass society. Related to this view is football's representation of a postethnic society in which helmets and alliances to the "unit" hide or sublimate players' racial and ethnic backgrounds, although some critics have complained that the rituals surrounding football reproduce patterns of inequality (Bissinger 1990; Foley 1990; Lindquist 2006; Oriard 1993, 2001; see also the message in the popular movies *The Blind Side* [2009] and *Remember the Titans* [2000]).

4. Football is a metaphor for civil or folk religion, which arose with the decline of organized religion as a moral arbiter and communal institution in America (Forney 2007; Hamilton 2008; Price 2001).

5. Football as a framed celebration of hypermasculinity is a metaphor for sexism and homophobia in American society. Fitting in with the idea of play as a distortion of society, football became a compensation for women's increasing power in society by becoming an instrument to sustain male, heterosexual hegemony (Falk 2005; Foley 1990; Hardin 2000; Kimmel 2008, 136–38; Nelson 1994).

6. Football is a metaphor for male adolescents' anxiety over developing or proving their masculinity. As a reflection of culture, it shows manliness by feminizing the opponent or withstanding homoerotic attack (Dundes 1978a).

Methodologically, the first four views provide rationales for the rise of football, whereas the fifth and sixth are distinguished by offering psychological explanations for the attraction to football. They seek the sources of football in boys' play development, while contextualizing the sport historically and sociologically. The last explanation, championed by folklorist Alan Dundes, shares with the fifth perspective the view that male anxiety originates in a feminizing social context, but it extends the interpretation (some critics say too far) by positing that developmental aspects of the homoerotic component of male display in big-time organized sports are rooted in male-dominated children's folk games such as "smear the queer," "piling on," and "king of the hill" (Dundes 1997a). Dundes's unprecedented contention, fitting in with his broader theory that traditions persist to provide socially sanctioned outlets for conflicts and ambiguities within a society, is that football is the American version of a ritual drive, found internationally among adolescent males, to display masculinity more than femininity by engaging in homoerotic activity within this frame of initiatory play. In his words, "The object of the game, simply stated, is to get into the opponent's endzone while preventing the opponent from getting into one's endzone" (Dundes 1978a, 81). Using expressive evidence in speech and custom to draw this conclusion, he offers the implication that sport can be linked structurally to war making by its action of feminizing an opponent in male combat to manifest victory and achieve self-fulfillment. Because it links the psychological explanation to other meanings grounded in historical and sociological explanation, his thesis deserves a closer look in relation to the others.

Homoeroticism and War

Dundes asserted that the tough demeanor and aggressive contact distinguishing football from other popular American team sports, such as baseball and basketball, owed to its heightened homosexual display, usually connected psychologically with emasculation. This elicited responses from popular as well as scholarly audiences. Dundes was featured in the popular press and was asked to speak on more talk shows as a result of this one article than for any of his other essays, numbering several hundred (Zumwalt 1995, 33–47). Although Dundes wanted to talk about the link between the game and war, popular interest hinged on the homoerotic components of a sport epitomizing manliness and popularly associated with aggressive heterosexuality (Dundes 1997d). It was as if Dundes had blown the whistle on some cover-up, implying that this whole toughness thing with hypermasculine bodies adored by sexy cheerleaders was one big ruse. He drew attention to the fact that football was the one big-time sport that began and ended every action with intimate male-to-male contact.

Had Dundes outed football players as homosexuals in denial? Hardly, he answered; instead, his point was that, as a metaphor, homosexuality is especially applicable to a situation in which proving masculinity creates anxiety. He might have nodded knowingly (had he lived to see it) at an advertising campaign by Spyware Doctor, a computer security program, that shows a scared, skinny young man wearing only his underwear and holding a football in front of his groin. A hefty, helmet-clad football player with hands outstretched is in the air, aiming to grab the man's football/phallus, while the young man cowers in fear. The caption for the image reads, "Do you have the right protection?" The ad conspicuously draws attention to male castration anxieties with an image of a subordinated man tackled or orally attacked in a homoerotic position. The ad even implies repressed homoerotic feelings in the sport by its reference to the football player as hidden, dangerous spyware. "Don't get hit by spyware; protect yourself," the text blares in an obvious appeal to the male fear of rape. If that is not enough, the text closes by reminding viewers that its "OnGuard" real-time protection, with its metaphor of warding off phallic penetration, will "keep your most precious assets covered" (PC Tools 2007).

Dundes was not strictly applying the universalist Freudian assumption that males possess a latent homosexual attraction and that its suppression results in socially sanctioned fantasies. Rather, his emphasis was on the cultural context of "proving" masculinity in America. While others maintained that football players convey a hyperheterosexuality, Dundes questioned how homoerotic elements compose this image (Hardin 2000, 36). What separated football in his mind from other sports was its highly ritualized nature, because it provides a socially sanctioned framework for male body contact. "Football, after all," he wrote, " is a so-called 'body contact' sport—is a form of homosexual behavior. . . . Sexual acts carried out in thinly disguised symbolic form by, and directed toward, males and males only, would seem to constitute ritual homosexuality" (Dundes 1978a, 87). Another possibility is that the hyperheterosexuality present in boasts of "sticking it to you" and derisions of "playing like girls" is compensation for the suspicion of homosexuality in a single-sex group. In the wake of the equal rights movement, all-male groups attracted the stigma of being either sexist or gay, yet as men's studies leader Michael Kimmel observes, "Football has gained in popularity in part because it remains so steadfastly single-sex" (2008, 138). Among the major sports, football is also the largest display of same-sex hugs, huddles, and hand-holding.

A check of the scholarly citation indexes with the keyword *football* reveals that Dundes's essay is cited more than any other, but this statistic is not necessarily a sign of his thesis's acceptance. He understood its controversial nature when he wrote, "I have no doubt that a good many football players and fans will be skeptical (to say the least) of the analysis proposed here. Even academics with presumably less personal investment in football will probably find implausible if not downright repugnant that American football could be a ritual combat between groups of males attempting to assert their masculinity by penetrating the endzones of their rivals" (1978a, 86). Although Dundes refers to anthropological literature treating football as a display of ritualized violence and compares it to events elsewhere, including bullfights and cockfights, he and other anthropologists are still at a loss to explain why America's primary text of play should take the form it does. Football in this kind of rhetoric appears to fill a structural slot rather than being a special kind of cultural practice. Dundes's academic complaint was that historical and sociological rhetorics of play are inadequate as meaning because they do not account for a cognition revealed by symbols that presumably guide action. The literal approach of tracing football's origins or positing its social functions offers an interpretation of the consequences of play rather than the motives that explain its action. The question left unanswered or intentionally avoided, Dundes contended, is the psychological rationale leading to the unexpected enthusiasm for the sport in the context of modernization (Dundes 1978a, 76–77).

Dundes claimed that the denial of football's homoerotic meaning is proof of its plausibility because of the assumption that it is the kind of disturbing thought that results in disguising or repressing conflict through the projection of symbols into fantasy and play. The meaning he brought to the fore was outside the awareness of participants, so that interviews and oral histories asking players and fans to reflect on the topic are of little consequence. He was less concerned with its American-ness than with the structure of its ritual, which can be cross-culturally compared, and he was less concerned with how the game is played and by whom than with the metaphors associated with play. These tendencies opened him up to criticism on methodological grounds even before dealing with the question of whether the explanation is valid.

The social phenomenon that Dundes addressed from his academic experience is that "in college athletics it is abundantly clear that
it is football which counts highest among both enrolled students and
alumni" (1978a, 75). This led him to observe that despite claims for the
national prominence of other sports, "No other American sport consistently draws fans in the numbers which are attracted to football" (1978a,
75). Having noted that football strikes, in his words "a most responsive
chord in the American psyche," he set out the problem: "What is it
about American football that could possibly account for its extraordinary popularity?" He implied that its popularity was indeed surprising
in the context of the feminist and civil rights movements, which questioned the social dominance (and what some critics have called the masculinist hegemony or national imperialism) of sport (Stempel 2006).

Constructionist and Ethnographic Interpretations

Prominent among football's academic followers, Michael Oriard provides a historical answer to the question of football's "extraordinary
popularity." In *Reading Football* (1993) and *King Football* (2001), he argues that football has risen to the level of spectacle because nineteenth-
century newspapers and magazines constructed it—indeed, willed it—
as a moral narrative about improving the national character. Although
concluding that sport is a place to invest the major issues of the day, he
finds the contemporary text of football too complex to decode. Unlike
the reductionist interpretation for sports writing in the nineteenth century, which set football as the location for showing one's toughness and
readiness for adult challenges, today's spectacle has it all, he summarizes in *Reading Football*, and he finds abundant examples of references
to race and class in football coverage to show that the sport acts as a
lightning rod for national social concerns about inequality. Or, stated
another way, as the major American cultural spectacle coming out of a
narrative of hardscrabble play and players, football is expected to fulfill
the American dream of social equity and mobility, and news is made
when it does not live up to that expectation (Lindquist 2006).

Other cultural critics extend the idea of football as a reflection of
society to claim that it is an agent of disturbing national trends, including the rise of date rape and male sexual coercion among college men;
the growing social inequality of race, gender, and class and patriarchal

hegemony; and support for the U.S. invasion of Iraq (Forbes, Adams-Curtis, Pakalka, and White 2006; Stempel 2006). Whereas Oriard thinks Americans draw their meanings of sport from myriad media, a host of scholars point the finger at television as the ringleader responsible for imposing, in the words of Carl Stempel, a "masculinist sport-militaristic nationalism complex" (2006, 82; see also Trujillo 1995). Indeed, one instrumental explanation for why football has eclipsed baseball is that it shows better on television, but that still leaves questions about other prime-time sports with continuous, explosive action such as basketball and hockey, which have not been raised to the level of cultural avatar. Countries outside of North America also have sports that draw avid televised attention with "close-up pictures and . . . slow-motion replays," to quote Michael Mandelbaum (2004). In his opinion, because the action of football occurs far from the stands and appears to the spectator to be merely a tangle of bodies on the field, television "can dissect the action and present each slice of it in a way that the naked eye cannot see" (Mandelbaum 2004, 177).

But during my time in Europe, avid television viewers said the same thing about soccer, especially the World Cup. In Japan, where per capita television ownership rivals that of the United States (678 per 1,000 in Japan, versus 740 per 1,000 in America), baseball, soccer, and sumo matches have a devoted television following (Paolantonio 2008, xii). Mandelbaum responds that football is a winter sport, and cold weather encourages more television viewing (2004, 176), but by that rationale, basketball should be more popular than it is. Football watching is also serious business in warm-weather climes of the Deep South and Texas, as the popular television series *Friday Night Lights*, about a high school football team, attests (running on network television between 2006 and 2011, before syndication; see also Bissinger 1990, on which the series is based). Football is the sport Americans watch rather than play, whereas basketball and baseball top the charts in surveys of American youth for *participation*. This suggests that football derives its hold from a framed drama unfolding before spectators to which Americans especially relate.

Besides the claim that the mass media make Americans embrace football, other social constructionist approaches have sought to explain football's unlikely rise by following its commercial development. They give credit or blame, through a Gramscian lens of crafty elites manipulating the unsuspecting masses, to entrepreneurial figures such as Pete Rozelle or headline-grabbing heroes such as Joe Namath for selling football better than baseball, soccer, or basketball to a consuming public (Oriard 2007). Viewing football as commodity rather than cultural text, some critics reduce its appeal to the fact that sex and violence are good sellers. Stephen Norwood writes, for example, "No NFL team, or college team for that matter, would sell any tickets if it played touch football" (2004, 4). Yet there are problems with this assertion, since a number of upstart football leagues have not sold tickets despite their promotion of sex and violence, and the exaltation of football has hardly been universally embraced, as entrepreneurs' failure to franchise football in Europe attests (Robertson 1980, 256).

Few critics look to traditions early in life that contextualize the appeal of football later on, although this material provides evidence of a continuity in the speech and ritual surrounding football. Dundes maintains that traditions in childhood undergird ritual male involvement to football. Games such as "king of the hill," "saloogie" (also known as "keep away"), and "piling on" all involve a person who is conferred superior status by the ability to withstand the physical assault of a gang. He asserts that this developmental link provides the basis for football's popularity among sports spectators, as well as establishing the homoerotic elements of the game. To be sure, football's division into a variety of organized "plays," each requiring an offensive plan working against a countering defensive scheme, differentiates it from the folk games. Football's heightened level of organization suggests adult sophistication, but the key competition is still "on the line," where the offense works to create a "hole" and the defense attempts to block it.

A breakdown of football's popularity by participant and spectator suggests that football has different functions for fan and player. According to a Harris poll conducted in 2005, football was the favorite sport of 46 percent of Americans, with baseball coming in second at 14 percent and basketball trailing at 9 percent. This was a marked change from 1985, when Harris reported the numbers as 34 percent for football, 23 percent for baseball, and 12 percent for basketball. Yet as far as participation, Scholastic Inc. (2008) reported that basketball predominates as the sport children want to compete in, and girls tend to be far less interested in team sports than boys are. In ethnographies, boys prefer chasing and physical games of social dominance, often exhibit packing behavior, and value toughness, whereas girls gravitate toward cooperative games that involve dyads and triads and value congeniality, repetition, and cooperation (Lever 1976; Pellegrini, Kato, Blatchford, and Baines 2002; Thorne 1993).

Behind-the-scenes glimpses of football teams often seek to answer the question why participants endure extreme pain and suffering for an activity labeled as fun. Is the implication that adoring fans confer more glory on football players if they risk injury in battle? Popular writers such as John Feinstein (2006) posit that money is the incentive for players to fight another day, but to get them motivated, they have to buy in to the master narrative of the satisfaction of vanquishing an opponent for a high-stakes triumph. This dominance is translated as a quest to be alone at the top of the standings or to hover over a fallen player, and satisfaction and even regeneration can come from strenuous battle. In *Next Man Up*, Feinstein highlights the message of the Baltimore Ravens' coach to encapsulate this moral imperative: "Fellas, this game, this setting is what your whole life is about. . . . A game like this is about commitment. It's about passion. It's about being willing to give yourself up for the cause if you have to. . . . If it were going to be easy, then nothing would be at stake" (2006, 444).

What makes the sport "hard" rather than easy is the risk of injury. Indeed, in Norwood's compilation of interviews with professional football players, injury is indexed more than commitment, the cause, money, or fame. Steve Zabel, one of the athletes interviewed, is especially introspective about whether taking this risk among football players is "normal" or is somehow a reflection of everyday life. He comments:

> Football players in general are not normal people. They don't do normal things. They walk a very fine line between reality and nonreality. If a football player really sat down and tried to introspectively examine what he was about to do, it would frighten the hell out of him. I mean, nobody in his right mind would do something, where the consequences of getting hit in the wrong position might be that you'd be crippled forever or that you might die. There's something that draws people like me to it, whether it's machismo or simply the lure of gratification. (Norwood 2004, 260)

Zabel appears to aver Dundes's point that the obsession with football is often outside of participants' awareness and that their gratification is related to proving masculinity, although he might not agree that in doing so he enacts a homoerotic display. One might further observe that, as a professional, the player is paid for what he performed ritually as an adolescent.

Ethnographies of adolescents engaged in football often point out the ritual display of masculinity in the staging of high school games. Douglas Foley provides an oft-cited ethnography of football in Texas, a state that prides itself on its passion for the game. According to Foley, for Texas high school football players, the game is about social prominence in and for their community. Foley concludes, "Many of them are willing to endure considerable physical pain and sacrifice to achieve social prominence in their community" (1990, 126). Their discourse shows the game's association with male display when they claim that football "makes a man out of you," and its association with hyperheterosexuality is shown in the statement that it "helps get you a cute chick" (Foley 1990, 126). Foley notes some discourse that reveals "psychological lessons," in his words; however, in what Dundes would call an academic aversion to psychological interpretation, Foley prefers to concentrate on the "contemporary system of class dominance and its archaic system of patriarchal dominance" (1990, 133; see also Foley 1994, 28–62). These lessons, though, support Dundes's query about why particular sexual and violent metaphors are expressed in football. Foley found that coaches' discourse is incorporated into players' folk speech, and what they talk about most is "hitting," "sticking," or "popping" someone. After a hard game, he observes, "the supreme compliment was having a particular 'lick' or 'hit' singled out. Folkloric immortality, endless stories about that one great hit in the big game, was what players secretly strove for. For most coaches and players, really 'laying a lick on' or 'knocking somebody's can off' or 'taking a real lick' was that quintessential football moment" (1990, 127). Players tend to portray themselves as primitive and hypersexualized, referring to themselves in the football play frame as studs, bulls, horses, gorillas, and animals. As animals, they are different, more powerful, and more manly than in real life, which is associated with the modernist ethics of egalitarianism and feminism. According to Foley, "A stud was a superior physical specimen who fearlessly dished out and took hits, *who liked the physical contact*, who could dominate other players physically" (1990, 127; emphasis added). Foley found that players "talked endlessly" about who is a real stud and whether the coach "really kicks butt," yet he concludes that all this talk shows only that pain is a badge of honor, rather than having any latent homoerotic component (1990, 127).

Looking for insight from players and the meaning they get from football, one school of thought is that football is not antithetical to modernism; rather, football has become popular because it embodies modernism (Adams 2001, 30; Norwood 2004, 3–19). The male predilection to invest in one or a few team sports, in contradistinction to American girls' attraction to a variety of activities usually involving small groups, suggests the importance of corporate identity and managing multiple roles and specialties, which some academics see as a model of exploitative capitalism. Male players tend to find value in loyalty, camaraderie, and ganging, which are intrinsic and incentive, in their view, to being part of the team. At the same time, this team spirit (there is no *I* in *team*) is underscored by the donning of a uniform, separating the sport from what is seen as the radical individualism and alienation of real life. One has to notice that *teammates*, despite the suggestion of intimacy, "pull together" less by close coordination than by beating an enemy through ritualized violence. In the introduction to *Real Football*, Norwood summarizes that "football's appeal derives in large part from its peculiar combination of highly modern qualities—an emphasis on order and precision, coordination within a group, and split-second timing—with more primitive elements, sublimated in bureaucracies, the open display of violence and aggression, which are involved in every play—in the bruising contact on the line, in the blocking and tackling in the open field" (2004, 4).

Mandelbaum extends the argument with a comparative observation about the extreme hierarchy in football: "Because it unfolds in defined, discrete sequences, and because for each sequence both the offense and the defense must coordinate the action of all eleven players, which cannot occur spontaneously but must be arranged in advance, football both requires and permits coordination from a single, central source, in a way that baseball and basketball do not" (2004, 164–65). Using an industrial metaphor, the coach is the engineer at the top of the hierarchy whose goal is to run the team like a well-oiled machine (Mandelbaum 2004, 164). Rituals and hollers in the stands, which the

Mud rush, Cornell University, early twentieth century. (Courtesy Jay Mechling)

spectacle of football supports, provide a different image, though. Spectators root for teams to scrap and fight, much like the collegiate class rushes—melees consisting of freshmen and sophomores colliding in a mass of bodies to push a ball over the line—that fed the campus craze for football in the early twentieth century (Krout 1929, 235). Contemporary ethnographies of football fan culture tend to reveal more fight than finesse. Shouts of "kill them," "you're getting killed," or "kill the ref" are heard more frequently in any stadium than comments about order and precision (see Smith 1983). References to the clockwork of teams come from the broadcasters or are reserved for the quiet moments of a review upstairs in the booth by sheltered and emasculated, if impartial, "officials," distant from the action on the field.

The Frontier of Football

The theme of regeneration through violence over turf is not just for coaches to spout in halftime pep talks or fans to scream in the heat of battle; it is also familiar from the American saga of expansion. Although commonly associated with the colonialist claim of taming virgin land and the frontier experience of nationalist America, the symbolism of land has been shown to permeate the American sense of mission into the modern period, including the notable value-laden slogans of John Kennedy's "new frontier" in politics and "new frontiers" in the popular culture of *Star Trek*, both emerging during the 1960s (Felkins and Goldman 1993; Slotkin 1993; Smith 1978; Williamson 1987). Yet for all the scholarship produced on football, the idea of virgin land or frontier experience as a context to explain its particularly American appeal receives scant attention. I would venture to say that this is not because it lacks validity but because, in the rush to set football in critical postmodern terms, the Americanness of the game is overlooked. Conversely, historians have typically not made the symbolic connection between sport and frontier experience because they are inclined to look for the notable event or influential person rather than a movement or cultural belief. As wonderful and sweeping a tome as Richard Slotkin's mammoth *Gunfighter Nation: The Myth of the Frontier in Twentieth-Century America* (1993) is, it lacks even a single mention of football among its abundant references to the frontier theme in popular culture.

Oriard provides a historical clue to the connection to frontier when he capably traces the sport's roots to the second half of the nineteenth century. He sees the significance of the period as the golden age of print and reads the football coverage of newspapers and magazines as signs of accelerating social changes, especially for the rise of a middle class. Yet popular literature of the period featured dime novels, many of them about the West, and historically, it was a time marked by rapid expansion and then the closing of the frontier. Talk of land, and violence to domesticate the land, pervaded the public's reading material and weighed heavily on the minds of Americans. Earlier, I asserted that football stood at the top of the sports heap after the 1960s, and it is worth noting that this period was replete with "new frontier" and war rhetoric. Observers of American culture should expect the frontier to be a symbolic part of football if, as Slotkin has insightfully argued, the frontier experience is inextricably tied to American identity, and central to that experience is the acquisition of land as a result of overcoming a hostile enemy in the character of the fearsome Indians.

Historian David Wallace Adams (2001) deserves notice for pointing out that the frontier theme was a factor in the public notoriety of the Carlisle Indians football team in the late nineteenth and early twentieth centuries, but he does not extend the analysis to the present day. He contextualizes the popularity of football in colleges during the period in the "cult of manliness" of Victorian America, caused by a desire to counter growing industrialization with activities serving as reminders of "an older frontier American [where] the opportunities for physical labor, wilderness adventure, and primitive expressions of violence, were not only available but frequently a precondition for survival. Denied these experiences, the rising generation of young men were in danger of becoming over-civilized, if not feminized" (Adams 2001, 29). Journalistic reporting of the highly publicized confrontations between the Carlisle team and major national powers such as Yale, Army, and Harvard blatantly referred to a battle for land between settlers and "the aborigine, the real son of the forest and plain" (Adams 2001, 31; see also Anderson 2007; Jenkins 2007).

Evoking frontier skirmishes in the play of football went well beyond the reporting of contests between the Carlisle Indians and the national collegiate powers of the Northeast. In the early twentieth century, President Theodore Roosevelt, who waxed poetic about the invigorating qualities of the great West, answered critics of the game's brutality by calling for reform of the rules, while making sure that it remained true to the ideals of "the strenuous life." He publicly declared that when he put together his band of "Rough Riders" for the foreign adventure of the Spanish-American War, he sought men who had played football because of their character as well as their old-fashioned fight, reminiscent of America's conquest of the frontier (Roosevelt 1899, 8–20). When the president of Harvard tried to abolish football at the school in 1907, Roosevelt angrily retorted, "As I emphatically disbelieve in seeing Harvard, or any other college, turn out mollycoddles instead of vigorous men I may add I do not in the least object to a sport because it is rough" (quoted in Rudolph 1990, 377).

Advocates thought of football's action as a throwback to a preindustrial age when one matched one's body and hands against the elements to reap the benefits of the land. Henry Davidson Sheldon, a respected commentator on the collegiate scene, observed that since football had become popular on campuses in the 1880s, it provided an antidote to the physical softness of a new postfrontier generation of students in elite schools, and it also compensated for the worrisome complexity, mechanization, and standardization in the rapidly industrializing America they seemed to embrace (1901, 251–52). Sheldon complimented football's "mass movements and general attitude of conflict which give zest to the latter," in contrast to "professional baseball in the cities," which "has become a business" (1901, 232). He thought that football owed its rise in the enervating collegiate context to a "human instinct" necessary for "physical combat" (1901, 233). More specific to the American experience, he saw intercollegiate football being adapted to the qualities of a mobile "frontier people—rude, boisterous, and over-assertive," and it matched "the conditions of frontier life favouring versatility and individual initiative" (Sheldon 1901, 90, 107).

Faculties that opposed the game as unbecoming of learned men still understood the communitarian spirit it fostered for the school as a whole. A faculty committee at Yale in 1902, taking up the problems of injury and cheating in football, considered the game's value in promoting selflessness among the students, characteristic of an earlier era of expansion and national feeling: "An impression is very strong and very prevalent that the athlete is working for Yale, the student for himself" (quoted in Rudolph 1990, 379). Commentaries of this kind led Frederick Rudolph, in his chronicle of the rise of football in the late nineteenth and early twentieth centuries, to pronounce that "the new game of football became an instrument of the past" (1990, 379).

Did the frontier rhetoric in football cease with the industrial era and the demise of the Carlisle Indian School? Hardly. In professional football, many of the names associated with the dramaturgical fantasy of the game come from frontier imagery: Braves, Redskins, Cowboys, Chiefs, Raiders, Forty-niners, Texans, Buffalo Bills. Other teams took their monikers from animals associated with the American wilderness: Eagles, Broncos, Bears, Panthers. In the college ranks, where football is the great symbol of big-time campuses, more than thirty schools' teams are called the Pioneers; others include the (Trail) Blazers, Braves, Cowboys, Highlanders, Hilltoppers, Mavericks, Mountaineers, Raiders, Ramblers, and Rangers. The highest concentration of nonanimal nicknames draws on the frontier experience (Smargon 2008). Typical of these teams are frontiersmen mascots, horses, and wagons that excite the crowd with their movements on the sidelines, especially after a touchdown. Many journalists have also taken notice of the Dallas Cowboys' designation as "America's team," at least in part because of the national appeal of the cowboy. Mandelbaum comments, for example, "In American mythology the Dallas mascot, the cowboy, symbolizes rugged individualism and courage. He is a repository of the virtues that the team itself embodied—or so it sought to suggest to the public, styling itself 'America's Team'" (2004, 187). Even in my hometown of Harrisburg, Pennsylvania—hardly a western outpost or a landscape that raises frontier images—the public voted in 2008 to call the city's arena football team the Stampede, with a picture of a steer's skull suggesting the western plains. Opinions left by fans on the team's message board (www.harrisburgstampede.com) impressed on the owners that football's action reminds them of western mythology involving the unfettered movement across the open range, translated into the modern context as the football field. On the Great Plains, meanwhile, professional football teams in Calgary and San Angelo, Texas, claim the names Stampeders and Stampede Express, respectively.

The terminology of football is replete with frontier imagery. Football commentators frequently note the importance of the "scout," who checks out the opponent's camp (Mandelbaum 2004, 131–32). The running back, a standout position on the offense, functions, according to Mandelbaum, as "the cavalry of the team—highly mobile agents of swift advance" (2004, 130). Indeed, among the memorable nicknames in the sport are equine metaphors assigned to Alan "The Horse" Ameche, Red "Galloping Ghost" Grange, and The Four Horsemen of Notre Dame. A key to success in the game is gaining ground, and the going gets tougher the deeper one moves into the opposition's territory. After a hotly contested game, reporters and players often refer to the game as "a good ol' fashioned Western" or a shoot-out, as Dallas quarterback Tony Romo did following a 41–37 victory on *Monday Night Football* in 2008 (Aron 2008). The previous weekend, Tennessee Titans linebacker Keith Bulluck said of his team's quarterback Kerry Collins, who led a winning march down the field, "I knew the old *gunslinger* was going to go out there and do his thing," even though Collins did not originally hail from the West (Kay 2008; emphasis added). Reflecting on popular football slang, journalist David Jones added, "The term 'gunslinger' is thrown around a lot in reference to lovably reckless quarterbacks. Brett Favre is said to be the prototype." He went on to make the case for George Blanda as a gunslinger in what he called the "Wild West" of the American Football League (Jones 2010).

ESPN correspondent Sal Paolantonio writes that firepower from the Old West is a powerful image for sportswriters because it most vividly connotes for Americans the conquest of land. In fact, he traces football's story line at the moment of important rule changes in 1882, which established the "first down" after gaining a certain number of yards, to the expansionist idea of "Manifest Destiny" (Paolantonio 2008, 7–8). The rule allows the team possessing the ball to advance it while holding on to the territory it has already captured. If it does not, it will be forced to "surrender" the ball. The successful team eliminates the opposing team and has the whole field, from end line to end line, to itself. With four tries to get ten yards, the offense relies on the methodical running game more than in Canada, where the rules call for three downs, resulting in what Mandelbaum calls "risky, spectacular plays" (2004, 144). With the close of the frontier in 1890, Paolantonio contends, "America, bursting at the seams, needed a game that had a chance to capture this haughtiness [of Manifest Destiny], that movement forward at all costs" (2008, 8).

The influence of land conquest lingered in the game, particularly among early shapers such as Walter Camp and Amos Alonzo Stagg. Many of the early rule changes emphasized advancement of the ball on the ground to emphasize a difference, in Camp's estimation, from the English rugby code, from which football apparently arose (Camp 1894, 1–22; Paolantonio 2008, 8). For Camp, the central feature that distinguishes the American game from the English is the scrimmage line, "the backbone to which the entire body of American football is attached" (1894, 9). The American game's action is organized around a series of skirmishes in land designated as territory. The quarterback has more control and more options than in the English game and thus is encouraged to create deceptions to advance the ball. To Camp, the American game shows "far more skill in the development of brilliant plays and carefully planned manoeuvres" (1894, 10). Although football has undergone many rule changes since Camp's time, the idea of the scrimmage line—with its function of establishing a movable border, drawing on the memory of the frontier in the late nineteenth century—remains critical to the game. Camp was proud of football's American-ness and the way it broke from the long-held English custom of the relatively immobile pile of bodies of the scrummage. Camp implies that football looks like his country when he writes, "Being bound by no traditions, and having seen no play, the American took the English rules for a starting-point, and almost immediately proceeded to add and subtract, according to what seemed his pressing needs" (1894, 8). Among those needs was a game with quick movement resulting in rewards for gaining ground. Much to Camp's satisfaction, the sport spread westward from the Northeast into the South and West, and he recognized its nationalism by initiating "All-America" honors as a distinctive accolade for football players (Mandelbaum 2004, 161).

James Oliver Robertson explains the resistance to football outside of North America in terms of the centrality of the frontier metaphor to the game. Unlike baseball and basketball, which have been taken up globally, football emphasizes lines that "must be defended, which must be penetrated, which must be moved" (Robertson 1980, 256). He astutely observes:

Steelton High School scrimmage, 1906–1907, in front of the steel plant; the field was known colloquially as "no-man's-land." (Courtesy Center for Pennsylvania Culture Studies, Pennsylvania State University at Harrisburg)

Cast from the movie *Life in College*, 1937. (Simon Bronner collection)

In football the entire game is built around the frontier, the line, the boundary. Football ritualizes the moving frontier, and the teamwork, cooperation, and individual heroism necessary to move that frontier; simultaneously, it also ritualizes the team-work, cooperation, and individual heroism necessary to resist the moving frontier (football players are pioneers *and* Indians at the same time). Ultimate victory in the game comes from moving the frontier more than the others do, crossing the goal line more frequently. There is little in such a ritual to appeal to the ideals and sensitivities of people who are not Americans. (Robertson 1980, 256)

Adolescent Masculinity on the Line

Robertson probably overstates the argument, because using violence to show manliness in response to the feminizing effects of moderniza-tion certainly extends beyond America's borders. If this is the case, can this historical consideration be reconciled with Dundes's psychoanalytic perspective, focusing on football's appeal as a demonstration of manliness? One symbolist overlap is the material significance of lines on the field and the conceptual emphasis on linearity (moving forward, expressed in the masculinist value placed on charging "straight ahead," "up the gut," or "up the middle"). As Robertson points out, the football "gridiron" is distinctive in the holy trinity of American sports by its profuse use of lines that players repeatedly cross (1980, 256). The lines structure the game as well as the field, because plays begin with the "lining up" of offensive and defensive "lines." The cultural significance of the gridiron is indicated by a commercial aired by wireless communications giant Verizon in 2010. A husky voice narrates a violent collision of football players that causes dirt to fly: "There is a reason it's called a gridiron, because the ground doesn't give up its yards without a fight." Gaining ground is important because an offense stays on the field by acquiring a "first down," measured in ten-yard increments. The team's objective is presented numerically by the number of yards remaining to get a first down, such as "second [down] and eight." Excitement builds when a third-down play has a short distance to go and teams close up their lines in anticipation of grappling bodies. The expectation in such situations is that the running back will be "shot through the line," suggesting a double meaning of gun and phallus. The pent-up, potent energy resulting in either a cheered release for the offense or a stop for the defense, thereby showing the offense's impotence, implies a male sexual praxis tying the acquisition of property to sexual gratification.

Ample cultural evidence exists for the association of linearity with masculinity, which is heightened by football's highly linear gridiron. Men are associated with "directness," in contrast to women's "roundness." For instance, in the military, soldiers (traditionally male) are honored by gaining stripes, and the humorous adage that "size matters" refers to a penile erection (Dundes 2004, 183–84). In contrast, girls' singing games tend to form circles; women are complimented for being "curvaceous" and are aligned with nature by having menstrual "cycles" (Dundes 2004, 184; Whiting and Ayres 1968, 128). In football strategy, the "end-around," "flea-flicker" (representing back-and-forth movement), and "double-reverse" are considered evasive tactics or even "junk plays." A quarterback who takes the ball ahead rather than handing it off to a halfback, who then rushes forward through the line, is said to dishonestly "sneak" across. In the praxis of crossing lines, men are arguably conquering nature as well as exhibiting sexual potency (Ortner 1974).

In his critical essay subtitled "Are Freudians Ever Right?" sociologist Gary Alan Fine (1984) raises doubts about the use of linguistic evidence to establish a link between violence and adolescent initiatory behavior in football. He finds that the expressive evidence is not consistent. Although he agrees that the rhetoric of sacking, making a pass, and penetrating have sexual undertones, he points out that hash marks, guard, punt, and field goal do not. Is it coincidental that all Fine's examples are references to land? He may not make the connection, but we can note the idea of a hash mark for a point on the field to spot the ball, a guard as protection for property, a punt for kicking the ball before it hits the ground, and a field goal for a ball kicked from the ground. Fine's point is that inconsistent symbolism indicates a weakness in the psychoanalytic argument, and he observes even less of a case on the basis of external validity, for he notes that most Americans do not play football and restricts it to a seasonal rather than a year-round activity. "Why," he asks, "aren't these drives present to be expressed throughout the calendar year; are they repressed the other nine months? . . . Are there other male activities in American culture which function in the same way?" Fine leaves the questions unanswered; their purpose is to "raise doubt as to the interpretation of football as ritual homosexuality" (Fine 1984, 16), and it appears that others share his skepticism, making Dundes's essay the most quotable citation on football and the article that academics and fans love to hate.

Let me suggest answers to Fine's questions by referring to the importance of the "ground" in football and its autumn play. Unlike other American team sports, the action in football is measured by players advancing across a line. The point of emphasis is the scrimmage line, which is movable. "Football is a game of inches" is a common adage indicating the importance of every piece of ground, and careful records are kept for yards gained (most total yards and yards per play). The defense wants to pin back the offensive players and drive or pound (a sexual double entendre) them to the turf, preferably putting them in a feminine position "on their butts." The defense wants to hold its ground or pin the offense back, "deep in its own territory." No team wants to "give ground" or be pushed around, knocked down, or thrown for a loss; coaches scream at players to hold their spots and get up. Particularly in American football, teams want to freely move up and down the field. Broadcasters like to talk about a team taking "real estate" or having "property" behind them as a sign of success. On sports talk shows, listeners know that callers are concerned when their team "sucks," in an obvious reference to taking a passive homoerotic position, but they are happy if their team kicks butt. They complain if their losing team looked like boys to the other team's men because they were crushed or, worse, nailed or sacked (with the explanation that the defensive line got "penetration in the *back*field"). In victory, though, spectators charge the field, occupying it with great jubilation, and they may tear down the goalposts as a sign of taking control of the land.

The property metaphor is critical to the drive toward victory. Each of the two teams is said to have "territory," and as a team advances, it acquires ground, even though the designation of territory is nowhere written on the field. A milestone is crossing into the other team's territory past the fifty-yard line, acquiring it by pushing the opponent off its turf. Dundes is right that one scores by eventually penetrating the other team's end zone on the ground or by sending a kick through the uprights, but one gains control in the game by "eating up big chunks of yardage." The goal is a piece of land. Scoring a goal implies that the other team has been eliminated, driven off the field. For the defense, the goal line is protected, and the ultimate test is the goal line stand, treating the end zone as precious ground that is distinguished from the field by stripes or decoration.

Accretion of power occurs as the offense gains ground, suggesting an Oedipal interpretation for the offense. Dundes notes that Adrian Stokes's observation of a male Oedipal complex in soccer also applies to American football, because each team defends the goal at its back: "In front is a new land, the new woman, whom they strive to possess in the interest of preserving the mother inviolate, in order, as it were, to progress from infancy to adulthood: at the same time, the defensive role is the father's; he opposes the forward youth of the opposition" (Dundes 1978a, 78–79; Stokes 1956, 185). In this view, both teams battle for possession of the father's phallus—that is, the ball—to "steer it through the archetypal vagina, the goal" (Stokes 1956, 187). But this may be too universalist a view, because an American context appears to be at work in observing the battle on the field as one between pioneer foes.

The importance of the ground game is its representation of battle with the goal of driving the other team off its land. This is coupled with a demonstration of social domination by emasculating the opponent in ritual performances of spiking the ball, engaging in war dances, and raising helmets or index fingers. Players are egged on to get the opponent on his back, showing that the team has "kicked ass." Invoking images of hunting, players on the run are chased down, and players are caught in the "open field." In a merger of hunter and soldier, quarterbacks are said to have a "rifle arm" and to be "on target." With the naturalistic image of a brown leather football, the thrower wants to hit his man "in the chest," while the defense, in sports talk, "brings down his prey." With some phallic implication, players in trouble are referred to as being "creamed," "shot down," and "hit hard."

When they are "slammed down to the ground," players are symbolically stuck in the mud or joined to feces. In describing the goal of football as carrying the ball into the end zone, Dundes misses that, on the way, ground is gained without the ball or one's body being brought down. Carriers have to keep the ball "clean"; that is, it cannot touch the ground, or else it becomes symbolically contaminated. The player who is dragged down to the ground is not just being overtly feminized; he is tainted by being stuck in infantile feces. The contrast is going into the end zone "untouched" or without being put down into the ground. Manhood is represented in such a case by overcoming the infantile desire to play with dirt or feces. Toughness is shown by "grinding out" or controlling "yards" (equivalent to dirt or land). The end zone is also known as the "house," and the runner who takes off down the field is said to be "bringing it to the house." As a frontier metaphor, this rhetoric suggests the transversal of hostile ground to create a settlement. Skill with the ball means that the prize possession is kept off the ground. Thus, time of possession, represented by control of the ball, allowing the offense to stay on the field, is an important statistic.

Adams insightfully observes that "part of football's appeal was in its capacity to tell stories, to convey meaning" (2001, 30). He suggests that journalistic attachment of the frontier story, as understood by white Americans in the 1890s, to the playing of football helped raise the game's profile (2001, 30–31). How can football be narratively structured? One answer is to trace its plot sequence to see whether it follows the functions of a story. Folklorists have found a common morphology that people recognize as narrative in the dramatic tension created by the establishment of something as missing, or a lack, to the consequence of something being restored, or a lack liquidated (Dundes 1964a, 1964b). In between, a struggle ensues to overcome challenges, summarized as an interdiction and a violation. For football, this morphology takes the following form:

	Lack	Interdiction	Violation	Consequence
Offense	Wants to go forward (into opponent's home or end zone)	Does not want to be stopped (dragged down, tackled to the ground)	Is stopped (or is not stopped, gains ground)	Loses game (or scores and wins game)
Defense	Wants to drive offense back (or recover ball and take it into opponent's home or end zone)	Keeps offense away from defense's home or end zone	Does not stop offense or gives ground (or stops offense)	Loses game (or scores and wins game)

Comparison between this narrative of the game sequence and other children's games is raised because, arguably, football takes on more of a linear sequence than baseball and basketball. In keeping with children's development as independent individuals who desire to move away from the maternal home as a sign of maturity and, at the same time, defend the home as social identity, childhood games frequently involve laying out "sides" that are thrust against each other; examples are "push ball" and "red rover," involving the crossing of an opposing team's line. Games that emphasize linear structures involving pushing and pulling, such as tug-of-war, are particularly associated with masculinity and demonstrations of toughness; it is no coincidence that its eliminative result of players falling to the ground raises images of war.

Another feature of the linear structure is that crossing a line signals triumph, represented by achieving a higher status or accomplishing a transformation. By doing this, the sequence marks maturity, particularly for an adolescent who recognizes the ritual components of an indi-

BIG DEEDS ARE OFTEN BORN IN DREAMS

Advertisement for Keds sneakers, circa 1920s, showing boys imagining themselves as football players.

vidual going through a transition to overcome obstacles (in the agent of a runner) and be "incorporated" with one's peers in celebration. Rather than contradicting the frontier thesis, this developmental perspective fits into the view that football became significant because it was perceived as emboldening at a time when modernization was equated with male infantilization. Yet it is also fair to say that, based on players' testimonies about their experience, the game provides participants with adolescent, masculine functions that are culturally distinct from the context of gaining property for the spectator.

The control of ground as a result of male adolescent initiation may be widespread in the play activities of many cultures, but there is an American social historical context that may help explain the United States' special investment in nationalistic as well as masculinist meanings in football after the 1970s. Much has been made of the loss of national prestige in the wake of the Vietnam War, especially to an Asian enemy that had been characterized in orientalist rhetoric as diminutive, feminine, and sneaky (Jeffords 1989). Associated with subversive guerrilla warfare that was not based on front lines and control of territory, the Vietcong were a source of frustration because of their use of hidden underground tunnels and their ability to blend into the population. American military leaders nonetheless used football metaphors for America's response, such as bombing campaigns named Operation Linebacker (Secretary of State Henry Kissinger was code-named "Quarterback" at the 1972 Paris peace talks) (MacCambridge 2004, 300). Writing on "post-Vietnam masculinity," Jerry Lembcke argues that the post-Vietnam era was peculiar in accentuating "the identity crises felt by many men." Identified as America's "first lost war," the Vietnam experience was blamed for male insecurities that reached, according to Lembcke, into age cohorts too young or too old for Vietnam (2004, 621). His explanation of how the blow to the male ego extended to national pride is that "military experience is a rite of passage, and for men who were in uniform during a war, there is an urge to connect as directly as possible to combat, the 'real thing' of war" (Lembcke 2004, 620; see also Gibson 1994; Lembcke 1998). War stories told by veterans did not help in the failed cause, especially because 85 percent of soldiers did not see combat, and televised reports on the national news dashed the ability to romanticize the war.

Other factors compounded the male and national identity crises. In the wake of civil rights legislation, the women's movement came to national attention by targeting the inequities of patriarchy and the dysfunction of the male provider role. Like other social movements of the time, sharing a commitment to progressivism and looking to break what was frequently referred to as traditionalism, it linked opposition to the Vietnam War to the failed militaristic policies of the traditional male "establishment." The United States suffered an economic downturn during the 1970s after two decades of prosperity. America's self-assurance as an industrial, commercial giant was shaken by competition from Japan and Germany, defeated foes from World War II. The specter of the Vietnam War loomed large in the search for American heroes who, like the Rambo character from the movies, could go out on their own, in frontier adventurer style, and redeem American pride; Saturday and Sunday heroes such as the superphysical stars of the *National* Football League and college teams seeking a *national* championship filled this void. Professional football catapulted in popularity with single-elimination playoffs that raised the stakes of imperial victory by advancing to the Super Bowl. At the local level, many women were attracted to the game, not only because of the publicity and celebrity status given to star players but also because victory elevated the community status of a campus, a region, or a city and appeared to trump the "bragging rights" earned in baseball, basketball, and other institutionalized sports. With the goal of going undefeated always in mind, collegiate and professional football tapped into, and helped expand, America's victory culture. Indeed, in the quest for a national college title, suffering a loss is considered fatal to one's chances for a championship.

A characteristic of the victory culture is that it is, in military terms, total and unconditional. In other words, the result is the elimination of the enemy. In football terms, it is expressed in the saying, "Winning isn't everything; it's the only thing." Though popularly attributed to legendary Green Bay Packers coach Vince Lombardi, there is evidence that former Vanderbilt and UCLA football coach Henry "Red" Sanders originated the saying in the 1930s (see Belliotti 2008, 7). Lombardi epitomized success, winning three consecutive league championships from 1965 to 1967, and his teams became models of dominance that others aspired to. Into the twenty-first century, John Madden, another coach known for his aggressive attitude on the field, elaborated on Lombardi's words for the society at large in this memorable quotation: "The only yardstick for success our society has is being a champion. No one remembers anything else" (Glenday 2008, 128). The eliminative characteristic of football is apparent in the oft-uttered statement that no one remembers who loses the Super Bowl, and after 1974, the National Football League instituted the "sudden death" system to decide a victor if the game ends in a tie (Rolfe 2008). Thus, only one team is left standing. Unlike the "Olympic spirit" of three medalists sharing a victory rostrum, in football, one winner takes all. There is no consolation prize. If this seems harsh, keep in mind that American political races are also run on a winner-take-all basis, rather than the proportional sharing of power typical of parliamentary systems in Europe and Japan.

I had a chance to view how cultural differences shape attitudes toward football when I spent a year in Japan in the late 1990s. Judging from the country's embrace of American baseball, I thought for sure that the Japanese would take to football fandom as well. The NFL had promoted its brand in Japan with preseason professional games and football clinics for interested high school players. I had a front-row seat to the development of football at Osaka University because its new team practiced virtually outside the window of my residence. I came down to watch the team's development and also to ask questions of the players and coaches. The first difference I noticed (besides the size difference between U.S. and Japanese players) was the emphasis on practice; the team did not have organized contests, but the game was attractive to participants because of an appeal to *doryoku*, roughly translating to "all-out effort." The Japanese players related the physically demanding drills on the football field to the *gattsu* ("guts") routines in Japanese baseball regimens (Whiting 1990, 65–66).

But in a society that values social harmony, the eliminative characteristic of the game troubled coaches and participants alike. The hostile quality of taking down an opponent seemed "shameful," they told me. Although sumo wrestling involves bodily contact, it is more ritually circumscribed, they observed, than the rough gang tackling of football. They worried about the social repercussions of a "sack" and the disgrace it brought. To be sure, they could be intensely competitive, but in a group-oriented society, they wanted to make sure that feelings of *wa*—a social unity without conflict or ill will, reflecting a social structure in which everyone knows their place—would be maintained. The physical as well as social dominance exuded in football praxis drew negative comments as unsportsmanlike or, in Japanese parlance, "impolite." In practice, they worked on the discipline of perfecting form, although when they watched games, they commented negatively that the plays looked disordered. They expressed a fondness for baseball's rigid structure of base paths and batting orders; they found the many options for a football "hit" frustrating. Another concern was the game's quick pace. To Americans, I reflected, "momentum" as an unstoppable surge is highly valued, but the Japanese are more cautious and favor the time allowed between innings and pitches in baseball to deliberate at length about strategy and tactics, often as a group (Whiting 1990, 50). Robert Hunt, a former offensive lineman for the Tampa Bay Buccaneers and international player development scout for the NFL, admitted the hard sell of football in Japan. He tried to encourage converts to football by advising youths, "No matter what your position is, you practice what you learned today in everyday life," but the players did not see the connection (Nagatsuka 2007).

Football's Rules of Engagement— Military, Industrial, and Urban

The American victory culture can be viewed in the growth of professional sports and big-time college athletics generally in the post–Vietnam War era, but a significant contribution of football as it moved into the public limelight was a change in the body image of the athlete. Desirable traits for the modern football player include being large and fast, as well as strong and gritty. In cartoons and humor during football's formative years, players were caricatured as slow, dumb, and flabby, as well as underpaid (Bronner 1995, 192–95). In the new post–Vietnam War context, the imposing sight of young, muscular, wide-bodied linemen in pads and helmets looking like buff titan warriors exudes power rather than grotesqueness. Players at other positions are attributed with "flash" and "cool" and are given nicknames such as "Broadway Joe" Namath (quarterback), "Cool Joe" Montana (quarterback), and "Primetime" or "Neon" Deion Sanders (cornerback). This turn from down-in-the-dirt frontier warfare on the football field to hip urban terms of engagement indicates that football adopted an urban sensibility in the post–Vietnam War era.

Mandelbaum credits Bill Walsh, coach of the San Francisco Fortyniners from 1979 to 1988, with initiating many changes in the game by introducing the "West Coast offense," which relies on short, precisely timed passes distributed among a variety of receivers (2004, 196–97). Walsh's personal laid-back style also drew notice for going against the image of the tough-as-nails authoritarian coach. Other teams at the college and professional levels, though, had already experienced a shift in the makeup of players—from those with rural and European ethnic backgrounds molded to the team's game plan of carefully orchestrated maneuvers to urban, African American athletes characterized as individualists with improvisational skills. As the change in play swept football programs, commentators referred to a new style of game they called "basketball in cleats" (Mandelbaum 2004, 198). It valued spontaneity, flexibility, and agility over the "plodding, grinding, rush-oriented style of football that had descended from the methods that Walter Camp had employed" (Mandelbaum 2004, 198).

Just as Camp had been proud of his break with English rugby, Walsh used the moniker "West Coast" to differentiate his new "wide-open" offensive scheme from the tight "up-the-gut" plays of the Northeast. The prominence of California suggested a close of the frontier and invited comparisons with the glitz of popular culture and the anything-goes imagery of Hollywood and the San Francisco Bay Area. The new style defied the strategies of field position and ground control associated with the frontier mentality of military-oriented coaches. The acceleration of the urban pace held more allure, while the battlefield fell into disrepute as a formula for action on the football field as well as in life. Mandelbaum observes the historical shift affecting football play when he writes, "the decline in the status of war in American society was accompanied by a devaluation of the norms and the practices that war cultivates and that football fosters as well: discipline, self-sacrifice, the acceptance of hierarchy as a principle of organization, and respect for authority. Their antitheses—spontaneity, self-indulgence, an insistence on equality, and the questioning of authority—became more acceptable and more widespread in American society" (2004, 196).

Arguably, the Wild West imagery of the game, with its associated folk narrative of possession, had already weakened by the time Super Bowls marked the ascendancy of the professional leagues. The first Super Bowl was held in Los Angeles in 1967 and was followed by venues in warm-weather climes, usually in major cities such as Miami, Tampa, New Orleans, and San Diego. Cities wanted a football team to represent them, and a number of them, including Indianapolis and St. Louis, erected huge stadiums right in the heart of their downtown districts. Halftime shows no longer stuck to the militaristic tradition of parading marching bands. Linking popular culture to the coolness of the sport, Super Bowls set the stage with elaborate concerts by megastars such as Bruce Springsteen, the Rolling Stones, and Prince. And what does it say about the commercial element that media attention focuses on the commercials aired during the Super Bowl, as well as the action on the field?

In a show of conspicuous consumption, football players given star status in the post–Vietnam War era were often depicted eating, weight lifting, and spending in excess. They embodied the idea of "to the victor belongs the spoils." Young people admired the apparent pinnacle of glory held by football players, and they aspired to the muscularity and athleticism of the football behemoths, rather than deriding them. Promoting this turn, the National Football League's youth program adopted the slogan "Dream Big, Play Big" to link aspiration with size. Yet it was not bulk but versatility and flexibility that press releases stressed when listing modern players' attributes. Some coaching holdouts of the old control game, featuring a rushing attack based on a few plays that

University of Pennsylvania coaches gather to diagram a play, 1937. (Simon Bronner collection)

Penn State offense lines up to do battle at the scrimmage line. (Courtesy University Archives, Pennsylvania State University)

were run and practiced repeatedly, drew criticism for being outmoded, even if they enjoyed success. For example, during the youth rebellion of 1968, arguments between the "Old Man" Woody Hayes at Ohio State University, who preferred the predictable T backfield, and young assistant George Chaump, who preferred the flexible and "sleek" I formation, drew press coverage (Rosenberg 2008, 30). Penn State's coach Joe Paterno, with more than sixty years on the sidelines, is another advocate of "grinding it out." Although he was criticized in his later years, he reportedly adjusted his style in 2008 to an explosive "spread HD" offense—using the parlance (HD stands for "high definition") of modern digital electronics. Along with it, though, his image of authority and running a "clean ship" suffered, with off-the-field issues involving defiant if light and speedy urban players who had run-ins with the law.

Football's metaphorical bow to technology, and its association with unruliness, went beyond the industrial overlays of clockwork precision and machine-like synchronization that marked football teamwork during the industrial era. Standout players made headlines, and individual records began to be kept—something that had never been experienced in the previous era when the team was all, or so it seemed. Mandelbaum sees a connection between the new individualism and the information technology industry of Silicon Valley, near where Walsh devised his eye-popping West Coast offense. To Mandelbaum, the organizational principles of the new industry emphasize collegiality over hierarchy and flexibility over rigid routine. The industry seeks to break the rules so that one can creatively, often spontaneously, think "outside the box." "Its products were light, versatile machines—personal computers—rather than heavy, bulky, powerful ones such as automobiles," Mandelbaum writes (2004, 198). This also means that football speaks less for tradition in the public imagination because it represents the continual changing of rules and strategies, in contrast to the nostalgia and constancy exuded by baseball and basketball. It appears more corporate than sandlot, more income generating than violently regenerative, more about being fully ready than about coming-of-age.

Voices occasionally say that the game needs to return to the tradition of a brutal contest over land. In 2008, Pittsburgh Steelers strong safety Troy Polamalu made headlines when he complained about fines imposed by the corporate NFL on a teammate for unnecessary roughness. Protesting fines is not exactly news, but his choice of words drew a rash of public responses. Polamalu said, "They're taking the physical nature of the game out of the game. It loses so much of its essence, and it really becomes like a *pansy game*" (Bouchette 2008; emphasis added). He laid blame for the game's degeneration on its rising commercialism. His ideal, he said, would be to make football "a real gladiator sport. We go there at a high speed, killing each other" (Bouchette 2008). He expressed admiration for the physical, down-in-the-trenches players of an earlier frontier era, calling them "raw, old-school, pound-it-out football players" (Bouchette 2008). His politically incorrect "pansy" reference drew public ire for its homophobic overtones, and the talk-show airwaves burned with questions of whether the celebrated violence of football is appropriate in a postmodern, postfrontier age.

Football and the Postmodern Crisis of Masculinity

Regardless of whether it has lost its regenerative qualities from the days of grit, as Polamalu claims, football in the twenty-first century still epitomizes hypermasculine aggression characteristic of war. Dur-

ing the second Iraq war, for example, American aggression was pridefully expressed in cartoons with football images. In 2008, a frequently
posted cartoon on the Internet showed a hefty football player running
through an Iraqi battlefield with a bomb under one arm and a clenched
fist. Another photo montage that made the rounds showed an oversized
bomber with the caption, "The terrorists have won the toss and elected
to receive!" The image of the airplane raised memories of the notorious
flying wedge offensive formations in football's early years, which were
outlawed because of the injurious force they hurled at defenders (Watterson 2000, 12–13). Football players and huge penetrative bombers
became joined as American icons, and both were portrayed as powerful
giants that positioned Americans, in socially dominant play terms, as
"king of the hill." Regardless of whether football players' positive body
image in the post–Vietnam War era had a symbolic component—valuing
size and speed because of the suggestion of abundance and control at a
time of economic scarcity and political-military threat—the fact is that
the appearance and skills of football players became models to aspire
to for many growing boys, although perhaps for different reasons than
they did in the pre–Vietnam War days.

In a postmodern era of self-development, football, more than other
sports, signifies the extremes of training and the possibility of transformation. Brandishing control over young men, larger-than-life football
coaches take the role of generals who, through boot/football camp,
turn individuals into a winning unit of titans. This has been a frequent
theme of movies, literature, and sports journalism. Many Hollywood
movies, such as *Necessary Roughness* (1991), *Little Giants* (1994), *Remember the Titans* (2000), and *Friday Night Lights* (2004), have presented
football to adoring audiences as the ultimate coming-of-age experience
for boys, who gain confidence and strength through the tough love of
an apparently uncaring, steely coach. On television, cameras focus on
surly coaches leading their player "armies" as they pace the sidelines
with a sense of urgency; like the talented players, they too became the
darlings of the press during football's ascendancy. Historian John Sayle
Watterson claims that "the Rambos of football already existed in the
NFL in the form of Vince Lombardi and George Allen, who emphasized that victory on the gridiron wasn't just important; to paraphrase
Lombardi, it was the only thing" (2000, 384). These legendary coaches
were honored for their victory-at-all-costs and take-no-prisoners men-

tality at a time when Americans longed to restore their position at the top of the heap. Such coaches conveyed an image that appeared to run counter to the equal rights movement. They underscored their total patriarchal control of the team and were seen as stern, punishing father figures (epitomized in nicknames such as George "Papa Bear" Halas of the Chicago Bears, Woody "The Old Man" Hayes at Ohio State University, Glenn "Pop" Warner at the University of Pittsburgh and the Carlisle Indian School, and Joe "Pa" Paterno at Penn State University). Also known as "field generals," these coaches whipped their boys into shape, linking the meanings of football as a youthful initiation into manhood, military victory by eliminating the enemy, and a control game meant to maximize the possession of territory.

Football as a location to compensate for a crisis of masculinity and a loss of patriarchal tradition in a progressive society continued into the twenty-first century. One indication is William Pollack's 1998 best seller *Real Boys: Rescuing Our Sons from the Myths of Boyhood*, followed by a host of popular titles beseeching the American public not to feminize boys to achieve a civil society (see Gilbert 2002; Iggulden and Iggulden 2007; Mansfield 2006; Sommers 2000). Pollack opens with a dire warning: "Boys today are in serious trouble, including many who seem 'normal' and to be doing just fine. Confused by society's mixed messages about what's expected of them as boys, and later as men, many feel a sadness and disconnection they cannot even name" (1998, xxi). He strikes a responsive chord by calling for the use of sports to express manly feelings rather than repressing them as overly competitive and hierarchical. Offering a perspective on play as therapy, Pollack underscores the "transformational" quality of sports: "our sons can go from being reserved, detached, and hardened to being expressive, affectionate, resilient" (1998, 274). Football especially allows for a grand spectacle of an all-male group that has been subjected to opprobrium in public discourse; for fans and players alike, football, more than other sports, is associated with an exuberant expression of emotion and brash display, whether in the chilly stands with shirts off, in a sports bar screaming at the screen, or on the field with war dances and spiked balls upon gaining a touchdown.

Particularly because of its initiatory characteristics, football is important in the American context because of the relative absence of public rites of passage for boys compared with girls. Referring to the

Exuberant shirtless fans at a Penn State football game, 2000. (Archives and Special Collections, Pennsylvania State University)

apparent disconnection between the primitiveness of traditional male-dominated sports and the progressivism of what he labels "liberated times," sociologist Ray Raphael observes that "the psychic needs of contemporary males have not always been able to keep pace with sex-role liberation and a computerized economy and nuclear warfare, all of which contribute to the apparent obsolescence of traditional initiations" (1988, xii). Although many traditional male initiations, such as hazing and subordination, went underground or disappeared as the twentieth century ended, football as a nationalistic sport became more acceptable as a location to fulfill what Raphael calls "an urge, a yearning, a mysterious drive to prove themselves as men in more primitive terms" (1988, xii). This drive hearkens back to the early days of the game, when reporters wondered about its hold among supposedly elite bastions of gentility at Harvard, Yale, Princeton, Swarthmore, and Columbia. Student chronicles show that the primitive game of contesting a piece of ground held initiatory qualities for players coming of age and, more than other sports, represented the collective identity of the whole class or institution (Bealle 1948, 17–78; Davis 1912, 33–43). For

fans, following football was a way to prepare for battle and tell "war stories" after the game in an enactment of ultimate male ritual transformation; it engaged a kind of talk that might be unacceptable in daily life.
Indeed, the magazine *Sporting News* distinguished football talk from
talk about other sports by locating it in a "War Room" section (Sporting News 2008; see also Nylund 2007, 40).

Abundant military references are linked to the acquisition and defense of property, which may be viewed as an outgrowth of the frontier
experience. In addition to the honor accorded a metaphorical kill, one
often hears the football field discussed as a battleground, the scrimmage
line as warfare in the trenches, quarterbacks (also called field generals)
throwing bombs, teams marching down the field, and running backs
accelerating as if shot out of a cannon. It was not uncommon, particularly during the formative period of football, for journalists to observe
that even if young men did not go off to war, they still had a need to
engage in combat that could be channeled into football. Writing in
Outing magazine in 1898, Price Collier observes, "as wars become less
frequent, gymnasiums and field sports increase in number and popularity" (383). David Wallace Adams reports this military metaphor's connection with the frontier in the words of sportswriter Harry Beecher,
who wrote of the 1900 Thanksgiving Day game between Carlisle and
Columbia, "Now it is brawn, muscle and speed scrapping over a slip-
pery football. Then it was tomahawks and rifles with lives at stake"
(Adams 2001, 31). In both cases, being outside on a field of battle vying
for turf, particularly during the fall (associated with earth tones and
hunting, rather than the feminine fertility of the spring), provided a
contrast to the sedentary domestic sphere (*Outing* magazine targeted a
male audience and constructed a binary between the exhilarating outdoors and the enervating indoors associated with domestication).

The military rhetoric expanded during the twentieth century with
the experience of the world wars in mind. Football strategies came to
include blitzes, formations on the front line, and battling linemen in
the trenches. There were more references to the modernization of the
game as well as war, with the "big strike" forward pass gaining ground
quickly, particularly with the modern "spread" offense and the quarterback in "shotgun" formation. As a result, more metaphors for avia-
tion came into play: quarterbacks throwing missiles, receivers catching
long bombs downfield, and coaches strategizing an aerial attack. Still,

the manly guts of football remained the ground game, as evidenced by an oft-repeated anecdote told by Purdue head coach Joe Tiller about an encounter with Penn State head coach Joe Paterno, known for his grind-it-out-on-the-ground style of play. As Tiller relates the story, "Joe looks at me and says, 'Tiller, you're not gonna spread the field and throw the ball all over the field today, are ya?' I said, 'Coach, we are what we are. We're gonna go out there and play *sissy* ball'" (Jones 2008b). In defense of the pass receiver—who is often viewed in feminine terms as an overly slim, spoiled, and flamboyant diva, contrary to the ethos of the game—Elmo Wright, an end for the Kansas City Chiefs, attempted to symbolically incorporate himself into the game's manly turf war by depicting himself locked in one-on-one combat with a defensive back: "Imagine me running a pattern. I make a break to the middle, and those few seconds that the ball is in the air, my life is on the line" (Craggs 2008).

The sport may have evolved into action taking place all over the field with small, lively encounters erupting simultaneously rather than a tight, forward-moving formation, but possession is still critical to the game's praxis. In the battle for the all-important line, teams are still expected to move oppositional forces; they dig in and get rough, suggesting that they become one with the land. Former coach and sportscaster John Madden became renowned for lauding the kind of player who shows his toughness by getting filthy during play. He praised players for wearing the earth they sought to conquer. His experience inspired a series of wildly popular video games emphasizing bodily collisions in football. The uniform, expected to get grimy, differs from baseball and basketball uniforms by its helmet and pads, which, like military attire, protect participants from attack. In these militaristic references, the contact in the sport is accentuated with instruments of war and violence that use phallic symbols to extend the power of the players and feminize their opponents. The context that makes sense to Americans is the property grab, so that owning land by eliminating its previous occupants is the sign of dominance.

Using animal and frontier names to rally around invokes what Richard Slotkin calls the "myth of the hunter" born out of frontier experience. The myth equates hunting in the wild to a heroic human pursuit involving a national, protective regeneration by destroying natural masters of the land. Slotkin asserts that, according to this worldview,

"Every American shares with Boone the love of the chase, the conflict, the kill" (1973, 426). The ground gained and controlled is that of the aggressive hunter figure, not the farmer-cultivator, because it is a representation of vanquishing an opponent, not developing the fertile land. There is a psychoanalytic connection because, as Slotkin notes, the hunted and hunter Indian on the frontier (and, I would add, the animal or titan in football) takes the image "of the American libido—the primitive source of sexual, conceptual, and creative energy" (1973, 560). In this view, however, people need not hunt to share in the hunter myth. In fact, it becomes more effective to ritualize the hunt by following it in activities such as sport rather than enacting it in a postfrontier society.

The difficulty with Europeans taking up American football, according to at least one European scholar, is the construction of football as a spectator spectacle, whereas the version of football known to Americans as soccer is more participatory and not as contact oriented as rugby or football. Some scholars consider the ritualization of violence in Europe to be located in the spectators in the stands rather than the players on the field. This raises another question about the location of sporting contests in the United States being either home or away, rather than being played at a neutral site, to emphasize imbalance. The away team is said to be playing in hostile surroundings, and violence tends to be minimized because the home-team crowd is unified behind its team as it immobilizes or crushes the opposition and drives it away (or, in slang, "runs the team out of town").

The neutral setting of the Super Bowl as a culminating event appears to diverge from this model, but it provides background for a grand festival surrounding the crowning of a "world champion" to emphasize the high stakes of elimination. Arguably, the folk celebrations that emerged in homes and bars for viewing the event verify the transgressive quality of football, even if, as Polamalu claims, the game has lost its folk "essence" of male combat to the death. The foods served signify unhealthiness and even danger: spicy chili, "hot" wings, sausage, pizza, chips, burgers, beer, and hot dogs. The finger foods emphasize communal sharing and, in many settings, male bonding. Further, among focus-group conversations about male-only activities, I often heard participants say that "spending a Sunday watching football with a bunch of guys is my idea of a perfect day." Hollering at the screen is expected, and attendees are asked, "Who are you going to root for?" suggesting the need for partiality at the event as one's team builds "momentum"—a feeling of mastery and unstoppable progress or forward movement (Letson 2008).

Does football's restriction to one season weaken the symbolist case, as Fine implies? It is true that, for most people, fall and winter constitute the football season, but I should point out that in the twenty-first century, football has become more of a year-round event. ESPN, beginning in 2005, has supported arena football, scheduled in the spring, and intrasquad games are another springtime ritual for big-time college sports, attracting as many as 50,000 fans to each event. If virtual play is taken into consideration, year-round involvement becomes even more evident. The Madden NFL football video game, aimed at the hard-core gamer segment of males aged eighteen to thirty-five, was the top-selling video game of 2006; almost 3 million copies were sold, outdistancing Gears of War at 1.8 million and far outpacing the popularity of any other sports game (Glenday 2008, 129; Wagner 2008). In 2007, Madden NFL set a new record by selling 2 million copies in its first week of release (Glenday 2008, 128). The Madden series is not alone in the football video market; other popular games include NFL Blitz and NFL Primetime. In the game versions, sacks and hits tend to be exaggerated with sound effects. In addition, cable TV and satellite radio stations devoted to football year-round burst on the scene with the dawn of the twenty-first century, enhancing the impact of sports talk rhetoric on the appreciation of football as masculine display well beyond when games are played (Eisenstock 2001; Nylund 2007).

More than the season played, football's hold on the American imagination in the postindustrial era derives from its claim as mass spectacle, which is another way of saying that it is something everyone can share in a postmodern era marked by social fragmentation and isolated individualism (Bellah, Madsen, Sullivan, Swidler, and Tipton 1996; McLean 2002; Putnam 2000). Football broadcasts a surfeit of social capital with its large teams and spectators in exaggerated proportions housed in oversized stadiums (10,000 for a high school game or 100,000 for a college contest), raising comparisons to classical coliseums as sporting centers of a civilization (Epting 2002; Reid 2008). Besides Polamalu's reference to male gladiator combat as football's essence, advertisements and sports journalism broadcast images of football players as "gladiators in the coliseum," suggesting the buildup of vicarious thrills for fans (Jones 2008a).

At the local high school level, the "big game" has significance in serving as a town commons because of the lack of communal institutions that bring residents—adults and children—together with a local identity. Institutions of church and municipality do not draw people together the way the ritualized football game does, especially in the era of consolidated schools and suburban sprawl. At the game, held outdoors on the "green" or "grounds," fans swirl about the field and socialize. Although the games may not always have the drama depicted in television shows such as *Friday Night Lights*, the message is similar: football cuts across and involves the community. In many regions that do not have major urban centers, the university football team (e.g., Syracuse University in upstate New York, the University of Nebraska in the upper plains, Penn State University in central Pennsylvania) represents the pride of the area; fan devotion, because it is not restricted to students and alumni, is compared to professional-level fervor. The passions that football raises for fans and players in America are reportedly unmatched. Sociologist Harry Edwards, for example, observes, "That kind of intensity brings out relationships, brings out a sense of commitment to each other and the game that you really don't see in other sports" (quoted in Paolantonio 2008, 190). That level of intensity for both fans and players is compared, not coincidentally, with the intensity found in other traditional institutions: "When those guys say, 'Hey, man, I really love you and I'm so happy that you're here,' they mean it. I mean they mean it at a level that you don't see in families. They mean it at a level that you only see by guys, from guys who have gone through war together or who will have each other's backs in a police department or fire department" (quoted in Paolantonio 2008, 191).

More Than a Game

If football has a ritual significance as an American tradition, then its spectacle should be related to the time it is played as well as its place. Many commentators wonder why, if football is binding and regenerative for players and fans, it is associated with the fall, a season of decay. Football's connection with autumn was apparent in its formative years, even before colleges took it up as a ritual opening of the academic year, often following the campus rushes (mentioned earlier) that set the whole freshman and sophomore classes against each other. As in football, the rushes or "scraps" often involved brutal contact as players tried to push a ball over a line and therefore declare the campus grounds as theirs (Bronner 2011, 11–46; Krout 1929, 235). Whereas baseball came to be the springtime ritual of going to the well-kept park, bask in the sun, and witness the blossoming greenery as a sign of renewal, football was meant to be dirty, befitting its gritty image of being played on grounds. It marked a time of natural decay, when sustenance would be gained by hunting rather than cultivating. Following the drama of the hunter myth, in the absence of greenery, humans looked beyond their domain and sought to expand. The narrative suggested for autumn endeavors is that adventurers show their courage under conditions of scarcity and decline, and they provide for their families, nations, and communities by venturing out and battling fauna, vying for survival (Paolantonio 2008, 15–32). As is common to hear in football narrative, the goal of the rugged warrior is to be the "last man standing," "laying on a big hit/score, "butting heads," and "dishing dirt" in a particularly "punishing sport." The prominent symbol is not the blooming garden but the dirt below their feet and its association with the untamed field of battle, where men engage in events greater than themselves. Arguably, the culmination of this process is the high-stakes championship or Super Bowl, held after the New Year. The "big game" has a finality to it, along with the anticipation of "next year." The Super Bowl—representing the priority of the professional version of the game, and held after the college championship, whose players will feed into the pros—is culturally marked as the preeminent sporting event with exuberant, even hyperbolic, festivity. It is not held all year but is scheduled in the dead of winter. It regenerates life, with an emphasis on masculine control of the land and labor to show the transition from adolescence to adulthood. Football shot up in appeal after the 1960s because it hybridized the regeneration of American frontier exploits with postindustrial characteristics of layered organization and urbane individuality in the midst of a social and political environment in which football provided a bounded cultural scene for an aggressive victory culture, a release from the pressures of routinized everyday life through vicarious spectator experience, and even a location for socially sanctioned immaturity. Rather than plateauing after this boost, football has grown in bursts, at least in America, through the enterprises of an advanced consumer culture, crises fueling a need for national identity, and the postmodern crisis of masculinity.

In sum, football—in its historical references to the frontier experience and urban-industrial synchronization; its invocation of tradition in an energetic, competitive, adolescent coming-of-age ritual; and its social context as a masculine response to modernization—is both a reflection and a distortion of culture. It has undergone many changes in rules as well as descriptive discourse over the years, including a shift from a nineteenth-century regional and campus folk game to a national spectacle of industrial, corporate, urban, and digital praxis in the twentieth and twenty-first centuries. With this norm of change, the game's reverence for the past is often questioned, suggesting that it lacks the constancy characteristic of tradition and that, more than other big-time sports, it embraces progress (Mandelbaum 2004, 124–26). Yet vital continuities exist between the sport's folk roots and modern versions in terms of the importance of possessing property and pushing occupants off theirs; inflicting bodily punishment with the crushing sack and the psychological humiliation of feminization; the military mind-set of intense preparation, strategizing, and battle; and its projection of adolescent masculine values and anxieties. American football has indeed engaged the prescriptive and connotative qualities of tradition in its ritualization of violence, passionate emotional release, and intense male bonding that connects the narrative of the game's gritty, grimy past to the cutting-edge technological wonders of the widely broadcast and watched present.

"More than a game," football constitutes for many spectators and participants an event working at various levels and often with contradictory symbolism. This tension within its practice—as modern and antimodern, normal and abnormal, refined and primitive, organized and chaotic—invites speculation not just on the final score but also on the various meanings that the hits, bangs, and blocks of the game entail. Instead of universalizing the end zone as Dundes did, we can understand the game structurally in the context of the field and the sidelines; we can link it historically and socially to Americanness and explain its enactment in mass spectacle as ritual and tradition. Dundes was on to something, though, by drawing attention to the way football provides metaphors to live and fight by on a field of play. Psychologically, the game as a male display related to adolescent development is crucial to its performance by players and the perception of its high stakes by spectators. In the stands, viewers are hardly passive; they actively engage and in many ways help construct the play frame of football that allows for violence and exuberant manly display. Spectators may be said to be playing at play, while players enact a dramatic battle over property. Getting down in their stances for a play, warriors on both sides of the ball anticipate a clash over turf that they can claim as their own. Whether pushing ahead or pulling back, manhood appears to be on the line. The key to control, and meaning, in the sport is gaining ground.

10

Virtual Tradition

On the Internet as a Folk System

Many people believe that traditions are all about being natural. In this view, traditions are down home, out in the fields, or back in the woods, where socializing, ritualizing, and storytelling occur unencumbered by machines or corporations. They raise images of family gathered around the dinner table at holidays or the neighborhood gang playing together, and this view might be imaginatively set in opposition to the socially alienating quality of modernity dominated by technology. The rhetoric of tradition cited in folkloristic annals is not far off from these characterizations, although it may broaden to include a variety of settings—urban as well as rural, industrial as well as agricultural—and encompass folk transmission via a host of technologies from printing press to photocopier (Blank 2009; Dundes and Pagter 1975, xiii–xxii; Georges and Jones 1995, 6–13). Still, a community's customs or face-to-face expressive encounters are typically referred to as *naturally* authentic and genuine, in contrast to the artificiality of technology. The folklorist's tradition signifies cultural production of earthy, artistic expressions from homey proverbs to handwrought pots that are said to be folk because they attach culturally to groups and repeat and vary. To be sure, the joke of the day or the latest rumor on the Internet may be pegged as lore or urban legend, but it is hard to shake the image of folk connections made around the campfire rather than through FireWire.

One test of tradition in modernity is to query whether the Internet has produced traditions and, if so, to ask how they are distinctive from other vernacular or mass-mediated forms. After all, grabbing a joke online from an unseen recipient is a far cry from gesturing and making eye contact with buddies huddled together at the usual gathering place. Pundits often appear to be surprised by the extent of the unofficial use of the Internet to share or create traditions, and in this chapter I explain why masses of people are attracted to the Internet not for business but as a folk system. I examine, as a cognitive basis for this attraction, the modernistic tendency to construct various cultural divisions or binaries to separate reality from fantasy or imagination, including natural and artificial, public and private, analog and digital, group and network, relational and analytical, and, especially, folk and official. Although folklorists have previously noted that various communication technologies emerging in the twentieth century, such as the telephone and the photocopier, have altered the way lore as well as information is spread, I find that the Internet, more so than other social conduits, has unsettled many of the prior cultural binaries, evident especially in the rise of what I call the transgressive folk Web. Using the Internet has become both an essential tool of everyday life and a cultural practice. Although use of the Internet as a cultural practice may simulate the naturalness of tradition, it is also distinguished by being envisioned as a separate location in which traditions arise and are constituted (Blank 2009; Dobler 2009; Howard 2005; McNeill 2009; Tucker 2009).

One description often applied to both cyberspace and natural space is the quality of being "free" and "open," in the sense of being unrestricted. Both invite involvement on common ground, and participants form social guidelines to organize themselves. From the perspective of the user, the Internet opens access and is an open medium. A formidable Internet social movement even advocates "open source culture," in which collectivity rather than acquisitive individualism dominates, and the communal spirit is manifested in creative, copyrightable works (including software) being made generally available to the masses (Truscello 2003). Unstructured in the cybercollective, the Internet could become one big, open mess were it not for organizational tools users put in place, consequently showing their orderliness in creating an "information system." Practices that especially tag the organization of information and become metaphors for vitality on the Internet are "searching," "surfing," and "marking." The thrill of the dynamo-proportion search engine driving the conspicuous consumption of information is downright intoxicating, until the sobering realization hits that one has to do some serious sorting and sifting of the results into a "personal desktop." For the individual, structuring one's knowledge allows, like a grammar of language, one to communicate—and think together—with others.

In the gathering on the digital commons, though, Internet users can only approximate an actual meeting, and when users talk of *virtual reality*, much of its meaning is wrapped up in a connection that is social as well as electronic, and this is where tradition comes in (Kirshenblatt-Gimblett 1995; Rheingold 2001; Swiss 2004; Žižek 2001). Perhaps most exciting, yet troublesome at the same time, is that individuals seated at screens can negotiate the isolation of the one-person/one–hard drive architecture of the virtual desktop with the wi-fi social networking breakthrough, which now allows digitally framed conversations out in the open. Examining the Web landscape from touch screens on the go or pads in cubicles, users recognize a fundamental difference between sites identified as "official" or corporate, usually controlling the content and broadcasting information to a passive viewing audience, and those that allow instant posting, "live" chats, and free exchange among users. For many users, the latter constitutes the folk universe of cyberspace, in contrast to an elite realm. The folk realm is not located in a socioeconomic sector or a particular nation; rather, it represents a participatory process that some posters refer to repeatedly as the democratic or open Web.

Now hold the phone. The traditional or folk Web is not just a place for simulating storytelling around the kitchen table or bull sessions in the dorm room. Noting that much of folklore research was premised on the social intimacy or familiarity of people engaging in oral communication during face-to-face contact, Barbara Kirshenblatt-Gimblett argues that rather than transposing premodern orality to the new media, the analysis of digital culture needs to start fresh with the premise that "computer mediated communication, at least in its present form is *between* speech and writing. Listers on X-CULT-X dub this kind of talk putation, and speak of puting or putating. The words on the screen neither precede nor follow speech, though they often feel more like talking than writing. Electronic messages are neither a play-script nor a transcript, particularly in the interactive chat programs. They *are* the event" (1995, 74). She describes the Internet lode as being mined typically for written texts of humor, although Internet veins abound with visual imagery, often in motion, that is layered, embedded, and juxtaposed with other messages into a multimedia assemblage.[1]

An expressive metaphor that can describe the Internet praxis between reading and writing, assembling and visualizing, is the folkloric reference of *relating* (and the interactive mode of *responding*). It carries the sense of doing more than scribing or sending information; it reaches someone by relating narrative and belief, and it also signifies the process of connection and assemblage by relating different sources and, in many cases, considering precedents in relation to the present.

Although it is tempting to see Internet communicative frames as mere conversations from which to extract traditions as rhetorical strategies, if not artifacts, surely something different is occurring when one is using a keyboard to "tell" a joke; it is a far cry from pecking out reports on the keys of a mechanical typewriter in a previous epoch. The computer screen has also been transformed from its previous incarnation as a television set in the couch potato–filled living rooms of the past. What happens when keyboard and monitor conjugate, and out of the union is born a vernacular communication form imitating the ease of conversation through tapping on keys or touching a screen? What happens when producer and consumer merge in a single interactive medium, becoming knowledge "prosumers" who can readily create as well as consume the message or the product (Toffler and Toffler 2006, 151–201)? Is it not a symbolic breakthrough when, instead of bowing to sacred icons, people can freely move them around on the screen, create their own avatars (drawing on Hindu mythology of the descent of a deity to earth), and, in ordinary, secular life, use a pointed cursor like the pointer handled by a cleric on sacred parchment scrolls (raising a further comparison of the hand symbol for locating a hyperlink with the revered *yad*, or "hand," in Jewish Torah readings)?

Maybe the big question (or byte) is whether, beyond offering unprecedented access to folklore materials amassed in the naturalistic field, the Internet *facilitates, mediates,* and *produces* tradition on the computer screen. Do some or all of the productions tailor made for the website phenomena of YouTube, Facebook, MySpace, and Twitter qualify as folk practices? And if they do, so what? What are the various "cultural" texts, and contexts, of e-mails, text messages, Listservs, blogs, vlogs, and home pages, and how do they diverge from the face-to-face, in situ experience of field-recorded material? Is disembodied storytelling on the Internet really folkloric, after all? Is it real, even if it is in "real time"? Or, in computer lingo, what happens when, in addition to digitizing folklore—that is, sending or posting jokes one has heard orally—people virtualize it? How do "new media" technologies utilizing the Internet—such as video game units, media players, iPods, iPads, and "smart" phones—relate to cyberculture?

These are key questions, because folklore as a fundamental, timeless form of communication is inextricably tangled up in the Web. Folklore as an expression of tradition has to be present on the Internet because it has become the primary way people "message," "connect," and "link" (if not talk) to one another; hence the Internet incorporates the symbolic and projective functions that folklore distinctively provides. And when people e-mail or post to a message board, they often invoke, and evoke, folklore as a cultural frame of reference for creatively relating experiences, particularly in narration and images that respond to ambiguity and anxiety. Although saying that folklore is *on* the Web or that folklore is produced *about it* is a relatively safe cultural call, the signal claim that the Internet acts folklorically may give pause (see Dundes 1980, 17–19; Dundes 2005, 406; Ellis 2006). Yet, upon reflection, the Internet as an expanding folkloric thoroughfare may help explain aspects that have confounded many technopundits who were sure that the vampire in the machine would suck users dry of their culture and creativity. And as an icon of mass media, the Internet, they said, was certain to alienate us all and obliterate our last semblances of community and art (Ronnell 2001; Ross 2001; see also Benjamin 2007). How, then, has it become a tool of social connection and, consequently, of new expressive lore engendering digital, or virtual, culture?

To begin answering these questions, I move from the manifest appeal of the Internet as a social networking tool to the less discussed but critical area of its folk system, steeped in a psychologically created frame of an open medium. In addition to suggesting concepts to guide the interpretation of folk Web practice and sources for the folk Web's social construction, I present a case study involving cultural responses to tragedy in analog and digital eras that allows me to compare folklore as oral and Internet traditions.

Social Factors and the Creation of Folklore

The basis of the claim that the Internet has folkloric features is the medium's interactive, instrumental quality, which differentiates it from radio and television, where people are divided between broadcasters and listeners or viewers. Internet users are captivated by the ability to simultaneously send and receive, produce and consume, read and write (Tabbi 1997; Zukin 2004, 227–52). Precedent can be found in vernacular uses of photography, photocopying, and faxing, which invited the manipulation of images and text to create a play frame in which humor, pathos, and memory were shared among members of a social network, often from an anonymous source. These commentaries, which we might call "metafolklore," touched on values and attitudes about the very technology and institutional contexts that made the images and text possible (Dundes 2007b; Dundes and Pagter 1975; Fineman 2004; Mechling 2004, 2005b; Preston 1994; Roemer 1994). Many of these broadside-type sheets, surreptitiously produced in and circulated from photocopy rooms, found their way to bulletin boards and office walls, giving a foundation to the humorous postings to websites' virtual display boards.

In my experience, folklore was present at the beginning of computing, even before the Internet and e-mail burst on the scene. I first began messing with computers back in the 1960s as a high school mathlete and part of a geek clique. The gargantuan machine we thought was wondrous in its power was barely capable of performing a few mathematical calculations, but it was light years ahead of our slide rules, and the idea of having a machine that could do what we did in our heads made us giddy. The machine was a *brain*, and we marveled at its symbolization of things automatic; it was self-acting and apparently had a life of its own. It suggested autonomy and, unlike the automobile, could run itself, evident in the digital installation of "autorun." It could speak with programmed message responses to actions by a user. I recall philosophical discussions of automorphism, the reproduction of forms, as a representative system. I wrote a program to generate automorphic numbers—those that, when multiplied, result in the original number appearing in the total (e.g., $5 \times 5 = 25$; see Kobayashi, Schmid, and Yang 2008)—maybe as a precursor to my folkloristic fascination with the repetition and variation of forms and actions.

Binary language, the programming fundament of 1s and 0s that spawned a new science, also gave rise to inside jokes written into notebooks: "There are only 10 types of people in the world—those who understand binary, and those who don't." Reflecting back on it, this humor laid the groundwork for the significance of multiple meanings in digital thinking as folklore. For the uninitiated, 10 refers to the number ten, but in binary, it means the number two, and in keeping with the praxis of writing programs, the joke makes sense only when written. It also has variations, which are often given serially, like a discussion thread: "There are only 10 types of people in the world—those who understand binary, and those who get laid." "There are three kinds of people in the world—those who can count, and those who can't." "I must have heard that joke 1100100 times." And "1010011010, the number of the Beast [the Devil, or 666 in binary]" (Beatty 1976; Binary Jokes 2008).

In response to the spate of lightbulb jokes that were all the rage at the time, these folks could imagine an automated lightbulb that changed lightbulbs: "How many lightbulbs does it take to change a lightbulb?" Answer: "One, if it knows its own Gödel number" (see Dundes and Renteln 2005, 187). Much of the discussion was about speed that, like acting out a heroic John Henry test, could be shown to outpace human effort. The buzz was about the advent of a new Pax Automatica age, besides the cultural revolution ushered in by youthful rebellion. The age was one in which society depended on information, and information gave youth power—or so we surmised from our memorization of Marshall McLuhan's work, which pronounced the revolutionary implication of instantaneous, automatically provided information mediated through technology (McLuhan 1994; see also Virilio 2001).[2]

At my high school, the room the computer occupied was papered with photocopied folk wisdom. This included "Garbage In, Garbage Out," made to look like a homespun motto; a flow chart beginning with the question "Does the Damn Thing Work?" with the arrow for "No" leading to a command box plainly advising "Shitcanit"; and an instructional graphic captioned "Understanding the Technology," which showed a toilet with arrows pointing to the input and output areas and a backup system consisting of a chamber pot (cf. Dundes and Pagter 1991b, 161–62; Dundes and Pagter 1996, 120–21). Perhaps inspired by this risqué gallery, which gave us and our geekiness a special status, some of our first deviations from the instructional text were cartoon characters made from computer-generated lines and circles. In an animated way, it showed we had a life and could humanize science. The material that represented our playing with the machine generated more excitement than the long printouts of calculations and data, truth be told. I do not recall talk of sneaky viruses at that time, but frequent reference was made to the ghost or the devil in the machine and the belief that the thing had a "mind of its own," sentiments still echoed today (Jennings 1991, 143–58). We did not call this material folklore, but it was significant to our fantasy about the control we exercised over the technology and the world we wrought, as we struggled to make the huge technological dragon do our bidding (see Dundes and Pagter 1996, 6–7, 58–61). Others made this folkloric connection about the artificial being that humans created and then sought to rein in, judging from the early supercomputer developed in the 1950s named "Golem," after the Jewish legend of a creature made from clay (Scholem 1966; Swaine and Freiberger 1983).

During the 1970s Alan Dundes was among the first scholars to spot the computer's leavening of folklore and commented, "So technology isn't stamping out folklore; rather it is becoming a vital factor in the transmission of folklore and it is providing an exciting source of inspiration for the generation of new folklore" (1980, 17). The folklore he reported as early as 1958 was about computing as a suspect occupational pursuit on the periphery, probably because of its potential to displace humans. Thus he documented the esoteric lore of computer programmers and an exoteric tradition in general society about the computer and its authorities. He explained the rise of this joke lore about computers and computer programmers as a function of anxiety: suspicious folks needed to symbolically project, and externalize, their worry about the changes wreaked by technology, which appeared to be part of the modern condition. In advance of security fears related to scams and identity theft via the Internet, Dundes noted, "there is widespread genuine anxiety that the use of the computer to gather personal data may bring us to the point where dossiers contain more information about a person than the person himself knows" (1980, 18).

The fear is that machines might replace humans in controlling daily life. Although technology promises users the "power of the Internet" in their hands, it also raises the fear that greedy multinational corporations will exact tolls on the information superhighway. Although Dundes did not predict that the Internet would become such a dominant interactive medium and common household appliance, he offered a hypothesis about vernacular human control in thematizing folklore about the computer. "It is folklore itself—including the joketelling process—that ultimately separates man from machine, or does it?" He closed with this example: "A super computer is built and all the world's knowledge is programmed into it. A gathering of top scientists punch in the question: 'Will the computer ever replace man?' Clickity, click, whir, whir, and the computer lights flash on and off. Finally a small printout emerges saying, 'That reminds me of a story'" (Dundes 1980, 18–19). The thing is, what constitutes a story in the new media is related differently in the context of humor sites, where viewers rate its funniness, respond with variations, or editorialize in blogs and chat rooms. Even more than identifying items classifiable as stories comparable to analogs in predigital form, people have developed emergent interactive practices represented by the "clickity, click, whir, whir, and the computer lights" that users in the Internet age identify with digital custom.

During the 1990s, when the graphical interface of the World Wide Web became widely available, the Internet took on the characteristics of a visual culture rather than an electronic post office or business tool. The development of Web 2.0, referring to the quantum leap from a display to a *platform* among users, resulted in an explosion of online expressive material. Platform development widened computing from self-isolating technogeeks to nonspecialists or ordinary users engaging in daily activities online. Arguably, it made the Internet more of a folkloric thoroughfare and mediator than when it was still conceived as a military or academic tool or as a desktop publication. It could easily be used to create public activity in the form of social networking sites, wikis, and blogs; it allowed uploading as well as downloading of videos, collaboration as well as individual tinkering. In my technological neolithic stage, folklore was outside of my and my fellow geeks' awareness, even if we engaged it, but by the time Web 2.0 burst on the scene with the new millennium, developers, not folklorists, were explicitly referring to the "folk" character of the Internet. *Folksonomy*, a portmanteau (one of many in digital culture indicating fusion and hybridization as technological evolution) of *folk* and *taxonomy*, entered Internet lingo for the emic, or user-generated, practice of collaboratively creating and managing tags to annotate content (Howard 2008; Mika 2007). Folksonomies are ubiquitous in popular social bookmarking and photography sites such as Flickr, Librarything, Esnips, and Del.icio.us, where users are aware of who created the tags and can see the other assigned tags. The vernacular implication is that this kind of taxonomy can provide an alternative to the corporate-controlled search engine with its monopolistic, industrial image. Another significant connotation of the growing, user-generated fondness for folksonomy is recognition that patterns of categorizing and organizing in the openness of cyberspace are key cultural practices defining boundaries and, hence, shared ways of thinking about information as markers of identity.

A key characteristic of the Internet that distinguishes it from face-to-face communication is its visual nature. Users look at a screen, allowing images and texts to be combined. Adherents of verbal communication might argue that this "visualness" takes away from the use of the imagination to picture episodes as they are being told. Yet visualness adds a level of suspicion about whether what one is looking at is "real." That is why, I contend, that people think of Internet information as simulated or *virtual*, deriving from the term *virtual image* in optics. Unlike touch, which can be used to verify physical evidence, sight identifies and is known to be manipulable. This can create suspicion that one is just "seeing things" or witnessing an "optical illusion" or that the image has been altered. If one of these claims is true, one might be accused of being "out of touch with reality." Facts are tangible, gripping, clinching, and hard. Knowledge from seeing, as the proverb "seeing is believing" attests, involves belief rather than certainty. To be sure, photographs are posted on the Internet as visual proof, but arguments and narratives can arise about activities outside the frame or the accuracy of the image inside the frame. Especially when images are broadcast from peer to peer in a play frame, the Internet becomes "folklorized" because the discourse of belief is involved. The perception that every picture tells a story, and that it may attract unseen viewers, only adds to the Internet's folkloric dimension.

The Internet's visual nature gives the impression that it broadens experience. One can see off into the distance, but touch is at hand. Locality—where one lives and interacts with others—is described in terms of touch as well as tradition: the earth beneath your feet, the feel of familiar furniture, the handshake on the street. Sight looks out on the horizon rather than feeling at home; ringing through one's head might be the reminders of expansive visualness—that one can "see the world" or "look to the future." The Internet carries this sensory implication further by reference to the World Wide Web and by the eyes in the Google logo, the largest search engine (following this idea of visual broadening, the first search engine was called the Wanderer). The rhetoric of the information superhighway and cyberspace expresses working the Internet as accelerating away from here and having the potential to take in everywhere and everything. As exhilarating as that sounds, it does not come without some anxiety about freedom and information overload. Questions of identity and security arise, for if one can be everywhere, then where and to whom does one belong? Where is the safe haven of home?

A formidable folk construction to temper the radically individualized world of the digital screen is the creation of places identified as groups, lists, and networks. Folklore arises among users, too, to caution others about unfamiliar sites and attachments as one wanders afield from the home page or gets too curious or lascivious about what is out there. They include stories of "attack" sites ("CNN News Alert," "Pictures of My Party"), virus-infested attachments ("Shakira's pictures," "Snow White and the Seven Dwarfs"), and worms released by virtual tokens from abroad ("An Internet Flower for You," "A Card for You") ("Virus Hoaxes & Realities" 2008).

The visual practice of Web posting differs from the vernacular use of photography, photocopying, and faxing because it is more widely available, but it can also be simultaneously personalized. In Dundes's joke, the machine runs by itself; on the Web, people imagine that they "personalize" the machine in their own image and often approach it like a workshop, with the screen constituting a virtual canvas or desktop. Material on the Web can be arranged and symbolized through virtual reality into a persona that is literally screened through postings and seeks kindred spirits. The wonder of the Web is the graphic material open to view—graphic in a visual sense and also in its uncensored quality, suggesting freedom of expression of a folk, or informal, commons in which participants regulate action through tradition rather than through arbitrarily imposed rules. Cognitively, a binary is constructed between analog print as the regulated, institutional world of censorship and digital Web as the open, uncensored folk domain.

Theoretically a wide-open field, the Internet's cultural hangout is especially attractive to youths. The public imagines that these young people better their elders with the informational capital of new media and often use it as a secret language outside of parental and professorial monitoring (Bronner 1995, 232–46; Sullivan 2005). In an individual-istic society that places faith in technological progress, the energy of youth is channeled into innovation that will displace the establishment culture of older stuffed shirts. Fashion, fads, and trends of the young dictate the popular culture, as media and retail outlets remind consum-ers. The Pew Research Center's study of the Internet and American life showed that in the first decade of the twenty-first century, adolescents aged twelve to seventeen were most likely to go online, and when they did, they logged on several times a day (Pew Research Center 2010). Youths supposedly embrace the communication potential of the folk Internet and shape it into their own image and culture because they are preoccupied with social and pubertal concerns rather than with busi-ness applications. Although adults increasingly use the computer for work, youths have extended the play functions of the Internet. Yet as I will show, digital technology fosters play and makes it accessible at all ages.

Youth has influenced the growing compactness of the Internet, which can be utilized on the run and in private away from home and away from the watchful eye of authority.[3] Young people are thought to engage the Internet because they have more to say and more to fan-tasize or worry about. They derive gratification from widening their circles of contacts into definable networked cliques. It enables their transition out of the home, giving them the physical mobility and social connections that are often associated with cultural passage into adult-hood. The openness of youthful endeavor is indicated by the number of electronic responses intended to tell others what one is doing. Face-book has a prominent feature that involves posting what one is doing now, and Twitter advertises itself as a service to stay connected through the exchange of quick, frequent answers to one simple question: what are you doing? This linkage of action to age is yet another way that the Internet mediates and alters tradition, for conspicuous on the Web are efforts to virtualize rituals of change, joy, and grief, such as vir-tual wedding chapels, church services, and cemeteries (Dobler 2009; Goethals 2003; Heagney 2009; Hutchings 2007). The folk Web has not replaced rites of passage in reality, but it often elaborates on them in virtual photo sites, and arguably, it has transformed the album keep-ing (and the related autograph album writing) and photocopying of humor into digital culture. As the folk Web is embraced by all ages, beginning before children can read, it becomes part of ritual routine, including the creation of electronic family albums, virtual cafés, and support groups for parents; niche sites for ethnic-religious networking; matchmaking and chat rooms to assuage the loneliness of singles; and memory making by older adults in scrapbook and memorial sites.

Don't get me wrong. I am sure that graybeards can 'pute with the best of the young whippersnappers, but my point is that cultural expectations have been created about who is wired and who is doing the wiring of society. The old pastoral model of folklore in which the wisdom of yore is "handed down" by a golden ager may lead us to think that digital culture displaces traditions in this mode. In fact, we might conceive of digital culture fostering a "handing up" of electronic practices by young computer wizards with mythic imagination and social ebullience. Modern parents marvel, "My kid knows more than I do about computers [or gadgets]" and "It's amazing what kids can do these days." Along with this comes the concern that "they spend all their time [playing or getting into trouble] online," spurring the need for parental control.

A dramatic tension is apparent in the metafolklore about the Internet concerning an unseen power that can spy one's codes and inscriptions (or even parents who want to peek at their children's e-mail exchanges). Theoretically, users have the power to select who can see their communications, but fear of unwanted viewers, lurkers, and hackers generates a folklore of its own. If the Internet is performative by virtue of the self-conscious act of "going to a site" for viewing or listening, it is surely different by virtualizing a context of security or secrecy that does not depend on a time and place of assembly (Laurel 1991; Simmel 1906). People presume that communication in this medium ripples outward like a wave and can be caught by any number of strangers. An important function of the folklorization of the Internet is the interpersonal controls people impose to secure the channels or conduits of interaction. The Internet's saturable, expansive features that facilitate the ability to log on anywhere and always be online raise images of defying nature and sleep in a 24/7 format; these are frequently mentioned as defining characteristics of the medium. "Speakers" on the Internet do not ask whether it is too late to call with a story. Those who post images appreciate that they "go up" instantaneously and are always retrievable. But more than following the actions of natural reality in posting a note or giving flowers to project feelings onto objects or language working in a structural form confined to three dimensions, the representation of the screen evokes in our minds the possibility of innovation, with expanded stringed dimensions and reconstitution of traditions in additional unforeseen or hidden perspectives that only the computer can reveal (Randall 2002; Waldrop 1985; Weingard 1988).

Besides freedom of expression, the Internet putatively liberates artistic communication from materiality. Hardly immaterial, the folklore of the Internet is the consequential stuff that invites human participation. Keeping this social factor in mind, it is conceivable to envision the differences in method and theory between natural and virtual reality that Kirshenblatt-Gimblett invited folklorists to contemplate by thinking about the betwixt and between characteristic of Internet communication. Start with the definition of folklore as artistic communication in small groups, as Dan Ben-Amos (1972) astutely suggested for a modern definition in a social context, and note that digital practices do not neatly fit his interpersonal delimitation. Although the communicative emphasis in the definition carries over to digital traditions, such practices appear as layered (and often nonlinear) symbolization in what has been described as multivariable, interactive networks that are distinctive to electronic communication (Dorst 1990; Joinson 2003, 1–24; Labbo 1996; Laske 1990; Sommerer and Mignonneau 1999).

Although naturalistic traditions are often associated with the precedent of way back when, the Internet's flattening, or disregard, of time in this manner affects the view that something being "on the Internet" is sufficient to show preexistence characteristic of tradition. The implication is that this something has its own independent existence and that it artificially involves a fusion of new and old, text and image, creativity and tradition. Folklorists and communications scholars may be concerned that, in this kind of tradition, the electronic tools of forwarding and copying and pasting standardize and stabilize texts, taking away the variability that marks cultural identities in "natural contexts," but the serial reproductive process of home pages and forums appears to foster commentary and communal alteration, often with the instrumentality of signifying cultural space (Baker and Bronner 2005, 346; Frank 2009).

The process of bricolage—that is, combining different images to create new forms—appears in the new media transmissions characteristic of a consumer society, and there is evidence of alterations and selections that show national and regional identities, such as the cultural divides in the global Internet phenomenon of 9/11 humor (Ellis 2003). Sources of this humor show that variable photo pastiches and riddle-jokes are divided between an American leitmotif of masculinist unity under stress against an exotic, feminized enemy and European satire deflating American leadership and arrogance. American jokes often express a militarist desire for revenge. For example: "What is Osama bin Laden going to be on Halloween?" Answer: "Dead!" British jokes, by contrast, blur the tragic events with images drawn from the media: "Bin Laden is going to be on [a cooking show] next week. He'll show how to make a big apple crumble" (Ellis 2006, 630; cf. Dundes and Pagter 1991a). Following the quick folkloric response on the Internet, folklorist Bill Ellis pointed out that "American jokes and British jokes were available to both cultures online, sometimes posted together on the same message boards. However, it seems clear that regionally generated social rules about humor continue to play an important part in determining which jokes spread and where they go" (2006, 630).

This symbolization of humor is a reminder of the function—indeed, the imperative—of folklore as a culturally variable frame in which to express or resolve feelings, ambiguities, and conflicts under conditions of stress. It also suggests that one should not quickly dismiss nationalistic and regional affiliations in the embrace of the Internet as a global village in cyberspace that subverts nation-states on land (Stratton 1997). The Internet incorporates folklore because it offers spontaneous transmission bounded by a number of social, localized configurations, and one might argue that it expands the folkloric frame because it extends the creative, reproductive (and often transgressive) capability of oral communication with visual imagery and instantaneous response. Indeed, to spotlight the interactive quality of the Internet, many sites encourage agonistic, rather than harmonious, relationships. On these pages, a button is frequently labeled with the folkloric reference "talk back," inviting an impudent reply that will form a heated exchange, virtualizing and ritualizing "getting in your face" (Millard 1997).

Symbolically, the Internet may be cast by Hollywood directors as a displacement "machine," reminiscent of industrial giants obliterating cottage-housed artisans, but it is also a tool of diverse subcultural maintenance because it allows for multilayered social interaction that would have been difficult to maintain in a dispersed society. In that sense, it is seen as "deep" as well as "open." Users often talk about subtexts and an archaeology of sites, with hidden links, clouds, and tags that reveal meanings not apparent on the surface (Wilbur 1997). Although users hail the openness of cyberspace, they also narrate dangers about fringe or nefarious groups latching on to the Internet and masking their predatory intentions with slick home pages. Although supposedly a tool of massification, the Internet has also spawned a belief that it expands social diversity by allowing communication about all sorts of interests or fetishes (Poster 2001).

To account for multifarious networks fostering *idiocultures* (cultures created through shared group interactions rather than through their place on the land), we can apply the multiconduit hypothesis from folkloristic theory, which holds that "folklore texts do not pass through an orderly, regulated trail from person to person but generate their own, specific linkages that carry messages through society" (Dégh 1997, 142; see also Dégh 1992; Dégh and Vázsonyi 1975). Thus, textual reproduction on the Internet does not necessarily homogenize cultural expression. The Internet's potential for free, spontaneous transmission fosters renewal and innovation by participants working within a traditional frame of reference. Indeed, the posting of sources in website counters, e-mails, and Listservs suggests a quantification of the multiple conduits of transmission that is onerous to attain in the naturalistic field and, when observed, often presumes degeneration (see Ellis 2003; Fine 1979, 1980b, 1983; Oring 1978). The belief is pervasive in cyberculture that expressive payloads launched into cyberspace are always new, intended "to boldly go where no man has gone before," to quote the television show *Star Trek*. Fear and a folkloric belief in conspiratorial, imperial deception reign among open source advocates; they fret that cyberspace will not always be open or deep, rhetorically representing virtual folklorization, as the state or corporation seeks to regulate it and bring it under its wing rather than letting the masses constitute it (Stelter 2008; Truscello 2003). Thus, the metafolklore of the Internet also refers to the possibility that the folk Web will be shut down or forced underground. Folk Web practice can change, and that leads to an examination of the characteristics that allow it to function for social and cultural purposes.

Digital and Analog, Analytical and Relational, Visual and Virtual

The Internet's means of transmission raise questions about what kind of cultural practice using digital equipment constitutes folkloric enactment. The association of generations and periods with technology, such as the computer age and the iPod generation, implies that lives are structured by what we own and do. These labels communicate that users harness tools for individualistic purposes; users are digital selectors, in a sense, who can create multiple personas suited for different Web events. People materialize digital power in everyday life by hanging equipment on their belts, reminiscent of emboldening gun holsters from the Wild West; opening laptops as if lifting the lid of a treasure chest or a secret spy code unit; and flipping open cell phones with sound effects like an attention-grabbing switchblade. Whereas going to the mailbox near one's house to send what computer geeks derisively call "snail mail" is an occasional, pastoral behavior, the instantaneous cyber-cultural experience of "checking" and "receiving" mail is constant and intrusive, especially when engaging in "instant messaging," with a rhetoric suggesting instant gratification. Although inexpensive webcams, often built into computers, make it possible to look our conversation mates in the eye, surprisingly, communicative practice on the Internet has resisted going live.[4] Or maybe this hesitation to show oneself is not so surprising if one considers the folkloric qualities people want to embed in their interactions. Being disembodied or immobilized allows for role playing, speech play, visual representation, bricolage, and sometimes anonymity that supports elaboration of the self—and connection to a group—through expressive material. The frame requires some boundaries to manage the risks inherent in communication, and although limitations are policed and legislated, a regulatory tradition of folk law has arisen governing transgressions voiced in the vernacular terms of flaming, snarking, lurking, spamming, phishing, socking, and thread bumping (Millard 1997; Stivale 1997). In other words, the Internet spawns behaviors that draw attention to themselves as repeatable *practices* related to logging on and rhetorically become ingrained in culture as *praxis*—representations for generalizable actions such as interfacing and downloading (Bernstein 1971; Bronner 1988b; Johnson 1999; Joinson 2003, 20–52; Lavazzi 2001).

Talk of an all-encompassing digital age and digital culture constructs a binary with analog culture that merits closer scrutiny. In this binary, which privileges the advancement of digitization, a number of structural oppositions are implied between digital and analog: large-small, new-old, artificial-natural, formal-informal, electronic-manual, and discontinuous-continuous. The implication of this rhetoric is that thinking has shifted from analog to digital as the technology and culture have evolved. Emblematic of the digital-analog difference is the clock. The analog version is understood by the positions of hands on a dial, based on the natural occurrence of lines and shadows formed by the sun and read by their relative positions. *O'clock* thus signifies the position of an observer in the center, with twelve o'clock considered straight ahead. The precise, and supposedly improved, digital clock takes the observer out of the equation. Time is represented in exact numbers or language and can be received anywhere and in any form. Its display is continuous, and it does not represent position as much as a code. Analog is considered more interpersonal and tactile because it can be equated with the process of sensation, which can be perceived directly (Gregory 1970, 162–66; Stewart and Bennett 1991, 24–29). Digital is conceived as artificial, perfectible, and visual, and it is usually depicted in alphanumeric symbols or icons framed in mechanistic rectangles, in contrast to analog's naturalistic circles.

Digital comes from the Latin *digitus*, for "finger," suggesting discrete counting; it involves converting real-world information into binary numeric form. *Analog* contains reference to the Greek *logos*, which comes from the term's related senses of "word" (or "say") and "reason"; folklorists' analog is an item in relative position to another. Further, the definitional strategy of holding up group and context as vital to folklore shows analog thinking because it is relational, emphasizing the immediacy and fragmentation of the event or performance, whereas the "repetition and variation" and "practice" more commonly applied to folklore in new technology, including the Internet, is digital because it underscores linear continuity and aggregate data (see Bronner 2002a, 58–61; Dégh 1994; Drout 2006; Dundes and Pagter 1975; Köstlin and Shrake 1997; Koven 2000). Analog culture, often attributed to the touch-oriented world of tradition, especially in premodern society, is one whose meaning comes from sensory aspects of perception (Bronner 1986b; Stewart and Bennett 1991, 28–32). Analog practices are circumscribed rather than delineated. People derive significance from analog face-to-face encounters because the appearance of people—what they do and how they do it—conveys an encircled, functional reality (Stewart and Bennett 1991, 29). Thus, storytelling in analog culture is an event defined not just by a text but also by a physical setting and the perceptions between teller and audience (Georges 1969; Oring 2008).

Digital culture emphasizes the representations of reality and the outcomes of "messages." Thus, it may seem to connect more people, but it judges meaning less from social relationships and appearances than from textual similarities. Arguably, in an analog context, meaning is attached to immediately perceived events within a small group; it is more sensitive to the "natural," immediate social context. Analog culture privileges the ground of turf, while digital culture values the action of surf. Both analog and digital cultures are capable of producing expressive traditions, but they may perceive them differently. Analog culture might be called relational and localized, with a high degree of sensitivity to experience, context, emotions, relationships, and status—within place. Digital culture, as indicated by its symbolic equivalence with "viral culture," is often described in terms of spread, immediacy, placelessness, and ubiquity (Wasik 2009). Digital culture relies on analytical, inductive thinking that takes observable events to form informational pieces linked in causal chains and categorized into universal criteria (Stewart and Bennett 1991, 41–42; Cohen 1969, 841–42; Jones 1971). As analytical thinker Alan Dundes points out, much of this linkage tends to be linear and is reflected in folklore, particularly folk speech oriented toward vision rather than touch, individual rather than group, outcome rather than process, future rather than past, and progress rather than stability (Bronner 2007; Dundes 2004; Lee 1968).

We can understand the misplaced perception that the Internet is devoid of folklore as a relational, evolutionary outlook in which digital equals machinery that replaces the human capacity to emote and embody. But viewed operationally or analytically, digital culture as represented by the Internet is replete with the "construction" and "assemblage" of multilayered messages into virtual, rather than natural, reality. One of those constructions is the binary itself, with the presumption that the digital pole is preferred because it is more efficient and objective, leading to a certain illusion that the digital world is culture free. It is indeed possible to analyze the folklorization of the

Internet as acts of organizing and tagging an ever-expanding array of messages. These acts are focused less on the immediacy of the event than on the spread, creativity, traditionality, simultaneity, and heterogeneity of transmission (see Bronner 1986a, 122–29; Lowe 1982; McCallum 2001).

Related to the Internet as daily practice rather than special performance is whether the Web structures perceptions outside of users' awareness. One can say that folk belief systems about Internet usage involve its global reach, classlessness, democratization, and gender neutrality (see Poster 2001; Wallace 1999). However, beliefs expressed about the Internet are not always consistently characterized. For instance, in the rhetoric of transmission, the Internet is frequently symbolized for its mass globalization and acquisitive individualism, as well as its freedom and collectivity, even by its most avid or addicted fans. When logging on, one can look for cultural expectations that affect the kinds of traditions created online. Through folkloristic investigation, geekdom is often cognitively associated with being emasculated yet holding cultural if not social capital. Country singer Brad Paisley had a chart-topping hit in 2008 with "Online," in which he sings over and over again, "I'm so much cooler online." He explains in the lyrics, "When you get my kind of stats, it's hard to get a date, let alone a real girlfriend, but I grow another foot and I lose a bunch of weight, every time I log in." As these lyrics indicate, the Internet lends itself to hyperbole, which can translate into rumor, legend, and humor often of tall-tale proportions.

In *The Greenwood Library of American Folktales*, a compilation organized by American regions, editor Thomas A. Green lists more than eighty discrete folkloric texts connected to cyberspace. Most are oral legends and chain letters adapted to the distributive medium of the Internet with the invitation to "forward asap," but several use the form of electronic communication to comment about its distinctive qualities. An example is the rumor that the federal government will charge a five-cent surcharge on every e-mail delivered to offset losses by the U.S. Postal Service (Green 2006, 4:262–64). A variant accuses newspapers and the popular press of repressing the story, and it invites users to harness the power of the Internet to "E-mail to EVERYONE on your list." It speaks to the Internet's ideal of democratizing freedom and, at the same time, the belief that superstructures representing the power elite flex control. As one variant states directly, "The whole point of the Internet is democracy and noninterference" (Green 2006, 4:264). This idealization of the Internet as an untethered, unbureaucratized "commons" suggests that although it is certainly viewed as postmodern in its transcendence of space and time, it is popularly constructed in the model of the premodern village, raising comparisons to a "global village" governed by tradition rather than the nationalistic rule of law. Indeed, its constructiveness is one of its culturally expected and addictive features (Joinson 2003, 55–64). Connecting this belief to the conduit hypothesis is the assertion made by folklorist Linda Dégh writing about face-to-face communication: "transmission of traditional messages in natural contexts is essentially free; arbitrary limitation of this freedom encroaches upon the normal functioning of the conduit" (1997, 143).

References to the democratization of the Internet in popular discourse raise the question about its Americanness or Westernness, which is associated with analytical thinking and democratization, especially considering that big-name developers such as Microsoft, Apple, and Google are American based (Stewart and Bennett 1991, 17–44; Cohen 1969; Jenkins and Thorburn 2003; Lee 1968).[5] One proposal to explain new media's special hold on Americans is that the American preoccupation with the constructiveness of culture counters the European emphasis on the rootedness and givenness of folk culture in the natural landscape and the Asian perception of groupness constituted by social homogeneity and historical antiquity (see Bronner 1998, 475–82; Dundes 1982; Schudson 2003). American conceptions of culture have often been distinguished by presenting culture as an outcome of social interaction, even if temporary and overlapping. Instead of appearing as a received tradition that is unself-consciously followed, culture—and websites—can be constructed, created anew, to meet the needs of the moment or person (Mechling 2006).

In a constructivist concept of culture, individuals choose with whom they affiliate and the customs in which they participate; they may hybridize different traditions to create a distinctive cultural persona. Dundes characterizes his definition of folk group, for instance, as a "modern" and "American concept" by the idea of social linkage rather than birthright: a folk group is *any group of people whatsoever* who share at least one common factor. It does not matter what the linking factor is—it could be a common occupation, language, or religion—but what is important is that a group formed for whatever reason will have some traditions which it calls its own" (Dundes 1965b, 2). His reference to "two or more persons" as the social minimum for a group rhetorically implies that these persons produce culture working in interaction with one another. This constructivist outlook, which does not have a baseline for the extent, location, economic status, literacy, or antiquity of the group, lends itself to the centrality of network as the social basis of folkloric communication on the Internet. In the words of folklorists Beth Blumenreich and Bari Lynn Polonsky before the advent of the Internet, the term *network* implies an understanding that "folklore is individually determined and based, not 'group' determined and based. Moreover, the individual folklore is determined by the nature of his interactions and experiences. This suggests that folklore can be most profitably studied in terms of interactional communicative and experiential networks—ICEN's, as we shall call them" (1974, 15; see also Augusto 1970; Fine 1983). Blumenreich and Polonsky conceptualize networks as face-to-face connections of choice in which obligations are decentered from family and community to a number of heterogeneous organizations that the individual chooses.

Unlike communities in which one resides or interacts with others, networks are infinitely expandable and transcend time and space. According to a dictionary of new keywords for the information age, virtual networks are central to the development of choices and are "imagined to be a means of establishing electronic communities (networks of people sharing beliefs and/or interests at a distance) at a time when long-term communities are said to be disappearing" (Webster 2005). Networks are integrally tied to technological change that facilitates increasing, simultaneous flows of information through accumulable, expandable social conduits. Although the buzzword *information* makes the communication sound like sterile minutiae, folklore is one of the strategies commonly employed to give a sense of tradition and hence identity to participants in the network.

Transmitting Tradition in Analog and Digital Eras: Lessons from the Budd Dwyer Saga

One way to test the production of traditions through interactive or mediated networks is to compare the use of lore in analog and digital eras.

I had a chance to do that when I found myself in the middle of an oral joke cycle that emerged in Pennsylvania in 1987 and was subsequently transmitted to a global audience on the Internet in the twentieth-first century. The subject of the humor was Pennsylvania state treasurer R. Budd Dwyer, who committed suicide at a televised news conference in the capitol building in Harrisburg. For months, regional media had been covering Dwyer's conviction for accepting a $300,000 bribe in exchange for a no-bid computer contract. Corruption trials were nothing new to the state capital, but Dwyer's prominent executive position made the story unusual.

Prosecutors had tried a parade of underlings for graft, but Dwyer was the highest official in the Dick Thornburgh administration to come to trial. If he made headlines as a big fish, he also drew notice for hanging around local watering holes. Preferring to be called by his chummy middle name, Budd, rather than his first name, Robert, Dwyer was known for his neighborly familiarity around town. His cherubic face and congenial style made him a social magnet. He came from the unassuming-sounding town of Meadville, and after starting out as a high school civics teacher, Dwyer worked his way up in the Republican Party from state senator to state treasurer. He was a regular sight on Harrisburg sidewalks, and he had the reputation for being approachable and affable. Some whispered that he was just a bumpkin who had gotten ahead by being the party's water carrier, but regardless, he was recognized as one of the state's political honchos.

January 22, 1987, looked like an ugly day to commuters descending on Pennsylvania's capital as dark, cheerless clouds hung over the city. Cleanup had wrapped up following inauguration celebrations two days earlier for the new Democratic administration of Robert P. Casey, and state workers settled back into their routines. The enormous State Farm Show in Harrisburg, an indoor agricultural fair attracting half a million visitors, had cleared out a few days before, and the winter holidays were a distant memory. The day started with one of those January frosts that brought frowns to the faces of the thousands who made their way to work for the area's largest employer—the state government. To top things off, a heavy snowfall began that morning, snarling traffic and keeping children home from school. As the snow depths increased, state workers were sent home, and most schoolchildren were seated in front of their televisions.

Budd Dwyer decided to go ahead with his scheduled press conference anyway. He faced sentencing the next day, and he was looking at the likelihood of a long stretch in prison for the federal crime. Most commentators expected Dwyer to use the occasion to reiterate his innocence and announce his resignation. Reporters, photographers, and television camera operators gathered in his office at 10:30 A.M. Several noticed that the furniture had been rearranged to create a barrier between where Dwyer was about to speak and the reporters, but no one protested the setup. When Dwyer entered the room, he insisted that the door to the adjacent room be closed, restricting the room to thirty or so reporters and a handful of aides. These were unusual actions, but the reporters on the state government beat figured that these were trying times for Dwyer, the state's highest fiscal officer now facing disgrace.

Dwyer read a long, rambling statement declaring his innocence. He opened by saying, "This has been like a nightmare, like a life in the twilight zone. It wouldn't surprise me to wake up this minute to find out I was home in my bed and had just had a terrible nightmare. That's how unbelievable this has been. I mean, I've never done anything wrong and yet all this horrible nightmare has occurred to me." Dwyer blamed former governor Dick Thornburgh for starting the probe because of a feud between them, and he criticized the press, FBI, judge, and jury for their handling of the case. But he saved his harshest words for James West, the aggressive, ambitious state prosecuting attorney. Dwyer then called for a review of the judicial system—a system that he felt had failed him. Occasionally he seemed to force back tears as he hurried through his speech. He skipped past pages of the text and told reporters they could read it later. Some of the TV reporters prepared to leave, but Dwyer called them back, saying, "I think you ought to stay, because we're not finished yet" (Cusick, Meyers, and Roche 1987).

After about twenty-five minutes, Dwyer came to the last page of his speech, but he did not read it. Instead, he handed three sealed envelopes to his aides.[6] He reached into his briefcase on the desk, removed a manila envelope, and pulled out a .357 Magnum revolver. He held the gun up and reached out with his other hand like a football quarterback fending off tacklers. Several reporters began to yell at him, "No, no, don't do this." Over the shouts, he announced, "Please leave the room as this will, as this will hurt someone." He looked like he was about

R. Budd Dwyer at his last press conference before publicly committing suicide, January 22, 1987. (Historical Society of Dauphin County)

to say something else, but as the reporters' shouts grew, he put the gun in his mouth and, holding it with both hands, pulled the trigger. Forty-seven-year-old Budd Dwyer died instantly. His body fell back against the wall and slouched down in full view of the whirring cameras. Blood splashed behind Dwyer's head and dripped down from his nose. Dwyer's press secretary closed out the event by stepping in front of the body and saying, "All right, show some decorum."

At 11:45 A.M., ABC affiliate WHTM, the largest of the midstate television stations, interrupted programming and reported the news of Dwyer's suicide. The footage broadcast included the gun firing, Dwyer's head jolting back, and his body falling to the floor. A flood of calls came into the station, protesting the airing of the tape when so many children were home watching. Drawing comparisons to coverage of the Kennedy assassination and the *Challenger* shuttle disaster, the station responded on the air that it was reporting the news as it happened, even if it was disturbing. WHTM showed a shortened version of the tape later, but this time it warned viewers about the graphic content. In Philadelphia, WPVI showed video of Dwyer pulling the trigger on its noon newscast (Bianculli and Shister 1987). Other stations also showed the video, but they edited out Dwyer pulling the trigger. They offered the phone numbers of crisis intervention centers to help those who had watched the earlier broadcast and were feeling anguish as a result.

The unread portion of Dwyer's statement revealed that his suicide in front of the cameras had been planned. It stated, "I am going to die in office in an effort to see if the shameful facts, spread out in all their shame, will not burn through our civic shamelessness and set fire to American pride. Please tell my story on every radio and television station and in every newspaper and magazine in the U.S. Please leave immediately if you have a weak stomach or mind, since I don't want to cause physical or mental distress." But he did cause distress among many viewers who phoned TV stations to request that they shelve the video.

The story quickly went national. NBC and CNN showed footage of Dwyer waving his gun, while CBS and ABC carried the news of the public suicide without showing the tape (Bianculli and Shister 1987). The Associated Press sent out photos showing the entire sequence of Dwyer's suicide, but it warned: "They are very graphic photos of Dwyer with the gun in his mouth and pulling the trigger. We call to your attention that they may be offensive to some readers." Newspapers across the country included stories on the event, but Pennsylvania's offered the most graphic depictions. Most notably, and to the chagrin of many readers, the *Philadelphia Inquirer* splashed photos of Dwyer putting the revolver in his mouth and falling to the floor (Cusick, Meyers, and

Roche 1987, 16A). Ironically, in many circles, the media's handling of the event became the story rather than Dwyer's message. *Time* magazine, for example, commented, "while most newspapers and TV stations carried only edited footage of the incident, two Pennsylvania stations aired the full sequence of the suicide—prompting hundreds of viewers to phone in protests" ("Milestones" 1987; see also Bianculli and Shister 1987; Smith 1987). The controversy was stirred a few days later when reports of a televised suicide by a public official in Australia, apparently in imitation of Dwyer's event, came on the air. A search of news archives, looking for precedents to mark the events as a pattern, uncovered the televised suicide in July 1975 of Christine Chubbuck, the host of a local variety show in Sarasota, Florida, but it did not receive worldwide attention. The Dwyer story resurfaced on June 19, 1987, in one of those "ripped from the headlines" fictional adaptations on the popular television series *Hard Copy*, broadcast by CBS. Perhaps the female lead replacing Dwyer was a nod to Chubbuck, but the plot clearly echoed the details of the Dwyer case. In the show, a public official is hounded by reporters for her alleged participation in a kickback-for-contract scheme. She calls a press conference, declares her innocence, pulls a gun out of her purse, and, in words reminiscent of Dwyer's, says, "Leave this room if you can't stand the sight of blood." The drama implies that media coverage drove her to ruin, and she gets back at the press by committing suicide in front of the reporters and cameras.

The show did not carry the story forward. In reality, the national networks gave the Dwyer story airtime for one night, although stations in Pennsylvania continued their coverage for weeks, reporting reactions from various officials, speeches at the funeral, and subsequent investigations. By most accounts, Dwyer's suicide hit Pennsylvanians, especially central Pennsylvanians, hard. The counseling center at Penn State–Harrisburg put out a statement five days after the suicide, reading, "We are aware that the events surrounding the recent public suicide of State Treasurer, R. 'Budd' Dwyer have generated considerable discussion and reaction in our community. We also know that a public and traumatic event of this kind may impact on individuals in different and sometimes unexpected ways." The center invited individuals to air their feelings with its counselors. Also venting their feelings were reporters on the capitol beat who had become part of the news rather than spectators to it. They were now the interviewees rather than the interviewers, and the questions were difficult: Could they have stopped it? Could they have known? Did they contribute to it? (Smith 1987; Parsons and Smith 1988).

During the weeks after Dwyer's suicide, reporters regularly queried psychiatrists for advice. Most commented on Dwyer's feeling of hopelessness, just when he thought he had achieved the pinnacle of success in his public life. Dr. John Fryer, deputy medical director of the Philadelphia Psychiatric Center, told the press, "To do it in this way is to really get back at everybody and make sure nobody will escape. The rage must have been overwhelming. The time-honored theory about suicide is aggression turned inward. But it was Dwyer's public expression of rage that separates him from most suicide victims." Dr. Steven Schwartz, chief of adult psychiatric services at Thomas Jefferson University Hospital, added, "It's a nice extra bonus to make others suffer like they tried to make him suffer. The act was directed at newspeople and the populace who hounded him giving them something to remember. If you're going to do such a grand act of autonomy and power, why not do it on the biggest stage you can? It's screaming to the world, 'You didn't do anything to me, *I* did to me!'" In addition to speaking on talk shows and news programs, psychiatrists went out to schools and spoke to schoolchildren who had witnessed the event (Herskowitz 1987; Lewis 1987).

Nowhere in the coverage was the rise of humor about Dwyer's suicide mentioned. Nowhere were the jokes circulating through youth networks cited as a way to adjust to the trauma of the event. Yet the lore was hard to miss. The jests began spreading the day after the event. They were brought to my attention by my students at Penn State–Harrisburg, where Dwyer's son was enrolled. A reporter had been interviewing me about the folk beliefs of central Pennsylvania and asked me if I had heard the jokes. When I asked him whether he was questioning me with regard to an article, he replied that he doubted his paper would run such a story because it might be considered in bad taste. Instead, he was asking me for personal reasons. He had gone to a journalism convention in South Carolina, and when the Pennsylvania reporters got together, he said, "All they did was tell these jokes. No one else knew them," he added, "just the Pennsylvania people."

Yet the Dwyer jests had the characteristics of other joke cycles based on televised tragedies such as the *Challenger* space shuttle disaster of January 28, 1986. Coincidentally, these jokes were gaining around again after replays of the event on its one-year anniversary (Bronner 1988a, 129–30; Oring 1987; Simons 1986; Smyth 1986). Jokes in the *Challenger* cycle, many of them referring to schoolteacher-astronaut Christa McAuliffe, had precedents in oral tradition. One joking question making the rounds after the tragedy was: "What was the last thing to go through Christa McAuliffe's mind?" Answer: "Ass, teeth, sheet metal, fuselage, tile." Similar jokes arose after Grace Kelly's fatal auto accident in 1982. Probably older is the bawdy, joking question often collected from youths: "What's the last thing to go through a bug's mind when he hits the windshield?" Answer: "His asshole" (Barrick 1987a; see also Barrick 1982). The central characters in these jokes were celebrities whose ordinariness was followed by a quick rise to fame, and all had connections to the technology that did them in (McAuliffe to the spacecraft, Kelly to a luxury automobile, and Dwyer to the computers involved in the scandal). Humor about all three also played on the unnatural deformity of their bodies as a result of the unexpected tragic events that were widely photographed or filmed.

Mac E. Barrick, a folklorist at Shippensburg University in central Pennsylvania, heard the Dwyer jokes too. We polled our classes immediately to trace the cycle of lore as it took its course, and compared our findings. When Barrick interviewed his students on February 4, all twenty-six had heard the jokes. On January 28, twenty-two of my twenty-six students had heard the jokes. Of those twenty-two, nineteen had seen the unedited version of the video (compared with eighteen of Barrick's students), and sixteen thought Dwyer was guilty (as did fifteen in Barrick's class). Fifteen of my twenty-two students knew at least two jokes, five knew three, and two knew one. From whom did they hear the jokes? They said other college students. Making other inquiries, I found that the jokes were not restricted to college-age youths. I heard them from children as young as sixth graders and from adults in their thirties, but I concluded that they were most popular among adolescents through those in their early twenties.

A total of 23 percent of respondents told me they had heard a Budd Dwyer joke the day after the suicide, but over 86 percent heard their jokes three to five days later. Both men and women heard the jokes, but men appeared to prefer telling them. In Barrick's class, divided equally between men and women, 36 percent had heard the jokes from both men and women, whereas 64 percent had heard them solely from men.

The joke cycle had two waves. During the first wave in the first five days after the event, the most popular jokes were questions playing on an answer that involved "shooting your mouth off." For instance: "What did Budd Dwyer's wife (mother, press secretary) say before his press conference?" or "How did you know Budd Dwyer was a politician?" Second in popularity were jokes playing on beer commercials or beer characteristics. For example: "What did Budd Dwyer's press secretary say to the coroner?" Answer: "This Bud's for you." Or "What do Dwyer and flat beer have in common?" Answer: "No head." Or "What kind of beer has no head?" Answer: "Budd-Dwyser." And finally, "What happens when you shake up a Bud?" Answer: "It blows its cap." Third in popularity were jokes offering another misplaced phrase or pun. "What were Dwyer's last words to his wife?" Answer: "I need this job like I need a hole in the head." Or "What's worse (or better) than a pistol in your washer?" Answer: "A bullet in your Dwyer." Other jokes took the form of joking remarks, such as "Budd Dwyer got so fed up at work the other day he shot his brains out, but now he has half a mind to go back to work." This might be rephrased as a joking question: "Did you hear that Budd Dwyer shot himself? Now he has half a mind to go back to work." These jokes apparently have cognates related to the head injury James Brady suffered during the assassination attempt on Ronald Reagan in 1981. The "hole in the head" answer to the Dwyer jokes has precedent in "What did James Brady say to Reagan that day?" Answer: "I need this job like I need a hole in the head." And the follow-up: "What did James Brady say later at the hospital?" Answer: "I have half a mind to go back to work."

During the second wave of orally circulated jokes, students composed new jokes or retooled *Challenger* disaster jokes. Typically offered at bar or dorm get-togethers, the jokes in this cycle rarely went beyond the group. Here are some examples of the newly composed jokes: "What did Budd Dwyer say to his secretary at the end of his press conference? The envelope please." "What did the guy say when he went into a bar? Gimme a Bud and blow the head off of it." "What's Budd Dwyer's favorite beer? Colt 45." "What's Budd Dwyer's favorite toothpaste? Aim." "Why did Budd Dwyer put money behind his head? He wanted to see his face on a dollar bill." "What's the Budd Dwyer memorial coin? A washer." A large share of the composed or adapted jokes were sexual in nature: "What does Budd Dwyer have in common with a good Catholic girl? No head." "What do Tom Selleck's girlfriend and Budd Dwyer have in common? They both had Magnums go off in their mouths." "What did Budd Dwyer and Liberace have in common? They both put things in their mouths they shouldn't have." "What's the difference between Budd Dwyer and Rock Hudson? Budd Dwyer put a bullet in his head and Rock Hudson put a head in his butt." The recycled *Challenger* jokes included: "What color were Budd Dwyer's (Christa McAuliffe's) eyes? Blue—one blew here, one blew there," and the aforementioned, "What was the last thing to go through Budd Dwyer's mind? A bullet." Still another joke went: "What's the new Capital Cocktail?" Answer: "Straight shot and a Bud" (whereas the Space Shuttle Cocktail was "7Up and a splash of Teacher's"). The second wave in the Budd Dwyer joke cycle subsided by the end of February, and when I asked about the jokes again in March, no one had heard any new ones.

The Budd Dwyer joke cycle took on the swift timing and mass-society characteristics of other celebrity tragedy humor, but the Dwyer jokes were restricted almost exclusively to central Pennsylvania. Although the entire nation had heard of Dwyer after the event, it was in central Pennsylvania where adjustment was called for. It was in central Pennsylvania where the suicide had been graphically displayed and where Dwyer's name and image were familiar. He was a person one might have run into in a local tavern or conversing on the street. The jokes thus created an incongruity between the unassuming figure and his celebrity status. There were overtones of the bumpkin overwhelmed by the city, but mainly, and especially to those living around Harrisburg, the jokes were understood in the context of political corruption in state government (Keisling and Kearns 1988). In addition to covering Dwyer's case, Harrisburg's media reported graft in contracts for the building of the capitol addition and the indictment of several state judges for accepting bribes. Along with Dwyer, the Republican Party chairman was convicted, and several other state officials were implicated. As Frank Lynch, a reporter who covered Dwyer's trial for the *Harrisburg Patriot-News*, told me, "Everyone did it, but Budd Dwyer just got caught, that's all. Budd became the symbol of Pennsylvania politics" (Bronner 1988c, 86).

But it was the way Dwyer left politics that attracted the humorous comment. It was the airing of the analog tape of Dwyer taking his own life and seeing the bloody result that forced young viewers to come to terms with the harshness of death. Perhaps especially wrenching for vulnerable adolescents was this public figure's ultimate statement of failure and hopelessness, an avowal that was repeated a few days later by a teenager in York, Pennsylvania, who took his own life by shooting himself in the mouth. In the first wave of jokes related during face-to-face encounters in the local setting, laughing at the community tragedy provided a kind of outlet, on the one hand. On the other hand, to many young men, telling these jokes was a sign of their toughness, an aggressive demonstration that they were unshaken by the horror of the graphic suicide. Still, most of the students I interviewed acknowledged that laughing about the event in the days following the suicide eased the tension in the air. Many of the students interviewed also considered the jokes irreverent and derived adolescent satisfaction from the rebelliousness of telling them, at least to one another. The event was a disaster to Pennsylvanians not only because of the loss of a life but also because the corruption that was running rampant and was taken lightly had a tragic end. It was a disaster because it brought death close to home, close to the children that American society tries hard to shelter (see Dundes 1987, 3–14).

The first wave of Budd Dwyer jokes gave rise to talk about the broadcast of his suicide, his guilt or innocence, and the context of political corruption around the city in general. The second wave focused on the act of joking itself. It played with the joking form rather than providing humorous comment on the historical and political context. In the second wave of jokes, a shift was apparent from Dwyer's predicament to the extension of word play and the realization of incongruity to create humor. The jokes emphasized the sexual and violent content that marks other joke-telling sessions during the college years. Dwyer became a temporary vehicle for varying the expression of these themes. But these jokes were not successful; they did not spread, and they often received a grudging reception when they were originally told.

The Budd Dwyer jokes that were spread orally had their limited time and place, but on the Internet, Dwyer lore has taken a different visual form and has gone global. Twenty years after Dwyer's death, a Google search of his name produced 37,600 sites. Among the sites are several memorial sites, MySpace and Facebook pages using his name (including a few rock bands), and lots of wikis on his biography, including gorewiki.org, where a clip of the shooting loops repeatedly. The jokes resurface, either on sites dealing with sick jokes in general or on humor sites (often under the subject category "suicide") that preface the jokes with explanations of Dwyer's conviction and press conference. Although some of the sites refer to the jokes as texts with particular meaning to Pennsylvanians, most are more generalized in networks such as the "Comedy and Jokes Community," which include Dwyer's death among a "list of crazy, weird and even funny deaths of prominent people in the last 100 years" (posted August 29, 2008). The most common joke listed on the different sites involves word play connecting Budd Dwyer with the commercial icon of Budweiser beer: "What's the difference between Budd Dwyer and Bud Lite? Bud Lite has a head." In fact, many sites misspell Budd's name as "Bud," assuming it was a nickname that fit his constructed persona of the victimized everyman.

Rather than repeating jokes, Internet chatters discussing Dwyer are fond of spouting a joking proverbial comparison: "Like Budd Dwyer, I'm going out with a bang" (Domi 2008). Reacting to a rumor that the Dwyer saga would be made into a movie, one discussion group started a thread of humorous comments: "He sure went out with a bang. Hahahahaha; Hey man, nice shot! Muhahaha; Now that's what I call a sack lunch" (Mencia 2008). A MySpace page repeated the line but used it to express gothic subculture by respecting Dwyer's "style" for going "out with a bang and make sure those who did you wrong remember it forever" (Laurelei 2008). Dwyer's name, along with the "bang" line, often comes up when a suicide makes the news. When a Pennsylvania district attorney went missing in 2005, a poster in a discussion thread commented, "I guess he didn't want to go out with a bang like Bud Dwyer" (Will 2005).

Different anonymous posters contributed to a parody of the typically "just-the-facts" Wikipedia entry for Dwyer in the "Uncyclopedia." The "out with a bang" line is there, expressed as "Dwyer's career had hit a rough spot, but he still managed to go out with a bang," and there is a spinoff at the end: "He then proceeded to give the audience a piece of his mind; those closest to him received that and more" ("Budd Dwyer: From Uncyclopedia" 2008). Whether functioning as "gross humor" to shock readers by its insensitivity and therefore question societal norms or to temper disturbing thoughts of death, the repetition and variation of the "out with a bang" remark resonate with viewers because of Dwyer's public death and subsequent celebrity status. If Dwyer jokes had previously been symbolic of a type of cultural communication one would not read in the newspapers, Dwyer images in the digital age signify the openness of the Internet and the ability and, in some cases, the obsession to make a public mark in cyberspace. Among the many suicides discussed, Dwyer's stands out because it was public, as is the Internet, and vivid footage challenging social norms is available.

For many viewers, Dwyer is known only on the Internet as someone who achieved cult status for engineering his own death on tape. Dwyer's parting sentence, "Stay back, this could hurt someone," is frequently cast in a play frame under a list of comical "famous last words throughout history" posted on many sites. Dwyer's name also rates recognition, along with celebrities Rosie O'Donnell, Michael Jackson, and Maury Povich, as an example, in chat jargon, of "IDIFTL" (I did it for the lulz), referring to an Internet drama one causes ("I Did It for the Lulz" 2008). Under the headline "Dwyer Suicide Lives On," the print version of the *Philadelphia Daily News* informed readers, "The former Pennsylvania state treasurer is an *Internet cult figure*, his final moments posted on Web pages as a curiosity or a *sick joke*" (Russell 1998; emphasis added). The reporter thought the main audience for the "gruesome suicide" would be youth, and the subtitle of the piece read: "Sex Isn't All that Parents Should Monitor on the Web" (Russell 1998).

In keeping with the untethered reputation of the Internet, many bloggers narrate the footage as evidence of a governmental conspiracy, suppression, or vendetta. Statements are posted, expressed like urban legends, that independent investigations have proved that Dwyer was framed and then hounded to death. Unlike television, which hides reality for the benefit of corporate suits or governmental higher-ups, the Internet opens access and invites commentary, much as oral tradition might. As culture critic Christie Davies expresses the contrast, "Television is hegemonic, the Internet libertarian" (2003, 30). She theorizes that "television, far from creating a global village, destroyed local communities and institutions, leaving behind a mass of atomized and alienated individuals, but the Internet is now enabling them to recreate virtual substitutes for the world they have lost . . . [the Internet] is a free, decentralized electronic medium in an otherwise controlled and restricted age" (Davies 2003, 34). Dwyer jokes in 1987 responded largely to television and commented on its moral authority to suppress the event of Dwyer's public suicide, as well as the public's adjustment to the images that leaked through. In the Internet age, the Dwyer tape is widely available and prompts more belief and narrative responses than textual production. It enhances the line between the folk Web and the official Web.

Another common reaction to Dwyer's footage on the Web that raises a comparison to folk communication systems is that it "haunts." It is narrated in terms reminiscent of ghost stories or spectral sightings, because the figure can appear to be a dubious image rather than a real person. At the time of Dwyer's suicide, when the jokes were first circulating, the connection to everyday life was clearer than it was years later when the footage was posted on the Internet. "Videotape instantly helps negate the 'real-ness' of any situation," journalist Daniel Krauss wrote of the Dwyer Internet tape thirteen years after the public suicide occurred. He observes that the Dwyer tape has a "friend-of-a-friend" validation because someone tells someone else to view it and "conjure up very similar scenarios time and time again" (Krauss 2000). As it shows up on various sites, the footage loses clarity each time it is copied and redubbed; the blurry man on the tape looks ghostly, several posters have commented. Like ghost hunters and legend trippers who go out in search of an encounter with the dead, the tape satisfies a morbid urge to view death while, at the same time, being repulsed by it. Seeing the footage invites narration about Dwyer's motivation or the forces at work on him that might also be at work on the viewer. Discussing the tape on MetaTalk, Phaedon writes, for example, "I couldn't believe what I saw at first was real," to which Vacapinta responds, "It's a video of a desperate man blowing his brains out in public. It's haunted me since" ("Suicide Video Link" 2007). On his MySpace page, Daniel independently writes, "This one haunted me . . . as desensitized as I thought I was, this one's been beating up my noggin for a couple of days." He narrates, "You basically see him make the decision to end his life in his eyes, and you hear the gunshot, and the next thing you see is his lifeless body" (Daniel 2008). Along with the feeling of being haunted by the Dwyer footage is disbelief at the action viewed and its lingering effects. Although the supernatural element is gone from most posted narratives, the footage is described as "unbelievable" and "incredible," leading to comments about the unnaturalness of the death. It suggests a "folk strategy" of ghost stories and beliefs to elicit responses about unnatural death and the vulnerability of mortals (see Thomas 2007).

Whether framed as sick, apparently insensitive humor or torment-ed, sensitive narrative, Dwyer's story apparently carries a different mes-sage on the Internet in the twenty-first century than it did in dorm talk sessions in the twentieth. In the oral communicative context of central Pennsylvania, discussions of Dwyer were often accompanied by comments on the problem of local corruption and the desperation of a popular public figure, whereas Internet discourse uses his name as a metaphor for a stupid or outlandish media act. With the Internet post-ing of his death tape, Dwyer, according to blogger David Eisenthal (2007), "became something of a . . . joke" in the two decades since his death. Eisenthal received several responses, many of which note how easy it is to view the video of Dwyer's death on the Internet, as it should be, in contrast to the controversy it created when it was shown on tele-vision. The implication in the digital age is that the prosumer Internet, unlike consumer media, is an open public commons where anyone can express an opinion, and this process comes to the fore in the posting of shocking images. Dwyer became a character rather than a biography in Web discourse. And that discourse takes on the characteristics of a backroom conversation that is instantaneous, even simultaneous; its content emphasizes the colloquial, often responding defiantly in the frame of the discussion thread to what elsewhere would be considered taboo or indecent.

The wiki and chat site *Urban Dictionary* lists six different defini-tions of "Budd Dwyer," arranged in a linear thread. The site has a participatory feature, allowing viewers to rate each definition, which reveals public perceptions of celebrities for cultural production. The first posted definition is "to commit suicide on television," and it gives the example of "they feared he could pull a Budd Dwyer." One reply worried that resigning New York governor Eliot Spitzer would "have a Budd Dwyer moment" in 2008. In the second definition, reference is made to the difference between understanding the event on television and on the Internet, with the comment, "this was pre-internet, mind you, so they weren't used to seeing stuff." It received the most votes of approval, perhaps because it reminded viewers of the openness of the folk Web. It assured contemporary users that they are wiser and more aware than in the days when the airwaves were censored. One poster complained that, as a term, Dwyer is not sympathetic; "he was an attention whore drama queen," Tien Duong baldly wrote, but his comment received more thumbs-down than thumbs-up symbols. Clearly not feeling pressure from any censors, Reservoir Dog got approvals for reporting the term used during fellatio. He explained, "When getting a blowjob from a hot girl, you cum so hard that it shoots out her nose simulating Budd Dwyer's public suicide" ("Budd Dwyer" 2008). The source of the usage was not so much Dwyer's status as a household name, which he was not, but the easy availability of the suicide video on the Web, which gave him notoriety for a new generation.

The visual material was grist for thread mills that impelled posters to express beliefs and metafolklore about modern mass media. Internet images of Dwyer's suicide invite evaluations of the immediacy, and even exhibitionism, of making a mark in postmodern digital culture.[7] On the blog *Modern Television*, filmmaker Phillip Patiris posted a photo of Dwyer but resisted showing the "cheap thrill" of the video clip. He explains that despite his "unassailable belief that the wide-open web as a culmination and synthesis of all previously existing media is a place where anything and everything should (must) be presented . . . it's about time that people were forced to develop for themselves that lost, civilized art of responsibility and *discerning* by giving them access to every temptation available" (Patiris 1999). He argues that the Internet is unbridled and uncensored in the spirit of oral communication, but restraints are developing to guide the use of the Web in the form of "netiquette" traditions. On the folk Web, accusations using folk terms, such as indicting posters for *flaming* (being intentionally provocative) or *snarking* (a portmanteau of *snide* and *remark*), are akin to jeers in children's folklore that keep group members in line by shaming them into conforming to standards of behavior (Knapp and Knapp 1976, 58–75). The disadvantage on the Web is that a jeerer cannot get in the culprit's face; however, group pressure is applied through the discussion thread, often using the power of the Internet's instantaneity. The spread of Dwyer as a character or metaphor led Patiris to comment, for example, "It's all so instant here in cyberspace . . . witness e-mail and newsgroup flaming and the rise of incivility as people give in to their immediate and emotional impulses, immediately transmitted to the whole world, a form of exhibitionism" (quoted in Lynch 1998).

The video of Dwyer's suicide appears in several versions, short and extended, on YouTube and other sites. Replacing the conversation in dorm rooms and offices in 1987 is a running thread debating whether the video is camp or creepy. The first post to the extended version stated, "I just pissed and shit my pants," one of several referring to the loss of control of bodily functions while watching it. Whether that was a positive or a negative statement, it was followed with the applauding line, "That was a good screamer! Good job!" and the not so laudatory "D* it that scared me!" Often posted as a link with an invitation to view it, the video also provoked some irate individuals to complain about the posters who "shit on them" or "fucked with their heads." Because it is a visual image without a historical context, some posters questioned the veracity of the footage and filled in a plausible narrative. RJAHaven, for instance, asked, "Does he really shoot himself in here or is this a spoof?" to which michaeldog responded that it is real: "he committed suicide so his family could reap off the benefits" (HurricanEAJW2 2008). As if to underscore the openness of the Internet, frequent reference was made to a sketch for a television pilot by comedian Norm MacDonald in 2005, mimicking Dwyer's comments before committing suicide at the press conference. The sketch never made it to television, as the story goes, but on the Internet, one can freely view and respond to videos about suicide, both comedic and serious.[8]

The understanding of the Internet as open and visual was apparent, for example, when "90 Day Jane" announced her intention on a blog to commit suicide on the Web in ninety days. She referred to Dwyer's and Chubbuck's televised public suicides as models for her act but insisted that she was not depressed or seeking attention. She did, however, intend to comment on the alienation of her young generation, whose "biggest obstacle is beating Halo 3" (Flumesday 2008). Responses ranged from sympathetic notes to vulgar accusations. She blogged each day leading up to her announced doomsday and received hundreds of comments on each of her posts. Word got around on the Web and apparently in college lounges, judging from the poster who wrote, "It was all my college spoke about in the last week" (Flumesday 2008). One curious fellow blogger wrote, "Like any site you hear about from a friend, there are thousands of other 'friends' out there telling their friends, and *your* friend is surely not the *first* friend to tell their friends" (Flumesday 2008). Alarmed by the reaction, Jane shut down the site and explained that her blog "was meant for me and (what I ignorantly thought would be) a small number of people who might find it on BlogSpot. It is the result of me tapping into the darkest part of myself and seeing where it led" (Douglas 2008). She imagined the site in a play frame, whereby the context would be understood by participants as if they were located in a social space, but as a viewed image, it spread quickly and was used to comment on the function of the Internet as a cultural location. Jane recognized that on the Internet people intensify their honesty and emotion. What began as a commentary on the "true human connection on the internet" ended up showing the extent of folkloric construction as the Internet distributes the material and image of disturbing topics such as suicide.

The classic theories to explain suicide are concerned with who is likely to take his or her life and the motivations for doing so. Emile Durkheim (1951) in particular argued that each society has a collective inclination toward suicide and posited social causes for its regularity. Dwyer's case fits into a combination of Durkheim's three categories of suicide—egoistic, altruistic, and anomic—and this encapsulation of social motive into a public declaration is partly responsible for its notoriety. In the egoistic category, the individual's underintegration into society is brought into question; altruism is at work in advancing a religious or political cause, reflecting a heightened sense of integration; and anomie results when a person has problems coping with new opportunities or developments, especially when that person was previously representative of societal beliefs and practices (Simpson 1951, 14–15). Coupled with this social perspective is the psychoanalytic view that suicidal individuals seek to internalize aggression they feel toward others. In either case, suicide draws attention to itself because it is considered unnatural, particularly with modernization and technological innovations premised on progress and greater ease of life. Suicide is intrusive and transgressive, therefore, because it uncovers the deep crisis in modern society (Simpson 1951, 17).

The Internet records folk commentary on suicide and makes it part of the process of questioning modernization. Arguably, the Internet brings suicide out into the open; in making it public through the Dwyer footage and 90 Day Jane blogs, it becomes more vivid and accessible. It raises conflicts that drive narrative and belief about the "collective conscience," to use Durkheim's term, at work in a cyberculture. On the

Internet, the circumstances of Dwyer's suicide became secondary to its perception by postmodern viewers. Memories of the act, especially in relation to historical corruption, were not solicited so much as ethical considerations of its disruption of public, bureaucratic life. The Dwyer tape came to symbolize the Internet itself and forced reactions as a metamessage about the cultural implications of the technology that allows viewing of the suicide tape. Whether treated as comical or haunting, the Dwyer footage is among the notable images on the Internet that compel a folk response as a way to deal with postmodern anxieties and ambiguities. Posters put themselves in Dwyer's shoes and create narratives that convey or subvert values for the present day. One frequent and telling response is that the footage makes people think about what it means when frustration leads them to say they want to "blow their brains out" or shoot themselves. They thus use the Internet as an imaginative platform to question the boundaries between fantasy and fact, virtuality and reality, life and death.

The Logic and Psychology of Internet Praxis

The Internet's distributive traits separate it as an electronic medium from the one-on-one communication of telephone calls and fax machines. The Internet layers messages with an assortment of captioned material—graphic and textual—brought together through the marvel of electronic cut and paste on a "page" or "site" (often "under construction," in computer lingo). This process raises comparisons with the *bricoleur*'s overlay technique in scrapbooking and album keeping of yore. The scrapbook is a personal document, yet it is made recognizable to others because at some point it is shared among a selected network of family and friends. Sites such as Facebook and MySpace virtualize, and folklorize, the scrapbook and album by encouraging users to make comments and effect designs for "friends" to view and post their own remarks. Blogs (a portmanteau of *web* and *log*) can have handles or tags rather than real names and often thematize the cultural frame of reference around special interests or identities (Lieber 2010).

Although bloggers have been compared to diarists and e-mail to postal mail, the distinctive features of visualizing discussion "threads" and leaving comments and responses for "posts" merits a different kind of comparison—that is, to the anonymous or tagged inscriptions in bathroom stalls known to folklorists and linguists as *latrinalia*. Defecation inspires writers to inscribe traditional verse on stalls, such as the following: "To the shithouse poet / In honor of his wit / May they build far and wide / Great monuments of shit." Or "Those who write on shithouse walls / Roll their shit in little balls / Those who read these words of wit / Eat the little balls of shit" (Dundes 2007a, 372–73). Inscriptions are often arranged in a vertical chain, with an initial message followed by different writers' responses below it. Linguist Allen Walker Read hypothesizes a motivation for the anonymous writers that can extend to Internet posting: "the well-known yearning to leave a record of one's presence or one's existence" (1935, 17). Writing in this individualized context is often associated with defecation, leading Dundes to relate this impulse to an infantile desire to play with feces displaced by "making one's mark" on the wall (2007a, 373).

An apparent analog to this scatological function is the posting of photocopied humor on bulletin boards and cubicle walls, which often subverts the machine-like corporate setting with visual references to bathroom behavior, where nature calls and people are naturally themselves. Users may also associate the bathroom with modern ritual beliefs, from children calling out revenants such as Bloody Mary in the mirror to narrating deaths and assaults occurring there during adulthood. My explanatory purpose is not to reduce all Internet usage to an expressive process apparent in latrinalia (one might call that "bullshit," but wouldn't that just be more evidence of the cultural trope?). It is to extend the Dundesian interpretation of graffiti as a projection of infantile repression of scatological taboo to the psychology of folk empowerment in the comparison of the technology-driven information age to the naturalistic context of toilets. Folklorist Jeannie Thomas noticed in 2007, for example, the preponderance of bathroom ghosts in modern folklore and theorized that their location in the home or institution is liminal: "it is simultaneously the unclean room and the room where we clean our bodies. As such, it is a place we feel ambivalent about, and it is associated with significant cultural issues: body functions that are seen as unclean, disease, sexuality, dirt, health, and intimacy" (Thomas 2007, 38). Of special significance to the computer metaphor is the notion of restrooms as public places where people rely on technology to do private things and therefore feel vulnerable. Many of the prime images offered on the open medium of the Internet—health, death, sex, and social connection—extend the issues Thomas mentions as being raised by the sequestered bathroom.

The computer's space is often envisioned as an artificial-sounding cubicle or station that is necessary to daily function but also may cause discomfort because of a person's inadequacy with the technology or the fear of being overwhelmed. Defecation can produce both relief and shame, and its product, known euphemistically as "presents" in childhood, is equated in folklore to official "paperwork" on a desk or a screen. In the corporate lore distributed by photocopiers, fax machines, and computers, for instance, is the image of an outhouse or a child on a potty with the caption, "The job is never finished until the paperwork is done!" (Dundes and Pagter 1975, 160–62). The action of the toilet is further symbolized as the model of information technology in humorous signs such as this: "We Welcome Advice and Criticism and always *Rush* Them through the Proper Channels (One flush usually does it!) (Dundes and Pagter 1991b, 102). The photocopied humor I recalled hanging in my high school computer room, relating parts of the toilet to computer hardware, is now a popular T-shirt sold over the Internet. Many humor sites carry this image, in addition to photos of a "toilet computer chair" ("Toilet Computer Chair" 2011).

Before you roll your analog eyes, consider this. Regardless of whether the Internet is hailed or reviled for enabling the rapid distribution of material, much of it is labeled rumor that is said to "smear" and slander (from the root for scandal or shameful conduct). As I noted in responses to the Dwyer suicide tape, many posters linked the presentation or viewing of the material to defecation ("I shit in my pants watching," "intense shit," "holy shit," "some kind of shit"). Of folkloristic significance is that Internet practice is widely viewed as yeast for *spreading* stories that call for an evaluation of truth (see Mikkelson and Mikkelson 2008; Oring 2008). Indeed, a website launched in 2008 with the domain name Fightthesmears.com was predicated on the presumption that the Internet fosters the "zooming" of hearsay, as reported in *Time*. Presidential candidate Barack Obama, particularly sensitive to "the blogosphere's superheated rumor mill," according to *Time*, referred to "dirt and lies . . . circulated in e-mails" being "pumped out" (Tumulty 2008, 40). Prime examples of popular Internet sites promoting verbal smearing are the-shit.net, JuicyCampus.net (replaced by collegeacb .com), and hecklerspray.com, replete with scatological references in

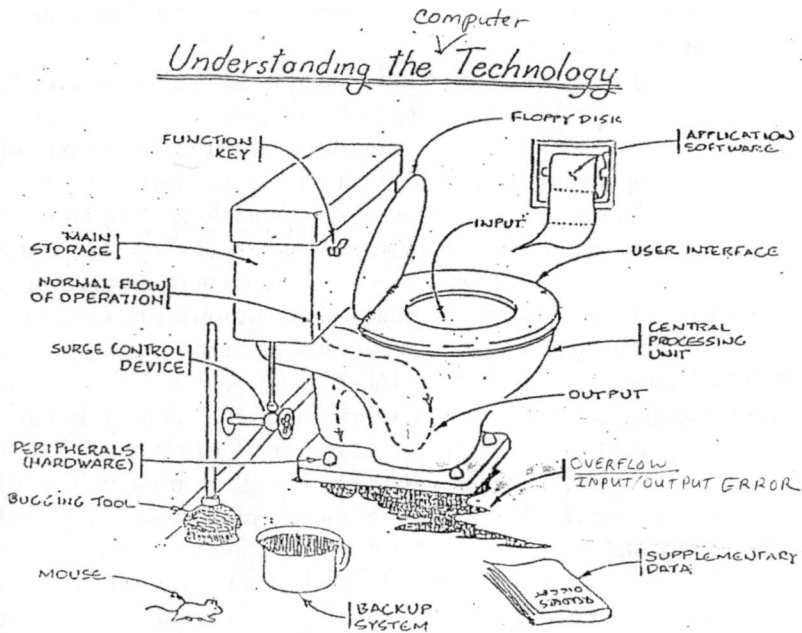

Understanding the Computer Technology.

Labels in figure: Computer · Understanding the Technology · FUNCTION KEY · FLOPPY DISK · APPLICATION SOFTWARE · MAIN STORAGE · INPUT · USER INTERFACE · NORMAL FLOW OF OPERATION · CENTRAL PROCESSING UNIT · SURGE CONTROL DEVICE · OUTPUT · PERIPHERALS (HARDWARE) · OVERFLOW INPUT/OUTPUT ERROR · BUGGING TOOL · SUPPLEMENTARY DATA · MOUSE · BACKUP SYSTEM

"Understanding the Computer Technology." Photocopied broadside hung in a college computer lab, 2001. (Simon Bronner collection)

their titles and aimed at youth. The home page of another, spokeo .com, which is advertised as a social network–based deep search engine, shows a string of teenage girls whispering in one another's ears, their hands over their mouths, above the text: "Want to see something juicy?" (Raphael 2009, 13). As of 2010, YouTube had featured 221,000 videos posted with titles that included the words "talking shit," and Facebook listed more than 500 groups using the phrase. Many of the posts and groups relate their sharing of *inside* or *juicy* information as providing the *straight poop*.

What is the connection to latrinalia? A play frame is established in the stall, released from the restraint of workaday mass society, and the wall becomes an open, uncensored discussion board and canvas on which creative messages and drawings are sequenced, similar to the heralded form and function of many blogs (Longenecker 1977). An individual in the stall, itself located within official space, connects to other people anonymously while engaging in a natural act. Many List-serv postings, too, are framed as informal rather than business and relay rumors with the invitation to give feedback. Accusations of "playing on the Internet" often imply that the user is engaging in idle "chatting" or rumor-mongering with others. The privatized context of defecation in a public institutional setting compels us to consider the psychoanalytic interpretation of graffiti and threading as the use of an infantile smearing impulse to signal human freedom, especially in the symbolic equation of playful writing and anality, which is applicable to the pose of sitting in front of a screen (Dundes 2007a).

Is there symbolic significance in the fact that Facebook's primary form of communication is privatized "writing on the wall"? Another clue to the folk logic of the Internet is MySpace's two standard "blurbs," in computer lingo: "About Me" and "Who I'd Like to Meet." Originally, *blurb* was an Americanism referring to an overblown advertisement for a book. In its reference to overblown writing, it has a connection in sound and meaning to the colloquial use of *blurt* (usually accompanied with *out*) for anal wind. In computer talk, it is common to refer to a flood of messages filling up a user's drive (which is periodically emptied), and the user feels anally impelled to organize accumulated material into boxes that can be emptied. Notably, odious messages are labeled junk or "spam" (from the stigmatized canned luncheon meat), suggesting a repulsion related to being defouled or smeared (expressed in the satire of the traditional proverb "To err is human, to really foul things up takes a computer"). Excretory references to digital work are also apparent in several common computer-age adages: "Garbage in, garbage out," "A program is a device to convert data [input] into error messages," and "A clean house is the sign of a broken computer." Early in computing, UNIX users assigned scatological names to certain characters, such as *splat* for the asterisk, and programmers' lore referred to the "bit bucket," a magical trash can in which computer gremlins stashed or excreted gobbled data (Beatty 1976; Jennings 1991, 105). Later, *bladder* or *bladderball* became terms for an obnoxious string of e-mails sent to a large list rather than being contained. Self-referential responses to rumors regarding the Internet, such as the one that Congress might allow phone companies to charge long-distance rates for Internet access, repeat variations of "When will people realize that they are spreading any shit they believe into?" "These people are full of crap," and, under the heading of "Polluting Internet," the "videos [on the rumor] are all a bunch of crap load of shit" (NESadvantage 2008; see also Green 2006, 4:262–64).

Anxiety that the folk character of the Internet will be lost comes through in a narrative directly relating defecation with computer use. In 2003, a story circulated that Microsoft was developing an Internet-capable toilet. In some reports, it was called an iLoo (from the British term *loo* for toilet). According to the narrative, the stall would be equipped with a wireless keyboard and an extensible, height-adjustable plasma screen located directly in front of the seated user. The story appeared to confirm that no place was immune from the Internet's reach, but some details also equated human control with wiping and smearing, such as the production of special paper imprinted with URLs that users may not have tried. Snopes.com, a reputable urban legend reference site, declared the story a hoax, but it quoted a newspaper interview with a Microsoft official who said, "People used to reach for a book or mag when they were on the loo, but now they'll be logging on! It's exciting to think that the smallest room can now be the gateway to the massive virtual world" ("iLoo" 2007). Arguably, that excitement extends to being seated at a screen within a cubicle, and the privatized "logging on" enacts the titillating smearing praxis of building "far and wide, great monuments of shit."

Responding to Twitter users' ability to state what they are doing at any given moment, hackers flooded the social networking site on July 5, 2009, in an orchestrated subversion of the corporate Web. Called "Operation Shitter," pranksters signed up for fake Twitter accounts and wrote nonsensical posts with the hashtag "#gorillapenis" (Paul 2009; the gorilla's penis is small relative to the animal's overall size, and in folk speech, it refers to human genitalia that are considered repulsively hairy or dirty, often drawing comparisons to the anus). Hashtagging is a user-developed method to search Twitter quickly for particular keywords. Here, *hash* refers to chopped meat, often compared to feces or, more generally, to a mess or a muddle. In computer lingo, it means meaningless or unwanted data or, more colloquially, garbage. The hackers managed to post a screen shot of their rogue hashtag perched atop Twitter's list of the most popular subjects on the social networking site in real time. Unlike other hacks that were the dirty work of one rogue geek, this prank had broad social participation. Making a connection between *guerrillas* and *gorillas*, the perpetrators of the "viral" Operation Shitter phenomenon also inspired posted comments about viruses lodged in abundant gorilla shit dropped all over the wild Internet jungle. *Shit* came to represent the vast body of knowledge out on the Web, as captured by the emergent folk text "Google that sh*t." The Facebook page using that title reminds students of the connection between googling and repeated practice: "Every single question EVER can be answered with Google. And you know it. And that's why you use it habitually." The "sh*t" rhetorically stands for the mess or hash of mass information out on the Internet.

A common reference to computer malfunctions is that "shit happens," understood widely in the texted initials "SH"; a related meaning is "same here," as if disembodied, diverse users share the natural act of defecation by sending cybermessages. Although linguists often note that folk initialisms are common in electronic communication, they rarely interpret the preponderance of scatological references in online chat lingo:

AS = ape shit
BAG = big ass grin
BS = bullshit, brain strain, big smile
BTSOOM = beats the shit out of me
CYA = cover your ass
DILLIGAS = do I look like I give a shit?
EE = electronic emission
ESAD = eat shit and die
FOS = full of shit
LMAO = laughing my ass off
PITA = pain in the ass
SEG = shit eating grin
SOGOP = shit or get off the pot
SOL = shit out of luck
SOS = same old shit
SSDD = same shit different day
TS = tough shit, totally stinks
TSFY = tough shit for you
UY = up yours
WTSDS = where the sun don't shine

WTSHTF = when the shit hits the fan
YGBSM = you got to be shitting me
YS = you stinker ("List of Chat Acronyms & Text Message Short-
hand" 2008)

Maybe some of this impulse comes from the ejective or retentive praxis
of users in a seated position. Much visual humor associates toilets and
electronic technology involving inputs and outputs. The position may
invite commentary because it brings into question boundaries of private and public, play and work, natural and technological, and freedom
and restraint that are of concern on the Internet. The common folkloric form of initialism is more than a linguistic device to save space;
it also signals a subversion of the usual institutional use of acronyms
in bureaucratized modern life (Jennings 1991, 91–108). The visualiza-
tion of the computer as toilet comments on the need to humanize the
technology and the institution, lest it replace or control humans, but
it is also congruent with the social negotiation between the pleasure
derived from ejection and the social restraint on its appearance (Jones
1961, 413–37). Moving beyond one-on-one communication, the Internet frequently makes use of an informal, scatological frame of reference for distributing playful material, tantamount to the smearing
of feces. References to the ease of "slinging mud," "dishing dirt," and
"spreading shit" online signify exhilaration, maybe compulsion, and a
certain amount of aggressive rebellion (Praeger 2007, 124–35). With
the writing-defecation equation, one leaves a potentially embarrassing
or satisfying remark, which becomes important to maintain a presence
in a youth-oriented, globalizing medium that blurs the divisions between private and public.

Make no mistake. I am not claiming that Internet users are imitating defecation. The point is that, rhetorically, scatological initialisms and symbolic references to smearing practices signal—indeed,
demarcate—the folk Web as a means of social control from the bottom up. Besides the smearing symbolism, invoking feces play brings
to mind youthful and often subversive activities of an anal stage of human development (Praeger 2007, 107–17). Precedents are apparent in
photocopied lore that contrasts the rotten swamp or pig sty and the
naturalized bathroom used by ordinary service and information workers in their cubicles. For instance, "When you are up to your ass in

alligators, it is difficult to remind yourself that your initial object was to drain the swamp" (Dundes and Pagter 1987, 91; the authors reproduce this motto under the heading "The Writing on the Walls") and "Never try to teach a pig to sing, it wastes your time and it annoys the pig" (Dundes and Pagter 1991b, 71). An intricate technical drawing that comments on the productivity urged by corporate bosses is the "output processer," which contains folds that reveal a simple toilet (Dundes and Pagter 1975, 193–94). Or before Operation Shitter, chain letters circulated inviting the recipient to "go to the address at the bottom of this list and shit on the lawn." Sounding like the expansion of a Facebook friends wheel, the result would be "3,216 people shitting on your lawn, if this chain is not broken." The "reward," the letter concludes, is a triumph of nature: "next summer's greenest lawn in your block" (Dundes and Pagter 1975, 7).

To be sure, users refer to other transgressive practices to locate the folk Web, such as the fact that information is most often viewed and that the act of reading or seeing the material fosters the emergence of a metalanguage for expressing gesture, emotion, veracity, and humor that typically accompanies face-to-face interaction. For example, on-line chat also has its noticeable share of phallic expressions transmitted by both men and women as *natural* symbols of aggression, particularly by teenage users (WTF = what the fuck, FFS = for fuck's sake, FOAD = fuck off and die, GFY = go fuck yourself, GTFO = get the fuck out, and STFU = shut the fuck up). When I discussed this penchant with users, they suggested that less stigma is attached to disembodied "swearing" online and that it marks messages as conversation, especially youthful talk associated with being brash and high-spirited. Like scatological references, this swearing also helps demarcate a traditional or play frame characteristic of the folk Web. In an analog world, typing is considered formal or institutionally supervised, whereas tapping out or texting WTF provides a "high" or feels transgressive, in a way that uttering the words, if one is inclined to do so, does not.

The transgressive rhetorical strategy raises questions about the symbolization of technology as phallic or pubertal power (essentialized, for instance, in lightbulb jokes with a double entendre for screwing) and, for many cultural critics, the gendering or patriarchal posturing of the Internet (Dundes 1981; Miller 2001). In relation to the previous argument for scatological impulses projected onto the Net (slang for Internet, which that draws attention to its function as a receptacle, as well as a linguistic clipping of *network*), the fear of being smeared is extended to the fear of being feminized sexually. This is evident in the motific slot filled by *fucked* or *fouled*: SNAFU (situation normal all fouled/fucked up), FUM (fucked/fouled up mess), and FUBAR (fouled/fucked up beyond all repair) (Jennings 1991, 107). The adoption of these terms from military lore may not be coincidental, because an analogy can be made between soldiers entering a vernacular cultural register with this speech and computer users as indoctrinated masculinized trainees using the computer as a phallicized weapon (Fleece 1946). In addition, the Internet has historical roots in military intelligence and is often associated with other institutionalized groups such as universities, hospitals, and corporations. Moreover, the Web can be construed in digital folk belief systems as representative of a formal, routinized organization that users need to humanize (often signified by creative variation and parody) and about which they need to vent aggression or even subvert.

Web-related folklore often creates, as its other, a money-grubbing, bullying elite aligned with corporate and scientific interests that seek to control, censor, and bureaucratize the Internet. Folklore in this construction represents the tradition of a democratic, participatory commons and the value of openness and inclusiveness. The cyberculture wars are imagined as a David-Goliath battle, or ordinary disempowered people affiliating with tradition against scientists carrying the brand of technology and modernity who would deracinate the Internet commons. Yet despite the cautionary tales and rumors of the end of the open Internet, the mass of user-generated data on the Web suggests the expansion of a folk system with the dawn of the twenty-first century, characterized by peer-to-peer sharing of handed-down wisdom and the priority of practice over scientism (Anderson 2010; Wolff 2010). A notable declaration of Internet user independence went by the headline "The End of Theory" (it read "The End of Science" on the cover) in the touchstone technology publication *Wired* magazine (Anderson 2008). The basis of the shift in authority, according to the magazine's editor Chris Anderson, is the "massive corpus" of reachable information as a sign of a new revolutionary epoch dubbed the "Petabyte Age." In previous iterations of data, organizational analogies were used: folders to file cabinets to libraries. "Petabytes," Anderson writes, "are stored in the clouds" (2008, 108). This cosmological analogy means that information is visualized in almost supernatural terms as being beyond human comprehension.

Technically, a petabyte is equal to one quadrillion bytes ($1,000^5$ or 10^{15}), and it symbolizes an extraordinary amount because of the significance of *quad* (from the root for "four") as a unit representing abundance if three in Western thought stands for completeness (Brandes 1985, 50–81; Bronner 2007, 7–8; Dundes 1968). It also refers to automorphism because of the fifth power (five being an automorphic number) to which the official measure of 1,000 is put. It relates to Internet usage because the vast extent of data can be expressed in petabytes: Google processes about twenty petabytes of data a day. "This is a world," Anderson philosophizes, "where massive amounts of data and applied mathematics replace every other tool that might be brought to bear. . . . Who knows why people do what they do? The point is they do it, and we can track and measure it with unprecedented fidelity" (2008, 108). Web phenomena are therefore described as patterns rather than models, rationalized in analytical terms as correlations rather than outlined relationally as causation. It may appear, as Anderson claims, to be "a whole new way of understanding the world" (2008, 109), but it also may be a virtualization of a mythic world in which one's experience is connected to everyone else's.

The essence of the mythic, as stated by anthropologist Eric Dardel, is placing oneself "in the current of the whole world's life." He contrasts the modern world, "dominated by logical and historical concerns, with our explanations ruled by the principle of causality," with the mythic, "which shows itself in convictions or in beliefs, in 'verities' which we declare to be true" (Dardel 1984, 229, 230). The mythic as seen on the Internet is *present*, not past or future; it is not set in place but occurs in repetitive patterns with a source in precedent that we might call tradition. This comes out in awe for the mass of data in its fantastical universe. Not envisioned as comprising things such as a file, a cabinet, or a library, it is ethereal, an "ethernet," and references the lights, whirrs, and clicks that manifest cosmic forces. There, people engage mythic meanings, especially through the Internet's responsive quality; users produce relational narratives in the play frames, commons, or *rooms* of the Web and raise discourse about the logic of virtuality.

Although an argument can be made that Internet communication simulates the mythic in online cafés or chat rooms, that does not necessarily result in the production of expressive lore. To be sure, many networks revel in their groups' thematized communications that result in initialisms, narratives, and beliefs, distinguishing each group and representing the Internet as a cultural space. The idea of constituting lore so as to give identity to the group is carried over from community life, and in this practice, the mode of communication on the Internet is culturally marked by the identification of self-referential genres. An example is the neologism *meme* for a digital file or hyperlink propagated quickly from peer to peer on the Net. Many memes are in fact folkloric because they often take the form of catchphrases, rumors, schemes, and legendary material; arguably, the word's praxis has a folkloric reference because it is taken from the Greek root *mime*, for "imitation" or "repetition," but altered to sound more like *gene* as the unit of cultural transmission on the Net (Jeffreys 2000). The invented term draws attention to both the Net's state of matter as data, reproducible and variable, and its difference from social forces in life. Such constructions force folklorists—and other scholars of culture—to think long and hard about standing on the shoulders of giants and restricting their concept of folklore to oral or naturalistic tradition.

How folklore is enabled by virtualization for its users and how it is differentiated from the face-to-face world referred to as analog culture demand a rethinking of assumptions, and questions, about the workings of tradition. Tradition was once thought to be a product or relic of the past, arising out of the land and group and belonging to "others," removed by a lack of technological advancement or cosmopolitanism. The issue with virtual tradition is not so much whether geeks, gamers, and bloggers constitute a folk group, the way a previous generation of cultural critics confronted with the modern phenomena of the assembly line, phonograph, and telephone asked, "Is there a folk in the city?" and "Is there a folk in the factory?" (Dégh 1985; Dorson 1970; Nickerson 1974). To be sure, that can be done with lists of computer slang, emoticons, and initialisms marking cultural knowledge and, consequently, identity for a group (Jennings 1991; Jordan 1997; Preston 1996).

The significance of rhetorically understanding the Internet as a folk system is its suggestion of how technology allows everyone in to enact and alter tradition in some form, whether digitally or analytically.

This is especially compelling as the Internet becomes more portable and pervasive and becomes the primary mediator of cultural connection or, potentially, as it becomes more incorporated or less "open" and is displaced as a folk medium by peer-to-peer communications (Anderson 2010; Wolff 2010). Either way, boundary maintenance appears to be less influenced by the corporeal traits of ethnicity, region, gender, and occupation, although they may enter into the communicative equation. One affiliates with any number of overlapping, often temporary global and local networks, lists, and interests, and these may correspond to age and organizational divisions that produce folklorized digital practices. These affiliations are often imagined through multiple avatars, roles, profiles, personalities, and addresses. So who is doing the talking—or connecting?

The answer to this question returns us to the original point about the significance of conceptually linking the Internet and tradition. As a fundamental human capacity and need, the production of folklore to represent tradition is a continuous vital force, and it is imperative to view how it is enacted with and problematized by media, old and new. Indeed, we may comprehend that folklore is digitized and virtualized in our new wired age, or we folklorize the age, often outside our awareness. Or, to quote a motto I have seen on the wall of the computer lab, "Oh, what a tangled Web we weave when first we practice."[9]

Notes

1. Defining Tradition

1. The Coalition for Traditional Values website emblazons its motto: "Empowering People of Faith Through Knowledge" (www.traditionalvalues .org; accessed September 12, 2010). Toward Tradition was active on the Web before 2006 and described its devotion to "faith-based American principles of constitutional and limited government; the rule of law; representative democracy; free markets; a strong military; and a moral public culture." The organization's founder, Rabbi Daniel Lapin, maintains a website at http:// www.rabbidaniellapin.com. The Citizens for Traditional Values website uses the motto "A Positive Voice for Your Values," and under its list of guiding principles posted on the "Faith and Family" site is "preserving the influence of faith and family as the great foundation of American freedom embodied in our Judeo-Christian heritage."

2. "Honesty: Zach's Tall Tale (*Adventures from The Book of Virtues*, No. 1)" was the opening of an animated prime-time series scheduled to debut over Labor Day weekend in 1997 on the Public Broadcasting System (PBS). Aladdin Paperbacks published an illustrated print version based on Bennett's story by Shelagh Canning in 1996.

2. Explaining Tradition

1. The procedure can also be rendered as circular to emphasize that the testing of the hypothesis leads to its revision, which in turn promotes building on the previous findings. Judy Kirscht and Mark Schlenz, in their textbook *Engaging Inquiry*, for example, illustrate the "scientific method" beginning with "observe" and proceeding circularly to "hypothesize," "experiment," and "revise hypothesis," before returning to "observe" at the top of the circle (2002, 13).

2. Many historians of American cultural anthropology have attributed the rising importance of interpretation since the 1960s to the influence of the subjectivist ethnography of Ward Goodenough and David Schneider, in addition to Clifford Geertz (see D'Andrade 1999; Winthrop 1991,146–49). As Ladislav Holy (1987) points out, the move to interpretation was guided by a post-structural focus on cultural specificities in place of a search for cross-cultural uniformities. Daniel Linger (2005) labels the preference for interpretation as the discursive "Geertzian tradition," which stands in contrast to the positivist "Durkheimian tradition." Robert Winthrop, in an entry on "Interpretation" in his *Dictionary of Concepts in Cultural Anthropology*, argues that

451

Geertzian interpretation displaced the historicism of Boasian anthropology. Citing Geertz, Winthrop writes, "From the interpretive perspective, in contrast, culture is not a 'power' determining behavior, but a context of meanings within which human action is made intelligible" (1991, 148). Paralleling the structural concerns I have raised, the resulting fate of generalization in anthropological research has also been debated. See, for example, the arguments over the proposition that "social anthropology is a generalizing science or it is nothing" in *Key Debates in Anthropology* (Ingold 1996, 15–54) and the controversy over the American Anthropological Association's removal of the word *science* from its self-description in a long-range planning document (Glenn 2010).

3. Recalling the paradigm shift in folkloristics during the 1970s, Roger Abrahams notes, "Goldstein's *A Guide for Fieldworkers* provided the center for gravity for the next generation. Fieldwork was now installed as the *sine qua non* of folklore as it had been in cultural anthropology and other ethnographic disciplines" (1993a, 385).

5. Adapting Tradition

1. The disease was not recognized in its epidemic form until 1887, when outbreaks were reported in Sweden. Since then, outbreaks of polio have been reported around the globe, including severe epidemics in Asia and central Europe. The disease was finally controlled by the introduction of the Salk vaccine in 1954.

2. American children are not unique in this preoccupation with games in which touch has a noxious effect. Iona and Peter Opie, in *Children's Games in Street and Playground* (1969, 75–78), describe various afflictions that European children playfully pass on by touching one another. In 1954, at the height of the polio epidemic, British children played a form of tag in which "the dreaded Lurgi" was the feared disease, and they would write "P.A.L." on their arms to protect themselves against it. The Opies write about other related chasing games: "In Liss children transmit something, which only they can understand, when they make the 'aggie touch'; and the touch may even be passed on by the deceit of shaking hands. In Wolstanton children play a game called 'Germ.' . . . In Lastonbury they play 'Minge.' In Swansea girls obtain a morbid thrill playing 'The Plague': in Cranford, Middlesex, the game is called 'Fever'; in Sale, Manchester, it is 'The Poo' ('the one that has it at the end of the day smells'); at Castel in Guernsey it is 'Poisonous Fungi'; and at St. Peter Port it is 'Lodgers.' And while these games are being played, and even afterwards, the suspension of disbelief in the game's pretence can be absolute: the feeling is unfeigned that the chaser's touch is unhealthy." The Opies also found the game in New Zealand, where it is called "the fleas," and in Italy, where it is known as "Peste." And in a nineteenth-century source, they found a reference to a chasing game in Madagascar in which the chaser was *boka*, a leper, "and when he touched someone his leprosy was conveyed to the one he touched, who in turn tried to rid himself of the disease on someone else."

7. Personalizing Tradition

1. Roger Abrahams, in *Deep Down in the Jungle*, reports a joke collected among African Americans in Philadelphia with a similar punch line but a different setting: "You ain't lying you sick, honey, your jaws are swollen like you have the mumps and your breath smells like shit" (1970, 216–17).

2. Folklorist Bruce Jackson recorded a similar toast from Texas prisons that he called "Stackolee" (1974, 51–52). For other versions from African American oral tradition, see Roberts 1965, 170–71; Abrahams 1970, 136–42; Jemie 2003, 207–8.

3. Dance (1978, 47–48) reports a similar joke among African Americans in Virginia but provides no information about the teller or the situation in which it was told. Legman (1968, 419) gives a version told by American whites with a Catholic priest in the preacher's role, which he traces to editions of *Oeuvres badines* by Alexis Piron, an eighteenth-century French erotic poet (Legman 1968, 36–37). A difference between the two variants is that the priest is involved in seduction during confession, as he gets closer and closer to the woman's vagina, whereas in the African American variant, the preacher is presented as already being involved in copulation. In the white versions, the man who gives the woman a venereal disease is called a "son of a bitch," whereas in the African American versions, a cultural signal is given by the epithet "motherfucker." An example of the former is a version I received from D. K. Wilgus of Los Angeles, California, in 1983:

> A young lady went to confession and confessed that she had called a man a dirty son-of-a-bitch. The priest asked her why she had done it. "Well, Father, he put his hand on my breast." "Like this?" "Yes." "Well, child, that's no reason to call a man a dirty son-of-a-bitch." "But, Father, he then put his hand on my knee." "Like this?" "Yes." "Now, child, that's no reason to call a man a dirty son-of-a-bitch." "But then he reached up my skirt and pulled down my panties." "Like this?" "Yes." "Child, that's no reason to call a man a dirty son-of-a-bitch." "But then he put his hand between my legs." "Like this?" "Yes." "Child, that's no reason to call a man a dirty son-of-a-bitch." "But then he took out his thing and put it inside me." "Like this?" "Yes." "Well, that's no reason to call a man a dirty son-of-a-bitch." "Then he told me he had the clap." "Oh, that dirty son-of-a-bitch!"

4. Similar behavior showing Shine's exaggerated sexual prowess—in this instance, getting the devil in the end—is reported by Abrahams (1970, 126). Legman calls these stories "potency jokes" and briefly discusses them in *Rationale of the Dirty Joke* (1968, 312–13). See also Bruce Jackson's consideration of Oedipal conflict and the rejection of white authority as paternal in "Circus and Street: Psychosocial Aspects of the Black Toast" (1972, 130–31). Allegorical and contextual aspects of the Shine character are discussed in Levine (1977, 427–29); Wepman, Newman, and Binderman (1974, 213–14); and Evans (1977, 136–37).

5. Although a widely reported joke, the reasons for its selection or the tellers' involvement with the text are not addressed by collectors. For other versions, see Dance 1978, 34–35; Abrahams 1970, 238–39; Dorson 1967, 327–28; Browne 1954, 130.

6. A variant of this story, with a policeman brandishing the blue steel that changes the driver's answers, is reported by Dance (1978, 80–81). In that story, Big Bimbo Bottom, the name he uses in New York City, is really "Thomas Lee," and his wife's name is Lucille; he drives an Oldsmobile (not a Cadillac), and he smokes Chesterfields (not "the best o' cigars"). When asked "What changed yo' mind?" he answers, "The blue steel." In the conclusion, when queried, "If I turn you loose, will you go home?" he replies in a hick accent, "I showly *wee-1-1*." The formula of one-word answers is evident in a story entitled "Of a Monk that Answered Altogether by Syllables" in the jest book "The Mirrour of Mirth" (1583); see Zall 1963, 385–86.

7. The structure of three girls talking about what makes them hot is often presented by African American tellers as an ethnic joke with characters of a white girl, a Chinese girl, and a black girl. Dance reports the punch line as, "Fuck me and don't pay me, that's what make me hot" (1978, 99).

8. Ernest's introductory narrative has elements of self-deprecating etiological tales such as "Why the Black Man's Hair Is Nappy" (Dance 1978, 8). It is followed by an attack on the testicles as women's revenge against men in a castration complex. Legman, for instance, reports a story about three men discussing the most terrible sound in the world. The third man tells of picking up a girl and returning to her apartment. When her husband comes home, he climbs out naked on the window ledge, seven stories up, and suddenly feels a large male hand grabbing him by the balls. The other men ask what that has to do with terrible sounds. He replies, "Just at that moment I heard the strangest scraping sound I ever in my life heard: the sound of him opening his pocketknife with his teeth!" (Legman 1975, 499).

9. Usually labeled "Oink Is Ugly," this story is reported widely among African Americans. See Dance 1978, 199–200; Dorson 1967, 184; Roberts 1965, 132–35; Jemie 2003, 278. Dorson, Roberts, and Dance relate the story to the Thompson (1955–1958) Motif K406, "Stolen animal disguised as person so that thief may escape detection" and Aarne-Thompson Type 1525H*, "Stolen sheep dressed as person sitting at helm of boat."

8. Symbolizing Tradition

1. Wherever possible I use the orthographic standard for Pennsylvania German (sometimes known as *Pennsylfanisch* or *Deitsch* in the dialect)—the Buffington-Barba system, used widely by linguists since the 1950s (see Buffington and Barba 1954). Since the dialect is primarily an oral language and was differentiated in the culture from the High German used in worship services, it did not develop a standard spelling for literature. The Buffington-Barba system uses an English system to represent the pronunciation of the language.

However, when quoting texts published by Brendle and Troxell (1944) and others, I preserve their original orthography.

2. Worth noting is that analysis and anality are not unrelated. The *Oxford English Dictionary* lists the roots of *anal* and *analysis* as the Latin *analis*, for "anus." The action of analysis constitutes the ejective action of loosening, the "breaking up of anything complex into its various simple elements, the opposite of synthesis" (i.e., tightening). The Pennsylvania German folklorists of the mid-twentieth century claimed to analyze in the sense of organizing collected material by themes, but they did not synthesize by giving a symbolic or metaphorical meaning.

3. Not all folkloristic collection efforts should be classified as anal-ejective. In "The Psychology of Collecting Folklore," Alan Dundes points out, "The anal retentive nature of some collectors is manifested by their putting their manuscripts or tapes in a secret or locked place, often denying others access to their materials. Frequently, they refuse to publish. By a curious verbal coincidence (which is probably no accident), one often hears such collectors described as 'sitting on' their material. ('Sitting tight' has somewhat the same connotation. 'Tight' commonly means stingy in the sense of being reluctant to part with something" (1975, 125). Further, the Pennsylvania German folklorists were averse to the formalistic classifications characteristic of the "historic-geographic" school of folkloristics, with its emphasis on global distributions. Dundes points out that this classificatory strategy fits into the "retaining-reaction formation" of anal erotic character, characterized by orderly, systematic arrangement (1975, 124). Brendle and Troxell (1944) did not annotate their collection with Aarne-Thompson tale type numbers or the Thompson motif numbers. By omitting such references, they gave the impression that the stories were not migratory but stayed within the Pennsylvania German culture. They appeared to be rooted in the culture's own fertile soil.

4. Alan Dundes, in his survey of scatological scholarship, finds that "the bulk of scholarship has been traditionally written in German or by Germans," suggesting that this interest arises from a German obsession with *dreck* (1984, 79–80). The connection of anality with ethnic separation may be related to the fact that the American folklife movement, centered in the distinctiveness of American traditional communities, was formulated by Pennsylvania German scholars. See Bronner 1998, 266–312.

5. Alan Dundes states that "the delight in pseudo-scatological names is a longstanding tradition in Germany." He points out that Wittenwiler's fifteenth-century mock epic *The Ring* has three peasants with names referring to cow dung: *Ochsenkäs* ("ox cheese"), *Fladenranft* ("cow pie"), and *Rindtaisch* ("cow dung"), while one of the hero's kinswomen is named *Jützin Scheissindpluomen* ("shit in the flowers"). He also quotes wordplay by Mozart in which he describes Duchess Smackbottom and Princess Dunghill (Dundes 1984, 72–73).

6. Folklorist Jan Harold Brunvand describes such narratives as "shaggy dog stories": "a nonsensical joke that employs in the punch line a psychological non sequitur, a punning variation of a familiar saying, or a hoax, to trick the

listener who expects conventional wit or humor" (Brunvand 1963, 44). In his classification, this narrative fits category "C1600–C1799. Punch Line States a Moral to Story—Comic Advice" (Brunvand 1963, 65). An example is "C1650, Don't Lose Your Head": A little worm (or a dog) has his tail chopped off by a passing train. He turns around and has his head chopped off as well. Moral: "Don't lose your head over a little piece of tail." Although the story that could be classified as "Don't Need Fancy Cars" clearly has a wide circulation outside the Pennsylvania German culture, its chicken imagery made it a favorite modern shaggy dog joke at the masculine joke-telling sessions I attended in Pennsylvania German settings.

7. There is a similarity with another pseudo-fable collected by Alan Dundes in Germany in 1979, although different animals are used as characters:

> *Eine Maus ist auf der Flucht vor einer Katze. Auf der Wiese steht eine Kuh, die gerade einen Kuhfladen macht, der glücklicherweise auf die Maus fällt. Nur die Schwanzspitze schaut noch heraus. Die Katze zieht die Maus am Schwanz aus dem Kuhfladen heraus, reinigt sie und frisst sie auf. Moral: 1. Nicht jeder, der dich bescheisst, meint es mit dir schlecht. 2. Nicht jeder, der dich aus der Scheisse zieht, meint es mit dir gut. 3. Wenn du schon in der Scheisse steckst, so ziehe wenigstens den Schwanz ein.* [A mouse was being chased by a cat. A cow was standing in the meadow and was dropping a cow pie, which, fortunately, fell on the mouse. Just the tail stuck out. The cat pulled the mouse out by the tail, cleaned it off, and ate it. The moral of the story is (1) Not everyone who shits on you means you ill. (2) Not everyone who pulls you out of the shit means you well. (3) If you find yourself in the shit, at least pull your tail in.] (Dundes 1984, 35–36)

10. Virtual Tradition

1. In my ethnic-religious background of Judaism, this assemblage is familiar rather than sui generis, as many Web aficionados would claim. Talmudic study involves navigating pages that have a central textual core surrounded by commentaries, often at odd angles, in different domains on the page. See Rosen 2000.

2. I argue in *American Folklore Studies: An Intellectual History* (Bronner 1986a, 106–29) that incorporation of the rhetoric of technology into the intellectualism of the 1960s, representing in part a shift in the history of science from natural history to physics in cultural applications, influenced the rise of *interaction, network,* and *dynamics* as keywords in folkloristics. Indeed, discourse on harnessing computers as an analytical tool goes back to this period (see Dundes 1965a; Holbek 1969; Maranda 1967; Petöfi and Szöllösy 1969; Sebeok 1965).

3. The miniaturization of Internet-equipped devices may also be a function of the influence of Japan's technological designers, who operate in what has been dubbed a "compact culture." Major Japanese computer manufacturers

such as Sony, Toshiba, and Hitachi cater to the demands of consuming Japanese youths, who do not have privacy in small dwelling spaces and use the devices on mass transit and in public areas. The pattern of compactness was prevalent in Japan before it became widespread in the Americas and Europe. See Lee 1992; Yoshida, Tanaka, and Sesoko 1982.

4. There is precedent for this cultural response in the history of technology. At the 1964 New York World's Fair, Bell Telephone hailed the "picturephone" as the next mass cultural appliance. Video technology allowed speakers on either end of the telephone to see each other, but despite a formidable marketing campaign, consumers did not buy into the vision. Historians of technology generally agree that consumers want to preserve the informality of appearance permitted when callers cannot see each other. See Lipartito 2003.

5. Stewart and Bennett (1991) culturally exemplify the difference between analog (relational) and digital (analytical) thinking as a contrast between Buddhist and Western approaches to perception. They offer different interpretations of a folk proverb to make their point:

> The American proverb, "still waters run deep," (as a way of describing a quiet, thoughtful person) would be rendered differently by the Chinese. In Mandarin, a profound thinker would be described as "great" or "valuable" rather than deep. Also, in Japanese, horizontal allusions to size, rank, or multiplicity more often render the quality of thought than vertical allusions to depth. Both for the Chinese and Japanese, the thinking process is seen as much less deep than it is by Americans and other Westerners. External social roles and relationships, for instance, receive much more emphasis than the nature of one's thought processes. Put differently, the Chinese and Japanese tend to have a highly developed sociological sense but make relatively little use of psychological analysis. (Stewart and Bennett 1991, 24–25)

Another difference is in ordering knowledge. As Stewart and Bennett explain, Buddhists' "perceptual theory minimized the distinction between direct sensory information and knowledge obtained through fantasy or inference, inducing them to treat perceptual objects and mental products similarly. Concrete objects and abstract concepts were situated side by side on a single dimension, and abstract ideas could be represented as concrete objects. The objective world was exhaustively described but without the rank ordering which Westerners impose on reality by classifying objects and events according to their importance" (1991, 24). For other comparisons of Asian and American thinking processes related to tradition, see Bronner 1998, 475–82; Nakamura 1964, 130–33; White 1994. In particular, Lee (1992) views technological differences as demonstrating a continuing cultural contrast.

6. Later it was revealed that one envelope contained instructions for Dwyer's funeral; another held his organ donor card; and the third contained a letter to

Governor Robert Casey asking him to appoint Dwyer's wife, Joanne, to succeed him as state treasurer. See Cusick, Meyers, and Roche 1987, 1.

7. As an example, see the digital folk art of a fictional Nintendo "shooting" game featuring Budd Dwyer (with an exploding pixelated face) as the main character: http://bluntobject.files.wordpress.com/2009/06/429px-budd_dwyer_nes.jpg (accessed June 30, 2009).

8. Although the suicide footage has not been replayed on television in the digital age, the image and audio track have been featured in a number of commercial films and CDs, most notably in the movie *Bowling for Columbine* (2002), directed by Michael Moore, and the singles "Hey Man, Nice Shot" (1995) by alternative rock band Filter and "Get Your Gunn" (1994) by Marilyn Manson. *Honest Man: The Life of R. Budd Dwyer* (2010), directed by James Dirschberger, was screened in Meadville and Harrisburg, Pennsylvania, with members of the Dwyer family in the audience, before going to DVD.

9. The phrase is a takeoff on Sir Walter Scott's *Marmion* (1933, canto vi, stanza 17). His poetic lines were, "Oh what a tangled web we weave, When first we practise to deceive!" A variation of the computer satire is, "Oh what a tangled website we weave."

References

Abernethy, Francis Edward. 1985. "Folk Art in General, Yard Art in Particular." In *Folk Art in Texas*, ed. Francis Edward Abernethy, 17–21. Dallas: Southern Methodist University Press.

Abrahams, Israel. 1958. *Jewish Life in the Middle Ages*. New York: Meridian Books.

Abrahams, Roger D. 1962. "Playing the Dozens." *Journal of American Folklore* 75: 209–20.

———. 1969. *Jump-Rope Rhymes: A Dictionary*. Austin: University of Texas Press.

———. 1970. *Deep Down in the Jungle: Negro Narrative Folklore from the Streets of Philadelphia*. Chicago: Aldine.

———. 1972. "Personal Power and Social Restraint in the Definition of Folklore." In *Toward New Perspectives in Folklore*, ed. Américo Paredes and Richard Bauman, 16–30. Austin: University of Texas Press.

———. 1980. "Folklore in the Definition of Ethnicity: An American and Jewish Perspective." In *Studies in Jewish Folklore*, ed. Frank Talmage, 13–20. Cambridge, Mass.: Association for Jewish Studies.

———. 1983. *The Man-of-Words in the West Indies: Performance and the Emergence of Creole Culture*. Baltimore: Johns Hopkins University Press.

———. 1993a. "After New Perspectives: Folklore Study in the Late Twentieth Century." *Western Folklore* 52: 379–400.

———. 1993b. "Phantoms of Romantic Nationalism in Folkloristics." *Journal of American Folklore* 106: 3–37.

———. 2005. *Everyday Life: A Poetics of Vernacular Practices*. Philadelphia: University of Pennsylvania Press.

Abrahams, Roger D., and Alan Dundes. 1969. "On Elephantasy and Elephanticide." *Psychoanalytic Review* 56: 225–41.

Abrahams, Roger D., and Lois Rankin. 1980. *Counting-out Rhymes: A Dictionary*. Austin: University of Texas Press.

Abrams, David M., and Brian Sutton-Smith. 1977. "The Development of the Trickster in Children's Narrative." *Journal of American Folklore* 90: 29–47.

Acton, H. B. 1952–1953. "Tradition and Some Other Forms of Order." *Proceedings of the Aristotelian Society*, n.s., 53: 1–28.

Adam, Robert, and Matthew Hardy, eds. 2008. *Tradition Today: Continuity in Architecture and Society*. Southampton, U.K.: WIT Press.

Adams, David Wallace. 2001. "More than a Game: The Carlisle Indians Take to the Gridiron, 1893–1917." *Western Historical Quarterly* 32: 25–53.

Addams, Jane. 1990 [1910]. *Twenty Years at Hull-House, with Autobiographical Notes*. Urbana: University of Illinois Press.

Adorno, Theodor W. 1993. "On Tradition." *Telos* 94: 75–82.

Allen, Barbara. 1996. "Regional Folklore." In *American Folklore: An Encyclopedia*, ed. Jan Harold Brunvand, 618–19. New York: Garland.

Allen, Barbara, and Thomas E. Schlereth, eds. 1990. *Sense of Place: American Regional Cultures.* Lexington: University Press of Kentucky.

Allison, Christine. 1993. *Teach Your Children Well: A Parent's Guide to the Stories, Poems, Fables, and Tales that Instill Traditional Values.* New York: Delacorte Press.

Allison, Randal S. 1997. "Tradition." In *Folklore: An Encyclopedia of Beliefs, Customs, Tales, Music, and Art*, 2 vols., ed. Thomas A. Green, 799–801. Santa Barbara, Calif.: ABC-CLIO.

Ames, Kenneth L. 1977. *Beyond Necessity: Art in the Folk Tradition.* New York: W. W. Norton for the Henry Francis du Pont Winterthur Museum.

Anderson, Chris. 2008. "The End of Theory." *Wired* (July): 108–9.

———. 2010. "The Web Is Dead, Who's to Blame: Us." *Wired* (September): 123–27.

Anderson, Lars. 2007. *Carlisle vs. Army: Jim Thorpe, Dwight Eisenhower, Pop Warner and the Forgotten Story of Football's Greatest Battle.* New York: Random House.

Anderson, Walter. 1951. *Ein volksundliches Experiment.* FF Communications 141. Helsinki: Academia Scientiarum Fennica.

———. 1956. *Eine neue Arbeit zur experimentellen Volkskunde.* FF Communications 168. Helsinki: Academia Scientiarum Fennica.

Applebaum, Charley. 1999. "Undser Lehrer Moshe" [Our Teacher Moses] *Der Onheib* 28: 3.

Aron, Jaime. 2008. "Cowboys Win Shootout." *Patriot-News* (Harrisburg, Pa.), September 16, Sports 3.

Associated Press. 2010. "Federal Appeals Court Rules against Utah Memorial Crosses along Highway." *FoxNews.com*, August 18. http://www.foxnews.com/us/2010/08/18/federal-appeals-court-rules-utah-memorial-crosses-highway/ (accessed September 2, 2010).

Augusto, David. 1970. "Network Analysis: A Contribution to the Theory of Folklore Transmission." *Folklore Forum* 3: 78–90.

Austin, J. L. 1961. *Philosophical Papers.* Oxford: Clarendon Press.

———. 1968. *How to Do Things with Words.* New York: Oxford University Press.

Austin, Michael W., ed. 2008. *Football and Philosophy: Going Deep.* Lexington: University Press of Kentucky.

Bacchilega, Cristina. 1997. *Postmodern Fairy Tales: Gender and Narrative Strategies.* Philadelphia: University of Pennsylvania Press.

Bachrach, Arthur J. 1962. "An Experimental Approach to Superstitious Behavior." *Journal of American Folklore* 75: 1–9.

Baker, Ronald L., and Simon J. Bronner. 2005. "'Letting Out Jack': Sex and Aggression in Manly Recitations." In *Manly Traditions: The Folk Roots of American Masculinities*, ed. Simon J. Bronner, 315–50. Bloomington: Indiana University Press.

Bar-Itzhak, Haya. 1990. "Modes of Characterization in Religious Narrative:

Jewish Folk Legends about Miracle Worker Rabbis." *Journal of Folklore Research* 27: 205–30.

———. 2001. *Jewish Poland—Legends of Origin: Ethnopoetics and Legendary Chronicles.* Detroit: Wayne State University Press.

Barone, Michael. 1994. "A History of Culture Wars." *U.S. News & World Report,* August 1, 40.

Barrick, Mac. 1969. "Pulpit Humor in Central Pennsylvania." *Pennsylvania Folklife* 19 (1): 28–36.

———. 1982. "Celebrity Sick Jokes." *Maledicta: International Journal of Verbal Aggression* 6: 57–62.

———. 1987a. Correspondence with Simon J. Bronner, October 8.

———. 1987b. *German-American Folklore.* Little Rock, Ark.: August House.

Barry, Phillips, and Fannie Hardy Eckstorm. 1930. "What Is Tradition?" *Bulletin of the Folk-Song Society of the Northeast* 1: 2–3.

Bartlett, F. C. 1965. "Some Experiments on the Reproduction of Folk Stories." In *The Study of Folklore,* ed. Alan Dundes, 243–64. Englewood Cliffs, N.J.: Prentice-Hall.

Bascom, William R. 1954. "Four Functions of Folklore." *Journal of American Folklore* 67: 333–49.

———. 1955. "Verbal Art." *Journal of American Folklore* 68: 245–52.

———. 1965 [1953]. "Folklore and Anthropology." In *The Study of Folklore,* ed. Alan Dundes, 25–33. Englewood Cliffs, N.J.: Prentice-Hall.

Bauman, Richard. 1969. "Towards a Behavioral Theory of Folklore." *Journal of American Folklore* 82: 167–70.

———. 1972. "Differential Identity and the Social Base of Folklore." In *Toward New Perspectives in Folklore,* ed. Américo Paredes and Richard Bauman, 31–41. Austin: University of Texas Press.

———. 1977. *Verbal Art as Performance.* Rowley, Mass.: Newbury House.

———. 1983. "Folklore and the Forces of Modernity." *Folklore Forum* 16: 153–58.

———. 1992a. "Folklore." In *Folklore, Cultural Performances, and Popular Entertainments: A Communications-Centered Handbook,* ed. Richard Bauman, 29–40. New York: Oxford University Press.

———. 1992b. "Performance." In *Folklore, Cultural Performances, and Popular Entertainments: A Communications-Centered Handbook,* ed. Richard Bauman, 41–49. New York: Oxford University Press.

Bauman, Richard, and Charles L. Briggs. 2003. *Voices of Modernity: Language Ideologies and the Politics of Inequality.* Cambridge: Cambridge University Press.

Bauman, Zygmunt. 1973. *Culture as Praxis.* London: Routledge & Kegan Paul.

Baver, Mrs. Russell S. 1953a. "Of Brooms and Cleaning." *Pennsylvania Dutchman* 5 (October): 5, 12.

———. 1953b. "Housebutzing." *Pennsylvania Dutchman* 5 (November): 7–8.

Bayard, Samuel. 1953. "The Materials of Folklore." *Journal of American Folklore* 66: 1–17.

Bealle, Morris A. 1948. *The History of Football at Harvard, 1874–1948.* Washington, D.C.: Columbia Publishing.

Beam, C. Richard, ed. 1995. *The Thomas R. Brendle Collection of Pennsylvania German Folklore*. Schaefferstown, Pa.: Historic Schaefferstown.

Beatty, Roger Dean. 1976. "Computerlore: The Bit Bucket." *New York Folklore* 2: 223–24.

Belden, Henry M., and Arthur Palmer Hudson, eds. 1952. *The Frank C. Brown Collection of North Carolina Folklore*. Vol. 3. *Folk Songs from North Carolina*. Durham, N.C.: Duke University Press.

Bellah, Robert N., Richard Madsen, William M. Sullivan, Ann Swidler, and Steven M. Tipton. 1996. *Habits of the Heart: Individualism and Commitment in American Life*. Updated ed. Berkeley: University of California Press.

Belliotti, Raymond Angelo. 2008. "Vince Lombardi and the Philosophy of Winning." In *Football and Philosophy: Going Deep*, ed. Michael W. Austin, 5–17. Lexington: University Press of Kentucky.

Ben-Amos, Dan. 1972. "Toward a Definition of Folklore in Context." In *Toward New Perspectives in Folklore*, ed. Américo Paredes and Richard Bauman, 3–15. Austin: University of Texas Press.

———. 1984. "The Seven Strands of *Tradition*: Varieties in Its Meaning in American Folklore Studies." *Journal of Folklore Research* 21: 97–131.

Bendix, Regina. 1997. *In Search for Authenticity: The Formation of Folklore Studies*. Madison: University of Wisconsin Press.

Benjamin, Walter. 2007 [1936]. "The Work of Art in the Age of Mechanical Reproduction." In *Illuminations: Essays and Reflections*, ed. Hannah Arendt, 217–52. New York: Schocken.

Bennett, William J., ed. 1993. *The Book of Virtues: A Treasury of Great Moral Stories*. New York: Simon & Schuster.

Berkhof, Hendrikus. 2002. *Christian Faith: An Introduction to the Study of the Faith*, trans. Sierd Woudstra. Rev. ed. Grand Rapids, Mich.: William B. Eerdmans.

Bernstein, Richard. 1971. *Praxis and Action: Contemporary Philosophies of Human Activity*. Philadelphia: University of Pennsylvania Press.

Bettelheim, Bruno. 1976. *The Uses of Enchantment: The Meaning and Importance of Fairy Tales*. New York: Knopf.

Bianculli, David, and Gail Shister. 1987. "How TV Covered the Dwyer Suicide." *Philadelphia Inquirer*, January 23, D1.

Bidell, Thomas R., and Kurt W. Fischer. 1992. "Beyond the Stage Debate: Action, Structure, and Variability in Piagetian Theory and Research." In *Intellectual Development*, ed. Robert J. Sternberg and Cynthia A. Berg, 100–140. Cambridge: Cambridge University Press.

Biedermann, Hans. 1994. *Dictionary of Symbolism: Cultural Icons and the Meanings behind Them*. New York: Penguin.

Binary Jokes. 2008. *Englishforums.com: The World's Largest EFL/TEFL Social Network*. Forum page. http://www.englishforums.com/English/BinaryJoke/2/kvbc/Post.htm (accessed June 13, 2008).

Bishop, Julia C., and Mavis Curtis, eds. 2001. *Play Today in the Primary School Playground*. Buckingham, U.K.: Open University Press.

Bissinger, H. G. 1990. *Friday Night Lights: A Town, a Team, and a Dream*. Reading, Mass.: Addison-Wesley.

Blank, Trevor J. 2009. "Toward a Conceptual Framework for the Study of Folklore and the Internet." In *Folklore and the Internet: Vernacular Expression in a Digital World*, ed. Trevor J. Blank, 1–20. Logan: Utah State University Press.

Blasdel, Gregg N. 1968. "The Grass-Roots Artist." *Art in America* 56: 24–41.

Blumenreich, Beth, and Bari Lynn Polonsky. 1974. "Re-evaluating the Concept of Group: ICEN as an Alternative." *Folklore Forum* (Bibliographic and Special Series No. 12): 12–18.

Boatright, Mody. 1949. *Folk Laughter on the American Frontier.* New York: Macmillan.

Bonneville, Patrick, ed. 2006. *The World Heritage.* Saint Hubert, Quebec: Bonneville Connection.

Bookstein, Jonah. 1995. Correspondence with Simon J. Bronner, January 17.

Boorstin, Daniel J. 1993. *The Lost World of Thomas Jefferson.* Rev. ed. Chicago: University of Chicago Press.

Borneman, Henry S. 1944. "Foreword." In *Pennsylvania German Folk Tales, Legends, Once-upon-a-Time Stories, Maxims, and Sayings: Spoken in the Dialect Popularly Known as Pennsylvania Dutch*, ed. Thomas R. Brendle and William S. Troxell, 5–7. Norristown, Pa.: Pennsylvania German Society.

Botkin, B. A. 1944. *A Treasury of American Folklore: Stories, Ballads, and Traditions of the People.* New York: Crown.

———. 1949. *A Treasury of Southern Folklore: Stories, Ballads, Traditions, and Folkways of the People of the South.* New York: Crown.

———. 1951. *A Treasury of Western Folklore.* New York: Crown.

Bottigheimer, Ruth B. 1985. Review of *Life Is Like a Chicken Coop Ladder: A Portrait of German Culture through Folklore* by Alan Dundes. *German Studies Review* 8: 527–28.

"Bottle Houses." 2010. http://www.bottlehouses.com/about.cfm#62 (accessed August 20, 2010).

Bouchette, Ed. 2008. "Steelers Notebook: Polamalu Criticizes Current State of NFL." *Pittsburgh Post-Gazette*, October 16. http://www.post-gazette.com/pg/08290/920304-66.stm (accessed February 10, 2009).

Bourdieu, Pierre. 1990. *The Logic of Practice*, trans. Richard Nice. Stanford, Calif.: Stanford University Press.

———. 1998. *Practical Reason: On the Theory of Action.* Stanford, Calif.: Stanford University Press.

Bourke, John G. 1891. *Scatalogic Rites of All Nations.* Washington, D.C.: W. H. Lowdermilk.

Boyer, Troy R. 1997. "The Forsaken Founder, William John Thoms: From Antiquities to Folklore." *Folklore Historian* 14: 55–61.

Brackman, Barbara. 1999. "Remember the Grotto: Individual and Community." In *Backyard Visionaries: Grassroots Art in the Midwest*, ed. Barbara Brackman and Cathy Dwigans, 20–28. Lawrence: University Press of Kansas.

Brackman, Barbara, and Cathy Dwigans, eds. 1999. *Backyard Visionaries: Grassroots Art in the Midwest.* Lawrence: University Press of Kansas.

Bradbery, Angela, and Robin Fields. 1997. "Memorial Markers Protested." January 1. http://articles.sun-sentinel.com/1997-01-01/news/9612310562_1_roadside-memorials-homemade-memorials-dot (accessed September 2, 2010).

Braid, Donald, and Moira Smith. 1993. "Cumulative Index 1979–1993." *Journal of Folklore Research* 30: 201–35.

Brandes, Stanley H. 1983. "Jewish-American Dialect Jokes and Jewish-American Identity." *Jewish Social Studies* 45: 233–40.

———. 1985. *Forty: The Age and the Symbol.* Knoxville: University of Tennessee Press.

Brendle, Thomas R. 1985. "*Unser Pennilfaanisch Deitsch Volk*/Our Pennsylvania German People." *Historic Schaefferstown Record* 19 (April): 20–35.

Brendle, Thomas R., and William S. Troxell, eds. 1944. *Pennsylvania German Folk Tales, Legends, Once-upon-a-Time Stories, Maxims, and Sayings: Spoken in the Dialect Popularly Known as Pennsylvania Dutch.* Norristown, Pa.: Pennsylvania German Society.

Brewster, Paul G. 1953. *American Nonsinging Games.* Norman: University of Oklahoma Press.

Brisson, Luc. 2000. *Plato the Myth Maker*, trans. Gerard Naddaf. Chicago: University of Chicago Press.

Britt, Steuart Henderson, and Margaret M. Balcom. 1941. "Jumping-Rope Rhymes and the Social Psychology of Play." *Journal of Genetic Psychology* 58: 289–306.

Bronner, Simon J. 1977. "Concrete Folklore: Sidewalk Box Games." *Western Folklore* 36:171–73.

———. 1978. "'Who Says?' A Further Investigation of Ritual Insults among White American Adolescents." *Midwestern Journal of Language and Folklore* 4: 53–69.

———. 1979a. "Concepts in the Study of Material Aspects of American Folk Culture." *Folklore Forum* 12: 117–32.

———. 1979b. "Eugene Powell: 'Sonny Boy Nelson.'" *Living Blues*, no. 43 (summer): 14–25.

———. 1982a. ". . . Feeling's the Truth." *Tennessee Folklore Society Bulletin* 48: 117–24.

———. 1982b. "Malaise or Revelation? Observations on the 'American Folklore' Polemic." *Western Folklore* 41: 52–61.

———. 1982c. "Special Section: Historical Methodology in Folkloristics." *Western Folklore* 41: 28–29.

———. 1984. "Toward a Philosophy of Folk Objects." In *Personal Places: Perspectives on Informal Art Environments*, ed. Daniel Franklin Ward, 171–77. Bowling Green, Ohio: Bowling Green State University Popular Press.

———. 1985a. "Researching Material Folk Culture in the Modern American City." In *American Material Culture and Folklife*, ed. Simon J. Bronner, 237–43. Ann Arbor, Mich.: UMI Research Press.

———. 1985b. "'What's Grosser than Gross?' New Sick Joke Cycles." *Midwestern Journal of Language and Folklore* 11: 39–49.

———. 1986a. *American Folklore Studies: An Intellectual History*. Lawrence: University Press of Kansas.

———. 1986b. *Grasping Things: Folk Material Culture and Mass Society in America*. Lexington: University Press of Kentucky.

———. 1988a. *American Children's Folklore*. Little Rock, Ark.: August House.

———. 1988b. "Art, Performance, and Praxis: The Rhetoric of Contemporary Folklore Studies." *Western Folklore* 47: 75–102.

———. 1988c. "Political Suicide: The Budd Dwyer Joke Cycle and the Humor of Disaster." *Midwestern Folklore* 14: 81–90.

———, ed. 1992a. *Creativity and Tradition in Folklore: New Directions*. Logan: Utah State University Press.

———. 1992b. "Elaborating Tradition: A Pennsylvania German Folk Artist Ministers to His Community." In *Creativity and Tradition in Folklore: New Directions*, ed. Simon J. Bronner, 277–326. Logan: Utah State University Press.

———. 1995. *Piled Higher and Deeper: The Folklore of Student Life*. Little Rock, Ark.: August House.

———. 1996a. *The Carver's Art: Crafting Meaning from Wood*. Lexington: University Press of Kentucky.

———. 1996b. "*Epes Tsoiberhaftes*: The Rhetoric of Folklore and History in Jacob Seifter's Memoirs of Auschwitz." *Yiddish* 10: 17–46.

———. 1996c. "Pennsylvania Germans ('Dutch')." In *American Folklore: An Encyclopedia*, ed. Jan Harold Brunvand, 549–54. New York: Garland.

———. 1998. *Following Tradition: Folklore in the Discourse of American Culture*. Logan: Utah State University Press.

———. 1999. "Cultural Historical Studies of Jews in Pennsylvania: A Review and Preview." *Pennsylvania History* 66: 311–38.

———. 2000a. "The American Concept of Tradition: Folklore in the Discourse of Traditional Values." *Western Folklore* 59: 143–70.

———. 2000b. "The Meanings of Tradition: An Introduction." *Western Folklore* 59: 87–104.

———, ed. 2000c. "The Meanings of Tradition." Special Issue, *Western Folklore* 59, no. 2 (winter).

———. 2002a. *Folk Nation: Folklore in the Creation of American Tradition*. Wilmington, Del.: SR Books.

———. 2002b. "Questioning the Future: Polling Americans at the Turn of the New Millennium." In *Prospects: An Annual of American Cultural Studies*, vol. 27, ed. Jack Salzman, 665–85. New York: Cambridge University Press.

———. 2005a. "Contesting Tradition: The Deep Play and Protest of Pigeon Shoots." *Journal of American Folklore* 118: 409–52.

———. 2005b. "Hidden Erections and Sexual Fabrications: Old Men Crafting Manliness." In *Manly Traditions: The Folk Roots of American Masculinities*, ed. Simon J. Bronner, 274–314. Bloomington: Indiana University Press.

———. 2005c. "Menfolk." In *Manly Traditions: The Folk Roots of American Masculinities*, ed. Simon J. Bronner, 1–60. Bloomington: Indiana University Press.

———. 2005d. "Plain Folk and Folk Society: John A. Hostetler's Legacy of the Little Community." In *Writing the Amish: The Worlds of John A. Hostetler,* ed. David Weaver-Zercher, 56–97. University Park: Pennsylvania State University Press.

———. 2006a. "Folk Logic: Interpretation and Explanation in Folkloristics." *Western Folklore* 65: 401–34.

———. 2006b. "Pennsylvania Culture Region." In *Encyclopedia of American Folklife,* ed. Simon J. Bronner, 942–44. Armonk, N.Y.: M. E. Sharpe.

———. 2007. "The Analytics of Alan Dundes." In *The Meaning of Folklore: The Analytic Essays of Alan Dundes,* ed. Simon J. Bronner, 1–50. Logan: Utah State University Press.

———. 2008. *Killing Tradition: Inside Hunting and Animal Rights Controversies.* Lexington: University Press of Kentucky.

———. 2008–2009. "Fathers and Sons: Rethinking the Bar Mitzvah as an American Rite of Passage." *Children's Folklore Review* 31: 7–34.

———. 2010. "Framing Folklore: An Introduction." *Western Folklore* 69: 5–27.

———. 2011. "The Rise and Fall—and Return—of the Class Rush: A Study of a Contested Tradition." *Western Folklore* 70: 5–67.

Brophy, John, and Eric Partridge. 1965. *The Long Trail: What the British Soldier Sang and Said in 1914–1918.* New York: London House & Maxwell.

Brown, Clifton. 2002. "Augusta Answers Critics on Policy." *New York Times,* July 10. http://query.nytimes.com/gst/fullpage.html?res=9906E0D61430 F933A25754C0A9649C8B63 (accessed January 16, 2009).

Brown, Marice C. 1979. *Amen, Brother Ben: A Mississippi Collection of Children's Rhymes.* Jackson: University Press of Mississippi.

Brown, Melissa. 2008. "Introduction: Developing a Scientific Paradigm for Understanding Culture." In *Explaining Culture Scientifically,* ed. Melissa J. Brown, 3–16. Seattle: University of Washington Press.

Browne, Ray B. 1954. "Negro Folktales from Alabama." *Southern Folklore Quarterly* 18: 129–34.

———. 1955. "Southern California Jump-Rope Rhymes: A Study in Variants." *Western Folklore* 14: 3–22.

Brunkhorst, Hauke. 2004. "Critical Theory and the Analysis of Contemporary Mass Society." In *The Cambridge Companion to Critical Theory,* ed. Fred Rush, 248–79. Cambridge: Cambridge University Press.

Brunvand, Jan Harold. 1963. "A Classification for Shaggy Dog Stories." *Journal of American Folklore* 76: 42–68.

———. 1998. *The Study of American Folklore: An Introduction.* 4th ed. New York: W. W. Norton.

———. 2001. *Encyclopedia of Urban Legends.* Santa Barbara, Calif.: ABC-CLIO.

"Budd Dwyer." 2008. *Urban Dictionary* website. http://www.urbandictionary .com/define.php?term=Budd+Dwyer&defid=2397819 (accessed September 22, 2008).

"Budd Dwyer: From Uncyclopedia, the Content-Free Encyclopedia." 2008. *Uncyclopedia.org,* July 24. Wiki. http://uncyclopedia.org/wiki/Budd_Dwyer (accessed July 26, 2008).

Buffington, Albert F., and Preston A. Barba. 1954. *A Pennsylvania German Grammar.* Allentown, Pa.: Schlechters.

Bulger, Peggy A. 1992. "Can't We Pass on Fairy Tales without Being Accused of Satanism?" *Atlanta Journal,* November 6, A11.

Burger, T. W. 2002. "Signs of Grieving: Crosses Help Families Mourn for Traffic Victims." *Sunday Patriot-News* (Harrisburg, Pa.), August 11, A1, A20.

Burnett, Jacquetta Hill. 1969. "Ceremony, Rites, Economy in the Student System of an American High School." *Human Organization* 28: 1–10.

Burnham, Smith, and Theodore H. Jack. 1934. *America, Our Country.* Philadelphia: John C. Winston.

Burns, Gerald L. 1991. "What Is Tradition?" *New Literary History* 22: 1–22.

Burns, Thomas A. 1977. "Folkloristics: A Conception of Theory." *Western Folklore* 36: 109–34.

Burr, Elizabeth, trans. 1994. *The Chiron Dictionary of Greek and Roman Mythology: Gods and Goddesses, Heroes, Places, and Events of Antiquity.* Wilmette, Ill.: Chiron.

Bushman, Richard. 1993. *The Refinement of America: Persons, Houses, Cities.* New York: Knopf.

Cahan, Y. L. 1938. *Yidisher folklor: Filogische shriftn fun YIVO.* Vilna: YIVO.

———. 1952. *Shtudies Vegn Yidisher Folksshafung.* New York: Yiddish Scientific Institute–YIVO.

Cahill, Holger. 1932. *American Folk Art: The Art of the Common Man in America, 1750–1900.* New York: Museum of Modern Art.

Camp, Walter. 1894. *American Football.* New York: Harper & Brothers.

Canning, Shelagh. 1996. *Honesty: Zach's Tall Tale.* New York: Aladdin Paperbacks.

Cannon, Hal, ed. 1980. *Utah Folk Art: A Catalog of Material Culture.* Provo, Utah: Brigham Young University Press.

Cantú, Norma E. 2002. "Chicana Life-Cycle Rituals." In *Chicana Traditions: Continuity and Change,* ed. Norma E. Cantú and Olga Nájera-Ramírez, 15–34. Urbana: University of Illinois Press.

———. 2005. "*Muy Macho:* Traditional Practices in the Formation of Latino Masculinity in South Texas Border Culture." In *Manly Traditions: The Folk Roots of American Masculinities,* ed. Simon J. Bronner, 116–33. Bloomington: Indiana University Press.

Carawan, Guy, and Candie Carawan, comps. and eds. 1990. *Sing for Freedom: The Story of the Civil Rights Movement through Its Songs.* Bethlehem, Pa.: Sing Out.

Cardinal, Roger. 1972. *Outsider Art.* New York: Praeger.

Carroll, Michael P. 1987. "'The Castrated Boy': Another Contribution to the Psychoanalytic Study of Urban Legends." *Folklore* 98: 216–25.

Childs, Peter. 2000. *Modernism.* London: Routledge.

Chisholm, Hugh, ed. 1910. *Encyclopaedia Britannica: A Dictionary of Arts, Sciences, Literature and General Information.* Cambridge: Cambridge University Press.

Cincotta, Nancy F. 2002. "The Journey of Middle Childhood: Who Are 'Latency'-Age Children?" In *Developmental Theories through the Life Cycle*, ed. Sonia G. Austrian, 69–122. New York: Columbia University Press.

Clark, Cindy Dell. 1995. *Flights of Fancy, Leaps of Faith: Children's Myths in Contemporary America.* Chicago: University of Chicago Press.

Clark, Michael D. 2005. *The American Discovery of Tradition, 1865–1942.* Baton Rouge: Louisiana State University Press.

Clements, William M. 1997. "Oikotype/Oicotype." In *Folklore: An Encyclopedia of Beliefs, Customs, Tales, Music, and Art*, 2 vols., ed. Thomas A. Green, 2:604–5. Santa Barbara, Calif.: ABC-CLIO.

Clinton, Hillary Rodham. 1996. *It Takes a Village: And Other Lessons Children Teach Us.* New York: Simon & Schuster.

Cochrane, Timothy. 1987. "The Concept of Ecotypes in American Folklore." *Journal of Folklore Research* 24: 33–55.

Cohen, Rosalie A. 1969. "Conceptual Styles, Cultural Conflict, and Nonverbal Tests of Intelligence." *American Anthropologist* 5: 828–56.

Coleman, James S. 1961. *The Adolescent Society: The Social Life of the Teenager and Its Impact on Education.* New York: Free Press.

Collier, Price. 1898. "Sport's Place in the Nation's Well-Being." *Outing* 32: 382–88.

Collins, Charles O., and Charles D. Rhine. 2003. "Roadside Memorials." *Omega: Journal of Death and Dying* 47: 221–44.

Collofino. 1939. *Non olet; oder, Die heiteren Tischgespräche des Collofino über den orbis cacatus, nebst den neuesten erkenntnistheoretischen Betrachtungen über das Leben in seiner phantastischen Wirklichkeit erzählt von ihm selbst.* Cologne: Privatdruck.

Congar, Yves. 2004 [1964]. *The Meaning of Tradition*, trans. A. N. Woodrow. San Francisco: Ignatius Press.

Conquerwood, Dwight. 1992. "Fabricating Culture: The Textile Art of Hmong Refugee Women." In *Performance, Culture, and Identity*, ed. Jean Haskell Speer, 206–48. New York: Praeger.

Cossar, Harper. 2005. "Televised Golf and the Creation of Narrative." *Film and History: An Interdisciplinary Journal of Film and Television Studies* 35: 52–59.

Craggs, Tommy. 2008. "Why Are Wide Receivers Such Flamboyant Egomaniacs?" *Play: The New York Times Sports Magazine*, September, 42–43.

Cray, Ed. 1970. "Jump-Rope Rhymes from Los Angeles." *Western Folklore* 29: 119–27.

———. 1992. *The Erotic Muse: American Bawdy Songs.* 2nd ed. Urbana: University of Illinois Press.

Cross, Gary S. 2004. *The Cute and the Cool: Wondrous Innocence and Modern American Children's Culture.* New York: Oxford University Press.

———. 2008. *Men to Boys: The Making of Modern Immaturity.* New York: Columbia University Press.

Crosswell, T. R. 1899. "Amusements of Worcester School Children." *Journal of Genetic Psychology* 6: 314–71.

Cunningham, Ken. 2004. "True Confessions of an Eight-Year-Old Warrior." *Qualitative Inquiry* 10: 706–14.

Cusick, Frederick, Dan Meyers, and Walter F. Roche Jr. 1987. "Treasurer Dwyer Kills Self: Suicide at News Session." *Philadelphia Inquirer,* January 23, 1, 16A.

Dance, Daryl Cumber. 1978. *Shuckin' and Jivin': Folklore from Contemporary Black Americans.* Bloomington: Indiana University Press.

D'Andrade, Roy. 1999. "Culture Is Not Everything." In *Anthropological Theory in North America,* ed. E. L. Cerroni-Long, 85–104. Westport, Conn.: Bergin & Garvey.

———. 2008. "Some Kinds of Causal Powers that Make up Culture." In *Explaining Culture Scientifically,* ed. Melissa J. Brown, 19–36. Seattle: University of Washington Press.

Daniel. 2008. MySpace blog, February 18. http://blog.myspace.com (accessed September 26, 2008).

Daniels, Ted. 1981. "A Philadelphia Squatter's Shack: Urban Pioneering." *Pioneer America: Journal of Historic American Material Culture* 13: 43–48.

Dardel, Eric. 1984 [1954]. "The Mythic." In *Sacred Narrative: Readings in the Theory of Myth,* ed. Alan Dundes, 225–43. Berkeley: University of California Press.

Dargan, Amanda, and Steven Zeitlin. 1990. *City Play.* New Brunswick, N.J.: Rutgers University Press.

Davies, Christie. 2003. "Jokes that Follow Mass-Mediated Disasters in a Global Electronic Age." In *Of Corpse: Death and Humor in Folklore and Popular Culture,* ed. Peter Narváez, 35–82. Logan: Utah State University Press.

Davis, Karen. 2002. "The Dignity, Beauty, and Abuse of Chickens: As Symbols and in Reality." Paper presented at the International Conference on "The Chicken: Its Biological, Social, Cultural, and Industrial History," Yale University, New Haven, Conn., May 17–19, 2002. Available at http://www.upc-online.org/thinking/dignity.html (accessed September 23, 2005).

Davis, Parke Hill. 1912. *Football: The American Intercollegiate Game.* New York: Scribner's.

Davison, Scott A. 2008. "Virtue and Violence: Can a Good Football Player Be a Good Person?" In *Football and Philosophy: Going Deep,* ed. Michael W. Austin, 67–79. Lexington: University Press of Kentucky.

De Caro, Francis A. 1976. "Concepts of the Past in Folkloristics." *Western Folklore* 35: 3–22.

De Certeau, Michel. 1984. *The Practice of Everyday Life,* trans. Steven Rendall. Berkeley: University of California Press.

Decker, Nancy M. 1986. Review of *Life Is Like a Chicken Coop Ladder: A Portrait of German Culture through Folklore* by Alan Dundes. *German Quarterly* 59: 343–44.

Decker, Theodore. 2002. "Man Charged in 6 Deaths Doesn't Grasp Reality of Horrific Area Crash, Father Says." *Patriot-News* (Harrisburg, Pa.), July 19, A1, 12.

Dégh, Linda. 1985. "Dial a Story, Dial an Audience: Two Rural Women Narrators in an Urban Setting." In *Women's Folklore, Women's Culture*, ed. Rosan A. Jordan and Susan J. Kalčik, 3–25. Philadelphia: University of Pennsylvania Press.

———. 1992. "The Legend Conduit." In *Creativity and Tradition: New Directions*, ed. Simon J. Bronner, 105–26. Logan: Utah State University Press.

———. 1994. *American Folklore and the Mass Media*. Bloomington: Indiana University Press.

———. 1997. "Conduit Theory/Multiconduit Theory." In *Folklore: An Encyclopedia of Beliefs, Customs, Tales, Music, and Art*, ed. Thomas A. Green, 142–44. Santa Barbara, Calif.: ABC-CLIO.

Dégh, Linda, and Andrew Vázsonyi. 1975. "The Hypothesis of Multi-Conduit Transmission of Folklore." In *Folklore: Performance and Communication*, ed. Dan Ben-Amos, and Kenneth Goldstein, 207–52. The Hague: Mouton.

Denisoff, R. Serge. 1971. *Great Day Coming: Folk Music and the American Left*. Urbana: University of Illinois Press.

Denzin, Norman K. 1975. "Play, Games and Interaction: The Contexts of Childhood Socialization." *Sociological Quarterly* 16: 458–78.

DeSantis, Alan D. 2007. *Inside Greek U: Fraternities, Sororities, and the Pursuit of Pleasure, Power, and Prestige*. Lexington: University Press of Kentucky.

De Saussure, Ferdinand. 1972. "Course in General Linguistics." In *The Structuralists from Marx to Lévi-Strauss*, ed. Richard DeGeorge and Fernande DeGeorge, 59–79. Garden City, N.Y.: Doubleday.

Dewhurst, C. Kurt. 1984. "The Arts of Working: Manipulating the Urban Work Environment." *Western Folklore* 43: 192–202.

———. 1986. *Grand Ledge Folk Pottery: Traditions at Work*. Ann Arbor. Mich.: UMI Research Press.

Dewhurst, C. Kurt, and Marsha MacDowell. 1983. "The Conduit Tile Buildings of Grand Ledge, Michigan." *Pioneer America: Journal of Historic Material Culture* 15: 91–104.

Dewhurst, Marit. 1996. "Beyond the Field: The Traditions of a High School Homecoming." *Michigan Folklife Annual*, 51–55.

Diffenderffer, Frank R. 1891. "Introductory." *The Pennsylvania-German Society: Sketch of Its Origin, with the Proceedings and Addresses at Its Organization, Lancaster, April 15th, 1891*, v–viii. Lancaster, Pa.: Pennsylvania German Society.

Dobler, Robert. 2009. "Ghosts in the Machine: Mourning the MySpace Dead." In *Folklore and the Internet: Vernacular Expression in a Digital World*, ed. Trevor J. Blank, 175–93. Logan: Utah State University Press.

Dodson, Victor. 1969. *The World's Dirtiest Jokes*. Los Angeles: Medco.

Dokupil, Susanna. 2005. "Thou Shalt Not Bear False Witness: 'Sham' Secular Purposes in Ten Commandments Displays." *Harvard Journal of Law and Public Policy* 28: 609–50.

Domi, Loser. 2008. *The Wonderful World of Loser Domi*. Blog, June 26. http://wwold.blogspot.com/2008_06_01_archive.html (accessed September 25, 2008).

Donald, Merlin. 1991. *Origins of the Modern Mind: Three Stages in the Evolution of Culture and Cognition.* Cambridge, Mass.: Harvard University Press.

Doroshkin, Milton. 1969. *Yiddish in America: Social and Cultural Foundations.* Rutherford, N.J.: Fairleigh Dickinson University Press.

Dorson, Richard M. 1949. "Dialect Stories of the Upper Peninsula: A New Form of American Folklore." *Journal of American Folklore* 61: 133–46.

———, ed. 1964. *Buying the Wind: Regional Folklore in the United States.* Chicago: University of Chicago Press.

———. 1967. *American Negro Folktales.* Greenwich, Conn.: Fawcett.

———. 1970. "Is There a Folk in the City?" *Journal of American Folklore* 83: 185–216.

———. 1971. *American Folklore and the Historian.* Chicago: University of Chicago Press.

———. 1972. "Introduction: Concepts of Folklore and Folklife Studies." In *Folklore and Folklife: An Introduction,* ed. Richard M. Dorson, 1–50. Chicago: University of Chicago Press.

———. 1975. "Comment on Williams." *Journal of the Folklore Institute* 11: 235–39.

———. 1976. *Folklore and Fakelore: Essays toward a Discipline of Folk Studies.* Cambridge, Mass.: Harvard University Press.

———. 1978a. "Folklore in the Modern World." In *Folklore in the Modern World,* ed. Richard M. Dorson, 11–54. The Hague: Mouton.

———. 1978b. "We All Need the Folk." *Journal of the Folklore Institute* 15: 267–69.

Dorst, John. 1990. "Tags and Burners, Cycles and Networks: Folklore in the Telectronic Age." *Journal of Folklore Research* 27: 179–89.

Dougherty, Barry, and H. Aaron Cohl. 2009. *The Friars Club Encyclopedia of Jokes.* New York: Black Dog & Leventhal.

Douglas, Ann. 1978. *The Feminization of American Culture.* New York: Anchor Press/Doubleday.

Douglas, Mary. 1975. *Implicit Meanings: Selected Essays in Anthropology.* London: Routledge & Kegan Paul.

Douglas, Nick. 2008. "90 Day Jane Not Killing Herself, Not as Hot as You Hoped." *Gawker,* February 13. http://gawker.com/356131/90-day-jane-not-killing-herself-not-as-hot-as-you-hoped (accessed September 22, 2008).

Dow, James R., and Hannjost Lixfeld, eds. 1994. *The Nazification of an Academic Discipline: Folklore in the Third Reich.* Bloomington: Indiana University Press.

Doyle, Charles Clay. 2009. "Fakelore: Richard Dorson and His Coinage." *Folklore Historian* 26: 51–58.

Doyon, Paul. 2001. "A Review of Higher Education Reform in Modern Japan." *Higher Education* 41: 443–70.

Drout, Michael D. C. 2006. "A Meme-Based Approach to Oral Traditional Theory." *Oral Tradition* 21: 269–94.

Dundes, Alan. 1962a. "Earth-Diver: Creation of the Mythopoeic Male." *American Anthropologist* 65: 1032–51.

———. 1962b. "From Etic to Emic Units in the Structural Study of Folktales." *Journal of American Folklore* 75: 95–105.

———. 1964a. "On Game Morphology: A Study of the Structure of Non-Verbal Folklore." *New York Folklore Quarterly* 20: 276–88.

———. 1964b. *The Morphology of North American Indian Folktales.* Helsinki: Academia Scientiarum Fennica.

———. 1965a. "The Study of Folklore in Literature and Culture: Identification and Interpretation." *Journal of American Folklore* 78: 136–42.

———. 1965b. "What Is Folklore?" In *The Study of Folklore*, ed. Alan Dundes, 1–3. Englewood Cliffs, N.J.: Prentice-Hall.

———. 1966. "The American Concept of Folklore." *Journal of the Folklore Institute* 3: 226–49.

———. 1968. "The Number Three in American Culture." In *Every Man His Way: Readings in Cultural Anthropology*, ed. Alan Dundes, 401–23. Englewood Cliffs, N.J.: Prentice-Hall.

———. 1969a. "The Devolutionary Premise in Folklore Theory." *Journal of the Folklore Institute* 6: 5–19.

———. 1969b. "Folklore as a Mirror of Culture." *Elementary English* 46: 471–82.

———. 1969c. "Thinking Ahead: A Folkloristic Reflection of the Future Orientation in American Worldview." *Anthropological Quarterly* 42: 53–72.

———. 1975. "The Psychology of Collecting Folklore." In *Analytic Essays in Folklore* by Alan Dundes, 121–29. The Hague: Mouton.

———. 1976. "Projection in Folklore: A Plea for Psychoanalytic Semiotics." *MLN* 91: 1500–1533.

———. 1978a. "Into the Endzone for a Touchdown: A Psychoanalytic Consideration of American Football." *Western Folklore* 37: 75–88.

———. 1978b [1976]. "Structuralism and Folklore." In *Essays in Folkloristics* by Alan Dundes, 178–206. Meerut, India: Folklore Institute.

———. 1980. *Interpreting Folklore.* Bloomington: Indiana University Press.

———. 1981. "Many Hands Make Light Work or Caught in the Act of Screwing in Light Bulbs." *Western Folklore* 40: 261–66.

———. 1982. "*Volkskunde, Völkerkunde* and the Study of German National Character." In *Europäische Ethnologie*, ed. Heide Nixdorff and Thomas Hauschild, 257–65. Berlin: Dietrich Reimer Verlag.

———. 1984. *Life Is Like a Chicken Coop Ladder: A Portrait of German Culture through Folklore.* New York: Columbia University Press.

———. 1987. *Cracking Jokes: Studies of Sick Humor Cycles and Stereotypes.* Berkeley, Calif.: Ten Speed Press.

———. 1994. "Towards a Metaphorical Reading of 'Break a Leg': A Note on the Folklore of the Stage." *Western Folklore* 53: 85–89.

———. 1997a. "The American Game of 'Smear the Queer' and the Homosexual Component of Male Competitive Sport and Warfare." In *Parsing through Customs: Essays by a Freudian Folklorist* by Alan Dundes, 178–96. Madison: University of Wisconsin Press.

———. 1997b. "The Motif-Index and the Tale Type Index: A Critique." *Journal of Folklore Research* 34: 195–202.

————. 1997c. "The Psychological Study of Folklore in the United States." In *From Game to War, and Other Psychoanalytic Essays on Folklore* by Alan Dundes, 1–24. Lexington: University Press of Kentucky.

————. 1997d. "Traditional Male Combat: From Game to War." In *From Game to War, and Other Psychoanalytic Essays on Folklore* by Alan Dundes, 25–45. Lexington: University Press of Kentucky.

————. 2002. *Bloody Mary in the Mirror: Essays in Psychoanalytic Folkloristics.* Jackson: University Press of Mississippi.

————. 2004. "As the Crow Flies: A Straightforward Study of Lineal Worldview in American Folk Speech." In *What Goes Around Comes Around: The Circulation of Proverbs in Contemporary Life*, ed. Kimberly J. Lau, Peter Tokofsky, and Stephen D. Winick, 171–87. Logan: Utah State University Press.

————. 2005. "Folkloristics in the Twenty-First Century." *Journal of American Folklore* 118: 385–408.

————. 2007a [1966]. "Here I Sit: A Study of American Latrinalia." In *The Meaning of Folklore: The Analytical Essays of Alan Dundes*, ed. Simon J. Bronner, 360–74. Logan: Utah State University Press.

————. 2007b [1966]. "Metafolklore and Oral Literary Criticism." In *The Meaning of Folklore: The Analytical Essays of Alan Dundes*, ed. Simon J. Bronner, 80–87. Logan: Utah State University Press.

Dundes, Alan, and Carl R. Pagter. 1975. *Urban Folklore from the Paperwork Empire.* Austin, Tex.: American Folklore Society.

————. 1987. *When You're Up to Your Ass in Alligators . . . : More Urban Folklore from the Paperwork Empire.* Detroit: Wayne State University Press.

————. 1991a. "The Mobile SCUD Missile Launcher and Other Persian Gulf Warlore: An American Folk Image of Saddam Hussein's Iraq." *Western Folklore* 50: 303–22.

————. 1991b. *Never Try to Teach a Pig to Sing: Still More Urban Folklore from the Paperwork Empire.* Detroit: Wayne State University Press.

————. 1996. *Sometimes the Dragon Wins: Yet More Urban Folklore from the Paperwork Empire.* Syracuse, N.Y.: Syracuse University Press.

Dundes, Alan, and Paul Renteln. 2005. "Foolproof: A Sampling of Mathematical Folk Humor." *Notices of the American Mathematical Society* 52: 24–34.

Durkheim, Emile. 1951. *Suicide: A Study in Sociology*, trans. Johna A. Spaulding and George Simpson. New York: Free Press.

Eaton, Allen. 1932. *Immigrant Gifts to American Life.* New York: Russell Sage Foundation.

————. 1937. *Handicrafts of the Southern Highlands.* New York: Russell Sage Foundation.

Editors of Roadside America. 2003. "The Flower Man." In *Roadside America*. http://www.roadsideamerica.com/attract/TXHOUflowerman.html (accessed July 31, 2007).

Egle, William H. 1892. "The Pennsylvania German: His Place in the History of the Commonwealth." *The Pennsylvania-German Society: Proceedings and Addresses*, 118–30. Lancaster, Pa.: Pennsylvania German Society.

Eidson, John R. 1984. Review of *Life Is Like a Chicken Coop Ladder: A Portrait of*

German Culture through Folklore by Alan Dundes. *Anthropological Quarterly* 57: 96–98.

Eisenstadt, S. N. 1969. "Some Observations on the Dynamics of Traditions." *Comparative Studies in Society and History* 11: 451–75.

Eisenstock, Alan. 2001. *Sports Talk: A Journey Inside the World of Sports Talk Radio.* New York: Pocket Books.

Eisenthal, David. 2007. "A Strange Case—R. Budd Dwyer." *Eisenthal Report* blog, January 19. http://davideisenthal.typepad.com/the_eisenthal_report/2007/01/a_strange_case_.html (accessed September 22, 2008).

Eizuru, Kazuko Miyashita. 1983. "High School Girls: A Comparison of Students in Japan and the United States." Master's thesis, Pennsylvania State University, Harrisburg.

Eliach, Yaffa. 1988. *Hasidic Tales of the Holocaust.* New York: Vintage.

Eliason, Eric A. 2004. *Celebrating Zion: Pioneers in Mormon Popular Historical Expression.* Provo, Utah: Brigham Young University Press.

Eliot, T. S. 1960. "Tradition and the Individual Talent." In *Selected Essays* by T. S. Eliot, 3–11. New York: Harcourt, Brace & World.

Ellingsgard, Nils. 1995. "Rosemaling: A Folk Art in Migration." In *Norwegian Folk Art: The Migration of a Tradition,* ed. Marion Nelson, 189–94. New York: Abbeville Press.

Ellis, Bill. 2000. *Raising the Devil: Satanism, New Religions, and the Media.* Lexington: University Press of Kentucky.

———. 2003. "Making a Big Apple Crumble: The Role of Humor in Constructing a Global Response to Disaster." In *Of Corpse: Death and Humor in Folklore and Popular Culture,* ed. Peter Narváez, 35–79. Logan: Utah State University Press.

———. 2006. "Internet." In *Encyclopedia of American Folklife,* ed. Simon J. Bronner, 627–30. Armonk, N.Y.: M. E. Sharpe.

Ennis, Michael. 2002. "Small Stuff." *Texas Monthly* (April). http://www.texasmonthly.com/mag/issues/2002–04–01/art.php (accessed July 31, 2007).

Ensminger, Robert F. 1992. *The Pennsylvania Barn: Its Origin, Evolution, and Distribution in North America.* Baltimore: Johns Hopkins University Press.

Epting, Chris. 2002. *Los Angeles Memorial Coliseum.* Charleston, S.C.: Arcadia.

Erikson, Erik H. 1950. *Childhood and Society.* New York: W. W. Norton.

Eskridge, William N., Jr. 1993. "A History of Same-Sex Marriage." *Virginia Law Review* 79: 1419–513.

Etzioni, Amitai. 1996. *The New Golden Rule: Community and Morality in a Democratic Society.* New York: Basic Books.

Evans, David. 1977. "The Toast in Context." *Journal of American Folklore* 90: 129–48.

———. 1982. *Big Road Blues: Tradition and Creativity in the Folk Blues.* Berkeley: University of California Press.

Everett, Holly. 2000. "Roadside Crosses and Memorial Complexes in Texas." *Folklore* 111: 91–103.

———. 2002. *Roadside Crosses in Contemporary Memorial Culture.* Denton: University of North Texas Press.

Falk, Gerhard. 2005. *Football and American Identity*. New York: Haworth Press.

Feinstein, John. 2006. *Next Man Up: A Year behind the Lines in Today's NFL*. New York: Little, Brown.

Felkins, Patricia K., and Irvin Goldman. 1993. "Political Myth as Subjective Narrative: Some Interpretations and Understandings of John F. Kennedy." *Political Psychology* 14: 447–67.

Fendley, Tony, and Red Level. 2009. "Judge Roy Moore Deserves a Chance." Letter to the editor, *Andalusia Star-News.com*. http://andalusiastarnews.com/news/2009/jan/28/judge-roy-moore-deserves-chance/ (accessed February 2, 2009).

Fenichel, Otto. 1954. "Trophy and Triumph." In *The Collected Papers of Otto Fenichel*, ed. Hanna Fenichel and David Rapaport, 141–62. New York: W. W. Norton.

Ferris, William. 1974. "Don't Throw It Away: Folk Culture and Our Dwindling Resources." *Yale Alumni Magazine* 37: 19–24.

Fife, Austin E. 1969. "Folklife and Folk Arts in the United States: Exhibit." In *Forms upon the Frontier: Folklife and Folk Arts in the United States*, ed. Austin Fife, Alta Fife, and Henry H. Glassie, 9–22. Logan: Utah State University Press.

Fine, Gary Alan. 1979. "Folklore Diffusion through Interactive Social Networks: Conduits in a Preadolescent Community." *New York Folklore* 5: 87–126.

———. 1980a. "Children and Their Culture: Exploring Newell's Paradox." *Western Folklore* 39: 170–84.

———. 1980b. "Multi-Conduit Transmission and Social Structure: Expanding a Folklore Classic." In *Folklore on Two Continents: Essays in Honor of Linda Dégh*, ed. Nikolai Burlakoff and Carl Lindahl, 300–309. Bloomington, Ind.: Trickster Press.

———. 1983. "Network and Meaning: An Interactionist Approach to Structure." *Symbolic Interaction* 6: 97–110.

———. 1984. "Evaluating Psychoanalytic Folklore: Are Freudians Ever Right?" *New York Folklore* 10: 5–20.

———. 1987. "Joseph Jacobs: A Sociological Folklorist." *Folklore* 98: 183–93.

———. 1989. "The Process of Tradition: Cultural Models of Change and Content." *Comparative Social Research* 11: 263–77.

———. 1992. "Folklore Diffusion through Interactive Social Networks: Conduits in a Preadolescent Community." In *Manufacturing Tales: Sex and Money in Contemporary Legends* by Gary Alan Fine, 86–119. Knoxville: University of Tennessee Press.

Fine, Gary Alan, and Patricia A. Turner. 2001. *Whispers on the Color Line: Rumor and Race in America*. Berkeley: University of California Press.

Fineman, Mia. 2004. "Photography, Vernacular." In *Encyclopedia of American Folk Art*, ed. Gerard C. Wertkin, 384–87. New York: Routledge.

Finnegan, Ruth. 1991. "Tradition, But What Tradition and for Whom?" *Oral Tradition* 6: 104–24.

Fischer, Claude S., and Greggor Mattson. 2009. "Is America Fragmenting?" *Annual Review of Sociology* 35: 435–55.

Fish, Lydia. 1972. "The Old Wife in the Dormitory—Sexual Folklore and Magical Practices from State University College." *New York Folklore Quarterly* 28: 30–36.

Flam, Gila. 1992. *Singing for Survival: Songs of the Lodz Ghetto, 1940–45*. Urbana: University of Illinois Press.

Fleece, Jeffery A. 1946. "Words in -FU." *American Speech* 21: 70–72.

Flumesday.com. 2008. "'90 Day Jane' a Hoax, Takes Down Site." Blog, February 13. http://www.flumesday.com/2008/02/13/90-day-jane-a-hoax-takes-down-site/ (accessed September 28, 2008).

Foley, Douglas E. 1990. "The Great American Football Ritual: Reproducing Race, Class, and Gender Inequality." *Sociology of Sport Journal* 7: 111–35.

————. 1994. *Learning Capitalist Culture: Deep in the Heart of Tejas*. Philadelphia: University of Pennsylvania Press.

Forbes, Gordon B., Leah E. Adams-Curtis, Alexis H. Pakalka, and Kay B. White. 2006. "Dating Aggression, Sexual Coercion, and Aggression-Supporting Attitudes among College Men as a Function of Participation in Aggressive High School Sports." *Violence against Women* 12: 441–55.

Forney, Craig A. 2007. *The Holy Trinity of American Sports: Civil Religion in Football, Baseball, and Basketball*. Macon, Ga.: Mercer University Press.

Foster, George M. 1953. "What Is Folk Culture?" *American Anthropologist* 55: 159–73.

Foster, Stephen C. 1984. "The Folk Environment: Some Methodological Considerations." In *Personal Places: Perspectives on Informal Art Environments*, ed. Daniel Franklin Ward, 5–14. Bowling Green, Ohio: Bowling Green State University Popular Press.

Fowke, Edith. 1969. *Sally Go Round the Sun: Three Hundred Children's Songs, Rhymes and Games*. Garden City, N.Y.: Doubleday.

Frank, Russell. 2009. "The *Forward* as Folklore: Studying E-Mailed Humor." In *Folklore and the Internet: Vernacular Expression in a Digital World*, ed. Trevor J. Blank, 98–122. Logan: Utah State University Press.

Franklin, Clyde W. 1992. "Surviving the Institutional Decimation of Black Males: Causes, Consequences, and Intervention." In *The Making of Masculinities: The New Men's Studies*, ed. Harry Brod, 155–69. New York: Routledge.

Frost, Joe L. 2010. *A History of Children's Play and Play Environments: Toward a Contemporary Child-Saving Movement*. New York: Routledge.

Freud, Sigmund. 1963 [1915]. "Symbolism in Dreams." In *The Standard Edition of the Complete Psychological Works of Sigmund Freud*, trans. and ed. James Strachey, 149–69. London: Hogarth Press.

————. 1999 [1900]. *The Interpretation of Dreams*. Oxford: Oxford University Press.

Freud, Sigmund, and D. E. Oppenheim. 1958. *Dreams in Folklore*. New York: International Universities Press.

Geertz, Clifford. 1973. "Thick Description: Toward an Interpretive Theory of Culture." In *The Interpretation of Cultures* by Clifford Geertz, 3–32. New York: Basic Books.

———. 2000. *Local Knowledge: Further Essays in Interpretive Anthropology.* New York: Basic Books.

Gensler, Harry J. 2002. *Introduction to Logic.* London: Routledge.

Georges, Robert A. 1969. "Toward an Understanding of Storytelling Events." *Journal of American Folklore* 82: 313–28.

Georges, Robert A., and Michael Owen Jones. 1995. *Folkloristics: An Introduction.* Bloomington: Indiana University Press.

Gibson, William James. 1994. *Warrior Dreams: Violence and Manhood in Post-Vietnam America.* New York: Hill & Wang.

Gilbert, Elizabeth. 2002. *The Last American Man.* New York: Penguin.

Glass, Joseph. 1986. *The Pennsylvania Culture Region: A View from the Barn.* Ann Arbor, Mich.: UMI Research Press.

Glassie, Henry. 1968. *Pattern in the Material Folk Culture of the Eastern United States.* Philadelphia: University of Pennsylvania Press.

———. 1972a. "Eighteenth-Century Cultural Process in Delaware Valley Folk Building." *Winterthur Portfolio* 7: 29–57.

———. 1972b. "Folk Art." In *Folklore and Folklife: An Introduction,* ed. Richard M. Dorson, 253–80. Chicago: University of Chicago Press.

———. 1974. "The Variation of Concepts within Tradition: Barn Building in Otsego County, New York." *Geoscience and Man* 5: 177–235.

———. 1983. "The Moral Lore of Folklore." *Folklore Forum* 16: 123–51.

———. 1985. "Artifact and Culture, Architecture and Society." In *American Material Culture and Folklife,* ed. Simon J. Bronner, 47–62. Ann Arbor, Mich.: UMI Research Press.

———. 1993. *Turkish Traditional Art Today.* 2nd ed. Bloomington: Indiana University Press.

———. 1995. "Tradition." *Journal of American Folklore* 108: 395–412.

Glazer, Nathan 1997. *We Are All Multiculturalists Now.* Cambridge, Mass.: Harvard University Press.

Glenday, Craig, ed. 2008. *Guinness World Records 2008: Gamer's Edition.* London: Guinness World Records Limited.

Glenn, David. 2010. "Anthropology Association Never Intended to Break with Science, Board Says." *Chronicle of Higher Education,* December 13. http://chronicle.com/article/Anthropology-Association-Never/125713/ (accessed March 28, 2011).

Goethals, Gregor. 2003. "Myth and Ritual in Cyberspace." In *Mediating Religion: Conversations in Media, Religion and Culture,* ed. Jolyon Mitchell and Sophia Marriage, 257–70. London: T& T Clark.

Goldin-Meadow, Susan. 2005. *Hearing Gesture: How Our Hands Help Us Think.* Cambridge, Mass.: Belknap Press.

Goldstein, Carolyn. 1998. *Do It Yourself: Home Improvement in 20th-Century America.* New York: Princeton Architectural Press.

Goldstein, Diane E. 2004. *Once upon a Virus: AIDS Legends and Vernacular Risk Perception.* Logan: Utah State University Press.

Goldstein, Kenneth S. 1964. *A Guide for Field Workers in Folklore.* Hatboro, Pa.: Folklore Associates.

———. 1971. "Strategy in Counting Out: An Ethnographic Folklore Field Study." In *The Study of Games*, ed. Elliott M. Avedon and Brian Sutton-Smith, 167–78. New York: John Wiley & Sons.

Goldstein, Sidney. 1992. "Profile of American Jewry: Insights from the 1990 National Jewish Population Survey." In *American Jewish Yearbook 1992*, ed. David Singer, 77–176. New York and Philadelphia: American Jewish Committee and Jewish Publication Society.

Gower, Barry. 1997. *Scientific Method: A Historical and Philosophical Introduction.* London: Routledge.

Graham, Andrea. 1989. "Railroad-Tie Architecture in Elko County, Nevada." In *Perspectives in Vernacular Architecture*, ed. Thomas Carter and Bernard L. Herman, 242. Columbia: University of Missouri Press.

Gramsci, Antonio. 1999. "Observations on Folklore." In *International Folkloristics: Classic Contributions by the Founders of Folklore*, ed. Alan Dundes, 131–36. Lanham, Md.: Rowman & Littlefield.

Granger, Byrd Howell. 1961. "Of the Teeth." *Journal of American Folklore* 74: 47–56.

Grawe, Sam. 2007. "Home Word Bound." *Dwell: At Home in the Modern World* (June): 41.

Green, Archie. 1983. "Interpreting Folklore Ideologically." In *Handbook of American Folklore*, ed. Richard M. Dorson, 351–58. Bloomington: Indiana University Press.

Green, Thomas A., ed. 2006. *The Greenwood Library of American Folktales*, 4 vols. Westport, Conn.: Greenwood Press.

Greenfield, Verni. 1986. *Making Do or Making Art: A Study of American Recycling.* Ann Arbor, Mich.: UMI Research Press.

Gregory, R. L. 1970. *The Intelligent Eye.* New York: McGraw-Hill.

Gross, David. 1992. *The Past in Ruins: Tradition and the Critique of Modernity.* Amherst: University of Massachusetts Press.

Grube, G. M. A., trans. 1992. *The Republic/Plato.* Revised by C. D. C. Reeve. Indianapolis: Hackett Publishing.

Guroian, Vigen. 1996. "Awakening the Moral Imagination: Teaching Virtues through Fairy Tales." *Intercollegiate Review* 32: 3–13.

Halleck, Reuben, and Juliette Frantz. 1925. *Our Nation's Heritage: What the Old World Contributed to the New.* New York: American Book Company.

Hamilton, Marci. 2003. "Judge Roy Moore and the Ten Commandments Controversy: Why He Was Not a Fit Justice, Won't Be a Fit Governor, and Belongs in the Private Sphere." *FindLaw.com* commentary website. http://writ.news.findlaw.com/hamilton/20031118.html (accessed September 12, 2010).

Hamilton, Mark. 2008. "Is the Gridiron Holy Ground?" In *Football and Philosophy: Going Deep*, ed. Michael W. Austin, 183–95. Lexington: University Press of Kentucky.

Hammersley, Martyn. 1992. *What's Wrong with Ethnography?* London: Routledge.

Hans, James S. 1987. *Imitation and the Image of Man.* Amsterdam: John Benjamins.

Hanson, Russell. 1995. "Tradition." In *A Companion to American Thought*, ed. Richard Wightman Fox and James T. Koppenberg, 681–83. Oxford: Basil Blackwell.

Hardin, Michael. 2000. "What Is the Word at Logos College? Homosocial Ritual or Homosexual Denial in Don Delillo's *End Zone?*" *Journal of Homosexuality* 40: 31–50.

Harmon, Mamie. 1949. "Folklore." In *Funk & Wagnalls Standard Dictionary of Folklore, Mythology, and Legend*, 2 vols., ed. Maria Leach, 399–400. New York: Funk & Wagnalls.

Harshav, Benjamin. 1990. *The Meaning of Yiddish*. Berkeley: University of California Press.

Hartland, Edwin Sidney. 1885. "The Science of Folklore." *Folk-Lore Journal* 3: 115–21.

———. 1891. *The Science of Fairy Tales: An Inquiry into Fairy Mythology*. London: Walter Scott.

———. 1894–1896. *The Legend of Perseus: A Study of Tradition in Story, Custom, and Belief*. London: D. Nutt.

———. 1904. *Folklore: What Is It and What Is the Good of It?* London: David Nutt.

———. 1968 [1899]. "Folklore: What Is It and What Is the Good of It?" In *Peasant Customs and Savage Myths: Selections from the British Folklorists*, ed. Richard M. Dorson, 1:230–51. Chicago: University of Chicago Press.

Hartmann, Douglas. 2003. "The Sanctity of Sunday Afternoon Football: Why Men Love Sports." *Contexts* 2: 13–21.

Hass, Kristin Ann. 1998. *Carried to the Wall: American Memory and the Vietnam Veterans Memorial*. Berkeley: University of California Press.

Hawes, Bess Lomax. 1968. "La Llorona in Juvenile Hall." *Western Folklore* 27: 153–70.

Heagney, Meredith. 2009. "Virtual Synagogue Serves Jews Online." *Columbus Dispatch*, September 18. http://www.dispatch.com/live/content/faith_values/stories/2009/09/18/FVonlineholiday.ART_ART_09-18-09_B4_NLF42MB.html (accessed September 10, 2010).

Hearn, Lafcadio. 1984. *Writings from Japan: An Anthology*, ed. Francis King. New York: Penguin.

Heath, Kingston Wm. 1988. "Defining the Nature of Vernacular." *Material Culture* 20: 1–8.

Henry, Jean. 1995. "Hmong and Pennsylvania German Textiles: Needlework Traditions in Transition in Lancaster County." *Folk Art* 20 (summer): 40–46.

Herbert, Wray. 1996. "The Moral Child. We're at Ground Zero in the Culture Wars: How to Raise Decent Kids When Traditional Ties to Church, School and Community Are Badly Frayed." *U.S. News & World Report*, June 3, 52–59.

Herman, Bernard L. 1985. "Time and Performance: Folk Houses in Delaware." In *American Material Culture and Folklife*, ed. Simon J. Bronner, 155–75. Ann Arbor, Mich.: UMI Research Press.

———. 1997. "The Bricoleur Revisited." In *American Material Culture: The Shape of the Field*, ed. Ann Smart Martin and J. Ritchie Garrison, 37–63. Knoxville: University of Tennessee Press for the Winterthur Museum.

Herskovits, Melville. 1948. *Man and His Works: The Science of Cultural Anthropology.* New York: Knopf.

———. 1949. "Folklore." In *Funk & Wagnalls Standard Dictionary of Folklore, Mythology and Legend*, ed. Maria Leach, 1:400. New York: Funk & Wagnalls.

Herskowitz, Linda. 1987. "Psychiatrists: An Act of Rage, Despair." *Philadelphia Inquirer*, January 23, 16a.

Hirsch, E. D., Jr. 1987. *Cultural Literacy: What Every American Needs to Know.* Boston: Houghton Mifflin.

———. 1989. *A First Dictionary of Cultural Literacy: What Our Children Need to Know.* Boston: Houghton Mifflin.

Hirsch, E. D., Jr., Joseph E. Kett, and James Trefil. 2002. *The New Dictionary of Cultural Literacy.* 3rd ed. Boston: Houghton Mifflin.

Hirsch, Jerrold. 1987. "Folklore in the Making: B. A. Botkin." *Journal of American Folklore* 100: 3–38.

Hobsbawm, Eric. 1983. "Introduction: Inventing Traditions." In *The Invention of Tradition*, ed. Eric Hobsbawm and Terence Ranger, 1–14. Cambridge: Cambridge University Press.

Hofer, Tamis. 1984. "The Perception of Tradition in European Ethnology." *Journal of Folklore Research* 21: 133–47.

Holbek, Bengt. 1969. "Computer Classification of Proverbs: Report on a Small Scale Experiment." *Proverbium* 14: 372–76.

Holy, Ladislav, ed. 1987. *Comparative Anthropology.* Oxford: Blackwell.

Hostetler, John A. 1963. *Amish Society.* Baltimore: Johns Hopkins University Press.

———. 1993. *Amish Society.* 4th ed. Baltimore: Johns Hopkins University Press.

Howard, Robert Glenn. 2005. "Toward a Theory of the World Wide Web Vernacular: The Case for Pet Cloning." *Journal of Folklore Research* 42: 323–60.

———. 2008. "Electronic Hybridity: The Persistent Processes of the Vernacular Web." *Journal of American Folklore* 121: 192–218.

Hubka, Thomas C. 1994. "The Americanization of the Barn." *Blueprints* 12: 2–7.

Huffines, Marion Lois. 1984. "The English of the Pennsylvania Germans: A Reflection of Ethnic Affiliation." *German Quarterly* 57: 173–82.

Hufford, David J., ed. 1970. *Teaching and Collecting Folklore at a Boys' Prep School.* Special Issue, *Keystone Folklore Quarterly* 15.

Hufford, Mary. 2002. "American Folklife: A Commonwealth of Cultures." In *Folk Nation: Folklore in the Creation of American Tradition*, ed. Simon J. Bronner, 237–47. Wilmington, Del.: Scholarly Resources.

Hultkrantz, Åke. 1960. *General Ethnological Concepts.* Copenhagen: Rosenkilde & Bagger.

Hunter, James Davison. 1991. *Culture Wars: The Struggle to Define America.* New York: Basic Books.

———. 1994. *Before the Shooting Begins: Searching for Democracy in America's Culture War.* New York: Free Press.

HurricanEAJW2. 2008. "Bud Dwyer—Extended Version." YouTube website, August 27. http://www.youtube.com/watch?v=0Y8ebVhlnBo (accessed September 22, 2008).

Hutchings, Tim. 2007. "Creating Church Online: A Case-Study Approach to Religious Experience." *Studies in World Christianity* 13: 243–60.

Hymes, Dell. 1972. "The Contribution of Folklore to Sociolinguistic Research." In *Toward New Perspectives in Folklore*, ed. Américo Paredes and Richard Bauman, 42–50. Austin: University of Texas Press.

"I Did It for the Lulz." 2008. *Encyclopaedia Dramatica.* http://www.encyclopediadramatica.com/I_did_it_for_the_lulz#Budd_Dwyer (accessed September 22, 2008).

Iggulden, Gonn, and Hal Iggulden. 2007. *The Dangerous Book for Boys.* New York: HarperCollins.

"ILoo." 2007. *Snopes.com.* Urban Legends References Pages. http://www.snopes.com/computer/internet/iloo.asp (accessed October 3, 2008).

Ingold, Tim, ed. 1996. *Key Debates in Anthropology.* London: Routledge.

In re Marriage Cases. 2008. Decision filed May 15 in Supreme Court of California. S147999. San Francisco County JCCP No. 4365.

Jackson, Bruce. 1972. "Circus and Street: Psychosocial Aspects of the Black Toast." *Journal of American Folklore* 85: 123–39.

———. 1974. *Get Your Ass in the Water and Swim Like Me: Narrative Poetry from Black Oral Tradition.* Cambridge, Mass.: Harvard University Press.

Jackson, Bruce, Michael Taft, and Havery S. Axlerod, comps. and eds. 1988. *The Centennial Index: One Hundred Years of the* Journal of American Folklore. Washington, D.C.: American Folklore Society.

Jacobs, Joseph. 1893. "The Folk." *Folk-Lore* 4: 233–38.

Jakobson, Roman, and Petr Bogatyrev. 1980. "Folklore as a Special Form of Creation." *Folklore Forum* 13: 1–21.

Jansen, William Hugh. 1959. "The Esoteric-Exoteric Factor in Folklore." *Fabula* 2: 205–11.

Japanese Pottery Information Center. 2005. "Living National Treasures List as of August 2005." Japanese Pottery Information Center website. www.e-yakimono.net/html/living-natl-treasures.htm (accessed July 29, 2007).

Jaspers, Karl. 1948. *Philosophie.* Berlin: Springer.

Jeffords, Susan. 1989. *The Remasculinization of America: Gender and the Vietnam War.* Bloomington: Indiana University Press.

Jeffreys, Mark. 2000. "The Meme Metaphor." *Perspectives in Biology and Medicine* 43: 227–42.

Jemie, Onwuchekwa. 2003. *Yo' Mama! New Raps, Toasts, Dozens, Jokes and Children's Rhymes from Urban Black America.* Philadelphia: Temple University Press.

Jencks, Charles, and Nathan Silver. 1972. *Adhocism: The Case for Improvisation.* New York: Doubleday.

Jenkins, Emyl. 1996. *The Book of American Traditions: Stories, Customs, and Rites of Passage to Celebrate Our Cultural Heritage.* New York: Crown.

Jenkins, Henry, and David Thorburn, eds. 2003. *Democracy and New Media.* Cambridge, Mass.: MIT Press.

Jenkins, Sally. 2007. *The Real All Americans: The Team that Changed a Game, a People, a Nation.* New York: Doubleday.

Jenkins, Virginia. 1994. *The Lawn: A History of an American Obsession.* Washington, D.C.: Smithsonian Books.

Jennings, Karla. 1991. *The Devouring Fungus: Tales of the Computer Age.* New York: W. W. Norton.

John Michael Kohler Arts Center. 1987. *From Hardanger to Harleys: A Survey of Wisconsin Folk Art.* Sheboygan, Wis.: John Michael Kohler Arts Center.

Johnson, Steven. 1999. *Interface Culture: How New Technology Transforms the Way We Create and Communicate.* New York: Basic Books.

Joinson, Adam N. 2003. *Understanding the Psychology of Internet Behaviour: Virtual Worlds, Real Lives.* New York: Palgrave Macmillan.

Jones, David. 2008a. "Gap Widens between Players, Fans." *Patriot-News* (Harrisburg, Pa.), September 26, Sports 20.

———. 2008b. "2 Joes Match Wits for Final Time." *Patriot-News* (Harrisburg, Pa.), October 3, Sports 20.

———. 2010. "Blanda Defined AFL Era." *Patriot-News* (Harrisburg, Pa.), October 1, Sports 28.

Jones, Ernest. 1961 [1912]. *Papers on Psycho-Analysis.* Boston: Beacon Press.

Jones, Louis C. 1946. Letter to Frances Gillmor, January 31. New York State Historical Association, Louis C. Jones Collection.

———. 1982. *Three Eyes on the Past: Exploring New York Folklife.* Syracuse, N.Y.: Syracuse University Press.

Jones, Michael Owen. 1971. "(PC + CB) × SD (R + I + E) = Hero." *New York Folklore Quarterly* 27: 243–60.

———. 1975. *The Hand Made Object and Its Maker.* Berkeley: University of California Press.

———. 1980a. "A Feeling for Form, as Illustrated by People at Work." In *Folklore on Two Continents: Essays in Honor of Linda Dégh*, ed. Nikolai Burlakoff and Carl Lindahl, 260–72. Bloomington, Ind.: Trickster Press.

———. 1980b. "L.A. Add-ons and Re-dos: Renovation in Folk Art and Architectural Design." In *Perspectives on American Folk Art*, ed. Ian M. G. Quimby and Scott T. Swank, 325–63. New York: W. W. Norton.

———. 1987. *Exploring Folk Art: Twenty Years of Thought on Craft, Work, and Aesthetics.* Logan: Utah State University Press.

———. 1989. *Craftsman of the Cumberlands: Tradition and Creativity.* Lexington: University Press of Kentucky.

———. 1993. "Why Take a Behavioral Approach to Folk Objects?" In *History from Things: Essays on Material Culture*, ed. Steven Lubar and W. David Kingery, 182–96. Washington, D.C.: Smithsonian Institution Press.

———. 1994. "Applying Folklore Studies: An Introduction." In *Putting*

Folklore to Use, ed. Michael Owen Jones, 1–44. Lexington: University Press of Kentucky.

———. 1995. "Why Make (Folk) Art?" *Western Folklore* 54: 253–76.

———. 1997. "How Can We Apply Event Analysis to Material Behavior, and Why Should We?" *Western Folklore* 56: 199–214.

———. 2000. "'Tradition' in Identity Discourses and an Individual's Symbolic Construction of Self." *Western Folklore* 59: 115–42.

———. 2001. "The Aesthetics of Everyday Life." In *Self-Taught Art: The Culture and Aesthetics of American Vernacular Art*, ed. Charles Russell, 129–45. Jackson: University Press of Mississippi.

Jones, Pamela. 1988. "'There Was a Woman': La Llorona in Oregon." *Western Folklore* 47: 195–211.

Jones, Suzi. 1976. "Regionalization: A Rhetorical Strategy." *Journal of the Folklore Institute* 13: 105–20.

Jordan, Rosan Augusta. 1997. "Computer-Mediated Folklore." In *Folklore: An Encyclopedia of Beliefs, Customs, Tales, Music, and Art*, ed. Thomas A. Green, 140–42. Santa Barbara, Calif.: ABC-CLIO.

Joselit, Jenna Weissman. 1994. *The Wonders of America: Reinventing Jewish Culture, 1880–1950*. New York: Hill & Wang.

Kalmar, Ivan Davidson, and Derek Penslar, eds. 2004. *Orientalism and the Jews*. Waltham, Mass.: Brandeis University Press.

Kammen, Michael. 1991. *Mystic Chords of Memory: The Transformation of Tradition in American Culture*. New York: Knopf.

———. 1999. *American Culture, American Tastes: Social Change and the 20th Century*. New York: Knopf.

Kanner, Leo. 1968 [1928]. *Folklore of the Teeth*. Detroit: Singing Tree Press.

Kapchan, Deborah. 2003. "Performance." In *Eight Words for the Study of Expressive Culture*, ed. Burt Feintuch, 121–45. Urbana: University of Illinois Press.

Kassovic, Julius Stephen. 1983. "Junk and Its Transformations." In *A Report from the Center for Folk Art and Contemporary Crafts*, vol. 3, ed. Margery Anneberg. San Francisco: Center for Folk Art and Contemporary Crafts.

Katoh, Amy Sylvester, and Shin Kimura. 2003. *Japan: The Art of Living*. Rev. ed. Boston: Tuttle.

Katz, Lilian G. 1991. "Are Fairy Tales Good for Kids?" *Parents* (November): 243.

Kay, Joe. 2008. "Collins Lead Titans over Bengals 24–7 in Wind." *Yahoo! Sports*, September 14. http://sports.yahoo.com/nfl/recap?gid=20080914004 (accessed September 16, 2008).

Kearney, Michael. 1969. "La Llorona as a Social Symbol." *Western Folklore* 28: 199–206.

Keil, Charles. 1978. "Who Needs the 'Folk'?" *Journal of the Folklore Institute* 15: 263–65.

Keisling, William, and Richard Kearns. 1988. *The Sins of Our Fathers: A Profile of Pennsylvania Attorney Leroy S. Zimmerman and a Historical Explanation of the Suicide of State Treasurer R. Budd Dwyer*. Harrisburg, Pa.: Privately printed.

Kemp, Alvin F. 1944. "The Pennsylvania German Versammlinge." *Publications of the Pennsylvania German Folklore Society* 9: 185–218.

————. 1978–1979. "Pennsylvania Dutch Dialect Stories." *Pennsylvania Folklife* 28 (2): 27–33.

Kemper, Kurt Edward. 2009. *College Football and American Culture in the Cold War Era.* Urbana: University of Illinois Press.

Ketner, Kenneth Laine. 1971. "Superstitious Pigeons, Hydrophobia, and Conventional Wisdom." *Western Folklore* 30: 1–17.

————. 1973. "The Role of Hypotheses in Folkloristics." *Journal of American Folklore* 86: 114–30.

————. 1975. "Hypotheses Fingo." *Journal of American Folklore* 88: 411–17.

————. 1976. "Identity and Existence in the Study of Human Traditions." *Folklore* 87: 192–200.

Kimmel, Michael. 1996. *Manhood in America: A Cultural History.* New York: Free Press.

————. 2008. *Guyland: The Perilous World Where Boys Become Men.* New York: HarperCollins.

Kirscht, Judy, and Mark Schlenz. 2002. *Engaging Inquiry: Research and Writing in the Disciplines.* Upper Saddle River, N.J.: Prentice-Hall.

Kirshenblatt-Gimblett, Barbara. 1975. "A Parable in Context." In *Folklore: Performance and Communication,* ed. Dan Ben-Amos and Kenneth Goldstein, 105–30. The Hague: Mouton.

————. 1983. "The Future of Folklore Studies in America: The Urban Frontier." *Folklore Forum* 16: 175–234.

————. 1988. "Mistaken Dichotomies." *Journal of American Folklore* 101: 140–55.

————. 1994. "On Difference." *Journal of American Folklore* 107: 233–38.

————. 1995. "From the Paperwork Empire to the Paperless Office: Testing the Limits of the 'Science of Tradition.'" In *Folklore Interpreted: Essays in Honor of Alan Dundes,* ed. Regina Bendix and Rosemary Lévy Zumwalt, 69–92. New York: Garland.

————. 1996a. "Coming of Age in the Thirties: Max Weinreich, Edward Sapir, and Jewish Social Science." *YIVO Annual* 23: 1–104.

————. 1996b. "Topic Drift: Negotiating the Gap between the Field and Our Name." *Journal of Folklore Research* 33: 245–54.

————. 1998. "Folklore's Crisis." *Journal of American Folklore* 111: 281–327.

Kirtley, Bacil F. 1960. "'La Llorona' and Related Themes." *Western Folklore* 19: 155–68.

Klaus, Mary. 2002. "MADD Members 'Devastated' by Wreck." *Patriot-News* (Harrisburg, Pa.), July 19, A1, 12.

Kliger, Hannah, ed. 1992. *Jewish Hometown Associations and Family Circles in New York: The WPA Yiddish Writers' Group Study.* Bloomington: Indiana University Press.

Kluckhohn, Florence Rockwood, and Fred L. Strodtbeck. 1973 [1961]. *Variations in Value Orientations.* Westport, Conn.: Greenwood Press.

Knapp, Mary, and Herbert Knapp. 1976. *One Potato, Two Potato . . . The Secret Education of American Children.* New York: W. W. Norton.

Knight, Douglas A. 2006. *Rediscovering the Traditions of Israel.* 3rd ed. Atlanta: Society of Biblical Literature.

Kobayashi, Toshiyuki, Wilfried Schmid, and Jae-Hyun Yang, eds. 2008. *Representation Theory and Automorphic Forms.* Boston: Birhäuser.

Kolakowski, Leszek. 1971. "On the Meaning of Tradition." *Evergreen Review* 15: 43–46.

Köstlin, Konrad, and Scott M. Shrake. 1997. "The Passion for the Whole: Interpreted Modernity or Modernity as Interpretation." *Journal of American Folklore* 110: 260–76.

Koven, Mikel J. 2000. "'Have I Got a Monster for You!' Some Thoughts on the Golem, 'The X-Files' and the Jewish Horror Movie." *Folklore* 111: 217–30.

Krauss, Daniel. 2000. "The Morbid Urge." *Gadfly Online* (August). http://www.gadflyonline.com/archive/JulyAugust00/archive-morbid.html (accessed September 26, 2008).

Kraybill, Don. 2001. *The Riddle of Amish Culture.* Rev. ed. Baltimore: Johns Hopkins University Press.

Kraybill, Don, and Steven M. Nolt. 1995. *Amish Enterprise: From Plows to Profits.* Baltimore: Johns Hopkins University Press.

Kristeller, Paul Oskar. 1983. "'Creativity' and 'Tradition.'" *Journal of the History of Ideas* 44: 105–14.

Kroeber, Alfred A. 1917. "The Superorganic." *American Anthropologist* 19: 163–213.

Krohn, Kaarle. 1999. "The Method of Julius Krohn." In *International Folkloristics: Classic Contributions by the Founders of Folklore,* ed. Alan Dundes, 37–46. Lanham, Md.: Rowman & Littlefield.

Krout, John Allen. 1929. *Annals of American Sport.* New Haven, Conn.: Yale University Press.

Kubie, Lawrence S. 1937. "The Fantasy of Dirt." *Psychoanalytical Quarterly* 6: 388–425.

Kurin, Richard. 2002. "Folklife in Contemporary Multicultural Society." In *Folk Nation: Folklore in the Creation of American Tradition,* ed. Simon J. Bronner, 249–63. Wilmington, Del.: Scholarly Resources.

Kutner, Philip. 2000. "Yiddish Survives the Millennium!" *Der Bay* 10: 1.

Labbo, Linda D. 1996. "A Semiotic Analysis of Young Children's Symbol Making in a Classroom Computer Center." *Reading Research Quarterly* 31: 356–85.

La Belle, Thomas J., and Christopher R. Ward. 1994. *Multiculturalism and Education: Diversity and Its Impact on Schools and Society.* Albany: State University of New York Press.

Lamm, Richard D. 1985. *The Immigration Time Bomb: The Fragmenting of America.* New York: Truman Talley Books.

Lane, Franklin K. 1912. "A Western View of Tradition." *University of Virginia Alumni Bulletin* (April): 3–10.

Lant, Antonia. 1992. "The Curse of the Pharaoh, or How Cinema Contracted Egyptomania." *October* 59: 86–112.

Lasch, Christopher. 1979. *The Culture of Narcissism: American Life in an Age of Diminishing Expectations.* New York: W. W. Norton.

Laske, Otto. 1990. "The Computer as the Artist's Alter Ego." *Leonardo* 23: 53–66.

Laurel, Brenda. 1991. *Computers as Theatre.* Reading, Mass.: Addison-Wesley.

Laurelei. 2008. MySpace blog. http://profile.myspace.com (accessed September 26, 2008).

Lavazzi, Tom. 2001. "Communication On(the)line." *South Atlantic Review* 66: 126–44.

Laver, John. 1975. "Communicative Functions of Phatic Communion." In *Organization of Behavior in Face-to-Face Interaction*, ed. Adam Kendon, Richard M. Harris, and Mary Ritchie Key, 215–40. The Hague: Mouton.

Leach, MacEdward. 1966. "Folklore in American Regional Literature." *Journal of the Folklore Institute* 3: 376–97.

Leach, Maria, ed. 1949. *Funk & Wagnalls Standard Dictionary of Folklore, Mythology, and Legend*, 2 vols. New York: Funk & Wagnalls.

Leddy, Betty. 1948. "La Llorona in Southern Arizona." *Western Folklore* 7: 272–77.

Lee, Dorothy. 1968 [1950]. "Codifications of Reality: Lineal and Nonlineal." In *Every Man His Way: Readings in Cultural Anthropology*, ed. Alan Dundes, 329–43. Englewood Cliffs, N.J.: Prentice-Hall.

Lee, O-Young. 1992. *The Compact Culture: The Japanese Tradition of "Smaller Is Better."* Tokyo: Kodansha International.

Legman, G. 1968. *Rationale of the Dirty Joke: An Analysis of Sexual Humor.* First series. New York: Grove Press.

———. 1975. *Rationale of the Dirty Joke: An Analysis of Sexual Humor.* New York: Breaking Point.

Lehman, Marjorie. 2010. "Reimagining Home, Rethinking Sukkah: Rabbinic Discourse and Its Contemporary Implications." In *Jews at Home: The Domestication of Identity*, ed. Simon J. Bronner, 107–39. Oxford: Littman.

Lembcke, Jerry. 1998. *The Spitting Image: Myth, Memory, and the Legacy of Vietnam.* New York: New York University Press.

———. 2004. "Post-Vietnam Masculinity." In *Men and Masculinities: A Social, Cultural, and Historical Encyclopedia*, ed. Michael Kimmel and Amy Aronson, 620–22. Santa Barbara, Calif.: ABC-CLIO.

Letson, Ben. 2008. "Feeling the Big Mo'." In *Football and Philosophy: Going Deep*, ed. Michael W. Austin, 209–18. Lexington: University Press of Kentucky.

Lever, Janet. 1976. "Sex Differences in the Games Children Play." *Social Problems* 23: 478–87.

Lévi-Strauss, Claude. 1966. *The Savage Mind.* Chicago: University of Chicago Press.

Levine, Faythe, and Corney Heimerl. 2008. *Handmade Nation: The Rise of DIY, Art, Craft, and Design.* New York: Princeton Architectural Press.

Levine, Lawrence W. 1977. *Black Culture and Black Consciousness: Afro-American Folk Thought from Slavery to Freedom.* New York: Oxford University Press.

Lewin, Chaim. 1999. *"Fun Redaktor Schreyb-Tish"* [From the Editor's Desk]. *Der Onheib* 28: 2.

Lewis, Jim. 1987. "Need Cited to Discuss Dwyer Death." *Patriot-News* (Harrisburg, Pa.), February 6, C1.

Lewis, Jim, and Kelly Bothum. 2002. "Their Story Is a Devastating Reminder that Life Can End 'In the Blink of an Eye.'" *Sunday Patriot-News* (Harrisburg, Pa.), July 21, A1, 18.

Lieber, Andrea. 2010. "Domesticity and the Home/Page: Blogging and the Blurring of Public and Private among Orthodox Jewish Women." In *Jews at Home: The Domestication of Identity*, ed. Simon J. Bronner, 257–82. Oxford: Littman.

Limón, José. 1983. "Western Marxism and Folklore: A Critical Introduction." *Journal of American Folklore* 96: 34–52.

Lindquist, Danille Christensen. 2006. "'Locating' the Nation: Football Game Day and American Dreams in Central Ohio." *Journal of American Folklore* 119: 444–88.

Lindstrom, Martin. 2009. "How Subliminal Advertising Works." *Parade*, January 4, 12–13.

Linger, Daniel Touro. 2005. *Anthropology through a Double Lens: Public and Personal Worlds in Human Theory*. Philadelphia: University of Pennsylvania Press.

Linnekin, Jocelyn S. 1983. "Defining Tradition: Variations on the Hawaiian Identity." *American Ethnologist* 10: 241–52.

Lipartito, Kenneth. 2003. "Picturephone and the Information Age: The Social Meaning of Failure." *Technology and Culture* 44: 50–81.

"List of Chat Acronyms & Text Message Shorthand." 2008. *Netlingo.* http://www.netlingo.com/emailsh.cfm (accessed November 14, 2008).

Lockwood, Yvonne R. 1984. "The Joy of Labor." *Western Folklore* 43: 202–11.

Logsdon, Gene. 1989. "The Barn Raising." In *Amish Roots*, ed. John A. Hostetler, 78–79. Baltimore: Johns Hopkins University Press.

Lomax, Alan. 1967. *Hard Hitting Songs for Hard-Hit People*. New York: Oak Publications.

———. 1993. *The Land Where the Blues Began*. New York: Pantheon.

Lomax, Joseph F. 1985a. "The Orange Show." In *Folk Art in Texas*, ed. Francis Edward Abernethy, 38–45. Dallas: Southern Methodist University Press.

———. 1985b. "Some People Call This Art." In *Folk Art in Texas*, ed. Francis Edward Abernethy, 17–21. Dallas: Southern Methodist University Press.

Longenecker, Gregory J. 1977. "Sequential Parody Graffiti." *Western Folklore* 36: 354–64.

Louden, Mark L. 2008. *"Die Alde un Neie Zeide:* Old and New Times for the Pennsylvania Dutch Language." *Der Reggeboge: Journal of the Pennsylvania German Society* 42: 3–18.

Lowe, Donald M. 1982. *History of Bourgeois Perception*. Chicago: University of Chicago Press.

Lowenthal, Marvin. 1942. *Henrietta Szold: Life and Letters*. New York: Viking Press.

Lowie, Robert H. 1965. "Some Cases of Repeated Reproduction." In *The Study of Folklore*, ed. Alan Dundes, 259–64. Englewood Cliffs, N.J.: Prentice-Hall.

Lupu, Ira C., David Masci, and Robert W. Tuttle. 2007. *Religious Displays and the Courts*. Washington, D.C.: Pew Forum on Religious and Public Life.

Lurie, Harry L., and Max Weinreich, eds. 1949. *Jewish Social Research in America: Status and Prospects*. New York: Yiddish Scientific Institute–YIVO.

Lynch, Annette. 1995. "Hmong American New Year's Dress: The Display of Ethnicity." In *Dress and Ethnicity: Change across Space and Time*, ed. Joanne B. Eicher, 255–68. Oxford: Berg.

Lynch, Dianne. 1998. "A Place on the Web for Self-Restraint." *Christian Science Monitor* website, March 9. http://www.csmonitor.com/atcsmonitor/cybercoverage/media/media0309.shtml (accessed September 25, 2008).

Lyons, John. 1968. *Introduction to Theoretical Linguistics*. Cambridge: Cambridge University Press.

MacCambridge, Michael. 2004. *America's Game: The Epic Story of How Pro Football Captured a Nation*. New York: Random House.

MacDowell, Marsha. 1989. *Stories in Thread: Hmong Pictorial Embroidery*. East Lansing: Michigan State University Museum.

Mandelbaum, Michael. 2004. *The Meaning of Sports: Why Americans Watch Baseball, Football, and Basketball and What They See When They Do*. New York: Public Affairs.

Manley, Roger. 1989. *Signs and Wonders: Outsider Art Inside North Carolina*. Raleigh: North Carolina Museum of Art.

Mansfield, Harvey C. 2006. *Manliness*. New Haven, Conn.: Yale University Press.

Maranda, Pierre. 1967. "Computers in the Bush: Tools for the Automatic Analysis of Myths." In *Essays on the Verbal and Visual Arts*, ed. June Helm, 77–83. Seattle: University of Washington Press.

Margry, Peter Jan, and Herman Roodenburg. 2007. "A History of Dutch Ethnology in 10½ Pages." In *Reframing Dutch Culture: Between Otherness and Authenticity*, ed. Peter Jan Margry and Herman Roodenburg, 261–72. Burlington, Vt.: Ashgate.

Margry, Peter Jan, and Cristina Sánchez-Carretero, eds. 2011. *Grassroots Memorials: The Politics of Memorializing Traumatic Death*. New York: Berghahn.

Marlow, Kristina. 1994. "For Politically Correct, Halloween Can Be Frightening." *Chicago Tribune*, September 30, 1:1.

Marshall, Howard W. 1982. *Missouri Artist Jesse Howard, with a Contemplation on Idiosyncratic Art*. Columbia: University of Missouri.

Martin, Charles E. 1983. "Howard Acree's Chimney: The Dilemma of Innovation." *Pioneer America: Journal of Historic American Material Culture* 15: 35–50.

Martin, Philip. 1989. *Rosemaling in the Upper Midwest*. Mount Horeb: Wisconsin Folk Museum.

Mathews, Mitford M. 1966. *Americanisms: A Dictionary of Selected Americanisms on Historical Principles*. Chicago: University of Chicago Press.

Matthiesen, F. O. 1941. *American Renaissance: Art and Expression in the Age of Emerson and Whitman.* New York: Oxford University Press.

Mayer, Egon, Barry Kosmin, and Ariela Keysar. 2003. *American Jewish Identity Survey 2001.* New York: Center for Cultural Judaism.

Mayhew, Henry. 1864. *German Life and Manners as Seen in Saxony at the Present Day.* 2 vols. London: Wm. H. Allen.

Mazo, Jeffrey Alan. 1996. "A Good Saxon Compound." *Folklore* 107: 107–8.

McCallum, E. L. 2001. "The Timezone Endgame." *CR: The New Centennial Review* 1: 141–73.

McClusky, Mark. 2003. "A Vehicle of Expression." *AAA World* (July/August): 45–49.

McCosh, Sandra. 1979. *Children's Humour.* London: Granada/Panther.

McCoy, Esther. 1974. "Grandma Prisbrey's Bottle Village." In *Naives and Visionaries,* ed. Walker Art Center, 77–85. New York: E. P. Dutton.

McDonald, Barry. 1997. "Tradition as a Personal Relationship." *Journal of American Folklore* 110: 47–67.

McDonald, Forest. 1994. "What Makes Right? The Theme Is Freedom: Religion, Politics, and the American Tradition." *National Review,* October 24, 62–64.

McGrory, Brian. 1997. "Quayle Attacks Gore's 'Hollywood Values' at N.H. Fund-Raiser." *Boston Globe,* October 27, A9.

McKeon, Michael. 2004. "Tacit Knowledge: Tradition and Its Aftermath." In *Questions of Tradition,* ed. Mark Salber Phillips and Gordon Schochet, 171–202. Toronto: University of Toronto Press.

McLean, Scott L. 2002. *Social Capital: Critical Perspectives on Community and "Bowling Alone."* New York: New York University Press.

McLuhan, Marshall. 1994 [1964]. *Understanding Media: The Extensions of Man.* Cambridge, Mass.: MIT Press.

McNeil, W. K. 1982. "History in American Folklore: An Historical Perspective." *Western Folklore* 41: 30–35.

———. 2005. "Mountain Masculinity: Jokes Southern Mountain Men Tell on Themselves." In *Manly Traditions: The Folk Roots of American Masculinities,* ed. Simon J. Bronner, 261–73. Bloomington: Indiana University Press.

McNeill, Lynne S. 2009. "The End of the Internet: A Folk Response to the Provision of Infinite Choice." In *Folklore and the Internet: Vernacular Expression in a Digital World,* ed. Trevor J. Blank, 80–97. Logan: Utah State University Press.

Mechling, Jay. 1980. "The Magic of the Boy Scout Campfire." *Journal of American Folklore* 93: 35–56.

———. 1986. "Children's Folklore." In *Folk Groups and Folklore Genres: An Introduction,* ed. Elliott Oring, 91–120. Logan: Utah State University Press.

———. 1989. "The Collecting Self and American Youth Movements." In *Consuming Visions: Accumulation and Display of Goods in America, 1880–1920,* ed. Simon J. Bronner, 255–86. New York: W. W. Norton.

———. 1993. "On Sharing Folklore and American Identity in a Multicultural Society." *Western Folklore* 52: 271–89.

———. 1997. "Some [New] Elementary Axioms for and American Cultur[al] Studies." *American Studies* 38: 9–30.

———. 1999. "Children's Folklore in Residential Institutions: Summer Camps, Boarding Schools, Hospitals, and Custodial Facilities." In *Children's Folklore: A Source Book*, ed. Brian Sutton-Smith, Jay Mechling, Thomas W. Johnson, and Felicia R. McMahon, 273–92. Logan: Utah State University Press.

———. 2004. "Picturing Hunting." *Western Folklore* 63: 51–78.

———. 2005a. "The Folklore of Mother-Raised Boys." In *Manly Traditions: The Folk Roots of American Masculinities*, ed. Simon J. Bronner, 211–27. Bloomington: Indiana University Press.

———. 2005b. "Found Photographs and Children's Folklore." *Children's Folklore Review* 27: 7–31.

———. 2006. "Solo Folklore." *Western Folklore* 65: 435–54.

Medved, Michael. 1992. *Hollywood vs. America: Popular Culture and the War on Traditional Values*. New York: HarperCollins.

Mencia, Carlos. 2008. "Re: The Biggest Tragedy in the World of Justice Will Soon Be a Movie." *Vindy.com*. Discussion Groups: Talk of the Valley, August 29. http:forums.vindy.com (accessed September 25, 2008).

Mergen, Bernard. 1999. "Children's Lore in School and Playgrounds." In *Children's Folklore: A Source Book*, ed. Brian Sutton-Smith, Jay Mechling, Thomas W. Johnson, and Felicia R. McMahon, 229–50. Logan: Utah State University Press.

Mieder, Wolfgang, ed. 1992. *A Dictionary of American Proverbs*. New York: Oxford University Press.

———. 2006. "'The Proof of the Proverb Is in the Probing': Alan Dundes as Pioneering Paremiologist." *Western Folklore* 65: 217–62.

———. 2011. "'It Takes a Village to Change the World': Proverbial Politics and the Ethics of Place." *Journal of American Folklore* 124: 217–62.

Mihailović, Kosta. 1989. "Tradition and Industrialization." In *Tradition and Modern Society*, ed. Sven Gustavsson, 27–38. Stockholm: Almqvist & Wiksell.

Mika, Peter. 2007. *Social Networks and the Semantic Web*. New York: Springer.

Mikkelson, Barbara, and David P. Mikkelson. 2008. "Snopes.com: Rumor Has It." *Snopes.com*. Urban Legends References Pages. http://snopes.com (accessed June 16, 2008).

"Milestones." 1987. *Time*, February 2, 68.

Millard, William B. 1997. "I Flamed Freud: A Case Study in Telextual Incendiarism." In *Internet Culture*, ed. David Porter, 145–60. New York: Routledge.

Miller, Dorothy C. 1939. "American Popular Art." In *Art in Our Time*. New York: Museum of Modern Art.

Miller, Laura. 2001. "Women and Children First: Gender and the Settling of the Electronic Frontier." In *Reading Digital Culture*, ed. David Trend, 214–20. Malden, Mass.: Blackwell.

Milspaw, Yvonne. 1983. "Reshaping Tradition: Changes to Pennsylvania German Folk Houses." *Pioneer America* 15: 67–84.

Mintz, Jerome R. 1992. *Hasidic People: A Place in the New World.* Cambridge, Mass.: Harvard University Press.

Mintz, Steven. 2004. *Huck's Raft: A History of American Childhood.* Cambridge, Mass.: Belknap Press of Harvard University Press.

Moore, Deborah Dash. 1994. *To the Golden Cities: Pursuing the American Jewish Dream in Miami and L.A.* New York: Free Press.

Moore, Roy S. v. Judicial Inquiry Commission of the State of Alabama. 2004. Petition for Writ of Certiorari in the Supreme Court of the United States, July 29.

Mordoh, Alice Morrison. 1981. "Analytical Index to the Journal of the Folklore Institute, Vols. 1–15." *Journal of the Folklore Institute* 18: 157–273.

———. 1989. "The Tradition of Geode Construction in Southern Indiana." In *The Old Traditional Way of Life: Essays in Honor of Warren E. Roberts,* ed. Robert E. Walls and George H. Schoemaker, 96–110. Bloomington, Ind.: Trickster Press.

Mulhern, Chieko Irie. 1980. "Japanese Cinderella as a Pubertal Girl's Fantasy." *Southern Folklore Quarterly* 44: 203–14.

Mullen, Patrick B. 1991. *Listening to Old Voices: Folklore, Life Stories, and the Elderly.* Urbana: University of Illinois Press.

Myerhoff, Barbara. 1980. *Number Our Days.* New York: Simon & Schuster.

———. 1982. "Rites of Passage: Process and Paradox." In *Celebration: Studies in Festivity and Ritual,* ed. Victor Turner, 109–35. Washington, D.C.: Smithsonian Institution Press.

———. 1992. *Remembered Lives: The Work of Ritual, Storytelling, and Growing Older.* Ann Arbor: University of Michigan Press.

Nagatsuka, Kaz. 2007. "NFL Japan Raising Level of Play: High School Students Tackle Football's Fundamentals." *Japan Times,* January 25. http://search.japantimes.co.jp/cgi-bin/sf20070125a1.html (accessed September 24, 2008).

Nakamura, Hajime. 1964. *Ways of Thinking of Eastern Peoples: India-China-Tibet-Japan.* Honolulu: East-West Center Press.

Nance, David B. 2004. "Descansos: Roadside Memorials on the American Highway." http://webpages.charter.net/dnance/descansos/ (accessed September 2, 2010).

National Endowment for the Arts. 2007. "Lifetime Honors: NEA National Heritage Fellowships." National Endowment for the Arts website. http://www.nea.gov/honors/heritage/index.html (accessed July 29, 2007).

National Football League. 2009. "NFL: America's Choice." National Football League Report, January. http://www.coldhardfootballfacts.com/Documents/Super_Bowl_1–09_popularity.pdf (accessed February 10, 2009).

Nelson, Maria Burton. 1994. *The Stronger Women Get, the More Men Love Football: Sexism and the American Culture of Sports.* New York: Avon.

Nelson, Marion. 1995. "Norwegian Folk Art in America." In *Norwegian Folk Art: The Migration of a Tradition,* ed. Marion Nelson, 89–100. New York: Abbeville Press.

NESadvantage. 2008. "2012: The Year the Internet Ends." *ScrewAttack.com* blog. http://www.screwattack.com/node/4003 (accessed November 14, 2008).

Newell, William Wells. 1963 [1883]. *Games and Songs of American Children.* New York: Dover.

Nickerson, Bruce E. 1974. "Is There a Folk in the Factory? *Journal of American Folklore* 87: 133–39.

Nicolaisen, W. F. H. 1979. "'Distorted Function' in Material Aspects of Culture." *Folklore Forum* 12: 223–36.

———. 1984. "Names and Narratives." *Journal of American Folklore* 97: 259–72.

———. 1990. "Why Tell Stories?" *Fabula* 31: 5–10.

Niles, John D. 1999. *Homo Narrans: The Poetics and Anthropology of Oral Literature.* Philadelphia: University of Pennsylvania Press.

Nnaemeka, Obioma. 2000. "The Clinton Controversies and the Africa (Igbo) World." *West Africa Review* 2. http://www.westafricareview.com/v012.1/nnaemeka.html (accessed July 23, 2010).

Noble, Allen G. 1984. *Wood, Brick, and Stone: The North American Settlement Landscape*, 2 vols. Amherst: University of Massachusetts Press.

Nolt, Steven M. 2002. *Foreigners in Their Own Land: Pennsylvania Germans in the Early Republic.* University Park: Pennsylvania State University Press.

Norkunas, Martha. 2004. "Narratives of Resistance and the Consequences of Resistance." *Journal of Folklore Research* 41: 105–23.

Norwood, Stephen H. 2004. *Real Football: Conversations on America's Game.* Jackson: University Press of Mississippi.

Noy, Dov Neuman. 1954. "Motif-Index of Talmudic-Midrashic Literature." Ph.D. dissertation, Indiana University.

Noyes, Dorothy. 2009. "Tradition: Three Traditions." *Journal of Folklore Research* 46: 233–68.

Nurge, Ethel. 1975. *Blue Light in the Village: Daily Life in a German Village in 1965–66.* Ann Arbor, Mich.: Published for University of Nebraska Press by University Microfilms International.

Nusbaum, Philip. 1979. "Some Notes on the Construction of the Jewish-American Dialect Story." *Keystone Folklore* 23: 28–52.

Nylund, David. 2003. "Taking a Slice at Sexism: The Controversy over the Exclusionary Membership Practices of the Augusta National Golf Club." *Journal of Sport and Social Issues* 27: 195–202.

———. 2007. *Beer, Babes, and Balls: Masculinity and Sports Talk Radio.* Albany: State University of New York Press.

Oakeshott, Michael. 1962. *Rationalism in Politics and Other Essays.* New York: Basic.

Oates, John, Clare Wood, and Andrew Grayson. 2005. *Psychological Development and Early Childhood.* Malden, Mass.: Blackwell.

Ochs, Peter. 1998. *Peirce, Pragmatism, and the Logic of Scripture.* Cambridge: Cambridge University Press.

Ochs, Vanessa. 2011. "Same-Sex Marriage Ceremonies in a Time of Coalescence." In *Revisioning Ritual: Traditions in Transition*, ed. Simon J. Bronner, 190–210. Oxford: Littman.

Ó Giolláin, Diarmuid. 2003. "Tradition, Modernity and Cultural Diversity."

In *Dynamics of Tradition: Perspectives on Oral Poetry and Folk Belief*, ed. Lotte Tarkka, 35–47. Helsinki: Finnish Literature Society.

Ohrn, Steven. 1984. "Faith into Stone: Grottoes and Monuments." In *Passing Time and Traditions: Contemporary Iowa Folk Artists*, ed. Steven Ohrn, 129–41. Ames: Iowa State University Press for the Iowa Arts Council.

Oinas, Felix, ed. 1978. *Folklore, Nationalism, and Politics*. Columbus, Ohio: Slavica Press.

Oliver, Paul. 1986. "Vernacular Know-how." *Material Culture* 18: 113–26.

———. 1989. "Handed Down Architecture: Tradition and Transmission." In *Dwellings, Settlements, and Tradition: Cross-Cultural Perspectives*, ed. Jean-Paul Bourdier and Nezar Alsayyad, 53–75. Lanham, Md.: University Press of America.

———. 1997a. "Introduction." In *Encyclopedia of Vernacular Architecture of the World*, xxi–xxviii. Cambridge: Cambridge University Press.

———. 1997b. "Tradition and Transmission." In *Encyclopedia of Vernacular Architecture of the World*, 117–18. Cambridge: Cambridge University Press.

———. 1999. "Vernacular Architecture in the Twenty-First Century." Typescript. Hepworth Lecture. London: Prince of Wales Institute.

———. 2006. *Built to Meet Needs: Cultural Issues in Vernacular Architecture*. Amsterdam: Architectural Press.

Ophir, Adi. 1991. *Plato's Invisible Cities: Discourse and Power in the Republic*. Savage, Md.: Barnes & Noble.

Opie, Iona, and Peter Opie. 1969. *Children's Games in Street and Playground*. Oxford: Clarendon.

———. 1985. *The Singing Game*. Oxford: Oxford University Press.

Orange Show Center for Visionary Art. 2010. "The Orange Show Is a Folk-Art Environment." http://www.orangeshow.org/orange-show-monument (accessed August 20, 2010).

Orenstein, Peggy. 2011. *Cinderella Ate My Daughter: Dispatches from the Front Lines of the New Girlie-Girl Culture*. New York: HarperCollins.

Oriard, Michael. 1993. *Reading Football: How the Popular Press Created an American Spectacle*. Chapel Hill: University of North Carolina Press.

———. 2001. *King Football: Sport and Spectacle in the Golden Age of Radio and Newsreels, Movies and Magazines, the Weekly and the Daily Press*. Chapel Hill: University of North Carolina Press.

———. 2007. *Brand NFL: Making and Selling America's Favorite Sport*. Chapel Hill: University of North Carolina Press.

Oring, Elliott. 1975. "Everything Is a Shade of Elephant: An Alternative to a Psychoanalysis of Humor." *New York Folklore* 1: 149–60.

———. 1976. "Three Functions of Folklore: Traditional Functionalism as Explanation in Folkloristics." *Journal of American Folklore* 89: 67–80.

———. 1978. "Transmission and Degeneration." *Fabula* 19: 193–210.

———. 1986. "On the Concepts of Folklore." In *Folk Groups and Folklore Genres*, ed. Elliott Oring, 1–22. Logan: Utah State University Press.

———. 1987. "Jokes and the Discourse on Disaster." *Journal of American Folklore* 100: 276–86.

———. 1989. "Documenting Folklore: The Annotation." In *Folk Groups and*

Folklore Genres: A Reader, ed. Elliott Oring, 358–73. Logan: Utah State University Press.

———. 1992. *Jokes and Their Relations*. Lexington: University Press of Kentucky.

———. 1994. "The Arts, Artifacts, and Artifices of Identity." *Journal of American Folklore* 107: 211–47.

———. 1996. "Folklorizing Theory." *Folklore Historian* 13: 30–32.

———. 2003. *Engaging Humor*. Urbana: University of Illinois Press.

———. 2006. "Missing Theory." *Western Folklore* 65: 455–65.

———. 2008. "Legendry and the Rhetoric of Truth." *Journal of American Folklore* 121: 127–66.

Ortner, Sherry B. 1974. "Is Female to Male as Nature Is to Culture?" In *Women, Culture and Society*, ed. Michelle Zimbalist Rosaldo and Louise Lamphere, 67–87. Stanford, Calif.: Stanford University Press.

Outten, Holly. 1988. "The Touch." Manuscript. Children's Folklore Section of the American Folklore Society Collection, Pennsylvania State University–Harrisburg Folklore Archives.

Oxreider, Julia. 1977. "The Slumber Party: Transition into Adolescence." *Tennessee Folklore Society Bulletin* 43: 128–34.

Paolantonio, Sal. 2008. *How Football Explains America*. Chicago: Triumph Books.

Paredes, Américo. 1972. "Foreword." In *Toward New Perspectives in Folklore*, ed. Américo Paredes and Richard Bauman, ix–x. Austin: University of Texas Press.

Paredes, Américo, and Richard Bauman, eds. 1972. *Toward New Perspectives in Folklore*. Austin: University of Texas Press.

Paredes, Américo, and Ellen Stekert, eds. 1971. *The Urban Experience and Folk Tradition*. Austin: University of Texas Press.

Parsons, Patrick R., and William E. Smith. 1988. "R. Budd Dwyer: A Case Study in Newsroom Decision Making." *Journal of Mass Media Ethics* 3: 84–94.

Partridge, Eric. 1970. *A Dictionary of Slang and Unconventional English*. New York: Macmillan.

Patiris, Phillip D. 1999. "The Budd Dwyer Suicide Clip: Communication Ethics . . . and a Change of Mind." *Modern Television* blog, November 20. http://www.moderntv.com/modtvweb/qtclips/buddintro.htm (accessed September 24, 2008).

Paul, Ian. 2009. "Twitter Travails: Pranks and Deleted Account Errors." *Today @PCWorld* blog. http://www.pcworld.com/article/167889/twitter_travails _pranks_and_deleted_account_errors.html (accessed September 12, 2010).

PC Tools Software. 2007. "Do You Have the Right Protection?" Advertisement for Spyware Doctor security program. *Game Informer* 176 (December): 15.

Pelikan, Jaroslav. 1984. *The Vindication of Tradition*. New Haven, Conn.: Yale University Press.

Pellegrini, Anthony D., ed. 1995. *The Future of Play: A Multidisciplinary Inquiry into the Contributions of Brian Sutton-Smith*. Albany: State University of New York Press.

Pellegrini, Anthony D., Kentaro Kato, Peter Blatchford, and Ed Baines. 2002. "A Short-Term Longitudinal Study of Children's Playground Games across the First Year of School: Implications for Social Competence and Adjustment to School." *American Educational Research Journal* 39: 991–1015.

Pells, Eddie. 2008. "Florida, Oklahoma Await Pairing for National Title." *ABC News*, December 7. http://abcnews.go.com/Sports/wireStory?id=6412399 (accessed January 8, 2009).

Peltz, Rakhmiel. 1998. *From Immigrant to Ethnic Culture: American Yiddish in South Philadelphia*. Stanford, Calif.: Stanford University Press.

Perez, Allie. 2008. "The Sports Tradition." *Cornell Daily Sun*, September 18. http://cornellsun.com/node/31920 (accessed January 8, 2009).

Pérez, Domino Renee. 2002. "Caminando Con La Llorona: Traditional and Contemporary Narrative." In *Chicana Traditions: Continuity and Change*, ed. Norma E. Cantú and Olga Nájera-Ramírez, 100–116. Urbana: University of Illinois Press.

Peterson, Sally. 1988a. "'They Know the Rule for What Will Make It Pretty': Hmong Material Traditions in Translation." In *Craft and Community: Traditional Arts in Contemporary Society*, ed. Shalom D. Staub, 107–18. Philadelphia and Harrisburg: Balch Institute for Ethnic Studies and Pennsylvania Heritage Affairs Commission.

———. 1988b. "Translating Experience and the Reading of a Story Cloth." *Journal of American Folklore* 101: 6–22.

Petőfi, János S., and Eva Szöllösy. 1969. "Computers in Folklore Research." *Computational Linguistics* 8: 65–70.

Pew Research Center. 2010. "Teen and Young Adult Internet Use." *Millennials: A Portrait of Generation Next*. http://pewresearch.org/millennials/teen-internet-use-graphic.php (accessed September 9, 2010).

Phillips, Donald G. 2000. *Post-National Patriotism and the Feasibility of Post-National Community in United Germany*. Westport, Conn.: Praeger.

Phillips, Mark Salber, and Gorden Schochet, eds. 2004. *Questions of Traditions*. Toronto: University of Toronto Press.

Phillips, Richard H. 1960. "The Nature and Function of Children's Formal Games." *Psychoanalytic Quarterly* 29: 200–207.

Pieper, Josef. 2008. *Tradition: Concept and Claim*. Wilmington, Del.: ISI Books.

Pleck, Elizabeth H. 2000. *Celebrating the Family: Ethnicity, Consumer Culture, and Family Rituals*. Cambridge, Mass.: Harvard University Press.

Pollack, William. 1998. *Real Boys: Rescuing Our Sons from the Myths of Boyhood*. New York: Henry Holt.

Popper, Dr. K. R. 1949. "Towards a Rational Theory of Tradition." *Rationalist Annual*, 36–55.

Posen, I. Sheldon, and Daniel Franklin Ward. 1985. "Watts Towers and the

Giglio Tradition." In *Folklife Annual 1985*, ed. Alan Jabbour and James Hardin, 143–57. Washington, D.C.: Library of Congress.

Poster, Mark. 2001. "Cyberdemocracy: The Internet and the Public Sphere." In *Reading Digital Culture*, ed. David Trend, 259–71. Malden, Mass.: Blackwell.

Praeger, Dave. 2007. *Poop Culture: How America Is Shaped by Its Grossest National Product*. Los Angeles: Feral House.

Preston, Michael J. 1994. "Traditional Humor from the Fax Machine: 'All of a Kind.'" *Western Folklore* 53: 147–69.

———. 1996. "Computer Folklore." In *American Folklore: An Encyclopedia*, ed. Jan Harold Brunvand, 154–55. New York: Garland.

Price, H. Wayne, and William D. Walters Jr. 1989. "Barn Raising at Metamora: A Photographic Essay." *Material Culture* 21: 47–56.

Price, Joseph L., ed. 2001. *From Season to Season: Sports as American Religion*. Macon, Ga.: Mercer University Press.

Propp, Vladimir. 1968. *Morphology of the Folktale*. 2nd rev. ed. Trans. Laurence Scott. Ed. Louis A. Wagner. Austin: University of Texas Press.

Pucin, Diane. 2008. "3-D TD Jumps Off Screen."*Los Angeles Times*, December 5. http://articles.latimes.com/2008/dec/05/sports/sp-media5 (accessed September 12, 2010).

Putnam, Robert D. 2000. *Bowling Alone: The Collapse and Revival of American Community*. New York: Touchstone.

Quillen, Ed. 1990. "Traditional American Values." *Denver Post*, December 30, sec. I, 3.

Rachlin, Howard. 1990. "Why Do People Gamble and Keep Gambling Despite Heavy Losses?" *Psychological Science* 1: 294–97.

Rader, Benjamin G. 1999. *American Sports: From the Age of Folk Games to the Age of Televised Sports*. Upper Saddle River, N.J.: Prentice-Hall.

Radin, Max. 1935. "Tradition." In *Encyclopedia of the Social Sciences*, ed. E. R. A. Seligman, 15: 62–67. New York: Macmillan.

Randall, Lisa. 2002. "Extra Dimensions and Warped Geometries." *Science* 296: 1422–27.

Raphael, J. R. 2009. "People Search Engines Tell Your Secrets." *PCWorld* (June): 12–14.

Raphael, Ray. 1988. *The Men from the Boys: Rites of Passage in Male America*. Lincoln: University of Nebraska Press.

Rapoport, Amos. 1989. "On the Attributes of 'Tradition.'" In *Dwellings, Settlements, and Tradition: Cross-Cultural Perspectives*, ed. Jean-Paul Bourdier and Nezar Alsayyad, 77–105. Lanham, Md.: University Press of America.

Read, Allen Walker. 1935. *Lexical Evidence from Folk Epigraphy in Western North America: A Glossarial Study of the Low Element in the English Vocabulary*. Paris: Privately printed.

Redfield, Robert. 1947. "The Folk Society." *American Journal of Sociology* 52: 293–308.

———. 1960. *The Little Community and Peasant Society and Culture*. Chicago: University of Chicago Press.

Reid, Heather L. 2008. "Heroes of the Coliseum." In *Football and Philosophy: Going Deep*, ed. Michael W. Austin, 128–40. Lexington: University Press of Kentucky.

Rheingold, Howard. 2001. "The Virtual Community." In *Reading Digital Culture*, ed. David Trend, 272–80. Malden, Mass.: Blackwell.

Rich, Tracey. 2002. "Sukkot." *Judaism 101*. http://www.jewfaq.org/holiday5 .htm (accessed July 28, 2007).

Richter, Alan. 1987. *The Language of Sexuality*. Jefferson, N.C.: McFarland.

Riesman, David. 1961 [1950]. *The Lonely Crowd*. New Haven, Conn.: Yale University Press.

Riesman, David, and Reuel Denney. 1951. "Football in America: A Study in Cultural Diffusion." *American Quarterly* 3: 309–25.

Robbins, Alexandra. 2004. *Pledged: The Secret Life of Sororities*. New York: Hyperion.

Roberts, John W. 1989. *From Trickster to Badman: The Black Folk Hero in Slavery and Freedom*. Philadelphia: University of Pennsylvania Press.

Roberts, Roderick J., Jr. 1965. "Negro Folklore in a Southwestern Industrial School." Master's thesis, Indiana University, Bloomington.

Roberts, Sam. 1995. *Who We Are: A Portrait of America Based on the Latest U.S. Census*. New York: Times Books.

Robertson, James Oliver. 1980. *American Myth, American Reality*. New York: Hill & Wang.

Robinson, John V. 2001. "The 'Topping Out' Traditions of the High-Steel Ironworkers." *Western Folklore* 60: 243–62.

Roemer, Danielle. 1994. "Photocopy Lore and the Naturalization of the Corporate Body." *Journal of American Folklore* 107: 121–38.

Rogers, Patricia Dane. 2003. "Drinks on the House: When the Root Beer Is Gone, the Can Lives On." *Washington Post*, May 8, H1.

Rolfe, John. 2008. "Beautiful Losers: Immortality Can Come with Losing the Super Bowl." *Sports Illustrated* website, January 22. http://sportsillustrated .cnn.com/2008/writers/john_rolfe/01/22/super.bowl.losers/index.html (accessed September 19, 2008).

Ronnell, Avital. 2001. "A Disappearance of Community.' In *Reading Digital Culture*, ed. David Trend, 287–93. Malden, Mass.: Blackwell.

Roosevelt, Theodore. 1899. *The Rough Riders*. New York: Review of Reviews.

Rosen, Jonathan. 2000. *The Talmud and the Internet: A Journey between Worlds*. New York: Farrar, Straus & Giroux.

Rosen, Seymour. 1979. *In Celebration of Ourselves*. San Francisco: California Living in association with San Francisco Museum of Modern Art.

Rosenberg, Michael. 2008. *War as They Knew It: Woody Hayes, Bo Schembechler, and America in a Time of Unrest*. New York: Grand Central Publishing.

Ross, Andrew. 2001. "The New Smartness." In *Reading Digital Culture*, ed. David Trend, 354–63. Malden, Mass.: Blackwell.

Ross, Edward Alsworth. 1909. *Social Psychology: An Outline and Source Book*. New York: Macmillan.

Roud, Steve. 2003. *The Penguin Guide to the Superstitions of Britain and Ireland*. New York: Penguin.

———. 2010. *The Lore of the Playground: One Hundred Years of Children's Games, Rhymes and Traditions*. London: Random House.

———. 2011. *Roud Folksong Index*. Vaughan Williams Memorial Library Website for the English Folk Dance and Song Society. http://library.efdss.org/cgi-bin/home.cgi?access=off (accessed March 25, 2011).

Rowe, John Carlos, ed. 2000. *Post-Nationalist American Studies*. Berkeley: University of California Press.

Rożek, Michał. 1990. *Jewish Monuments of Kraków's Kazimierz*. Kraków: Oficyna Cracovia.

Rubin, David C. 1995. *Memory in Oral Traditions: The Cognitive Psychology of Epic, Ballads, and Counting-out Rhymes*. New York: Oxford University Press.

Rudolph, Frederick. 1990 [1962]. *The American College & University: A History*. Athens: University of Georgia Press.

Rumford, Beatrix T. 1980. "Uncommon Art of the Common People: A Review of Trends in the Collecting and Exhibiting of American Folk Art." In *Perspectives on American Folk Art*, ed. Ian M. G. Quimby and Scott T. Swank, 13–53. New York: W. W. Norton.

Russell, Don. 1998. "Dwyer Suicide Lives On: Sex Isn't All that Parents Should Monitor on the Web." *Philadelphia Daily News* website, February 16. http://www.moderntv.com/modtvweb/budd/buddpress/budd16b.htm (accessed September 25, 2008).

Sabbath, Dan, and Mandel Hall. 1977. *End Product: The First Taboo*. New York: Urizen Books.

Said, Edward. 1993. *Culture and Imperialism*. London: Chatto & Windus.

———. 1994. *Orientalism: Western Conceptions of the Orient*. New York: Vintage.

Salmons, Joe. 1988. "On the Social Function of Some Southern Indiana German-American Dialect Stories." *Humor: International Journal of Humor Research* 1: 159–75.

Samuelson, Sue. 1980. "The Cooties Complex." *Western Folklore* 39: 198–210.

———. 1983. "Notes on a Sociology of Folklore as a Science." *New York Folklore* 9: 13–20.

Sanders, Irwin T. 1958. *The Community: An Introduction to a Social System*. New York: Ronald Press.

Santino, Jack. 1986. "The Folk *Assemblage* of Autumn: Tradition and Creativity in Halloween Folk Art." In *Folk Art and Art Worlds*, ed. John Michael Vlach and Simon J. Bronner, 151–70. Ann Arbor, Mich.: UMI Research Press.

———. 2006a. "Performative Commemoratives: Spontaneous Shrines and the Public Memorialization of Death." In *Spontaneous Shrines and the Public Memorialization of Death*, ed. Jack Santino, 5–16. New York: Palgrave Macmillan.

———, ed. 2006b. *Spontaneous Shrines and the Public Memorialization of Death*. New York: Palgrave Macmillan.

Sapir, Edward. 1917. "Do We Need a 'Superorganic'?" *American Anthropologist* 19: 441–47.

Schertz, Chaim. 2005. "Orthodoxy on the Periphery—Where It Counts." *Jewish Action* (summer): 22–24.

Schlereth, Thomas J. 1990. *Cultural History and Material Culture: Everyday Life, Landscapes, Museums.* Ann Arbor, Mich.: UMI Research Press.

Schlesinger, Arthur M. 1998. *The Disuniting of America: Reflections on a Multicultural Society.* 2nd ed. New York: W. W. Norton.

Schneider, Mark A. 1987. "Culture-as-Text in the Work of Clifford Geertz." *Theory and Society* 16: 809–39.

Scholastic Inc. 2008. "Kids USA Survey: Favorite Sports." http://teacher.scholastic.com/kidusasu/favsport/index.htm (accessed March 27, 2011).

Scholem, Gershom. 1966. "The Golem of Prague and the Golem of Rehovoth." *Commentary* 41 (January): 62–65.

Schudson, Michael. 2003. "Click Here for Democracy: A History and Critique of an Information-Based Model of Citizenship." In *Democracy and New Media,* ed. Henry Jenkins and David Thorburn, 49–60. Cambridge, Mass.: MIT Press.

Schwendener, Norma. 1932. *Game Preferences of 10,000 Fourth Grade Children.* New York: Columbia University.

Sciorra, Joseph. 1989. "Yard Shrines and Sidewalk Altars of New York's Italian Americans." In *Perspectives in Vernacular Architecture, III,* ed. Thomas Carter and Bernard L. Herman, 185–98. Columbia: University of Missouri Press.

Scott, Janny. 1997. "An Appomattox in the Culture Wars." *New York Times Weekly Review,* May 25, 1–4.

Scott, Walter. 1933 [1808]. *Marmion: A Tale of Flodden Field, in Six Cantos.* New York: Macmillan.

Sebeok, Thomas A. 1965. "The Computer as a Tool in Folklore Research." In *The Use of Computers in Anthropology,* ed. Dell Hymes, 255–72. The Hague: Mouton.

Seifter, Jacob. 1977. "Die Stadt Ospitsin." In *Sefer Oshpitsin,* ed. Ch. Wolnerman, A. Burstin, and M. S. Geshuri, 355–61. Jerusalem: Irgun Yotzey Oswiecim.

Seltzer, Debra Jane. 2000. "Bottle Houses." *Roadside Architecture.* http://www.agilitynut.com/bh.html (accessed July 28, 2007).

Sewell, Ernestine P., and Charles E. Linck Jr. 1985. "The Rural Mailbox." In *Folk Art in Texas,* ed. Francis Edward Abernethy, 22–25. Dallas: Southern Methodist University Press.

Sheehy, Colleen J. 1998. *The Flamingo in the Garden: American Yard Art and the Vernacular Landscape.* New York: Garland.

Sheldon, Henry Davidson. 1901. *The History and Pedagogy of American Student Societies.* New York: D. Appleton.

Shepard, Richard F., and Vicki Gold Levi. 1982. *Live and Be Well: A Celebration of Yiddish Culture in America.* New York: Ballantine.

Sherman, Josepha. 1992. *A Sampler of Jewish American Folklore.* Little Rock, Ark.: August House.

Sherman, Josepha, and T. K. F. Weisskopf. 1995. *Greasy Grimy Gopher Guts: The Subversive Folklore of Childhood.* Little Rock, Ark.: August House.

Sherzer, Joel. 1993. "On Puns, Comebacks, Verbal Dueling, and Play

Languages: Speech Play in Balinese Verbal Life." *Language in Society* 22: 217–33.

Shils, Edward. 1958. "Tradition and Liberty: Antinomy and Interdependence." *Ethics* 68: 153–65.

———. 1981. *Tradition*. Chicago: University of Chicago Press.

Shimamura, Takanori. 2003. "Cultural Diversity and Folklore Studies in Japan: A Multicultural Approach." *Asian Folklore Studies* 62: 195–224.

Shin, Hyon B., and Robert A. Kominski. 2010. *Language Use in the United States: 2007*. American Community Survey Reports, ACS-12. Washington, D.C.: U.S. Census Bureau.

Shubnell, Thomas F. 2008. *Greatest Jokes of the Century Book 1*. Scotts Valley, Calif.: CreateSpace.

Shulman, Yaakov David. 1991. *The Rema: The Story of Rabbi Moshe Isserles*. New York: C. I. S. Publishers.

Shuman, Amy, and Charles L. Briggs. 1993. "Introduction." In *Theorizing Folklore: Toward New Perspectives on the Politics of Culture*, ed. Charles Briggs and Amy Shuman, 109–34. Los Angeles: California Folklore Society.

Sider, Gerald. 1986. *Culture and Class in Anthropology and History: A Newfoundland Illustration*. Cambridge: Cambridge University Press.

Silverman, Carol. 1983. "The Politics of Folklore in Bulgaria." *Anthropological Quarterly* 56: 55–61.

Simmel, Georg. 1906. "The Sociology of Secrecy and of Secret Societies." *American Journal of Sociology* 11: 441–98.

Simons, Elizabeth Radin. 1986. "The NASA Joke Cycle: The Astronauts and the Teacher." *Western Folklore* 45: 261–77.

Simpson, George. 1951. "Editor's Introduction." In *Suicide: A Study in Sociology* by Emile Durkheim, ed. George Simpson, 13–32. New York: Free Press.

Singer, Isaac Bashevis. 1978. *Nobel Lecture*. New York: Farrar, Straus & Giroux.

Siporin, Steve. 1992. *American Folk Masters: The National Heritage Fellows*. New York: Harry N. Abrams.

Slotkin, Richard. 1973. *Regeneration through Violence: The Mythology of the American Frontier, 1600–1860*. Middletown, Conn.: Wesleyan University Press.

———. 1993. *Gunfighter Nation: The Myth of the Frontier in Twentieth-Century America*. New York: HarperCollins.

Smargon, Adam Joshua. 2008. "College Nicknames." http:www.smargon.net/nicknames (accessed February 10, 2009).

Smith, Bubba. 1983. *Kill, Bubba, Kill*. New York: Simon & Schuster.

Smith, Craig. 1995. "Dan Quayle and Family Values: Epideictic Appeals in Political Campaigns." *Southern Communication Journal* 60: 152–64.

Smith, Elmer Lewis. 1958. *The Amish People: Seventeenth-Century Tradition in Modern America*. New York: Exposition Press.

———. 1960. *The Amish Today: An Analysis of Their Beliefs, Behavior and Contemporary Problems*. Allentown, Pa.: Pennsylvania German Society.

Smith, Elmer Lewis, and Grant M. Stoltzfus. 1959. "The Community Barn-Raising." *Historical Review of Berks County* 24: 37–43.

Smith, Henry Nash. 1978 [1950]. *Virgin Land: The American West as Symbol and Myth*. Cambridge, Mass.: Harvard University Press.

Smith, Michael R. 1987. "Newsroom Dilemma." *Editor & Publisher*, January 31, 9–11.

Smith, Winifred. 1926. "A Modern Child's Game Rhymes." *Journal of American Folklore* 39: 82–85.

Smyth, Willie. 1986. "*Challenger* Jokes and the Humor of Disaster." *Western Folklore* 45: 243–60.

Sommerer, Christa, and Laurent Mignonneau. 1999. "Art as a Living System: Interactive Computer Artworks." *Leonardo* 32: 165–73.

Sommers, Christina Hoff. 2000. *The War against Boys: How Misguided Feminism Is Harming Our Young Men*. New York: Simon & Schuster.

Spencer, Martin E. 1994. "Multiculturalism, 'Political Correctness,' and the Politics of Identity." *Sociological Forum* 9: 547–67.

Sporting News. 2008. "Pro Football War Room." http://warroom.sportingnews.com/promo.html (accessed September 12, 2008).

Stanley, Tom. 1984. "Two South Carolina Folk Environments." In *Personal Places: Perspectives on Informal Art Environments*, ed. Daniel Franklin Ward, 62–71. Bowling Green, Ohio: Bowling Green State University Popular Press.

Staples, Andy. 2010. "Shift to 3-D TV Broadcasts Will Begin with College Football Fans." *SI.com*, March 3. http://sportsillustrated.cnn.com/2010/writers/andy_staples/03/02/3d-tv/index.html (accessed September 12, 2010).

Starbucks Newsroom. 2008. "Steeped in Coffeehouse Tradition, Starbucks Introduces New Handcrafted Tea Beverages and Encourages Consumers Take a Much Needed Break." http://news.starbucks.com/article_display.cfm?article_id=3 (accessed March 23, 2011).

Staub, Shalom. 1988. "Folklore and Authenticity: A Myopic Marriage in Public Sector Programs." In *The Conservation of Culture: Folklorists and the Public Sector*, ed. Burt Feintuch, 166–79. Lexington: University Press of Kentucky.

Steinberg, Theodore. 2006. *American Green: The Obsessive Quest for the Perfect Lawn*. New York: W. W. Norton.

Steinmetz, Sol. 1986. *Yiddish and English: A Century of Yiddish in America*. Tuscaloosa: University of Alabama Press.

Stelter, Brian. 2008. "Charging by the Byte to Curb Internet Traffic." *New York Times*, June 15, 1, 21.

Stempel, Carl. 2006. "Televised Sports, Masculinist Moral Capital, and Support for the U.S. Invasion of Iraq." *Journal of Sport and Social Issues* 30: 79–106.

Stephens, John Richard. 2001. *Into the Mummy's Tomb*. New York: Berkley.

Stewart, Edward C., and Milton J. Bennett. 1991. *American Cultural Patterns*. Rev. ed. Yarmouth, Me.: Intercultural Press.

Stivale, Charles J. 1997. "Spam: Heteroglossia and Harassment in Cyberspace." In *Internet Culture*, ed. David Porter, 133–44. New York: Routledge.

Stokes, Adrian. 1956. "Psycho-Analytic Reflections on the Development of

Ball Games, Particularly Cricket." *International Journal of Psycho-Analysis* 37: 185–92.

"The Stoll Report." 1997. *Forward*, March 28, 5.

Stone, Lisa, Jim Zanzi, and Earl Iversen. 1999. "In Imitation of Nature: Father P. M. Dobberstein's Grottoes in Iowa and Wisconsin." In *Backyard Visionaries: Grassroots Art in the Midwest*, ed. Barbara Brackman and Cathy Dwigans, 50–69. Lawrence: University Press of Kansas.

Stoudt, John Baer. 1915. *The Folklore of the Pennsylvania-German*. Lancaster, Pa.: Pennsylvania German Society.

Stratton, Jon. 1997. "Cyberspace and the Globalization of Culture." In *Internet Culture*, ed. David Porter, 253–76. New York: Routledge.

Su, Rick. 2010. "The Overlooked Significance of Arizona's New Immigration Law." *Michigan Law Review* 76. http://www.michiganlawreview.org/assets/fi/108/su.pdf (accessed July 30, 2010).

"Suicide Video Link." 2007. *MetaTalk*, April 28. Discussion thread. http://metatalk.metafilter.com/14104/suicide-video-link (accessed September 26, 2008).

Sullivan, Bob. 2005. "Kids, Blogs and Too Much Information." msnbc website. http://www.msnbc.msn.com/id/7668788/ (accessed June 15, 2008).

Sullivan, C. W., III. 1987. "Johnny Says His ABCs." *Western Folklore* 46: 36–41.

Sussman, Bernard. 1995a. Correspondence with Simon J. Bronner, March 9.

———. 1995b. Correspondence with Simon J. Bronner, March 13.

Sutton-Smith, Brian. 1959. *Games of New Zealand Children*. Berkeley: University of California Press.

———. 1970. "Psychology of Childlore: The Triviality Barrier." *Western Folklore* 29: 1–8.

———. 1971. "A Developmental Psychology of Play and the Arts." *Perspectives on Education* (spring): 8–17.

———. 1972. "The Expressive Profile." In *Toward New Perspectives in Folklore*, ed. Américo Paredes and Richard Bauman, 80–92. Austin: University of Texas Press.

———. 1979a. "The Importance of Children's Folklore." In *Festival of American Folklife 1979*, ed. Peter Seitel, 5–6. Washington, D.C.: Smithsonian Institution.

———. 1979b. "The Play of Girls. In *Becoming Female: Perspectives on Development*, ed. Claire B. Kopp, 229–57. New York: Plenum.

———. 1980. "The Playground as Zoo." *Newsletter of the Association for the Anthropological Study of Play* 7: 4–8.

———. 1981. *A History of Children's Play: The New Zealand Playground, 1840–1950*. Philadelphia: University of Pennsylvania Press.

———. 1986. *Toys as Culture*. New York: Gardner Press.

———. 1990a. "The Future Agenda of Child Study and the Implications for the Study of Children's Folklore." *Children's Folklore Review* 1: 117–21.

———. 1990b. "School Playground as Festival." *Children's Environments Quarterly* 7: 3–7.

———. 1992. "Tradition from the Perspective of Children's Games." *Children's Folklore Review* 14: 3–16.

———. 1995. "History of Children's Folklore." In *Children's Folklore: A Source Book*, ed. Brian Sutton-Smith, Jay Mechling, Thomas W. Johnson, and Felicia R. McMahon, 20–22. New York: Garland.

———. 1997. *The Ambiguity of Play*. Cambridge, Mass.: Harvard University Press.

Sutton-Smith, Brian, and John M. Roberts. 1972. "The Cross-Cultural and Psychological Study of Games." In *The Folkgames of Children* by Brian Sutton-Smith, 331–40. Austin: University of Texas Press.

Sutton-Smith, Brian, John M. Roberts, and Adam Kendon. 1972. In *The Folkgames of Children* by Brian Sutton-Smith, 341–58. Austin: University of Texas Press.

Swaine, Michael, and Paul Freiberger. 1983. "Lee Felsenstein: Populist Engineer." *InfoWorld* 5 (November 7): 105–7.

Swinson, Angela P. 2000. "Parents Salvage Holiday Custom." *Patriot-News* (Harrisburg, Pa.), October 7, A1.

Swiss, Thomas. 2004. "Electronic Literature: Discourses, Communities, Traditions." In *Memory Bytes: History, Technology, and Digital Culture*, ed. Lauren Rabinovitz and Abraham Geil, 283–304. Durham, N.C.: Duke University Press.

Tabbi, Joseph. 1997. "Reading, Writing, Hypertext: Democratic Politics in the Virtual Classroom." In *Internet Culture*, ed. David Porter, 233–52. New York: Routledge.

Tallis, Raymond. 2005. "The Linguistic Unconscious: Saussure and the Post-Saussureans." In *Theory's Empire: An Anthology of Dissent*, ed. Daphne Patai and Will H. Corral, 126–46. New York: Columbia University Press.

Taylor, Archer. 1994. "The Wisdom of Many and the Wit of One." In *The Wisdom of Many: Essays on the Proverb*, ed. Wolfgang Mieder and Alan Dundes, 3–9. Madison: University of Wisconsin Press.

Teyssot, Georges. 1999. *The American Lawn*. New York: Princeton Architectural Press.

Theis, Susanne. 1998. "The Drive to Create: Three Handmade Personal Spaces in Houston." *Folk Art Messenger* 11, no. 2. http://www.folkart.org/mag/drive/drivetocreate.html (accessed September 12, 2010).

Thomas, Jeannie B. 2007. "The Usefulness of Ghost Stories." In *Haunting Experiences: Ghosts in Contemporary Folklore* by Diane E. Goldstein, Sylvia Ann Grider, and Jeannie Banks Thomas, 25–59. Logan: Utah State University Press.

Thompson, Stith. 1951. "Folklore at Midcentury." *Midwest Folklore* 1: 5–12.

———. 1955–1958. *Motif-Index of Folk-Literature: A Classification of Narrative Elements in Folktales, Ballads, Myths, Fables, Mediaeval Romances, Exempla, Fabiaux, Jest-books, and Local Legends*. Rev. and enlarged ed. Bloomington: Indiana University Press.

Thoms, William. 1965 [1846]. "Folklore." In *The Study of Folklore*, ed. Alan Dundes, 4–6. Englewood Cliffs, N.J.: Prentice-Hall.

Thorne, Barrie. 1993. *Gender Play: Girls and Boys in School*. New Brunswick, N.J.: Rutgers University Press.

Tilly, Charles. 2006. *Why? What Happens When People Give Reasons . . . and Why.* Princeton, N.J.: Princeton University Press.

"Tinkering with Iron: Recycling Skills and Materials." 1984. In *Passing Time and Traditions: Contemporary Iowa Folk Artists,* ed. Steven Ohrn, 142–48. Ames: Iowa State University Press for the Iowa Arts Council.

Tishler, William H. 1982. "Stovewood Construction in the Upper Midwest and Canada: A Regional Vernacular Architectural Tradition." In *Perspectives in Vernacular Architecture,* ed. Camille Wells, 125–36. Annapolis, Md.: Vernacular Architecture Forum.

Toelken, Barre. 1979. *The Dynamics of Folklore.* Boston: Houghton Mifflin.

———. 1995. *Morning Dew and Roses: Nuance, Metaphor, and Meaning in Folksongs.* Urbana: University of Illinois Press.

———. 1996. *The Dynamics of Folklore.* Rev. and expanded ed. Logan: Utah State University Press.

Toffler, Alvin, and Heidi Toffler. 2006. *Revolutionary Wealth: How It Will Be Created and How It Will Change Our Lives.* New York: Doubleday.

"Toilet Computer Chair." 2011. *CoolFunPics.com.* http://www.coolfunpics .com/slides/Toilet_Computer_Chair.html (accessed March 28, 2011).

Tolson, Jay. 2007. "A Return to Tradition." *U.S. News & World Report,* December 13. http://www.usnews.com/articles/news/national/2007/12/13/a-return -to-tradition.html (accessed December 12, 2008).

Tortora, Vincent R. 1980. *The Amish Folk of Pennsylvania Dutch Country: Their Life, Manners, Customs and Costumes.* Manheim, Pa.: Photo Arts Press.

Trachtenberg, Joshua. 1979 [1939]. *Jewish Magic and Superstition: A Study in Folk Religion.* New York: Atheneum.

Trujillo, Nick. 1995. "Machines, Missiles, and Men: Images of the Male Body on ABC's *Monday Night Football.*" *Sociology of Sport Journal* 12: 403–23.

Truscello, Michael. 2003. "The Architecture of Information: Open Source Software and Tactical Poststructuralist Anarchism." *Postmodern Culture* 13 (May). http://muse.jhu.edu/journals/postmodern_culture/toc/pmc13.3.htm (accessed June 12, 2008).

Tuan, Yi-Fu. 1989. "Traditional: What Does It Mean?" In *Dwellings, Settlements, and Tradition: Cross-Cultural Perspectives,* ed. Jean-Paul Bourdier and Nezar Alsayyad, 27–34. Lanham, Md.: University Press of America.

Tucker, Elizabeth. 1984. "Levitation and Trance Sessions at Preadolescent Girls' Slumber Parties." In *The Masks of Play,* ed. Brian Sutton-Smith and Diana Kelly-Byrne, 125–33. New York: Leisure Press.

———. 2007–2008. "Levitation Revisited." *Children's Folklore Review* 30: 47–60.

———. 2009. "Guardians of the Living: Characterization of Missing Women on the Internet." In *Folklore and the Internet: Vernacular Expression in a Digital World,* ed. Trevor J. Blank, 67–79. Logan: Utah State University Press.

Tucker, Nicholas. 1985. Review of *Life Is Like a Chicken Coop Ladder: A Portrait of German Culture through Folklore* by Alan Dundes. *Folklore* 96: 262.

Tuleja, Tad. 1991. "The Tooth Fairy: Perspectives on Money and Magic." In *The Good People: New Fairylore Essays,* ed. Peter Narváez, 406–25. Lexington: University Press of Kentucky.

————, ed. 1997. *Usable Pasts: Traditions and Group Expressions in North America.* Logan: Utah State University Press.

Tumulty, Karen. 2008. "Can Obama Shred the Rumors?" *Time*, June 23, 40–41.

Turner, Stephen. 1994. *The Social Theory of Practices: Tradition, Tacit Knowledge, and Presuppositions.* Chicago: University of Chicago Press.

Tyron, Rolla M., and Charles R. Lingley. 1927. *The American People and Nation.* Boston: Ginn & Co.

Ueda, Reed. 1987. *Avenues to Adulthood: The Origins of the High School and Social Mobility in an American Suburb.* New York: Cambridge University Press.

UNESCO. "Itsukushima Shinto Shrine." World Heritage website. http://whc.unesco.org/pg.cfm?cid=31&id_site=776 (accessed July 29, 2007).

United Synagogue of Conservative Judaism. 2003. "Sukkot." http://www.uscj.org/scripts/uscj/paper/ARticle.asp?ArticleID=286 (accessed August 10, 2010).

Unterman, Alan. 1991. *Dictionary of Jewish Lore and Legend.* London: Thames & Hudson.

Upton, Dell. 1979. "Toward a Performance Theory of Vernacular Architecture: Early Tidewater Virginia as a Case Study." *Folklore Forum* 12: 173–98.

————. 1985. "The Preconditions for a Performance Theory of Architecture." In *American Material Culture and Folklife*, ed. Simon J. Bronner, 182–85. Ann Arbor, Mich.: UMI Research Press.

Uther, Hans-Jörg. 2004. *The Types of International Folktales: A Classification and Bibliography.* 3 vols. Helsinki: Suomalainen Tiedeakatemia.

Van Gennep, Arnold. 1960. *The Rites of Passage.* Trans. Monika B. Vizedom and Gabrielle L. Caffee. Chicago: University of Chicago Press.

————. 1999. "The Rites of Passage." In *International Folkloristics: Classic Contributions by the Founders of Folklore*, ed. Alan Dundes, 99–108. Lanham, Md.: Rowman & Littlefield.

Van Wagenen, Jared. 1953. *The Golden Age of Homespun.* Ithaca, N.Y.: Cornell University Press.

Veblen, Thorstein. 1899. *The Theory of the Leisure Class: An Economic Study of Institutions.* New York: Macmillan.

Vermeulen, Han F. 1995. "Origins and Institutionalization of Ethnography and Ethnology in Europe and the USA, 1771–1845." In *Fieldwork and Footnotes: Studies in the History of European Anthropology*, ed. Han F. Vermeulen and Arturo Alvarez Roldán, 39–59. London: Routledge.

Vinecour, Earl. 1977. *Polish Jews: The Final Chapter.* New York: New York University Press.

Virilio, Paul. 2001. "Speed and Information: Cyberspace Alarm!" In *Reading Digital Culture*, ed. David Trend, 23–27. Malden, Mass.: Blackwell.

"Virus Hoaxes & Realities." 2008. *Snopes.com.* Urban Legends References Pages. http://snopes.com/computer/virus/virus.asp (accessed October 3, 2008).

Vlach, John Michael. 1985a. "The Concept of Community and Folklife Study." In *American Material Culture and Folklife*, ed. Simon J. Bronner, 63–75. Ann Arbor, Mich.: UMI Research Press.

———. 1985b. "Holger Cahill as Folklorist." *Journal of American Folklore* 98: 148–62.

———. 1986. "'Properly Speaking': The Need for Plain Talk about Folk Art." In *Folk Art and Art Worlds*, ed. John Michael Vlach and Simon J. Bronner, 13–26. Ann Arbor, Mich.: UMI Research Press.

———. 1989. "Morality as Folk Aesthetic." In *The Old Traditional Way of Life: Essays in Honor of Warren E. Roberts*, ed. Robert E. Walls and George Schoemaker, 28–39. Bloomington, Ind.: Trickster Press.

———. 2003. *Barns.* New York: W. W. Norton.

Von Sydow, Carl Wilhelm. 1948. *Selected Papers on Folklore.* Copenhagen: Rosenkilde & Bagger.

———. 1999 [1932]. "Geography and Folk-Tale Oicotypes." In *International Folkloristics: Classic Contributions by the Founders of* Folklore, ed. Alan Dundes, 137–52. Lanham, Md.: Rowman & Littlefield.

Wagner, James. 2008. "Top-Selling Video Games Show Growing Casual/ Crossover Trend." *Gigaom* website. http://gigaom.com/2008/01/24/top-selling-video-games-show-growing-casualcrossover-trend/ (accessed April 2, 2008).

Walbert, David. 2002. *Garden Spot: Lancaster County, the Old Order Amish, and the Selling of Rural America.* New York: Oxford University Press.

Waldrop, M. Mitchell. 1985. "String as a Theory of Everything." *Science* 229: 1251–53.

Walker Art Center. 1974. *Naives and Visionaries.* New York: E. P. Dutton.

Wallace, Patricia. 1999. *The Psychology of the Internet.* Cambridge: Cambridge University Press.

Walzer, Michael. 2000. "Philosophy, History, and the Recovery of Tradition." *Chronicle of Higher Education*, June 16, A56.

Wampler, Jan. 1978. *All Their Own: People and the Places They Build.* Oxford: Oxford University Press.

Ward, Daniel Franklin. 1984. *Personal Places: Perspectives on Informal Art Environments.* Bowling Green, Ohio: Bowling Green State University Popular Press.

Warnock, G. J. 1989. *J. L. Austin: The Arguments of the Philosophers.* London: Routledge.

Wasik, Bill. 2009. *And There's This: How Stories Live and Die in Viral Culture.* New York: Penguin.

Wattenberg, Ben J. 1995. *Values Matter Most: How Democrats or Republicans or a Third Party Can Win and Renew the American Way of Life.* Washington, D.C.: Regnery Publishing.

Watterson, John Sayle. 2000. *College Football: History, Spectacle, Controversy.* Baltimore: Johns Hopkins University Press.

Weaver-Zercher, David. 2001. *The Amish in the American Imagination.* Baltimore: Johns Hopkins University Press.

Weber, Nicholas Fox. 2007. *The Clarks of Cooperstown.* New York: Knopf.

Webster, Frank. 2005. "Network." In *New Keywords: A Revised Vocabulary of Culture and Society*, ed. Tony Bennett, Lawrence Grossberg, and Meaghan Morris, 239–41. Malden, Mass.: Blackwell.

Weidlich, Loree. 1974. "'. . . To See Who Had the Longest, Uh, Organ': Hedging One's Way through the Dirty Joke." *Folklore Annual of the Folklore Association of the University of Texas* 6: 46–57.

Weingard, Robert. 1988. "A Philosopher Looks at String Theory." *PSA: Proceedings of the Biennial Meeting of the Philosophy of Science Association* 2: 95–106.

Weinreich, Beatrice Silverman. 1988. *Yiddish Folktales*. New York: Pantheon.

Weiss, Moshe. 1994. *From Oswiecim to Auschwitz: Poland Revisited*. Oakville, Ontario: Mosaic Press.

Wells, Rosemary. 1991. "The Making of an Icon: The Tooth Fairy in North American Folklore and Popular Culture." In *The Good People: New Fairylore Essays*, ed. Peter Narváez, 426–54. Lexington: University Press of Kentucky.

Welsch, Roger L. 1970. "Sandhill Baled-Hay Construction." *Keystone Folklore* 15: 16–34.

———. 1976. "Railroad-Tie Construction on the Pioneer Plains." *Western Folklore* 35: 149–56.

Wepman, Dennis, Ronald B. Newman, and Murray B. Binderman. 1974. "Toasts: The Black Urban Folk Poetry." *Journal of American Folklore* 87: 208–24.

Whatley, Mariamne H., and Elissa R. Henken. 2000. *Did You Hear about the Girl Who . . . ? Contemporary Legends, Folklore, and Human Sexuality*. New York: New York University Press.

White, Merry. 1994. *The Material Child: Coming of Age in Japan and America*. Berkeley: University of California Press.

Whiting, John W. M., and Barbara Ayres. 1968. "Inferences from the Shape of Dwellings." In *Settlement Archaeology*, ed. K. C. Chang, 117–33. Palo Alto, Calif.: National Book Press.

Whiting, Robert. 1990. *You Gotta Have Wa*. New York: Vintage.

Wieand, Paul R. 1984. "Where the Groundhog Is King." *Pennsylvania Folklife* 33 (3): 129–33.

Wilbur, Shawn P. 1997. "An Archaeology of Cyberspaces: Virtuality, Community, Identity." In *Internet Culture*, ed. David Porter, 5–22. New York: Routledge.

Wilgus, D. K. 1983. Letter to Simon J. Bronner, February 15, Los Angeles, Calif.

Will. 2005. Response to "Ray Gricar Missing." *StateCollege.com*. Discussion thread on Townhall Forum, April 21. http://www.statecollege.com/townhall (accessed September 26, 2008).

Williams, John Alexander. 1975. "Radicalism and Professionalism in Folklore Studies: A Comparative Perspective." *Journal of the Folklore Institute* 11: 211–34.

Williams, Raymond. 1983. *Keywords: A Vocabulary of Culture and Society*. Rev. ed. New York: Oxford University Press.

Williamson, Ray A. 1987. "Outer Space as Frontier: Lessons for Today." *Western Folklore* 46: 255–67.

Wilson, E. Bright. 1991. *An Introduction to Scientific Research*. Mineola, N.Y.: Dover.

Wilson, Frank R. 1999. *The Hand: How Its Use Shapes the Brain, Language, and Human Culture*. New York: Vintage.

Wilson, William A. 1976. *Folklore and Nationalism in Modern Finland.* Bloomington: Indiana University Press.

———. 1988. "The Deeper Necessity: Folklore and the Humanities." *Journal of American Folklore* 101: 156–67.

———. 2006. *The Marrow of Human Experience: Essays on Folklore,* ed. Jill Terry Rudy. Logan: Utah State University Press.

Winthrop, Robert H. 1991. *Dictionary of Concepts in Cultural Anthropology.* New York: Greenwood Press.

Wolff, Michael. 2010. "The Web Is Dead, Who's to Blame: Them." *Wired* (September): 123–27.

Yoachum, Susan. 1993. "Powerhouse behind Lobbying Effort for 'Traditional Values.'" *San Francisco Chronicle,* September 13, A17.

Yoder, Don. 1990. *Discovering American Folklife: Studies in Ethnic, Religious, and Regional Culture.* Ann Arbor, Mich.: UMI Research Press.

———. 2003. *Groundhog Day.* Mechanicsburg, Pa.: Stackpole.

———. 2005. *The Pennsylvania German Broadside: A History and Guide.* University Park: Pennsylvania State University Press.

Yoder, Don, and Thomas E. Graves. 1989. *Hex Signs: Pennsylvania Dutch Barn Symbols and Their Meaning.* New York: E. P. Dutton.

Yoffie, Leah Rachel Clara. 1947. "Three Generations of Children's Singing Games in St. Louis." *Journal of American Folklore* 60: 1–51.

Yoshida Kei. 2007. "Defending Scientific Study of the Social Against Clifford Geertz (and His Critics)." *Philosophy of the Social Sciences* 37: 289–314.

Yoshida Mitsukuni, Tanaka Ikko, and Sesoko Tsune, eds. 1982. *The Compact Culture: The Ethos of Japanese Life.* Hiroshima: Toyo Kogyo.

Zall, Paul M. 1963. *A Hundred Merry Tales, and Other English Jestbooks of the Fifteenth and Sixteenth Centuries.* Lincoln: University of Nebraska Press.

Zaretzke, Kenneth. 1982. "The Idea of Tradition." *Intercollegiate Review* 17: 85–96.

Zelinsky, Wilburg. 1977. "The Pennsylvania Town: An Overdue Geographical Account." *Geographical Review* 67: 127–47.

Zemljanova, L. M. 1963. "The Struggle between the Reactionary and the Progressive Forces in Contemporary American Folkloristics." *Journal of the Folklore Institute* 1: 130–44.

Zercher, Wendell R. 1992–1993. "Charles E. Starry, Adams County Chair Maker." *Pennsylvania Folklife* 42 (winter): 50–63.

Zerubavel, Yael. 1995. *Recovered Roots: Collective Memory and the Making of Israeli National Tradition.* Chicago: University of Chicago Press.

Žižek, Slavoj. 2001. "From Virtual Reality to the Virtualization of Reality." In *Reading Digital Culture,* ed. David Trend, 17–22. Malden, Mass.: Blackwell.

Zukin, Sharon. 2004. *Point of Purchase: How Shopping Changed American Culture.* New York: Routledge.

Zumwalt, Rosemary. 1976. "Plain and Fancy: A Content Analysis of Children's Jokes Dealing with Adult Sexuality." *Western Folklore* 35: 258–67.

———. 1995. "Alan Dundes: Folklorist and Mentor." In *Folklore Interpreted: Essays in Honor of Alan Dundes,* ed. Regina Bendix and Rosemary Lévy Zumwalt, 1–48. New York: Garland.

Index